"What a spectacular achievement! In 'an ecstasy of exploration,' to use Sherrill Grace's lovely description of Findley's dogs criss-crossing a frozen river, one of Canada's leading critics has created a definitive biography (there can never be only one) of a giant in Canadian literature. 'We are what we keep' is the mantra informing her exhaustive attention to the details that shape and reflect the turbulent life of Timothy Findley or Tiff, as he was generally known. Sherrill Grace illuminates the private personal past that Findley's fiction transforms into an urgent and unforgettable presence."

—JOHN MOSS, AUTHOR OF *A READER'S GUIDE TO THE CANADIAN NOVEL*

"Sherrill Grace's meticulously researched biography accesses 'Tiff's' extensive personal diaries and dozens of interviews to reveal the stories behind the Timothy Findley we thought we knew. One of Canada's most perceptive literary scholars, Grace explores the genesis of Findley's writing, provides astute analyses of all his fiction, and an illuminating, long overdue reassessment of Findley's acting and playwriting. She traces his personal and artistic friendships with some of the giants of twentieth-century culture, from Margaret Atwood to Sir Alec Guinness, and unpacks the complex family history that inspired the work and troubled the man. A powerful, eye-opening portrait of the artist as an anguished man who tried desperately to live by his motto: Against despair."

—JERRY WASSERMAN, EMERITUS PROFESSOR OF ENGLISH AND THEATRE, UBC, EDITOR OF *MODERN CANADIAN PLAYS*

"Memory and remembering, central to Timothy Findley's life and work, are equally so to Sherrill Grace's outstanding biography of this celebrated Canadian author. Drawing impressively and insightfully on a vast archive of letters, photos, journals, diaries, and interviews, and on her own towering talents as one of Canada's foremost literary scholars, Grace presents a compelling portrait of a complex man and brilliant multi-faceted writer— himself a master of auto/biography."

—CHRISTL VERDUYN, MOUNT ALLISON UNIVERSITY, AUTHOR OF *LIFELINES: MARIAN ENGEL'S WRITINGS*

SHERRILL GRACE

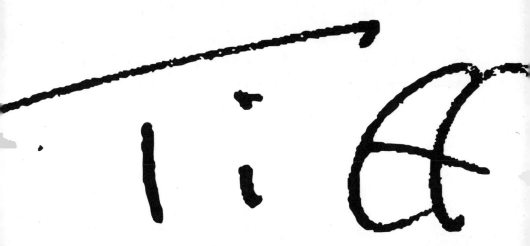

A LIFE OF
TIMOTHY FINDLEY

WILFRID LAURIER
UNIVERSITY PRESS

Wilfrid Laurier University Press acknowledges the support of the Canada Council for the Arts for our publishing program. We acknowledge the financial support of the Government of Canada. This work was supported by the Research Support Fund.

LIBRARY AND ARCHIVES CANADA CATALOGUING IN PUBLICATION

Title: Tiff : a life of Timothy Findley / Sherrill Grace.
Names: Grace, Sherrill, 1944– author.
Description: Includes bibliographical references and index.

Identifiers: Canadiana (print) 20200165690 | Canadiana (ebook) 20200165704 |
ISBN 9781771124539 (hardcover) | ISBN 9781771124553 (EPUB) | ISBN 9781771124560 (PDF)

Subjects: LCSH: Findley, Timothy. | CSH: Authors, Canadian (English)—20th century—
Biography | LCGFT: Biographies.

Classification: LCC PS8511.I38 Z64 2020 | DDC C813/.54—dc23

Front cover photo © Elisabeth Feryn. Frontispiece: A relaxed Timothy Findley at Stone Orchard, 1984. Photograph reproduced with permission of Elisabeth Feryn, who recalls the photo shoot "on a lovely, warm summer afternoon; while we were shooting, Findley would tell me about the book he was writing, tell stories about the farm animals, and quiz me about my life. He was such a warm and empathetic soul." Cover and interior design by Lime Design.

© 2020 Wilfrid Laurier University Press
Waterloo, Ontario, Canada
www.wlupress.wlu.ca

This book is printed on FSC˚ certified paper. It contains recycled materials and other controlled sources, is processed chlorine free, and is manufactured using biogas energy.

Printed in Canada

In Memory of Bill Whitehead (1931–2018),

who made so much possible

"I KNOW THAT HUMAN IMAGINATION CAN SAVE US; SAVE THE
HUMAN RACE AND SAVE ALL THE REST OF WHAT IS ALIVE AND
SAVE THIS PLACE—THE EARTH—THAT IS ITSELF ALIVE.
IMAGINATION IS OUR GREATEST GIFT."

(Timothy Findley, *Inside Memory* 314)

Contents

Illustrations xi

Acknowledgements xiii

Abbreviations xxi

INTRODUCTION | Remembering Timothy Findley 1

One

THE LANDSCAPE OF MEMORY—1870 TO 1949

One Inside Findley's Memory 13

Two Living with the Dead 31

Three Going up to Rosedale 60

Two

THE CANADIAN PROTEGE—1950 TO 1962

Four Leaving Home 87

Five Actor or Writer? 125

Six Beginning Again—and Again 151

Three

CAN YOU SEE ME NOW?—1962 TO 1989

Seven Becoming a Writer 175
Eight The Golden Age of Canadian Writing 208
Nine The Second World War and the Faces of Fascism 260
Ten Staring Down Despair: Stories, Lectures, and *The Telling of Lies* 293

Four

STILL PAYING ATTENTION—1990 TO 2002

Eleven The Canadian Findley 321
Twelve Not Yet 368

AFTERWORD | Back to Stone Orchard 401
APPENDIX ONE | Timothy Findley Chronology 405
APPENDIX TWO | Family Tree 416
NOTES 419
BIBLIOGRAPHY 445
COPYRIGHT ACKNOWLEDGEMENTS 489
INDEX 491

LIST OF ILLUSTRATIONS

1   Frontispiece: Timothy Findley at Stone Orchard, 1984

2   Thomas Findley, Findley's paternal grandfather, ca. 1920

3   Phoebe Findley, Findley's paternal grandmother "Goggie," ca. 1925

4   The Thomas Findley family, Kingston, 1915

5   Thomas Irving Findley, Uncle Tif, ca. 1916

6   Edith Maude Fagan Bull, Findley's maternal grandmother, ca. 1907

7   Frederick Bull, Findley's maternal grandfather, with daughters
    Ruth and Margaret, ca. 1922

8   Detail from the endpapers of *The Piano Man's Daughter*

9   Tiff at Crescent Road home, ca. 1937

10 Timothy Findley in Grade 5, Rosedale Public School, 1942

11 Margaret and Allan Findley in 1944, with Findley's annotation

12 Allan Findley with Tiff and Michael, 1944

13 Janet Baldwin, ca. 1950

14 Timothy Findley at Stratford, 1953, painting by Grant Macdonald

15 Janet Baldwin and Timothy Findley, Cambridge, England, ca. 1954

16 Timothy Findley and Alec McCowen in *The Matchmaker*, 1954

17 Timothy Findley's makeup box, 1954 gift of Alec Guinness

18 Bill Whitehead as "Fredric Whitehead," ca. 1960

19 Actors with the Red Barn Theatre, 1961

20 Dr. R. Edward Turner, ca. 1975

21 Timothy Findley with Louis Applebaum and Bill Whitehead,
    working on *The National Dream*, 1973–74

22 Timothy Findley and Bill Whitehead in Yukon, 1974

23 Timothy Findley drawing, self-portrait, ca. 1976

24 Nancy Colbert, 1983

25 William Hutt as Sir John A. Macdonald in *John A.—Himself!* 1979

26 Bill Whitehead, Len Collins, Anne Collins, and Timothy Findley,
    Stone Orchard, 1980

27 Remains of the root cellar at Stone Orchard, 2011

28 Findley's LLD, Trent University, 1982

29 William Hutt and Martha Henry in *The Stillborn Lover*, Stratford, 1995

30 Timothy Findley and Bill Whitehead with Nésida Loyer, 1996

31 Timothy Findley's study and desk, Stratford condominium, 2001

32 House in Cotignac, 2001

33 Tiff's study in Cotignac, 2001

34 Tiff and Bill, Stratford condominium, 2001

35 Field and path at Stone Orchard, 2018

ACKNOWLEDGEMENTS

I t is important to acknowledge the funding that has made this book possible. To the SSHRC (Social Sciences and Humanities Research Council) and the Killam Foundation, therefore, I offer my most sincere thanks. These funds enabled me to hire and train graduate students in archival work; to spend many weeks in Ottawa with the Findley fonds at Library and Archives Canada (LAC); to travel to Stratford several times for meetings with Bill Whitehead and for work in the Stratford Festival Archives; to travel to many places of importance to Findley in Canada, the USA, England, and France; to present work at several conferences; and to cover the permissions fees required for this book. Without this kind of funding support, research in the Humanities would be difficult if not impossible to undertake.

I am grateful to all those individuals who have shared their "Tiffs" with me or helped in other ways. They are named below, and I sincerely hope I have not forgotten anyone. Two people, however, deserve more thanks than I can express. Bill Whitehead, Tiff's partner, was enormously supportive throughout my research and writing; he granted me full access to materials, including photographs, memorabilia, and audiotapes, and permission to quote from manuscripts, diaries, journals, and letters, he patiently endured many interviews in person, by phone, and on Skype, and he prepared dozens of pages with answers to my questions over the years. Unless otherwise cited, my quotations of Bill's recollections come from eight years of lively conversations and correspondence. He introduced me to theatre people I needed to meet, encouraged others to help me with inquiries, and on one unforgettable occasion made his delicious pear torte for me. He read the entire manuscript in its first version, sent me his congratulations, and never once interfered with my interpretation of Findley's life. Erin Ramlo worked as my research assistant through most of the work and her help has been invaluable—from fact-finding, transcription of audiotapes, and archival tasks to the search for "Nicolas Fagan," which was a most memorable research adventure, not least because it was shared. But the term *research assistant* does not really capture the extent of her presence in my life over many years: we had fun working on Findley, even when confronting the challenges of his fonds; we discussed his work on many occasions; and we shared frustration and then excitement when something suddenly became clear.

There are a few more people whom I wish to single out for special thanks. Trevor Greene, Bill Whitehead's partner, has provided much badly needed help over the years. Thank you, Trevor, for finding Findley family letters, sending me boxes of materials, photographing a selection of pictures in Timothy Findley's family albums, arranging voice-mail communications for me and Bill (both of us sad Luddites); for listening patiently or disappearing quietly on many occasions when Bill and I were talking; and for sharing precious moments with me at Stone Orchard. Susanna Egan and K Edgington, scholars and friends, read early versions of the entire manuscript; each provided helpful feedback and asked many questions that sent me searching for more answers, but most importantly, at times when it was needed, they offered enthusiastic support. Another colleague, Harry Lane, stepped onto the stage with practical help on two occasions, for which my profound thanks, and blessings on Jan Lermitte for help on the index. Readers' reports on manuscripts are blind (the author's name is known, but the reader's is not), and one of my readers engaged thoughtfully with the manuscript and wrote many pages of precise, useful suggestions and comments. I wish all writers such valuable readers and offer mine my sincere thanks. My editor Kel Pero was a joy to work with, although there are still many Findley matters we could discuss for hours. Thank you, Kel—for your engaging commentary, practical advice, and much more. To my editor at WLUP, Siobhan McMenemy, my sincere thanks for her thoughtful reading of an early draft of the manuscript and for her belief in the importance of this project. To my copy editor, Margaret Crammond, for her meticulous work, to Murray Tong for his expert care, to others at WLUP, and to Lara Minja, who contributed to the design of the book, my thanks for a job well done.

During the protracted research for a biography, an author meets people with whom one wants to stay in touch. In my case, with this biography, I am grateful to Carol Roberts, Findley's first biographer, and her husband, Ken, for their hospitality and regular messages. Marian Hebb, literary trustee for the Findley and Whitehead estates and Pebble Productions Inc., has supported this biography with interest and enthusiasm; it has been a privilege to work with you, Marian. Nancy Colbert is another special person with whom I like to stay in touch and to whom I owe thanks. As Findley's literary agent and friend and as a major presence in Canadian publishing, she was creative, clear-sighted, fair, and indomitable. Findley adored her and with good reason. She helped him build his career, shared many of his interests, and cared deeply for the man as well as the writer. Several individuals shared their private collections, as well as their memories, with me, and for this generosity I am deeply grateful to John Bull, Dick Cousland, Mary Lou Finlay, Joann Guthrie, Elizabeth Hay, Alan Lawson, Matt Mackay, and Veronica Tennant.

Finally, I want to thank my personal support team and my family. Authors always do this, but there is nothing merely pro forma about my appreciation. Research and the writing of books, which require long hours bent over archival files and tied to desks and computers, are always team efforts, but I have relied enormously for years on the regular help of Fátima Amado, Beverley Kosuljandic, and Dr. Jeffrey Quon, who have, quite literally, kept me functioning. My daughter, Elizabeth Grace, has taken time from her busy legal practice to drive me to several out-of-the-way places connected with my research and, with her partner Susan Vella, provided accommodation, good food, fine red wine (Findley would have approved), and photographic services on my many extended research trips to Toronto. (By the way, we still need to tour the old cemeteries in Prince

Edward County to check for pioneer Fagans.) My husband, John Grace, has also accompanied me on several Findley adventures to Cannington, Stratford, Dieppe, and London (UK). The most challenging and memorable, however, was our drive to Cotignac, but once we found it we enjoyed the country roads, restaurants, and cobbled streets—one of which, after much perseverance, finally led to a man who had known Findley and Whitehead well: John Bertram. Sharing this fieldwork, as I call it, makes up for the long weeks, months, and years of solitary writing. Thank you, Elizabeth and John, for the companionship and memories.

It is a pleasure to thank the following individuals for their help on this long journey. Any errors in this biography are mine alone.

Albert Abitbol
Mary Adachi
Fátima Amado
Mia Anderson
Rick Asals
Amanda Attrell
Margaret Atwood
Agatha Barc
Renu Barrett
Nishi Bassi
Jan Bauer
Bev Bayzat
John Bertram
E. D. Blodgett
Helen Bradfield
Pat Brennan
William E. Britnell
Diana Brydon
Eric Bull
Lloyd Burritt
Steven Bush

Elspeth Cameron
Brent Carver
Mary Chapman
Marigold Charlesworth
Adrienne Clarkson
Sheilagh Clucas
Katrina Cohen-Palacios
David Colbert
Nancy Colbert
Anne and Len Collins
Marc Coté
John Court
Dick Cousland
Margaret Crammond
Susan Dalton
Diane D'Aquila
Hilary Dawson
Mary Doig
Dennis Duffy
Julia Emberley
Charlotte Engel

Howard Engel
Alicia Fahey
Elisabeth Feryn
Mary Lou Finlay
Ted Foster
Graeme Gibson
Cynthia Good
Andrea Gordon
Trevor Greene
Joann Guthrie
Annemarie Hagan
Bonnie Hamburgh
Denis and Deborah
   Harrison
Kathryn Harvey
Elizabeth Hay
Sue Hayter
Marian Hebb
Martha Henry
Catherine Hobbs
Heather Home

Acknowledgements

Nick Hudson

John Hulcoop

Peter Hutt

Dr. Paula Iriarte

Tiffany Johnstone

Nora Joyce

Joe Kertes

Ric Knowles

Martin Kuester

Martha Kumsa

Harry Lane

Debra Latcham

Alan Lawson

Alma Lee

Jan Lermitte

Karen Levine

Nésida and Alain Loyer

Viola Lyons

Terence Macartney-
    Filgate

Louise MacCallum

Matthew Mackay

Alberto Manguel

Juliet Mannock

Alec McCowen

Alexandra McEwan

Laurie McNeill

Barb and Doug Minett

Peter Moss

William Needles

Léa and Pierre Nicolas

Mary O'Regan

Dr. Wayne Parsons

John Pearce

Kel Pero

Michael Peterman

Marilyn Powell

Jeffrey Quon

Erin Ramlo

Frances Reilly

Carol and Ken Roberts

Jean Roberts

Shelagh Rogers

Sabine Roth

Margarida Santos

Christine Schindler

Kelly and Terry Sellers

Elizabeth Semmelhack

Patrick Sisam

Brian Skerrett

David Staines

Rick Stapleton

Anna St. Onge

Paul Stuewe

Rosemary Sullivan

Anne Tait

Dr. David Tamblyn

Sophie Tellier

Paul Thompson

Vincent Tovell

Iris Tupholme

Sylvia Tyson

Jane Urquhart

Guy Vanderhaeghe

Susan Vella

Héliane Ventura

Jacqueline Vincent

Allison Wagner

Phyllis Webb

William Whitehead

Martha Wilson

Dominique Yupangco

Waldemar
    Zacharasiewicz

Cynthia Zimmerman

Archives Consulted

Archives are precious, and the following archives have been invaluable for my work. My thanks to them and to the archivists who have been so helpful in finding documents, taking photographs, and cheering when a discovery was made.

Bata Shoe Museum, Toronto: Timothy Findley's boots

British Library, London: Alec Guinness fonds

Brock Township Public Library: historical documents

Canadian Broadcasting Corporation (CBC): Still Photo Archive

Cannington & Area Historical Society: records

Centre for Addiction and Mental Health (CAMH): Clarke Institute fonds; historical records; R. Edward Turner fonds

City of Toronto Archives: historical documents

Estate of Garson Kanin, New York: Ruth Gordon papers

Elisabeth Feryn: photography archive

Mary Lou Finlay: private papers

Sherrill Grace: private papers

Grace Church on-the-Hill, Toronto: records

Joann Guthrie: private papers

Havergal College, Toronto: records

Elizabeth Hay: private papers

Alan Lawson: private papers

Library and Archives Canada (LAC): Timothy Findley and William Whitehead fonds; Colbert Agency fonds; Phyllis Webb fonds; Veterans Affairs personnel records

Matthew Mackey: private papers

McMaster University, Hamilton: Pierre Berton fonds; Clarke, Irwin & Company Limited fonds; Marian Engel fonds; David Helwig fonds; Writers' Union of Canada fonds

Mount Pleasant Cemetery, Toronto: records

Oshawa Public Library: Williams Piano Company collection

Queen's University and the Agnes Etherington Art Centre: Grant Macdonald collection; Isabel McLaughlin fonds

St. Andrew's College, Aurora: Findley records

Acknowledgements

St. James Cemetery, Toronto: records

Stratford Festival Archives: historical documents, 1953–55

Toronto Municipal Library: historical records

Toronto Public Library: *Mail and Empire* microfilm archives; Janet Baldwin papers

Trent University, Peterborough: Richard Dellamora fonds; convocation records

Trinity College School, Port Hope: Alan Bull records

University of British Columbia, Vancouver: Jane Rule fonds; Alan Twigg fonds; David Watmough fonds

University of Calgary: Whitehead/Findley book collection (in storage); Hugh Hood fonds; Robert Kroetsch fonds; W. O. Mitchell fonds; Alice Munro fonds; Mordecai Richler fonds; Guy Vanderhaeghe fonds

University of Guelph: Timothy Findley and William Whitehead collection; William Hutt fonds; Massey-Harris fonds; Stephen Bush fonds

University of Toronto: Graeme Gibson fonds (Thomas Fisher Rare Book Library); David Gardner fonds (Thomas Fisher Rare Book Library); Northrop Frye fonds (Victoria College); Sheila Watson fonds (St. Michael's College)

University of Victoria: Timothy Findley collection donated by Moira Troup; Robin Skelton fonds

William Whitehead (WFW): private papers, including Findley family letters, photographs, and several unique cassette tapes (TF's 1993 conversation with his cousin, Isobelle Guthrie; TF's recollections of his life for WFW; and TF's audiotape letters to friends). These materials, given to me by WFW, are now with my private papers.

Yale University: Thornton Wilder collection

York University: Margaret Laurence fonds; Herbert Whittaker fonds

LIST OF ABBREVIATIONS

———

The following abbreviations are used in citations in the text; all are for works by Timothy Findley, except as noted.

BP	The Butterfly Plague		All references are to the box
CYSM	Can You See Me Yet?		number followed by the file
DAA	Dinner Along the Amazon		number, where relevant; most
DD	Dust to Dust		documents are unpaginated.
ER	Elizabeth Rex	LCP	The Last of the Crazy People
FLW	Famous Last Words	NWV	Not Wanted on the Voyage
FSO	From Stone Orchard:	P	Pilgrim
	A Collection of Memories	PMD	The Piano Man's Daughter
H	Headhunter	SBL	The Stillborn Lover
IM	Inside Memory: Pages	TEP	The Trials of Ezra Pound
	from a Writer's Workbook	TW	The Wars
J	Journeyman: Travels of a Writer	WLB	Words to Live By
LAC	Findley's journals, diaries,		(William Whitehead)
	calendars, and workbooks in	YWA	You Went Away
	Library and Archives Canada.		

Remembering Timothy Findley

———

I have returned to Stone Orchard, Timothy Findley's home, many times over the years of research for this biography, each time learning more about the man who lived and wrote there, but one damp November day remains with me as only a first, impressive experience can. As I walked through the fields, surrounded by the scent of damp vegetation and fresh air—memory inhaled—I could situate Timothy Findley on this, for him, home ground, where he struggled against despair and experienced peace, joy, and great success. I remember that day well. It was 11 November 2011, spitting rain, chilly, with low grey clouds—my first visit to the farm called Stone Orchard, where Findley had lived for thirty years and where he wrote most of his fiction and plays. I knew how important landscape and place were to him and how necessary they were for the biography I would write, and no place was more significant to him than this home.

I was especially grateful, therefore, to the current owners, who gave me a tour of the old house, beginning with the spacious kitchen where Findley often sat with tea or coffee while reading his latest draft aloud to his lifelong partner, Bill Whitehead. The large living room had been reno-vated, but photographs show that in Findley's time the walls were lined with books and the room contained two large sofas and his beloved piano. Upstairs there were still traces of the cerulean blue walls that he liked to have around him. (As I later discovered, Findley often said that "blue was the colour of hope.") I was allowed to roam the grounds of Stone Orchard and to explore the fields: *there* was the old root cellar, refurbished to give him a writing place in good weather; *there* was the barn that housed so many dogs and horses he and Whitehead rescued; *there* was the low stone wall running beside the property (within which he had placed a sealed bottle carrying a message for the future); farther off was the pond that they created to attract migrating birds. Beyond the grounds, the fields, now wet from the rain, stretched to distant woods and the Beaver River, places where Findley walked the dogs, landscapes that found their way into his writing and stimulated his imagination. Above all, this place was his home.

Some of Timothy Findley's ashes were scattered here in the autumn of 2002, and the ashes of many family members and of his animal "significant others" were also scattered in these fields he loved and in the herb garden he tended. Stone Orchard provides much insight into the person behind the art: a man for whom ancestors, memory, and home were crucially important, a man who achieved so much and yet remained tormented by fear of failure, of rejection, and of dying before he had said all he felt compelled to say.

Timothy Findley (1930–2002) was a celebrated author and an astute witness to Canadian culture and society from the 1960s to his death. He wrote award-winning, iconic novels like *The Wars*, *Famous Last Words*, and *Headhunter*, hugely popular ones like *Not Wanted on the Voyage* and *The Telling of Lies*, major historical fictions like *The Piano Man's Daughter*, several award-winning plays, and some very fine short stories. He contributed to important developments in Canadian writing and publishing during the 1970s and '80s and was a founding member of the Writers' Union of Canada. His voice was raised, with passion and conviction, on crucial issues during those years, from war and human rights abroad to environmental degradation and censorship at home. His story is, in no small part, Canada's cultural story during the last thirty years of the twentieth century, and his life's path intersected with many major artists of his time, from Alec Guinness, Peter Brook, and Thornton Wilder to Glenn Gould, William Hutt, and Margaret Laurence.

Although I read each of his works as it was published and saw his plays in performance, I never met him. His fiction fascinated and haunted me—it still does—but I did not know the human being who could write and move me so profoundly. And I wanted to know him, to understand, if I could, what shaped this man into the writer and witness he was. This question came to a head in 2007 while I was teaching *The Wars*. Despite my long-standing appreciation of the novel, I had not yet paused to consider its author or his reasons for writing the book; I had been trained to focus on the text and ignore the author. But the times and critical approaches had changed, and my students were curious, with questions I could not answer. A few years later I taught a graduate seminar exclusively on Timothy Findley and quickly realized that these students were also swept away by his writing; they were no more than twenty-five years old, but they became hooked because they saw Findley as speaking to their generation. Again there were the questions: why had they not discovered him before and how could they learn more about the author's life? In 2010 I cleared my desk and began my search for Timothy Findley, the man, in his time and place. I too wanted answers.

Caveat lector: a biography cannot capture its subject whole; it should not claim to have the Truth or all the answers. Happily, a biographee slips through a biographer's net, preserving a core of privacy. This is true even for a person like Findley who published two memoirs, kept exhaustive journals (surely intended for his biographer to find), drew on his family's and his own experiences for his fiction, gave many revealing interviews, and wrote frank letters to close friends. This is, moreover, a literary biography because Findley was a major writer whose life intersected with some of the most fascinating people and momentous events of the twentieth century. What he had to say about his century was important during his lifetime, but it remains relevant—urgently so—today. His advice to himself and to all who read him was this: no matter how violent and dangerous the world becomes, do not give in to despair but pay close attention to the possibilities and joys of life. To resist despair, he employed creative imagination in his life, and he invited his readers to do the same because he believed that "imagination can save us." He was often angry with this world, most especially with human beings and with himself; he could be violent when drunk and he drank a lot, but he was also full of laughter and joy. He had fun—enjoying his friends, his family, his garden and animal companions, good food and wine—when he wasn't working extremely hard to give us the novels, plays, and stories that are his legacy.

The life of a serious artist—painter, writer, composer—is a solitary one, and Findley constantly faced a paralyzing loneliness compounded by his search for artistic perfection. In Bill Whitehead, however, he was blessed with a partner's love and support, and he knew he was blessed. He was deeply loved by his mother and, eventually, by his father, even though Allan Findley never fully understood him and inflicted lasting emotional scars. Extended family members also provided loving support, as did many close long-time friends through the friendships he cultivated and treasured. He was admired and respected even by those who observed how difficult he could be, and young people who attended his readings have told me that he charmed them because he took them seriously and listened attentively to them. He was, in short, a complex, generous, formidably intelligent, volatile, acutely sensitive person. But in the final analysis, he lived to write and to communicate, and he has left us with his vision of a world in need of our attention, love, and imagination.

In telling this story, I sometimes call Findley "Tiff," and there are several reasons for this informal address. Tiff, which stands for his full name—Timothy Irving Frederick Findley—was how he thought of himself, and everyone who knew him even a little called him Tiff; in interviews and on other public occasions he was often addressed as Tiff. This name, as we shall see, carried important family associations for him. Nevertheless, he was, and still is, the writer, Timothy Findley, and the formal name meant a great deal to him as well. He was also adamant about another form of address: he spoke of himself as "homosexual" and disliked the word "gay." He resented being called gay, rejected the notion that he and Whitehead were "poster boys" for gay marriage, and vehemently refused to be categorized as a "gay writer." Nevertheless, his homosexuality must be considered carefully because of the ridicule and trauma he suffered as a young man, the particular social and legal context for homosexuality between 1940 and 1970, and the relevance of these experiences for his work. That said, my primary focus is on his life as a writer, a great one, I believe, who happened to be Canadian, to live most of his life in southern Ontario, and to be gay. His audience was the world; his subject was the human species and other living creatures; and his message was always to maintain hope.

In his review of Otto Friedrich's biography of Glenn Gould, Findley wrote something that has remained at the back of my mind while writing this book. He warned that "the creation of any successful biography involves, of necessity, encounters with any number of nightmares for a writer: facts that cannot be verified; people you need to interview who die two days before you arrive; intransigent keepers of the flame who refuse to divulge the one vital thing you must have access to" (*IM* 279). Findley could scarcely have summarized the hurdles a biographer faces more succinctly. Other writers have made similar comments and warned against a biographer trusting their subject's duplicities, the faulty memories of well-intentioned friends or the skewed perspective of enemies, and the frustration of arriving after a key person has died or finding that vital information has been lost or destroyed. But not all writers are as interested in autobiography and biography as Findley was, as skilled at creating fictional biographers and autobiographies as he was, and as insistent that memory, whether faulty or not, is fundamental to human identity and survival. Moreover, Timothy Findley understood the slipperiness of life stories and made telling the difference between truth and lies a central theme in his fiction.

The truth is—and here I am certain it is the truth—he enjoyed performing, and, as a former actor, then a public intellectual, he was always the consummate performer. Performance was integral to the man and the artist even when, I have come to believe, he wrote in his personal journals. I have had to tread carefully, therefore, through the private landscape of his journals and the public presentation of himself in readings and interviews to detect the person behind the role and to expose the vital capillary links between the two. But this journey has always been exhilarating, with moments of frustration when I arrived at a dead end and moments of delight when I turned a journal page to find an answer to a question, a drawing of cats, a single dried and pressed flower, or a quickly sketched self-portrait—Tiff as the all-night, early morning artist with cat companion and coffee cup and, tellingly, with his back to the viewer.

Finding Timothy Findley has produced all the nightmares he mentions in the Gould review and a few more besides. If I could have interviewed him before he died, I would have tried to confirm certain details. He, of course, might not have answered my questions about his aunt, Ruth Bull Carlyle, and her medical condition or why she meant so much to him, and he may not have known if he had a distant Fagan relative in Ireland who suffered from a mental illness that had been passed down through the generations. I would have asked him about his interest in the writer Malcolm Lowry, in the painter Attila Richard Lukacs, and in the composer Franz Schubert, especially his fascination with Schubert's last piano sonata. I wish I could ask him if he actually owned a recording of Alfred Cortot performing the piece and, if not, why he invented such a record for *Famous Last Words*. My reading of his journals suggests that there was a psychiatrist who subjected him to grotesque treatment in the late fifties, but he may not have been willing to discuss that episode in his life or able to remember how he came to be treated by this doctor. Although he might well have balked at my inquisitiveness, I would certainly have asked him about being persecuted at school and if he was sexually abused at some point in his youth because so much in his fiction suggests that he was. One must be careful, however, not to read the fiction back into the life.

Among the many people who died before I could speak with them, a number stand out. The most important person is the psychiatrist Dr. Edward Turner, who would not have divulged patient information from his years of treating Timothy Findley but who, I feel certain, would have shed light on the kind of private, inner person he believed Tiff was and on the challenges faced by the psychiatric profession as it reformed its views on homosexuality during the latter half of the twentieth century. Turner's patient records (if he did not destroy them all) have not been located, but meeting Turner would have helped me understand Findley's respect for this psychiatrist and how this doctor had helped him. There are others who were important in Timothy Findley's life and whom I would have contacted: Alec Guinness, Robin Phillips, Janet Reid, Pierre Berton, and Marian Engel, for example. Thornton Wilder is a special case, not simply because he died before I dreamed of writing this book, but because it appears that much of the Findley/Wilder correspondence has either been lost or destroyed. For years Findley kept twenty letters from Wilder in his safety deposit box, but at Wilder's funeral, his sister Isabel asked Tiff to be "careful" of Wilder's letters to him and he promised he would be (*IM* 288–89). In a letter that he wrote to Isabel shortly after Wilder's death, he acknowledged her desire to destroy the Findley/Wilder correspondence, and yet he did not destroy all of Wilder's letters to him. As some of these letters show, Wilder not only was an early influence on Findley's career, but he also had sage advice for Findley the man. I have found one important letter to Alec Guinness, and I discuss it in chapter 12, but Findley's early letters to Guinness seem to have disappeared, and I have no evidence to suggest that he and Guinness agreed to destroy or suppress their correspondence. Inevitably, as Findley knew, there have been a few "intransigent keepers of the flame," who either refused to speak with me at all or refused to answer certain questions, as was their prerogative.

Perhaps my most fascinating challenge—I would not call it a nightmare—has been the existence of so many volumes of private journals. There are thousands of pages of autograph journals, as well as diaries, annotated calendars, and workbooks, in the Timothy Findley/William Whitehead fonds housed in Library and Archives Canada. From 1950 until shortly before his death, he kept journals, wrote in them constantly and at considerable length, and carefully preserved them. They were important sources of information for him, and when he was away from Stone Orchard he took photocopies of journal material that he needed to consult for works-in-progress. These journals have been invaluable for my research, and I have no doubt that Findley preserved them, in part, so that his biographer could use them. But therein rests my challenge: how much should I rely on them, and how complete are they? Timothy Findley, the man and the artist, placed enormous weight on journals as a genre. In his early journals one can follow his almost daily battle with loneliness, even when he realized the necessity for being alone as he wrestled with the blank page. Reading these journals enables one to watch him, rather like a voyeur—slowly and hesitantly at first, yet surely—discover his identity as a writer; they then show him struggling, sometimes with excitement, sometimes with crushing self-doubt, but always with passion, to find his characters, their story, and the exact word or phrase he needs. His journals became a companion of sorts, a safe place for describing his ambitions and expressing his self-doubt and despair, and he delighted in creating fictional journals and diaries for his characters and fictional biographers. They also provide an irresistible thread to follow through the daunting maze of Findley's life.

Early on I decided to trust these journals for insights into his life and state of mind, and I often quote from them or summarize what he confided to them. At the same time, I read them with caution because there are obvious lacunae in his journal entries; sometimes, many journal pages are left blank, and in a small number of places a few pages have been torn out. This actual excision of pages is rare with Findley, but the number of blank pages left in some journals is more common. Were there things he was unwilling to record? Or was there simply an innocuous reason for abandoning those pages and starting a new journal? On one matter in particular, Findley was circumspect, even in his journals: he rarely reflected openly, or with any specifics, on his sex life, which leaves one to rely on his guarded comments in interviews for information. In short, these journals cannot be taken as revealing everything or answering every question. At times, especially in the early journals, the page serves as a mirror in which he observes himself posing, performing, talking to himself, or trying out a gesture or a phrase. The journals are also the repository of his memories, making them *the* essential source in his search for identity, for the significance to him of family and ancestors, and for the major themes he developed in his work. Consequently, I have treated these journals as the connective tissue between the external facts of his life and the transformation of personal memory and experience in his art.

Many famous people—artists and politicians such as Johannes Brahms and William Lyon Mackenzie King, for example—try to destroy as much autobiographical evidence as possible, either while they are alive (as in Brahms's case) or in their wills (as with King) because they want to control their life story and forestall nosey biographers. Findley, however, was an obsessive collector: he tried to keep every letter, gift, book, record, and draft of his many novels, stories, plays, and other writing. His study shelves and desk were filled with many precious mementoes that held special meaning for him: a picture of Elizabeth Taylor, a crucifix, a small stuffed silvery-grey unicorn, family photographs, a teddy bear called Sebastian, and much more. This need to preserve his possessions, no matter how ephemeral, predates his life with Bill Whitehead and represents, I think, his need to confirm his identity: we are all, to some degree, what we keep, and Findley saw himself in his possessions. Bill fell into line by helping him preserve every draft of his writing and then sending the great majority of this material to LAC, Canada's national archive, where it would be preserved for posterity.

Like the rest of his family, Findley collected and preserved professional photographs and family snapshots. These too were treasured heirlooms to be kept safe. During the process of writing this biography, I studied hundreds of these photographs. When the time came to choose a few to include here, I realized that the very act of selection would influence the picture of Timothy Findley that I have created. I also know that photographs were powerful sources of inspiration for his imagination and a stimulus for his memories: he reproduced and described family pictures in his fiction, pasted actual photographs into his journals, created imaginary ones for his novels, and in the journals he often reflected on the difficulty of interpreting what a photograph told him. Some of the photographs I have chosen are central to any biography—photos of ancestors, places where he lived, his study, a few key events, and important ones of Tiff and Bill. Others are useful for understanding his fiction and life—pictures of Aunt Ruth, of Uncle Tif, of the Findley family with Allan Findley, Tiff's father, in uniform, and others that show Tiff in a play or at the Red Barn Theatre. Then there are those snapshots that cast interesting sidelights on his life, like the image of him huddled against the Yukon cold with a film crew. Some of these photographs suggest that his was a happy family and that life after Stone Orchard was sustaining; however, his journals tell a more complex story. As do his novels, stories, and plays.

And that's the challenge—the fundamental role of biography, and of the biographer's exhilarating, at times maddening, search through an immense and varied archive—that I have experienced and chart here as I searched for this man. Findley was too self-conscious, even in his journals, too wary of bare facts, and far too clever to be captured by a single version of Truth, which makes him all the more intriguing. In the final analysis, there are many public and private Tiffs, but the most important Timothy Findley exists in his creative work, in his admonition to pay attention because "imagination can save us," and in his message: "Make prayers against despair, I am alive in everything I touch" (*TW* 135).

THE LANDSCAPE OF MEMORY—

1870 TO 1949

—

CHAPTER ONE

Inside Findley's Memory

PEOPLE ARE THE LANDSCAPE OF MEMORY. WITHOUT THE BENEFIT
OF TIME AND PLACE, THEY ARE FORCED TO PLAY THE SCENERY
THEMSELVES. ALL THE INFORMATION THEY CAN GIVE YOU IS
THERE IN THEIR FACES AND IN THEIR NAMES.

(Timothy Findley, *Inside Memory* 11)

I f you are approaching Timothy Findley for the first time, if all you
know about him is his name and that he was an important writer,
then there are two ways to begin. You can start by reading his fiction, as I did in 1977, or you can start with his life, here, in *Tiff: A Life
of Timothy Findley*. As I noted in the introduction, my biographical
search for Findley took me first to the places where he lived, then to his
private journals, workbooks, and letters (his archive), and to many people
he knew, but I begin this biography with his version of his life in *Inside
Memory: Pages from a Writer's Workbook* because to begin here means
to start with a special kind of fiction—a life story presented in a carefully selected and structured form. *Inside Memory* was published in 1990,
but Findley lived for another twelve years and wrote several more major
works. As a memoir, then, it is far from complete, and it is by no means
a casual collection of "pages" from his "workbook." It may seem to promise secrets from behind the scenes—a private workbook—but there are

surprisingly few personal secrets or salacious tidbits in this work. In fact, it is an autobiographical exercise that has as much to say about other people as it has about Timothy Findley. That, however, is my point. For Findley, and thus for his biographer, those other people and his vivid memories of them are essential aspects of who he was and of the person he understood himself to be. This memoir is valuable for what it tells us about its author and about the construction of autobiography, especially for a writer as self-conscious as Findley, because he reveals a lot about family, friends, and places that mattered deeply to him and inspired his writing, and he has much to say about key experiences that influenced his views on life. It is in these selected pages from his workbook (and other sources) that he defines himself as a writer with important things to say about imagination, despair and hope, and the writing process, and he acknowledges his fear of failure and of death, fears we all face to some degree, but ones that haunted him for most of his life and would surface again and again in his writing. Above all, in this memoir he celebrates memory, his personal memories and the general human reliance on memory.

Inside Memory is organized into eleven sections, the first and last of which frame those in between. The framing sections, "Remembrance" and "Inside Memory," are primarily concerned with remembering as a process and with memory as a fundamental component of individual and collective identity. They balance each other in certain ways and hold a reader inside the writer's memory as he recalls people and places important to his life and work. The first entry in "Remembrance" is his script for a radio talk about Chekhov and Remembrance Day dated "Stone Orchard, November 11, 1970." The name Stone Orchard, which he gave his farm, was inspired by Chekhov's *The Cherry Orchard*, and Remembrance Day holds special significance for him. He tells us that he wishes Remembrance Day were "a day of happiness" (6), but that November 11 always reminds him of an uncle, Lt. Thomas Irving Findley, who played an important role in his life and is buried in Toronto's Mount Pleasant Cemetery. This short opening section closes with an establishing shot—a keynote—for everything that follows. "Remembrance is more than honouring the dead," he tells us. "Remembrance is joining them—being one with them in memory" (7). By the time we reach the final section, called "Inside Memory," we have met many of Findley's dead through his stories about them, but, as a conclusion to the memoir, this section is unusual because, instead of tying up loose ends, he circles back through memory to his dead—Thornton Wilder, his mother's Bull family ancestors, and many beloved fellow artists and friends. Then he returns to Mount Pleasant Cemetery and stops to admire the large, impressive Massey family mausoleum, where he imagines that vines now cover "a mass of scars" (264) created by a young Tiff Findley when he crashed into the monument while learning how to drive (he never did learn). Finally, he visits his Findley ancestors, who are "buried in the [main] mausoleum," where he can "reach in past the iron rails and touch [his] father's father's name: *Thomas*" (267).

The most revealing and moving part of this closing section, however, is a speech he gave at Trent University in 1987. The lecture series bore the general title "My Final Hour," and speakers were asked to consider what they might have to say toward the end of their lives. As a public performance, which is also intensely private in its revelations, this published text captures the writer, Timothy Findley, moving back and forth across living memory to reflect on life and death, and it illustrates his self-conscious presentation of his life—"here it is: my final hour. And what do I have to say for myself" (*IM* 301). It is here that he recalls the significance of Phyllis Webb's poetry for him and quotes from "I Daniel," which she dedicated to him, because in this poem she captures "what it means to be that most ill-defined and imprecise embodiment of humankind—the writer" (301); it is here that he confesses his youthful identification with Richard III—"the most *aberrant* human being in all of English Literature" (304)—and his early realization that he was gay, which caused others to reject him. In this speech he describes an experience from 1957 at the home of a Hollywood screenwriter that would profoundly affect the rest of his life, and it is here, in this speech, that he offers his most precise ethical statements on how to live imaginatively and creatively by reconciling ourselves with who we are and, above all, by resisting despair: "Nothing is harder, now in the present time, than staring down despair. But stare it down we must" (*IM* 318).

With one exception, each of the nine sections inside the memory frame recalls a working period in his life, or a specific novel. He begins in the 1950s in London, England, where he tried to be an actor and discovered he was a writer, and he ends the ninth section with some context for his novel *The Telling of Lies* (1986). The exception comes almost at the midpoint of the memoir with a piece called "Alice Drops Her Cigarette on the Floor," one of the most amusing interviews that Findley ever gave. Asked by the journal *Canadian Literature* to write a piece about himself and his work, he balked because "if you're a fiction writer—most of you is already out there. [...] And the rest of you is [...] so obliquely private that it's very hard to get at" (*IM* 167). If he knew how to begin or what to say, he protests, he would not "be sitting here worried to death about how to write this article" (167). "Here" is Stone Orchard; the date is October 1981. The solution to his problem is Bill Whitehead, who decides to perform the role of "Timothy Findley," while Findley "will be a character—and try to give the answers" (168). Wonderful.

In this cleverly staged interview, we never learn who Alice is (Alice B. Toklas? Lewis Carroll's Alice?) because she and her cigarette are merely stage business, but we do learn a little about what the real Findley thinks of Chekhov ("I like Chekhov because of the famous *pauses*" [170]) and painting ("I have visions of huge canvases [with] masses of people [...] very colourful [but] I'm not accomplished enough" [169]), and we gain insight into his first published and performed play, *Can You See Me Yet?* As for the private Findley, he remains "very hard to get at" (*IM* 167) and, for the most part, in the wings, from where he grants us a few prompts and some noises off. Nestled within the memoir, this interview is like a play. Although this speech certainly represents the public Timothy Findley, the person we watch is a character in costume, posing, performing, and hiding more than he reveals, and as such it warns the reader not to mistake a performance for the real man, who had been an actor. It challenges me, as his biographer, to look more closely, to search backstage for this writer who shrank from autobiography, even while writing one, and revelled in the biographies of family, friends, and historical figures who influenced him and inspired his work.

The sources Findley drew upon for *Inside Memory* range from his published pieces, like the "Alice" interview or obituaries he wrote, to public presentations, like the Remembrance Day broadcast and "My Final Hour," to excerpts from his personal letters and private journals. The result is a fragmented, multi-faceted narrative collage in which public and private documents carry the same degree of authenticity: one is no more private or public than the other. In his novels, he uses this strategy to suggest that one story is no less fictional than another, although, as Mauberley, one of his most infamous characters, warns us in *Famous Last Words*: "*All I have written here is true: except the lies*" (59). The handling of dates is similarly deliberate and unsettling. One entry, dated 1986, is followed by a 1976 journal excerpt, which is followed by another journal entry from 1970. Thoughts and memories recorded in 1990 sit side by side with a journal entry from April 1968 because they both bear on his novel *The Butterfly Plague*. This anti-chronological structure keeps readers on their toes and reflects Findley's process of remembering, which obeys its own rules to evoke and then locate a particular story, person, or image within a present remembering context.

"Memory is a form of hope" (*IM* 4). "Memory is survival" (*IM* 7). It would be hard to overemphasize the importance of memory for Findley. Although *Inside Memory* presents a rich store of personal memories, which he draws on for his fiction and plays, in his work he also mines the cultural memory of his time and place, of Western history, and especially of major events in the twentieth century. "Memory is making peace with time" (*IM* 5), he tells us, and this idea of making peace is crucial to understanding the man, his capacity for reconciliation, and his choice of themes and characters for his work. "We *are* what we remember," he insists, and he reminds us that "memory is other people—it is little of ourselves" (5–6). In the life story that follows, I explore how Findley used memory in his work and performed remembering throughout his life because *The Wars* cannot be fully appreciated unless a reader surrenders to a set of remembering voices and to fading images recalled from the First World War. Likewise, *Elizabeth Rex* would not exist on page or stage if the fictional playwright within the play—one Will Shakespeare—refused to remember.

The cast of characters remembered in *Inside Memory* does not include all the people in the Findley landscape. One "WFW" appears from time to time, but he is rarely seen at centre stage or drawn into the spotlight. Yet William Frederick Whitehead was the most important person in Findley's adult life, the man without whom we would not have the writer Timothy Findley or the private human being called Tiff. I cannot tell this life story without Bill Whitehead, who appears often in this biography as Bill, just as I cannot write this story without sometimes calling its subject Tiff, who stresses the importance of this name by telling us about one of the most influential people in his life—American playwright and novelist Thornton Wilder. Wilder always called him Timothy or Findley because, as far as Wilder was concerned, *Tiff* was a verb, not a real name (*IM* 14). But for Tiff this name carried important family associations and linked him with his father's brother. Several family members are remembered in *Inside Memory*. His father comes on stage briefly, mostly in a positive light, because by the time Tiff remembered Allan Findley for this memoir he was largely reconciled to the man. His mother, Margaret, is recalled as an image in white, mourning the death of her father. Another family member of special significance to him is his mother's sister; Ruth Bull Carlyle is not named, but she was central to what he called "the first truly profound experience of my consciousness. I was seven. Maybe six" (179). She was so important to Findley that I will come back to her, as I will to Thomas Irving Findley, Uncle Tif (for whom Tiff was named), his father's only surviving brother, who also makes a brief appearance in *Inside Memory*, but is an important figure in this biography and a major inspiration for *The Wars*.

The other people who receive more attention than Findley grants himself are close friends, colleagues he admired and learned from, theatre people and fellow writers. It was Wilder who pointed him towards his true vocation: "You are a writer, Findley. That's a certainty" (*IM* 29). Wilder also gave him some of the most useful advice a writer can have, advice that Findley would often repeat: "Pay attention" (31). Two actors from his years in London, England, in the 1950s made deep and lasting impressions on him: American actress Ruth Gordon and British First World War veteran and actor Ernest Thesiger. Each comes to life in vivid scenes and through amusing and poignant stories as Findley remembers them and writes them into his life. "Ruth is small. She ticks [...] like a watch," noting that, if the watch "stops ticking, everyone runs for cover. You wait for the explosion" (*IM* 11); Ernest "was the person whose appearance always made you smile with anticipation [...]. The minute Ernest turned up, you knew the hero was about to be caught in a diabolical trap" (*IM* 41). In Canada Findley developed many precious relationships with fellow writers—all important figures in Canadian cultural history—and he captures them as if they were sitting for a portrait: Pierre Berton, Marian Engel, Margaret Laurence, Ken Adachi, and Gwendolyn MacEwen, to name a few. Phyllis Webb, who played a decisive role in his writing life, is remembered here through her poetry and its strategic influence on *Not Wanted on the Voyage* and *Famous Last Words*.

Relationships with others whom he holds dear serve as a set of lenses through which to view the human being who cherished them: Mottle, the blind cat who stumbled into his life, became a close companion with whom (yes, *whom*) he played "silver-paper hockey" on the kitchen floor at two a.m. (*IM* 94), and with whom he felt a "relationship that is as complex" as it can be with another human being (*IM* 223); Janet Baldwin, a close family friend and his ballet instructor, who inspired the character of Ruth Damarosch in *The Butterfly Plague*, occupied a special position in his personal landscape. Glenn Gould, with whom Findley talked—to whom he listened—in late-night and early morning telephone calls, is captured in an especially moving vignette about the filming of *The Wars*; we see Gould as Findley saw him, and through Gould we catch a glimpse of Timothy Findley remembering and celebrating a personal friend, a lover of animals (like Tiff), and a fellow insomniac, as well as a musical genius.

Samuel Johnson, who gave Findley his personal motto—"Against Despair"—(*IM* 318) is acknowledged. So are his literary agents, Nancy and Stan Colbert, and an early publisher, Grace Bechtold, whom he remembers by telling stories about his own fumbles and foibles—reluctantly following Stan Colbert's stern advice to burn a failed manuscript so he could start afresh, or arriving drunk, dishevelled, and with loose manuscript pages floating about him in Bechtold's New York office. British screenwriter and

Hollywood producer Ivan Moffat also makes a brief appearance, but this time Findley's memories are anything but lighthearted. Moffat had joined the American army in 1943, and, after a dinner at Moffat's Hollywood home in 1958, Findley discovered Moffat's photographs of the liberation of Dachau at the end of the Second World War. Although he devotes only a few pages to this memory, its significance cannot be overstated; the impact on his psyche was not unlike a child's exposure to a primal scene. Left alone for an hour or so, he explored Moffat's library and happened upon these appalling images: "I was looking into hell—and hell was real. [...] I never recovered from what I saw that night" (*IM* 310–11).

Inside Memory also throws light on why and how Findley wrote. At one point, he describes writing as "like talking to yourself" (155), and while this may not reflect what other writers think or do, it is most certainly what Timothy Findley did. At another point, he insists that "words in a sentence are a written gesture. And if the cadence is wrong—if a single syllable is out of place—the sentence fails ... the book fails" (184). Reading his novels, stories, or private journals, one is always aware of listening to a storyteller, to a voice that addresses one directly or that one seems to be overhearing as the speaker talks to himself. "The writer is a *voyeur*," he warns us, a voyeur and an eavesdropper (171), which makes us his accomplices. But such talking to oneself is never merely private or idiosyncratic for Findley. There is always a strong ethical imperative to this talking. "A writer is a witness," he insists. "Memory provides that witness with veracity" (313). In his fiction, the writer is often a character who bears witness to events and guides the reader, who must in turn bear witness by listening carefully to what they're being told. And yet, "Writing isn't therapy" for a writer or a reader because the writer enters "the other world of hell" (181) and comes back to tell the rest of us about it. Writing then, like reading, exists to open doors for the imagination; to make us *see*, as Joseph Conrad once said; to show us truths we prefer not to face, as Malcolm Lowry also knew. For James Joyce, the ideal reader was an insomniac; for Timothy Findley, this reader is a witness who pays attention.

Findley has other, less portentous things to say about writing in *Inside Memory*, and one of his most inviting analogies involves music. He loved music and played the piano by ear. After a long day's work in his upstairs studio at Stone Orchard, with a Schubert sonata or perhaps something by Poulenc on the record player, he would come downstairs to his piano. Mottle would sit beside him, her paws near the keyboard, and purr while he played. Classical music made a profound impact on him, but his tastes were catholic, as the many allusions in his work to popular songs, ballads, and film scores demonstrate. Nevertheless, to describe how writing—for him—functions, he turns to classical forms: the "first draft is the unaccompanied piano—and the other drafts are the orchestration. Ultimately, it is all one concerto—but the *reader* plays the solo part—which, in the beginning, the writer played" (155). On other occasions, he describes the importance of rhythm in his writing through a comparison with dance and with breathing; all three—music, dance, breath—he believed, had to come from the solar plexus. Clearly then, rhythm and breath are features of his writing to watch for, but the bigger picture depends on landscape, which I see as a governing metaphor for his life and art.

Events, people, memories, are always *placed* in the Findley world. And places inform everything he loved and created; places grounded him. Landscapes of memory, as well as actual lived-in landscapes, were his spiritual home. As I noted in the introduction, I began my research not in his archives but in his places, with *Inside Memory* as my guidebook. One treasured landscape was an old beach hotel in Maine: Atlantic House. The hotel is long gone now, but the beach remains. When I walked that beach in 2011, I had to trespass into a gated community of luxury condos, but the ghost of Timothy Findley was still there to greet me and no one blocked my way. The senior Findley family had made annual summer visits to this rambling, elegant hotel; Tiff's father played there as a boy; Tiff and his brother swam and played along those beaches; Tiff brought Bill to Atlantic House for several summers until the place was sold and slated for demolition. When the time came, Tiff scattered his father's ashes in the Atlantic waters just offshore, and he set *The Telling of Lies* in that loved and lost hotel and along those stretches of beach. Beaches were a favourite landscape, never more so than at Dieppe, which held a unique importance for him, and in one of his finest stories, "Stones," he created a profoundly moving visit to those beaches. Saltspring Island in British Columbia also drew him spiritually and imaginatively. Phyllis Webb may have been the original attraction, but he found much to enchant him there, from slugs trying to cross a highway to a unicorn. He first spotted this magical beast, disguised as a white horse, with marble hoofs and a horn-like marking on its forehead, in 1985, and thereafter added apples for the unicorn to the shopping list.

If Rosedale, where he grew up, and the larger urban landscape of Toronto formed an inescapable and often nightmarish landscape for Findley, a terrain far removed from that city came to matter in a very different way. In a November 1969 letter to Thornton Wilder, an excerpt from which appears in *Inside Memory* (215–16), he describes his one visit to the Northwest Territories with Bill in the summer of that year in almost mystical terms. "Nothing else I can imagine doing could have had more effect on me than our trip to the Northwest Territories this summer," he told Wilder: "how deeply I am affected by nature" (215). There is nothing sentimental about this for him; it was, quite simply, a life-altering experience, an antidote to Ivan Moffat's Dachau photographs. "I gained access to my biological past [in the NWT] and I was linked—not just to other human beings—but to life itself" (215). Of course, this spiritual connection with wilderness could not erase the influence of Rosedale. Toronto and that privileged enclave where the Findleys lived, even if only on its edges at times, was far too deeply engrained in his memory to be left behind. He began his writing life in that landscape, and he was still wrestling with it in several works from the nineties: Rosedale, family, fathers and sons— and mothers—are the figures in the ground of *The Last of the Crazy People* (1967), *The Piano Man's Daughter* (1995), and *You Went Away* (1996). Rosedale and the surrounding city represent his terrifying, personal heart of darkness in *Headhunter* (1993). Stratford would enter his life and work in the late nineties, and Cotignac—or more generally southern France— made tentative inroads on his imagination, most notably in the short story "The Madonna of the Cherry Trees." But Findley's biography begins in and returns to Ontario. He was never a Canadian writer in a narrow or nationalistic sense; however, he was inseparable from his homes: Rosedale, Stone Orchard, and the fields and roads around Cannington.

The town of Cannington, a ninety-minute drive north of Toronto and a few miles south of Lake Simcoe, is the most important of his landscapes. Stone Orchard, the old farm on the outskirts of Cannington, is described in lyrical detail in *Inside Memory* and in *From Stone Orchard: A Collection of Memories* (1998). He creates this deeply loved landscape through descriptions of the animals with which he shared his life there: domestic pets, many cherished dogs, dozens of cats (some of which, like Mottle, are personalities in their own right), birds, farm animals, raccoons, deer and, yes, mice. He describes the coordinates, the topography, with precision: you could go to the old farm as I did and trace Findley's footsteps through the fields and along the 11th Concession Road in Brock Township.

So vivid are his images that he makes us see Bill in an orange sweater skating on the Beaver River, flanked by the dark forest—a "pure Northland vista" (99) that recalls the canvases of Tom Thomson—and accompanied by their dogs, who criss-cross the frozen river in an ecstasy of exploration and freedom. "Then back home to fire and coffee—the safety symbols of all Canadians" (99). And "home" is the key word here. Stone Orchard was Findley's home in the most profound sense. "I truly believe that each of us has a natural home," he explains:

> It may or may not be where we are born. We make it—yes. But we cannot make it perfect unless we discover where it belongs. My home is here. I'm lucky—and I know that. And this is what I have that feeds me—both as a person and as a writer: the curve of these hills, the lines of these horizons, the shapes and the smells of these trees, the hardness of these stones, the ghosts within these walls, the harshness of this climate—and all its weathers—and the sounds which fill my ears. (*IM* 88)

This is where I want to be, he writes, "until I die" (81).

Allusions to his own mortality are rare in *Inside Memory*, but remembering the dead is the motivating theme of the book. His exposure to the reality of dying came early with the loss of a baby brother and then of Uncle Tif, and his fear of death was reinforced from an early age by his surroundings. Near the beginning of *Inside Memory*, he recalls himself as a small boy leaning over the backyard fence at his grandmother Findley's Toronto home at 27 Foxbar Road to study the headstones in St. Michael's Cemetery: "what I remember [is that] I am all the gravestones I was looking at [...]. And the fence boards that supported me. And the sun on my back" (5). He does not say he remembers seeing the gravestones or feeling the boards and the sun, but that he *is* all the gravestones, the boards, and the sun. Toward the end of the memoir, he describes his "earliest memory of death" (311). He was seven when his maternal grandfather, Fred Bull, died, and he remembers watching his mother, with her two sisters-in-law, all three dressed in white "standing in the sunlight" and caught in an embrace of comfort and mourning. In this scene, "lifted from mythology," he recognized "a view of grief as old as time" and understood that "we can embrace, in spite of death" (311–12). Death and the dead haunted Findley, but instead of denying this, or viewing these ghosts as evil or negative, he turned that haunting into art.

On 9 August 2001, however, when he signed a living will, he left his estate to Bill, but on one important point he had no instructions for surviving family (in his case, cousins) or his doctors. After the blunt sentence—"If the time comes when I, Timothy Irving Frederick Findley, can no longer take part in decisions for my own future, let this statement stand as an expression of my wishes, while I am of sound mind"—there is a blank space, but he had nothing to say.[1] The form continued with questions about his wishes if there were "no reasonable expectation of my recovery" or whether he "be allowed to die and not kept alive by artificial means." Here Timothy Findley, this man who was so eloquent with words, wrote just one word in the allotted space: "none." There could be a number of reasons for this silence, this refusal to comply. He may simply have had no idea what to say. He may have felt his wishes were private. Or he may have been superstitious; completing that form may have struck him as tempting fate. Timothy Findley was afraid of death, of dying before his time as so many of his friends had, and, unlike *Inside Memory*, his private journals reveal this fear. In an April 1968 entry he confessed: "I am afraid of death ... I am afraid of pain—and I am afraid of 'stopping'" (qtd. in *J* 73), that is—of stopping his work when he still had so much to say. By the late winter and early spring of 2002, he knew he was being stalked by death. He *knew*, and with reason. In the fall of 2001, he noted that he felt poorly: "stomach not right ... lower back gone ... legs wobbly .... Well—I'm seventy-one, over-tired, overworked and with a powerful stress load. (So many friends have dire health problems.) I was going to write: *but that's life, Tiff*—and yet there are moments when it feels more appropriate to write: *that's death*. Must not allow depression to take over. *That* is death" (*J* 309–10).

His description of his health that autumn was prescient. He was in very poor shape, worse than he or Bill realized. The hard work, constant travelling, insistent demands and deadlines, not to mention the heavy smoking and booze, the barrage of pills and lack of exercise, had caught up with him. At 8:41 a.m. on 22 February 2002 he was admitted to Emergency at the Stratford General Hospital with hypertension and respiratory failure. After five days of treatment, his medications were adjusted; he was warned to stop smoking and reduce alcohol consumption and was discharged. But his doctors knew, as did he, that his overall condition was not good. His heart, lungs, and kidneys were failing. He was exhausted. He had trouble breathing, sleeping, and walking. He was overweight. He admitted to his family physician, Dr. Wayne Parsons, that he was sick of being old and a burden and "quite frightened."[2] And yet, despite this fear, he did not change his habits. In his 1 July 2002 obituary for Findley, the Stratford Festival's artistic director, Richard Monette, recalled the last time he spoke to him. He and Bill were eating pizza at Pazzo Taverna in Stratford, with Findley wreathed in smoke and drinking red wine. He "grabbed [Monette's] arm and greeted [him] with the startling words— 'You know, I'm dying.'" Monette replied, "Mr. Beckett, we are all dying." To which Findley answered: "That's a good line. I think I'll use it."

He and Bill left for France in late March 2002, hoping that the peace and quiet of their Cotignac retreat would be restorative. Findley had a commission from Stratford to write an adaptation of *The Trojan Women*, and his play *Shadows* needed polishing. When he fell in the bathroom on the night of March 31, these plans were halted. At first, he and Bill thought that bedrest was all he needed, but by April 3 he was in severe pain and

Bill called a local doctor, who advised that Findley be taken to hospital. By now the problem was urgent, and, on April 4, Bill got him by ambulance to the nearest hospital, twenty-one kilometres away in Brignoles. He had fractured his pelvis on the right side near the groin and there was internal bleeding. After a week he was sent home; however, his doctors had not stopped an infection resulting from the bleeding. Once this set in, he became rapidly worse, and two days later he was in a crisis, but the paramedics from Brignoles did not want to risk moving him. The logistics of the Cotignac house (down a steep driveway approached from a narrow country road), the distance from there to the hospital, and Findley's severely compromised condition made for a precarious situation. Bill protested and called the head of the Emergency department at Brignoles, who visited the house in person and sedated Findley for the journey. From Brignoles he was taken by ambulance to the Saint-Anne Military Hospital in Toulon, fifty kilometres from Brignoles on the Mediterranean coast east of Marseilles. There he was immediately put on dialysis because his kidneys had failed in Brignoles and given a tracheotomy to assist his breathing. He was kept in an induced coma for over two months, during which time he suffered several cardiac arrests and kidney failure. He regained consciousness sufficiently to recognize Bill on one occasion. Moreover, as the autopsy confirmed and as Bill already suspected, the cardiac arrests had caused brain damage.

For Bill, the situation was a nightmare. Driving between Cotignac and Toulon took well over two hours each way on winding, hilly roads, and hospital visiting hours were strictly limited to one hour a day. On the night of June 20, Bill had returned to the house exhausted. He was awakened from a deep sleep shortly after one a.m. by a phone call, and he remembered a voice saying: "Monsieur Findley est décédé." His first thought was—what? What has Mr. Findley decided? Then he awoke enough to understand: Timothy Findley had died. The time of death was just before one a.m. on June 21. Bill was also informed that he had thirteen hours to make arrangements and retrieve the body, but he had foreseen this eventuality and had already arranged for Tiff to be transferred to the nearest crematorium. It was at Pompes Funèbres Claude Pianetti in

Vidauban (northeast of Toulon) that he was cremated on June 26, with Bill and nine others in attendance. Their dearest old friends from theatre days in Canada, Jean Roberts and Marigold Charlesworth, were there. Jean and Marigold, who had lived in Bagnols-en-Forêt (north of Cotignac) for several years, had helped Bill and Tiff find their Cotignac retreat, and they were a great comfort to Bill. The other people present were the handyman, John Bertram; the housekeeper, Nadine Mensenqual; their Cotignac neighbours, Ursula and Harry Chandor; Italian scholar Christina Saviola; and Léa and Pierre Nicolas, the couple who owned Tiff and Bill's favourite restaurant, La Fourchette. After the service, the mourners gathered at a restaurant for lunch with red wine, and Léa later planted a mimosa tree in the garden of the Cotignac house in memory of Tiff.

In the hours immediately after Findley's death, Bill began phoning his list of friends in Canada, but he could not reach many of them in person. He left voice messages instead, which was small comfort. By the morning of June 21 in Ontario, however, the news was spreading quickly. Obituaries began to appear in Canadian newspapers the next day: "An incomparable friend and a remarkable writer" (Sandra Martin); "Homage to a literary giant" (Robert Crew); and in Cannington, "Village mourns 'Tiff' Findley" (Jeff Bower) capture some sense of the public's initial reaction to the loss. On June 23 *Le Monde* published a major piece by Raphaëlle Rérolle under the heading "Disparition de Timothy Findley, une grande figure de la littérature canadienne." The time had come to mark his passing and reflect upon his contribution to the arts.

The Stratford memorial held in the Festival Theatre on July 14 was profoundly moving and ideally suited to the character and talent of the man being celebrated. If the manner of his dying had not been kind, this service was full of love, funny at times, perfect in every detail, and staged with a degree of theatrical panache that would have delighted Findley. There was a full house. Friends came from Toronto, Cannington, Ottawa, London, Peterborough, Guelph, and further afield. There was music too, just as he would have wanted—recordings of Glenn Gould playing the Largo from Richard Strauss's Fünf Klavierstücke, op. 3 and the Brahms Intermezzo in E-flat Major, op. 117, no. 1. Gould had performed both works for the soundtrack of the 1981 film adaptation of *The Wars*. And so it was that Gould appeared at Findley's memorial, in balance with Findley's presence in St. Paul's Anglican Church on Bloor Street East for Gould's memorial service twenty years earlier.

The house program was beautifully put together. It featured a serious Timothy Findley, photographed in the Stratford condo with his Order of Canada pin clearly visible on his left lapel and a cigarette dangling from his right hand. His hair is white, and he has a trim white beard and moustache; he looks composed, gracious, and well. Beneath the photograph is simply: "Timothy Findley 1930–2002." Richard Monette opened and closed the service and read from the last Findley play, *Shadows*. Martha Henry read from *The Wars*; William Hutt, still shattered by the loss of a man, younger than himself, whom he had loved and respected for fifty years, also read; and Brent Carver and Diane D'Aquila read a scene from *Elizabeth Rex*, after which Carver sang "Fear no more the heat o' the sun" (a song from *Cymbeline* that Findley used in *Elizabeth Rex*). Adrienne Clarkson, Canada's Governor General at the time, had awarded him the Governor General's medal for *Elizabeth Rex* just two years before, and now she praised her friend's gentleness and great creative gifts. Bill spoke last and managed well despite his grief. He had Tiff's signature red bandana with him, and he summoned his experience as an actor to tell everyone the story of how he and Tiff came together in Toronto in 1962. Tiff had a role in a television production, but he didn't own a television. Bill owned a television, so he invited Tiff over to watch the program. When the broadcast was over, Bill asked if it were not time for Tiff to go home, but he stayed … for the next forty years. Now, he had left, and a remarkable partnership had come to its end.

The second memorial was held at the University of Toronto's Convocation Hall on September 29. HarperCollins, Findley's publisher, assisted with publicity for the service, but many aspects were planned by Bill or by special guests who wished to participate. William Hutt wanted to read, so Bill selected a passage for him from *Not Wanted on the Voyage*, and Margaret Atwood and Graeme Gibson spoke. So did Veronica Tennant, who had played an important role in Findley's 1997 tour of *The Piano Man's*

Daughter and Others. Sylvia Tyson sang one of his favourite songs, *You'll Never Know*, with its haunting phrase "You went away, / And my heart went with you," accompanied by pianist Joe Sealy, and the song left everyone in tears. Bill was especially moved by June Callwood's comments; he recalled her saying that "a part of Bill died when Tiff died [and] a part of Tiff lives on in Bill." Once again, Bill organized a meal after the ceremony. Twenty-five celebrants joined him at a restaurant for lunch, and this time he was prepared with gifts for each person. Sylvia Tyson received Tiff's favourite carved wooden Canada goose; Bruce Westwood received Tiff's red bandana, which he had admired; Veronica Tennant's special gift was a brass horse, an object rich in Findley symbolism; Iris Tupholme received Tiff's maternal grandmother's silver visiting-card case. For Mary Adachi, Bill prepared a box with a unicorn and a photograph of Mottle—two important Findley symbols. "Pass it on" is Lily's motto in *The Piano Man's Daughter*, and Bill did exactly that with these mementoes.

Writing from Stone Orchard in 1997, Findley had set down his own wishes for his end of life: "Name one who does not hope that life will end *at home.* Where else? *Down in the woods*—my second choice. *In a hospice*—my third. But first and foremost—*at home*" ("Of Trunks and Burning Barns" 66). And for Findley, home was Stone Orchard—southern Ontario—Canada. Earlier in September, Bill had scattered some of Tiff's ashes at Stone Orchard, and when he returned to Cotignac that winter he scattered some ashes there as well. However, the little house with its terraced gardens, bright colours, and warm sunshine was no longer a haven. Without Tiff, the joy was gone. As 2002 stretched into 2003, Bill came back to Stratford and their condo on Ontario Street, determined to sell the Cotignac property, which he did in 2005. He had kept a portion of Tiff's ashes, some to be scattered in Stratford, and some to be mingled with his own at Stone Orchard when the time came, which it did in April 2018.

"Never that which is shall die"—the haunting epigraph from Euripides that Timothy Findley chose for *The Wars*—comes to mind now, as I contemplate his death; therefore, I have described this death at the start of his story so it can be put aside. The facts of what happened do not capture what is important about Timothy Findley. This biography is about a remarkable life, not a death; it explores an extraordinary career and an oeuvre left for posterity—for readers, actors, theatregoers. To understand what mattered most to him I first turn to those haunting, inspiring ancestors whom he remembered in *Inside Memory* and recreated in his fiction. Only after they have been placed in his biographical landscape of memory can I begin looking for the boy and the man who grew up there.

CHAPTER TWO

Living with the Dead

THE DESIGN OF GENES, DRAWN IN BLOODLINES—THE

INFORMANT—*THE TELLER.* [...] A CONGREGATION OF ANCESTORS

GATHERED TO REMIND ME: NO ONE IS HIMSELF, ALONE.

(Timothy Findley, *Journeyman* 78)

The Findleys

In a speech called "Riding Off in All Directions," given to the Leacock Symposium at the University of Ottawa in 1985, Findley surprised his audience by announcing that he was "none other than the grandson of Stephen Leacock" (*J* 190). He supported this astonishing claim by explaining why his "so-called" grandfather, Thomas Findley, "refused to be buried in the graveyard at Sibbald Point along with Mazo de la Roche ["little Maisie Roach" from nearby Roach's point] and Stephen Leacock" (*J* 190). Grandfather Findley had a summer residence at Jackson's Point, on the south shore of Lake Simcoe just west of Sibbald Point, and he must have known "Roach" and Leacock; therefore, it was difficult for Findley to understand why his grandfather would refuse to be buried in their company. After careful genealogical research and the teasing out of literary connections that linked him with de la Roche and Leacock, he came to the only possible conclusion: "that I am not descended from Thomas Findley, but from that unsuspected and illicit union of literary giants" (*J* 190).

The actual Findley genealogy may not be as entertaining as this spoof, but it is certainly important because his ancestors played such a significant role in his imagination and his writing. The Canadian roots for his branch of the Findleys stretch back to his great-grandfather, Thomas Findley, who was born in Scotland in 1839, in the village of Ecclefechan, and emigrated in the late 1840s or early 1850s. A staunch Presbyterian, he settled in the Sutton West area, York County, in southern Ontario, amongst other Scots Presbyterian farming families. Great-grandfather Findley was twenty-five when he married Agnes Thompson, the sixteen-year-old eldest daughter of James and Elizabeth (Fraser) Thompson, on 20 November 1866 in the Presbyterian Church at Chatham. Canadian census records confirm that Thomas died in February 1871, age 32, from "consumption," a wasting disease (probably tuberculosis) and a leading cause of death at the time. According to the family, great-grandfather Findley's death followed a severe chill he received while seeking medical assistance for Agnes when she went into labour. It was winter. They lived on a farm near Oak Ridges at Bond Lake, where the roads were poor, and he may have been on foot. He left his widow with one surviving child, who would be Findley's grandfather—baby Thomas, born 12 December 1870. After her husband's death, Agnes and the baby moved back to her parents' home. Findley's copy of the Findley clan's coat of arms gives the family motto as "*Fortis in arduis*": strength in adversity. And his Findley ancestors would need much strength to overcome the adversities that lay ahead.

Although Agnes disappeared from York County records by the late 1870s, Thomas stayed with his maternal grandparents and was raised by his mother's sister until 1886, when he moved to Sutton West, where he worked in the village store. At the store he learned to use Morse code and operated the newly acquired telegraph system. In 1890 he moved to Toronto, hoping to do more with his life than be a village postal clerk and telegraph operator. His knowledge of the new telegraph technology gave him an important skill, and his first-hand experience with farming made joining the Massey Company, which specialized in the manufacture of farm machinery, an obvious choice for him. In 1891 Hart Massey merged the company with the Harris family business to form Massey-Harris, one of most important and successful businesses in Canadian history, and after 1891 Grandfather Findley's life is easy to follow. He presented himself at the factory and was hired on the spot as a telegraph operator at a salary of six dollars per week. From the telegraph operator's desk, and with his understanding of farming, he quickly realized the opportunities ahead for the business, but without more education or formal training he knew his chances for advancement were limited. Therefore, he set out to educate himself and took night classes in business accounting at the YMCA. By 1895 he had risen from the bottom of the corporate ladder to the position of chief accountant, then to assistant general manager in 1907, from which position he rose rapidly to become a company director, then the vice-president, and finally the president and general manager. Thomas Findley had come a long way from his birth on an Oak Ridges farm.

Upon his arrival in the city in 1890, he joined St. Mark's Presbyterian Church, located on the northeast corner of King Street West and Tecumseth, where he began teaching Sunday school and where he met his future wife, Phoebe Constance Smith. Tracing Phoebe's ancestors has proven more difficult than following the Canadian Findley line. The genealogical notes gathered by Timothy Findley's parents extend back to her grandfather, Andrew Smith, who lived in Quebec City and was sufficiently well off to leave property to his widow and money for his grandchildren. His son, Samuel, moved to Upper Canada and settled in Kingston, where he and his wife had at least two surviving children: a son called Andrew and Phoebe, born in 1869. By 1893 Phoebe had moved to Toronto to live with her brother Andrew, and she attended St Mark's. Like Thomas Findley, her social life centred on this church, where she became the organist and a teacher, and she and Thomas married in St. Mark's on 24 April 1894. Judging from surviving pictures, they made a handsome couple: Phoebe was strikingly beautiful and Thomas, although serious, had the blue eyes and shape of face that would show up two generations later in his grandson.

Their first home was at 205 Crawford Street, facing Trinity-Bellwoods Park, just a short walk from their simple, unadorned wooden church and the Massey-Harris factory at King and Strachan. As their family grew, they moved to a larger house at 183 Crawford, which was a respectable, if not an affluent, address. At this time, the Parkdale area to the west was little more than a village; the new railway lines lay to the south next to the Lake Ontario shore; and there were five taverns on King near the factory entrance. For stern Presbyterians like the young Findleys, this was hardly the most salubrious of surroundings. By 1906 they were living at 130 Walmer Road, further north and just south of Dupont Street, and they had four children: the twins Thomas Irving (nicknamed Tif) and Phoebe Margaret were born on 24 January 1895; a second son, Stuart Eadie, arrived on 2 June 1896; and Timothy Findley's father, Allan Gilmour, was born on 30 September 1902. The Findleys were now a solid middle-class urban family rising steadily in Toronto social circles. They were still at the Walmer Road house in 1907, when eleven-year-old Stuart died during an operation, conducted on the kitchen table, to remove a brain tumour, and Stuart's tragic death provided Findley with the source for a terrifying episode in *The Piano Man's Daughter*. But life had to go on, and about two years after Stuart's death, Thomas moved the family again, this time to a more prestigious address and an elegant house at 88 Admiral Road.

Several factors would have prompted this decision to move, not least the wrenching grief at the loss of a child and the inevitable association of that loss with the rooms of the Walmer Road house, but Thomas could now afford to provide some luxuries for his family. As the vice-president at Massey-Harris, he and Phoebe needed the right address and the proper type of home for a man in his position. In the 1913 *Society Blue Book* for Toronto, the Findleys are listed as receiving guests on Fridays and as belonging to the Canadian Club of Toronto, the Women's Art Association of Canada, the Women's Canadian Club, and the Victoria Club, as well as the prestigious, private Lambton Golf and Country Club. For Findley's father, Allan, and for Findley himself, the family's loss of wealth and status after Thomas Findley's death would have traumatic consequences, but, as we shall see, Findley drew on many aspects of this period in the Findley family for his fiction.

The history of Toronto at the start of the nineteenth century and in the years leading up to the First World War provides important context for the Findley family story. The city was well on its way to becoming a powerful commercial, railway, and banking centre with a population of 181,000 by 1891, more than three times what it had been twenty years earlier. Many businesses were moving to Toronto, and Hart Massey built his four-storey factory on King Street West in 1884. Retail magnates like Timothy Eaton and Robert Simpson were based in Toronto but already branching out across Canada. Electric streetcars arrived on Toronto streets in the 1890s. Prestigious hotels were in operation: the King Edward Hotel on King Street East opened in 1903, and the Queen's Hotel, across from Union Station, would soon be replaced by the larger Royal York. Toronto had four major newspapers, one of which, the *Mail and Empire*, would play a role in the wartime Findley family story. The Ontario Society of Artists formed in 1872; the Grand Opera House opened in 1874, and Massey Hall opened in 1894. The great fire of 1904, which Findley describes in *The Piano Man's Daughter*, was a setback because many businesses along Front Street and in the downtown core were destroyed, but the city was quick to restore and rebuild.

Through the early years of the twentieth century, Toronto continued to grow. Upper Canada College, founded in 1829 (the oldest private boys' school in Canada), was Anglican, elite, and wealthy; St. Andrew's College (SAC), founded in 1899, appealed to well-off Presbyterian families, and the Findley sons were sent there. The daughters of the well-to-do could choose from Bishop Strachan, Havergal (founded in 1894 and where Findley's mother and Aunt Ruth were educated), St. Margaret's College, and Branksome Hall. Upscale residential areas developed north of old Rosedale, up to St. Clair Avenue and beyond to what is, today, Forest Hill, in order to accommodate newly rich business elites like Thomas and Phoebe Findley. Bloor Street Presbyterian Church or the Cathedral Church of St. James (Anglican), on Church Street at King, catered to the souls of the wealthy. The Mendelssohn Choir, begun in 1894, quickly achieved excellence and is still a source of pride. The Art Gallery of Ontario was founded in 1900, the Royal Ontario Museum (ROM) in 1912, the Toronto General Hospital opened its doors in 1913, and Hart House was established by Vincent Massey, in honour of his grandfather, in 1919. Thomas Findley, president of Massey-Harris at the time, was present. "Toronto the Good" may not have been Paris, London, or even New York, but it was most definitely prosperous, with cultural aspirations and strong British loyalties that would soon be tested by war.

By 1910, Thomas and Phoebe were installed in their large, red brick Victorian-style house on Admiral Road, where they stayed until 1918. They had at least one maid—Annie Brant—as well as a cook, a chauffeur, and more than one car. They had their place in the *Blue Book*, belonged to the Lambton Golf Club, and placed their children in private schools; Irving was at SAC and Margaret attended St. Margaret's. They had also acquired a summer cottage at Jackson's Point on Lake Simcoe, which they could reach in a couple of hours by car or rail. Thomas travelled on business a good deal, with frequent trips to England and the continent, but he also financed holidays abroad for Phoebe and the children. Surviving letters exchanged on two of these trips shed light on the style in which the family lived and the affection between husband and wife. Life was good. Sadness at the loss of a child had faded somewhat with time and the dogs of war were distant and easy to ignore.

What lay ahead was impossible to imagine from the perspective of the winter and summer of 1914. Skating parties for the winter months and summer picnics and swimming parties were the high points of young, well-to-do peoples' social lives right up to August. Despite warning signs in newspapers and political circles, and certainly within the network of business and industry, most Canadians were optimistic. As Sandra Gwyn notes, it was "silly to be gloomy, when all the way from Cape Breton to Vancouver Island this was the loveliest summer anyone could remember" (12). Thomas and Phoebe, however, must have seen what was coming. As late as 1913 the family spent weeks in the United Kingdom; they had friends in England, and Thomas had business connections in Europe. He, especially, must have watched anxiously as France, Germany, Russia, and Austria-Hungary repeatedly threatened war and then backed off, only to resume aggressive moves a few months later. He had, after all, the business to think about and a son of the right age. Moreover, the Findleys and Smiths were staunch royalists and proud of their British ancestry. Massey-Harris stood to gain, or lose, a lot should war come, and Thomas would help steer the company safely through the war years and the difficult postwar years of recession and labour unrest.

Surviving photographs from the pre-war and war years provide glimpses of the family's life. Findley's grandparents, his father, Allan Findley, and then Tiff himself collected and preserved such photographs. At one time, they were carefully inserted in standard photograph albums, but when Allan Findley inherited these albums, he made changes. He cut pictures from their original frames, reassembled and annotated them, and pasted them onto pages of heavy paper held in ring binders. They shared space with the poems, assorted magazine clippings and illustrations, and drawings that Allan added. Many of the images carry dates, and some have captions, or brief commentaries, in Allan Findley's handwriting. Findley inherited these binders, and when it came time to design *The Piano Man's Daughter*, he turned to this personal archive for the images reproduced on the endpapers of the first edition of the novel. These binder collections are a fascinating visual archive. Several pictures show smiling family groups, gatherings of children at Jackson's Point, snaps of children riding the family's pony "Queenie," and of young adults posing with the latest model of car or running what appears to be a three-legged race. Two photographs show a dozen young people posed beside a picturesque split-rail fence and suggest a cheerful, carefree camaraderie on a fine summer's day in a typical Ontario field. When I examined the binder that Bill showed me, however, it was a faded sticky note beside these pictures that caught my eye; it is in Tiff's hand: "Summer 1912—And all their voices stilled. How can it be?" Decades had passed between that summer and the sticky note, of course, but the answer involves so much more than time. The simplicity, innocence, relaxation, friendships, and sunshine would be swept away and lost in the approaching war.

The Findleys' eldest son, Irving, survived his war, but the young man he had been before he enlisted did not. The old photographs show him as a stiff, serious, and unsmiling schoolboy, teenager, and young officer of twenty off to the wars. The diaries he started to keep in 1913, his war letters from England and France, his war record, injuries, decorations, and finally his obituaries, help to flesh out a larger, more interesting picture of the man, and they provided sources of information for Findley when he was writing *The Wars*. Irving began his schooling at Givens Street Public School before entering SAC as a day boy in 1906. In those years, SAC was the private school of choice for the sons of wealthy Presbyterian and Methodist families, and some future Canadian leaders were "Old Boys," among them Lawren Harris, a founding member of the Group of Seven and a scion of the Harris family, and Vincent Massey, a Massey grandson and the first Canadian-born Governor General of Canada. Academic subjects were neither Irving's strong suit nor his interest. His senior matriculation marks were too low to reserve him a place in the university, so he was obliged to write supplemental exams. Judging from his 1913 diary, he did not seem bothered by his poor standing; studying was a struggle and a bore.[1] He played several team sports, however, and enjoyed fencing, track and field, and cross-country running. He went to dances, liked live theatre, and made frequent diary entries about his "good times" at Jackson's Point playing tennis, swimming, and rowing. But Irving had a serious side that also surfaces in this diary. He attended bible classes regularly, went to church every Sunday, and listened to guest speakers at "Knox Church" and "at Riverdale."

The most striking aspect of this short diary record of a young man's life in that period is what he does not mention. Although he was active in the SAC cadet corps, nowhere does the word "war" appear in his entries. Did he hear nothing about the possibility of war at this school? Was nothing said around the family dinner table? Did he read nothing in the Toronto newspapers about the German buildup of their navy? Through much of 1912 and 1913, the Canadian government was locked in public debate over a bill to support the British navy by funding new warships. If there was talk around the dinner table at 88 Admiral Road or at Jackson's Point—and there must have been—then it would have stressed support for the mother country and the glory of the British Empire. Whatever their private qualms, families like the Findleys expected their sons "to play up, and play the game." Irving completed his final year at SAC in June 1914 and was accepted into University College at the University of Toronto. War was declared on 4 August 1914, and that fall Irving listened as the principal of University College assured the young volunteers that, "when you return your romance will not vanish with your youth. You will have fought in the great war, you will have joined in the liberation of the world" (qtd. in Berton, *Marching as to War* 133). No mention of death or of wounds, trauma, and mutilation. Crowds took to the streets in Toronto and Montreal and spontaneous parades broke out in support of war during that first week of August. Thomas Irving Findley was among the first students to volunteer.

There is a photograph in one of Timothy Findley's photograph albums that shows his grandparents' family together in Kingston on 24 May 1915 (ill. 4). It is a poignant image representing what so many families faced. Irving looks even younger than his twenty years, despite the uniform. Phoebe, who stands on his right, is inscrutable. Margaret stands close to her brother with her hands behind her back and her face partially shadowed by her hat. Twelve-year-old Allan, Findley's father, looks somewhat confrontational (an early sign of the man he became), and Grandfather Thomas stands slightly apart from the group looking grim. No one appears happy or proud. But then, no one seems anxious or apprehensive either. The young soldier is clearly the important figure, and this photograph may have been taken so he would have a keepsake to carry with him through the separation ahead. By November he had arrived in Lethbridge for training, and in the journal he began at this time he notes that he goes running before breakfast and attends the local Presbyterian church. This war journal is the one Findley inherited after his uncle's death, and it consists of dated entries and letters organized chronologically to form a record of Irving's wartime experience.[2] The information it provides is invaluable for several reasons. The dates make it possible to track Irving's activities, and they supplement his official army record; the narrative threads caught up by the entries shed light on what life and the war were like for these young men—they produce a type of eyewitnessing common to many first-hand accounts of the war. For the purposes of this biography, and for anyone interested in Findley's sources for *The Wars*, this journal is fascinating for the light it casts on Irving's role in the lives of his family and in his nephew's imagination. Many details from the journal reappear in the novel, transformed but recognizable. For example, on November 20, Irving wrote his father, Thomas Findley, to explain that his father had sent the wrong revolver and to say that he hoped to see his parents briefly in Montreal, where his troop train would stop. When Lieutenant Findley sailed on the *Missanabie* from Saint John, New Brunswick, with the 39th Battery in the Canadian Expeditionary Force on 18 December 1915, a soldier called Harris shared his cabin and this young man would be hospitalized in London with severe bronchitis. By February and March, Irving was "somewhere in Belgium," and among his fellow officers were Captain Leather and an officer called Guy Purchas. In *The Wars*, these scenes, places, and names become part of Robert Ross's life.

At Ypres, on July 23, Irving received a shrapnel wound in his right foot and was granted a four-month furlough, three months of which he spent at home receiving medical attention. By December 1916 he was back in France to prepare for action with the 25th Battery of the 2nd Division of the Canadian Field Artillery in one of Canada's most famous battles: Vimy Ridge. For Lieutenant Findley, as for the Canadian army, Vimy was a high point. On 6 April 1917 (Good Friday), Irving wrote to his father:

> Well, Dad, by the time you receive this you will know everything I can
> tell you and perhaps quite a lot more, so this ought to get by the Censor.
> Anyway, the old Hun knows all about it. He put up a sign on his front
> line two days ago, saying, "Anybody can take Vimy Ridge, but all the
> Canadians in Canada can't hold it." We're going to show him that we
> can. (LAC 332:2 np)

Six days later he wrote again: "As you probably saw, the Canucks pulled off one of the finest shows in the Big War."

One hundred thousand Canadians fought together under Arthur Currie, later Major-General Sir Arthur Currie, at Vimy. By the time the four-day battle was over, however, the site was an unrecognizable sea of mud, blood, human limbs, broken weapons, and gear, with thousands of rifles jammed in the mud to mark the spot where a wounded man lay. For *Vimy*, his book about the battle, Pierre Berton borrowed Irving's journal from

Findley for research and quoted Irving's 6 April 1917 letter to his father. Berton concluded that the battle "cost Canada twenty thousand casualties … a quarter of which would never go home" (278). Irving was fortunate to survive, and in August he joined the Royal Flying Corps (RFC) as an observer with the 82nd Squadron, doing contact patrols and reconnaissance flights. However, these flights ended abruptly on 2 April 1918 when Irving's plane was shot down over no man's land by German machine-gun fire. He was reported as missing in action, and it would be several days before word filtered out that he had survived. French troops had rescued him, and he was transported to the military hospital in Ris-Orangis, where he was tracked down by one of Grandfather Findley's assistants. His injuries were severe: one bullet had damaged his right arm; another had shattered his left leg below the knee and "carried away" a large piece of tibia. From Ris-Orangis, he was taken to Paris, then to Le Havre and across the Channel to the RFC hospital in Hampstead for major surgery. In July 1918 he was awarded the Military Cross and cited "for conspicuous gallantry and devotion to duty."

One of the letters, dated 9 April 1918, included in Irving's war journal is written by C. M. Davison, a Canadian nurse at Ris-Orangis, to her mother (LAC 332:2 np). She reports that the nurses had just received several wounded men: "One is a Lieut in the Flying Corps, his name is Findley, from Toronto, used to work in Massey-Harris. The poor kid is very young, has a bullet wound in his right arm and I am afraid it is ruined for life, and he has a very bad fracture of right leg [it was the left], in fact, it is pretty badly smashed up, and the poor kid's nerve is pretty well gone."[3] The family on Admiral Road knew nothing of this, or whether their son was even alive, until a telegraph arrived from the Massey-Harris representative in London, Mr. C. W. Dawkins, who informed them that Irving's plane had been shot down but that he had been rescued and that they were all "greatly indebted to Miss C. M. Davison for promptness in obtaining news about Irving." Presumably, Mr. Dawkins also forwarded an undated letter (also in the journal) from Miss Davison to the Findleys, with her explanation of Irving's condition and the hospital's address. In an April 16 letter to Mr. Dawkins, Irving described what had happened and praised the two

French officers who rescued him at great risk to their own lives. In the first letter that Irving wrote himself, his writing is virtually indecipherable because he was using his left hand. The date is 8 April 1918, and just the sight of her son's scrawl must have shocked Phoebe: "Dear Mother," he wrote, "this is absolutely the first day I have been able to think of anything but my wounds, so please excuse delay in writing" (LAC 332:2 np). Irving returned home in September and for the next six years he endured various treatments in the effort to save his leg. He lived with Phoebe and his siblings until he married Dorothy Candee in 1920, and after the amputation of his leg in 1924 he joined Massey-Harris to work in the export branch of the company. He was soon managing well enough financially to move his wife and children to 39 South Drive in Rosedale, where a young Tiff Findley retained vivid memories of visiting him. However, by 1932 Irving was back in hospital and nothing further could be done; he died at home at thirty-eight years of age and was buried in Mount Pleasant Cemetery.

Phoebe Margaret Findley is much harder to trace than her twin brother. As far as I can tell, she never used her first given name, Phoebe: Irving called her "the Kid," her friends called her "Finney," and Tiff called her Aunt Marg. The woman herself rarely appears in surviving documents, and in photographs she seems shy and withdrawn. But she was intelligent and earned better marks at St. Margaret's than Irving did at SAC. A few of her letters to her father have survived, but they reveal little about her interests or her personality.[4] In one, she reports that they are spending a lot of his money in London, but have not yet seen the king and queen, and she tells him that "Irving is keeping a dairy, in other words a diary." If she was also keeping a diary, she does not say so. The *Toronto Society Blue Book* for 1915 lists Margaret Findley as a "shareholder" in the Lambton Golf and Country Club, and by 1917 she owned a car. However, some health problem (unspecified in surviving letters, but possibly a stroke) indicates that by late 1917 she was at the Mayo Clinic in Rochester, Minnesota, for an operation. Something fairly serious was obviously amiss because Phoebe accompanied her daughter and the two were away for several weeks; for the rest of her life, Margaret had facial damage that affected her speech. Margaret never married, and, in later life, she lived with Phoebe on Foxbar Road and worked as an administrator with the St. George's School for Child Study (now the Dr. Eric Jackman Institute of Child Study) at the University of Toronto. She was loved and admired by her colleagues, and Tiff saw her often at the Foxbar Road house and later, when she moved to a Heath Street apartment in the same building as his mother. In his diary for December 1971, he listed his Aunt Marg as one of his friends and described her as "a unique woman ... and a great source of material. Every writer should have an Aunt Marg [who] appears in one guise or another in nearly everything I write" (LAC 86:8). However, as I note in my discussion of *The Last of the Crazy People*, when he made Aunt Marg the model for one of the novel's characters, he infuriated his father and precipitated a nasty family quarrel.

Apart from a few pictures and a marker in the Findley vault in the Mount Pleasant Mausoleum, Stuart disappeared from the family's life until Findley recreated him as young Lizzie Wyatt in *The Piano Man's Daughter*. Given the power of the scene in which this character dies on the kitchen table during a primitive operation to remove a tumour from his brain, it seems likely that Stuart's death haunted Phoebe and became one of the tales she told her children and grandchildren. Unlike Uncle Irving and Aunt Marg, Stuart's influence on Findley's work is limited to this memorable Lizzie Wyatt character. However, Phoebe's youngest son (Tiff's father), Allan, plays a critical role in this biography. Although in the surviving letters he is rarely described or even referred to by his parents or siblings, he does appear in family photographs, usually with legs apart and hands in pockets in a defiant stance, as if daring the viewer to ignore him. In a 1912 picture, taken with his family at Jackson's Point, Allan poses in the foreground drawing a bow and arrow, and in another picture he stands alone in front of the Admiral Road house, wearing a fringed cowboy shirt, holding a fully drawn bow and arrow aimed just beyond the photographer. Allan followed Irving to SAC in 1914, and, like his brother, he was weak in academic subjects but enjoyed sports and did well in the cadet corps. He excelled in hockey, and in his final year he was captain of the school's second hockey team, served on the athletics committee, and was made a prefect. He completed four upper-level years to graduate in

1922, despite failing grades in algebra, geometry, and French composition. He left SAC in June that year without the marks for university entrance, so he joined the A. E. Ames Insurance Company on Bay Street to work in stocks and bonds investment. Between 1914 and 1922, Allan Findley was sidelined by events beyond his control—the war, Irving's injuries and honours, his sister's health problems, and, most importantly, his father's death—and he bore lasting psychological scars from these years.

After Thomas Findley's death from cancer in 1921, aged just fifty-one, Massey-Harris general manager Thomas Bradshaw published an "Appreciation" in the *M-H Weekly* and stressed how "beloved" Findley had been by both the workmen on the factory shop floor and the children in the Sunday school where he had taught for many years. He had actively supported the YMCA and worked tirelessly for the Presbyterian missionary movement. In his 1909 address to the Missionary Congress of the Presbyterian Church of Canada, called "The Only Way to Reach Every Member," Findley had encouraged the four thousand gentlemen who were present to advance the missionary work of the church through door-to-door "personal canvass." As one historian put it, "the list of leaders in the Layman's Missionary Movement reads like a *Who's Who* of the financial, industrial, legal and political 'establishment' of Canada in the pre-war days" (Moir 134). Thomas Findley was on that list, and taking a personal interest in people was his hallmark. Bradshaw called him a "sympathetic employer" with "a deep and abiding interest in his employees," and in his history of the company, *Harvest Triumphant*, Merrill Denison credited him with steering the company safely through a difficult postwar period and for introducing "progressive labour policies" (229). When Timothy Findley worked briefly for Massey-Harris in the 1940s, the older workers remembered his grandfather and praised him warmly. It was Tom Findley who installed their cafeteria, Tom Findley who arranged medical care for workers and their families, and Tom Findley who inaugurated their pension plan and established fair and reasonable wages. His funeral was held at Bloor Street Presbyterian Church, which he had supported for years, and the church was full.

The family was living in south Forest Hill on Warren Road during the last years of Thomas's life, and in the *Society Blue Book* for 1920 they were listed as belonging to seven clubs, but much of this social profile and prosperity was lost after Thomas died. By 1929, Phoebe and Marg had moved to a more modest house at 27 Foxbar Road, where Phoebe lived until her death in 1953, and where Findley so vividly remembered himself as a little boy leaning over the fence to contemplate the graves in St. Michael's Cemetery (*IM* 5–6). But it was the living room at Foxbar that held the family memories he most often recalled. Every Sunday, "Goggie" (as Grandmother Findley was called) served afternoon tea in that room, surrounded by photographs of her men. Thomas was a palpable presence, of course, but so was Irving, who appeared in several photographs, most notably in a framed formal image as the young soldier. Of her four children, Allan did not figure prominently in this display because, so the story goes, he disappointed his mother; he could never measure up to her husband or her war hero son. Years later, Findley described those afternoon teas in great detail, on one occasion imitating his grandmother's prim, disapproving demeanour.[5] He, his brother, and their cousins (Irving's three daughters) were dressed in their best clothes and were expected to sit quietly while Phoebe presided, sipping tea laced with sherry and reminiscing about her beloved Tom and heroic Irving. Such performances were stressful for Allan and his sons because, as Bill recalled, they were all expected to acknowledge Irving as a saint and Tom as a legend.

In 2000 Findley published a short story in the *Globe and Mail* that suggests how Allan must have felt as a boy growing up under his mother's roof, and as such it reveals his effort to understand and sympathize with his father. It is called "We Must Prepare for a New Plague" and is set in late 1918 in the Rosedale home of Ned and Phoebe Hart, after their eldest, favourite son, Tom, has returned safely from the war. By November, however, Tom has died from the Spanish flu, and his mother has withdrawn into silence and alcohol. Although this devastating little story recalls *The Last of the Crazy People*, *The Wars*, and even *The Piano Man's Daughter*, it is neither the mother nor the war hero son who attracts a reader's attention. The Harts have a younger son called Graeme, and he is the character to notice. Graeme is a deeply troubled boy who lives on the margins of his family, overshadowed by his big brother. He has become a bully at his private school and is obsessed with "weapons ... wars ... his brother's tormented flesh [and] guns." He sees himself as a failure and is jealous of his adored brother, who he sees as having *"everything,"* while he has *"nothing. Not even wounds."* Graeme Hart is one of Timothy Findley's thinly disguised, sharply etched pictures of Allan Findley as a boy who lived in the shadow of his father and brother and who, as an adult, was never able to gain a mother's approval.

After her death, Grandmother Findley's ashes were placed in the family vault in the Mount Pleasant Mausoleum. The top marble tablet bears the inscription "Thomas Findley. Born December 16 1870. Died December 19 1921. 'Until the day break and the shadows flee away.'" Beneath his stone is "Phoebe Constance Smith. Beloved wife of Thomas Findley," and in heavy black letters inscribed beneath her marker is the name: FINDLEY. The vault also contains the sad reminder of a youngster's death: "In loving memory of Stuart Eadie Findley. Died Oct. 12 1907. Aged 11 years." Years later it received just one more Findley—Timothy Findley's baby brother— who was named for their father: "Allan G. L. Findley. Died 1932."

The Bulls and Fagans

There is a striking passage in a speech that Findley gave at Harbourfront in 1997 in which he imagined his mother's ancestors by contemplating their photographs. In the published text, *A Nation of One*, he remembers himself as a teenager studying these old photographs and being fascinated by one particular image from 1916: "In the photograph, my mother is the very same age as I am, gazing down at her. She is standing looking up at her father. Also in the photograph are her sister, her brother and mother. It is a pleasing photograph" (11). Hidden in this photograph, however, are other ancestors, other memories, and many not so pleasing family stories that Findley would not forget (and that I will return to), especially about Edith Maude Bull, his maternal grandmother, who was born a

Fagan. These Bull and Fagan ancestors come alive as characters in *The Piano Man's Daughter*, as they do through the stories he tells in essays like *A Nation of One* or in *Journeyman*. Margaret Bull Findley, his mother, believed that her father's family had descended from a Dutch Von Boel (or Buell) patriarch, a Huguenot perhaps, who fled to England in the sixteenth century to become a court musician for Elizabeth I. This story of escape, prestige, and musical talent appealed to Findley's Canadian ancestors and lingered in the margins of the Bull genealogy, adding a touch of glamour to an otherwise common English surname. Music was central to the lives of the Bull family; they sang, they played instruments, and they sold and made pianos. The story of Great-Uncle Frank is especially dramatic. He is the one who ran off with a beautiful young woman (in a horse-drawn sleigh in a snowstorm, with her father in angry pursuit), married her, and set himself up in the United States as a music teacher. As Findley told his cousin, John Bull, Frank's business cards read: "*Maestro François von Buell. Vocal Coach to the Royal Houses of Europe,*" and he described his great-uncle as "a dashing white-haired 'impressario' with walking stick and cape" and his aunt, who was always dressed in "flowing chiffon," as "one of the most beautiful women I've ever met."[6]

Current Bull family members trace their line back to a Reverend Abraham Bull, who was born in England in 1760.[7] This man emigrated, with his wife and children, around the turn of the century, and one of his sons, John Gurnsey Bull, appears in the 1851 census as born in Mountain, Dundas County, Ontario. John G. Bull was a minister with the Methodist Episcopal Church of Canada, and he and his wife, Rachel Napp Bull, were Tiff's great-great-grandparents. They lived and worked in towns east of Toronto, where the Rev. Bull served as a circuit minister in 1847, a deacon by 1849, and an elder by 1850, until he retired in 1868 to become a dentist in Newburgh, twenty-five miles northwest of Kingston. He died on 28 October 1877 at the age of sixty-three, leaving his wife and eight children, one of whom was Henry Bull, Findley's great-grandfather. The Bull family story becomes more interesting and certainly more relevant and useful to Timothy Findley with his musical great-grandfather Henry Bull. A Methodist like his father, he married Emily Augusta Vader, also a Methodist, and the couple had at least nine children. Of the seven who reached adulthood, there were two daughters, Bertha and Grace, and five sons: Frederick, Claude, Henry, Clarence, and Frank. Henry Bull Sr. turned his hand to several occupations. At one point, he was a farmer; at another he was a merchant living in Brighton, Ontario, and he owned medical patents that he purchased in Belleville in the 1890s. But most importantly, Henry Bull was a "Dealer in Pianos and Organs." By the time Henry died in 1913, he was a successful businessman with a home in Belleville and a summer cottage in Brighton, and his musical, entrepreneurial spirit lived on in his sons.

The eldest of these sons, Findley's grandfather Frederick Bull, followed his father into the piano business. He began by selling pianos for his father before joining the Nordheimer Piano Company in Toronto in the late 1880s or early 1890s, but to sell pianos Frederick had to travel, with sample instruments, on a circuit of southern Ontario towns. At that time, pianos were a status symbol testifying to a family's social success and cultural refinement; they were also important in schools, hotels, and church halls. On one sales trip, Frederick Bull visited the town of Collingwood to play a Nordheimer piano, take orders from local families, and fall in love with an Irish-Canadian beauty called Edith Maude Fagan. In the 1996 letter to his cousin John Bull, Findley described his grandparents' meeting as love at first sight. "Salesmen would travel by train in the 1880s," he explained, and

> sometimes they gave demonstrations that were quite entertaining— either playing themselves, as Fred did, or hiring a local pianist. Fred, who was extremely handsome in his youth, met Edith Maude Fagan at a party in Collingwood, where her father was a fairly prominent merchant. [...] When the salesmen came to town, [...] they set up their wares in special show rooms in local hotels and the whole town turned out to see them. In the evenings, parties were given, with food, music, and dancing. E.M.F. caught Fred's eye and he pursued her hotly.

As he went on to say, "all this is set out in *The Piano Man's Daughter*."

Frederick and Maude (her preferred name) married in 1890 and settled down in a house at 82 Sorauren Avenue in the Parkdale area of

Toronto. Their first surviving child was Emily Ruth, born on 12 May 1893. A son, Alan Talbot, arrived on 31 March 1899, and Margaret Maude (Findley's mother) was born on 21 August 1902. Fred Bull was ambitious as well as talented, and by the turn of the century he had left Nordheimer's to become sales manager for the Mason & Risch Piano Company. From that position he changed companies once more to join the larger, more prestigious Williams Piano Company, which had its family-operated base in Toronto, with a factory in Oshawa.[8] The Bulls moved to Simcoe Street North, in Oshawa, and Frederick advanced quickly with the company to become president and then owner of the factory in 1907. Two of his brothers, Henry P. and glamorous Frank W., joined the company during the war, and Frank invented a device called the "Master-Touch" for the player piano, the hottest new item on the musical instrument market during the war. But the parlour piano, like the horse and buggy, was on the way out, and by the 1920s phonographs, talking records, talking movies, and radios were rapidly changing the way the average person lived. Nevertheless, for about three decades, Findley's grandfather Frederick Bull and his uncle Frank Bull were at the helm of an important Canadian business, just as his Findley grandfather had been central to another major Canadian manufacturing industry.

The year 1918 was not a good one for Frederick and Maude Bull, however. The war was over, but the Spanish flu epidemic had arrived to decimate populations across Europe and North America. One of the casualties was the couple's only son. Alan Talbot Bull is a minor player in this biography, but the impact of his death on his parents and, through them, on his surviving sisters and on Findley was significant. Alan had tried to enlist before the legal age, but was sent instead to Trinity College School, an Anglican private school for boys in Port Hope, from 1914 to 1917, and after graduation he entered the University of Toronto. Alan escaped the war but he caught the flu and died of pneumonia, after several agonizing days in a primitive iron lung, with his parents and sisters listening in horror for the sound of the machine, which helped the young man to breathe, to fall silent. This is just one of the family's tragedies, and it is vividly remembered in Findley's story "We Must Prepare for a New Plague."

There are many branches of the Irish Fagans in Canada, but the Fagan line that led to Edith Maude Fagan Bull and to Timothy Findley is descended from a Nicholas Fagan, who was born just north of Dublin in County Meath, Ireland, and married Elizabeth Cusac Ryan from the same county. This couple, Findley's great-great-grandparents, immigrated to New York City before moving to Upper Canada in 1857. They settled in Prince Edward County with three children: James Talbot, Victoria Elizabeth, and Nicholas Jr., who died in his twenties from tuberculosis. The Fagans were Roman Catholic, and Nicholas Sr. taught school in Prince Edward County for thirteen years before moving to Collingwood, where the family had relocated by 1872. Their son, James Talbot Fagan, Maude's father and Findley's great-grandfather, stayed in Collingwood until the 1920s and became a successful merchant there. He and his wife, Margaret Ann Mouck, had two surviving children—Maude and her younger brother John, who worked on the lake boats—but as Findley explained in his 19 February 1996 letter to his cousin John Bull, John James Fagan drowned in a boat accident at the age of twenty. Edith Maude, always called Maude, is the grandmother in the 1916 family photograph that Findley described in *A Nation of One*, the mother of Tiff's mother and of Tiff's Aunt Ruth. Of all his relatives, apart from his immediate family, this aunt is the one who must be carefully situated in his biography because she haunted Findley, and, as I will explain, she inspired the character of Lily in *The Piano Man's Daughter*.

To all intents and purposes, Findley's Aunt Ruth has been erased from the public record, and my search for her has taken me to archives, early twentieth-century newspapers, and her family's memories. Under "C" in volume 1 of *Who Was Who among North American Authors, 1921–1939*, there is an entry for "Carlyle, Emily Ruth Bull: poet," and this woman is Findley's aunt. All the basic facts are there: Emily Ruth Bull, born in Toronto on 12 May 1893, the daughter of Frederick and Edith Maude (Fagan) Bull. Educated at Bishop Bethune College in Oshawa, a private Anglican school for girls, and then at Havergal College in Toronto. Married David Brainerd Carlyle on 5 May 1920 and is "the mother of triplet sons and one daughter, all living and healthy." Address: 309 Golf Street, Oshawa, Ontario,

Canada. She was a "writer of poems. Contributor to Toronto *Globe* (Mail and Editorial Page, 1915–), *Oshawa Reformer*," and her writing is described as "General character writing, imaginative." There is more to say, however, about Aunt Ruth's life and about the stories behind that Bull family photograph from 1916 that captivated the adult writer Timothy Findley. As his eyes shift from his young mother to her older sister, he explains how, "looking down at them, I rehearse their fates. The parents divorced. The brother and the father tragically dead. The sister in an institution. *Mad*. Their word for it, not mine" (*J* 77). Findley never described Ruth as mad because to him she was an enchanting storyteller, an almost mythic presence. His childhood encounters with her were "magical." However, at some point in her early forties, between 1934 and 1936, Ruth was institutionalized and banned from further contact with him, or, to put it another way, he was removed from her disturbing and unhealthy influence. She was later diagnosed as schizophrenic.

Findley saw things differently. In an essay included in *Journeyman* (89–95), he remembered his "tall, somnambulistic, reticent—and beautiful" aunt:

> When I was a child, my aunt was still in the world-at-large, and I adored her. I was in awe of her. Her stories, her explanations of the world that children inhabit and her versions of reality were mesmerizing. [...] She was, I am certain, a shaman, a medium, a mystic.
>
> She was also damaged, betrayed, abandoned, and, in some ways, destructive. As the disease increased its hold on my aunt, it drove her to fight back in sometimes alarming ways: disappearances, violent gestures, silences. But I loved her. So did her children, so did her mother—and so did my mother, her sister. (*J* 91)

Today we know that schizophrenia usually manifests itself in a person's late teens or twenties, and perhaps Ruth did show early signs of being different, of seeing things differently from other people. Certainly Findley looked for such signs in trying to understand what happened to her. In another passage from *Journeyman* (85–87), he analyzes several photographs of his aunt in the effort to understand—to *find*—her: as a baby, she is "serious" and questioning; as a thirteen-year-old girl, she sits for her picture with "an almost alarming poise." He sees that she is a beautiful girl, but he believes that she is hiding behind a mask because she has been lied to by her parents, her teachers, and society. In a 1917 picture, he thinks that her "mask is slipping," and that "her mind wants out." Ruth is now twenty-four: the Great War is still raging; the man she will marry is away fighting; and for days she listens, with dread, as her brother Alan gasps for breath in the iron lung and finally dies. In a 1919 picture, the mask "is finally back in place," but in Findley's reading of the woman in these photographs, Ruth has found an outlet for her mind and imagination; she has found a voice and a name. "'I am Nicholas Fagan,' the woman's mind said and [so Findley imagined] the hand wrote. 'I have waited long enough for what I have known and what I have seen to be matched by what I have been told'" (*J* 87).

My search for Ruth involved trips to several archives, hours spent scanning old newspaper microfilm, listening many times to a 1993 taped conversation (made and given to me by Bill Whitehead) that Findley had with his cousin Isobelle, Ruth's daughter, and reading a selection of her poems lent to me by her granddaughter.[9] Bishop Bethune College, where she was sent after her parents moved to Oshawa, was an Anglican boarding and day school for girls, run by nuns from the Toronto Community Convent for the Sisterhood of St. John the Divine. Classes were small, discipline was strict, and the food served was "plain." Although they received a general education, the aim of the school was "to fit its pupils to carry out with credit the manifold family and social duties which are expected of every Canadian girl of good position." Pupils were warned that they "must conscientiously endeavor to conform ... and they must live the life of the school."[10] Must. This message was uncompromising, and it meant *behave, follow the rules—or else*. According to Olive French, an Oshawa pianist and teacher, "students were not allowed to talk during breakfast" and, when the girls protested this oppressive rule, the bishop of the day rejected their request, saying, "I think it is a very good thing, you know, my dear girls, that women should be taught to hold their tongues sometimes."

In 1907 Ruth entered Havergal, where life was regimented, to be sure, but where the opportunities for growth were much richer and she received a good education in privileged surroundings. A liberal arts education, with an emphasis on music and performing arts, was the core curriculum. The school motto was (and still is) *Vitai Lampada Tradens*—passing on the torch of life—and Findley gave a similar motto to Lily in *The Piano Man's Daughter*. Among the earliest Havergal alumnae of distinction was Dora Mavor Moore, a pioneer in Canadian theatre and the mother of Mavor Moore. Later the school would add great actors like Kate Reid and Margot Kidder and distinguished novelist Jane Urquhart to their list of notable graduates. Excellence in the arts has indeed been passed on through the generations at Havergal, but Ruth Bull was not destined for a career as a writer. Instead, she sent several of her poems to the *Mail and Empire* between 1914 and 1917, signed them "Nicholas Fagan," and, with the exception of that entry in volume 1 of *Who Was Who among North American Authors*, disappeared from public view. The greatest concentration of her published verse was in 1917, when a poem appeared at the bottom of the editorial page of the *Mail and Empire* on average twice a month, and some of these poems refer to the Great War. None of them is remarkable as poetry; they all suffer from the use of clichés, archaic rhetoric, and sentimentality. However, in her taped conversation with Tiff, cousin Isobelle told him that her mother had never stopped writing, and this revelation disturbed and intrigued him. He wanted to know when and why she had ceased trying to publish her work, but above all, he wanted to understand her choice of *nom de plume*: Nicholas Fagan, the name of her great-grandfather and of his son, Nicholas Jr. Isobelle did not have the answers, which left him to imagine his way toward them.

Ruth Bull married David Brainerd Carlyle on 5 May 1920 and her children arrived in rapid succession—a daughter (Isobelle Ruth) on 18 February 1921 and triplet sons (Alan Talbot—in memory of her dead brother—William Mackay, and David Brainerd) on 26 July 1923. The birth of her triplets coincided with a serious blow to the family that had a lasting impact on Findley's mother, Margaret, and on Ruth. In 1925–26, their father, Frederick Bull, confessed to having an affair with a younger woman, who was about the age of his own daughter Margaret. He demanded a divorce because the other woman was pregnant and he wanted to make the child legitimate. Maude was devastated but, despite the contemporary stigma attached to divorce and the difficulty in securing one, she agreed to his demand and presented a petition for divorce to the Senate in Ottawa in December 1926. Her petition was granted in March 1927, and Frederick remarried that June.[11] By 1930 he was living in Whitby with his second wife, Amy Maude (Peggy) Douse (later Peggy Fortune), and they had two children before Frederick died on 2 May 1937 after a painful struggle with cancer. The years from 1918, when the Bulls' only son, Alan, died in the Spanish flu epidemic, through the mid-1920s and the wrenching breakup of the Bull family, with the cruel gossip that followed in small-town upper-middle-class Oshawa circles, and the collapse of the piano industry, were extremely traumatic. As we shall see, Findley's mother carried deep scars from those years, and Ruth's eventual breakdown may have been precipitated by this sequence of family tragedies.

The family's collection of Ruth's poems is dedicated to Ruth's daughter Isobelle, one of her sons, Alan Talbot Carlyle, and Timothy Findley, and he kept a photocopy of these poems with his notebooks for *The Piano Man's Daughter*. Some of them, when read retrospectively, do raise questions—not about her mental state but about her sharp observations of the distinctly biased world around her and the restrictive, gendered conduct expected of women. For example, in a dramatic monologue called "Parmesian Violets," a poem clearly inspired by Robert Browning's "My Last Duchess," a jealous husband drowns his wife "by pressing her face in a glass bowl of water," and then exclaims: "God! But her maddening body / Which ne'er was mine in Life / Now lies as quiet in my arms / As the most docile wife" (TS 33). Scenes of such violence, however, are not a dominant feature of Ruth's surviving poems. A subject that does recur in both the published and chapbook poems is the war. Two poems from the chapbook are particularly representative of patriotic Canadian verses from the period, when patriotism meant loyalty to the mother country as much as to Canada. In "The Call," we are told that a "voice came out of England, and it said / 'Arise my sons … / kill off'" the Germans, who boast of their

"Kultur" but "Desecrate churches, and fling Louvain low!" In "The Answer," the sons predictably reply: "Mother we come [...] Marching, fighting, shouting, 'ENGLAND, and the RIGHT'" (TS 25–26). In "The Year 1915," published on 1 February 1917 in the *Mail and Empire* and signed "Nicholas Fagan," she wrote a neatly rhymed and balanced verse lamenting the heavy losses in France and concluding with the thought that "Lilies for the Dead" sums up the meaning of the year. In her conversation with Tiff, Isobelle remembers her mother as a suffragette and an active member of Toronto's Junior League, but Emily Ruth Carlyle only emerges briefly within her poetry and never directly or completely. The speaking voices in the poems are derivative and conventional, and the person of the poet is doubly absent—occluded by borrowed techniques and by the signature of a man.

Ruth's husband, David Brainerd Carlyle (1895–1992), was born in Toronto, lived in the Rosedale area on Mount Pleasant Road, and attended St. Andrew's College from 1908 to 1912. He entered the University of Toronto to study medicine, but the war interrupted his plans, and like many young men, he joined the Canadian Officers Training Corps at university and enlisted in 1915; by November he had left for overseas. After his demobilization, he settled down in Oshawa to work with Frederick Bull at the Williams Piano factory, and he went on to become president of the Canadian Piano Manufacturers' Association. When the Williams factory closed operations for good in 1932, the Carlyles lost almost everything. Brainerd, who was vice-president by this time, was suddenly unemployed, and the family had to sell their elegant home, with the grand piano that Frederick Bull had given to his daughter. They moved to Belleville, where Brainerd had found work, and it was at this time, Isobelle told Tiff, that she recalled noticing a definite change in her mother. Ruth, who had spent most days in her Oshawa home writing and playing the piano (Beethoven and Chopin were favourites), who entertained, read regularly to her children, and listened to the Saturday opera on a crystal set with her daughter, was now comparatively poor and with few friends. Brainerd, never a compassionate or kind husband, was resentful and unhappy; within a year he lost the Belleville job and moved his family to Toronto to live with his mother. As Isobelle told Tiff, when Ruth attempted to talk to her husband about her life, their marriage, or the family's affairs, Brainerd would silence her, and he would not permit the children to speak at the dinner table, except on Sundays, when French only was allowed. Shortly after the move to Toronto in 1934, Ruth walked out. With her father's help, she moved into a Toronto boarding house to continue her writing, make her regular visits to the library, and maintain her connection with her children, especially Isobelle and Alan.

The crisis came after Brainerd moved once more, this time into a dark house on Moore Avenue, north of St. Clair, on the southern boundary of Mount Pleasant Cemetery, and Ruth rejoined her family. In her conversation with Tiff, Isobelle wondered if an early onset of menopause might have contributed to her mother's health problems, and she also told him that there had been another pregnancy that miscarried. Whatever factors contributed to Ruth's state of mind in the mid-1930s, she was desperately unhappy. One day, feeling apprehensive, Isobelle rushed home from school to find, as she told Findley, that her mother had attempted suicide by swallowing a distemper medicine for cats. In what could only have been a thoroughly terrifying scene, Isobelle found Ruth gagging and foaming at the mouth. With great presence of mind, she helped her mother before calling the family doctor and her father, and Ruth was saved. However, Brainerd decided to have his wife committed, and she was taken away in a straitjacket, protesting against his decision, with her children looking on. Necessary or not, such a drastic step was one her daughter never forgot; Isobelle believed that her father had bullied his wife into believing she was unbalanced. Following the suicide attempt, Ruth was taken to the Queen Street Mental Hospital, and after a period of incarceration there, she was sent to the asylum in Whitby.[12] "Sometimes, though rarely," Findley tells us in *Journeyman*, "I was taken to see her in the asylum. Green lawns, trees, and park benches—buildings that had been created as army barracks. Gates—walls—many people wearing white. These are seminal images for me of those visits. And of my aunt: tall, somnambulistic, reticent—and beautiful" (91). Aspects of these appalling events and asylum scenes stayed with him to surface frequently in his writing and to be fully recreated in *The Piano Man's Daughter.*

By the 1950s Whitby's patients began to be released into community settings for assisted care. Eventually it was determined that Emily Ruth (Bull) Carlyle belonged in this category of patient, and she lived in two such facilities in Toronto. This relative freedom enabled her to resume her writing and make daily trips to the library. In 1972 her name appeared on the resident voters' list for the halfway home called Hilltop Acres at 1088 Davenport Road in Toronto. On 5 September 1984, a brief notice of her death appeared in the *Globe and Mail*, and a private family service was held. Brainerd Carlyle is not mentioned in this notice because he had not been part of Ruth's life for many years; he had obtained a divorce and remarried. Ruth was buried beside her father and brother in Oshawa's Union Cemetery. Ruth Bull (a.k.a. Nicholas Fagan) was dead and gone. Until, that is, the man who remembered her voice, her face, and her stories decided that "Nicholas Fagan wasn't going to die without having said a few words aloud, beyond the secrecy of her notebooks and letters" (*J* 88). And if you examine the endpapers of *The Piano Man's Daughter* carefully, you will also find her there, in the lower left-hand corner, smiling, between her father and younger sister (ill. 8).

That sister, Margaret Maude Bull, was born into the Bull family just when her father's success and the family's position were on the rise and the move to Oshawa guaranteed their prosperity and status. Margie (as she was called by her husband and friends) also attended Bishop Bethune School and went on to Havergal, from which she graduated in 1922. She grew up surrounded by material comfort, the sounds of piano music and song, the warmth of a loving, storytelling mother, and the affection of her older siblings. For her first sixteen years, her world was privileged and secure. There seems to have been no sign that the First World War intruded on her world until her brother Alan's death from the flu in 1918, but after that she experienced shocks that would scar her for life. Chief among these was the breakup of her parents' marriage and the revelation of her father's betrayal. Before she died, Margaret told Tiff how she had learned about her father's infidelity and, more troubling still, she described the circumstances and implications of his affair—at least as she perceived them to be and as they haunted her. Apparently, Frederick had introduced her to his pregnant lover before the divorce and had done it without explaining whom it was that he was taking her to meet. Margaret was stunned. But worse still, she saw that this other woman was not much older than herself, and she suspected that her father may have been sexually attracted to her—his own daughter; in fact, Margaret told Tiff that, as a teenaged girl, she had felt uneasy in her father's company and with the way he looked at her. What, if anything, occurred in the Bull family home prior to Frederick's departure and divorce from Maude, is now impossible to know. In 1988 Findley published "Almeyer's Mother," one of his most biographical stories, about his grandfather Bull's behaviour and his mother's reaction. The clear implication in the story is that the mother character felt so sexually threatened by her father that she tried to excise him from her life.

Findley's grandmother, Edith Maude Fagan Bull, made a lasting impression on her grandson because she spent considerable time with his family and entertained them with her Irish gift for storytelling. Although he was raised in a Protestant home and environment, his Irish Roman Catholic granny gave him her crucifix, which he carried with him all his life. During his acting years in England and the many tours he had to take with a production, he would try to make his actor's shabby digs more like a home by setting out his few personal treasures—family photographs, books, some postcards—and this crucifix. In 1996, Findley wrote that this "crucifix was the last surviving remnant of my grandmother's Irish Catholicism, and it still sits beside my bed, protecting me" (*J* 240). On one of the last occasions that he saw and spoke with her, she was in Toronto General Hospital with a broken hip. He was sure she was dying because she was very confused and clutched his hand, repeating that "they took something lovely away from Maudie" (*J* 74). As it turned out, Maude lived for another fifteen months and died on 16 August 1963, aged ninety-four. Her remains were cremated in a private service at St. James Crematorium on August 19 and her headstone is in Mount Pleasant Cemetery.

In his journal, Findley described his last hospital visit with his grandmother and wrote that he would "never forget" it, and then he repeated her words: "'I went in somewhere and they took something lovely away from Maudie and I don't know what I am going to do'" (*J* 75). But Findley did. He transformed Granny Bull, along with other ancestors, into fiction because "fiction is not an extension ...[but] a distillation of reality" (*J* 209). "Fiction articulates," he insisted, "by telling us stories, it keeps our imagination alive and functioning" (*J* 209). "*Fiction never bears false witness*" (*J* 76). By living with his dead, by preserving and contemplating their photographs, by listening carefully to their words and remembering their stories, Timothy Findley amassed a writer's archive of knowledge about life and death, passion and human frailty, about war, betrayal, and human endurance. To the extent that we are what we keep, then Timothy Findley is to be found in these personal treasures, that crucifix, his photographs of his ancestors, and his indelible memories of past events, of scenes caught in a shaft of sunlight, of faces, voices, images, and stories.

CHAPTER THREE

Going up to Rosedale

———

WEEKENDS, OUR PARENTS USED TO TAKE US WALKING UNDER

THE TREES ON CRESCENT ROAD. THIS WAS ON THE ROSEDALE SIDE

OF YONGE STREET [WHERE] THE HOUSES SAT UP NEAT AS PINS

BEYOND THEIR LAWNS, [...] HAVENS OF WEALTH AND

ALL THE MYSTERIES OF WEALTH.

(Timothy Findley, *Stones* 220)

Rosedale

*A*ccording to the family story, Findley's parents met at a Rosedale party. Allan was playing the piano and Margaret sat down beside him on the bench; they sang together, fell in love, and married. But theirs was not an easy, or especially happy, story, and the strains in the marriage, coupled with the psychological baggage carried by both parents, made a significant impact on their sons. Allan Findley lived all his life in the shadow of his beloved, successful father and war hero brother. Margaret Bull reached adulthood knowing that husbands betray and leave their wives and that there was a strain of mental instability in her family. Moreover, by the time Allan and Margaret met in 1928 both families had lost their financial security, and the 1929 stock market crash followed by the Great Depression meant that they began married life and started a family during difficult economic times.

Judging from photographs, Allan Findley was handsome. He was tall and well built—six feet in height and about 170 pounds—with blue eyes, wavy hair, and a neat moustache. But he was unpredictable—he could be charming and entertaining or moody and violent. On the one hand, he recited poetry for his sons and read them stories; on the other, he was usually shrouded in cigarette smoke, tipsy or drunk, and often aggressive. By the mid-1930s, he was becoming an alcoholic and a bully who lashed out at his wife and children one moment and sang sentimental songs or recited Tennyson the next. Margaret Findley was as strong and stable as her husband was weak and unpredictable. After graduating from Havergal, she did not enter university, hold a job, or pursue a profession, but she circulated in the same social milieu as the Findleys and the Carlyles, and she retained close friendships with Oshawa friends like the painter Isabel McLaughlin (1903–2002) from the wealthy Oshawa McLaughlin family. Parties and family gatherings were an important part of her upper-middle-class life before and after her marriage. It would be a mistake, however, to dismiss Margaret as a flighty socialite. She was an intelligent, courageous, outspoken woman, devoted to her family and with an active interest in music and literature.

At the time of her wedding in St. Paul's Anglican Church on Bloor Street East on 6 June 1928, Margaret was an attractive twenty-five-year-old woman. Ruth was her matron of honour, and Brainerd Carlyle gave the bride away. Fred Bull was seen at the back of the church during the service, but he was not invited to the reception for 250 guests, which was held on the lawns of an elegant Georgian mansion, called "Iverholme," at 74 St. George Street. Maude Bull lived at Iverholme, a private boarding house for ladies (recreated in *The Piano Man's Daughter*), during this period after the divorce, and Margaret was staying with her. No expense was spared on this wedding. Maude wanted her daughter to be married in a style befitting her social class and upbringing, even though that style was now rented and her father was *persona non grata*. After their honeymoon, the couple moved into a rented house on Meredith Crescent in Rosedale, the first of at least eight houses they rented or owned over the next fifty years. Living in, or on the edge of, Rosedale, having a maid, mixing with the right people, attending the right schools and churches, and dressing well soon became Margaret's chief concerns. As the years passed and her husband failed to provide well, Findley recalled that maintaining appearances meant buying clothes from "the Junior League secondhand shop" and hoping the neighbours believed they came from the upscale Ely's shop (qtd. in McIvor, 81). To make matters worse, they were frequently obliged to move in with relatives, and Findley never forgot the unhappiness and sense of insecurity he felt because of his mother's pretense and the lack of a stable home. As he told Jack McIvor, when the family moved from their Glenrose Avenue house, "a lot of things didn't come with us" (81).

Margaret and Allan Findley had three sons in rapid succession, all born while they were living in the house, which the Findleys had purchased, at 91 Glenrose Avenue. Thomas Michael arrived on 14 April 1929; Timothy Irving Frederick on 30 October 1930; and Allan Gilmour Lyon on 22 January 1932. The eldest son, who was named for his paternal grandfather, was always called Michael. Findley received his uncle's name, Irving, but he was always called Tiff in remembrance of Uncle Tif. The third boy was named for his own father. This passing on of family names celebrated the paternal line, with its promise of blessings and pride, but the boys' futures would prove complicated and, in the case of two of them, tragic. Michael Findley, who died in November 1994, aged 65, became a self-destructive alcoholic who was violent when drunk, self-absorbed, possibly schizophrenic, and never able to hold a job. An aggressive "boy's boy," in many ways like his father, he was the son Allan favoured, at least until Tiff became famous. Michael nursed a deep resentment over the loss of the family's status and wealth that, he believed, should have come to him as the eldest son. As Findley told Ann-Marie MacDonald in a 1999 interview, Michael spurned him if he tried to tag along and when they did play games together as children, Michael had to win: "that was our *relationship*." Although Findley insisted that he had always loved his brother, he also knew—and said so—that Michael "was not a nice man." The third son brought a different kind of grief, especially for Margaret. Allan lived for just four weeks before dying in hospital and leaving Margaret terrified of losing her children—with good reason. Timothy was a delicate baby. At about sixteen months, in late February or early March 1932 and close upon the death of baby Allan, Timothy fell ill with pneumonia. He was hospitalized in Toronto's Hospital for Sick Children, and his parents were told he would not live. The story Findley often told about his first brush with death cast Margaret as the hero because she insisted on taking him home. If he was going to die, she said, he was not going to die in a hospital the way Allan had; he would die or survive at home. And so she carried him home, bundled him up warmly in his pram, and put him out on the back porch in the fresh air and sunshine.

The family's problems, however, were only beginning. As the Depression took hold, Allan Findley's career with the Ames Insurance Company floundered. They had to sell their Glenrose house and rent a house on Delisle Avenue, just north of St. Clair Avenue West and well beyond the borders of Rosedale. The year 1933 was a bad one for the Findleys: Allan's war hero brother, Irving, died in August; Tiff went back to Sick Kids, this time with a double mastoid infection that nearly killed him, and his parents' marriage was in serious trouble: as Allan sank further into alcohol and depression, he started seeing other women, and thus began a pattern that would worsen over the years ahead. The family was obliged to move in with Grandmother Findley on Foxbar Road, which returned them a few blocks nearer to Rosedale but also placed Allan under the critical gaze of his mother. At some point between 1932, with the loss of the Glenrose house, and 1937, when they moved into a rented house on Crescent Road, Margaret packed her bags and left the boys in her mother's care because she could no longer tolerate her husband's drinking and violent outbursts. However, after a few hours she caught her breath and returned to her children and the task of keeping her marriage together. Many factors influenced Margaret's decision to stay in the marriage, a decision she made again during the war years. There were appearances to maintain, family reputation and pride to protect, and dependent children to raise. It was bad enough that her parents' marriage had failed, and by the early 1930s it was increasingly clear that the Carlyle marriage was in trouble and that

Ruth was unwell. In any case, where could she go? She had little or no money of her own, two small children, and no employable skills, but she did have strength, courage, religious conviction, and determination. She loved her husband and resolved to keep her family together despite the emotional and psychological cost. When the family moved to 27 Crescent Road in 1937, she believed they had finally found a home. What I have found no hint of, however, is that Allan Findley sought help for his drinking problem, either at this point in the 1930s or later. It would be Margaret who looked for answers.

If one relies on a few emphatic comments about his childhood that Findley made later in life, it would be easy to conclude that he suffered one ghastly experience after another. True, he was often seriously ill and missed a lot of school; he was often lonely and lived in his own very private world. Yes, Michael thought he was a sissy nuisance. Yes, his father often ignored him. And listening to church sermons frightened him. Most important is the fact that, even as a child, he deeply resented living in other peoples' houses and not having a secure place of his own. In high school, at Jarvis Collegiate, he quickly realized that, as a gay teenager with artistic interests, he didn't fit in, and he was desperate to leave the school. He described his childhood and early youth as an "unmitigated hell" (E. Cameron, 1985, 27), and in the journals from his adult years, he often recorded feeling a degree of condemnation and hostility towards his father that amounted to hatred. Although Allan Findley was physically and emotionally abusive with his wife and with Michael, for reasons Findley did not understand his father never struck him when he was a child, and he was never physically afraid of the man. Years later, however, he told Marian Engel that in his late teens he did come to blows with both his father and his brother (TF to ME, 5 April 1978, Engel fonds B36 F25).

Findley's deep resentment of his father came, as we shall see, partly from Allan's treatment of Margaret, but even more from Allan's open hostility to Tiff's homosexuality, which amounted to rejecting his son's full identity. When Tiff told his mother that he was gay in 1944, she accepted the news, despite her concern for appearances and her desire for grandchildren. When he told his father, shortly after he returned home from military service in 1945, Allan was appalled. Such an admission was a disgrace and a blow to male Findley honour. To add to Tiff's pain, brother Michael was derisive. Timothy Findley's coming out to his parents was a remarkably brave thing for a fourteen-year-old boy to do at a time when homosexuality was a social disgrace and a crime. Such an admission confirms that he was determined to be recognized and, hopefully, accepted for who he understood himself to be. Here was a boy who took an enormous risk, trusting that he would not be rejected by those he loved; his father's reaction, therefore, must have been an indescribable blow.

Nevertheless, Timothy Findley was not a David Copperfield. He was loved by both parents, even though Allan caused him acute distress. Margaret doted on him and was immensely proud of his accomplishments—as Allan eventually came to be. In his extended family, he had two loving grandmothers who were active presences in his young life. Granny Bull adored him, a feeling he returned. Her stories and songs provided some of his happiest memories, which would last a lifetime and find their way into his writing. "Goggie" (Grandmother Findley) was more aloof and more critical. Michael was her favourite grandson, but she was always kindly and affectionate, and Tiff loved her from a distance. On days when the family visited her on Foxbar Road and she had withdrawn to her bedroom, he would go upstairs to see her and she would ask her "Tiffy dear" to retrieve the bottle of sherry from her dresser and refill her cup. (No doubt a good deal of decorous tippling went on behind Rosedale's lace curtains, as did more serious drinking, but Phoebe's fondness for sherry does make me wonder if problems with alcohol ran in this seemingly stern Presbyterian family.) Moreover, Findley was not always alone. He had cousins to play with, especially on summer trips to the cottage at Shanty Bay on Lake Simcoe, and a few good friends at Rosedale Public School. One boyhood pal, Dick Cousland, joined him in exploring the Rosedale Ravine or riding horses from the Whitewood Stables in the Don Valley. Dick remembers that he and his sister, with Tiff and two other girls, formed a sort of kids' riding club that would hang out around the stables. They loved the horses, the ravines and valley, and the freedom. At other times, the two boys would head off to Britnell's bookstore near the corner of Yonge and Bloor to browse through Arthur Ransome's *Swallows and Amazons*, and they had fun with a joint writing venture in which they wrote alternate chapters of a book. Another friend from Rosedale Public School was Greg Leishman, and Tiff, Dick, and Greg spent a few weeks together in the summers of 1945 and 1946 at Camp Kagawong on Balsam Lake in the Kawartha Lakes district north of Toronto.[1]

In the summer of 1944, Findley spent much of June on a farm, owned by the Kett family, near Washago at Severn Bridge, south of Gravenhurst, and he kept a detailed account of his time there in a school scribbler, which is the earliest surviving example of his interest in writing.[2] He wrote down his thoughts, his experiences, and even scraps of dialogue, and his descriptions of nature are lovingly observed; his lists—a method of record keeping he would retain throughout his life—include not only every item of clothing he had packed but also his drawing and painting materials. The scribbler contains several of his sketches of the fields, woods, and wildlife and some attempts at portraits. The most interesting features of this early example of his writing, however, are his capacity to observe things around him and his attraction to narrative. Findley at fourteen did not simply record facts; he looked closely and then told a story. Above all, he was happy. Helping to herd the cows was exciting for a city boy, and there was a piano he could play: "I've simply loved it here," he noted (LAC 82:1).

Findley's appreciation for nature extended to a love of animals. His family always had dogs and as a boy he turned to these creatures for affection and companionship. Horses were another source of pleasure. Those rides in the Rosedale ravines and the Don Valley, for which he saved his allowance (fifty cents for an hour's ride), allowed him to connect with the peace and beauty of the natural world, and in the 1930s and early '40s, that world lay just beyond the Crescent Road garden. He was fascinated by the ants in the garden, as is young Lily in *The Piano Man's Daughter*, and he kept a pet rabbit in a hutch there, occasionally letting it out to run around. He would never forget the day an older boy, one of Michael's friends, came to see the rabbit and thrust a curtain rod through the bars, killing the creature (Meyer and O'Riordan, 51). Findley, who saw many animals as his "significant others," was devastated by this senseless act, and rabbits would become symbols of innocence and vulnerability in his fiction. Nevertheless, the rented house at 27 Crescent Road was the closest thing to a permanent home that Findley would have until he and Bill settled into Stone Orchard nearly thirty years later. He remembered it as having "almost everything a child could want: a garden to play in, a wall at the back, over which you climbed to enter a deep ravine that was like a park. The rooms in the house had leaded windows, plastered ceilings with ornate medallions, fireplaces, window seats, and one of the rooms even had a skylight" ("My Mother, My Friend" 47). It also had shelves full of books and a piano. "Reading and being read to were everyday events," he recalled, and music was part of the air he breathed ("Significant Others" 153). His parents subscribed to magazines like the *Saturday Evening Post* and *Esquire*, which published the work of important contemporary American writers, and he eyed with interest the shelves beyond his reach with rows of serious adult fiction that he would discover years later: Thomas Wolfe, Sherwood Anderson, Thomas Hardy, Sinclair Lewis, H. G. Wells, Virginia Woolf, Thomas Mann, Stefan Zweig, and Katherine Mansfield. There were also books by the Canadian authors—Charles G. D. Roberts, Ernest Thompson Seton, Morley Callaghan, and Mazo de la Roche. Seton and Roberts made a lasting impression. He remembered listening to Roberts, who lived in Toronto at this time and was his parents' guest, "roaring in the living room after [he] had gone to bed," declaiming his poetry. On Saturday afternoons before the war, Allan would take Michael and Tiff into the Rosedale Ravine and along the Don Valley to read Seton's animal stories and introduce the boys to the landscape and habitat of Raggylug, the rabbit, Silverspot, the crow, and Redruff, the partridge: "Seton's animals, then, and Ernest Thompson Seton himself, became the first of my Canadian 'others'" ("Significant Others" 153). When he read to himself, he would "hide" in these books "and pull the characters away from their reality and out into mine." Among those early favourites were *The Tale of Peter Rabbit, The Wind in the Willows, Alice in Wonderland, National Velvet, Kidnapped,* and *Huckleberry Finn.* This reading enabled him to populate his world with imaginary companions and to survive during periods of illness and loneliness. When Enid Bagnold's novel *National Velvet* was made into a film in 1944, it starred a young Elizabeth Taylor, who instantly became one of Findley's female idols, and Beatrix Potter's *Peter Rabbit* would stay in Findley's mind to surface with an important role in *Head-hunter*, which I discuss in chapter 11.

During the thirties, Sunday afternoon walks along the Rosedale streets were very pleasant. The houses were stately, the lawns and gardens groomed, the cars in the driveways expensive, and in a short story he remembered them as "havens of wealth and all the mysteries of wealth" (*Stones* 220). Rosedale's streets, along with nearby Yonge and Bloor, were of further interest. Farther north, on Glenrose Avenue, where the Findleys lived when their children were born, the sculptors Florence Wyle and Frances Loring had their studio in an old wooden church building, and Allan once pointed the two women out to him: "one day you will remember those two women," he said, "and you will understand how wonderful they are" (Introduction to *Art for Enlightenment* 4). Other artists walking his neighbourhood streets in the 1930s and '40s were the writers Mazo de la Roche, Charles G. D. Roberts, Morley Callaghan, and Lucy Maud Montgomery, and some of Canada's famous painters—Yvonne McKague Housser, Paraskeva Clark, who always cut a dashing, elegant figure, Charles Comfort, who lived at one end of the Findleys' street, Lawren Harris, and A. Y. Jackson. He remembered seeing "Tom Thomson's old grey barn-board studio" in a nearby park, where he played.[3] As a boy, he was once taken to see a Frederick Varley portrait in a friend's house, an experience he never forgot: "I make a pilgrimage where ever his paintings hang the moment I know one is near" (1). Silkscreened reproductions of selected paintings by the Group of Seven and other Canadian artists hung in the schools he attended, as they did in schools across Canada.

Although books and paintings were important in his early life, music was a pervasive, shaping influence. In the evenings, his parents' voices singing popular songs at parties would drift upstairs while he and Michael were falling asleep: "Keep the Home Fires Burning," "Till We Meet Again," "Roses of Picardy," "Till the Clouds Roll By," "As Time Goes By." Church music and song moved him deeply—the only aspect of organized religion that did. His aunts loved classical music, which he heard them play on occasion, and the family owned early gramophone records featuring the great opera singers of the day. His parents also took him to concerts at Massey Hall, and they listened to the Saturday afternoon radio broadcasts from the Metropolitan Opera, a habit Findley continued through his adult life. Early on he learned to play the piano by ear, and for the rest of his life access to a piano was essential to his happiness. But all this was before the war, and the war years were profoundly traumatic for him; they lie open in his life story like an abyss. Before the war there were bedtime stories, songs, and adventures in the ravine. Before the war there were housemaids with whom Tiff spent hours in the kitchen. Before the war there was a family.

Allan Findley's enlistment left a deep and lasting scar on his son's psyche. He applied to the Royal Canadian Air Force (RCAF) on 12 July 1940, and, whatever the man's reasons for doing so, Findley believed that his father simply wanted to escape the family and its obligations. Allan would turn thirty-eight on September 30 that year and he had a dependent wife and two young sons—an age and family circumstances that were not common for military recruits (nor for conscripts, after home conscription was later introduced); in other words, Allan Findley was under no external pressure to sign up. What's more, he had no particular skills, no previous service, and no education to offer the military.[4] The officer who interviewed him reported that he was "not recommended" for service. Nevertheless, he persevered and was finally accepted into the administrative branch of the RCAF as an adjutant. He served briefly as an intelligence officer, had several postings within Canada, with the longest period spent at RCAF Station Trenton just east of Toronto, and had one posting to England, from 13 April to 22 October 1945. Allan Findley did not have a distinguished military career. Like the father in *You Went Away*, he did little more than "fly a desk," which, as Findley came to understand, was a cruel disappointment for Allan. If his decision to enlist was motivated, even in part, by a desire to emulate his war hero brother, then he fell far short of that mark. Nowhere in Allan's surviving letters to his son or in the scrapbooks he kept is there any suggestion that he was politically or ethically motivated to fight. Patriotism must have been a factor in his decision, inculcated by the Findleys' loyalty to Great Britain, but from

Findley's perspective his father seemed utterly indifferent to the impact of his actions on his wife and children.

Although the First World War continued to cast a long, troubling shadow over Findley's adult life, the Second World War defined him and his generation in ways difficult for later generations to fully appreciate. "Mine was the generation whose childhood had been interrupted by the war," he said: "We grew up through that time, deprived, one way and another, of normal life. Our fathers went to war. Our cities were bombed. And some of us went to Auschwitz. Our childhood ended with the dropping of the Hiroshima bomb. What darkened our moods [...] was the vision we had been forced to endure of what people really do to one another" (*IM* 19). He often recalled feeling powerless and fearful. While walking to school one day when he was ten, he thought about kids his age being killed overseas: "I vividly recall [...] thinking *right this very minute* someone my age is dying in a prison" (qtd. in McIvor, 76). He knew precisely where he was when the news broke that Pearl Harbor had been bombed: it was 7 December 1941, something by Brahms was playing on the radio, and he was tying up his shoes when the lace snapped; his first thought was that Pearl Harbor was in the St. Lawrence River and he was terrified. But most of all he remembered his father's eagerness to get away, the sight of him arriving at the house one evening with some tipsy buddies to celebrate enlisting, or a later scene when this adult man leapt onto the bed with joy because he was being posted somewhere away from home. Findley watched these childish performances, registered them in his memory, and believed his father "hated" him. At the age of eleven he saw this father as "absolutely my enemy" (MacDonald interview).

The early autobiographical short story "War" conveyed Findley's childhood response to his father's behaviour especially well. Written in 1954–55 in England, it is one of his earliest extant fictions, but it was not published until 1984, after Allan Findley's death. Neil Cable is the twelve-year-old, first-person narrator who remembers "a Saturday, two years ago. August, 1940" (*DAA* 65). He had arrived at a farm near Orillia to join his brother Bud, who was also staying there for a summer holiday. In an argument with a friend, Bud boasts that "our dad's joined the army" (69). And that, Neil tells us, was how he heard. He is stunned by this announcement and leaves the two older boys to hide in the barn. Neil knows that "in the army you always went in a trench and got hurt or killed" because he saw his uncle, who "got hit in his stomach" in the first war, suffer and die. This uncle "was always in a big white bed, and he gave us candies from a glass jar" (69), just as Irving had done for his nephews. As time passes and night falls, Neil climbs into the hayloft to hide, and when his father enters the barn to search for him, Neil throws stones at the man and knocks him out. Neil's father is not seriously injured, but if the father understands why his son is so angry, he does not let on, and the boy feels that "the thing never got settled. Not in words, anyway" (81). Instead, his father asks for a family picture to take with him when he leaves for Ottawa the next day, and so a photograph is taken. Neil begins his story with a description of this photograph: "That's my dad in the middle. We were just kids then" (65), and in the last sentence of the story, Neil assures us that "there was a photograph. There still is" (81; ill. 12).

There were, in fact, three Findley photographs taken in the fall of 1944.[5] In one, Margaret has turned to her right and is speaking to Michael; Allan is on her left smiling for the camera. On Allan's left, Tiff leans into his father's side with a broad smile on his face. In another, Allan stands alone between his two sons, his arms hooked through theirs, his gaze on something off to his left. All three are smiling, although Michael seems tense and reluctant. Tiff is actually laughing. The third snapshot is of Allan and Margaret together, and all these photographs seem to show a proud father in uniform, with his wife and sons. Details in the short story are not a precise match with the facts—Allan joined the air force, and the photograph he asked for was taken before his posting to England in 1944—but the parallels between the fiction and real life are obvious. When Findley went to England a decade later, he took one or all of these pictures with him, and if the story "War" tells us anything about him, it emphasizes the complex memories and emotions evoked by the smiling performance in these photographs and the regret Findley carried with him because he and his father did not discuss these hurts until it was almost too late. Moreover, this story foreshadows the disturbing portraits of father figures in many of his later works.

Throughout his life, in interviews and in his fiction, Findley returned to the shock of these scenes. Not being told was shattering, but he felt the physical absence of his father as an abandonment. To make matters worse, in 1942 he and Michael were shipped off to SAC, which had moved north of the city to Aurora, and he felt marooned there. Allan's absences during the war years meant that Margaret was the stable centre of her family, and they enabled Findley "to see her as herself, as a person independent of her husband and her children," and as someone "who had a life of her own and whose resources, hitherto a mystery, slowly came into focus" ("My Mother, My Friend" 47). Unfortunately, Allan's absences also precipitated Margaret's. The boys were left behind on several occasions when she joined her husband in Halifax or Ottawa or Kingston. What her sons learned much later was that she was trying to save a failing marriage. Christmas 1942 marked the nadir for Margaret and the boys. Allan was away on an assignment in Halifax and had not seen his children for a year. Michael had come down with rheumatic fever and been brought back to Toronto from SAC to stay in Grandmother Findley's house for medical care. When Tiff came home for the holidays, he had no *home* to go to.[6] "When I went through the door," he recalled, "the first thing I was told was to be quiet" ("Christmas Remembered" 80). When he was allowed to go to his brother's bedside, he watched Michael lying there and struggling to breathe. Tiff thought his brother was about to die and felt frightened and miserable. On Christmas morning, Michael was able to come downstairs to open presents, but the gifts were very few: two books, a pair of socks, a hockey stick, and some candy for each boy: "No skates. No pucks": "We stood there, looking like refugees, standing in the middle of the floor. Huddled like the team that just lost the game. Sheep in a storm. Emigrants in a foreign country. Anything but a family. We didn't even seem to belong to one another." Then Margaret began to weep and fled to the kitchen. Findley waited twelve years for her explanation of what had gone wrong. Not only was Allan away, but he had failed to send her the promised Christmas money, and he was having an affair with a woman in Halifax. Margaret had pawned the stone in her engagement ring to raise a little cash for the boys' meagre gifts, and for the time being she and the boys were homeless and virtually penniless.

Findley summed up the situation well in "Christmas Remembered" when he described his Christmas of 1942 as "null and void" (80). The Findleys had lost the "cohesion," as he called it, to sustain a family. In early 1943, Margaret took the train to Halifax to deal with the other woman in the kind of brave move few betrayed wives would be able, or willing, to make. Michael recovered from what Findley would always call his "romantic fever"; Tiff returned to his exile at SAC; and Margaret came back to Toronto with a new ring and moved back into the rented house at 27 Crescent Road. As for Allan, he had another year and a half with the air force before his discharge. On his leaves, he visited his family in Toronto but was eager to get away again as soon as possible. Insofar as the portrait of the husband and father in *You Went Away* is drawn from life, it strongly suggests that Allan Findley continued to womanize and drink heavily. Meanwhile, back on Crescent Road another axe was about to descend. The landlord was selling the house, and, despite her efforts, Margaret could not raise enough money to buy it.

Apparently Tiff and Michael never discussed their parents' marital trouble, although they both knew there were problems. Tiff loved them both and desperately wanted them to stay together because a separation would further shake his already very fragile sense of safety and stability. Certainly the years between 1945 and 1950 continued to be strained. No one in the family would forget the sight of their husband and father arriving home by train on 30 October 1945 (Findley's birthday) drunk, dishevelled, and aggressive. Allan refused to buy a house, so when they weren't living with relatives or friends, they rented. One rented house was especially dark and depressing, and to make matters worse, for close to two years Allan would lie on the sofa, eating sardines, drinking, smoking, and complaining bitterly about his dismal lot in life. It was at this point, in 1945, shortly after his father's return and his completion of Grade 8, that Findley told his father he was gay, and this declaration gave his father further cause for resentment. Allan's war had not made him a hero; he was not holding down a good job and making enough money to live in the Rosedale style; he was tied to a family and a wife who wanted to pin him down further by buying a house; he was aging; and now this—in Allan's words, a "queer" son. In a

1984 interview, Findley recalled that his mother "didn't react badly, there was no 'How could you be, how awful.' But my father … it was very hard [because] it was his responsibility, as he saw it, to carry on the honour that had died with his father and his wonderful brother" (Montador, 28).

By the time he left SAC in June 1943, Findley knew he was gay, even if the other boys did not. When he returned to Rosedale Public School for Grades 7 and 8, he may have felt uncomfortable, but certainly by the time he reached Jarvis Collegiate for Grades 9 and 10 he and his classmates were well into puberty and he found it impossible to pretend. One of Tiff's friends, who struggled to hide his orientation, was terrified of being persecuted and was going through hell because he tried to pretend he was heterosexual. The pain Tiff watched his friend suffer angered him because he spurned the need for such crippling pretense. As a result, he was very likely taunted for being a "fairy," ostracized, and bullied to a degree that society would not begin to recognize and address for decades. Later in his life, Findley would try to pretend—with devastating consequences—but as a teenager these anxieties, combined with illnesses, including minor bowel surgery, caused him extended periods of absence from classes, during which he stayed at home and withdrew into books, reading, and his earliest attempts at writing. He struggled through Grade 9 at Jarvis, with some tutoring help at home, and entered Grade 10 in the fall of 1946, shortly before his sixteenth birthday. However, he was fundamentally unhappy and desperate to get away from the school. If there was a particular event that prompted his decision to leave, he did not mention it later in life in his journals or interviews; however, an understanding teacher assured his parents that their son was not cut out for high school but was very intelligent and would find his own way in life. Partway through Grade 10 he left, and many years later he stated that he "had no business being in that school [and] didn't want to be there" (Black, 1994, 43). Nevertheless, this abrupt termination of his formal education was a massive step, representing his rejection of a bigoted world that had not accepted him, but it would always be a source of regret to him. For the rest of his life Findley felt deeply his lack of a university education and frequently lamented this lack in his journals.

Crisis: "I am myself alone."

Without a formal education, at least to matriculation, Findley had no idea what his life's work would be. Because he enjoyed music and dance, he considered acquiring some training in the arts, but there were few options in the Toronto of 1947. Dance, in particular, appealed to him, but for lessons he needed money. Being a Findley, however, helped him land his first job in the factory where his grandfather Findley got his start in life. For several months, he caught the streetcar south on Yonge and west along Adelaide to the new Massey-Harris foundry at 67 Adelaide Street West, where he put in a day's work delivering "roughly finished bits of metal to other parts of the factory" ("My First Job"). The heat was intense and the noise deafening; as he told Carol Roberts, the foundry was "a raging, blazing red place filled with fire [and the] workers were all deaf" (1994, 22). At the end of his shift, he emerged from the factory in workboots and dirty clothes and rushed home to change for a ballet lesson. Findley's life at home, however, was difficult. Although Margaret had found a Rosedale house they could afford at 97 Whitehall Road and Allan had grudgingly agreed to the purchase, thereby providing a degree of stability for the next few years, nothing existed in the Findleys' experience of life or in society at large to help them understand their son's orientation.

In the 1940s, Canadian law and social convention considered homosexuality a crime, a psychological illness, a social aberration, and a religious sin. Consequently, Allan and Margaret tried repeatedly to set their son up with suitable young ladies from Rosedale, and they expected him to become a heterosexual teenager.[7] As for his work and activities, a job at Massey-Harris was acceptable, in the short run, but the arts were not. Although his family appreciated the arts, his father did not consider them suitable for a profession. Allan enjoyed knowing artists, fancied himself a poet, and liked to draw, but he considered these activities the accoutrements of a gentleman, not the serious work of a proper adult male. "I'll be damned if I will pay for ballet lessons for a son of mine" was how Findley recalled his father's reaction (E. Cameron, 1985, 28). Margaret's response to his early attempts to find his way was more complex; she had once wanted a career in dance (forbidden as unacceptable by her father) and she sympathized with his artistic interests, but she could not understand his sexual orientation. After her death, however, Findley said that she had never turned her back on him as his father had. Securing the Massey-Harris job enabled him to flout his father's disapproval and pay for ballet lessons with Boris Volkoff (1900–74), a harsh disciplinarian who had married a close family friend of the Findleys', Toronto dancer Janet Baldwin (1912–90). Studying with Volkoff was an ordeal but, when Findley shifted to working with Janet, he not only enjoyed the dancing but also found in Janet a personal friend and mentor for life.

After back problems put a stop to his dream of a career in dance, he turned to the amateur theatre and a part-time job at the Toronto Stock Exchange, which gave him flexible hours, some cash, and the freedom to accept bit parts with the Earle Grey Players, who performed Shakespeare in the Trinity College quad at the University of Toronto. When the Players staged an Easter play in a downtown church in 1948, he landed a role as a member of the crowd screaming for Christ's crucifixion. As he told Elspeth Cameron, screaming "Crucify him!" gave him "an outlet for self-expression," as well as for pent-up anger and frustration with his parents and with what he saw as his miserable prospects in life. After leaving Jarvis he had begun visiting the Toronto ravines for sex with older boys and men. At sixteen he was still a minor, and this secretive activity was illegal and dangerous. In strict Christian circles it was a grave sin. Worse still, it meant hiding who he was, and the double life was becoming too much to bear. Years later, he would say that during this period he felt "the sorrow of the leper and the rage of the outcast" and feared he would never find "reconciliation between [him]self and others":

> Everything *else* that I was—which felt to be about 99.9 percent of who I was and what I was about—went into exile with the .1 percent of aberration. But I could not tell the others in my life—I could not explain to those who had set me apart—and I could not even tell or explain to myself what it was that I felt, because I had no words: I had no means of articulation. ("My Final Hour" 7)

Raging at the world—screaming "Crucify him!"—was no help.

In 1950, the stress produced by anger, frustration, rejection, and the isolation he was experiencing led to some form of breakdown during which he tried to run away—from his father's criticism, from the nice Rosedale girls he was supposed to date, from a host of expectations he could not live up to, and from the pressure to be what he knew he was not. If Findley saw a doctor at this time, I have found no mention of such a consultation in his journals or surviving family correspondence, and it was not until 1955 that he recorded fearing a recurrence of the 1950 breakdown in his journal, but without adding any details. However, his parents were sufficiently worried to send him on a trip to Europe. In July 1950, they saw him off from Montreal on the *Mont Gaspé* for what they hoped would be a recuperative voyage to France, where he visited Paris and Caen in Normandy before going to Caux (near Geneva) in Switzerland, and from there to Rossinière. In Rossinière he lived and worked with a local farming family for close to two months. His parents must have hoped that these months away would improve his health and that the trip would somehow make him think differently about his sexuality. But it is not fair to suggest that only Allan wanted to straighten out his son. Findley's stop in Caux, Switzerland, in the early fall of 1950 had a particular and, in retrospect, a disturbing purpose.

Sometime during the Second World War, Margaret Findley became a member of the Moral Re-Armament movement (MRA), led by the American cult figure Frank Buchman.[8] When Buchman and his followers organized the highly publicized cross-Canada propaganda tour called "Pull Together Canada" in 1941, two tenets of this extreme right-wing evangelical movement caught her attention: first, their loudly proclaimed attack on sexual sin among young men and, second, their opposition to the use of alcohol, which had produced a sub-branch of the MRA that began Alcoholics Anonymous in 1935. From the 1930s to the 1960s, the MRA was very popular in North America and in Europe, where it set up its headquarters in Caux, Switzerland. Between the wars Buchman and his followers enjoyed the vigorous support of Protestant churches, especially the Presbyterian Church, and of a network of wealthy elites associated with universities and the YMCA. Their target group was young men, preferably from leading families, and this exclusive focus on male youth provided a link with Hitler and the Nazi movement. Buchman, in fact, admired Hitler, and shared his extreme ideology of purity, the idealization of youth, and the desire for world domination. The MRA adopted the Nazi propaganda tools of mass rallies, spectacular revues, and proselytizing through the media and by means of their magazine called *Rising Tide*. Hundreds of thousands of people, including politicians, academics, and religious leaders, were members and gave large sums of money to support the movement. Many Findley family friends and associates also joined, supported the movement financially, and attended its rallies. Clearly, the key prohibitions proclaimed by the MRA against sexual sin and alcohol resonated with Margaret Findley's personal situation. For years she had been coping with a husband who was both an alcoholic and an adulterer, and after her son declared he was gay and her husband returned from the war embittered, she needed all the support she could find.

In a letter written in the mid-1940s to her closest friend, Isabel McLaughlin, Margaret described her attendance at an MRA meeting in London, Ontario, where she spoke about her experiences. She told Isabel that she found "proof that if *guided living* works for our diverse dispositions [her mixed group of fellow testifiers] it would work for anyone," and that "to give of our best we must have a vision of what the world should be in the future."[9] This belief in a vision for improving the world along evangelical Christian lines of *guidance* confirms her faith in MRA precepts, but it also testifies to her search for spiritual strength. In a 1991 letter to Isabel after his mother's death, Findley reflected on this period in his mother's life with understanding. "I agree [with you] about the Oxford Group [the early name for the movement]," he wrote. "I *hated* it":

When I got old enough to understand such things, it seemed to me to be politically dangerous—aligned with figures in public and political life I did not trust. They were very right-wing. (To say the least!) Still—it gave mother one good aspect and that was something she found in herself having to do with courage. She learned to stand up for her rights in areas where Dad was concerned—and she gained self-respect by learning to challenge some of his decisions. (27 January 1991, McLaughlin fonds)

Findley's direct exposure to the MRA came on his 1950 trip to Europe. After a few days in France that August, he caught a train to Switzerland to spend time in Caux before continuing on to Rossinière, where he spent his first night in the famous Grand Chalet. In a letter to his "Dear Family" dated 1 September 1950, he informed them that he stayed in Caux for three days, "saw all our friends and had a good time" (LAC 97:6). He named several of these family friends, then admitted that, although it "was certainly like old times ... I wasn't changed." Later in this letter, after he had been working at the Henchoz family farm in Rossinière for a week, he described his situation more clearly. "The main thing," he told his parents, "is that I can rely on guidance to carry me each step of the way," and he called Daniel Henchoz "a bit of a socialist," who identified Caux and the MRA with Nazism: "They [Daniel and Rachel Henchoz] know I've been to Caux but don't mention it" (LAC 97:6). During his years in England in the fifties, his parents encouraged him to visit Caux again, and they also tried to get his brother Michael involved. Although Findley came to understand and deplore the fascist characteristics of Buchman and his movement, in his early twenties he was still swayed by his mother's convictions and still deeply unsure about his own. The contradictory remarks in this 1950 letter home—"I wasn't changed" and "I can rely on guidance" (a key MRA term)—make his youthful confusion very clear, and this philosophical and ethical uncertainty tormented him until he learned how to turn his hatred for extreme ideological and religious positions into art. Long before he told Isabel McLaughlin that he hated the Oxford Group, he had written *Famous Last Words* and *Not Wanted on the Voyage*. And both novels are, in no small part, his condemnation of fascism and an authoritarian, homophobic cult like the MRA.

The MRA aside, this journey to Europe, working his way across in the ship's storeroom, and his time in Switzerland would be productive in other, more positive, ways. From the start he kept a scrapbook titled the "1950 Journal of Timothy Findley" (LAC 332:3). He dated his entries and kept a meticulous record of whom and what he saw. He recorded his opinions of people he met, details of conversations about books and politics, the food, and the places he visited. He also filled this large book with photographs, some of his early poems, carefully labelled and coloured maps of Europe, and his itinerary for the months of August, September, and October.[10] Although this journal is neither as personal nor as extensive as his later journals would be, it does represent a practice he continued through the rest of his life. Moreover, he went back over the journal to fill in details after the fact because he already recognized the importance of preserving this information for future reference. Beside his photographs of the ship's approach to France and of his first view of Dunkirk on August 7, he wrote: "for future reference [...] so I will remember." On board ship he was befriended by Philippe Lemaistre, a young Frenchman who had been studying fruit farming in Quebec, and his family invited Findley to stay with them in Paris and at their home in Lillebonne (near Rouen). Through this family he learned a lot about the Second World War and its impact on France, and he noted, with concern, the terrible destruction of Dunkirk in 1940. When he sighted the Vimy Monument from the train, he wrote: "I have seen it at last, one of the greatest memorials ever built in honour of Canadians [and] possibly the very spot where Uncle Tif once walked."

During this time away he tried to budget his money (something he would never master), and he reported that his French was improving but that he found the physical farm work exhausting: Daniel Henchoz "makes me work so hard ... when he knows I am nearly dropping" (LAC 97:6). Heavy manual labour was never something Findley enjoyed, but his parents no doubt thought it would distract, possibly cure, their son; it was a case of *mens sana in corpore sano*. He told his parents that he could not wait to get home, go to his own room, and listen to his records—"My heavens, how I miss the music. I've heard so little." The return voyage in October was smooth until the *Mont Gaspé* hit a violent storm off the Labrador coast, but he kept his mind occupied by reading Gabrielle Roy's 1947 novel *The Tin Flute* and, as soon as he was able, writing down a description of the

storm. The most intriguing influence from this trip, however, would surface years later. Rising from the forested mountainside above Rossinière
is one of the oldest and most impressive chalets in Switzerland, the one
he had stayed in on his first night there: le Grand Chalet, with its facade
covered in writing. Originally built in the 1750s by the Henchoz family, it
became a famous hotel popular with an international clientele, including
important writers like Victor Hugo and famous figures like Alfred Drey-
fus. From the village of Rossinière, Findley could see this hotel, which may
well have inspired the hotel in the Austrian Alps, with its writing on the
walls, that he created as the setting for *Famous Last Words*.

For the time being, however, he had no career, no job, and no clear
sense of what he could do with his life. He was at loose ends, a Rosedale
boy with very little practical experience of the world. Back in Toronto he
returned to his room in the family home but continued to feel criticized and
misunderstood. He confessed to this 1950 journal that he was full of anxiety about his future, about a choice of career in which he could be himself
and make a contribution, something he already believed he was destined to
do. Finally, he decided to look for acting jobs, but he knew he needed training to prepare for a theatre career. Toronto had little professional work to
offer at that time, but there was one possibility for training: the Sterndale
Bennett School.[11] He enrolled, and he also began speech lessons with Clara
Baker at the Royal Conservatory of Music. This time his parents agreed to
pay for the lessons. Findley was in awe of Mrs. Baker, and he learned from
the Sterndale Bennetts that the theatre was a serious business of discipline,
hard work, and total commitment to artistic perfection—all valuable lessons he needed and that would stay with him. These were the days before
the Crest Theatre or Stratford, but the students were encouraged to take
in every touring show at Toronto's venerable Royal Alexandra Theatre, the
oldest continuously operating theatre in North America and now a designated national historic site. When they put on plays in their tiny performance space above a store on Church Street, they made their own sets
and costumes and performed for a paying public. Findley continued with
the Sterndale Bennetts until the spring of 1951, followed their regimen of
reading and studying scripts, and played bit parts in several productions.

As 1950 drew to a close, his private life was once more in crisis because he could not find a community of people like himself. Much as he cared for and needed his parents and extended family, he knew they wanted him to get over being gay, fall in love with a woman, marry, and have children, which meant he had to seek what he called "the very secret company of men in parks," in Allan Gardens, in the ravines, or in a few bars (Montador, 28). From today's perspective it may come as a shock to be reminded that homosexual acts were illegal at the time, that the Toronto police raided places where gay men met, and that extreme homophobia and persecution were the order of the day through the fifties, sixties, and seventies. During the mid-1950s, when a serial killer was preying on children, the newspapers blamed a "sex pervert" and, as late as 1977, the murder of a twelve-year-old Toronto boy elicited virulent attacks in the tabloid press damning all gays as perverts and murderers. In their study *The Canadian War on Queers*, Kinsman and Gentile remind readers that through these decades psychiatrists blamed bad mothering for producing character weakness and sexual deviance (55–56), and they explore, in depth, the entrenched homophobia in all branches of the Canadian military, a prejudice that must have reinforced Allan Findley's rejection of his son. Although the Church and Wellesley area has long been a centre for gay life in the city, in Findley's youth an event like Pride Toronto was undreamt of, and openly gay publications did not really begin to circulate until 1964 (see Lorinc et al.). It was not until late in 1950 that Findley discovered the Letros Tavern, a restaurant with fine cuisine and a gay bar, on King Street across from the King Edward Hotel. The King Eddie also had a bar on their mezzanine that was popular with those who were able to patronize elegant places and dress well; lesbians were often accompanied by gay men because they had to masquerade as heterosexual couples to enter the hotel. Slowly Findley gathered up the courage to go to these public places, where he "began to meet the most wonderful people ... and they were artists" (Montador, 28). Nevertheless, the stigma remained, as well as the risk. Wisely, Findley was reluctant to be seen entering these bars; he was understandably fearful of the consequences of this illegal activity and tormented by the isolation he felt when leading this life of secrecy and pretense.

At about this time, while studying with the Sterndale Bennetts, Findley discovered Shakespeare's Richard, Duke of Gloucester (King Richard III), whom he later described as "perhaps the most *aberrant* human being in all of English literature":

> I devoured him whole. It seemed that I was already intimate with all his dreams and aspirations as a man. I understood—acutely—what it was that drove him to divorce himself from decency. And I remember to this day my reaction to that first encounter. I blushed. I blushed because I thought I had been seen. And then I felt a rush of immense excitement. The more of Gloucester I read, the more I understood that I was reading the definitive articulation of everything I had not been able to articulate about myself and how it felt to be *my* self alone. ("My Final Hour" 7-8)

A heartbreaking confession this, to have seen himself at twenty in the shape of Shakespeare's deformed monster and regicide, who vows to make his mind mirror his body's crookedness. And yet it was not only deformity and aberration that Findley recognized (this admission that he blushed at the thought of being "seen" implies that he saw the king as homosexual and, for that reason, aberrant), but also the aloneness of Richard. In his lecture, "My Final Hour," prepared more than forty years later, he returned to Gloucester's words in *King Henry VI, Part III* (act 5, scene 6):

> I have no brother, I am like no brother;
> And this word 'love,' which greybeards call divine,
> Be resident in men like one another,
> And not in me: *I am myself alone.*

In 1950s Toronto, with his Rosedale background, he *felt* alone and unseen, and he was tormented by his perceived failure to be like his family members, who surrounded him in person and in memory.

THE CANADIAN PROTEGE—

1950 TO 1962

CHAPTER FOUR

Leaving Home

———

MAKE PRAYERS AGAINST DESPAIR.

(Samuel Johnson)

Early Theatre Experiences: Toronto to Stratford

In many ways the 1950s were Findley's decade from hell. He was often filled with self-doubt, acute self-criticism, and even self-loathing, and he complained bitterly in his journals about his failures, defeats, and loneliness. Although he desperately needed stability, he was restless and constantly on the move from one place, or one person, to another. It was at this time that he discovered Samuel Johnson's words, "Against Despair," and this became his personal motto.[1] And yet, despite the despair and self-criticism, the 1950s were packed with valuable professional theatre experience, with love and support from many quarters, and with opportunities to make up for the formal education he lacked. Even in his darkest moments, he realized he was gaining knowledge and strength, and his theatre work between 1950 and 1956 would prove influential for his future career as a writer. Equally important, especially for the kind of writer he became, he began recording his experiences and feelings in meticulous detail in a series of journals and workbooks.

At the start of 1950 he was treading water and searching for opportunities to act. While studying with the Sterndale Bennetts and taking speech classes with Clara Baker at Toronto's Royal Conservatory of

Music, he met William Hutt and Kate Reid, two actors whose example inspired him. When an amateur group called the International Players called the Sterndale Bennetts looking for a young male actor, Findley got his chance. The play was Sidney Howard's *The Silver Cord*, directed by William Hutt and starring Charmian King, who became a regular performer on Toronto stages and on Broadway. He was asked to read for the role of a neurotic young man, one of the two sons dominated by a possessive mother in a dysfunctional family, and he got the part of Robert. *The Silver Cord* gave him a chance to be well directed in a popular American play opposite a more experienced actor like King. It was a start, and a decided improvement on the twenty-five dollars a week he earned helping to stage Shakespeare in the Trinity College quad (Brooks et al., 27). Findley stayed with the International Players for their 1951–52 season, performing in the Kingston summer production of Priestley's *Dangerous Corner* and Robertson Davies's *At My Heart's Core*. Later in life, he remembered his time in Kingston with mixed feelings. On the one hand, he was gaining theatre experience and meeting interesting people. It was during 1951–52 that he became close to Hutt and that he met Grant Macdonald, an artist based in Kingston who painted portraits of the actors from the 1953 company at Stratford; Timothy Findley would be one of his subjects (ill. 14). On the other hand, he was desperately unhappy, drinking heavily, getting only minor roles, and hiding his full identity. Grant Macdonald was gay, but reticent and cautious. According to William Hutt's biographer, Hutt's "sexual preference for males remained a closely guarded secret" (Garebian, 2017, 57). These two older men whom Findley admired seemed to epitomize the necessity of leading a double life. Ironically, as if art were imitating life, Priestley's play involved both murder and many secrets, including a clandestine homosexual affair, and Findley was cast as the young married man, Gordon Whitehouse, who had secretly loved and been loved by the murdered man. Describing his earliest theatre experiences years later, Findley claimed that the audience gasped audibly when this liaison was revealed and that the play received a negative review in the *Kingston Whig-Standard* because of this revelation. If he needed proof that gay men had to be secretive, this response to the play was it.

Performing in Davies's *At My Heart's Core* was a happier experience. This satirical play about settlers in Upper Canada takes place during the 1837 rebellion. Most loyal British men are off fighting, while their wives maintain domestic order. Two of these women are Susanna Moodie and Catharine Parr Traill, who are tempted by a smooth-talking neighbour to reveal their frustrated vanity and ambitions—Traill as a scientist, Moodie as an author—until their complaints are interrupted by an inebriated man called Phelim Brady. The role of Phelim, "an elderly, but not decrepit, Irishman in breeches, stockings, and lace-up boots [. . . with] a shrewd and even noble face, framed in Galway whiskers" (18), was played by the not-quite-twenty-two-year-old Timothy Findley. As he later recalled, his "beard kept falling off," and on opening night the artificial snow, held in a hammock-like affair up in the flies, refused to float down over the final scene. Due to the sweltering summer heat, "the flakes that were supposed to drift gently down through the light … were all sticking together like glue … until in one appalling moment, they all came down *en masse*" dumping Lux soap on the actors' heads (Green and Moore, 105). Such theatrical indignities aside, Findley enjoyed himself and admired Davies, who had attended rehearsals.

By 1952 or early 1953, he had moved out of his parents' house and into a small apartment on Avenue Road in Toronto's Yorkville district, which he shared with a number of University of Toronto students, one of whom was Hugh Hood.[2] He continued to drink heavily, but succeeded in obtaining roles in live theatre and with the newly launched television arm of the CBC (Canadian Broadcasting Corporation), and he kept in close touch with William Hutt. For a brief period in 1952, he and Hutt tried living together, but for a number of reasons (never specified by either man) this more intimate relationship did not work. Hutt terminated it, but he remained one of Findley's most valued friends. When the two men attended a performance of Carson McCullers's *The Member of the Wedding* at the Royal Alexandra Theatre, Tiff was deeply hurt because, during the intermission, his parents, who were also at the play, saw the two men together and studiously avoided them. As far as Timothy Findley was concerned, their reaction confirmed that he was a public embarrassment to them. The play stayed in his mind for more constructive reasons, however, because in it he recognized an image of his childhood: as he told Eugene Benson in 1986, "that kitchen and that garden in that play were the kitchen and the garden of my childhood, of my real childhood. I sat in kitchens with the maid all through my own childhood, the maid was my companion" (108).[3] When the right time arrived, Findley drew on the inspiration of this play to fictionalize his childhood in the story "About Effie" and in *The Last of the Crazy People*. And there were other acting gigs. He landed the role of Pupkin in the 1952 CBC television production of Leacock's *Sunshine Sketches of a Little Town*, thereby gaining an important connection with this new medium and with CBC people who were interested in drama. He also played Leo Hubbard in Lillian Hellman's *The Little Foxes*, supporting parts in *O Mistress Mine* by Terence Rattigan and *Ladies in Retirement* by Edward Percy and Reginald Denham, and the male lead in the Jupiter Theatre's production of Eugene O'Neill's *Anna Christie*. But such temporary, poorly paid work was neither enough to keep body and soul together nor to encourage hope for a future career. He moved back in with his parents, where he felt obliged to resume a double life. Findley rarely discussed this period in his life, and when he did he was cautious about what he revealed; if he kept a journal from 1951 to 1952, it does not appear to have survived. But he did not give up, and his life was about to change for the better through an opportunity that lay just ahead in the small town of Stratford, Ontario.

The story of the Stratford Festival is a Canadian legend.[4] The original idea for a Shakespearean Festival came from a young Stratford journalist, Tom Patterson, a Second World War veteran who had seen European productions during the war and become a theatre enthusiast. When Stratford experienced an economic slump after the war, he thought that a festival might revive his town's fortunes. The mayor and city council agreed to support Patterson's idea with a modest grant, and he set forth on his quest. Seasoned theatre people like Robertson Davies and Mavor Moore suggested that he contact Tyrone Guthrie at London's Old Vic Theatre, which he did. Guthrie, intrigued by the image of Shakespeare being performed in sleepy Ontario's Stratford, agreed to come. He fell in love with Patterson's dream, and the nascent Stratford festival could not have recruited a more charismatic, energetic, and talented champion. Guthrie hired one of Britain's top stage actors, Alec Guinness, three other leading British actors, and his own long-time set designer, Tanya Moiseiwitsch, to help him turn the opening summer season of 1953 into a stunning success. The lack of a suitable performance space did not faze Guthrie, who opted for a large tent. The tent went up, the theatre patrons arrived, and the show went on. Alec Guinness was sensational in the title role of *Richard III*, and *All's Well That Ends Well* was so popular that its run was extended for a week. Guests enjoyed their picnics on the lawn beside the Avon River, and Glenn Gould, among other celebrated musicians, presented afternoon concerts. The Stratford Shakespearean Festival was launched to ringing applause from audiences, Toronto critics, and New York pundits.

During the winter of 1952–53, word had spread through the tightly knit Ontario theatre community that Guthrie was coming from London to direct a festival in Stratford. Canadian actors would be needed, auditions would be held through the spring of 1953, and Timothy Findley applied. In an undated letter from late 1952 or early 1953, now held in the Stratford Festival Archives, he wrote to Patterson describing his acting experience and enclosing a photograph: "Dear Sir," he began, "I am writing to apply for [an] appointment with Mr. Guthrie in regards to the Shakespeare Festival which I understand will take place in your city this summer." And he continued—

Briefly my experience has been as follows:

  Gordon Whitehouse—"Dangerous Corners" [sic]
  Leo Hubbard—"The Little Foxes"
  Michael—"Oh Mistress Mine"
  Albert Feather—"Ladies in Retirement"
  Matt Burke—"Anna Christie."

As well I have played character and character juvenile roles in twenty-three weeks of stock with the "International Players."

I have been playing on television for the C.B.C. since this medium was first introduced. Principally this work has been on the series program "Sunshine Sketches." That is the extent of my professional work. Also I have played Shakespeare with Mr. Earle Grey for several years. I have studied with both Mr. Sterndale Bennett and Clara Baker in Toronto. I am sorry that the picture I attach is not a professional study but my stock of prints has run out, and I want to send you this application as soon as possible.

Statistically, I am five feet eleven inches tall, light brown hair and approximately 150 pounds in weight. I might add that I have a good command of the British dialect, as well as Cockney and the Northern dialects.

I should very much appreciate the opportunity of having an interview with Mr. Guthrie and to audition for him.

And so until I hear from you I am

Sincerely

Timothy Findley

Findley was called to audition with Guthrie in the old dance studio on Yonge Street where he had once studied ballet, and he recalled that "Guthrie sat at the far end, at a table, and you had to walk in and present yourself all the way down to the table" (Ouzounian, "Timothy Findley's Stratford Memories"). Daunting as this was, he must have presented himself well because in March he received a letter from Cecil Clarke, Guthrie's assistant director, offering him the part of Sir William Catesby in *Richard III* and the walk-on role of the Second Gentleman in act 3 of *All's Well*. About the latter, Clarke explained that "we intend to make him an officer and he will also appear in various court scenes throughout the play" (16 March 1953, Stratford Festival Archives). Rehearsals would start on the first of June, with *Richard* opening the season on July 13. Findley replied immediately that he was "thrilled": "I would most certainly enjoy to take part in the festival and the parts you offer me are most satisfactory to me as I feel you have been more than generous in the case of *Richard III*." He signed his contract on 8 May 1953 and was paid $750 for the season, which included rehearsals. From this sum, he was expected to cover his room and board, plus other living expenses, and he agreed to provide the modern clothes required for this production of *All's Well That Ends Well*. By all accounts, Guthrie was a demanding director who did not hesitate to exercise his sharp wit in chastising his actors. On one occasion, he stopped "Findley" in his tracks, and in front of the others, to ask: "Haven't you learned yet that you don't have to tell your face what to do—that it will do it on its own?" (Garebian, 1988, 92). On another, he nagged Frances Hyland to speak louder until she grew angry and shouted her lines. "Very nice, Fran," said Guthrie. "Not very interesting, but I can hear every word" (Garebian, 1988, 93). But Guthrie knew his business and expected the absolute best from his cast. He rehearsed twelve hours a day, seven days a week in an old building in the countryside with poor ventilation, an echo, and a tin roof. "If it rained," Findley recalled, "you couldn't hear a thing. And there were all these damn sparrows that ... shat on you the whole time you were working" (Brooks et al. 28).

Dress rehearsals in the tent were not much better. The humidity and heat were so intense that Guthrie took to wearing canvas shoes, a bathing suit held up with a rope, and a see-through plastic raincoat. He was always on the move, lining up sightlines, clambering over seats, and Findley remembered that he "kept looking up and seeing this giant"—Guthrie was very tall—"looming in his plastic raincoat" (Brooks et al. 28). On one especially memorable occasion, Guthrie decided that a crucial scene in *Richard III* would be vastly improved if Catesby leapt onto the stage. The scene (act 5, scene 4) is already one of high drama; Richard is losing the battle and is alone on a dark stage crying out, "A horse, a horse, my kingdom for a horse." Guthrie wanted Catesby, Richard's loyal henchman, to appear suddenly on the balcony ten feet above the stage and, without a pause, leap down beside Richard. "How would you feel, Findley," the great man asked, "if you jumped off the balcony. We want a surprise entrance" (Ouzounian, 2002). Well. Findley hadn't much choice. He climbed up the stairs, broke through the curtain, ran onto the balcony and ... took a flying leap into the dark. "I had to do it like that. I couldn't look.... I never landed on Guinness and I never broke my legs, but it was really scary" (Ouzounian, 2002). Findley often recalled that scene, that first leap in the dark, and the commanding personality of Tyrone Guthrie. He "was a magical character," Findley said; "one of the great theatre people and thank God I worked with him" (Brooks et al. 28). What Findley did not recall, as far as I can tell, in interviews or his later journals, was the complex irony of his playing Catesby to Guinness's Richard, that deformed, aberrant creature, with whom Findley had identified just three years before, and the actor who was about to play an important role in his life.

Although there were challenges, less-than-ideal working conditions, and some personal disappointments, that first season was an adventure and Findley cherished those months with the Festival. The portrait Grant Macdonald painted, showing him in his cadet-style jacket for *All's Well That Ends Well*, was reproduced in Guthrie's first book about the festival, *Renown at Stratford*, and eventually bought by his parents. Sitting for the artist, however, was an ordeal because Macdonald worked in a hot, airless space under the stage, while Findley sat in his swim trunks, wearing only the jacket. The portrait experience made for a good story after the fact, as did his theatrical attempt to drown himself one evening by leaping from the Waterloo Street bridge (now the William Hutt bridge) into the Avon, where the water was only two feet deep. This may have been his first lame attempt at suicide but, as we shall see, it was not his last, even though he always downplayed suicidal thoughts by stressing his deep love of life. And there were romantic liaisons that did not turn out well, one of which may have precipitated his leap from the bridge. Most of the sixty-eight actors were Canadians—people like Richard Easton, Douglas Rain, Amelia Hall, Frances Hyland, Don Harron, William Needles, and, of course, Bill Hutt—and many of them became fine professionals or, as in Hutt's case, major stars by staying in Canada and performing regularly with the Festival.

Going into the profession was rapidly becoming Findley's ambition. There is a brief sequence from *The Stratford Adventure*, a National Film Board (NFB) documentary film about the founding season of 1953, in which Timothy Findley and Alec Guinness appear together as Findley repeats some lines and Guinness comments on his delivery and the importance of breath control for an actor. This brief clip represents a symbolic moment in Findley's early career: young, inexperienced Canadian lad interacts with older experienced British star; young man leans against the tent's guy ropes, his head resting on his arm, looking worshipfully at the older man, hanging on his every word, and the man smiles kindly, with a degree of indulgence. The two seem close, almost intimate: father and son; teacher and student; master and acolyte. On one occasion, when Guinness asked him for help rehearsing his lines, Findley was very nervous, but the practice went well; he read all the other roles so Guinness could work on his. Before the season ended, Guinness issued an invitation that would introduce Findley to an artistic and cultural milieu he could only imagine. "How would you feel about coming to London to study?" he asked; "You have talent and I think it's worth getting the voice right as early as possible" (Ouzounian, 2002). An eager Tiff Findley said he would love to go, so Guinness called Margaret Findley to explain that her son would live with the Guinness family in London, and that he would support Tiff's studies at the Central School of Speech and Drama. Findley's friend and fellow actor, Richard Easton, accepted a similar offer. On 6 September 1953 his parents drove him to Quebec City, and he sailed for England on the RMS *Scythia*, leaving his mother in tears.

To appreciate the significance of the Guinness offer, it helps to remember what opportunities were available in Canada prior to the Stratford Festival. The CBC, begun in 1932 as the Canadian Radio Broadcasting Commission (CRBC), played a crucial supporting role for many Canadian artists, including Findley. After 1943, CBC radio began drama programming, which flourished under Andrew Allan, who developed the Sunday night *Stage* series that provided Canadians with a form of national theatre for several decades. The Dominion Drama Festival held amateur festivals and adjudications from 1933 to 1978. The Banff School of Drama also opened in 1933, but it took years to develop into its current professional status as the Banff Centre for Arts and Creativity. Dora Mavor Moore (Mavor Moore's mother) established her New Play Society in Toronto in 1946, and two years later Arthur Sutherland founded the International Players in Kingston. The Straw Hat Players, an Ontario summer theatre troupe, began in 1948, and in 1949 the Red Barn Theatre opened in Sutton, Ontario, not far from Jackson's Point and about an hour's drive north of Toronto. Until it burned down in 2009, the Red Barn was Canada's oldest professional summer theatre. In the immediate postwar period, Canada was beginning to value the arts and the presence of artists on home ground, and during the fifties the momentum increased, with both Hart House and Trinity College, in the University of Toronto, staging plays and providing training and experience for ambitious young actors like William Hutt.

One of the most significant events for the future of the arts in Canada was the submission to the federal government of the 1951 Report of the Royal Commission on National Development in the Arts, Letters, Humanities, and Social Sciences (more familiarly known after its co-chairmen as the Massey/Levesque Report). The report championed Canadian cultural nationalism, with particular emphasis on the theatre, in which Vincent Massey had a personal interest.[5] And it led directly to the formation of the Canada Council for the Arts in 1957. Ballet would also begin a national life when Celia Franca arrived in Toronto in 1951 to establish the National Ballet of Canada; the Royal Winnipeg Ballet started up in 1953. CBC television, which began broadcasting in Toronto in 1952, brought Elvis Presley and Ed Sullivan into Canadian living rooms; Broadway musicals were coming north; and by the end of the decade Ottawa's own Paul Anka was crooning to radio listeners, "I'm just a lonely boy," a song that resonated with Tiff. The CBC founded its Symphony Orchestra in 1952, and Sir Ernest MacMillan, renowned conductor of the Toronto Symphony Orchestra, composer, and educator, published *Music in Canada* in 1956. By 1957, when Glenn Gould made his famous concert tour of the Soviet Union, it was clear that Canadian classical musicians had arrived.

Many new novelists, poets, and short story writers were beginning to publish during the fifties, among them Margaret Laurence, Mordecai Richler, Alice Munro, Earle Birney, and Dorothy Livesay. *Tamarack Review*, the first literary magazine to publish a Findley work, the story "About Effie," began publication in 1956, and in 1957 Jack McClelland announced his New Canadian Library series, which he launched in 1958 with works by Callaghan, Grove, Leacock, and Sinclair Ross. The premier scholarly journal in the field, *Canadian Literature*, was founded at the University of British Columbia and began publishing under George

Woodcock's editorship in 1959. The year 1959 was also notable for other reasons: Hugh MacLennan won the Governor General's Award for Fiction that year for *The Watch That Ends the Night*, and Sheila Watson's modernist classic *The Double Hook* was released by McClelland and Stewart. These developments meant that essential groundwork profiling the arts was preparing the way for a blossoming of Canadian literature in the late sixties and seventies. A lively arts scene was developing in the "village" area near the University of Toronto, where people could sing along with Ian Tyson or listen to young poets give readings in crowded, smoke-filled cafés, where everyone dressed in bohemian black. Theatre was also becoming increasingly visible, and not simply because of imported musicals. Jean Gascon helped found Montreal's Théâtre du Nouveau Monde in 1951; the Canadian Theatre Centre in Toronto opened in 1956, with Mavor Moore as its first chair; and John Hirsch and Tom Hendry started the Manitoba Theatre Centre in 1958. To meet this upsurge in professional theatre, a Canadian branch of Actors' Equity, an American organization, was established in 1955. The Toronto—indeed, the Canada—that Findley left behind in 1953 was by no measure culturally asleep, but going away helped him see what was needed and how he could contribute to the exciting growth ahead. Young Tiff Findley was about to be educated.

The London Journals

Between September 1953 and April 1956, when he returned to Canada, Findley filled seven large journals, each one bound, dated, titled, and signed. He also kept a separate collection of small notebooks and some tiny, pocket-sized diaries. For someone destined to become a writer, these records proved invaluable, and of the three categories of record, the journals provide the biographer with a remarkable self-portrait of the artist as a young man. Looking back on this lifelong practice four decades later, he confessed—"I love writing my journal," and "there's lots of stuff I go back for" (Richards, 1999). On another occasion, he speculated that even on his deathbed he would ask: "Where's the notebook? This is what it's like"

(Mumford). These journals were another genre for Findley and a distinct advance on the travel journal he kept in 1950 because, from the first entry on 4 September 1953 to the last in 1956, he was often self-consciously composing prose. He was also describing people, events, and places; noting down books, concerts, and interesting quotations; and making lists.[6] Regular journalling became a necessary practice for him at this time: he loved the writing; he loved the sound, the rhythm, and the heft of language. The surviving diaries supplement the journals, and, increasingly with time and the development of the professional writer, the workbooks support the fiction writing. Findley's use of journals inside his fiction further demonstrates that, for him, journals were strategic narrative devices.

The London journals all contain a mixture of lengthy, objective descriptions of things he saw or experienced and intimate, subjective passages of reflection on his ambition and creative gifts; he recorded his perceived failings and sins, his frustration with what he believed were obstacles in his way—stupid mistakes, lack of higher education, a colonial Canadian accent—and his, at times, almost paralyzing loneliness. Protestations about the pain of being alone, coupled with his impatience at needing other people and needing to be loved, recur obsessively. For the young Findley, who turned twenty-three in London with the Guinness family, this was much more serious than homesickness, although he was often very homesick. His dread of being alone and lonely took on existential dimensions. He frequently felt spiritually isolated, abandoned by God and his fellow human beings, and when offered affection or companionship he was suspicious of the other person's sincerity and motives. While he had a real basis for his fear of loneliness—he was after all the proverbial stranger in a strange land, insecure in many ways, and lacking friends of his own age—the intense feeling of abandonment and fear of rejection go back to the anxiety caused by his traumatic separation, as he always saw it, from his parents, especially his father, during the Second World War, further exacerbated by Allan's negative reaction to having a gay son. But he had objective reasons for mistrusting peoples' motives when they seemed to offer friendship. He struggled constantly with his sexual urges, drank heavily, and, as the journals make clear, he despised being courted for that fraction of himself that was gay and loathed himself for getting so drunk at times that he couldn't remember his actions from the night before.

Such personal passages read as if he were talking to himself, and there are indications that he saw the journal almost as an interlocutor, a companion, and a sympathetic listener. Early in the first journal he wrote that he was pleased to know that he could "safely reveal myself to myself without fear of being spied upon," and somewhat later, after settling in with the Guinness family, he realized that "this writing has been good for me. Some of my fears have been written away" (LAC 332:3). Sometimes he rose to peaks of self-castigation and frantic doubt about his future; at others he relaxed into spontaneous delight over a beautiful piece of music, a rewarding film or play he had seen, or a book he was reading that moved and inspired him. And he made lists of quotations from his reading, lists of books he must read, lists of his records, lists of his favourite writers, and lists of things in nature that pleased him. There are equally long lists of his sins and failings, but he was cautious, self-censoring, about explicit sexual confessions: "Sin abounds in my loins," he lamented, but the particulars are left unwritten.

Sin is Findley's word; he uses it frequently in these journals. The word seems old-fashioned in contemporary, secular society, where people rarely lament their sins, but Findley was almost biblical in his views at this time. Having grown up in a stern Protestant environment, he believed that sin was real and that punishment was deserved and inevitable. He read his Bible and tried to stay on the straight and narrow path to purity, hard work, and worldly success. In January 1954, full of anguish and doubt, he wondered what he would become: "An alcoholic wreck? A dissipated has been of the arts? A dabbler in all things; a reality in none?" (LAC 83:9). At times, his journal writing assumed a kind of religious introspective function, and the journals often read like the spiritual agonizing of an individual wrestling with God who repeats his *mea culpa* and promises to improve. He was terrified of being found wanting and desperate to lead a worthy life. While these passages in the journals, shot through with guilt, rage, and fear, are painful to read, there are many other passages that astonish and delight with their sheer exuberance and capacity to entertain. Together they provide clear evidence of his talent, his individual voice, and his ability to use language. All protestations of guilt and failure aside, Timothy Findley at twenty-two knew he had creative gifts and wanted nothing more than to use those gifts to the full. He was very ambitious and believed emphatically in his artistic mission.

———————

Findley began volume 1 of his London journals on 4 September 1953 while sitting in his parents' living room in Toronto. He was in a reflective frame of mind, concerned for the well-being of his family and full of admonishments about his own behaviour. He wrote at length about his brother Michael, who was already in serious trouble with alcohol, and he ruminated on a failed relationship with a man in Stratford whom he identified as "D."[7] He also wrote about the temptation of suicide; however, he knew that he loved life too passionately to give it up: "life to me is wonderful," he wrote, "and ordinarily I can see every reason to preserve myself with great care" (LAC 332:3). He knew liquor could defeat him, and he also knew he was an "artist" and "destined for greatness," and that he must not give in to alcoholic escapes. At 1:45 a.m. on September 5, still writing down his worries about Michael, his thoughts turned to his parents and to the home they had created—"the real peace of this home—the total giving that I feel as I sit here—the sense of having been given a great deal of love." Although he was leaving this love behind, he knew he was taking "something worthwhile from this home," and he wanted to give back his best. There is no hint here of the anger and resentment he so often expressed against his father in his journals. Perhaps knowing that he was on the verge of leaving the parental home, where he had to hide his identity, enabled him to see that he also had much for which to be grateful.

He devoted sixteen journal pages to the nine-day Atlantic crossing on the *Scythia*, where he was attracted to a beautiful woman, partly because of her inner beauty and partly because she so clearly adored her husband. "I want some day to have such a companion," he said, "and oh it is too bad it may not happen. The well of loneliness is deep."[8] He found most of the other passengers boring, and he criticized a group of newly graduated university students because they appeared to think they knew it all. Findley was already a writer at work: watching others, standing apart, observing without being observed, and then imagining identities for those individuals he found noteworthy. Sometimes he created mini-stories about these strangers, who became characters with invented desires and motivations. When his attention turned inward, he pondered what it took to be a great actor and decided that, most of all, he wanted "to become totally myself. I do not want to become Alec [Guinness] or Tony Guthrie or Lawrence of Arabia or James Joyce or W. H. Auden. I want to form the intended me." The "'priesthood' of the arts," he concluded, "is what I do seek." Even at this stage his ambitions were far from modest: Guthrie, Joyce, and Auden set a benchmark he planned to meet in his own way.

After the *Scythia* docked at Southampton on September 17, Findley travelled by train to London to stay with the Guinnesses in their large, elegant, rented house at 7 St. Peter's Square. Guinness was in France for a film shoot, but his wife, Merula, greeted him warmly, thereby starting a friendship that he cherished. Despite her warm welcome, however, he was nervous. He was constantly homesick, especially for his mother's companionship, and terrified of Guthrie, Michael Redgrave, Sir John Gielgud, and other famous actors and writers who visited the Guinness home. He felt embarrassed by his Canadian accent, his lack of education, and his inability to say anything appropriate in a conversation. The prospect of starting classes at the Central School for Speech and Drama overwhelmed him. To the journal he confessed that he had to stick it out and not retreat to Toronto and television work, but—"Oh how I wish I had gone to school—what a god-damn—bloody—fool I was not to keep on no matter what happened." Then he suddenly shifted to a brighter key: he had seen Redgrave in *Antony and Cleopatra* and in *Lear* and he focused on an analysis of both performances, which were, he decided, too controlled and intellectual, "neither truly great nor convincing." After the first two days of classes he admitted that he was more happy than terrified and that he was "thrilled" with the attention given to voice production and breath control.

Without question, Alec Guinness (1914–2000) was an important presence in Timothy Findley's life over the next two-and-a-half years, but his influence was not always benign. Guinness was generous and supportive of Findley's career, and he introduced his young protege to a world of books, art, music, and theatre culture beyond anything Findley had access to in Toronto. But Guinness was complex, with a troubled past, and his biographers concur that his childhood of "flitting" produced an adult man who cultivated disguise in his private and professional life.[9] When Timothy Findley joined the household, the home was full; in addition to Merula Salaman Guinness (from a distinguished, well-to-do secular Jewish family) and their young son, Matthew, there was a housekeeper, Alec Guinness's private secretary, a chauffeur (Guinness always used a chauffeur), from time to time Guinness's mother (whom Guinness disliked and mocked), and several pets—two dogs, a cat, and a parrot. Findley was impressed by this cultured home. The animals immediately helped him to feel comfortable, and during 1953–54 Dick Easton sometimes stayed in the Guinness home, so he had a fellow Canadian for company. Soon after his arrival, Findley discovered that Alec Guinness was in the process of converting from his Anglican faith to Roman Catholicism (he entered the church formally in March 1956), and Guinness introduced Findley to the saints, notably Teresa of Avila (a favourite Findley saint, whom we will meet again). On evenings when Guinness read aloud from various religious texts, he expected Findley to join the family.

As Guinness's career progressed, with successful stage and film work, he became wealthy and increasingly intent on controlling his life and the lives of those around him. Biographer Garry O'Connor describes him as a man who wanted power over himself and others to such an extent that people grew to fear he would withdraw his "favour" (238) if they dared resist him. Guinness called his autobiography *Blessings in Disguise*, an apt title for a life that involved many disguises—on stage, in films, and in private. His highly successful life, which on the surface comprised wealth, fame, and a happy home, was much less attractive behind the scenes. Both biographers Garry O'Connor and Piers Paul Read describe him as nasty, even cruel, to his wife and son; the home revolved around him and conformed to his wishes. Moreover, Guinness was bisexual and, according to O'Connor, he "had love affairs with men" and possibly sought casual sex with younger men. In fact, although this was not public knowledge during his lifetime, Guinness had been arrested, charged, and fined in 1946 for homosexual activity in a public lavatory. Read claims that Dick Easton was one of these young men (249), and that Merula knew why her husband brought young men into their home. At some point, Findley realized that he too was expected to be one of these young men. Was he? What did his private relationship with Guinness entail? Guinness was extremely guarded about many aspects of his life, including sex, so what did Timothy Findley, who despised the double life, think about his mentor's secrecy? It was not until 1955 that he confided, in some detail, to his journal that he finally rejected Guinness's overtures, so I shall come back to these questions in due course.

Once Guinness returned from filming scenes for *Father Brown* in France, however, everything seemed wonderful: the family dined out and took Findley to various sights in London and further afield through the countryside. Guinness brought gifts from Paris for everyone, including Findley (a new tie), and he bought a portable watercolour paintbox for him on a West End jaunt. But when Guinness mentioned sending him to see Hugh "Binkie" Beaumont, the famous London éminence grise and theatre manager/producer of the H. M. Tennent Company, who controlled many actors' careers, Findley froze in terror. He was in London to pursue an acting career and grateful for Alec Guinness's mentorship, but he was certain he would "flumoxe the whole meeting" and that he needed "hours of prayer for courage" to prepare for this interview. Getting an appointment was extremely difficult, Guinness warned, and a young actor's future depended on Beaumont's good opinion. During those first few months in London, as he waited for the summons to Beaumont's office, Findley worked hard to improve his acting and expand his education. He read scenes from *Hamlet* under Guinness's guidance, met famous actors like Sir John Gielgud, Peter Glenville, and Richard "Dickie" Burton at the Guinness dinner parties, and attended plays and concerts. After copying Coleridge's "The Pains of Sleep" into his journal, he began one of his lists:

"I want more and more, these days, to read and read and read . . . I have not yet touched Dickens or Thackeray, Tolstoy, Dostoevsky, Pope, Dryden, nor yet conscientiously, even the mighty Bible" (LAC 332:3). Timothy Findley was finally catching up on the education he knew he lacked.

In the midst of all this activity and preparation for the dreaded Beaumont interview, however, a dark cloud gathered over the entire Guinness household and the British theatre community at large: Gielgud was arrested on charges of soliciting (or as the authorities put it in the fifties, "importuning male persons for immoral purposes"). As Findley explained in a 26 September 1985 letter to Mary Lou Finlay (who was working at the CBC and had become a good friend), it was teatime at the Guinnesses' on the afternoon of 22 October 1953 when the phone rang. Guinness answered it—"The 'phone was offstage' in another room—and all we could hear was: 'dear god—oh the poor man—' and then silence."[10] When he returned to Merula and Tiff, he told them the terrible news: "John has been arrested. It's on all the front pages." No one in the London theatre community of the 1950s would have been surprised to learn that Gielgud was gay, and Alec Guinness certainly knew that his friend took risks, but the impact of Gielgud's arrest and the subsequent scandal was especially chilling because the professional theatre included many gay men. Moreover, the 1950s saw aggressive witch hunts against suspected homosexuals, who were viewed as dangerous perverts or likely spies. This was, after all, the time of the Cambridge Five. Guy Burgess and Donald Maclean had defected, and even a brilliant mathematician like Alan Turing, who had served his country during the war, could be driven to commit suicide because of his homosexuality. It stands to reason, then, that those in the theatre business were extremely worried that a wider public investigation would catch them in its net.

This thought crossed Merula's mind the moment her husband broke the news. As Tiff told Mary Lou Finlay:

We sat without words—and then Alec excused himself. He just left the room. I looked at Merry. She was white and her hands were shaking on the table. We'd been friends and very close from the moment of our meeting—but we both knew why I was there and the next thought we had—together—was "What if there's an investigation ...? We would all fall down."

Surely this admission (made thirty years later) that both he and Merula "knew why I was there," clears up any doubt about Findley's relations with his mentor, but his 1953 journal is silent on the matter. Instead, he focused on Gielgud and commented at length about the scandal: he worried about Gielgud's future career, railed against the newspapers responsible for creating a scandal—they "should be burnt to the ground and their bloody editors shot"—and then reflected on the general hypocrisy about sex, homosexual and heterosexual, and the vicious intolerance of most people. "The mystery of perversion," he wrote, "is so far beyond our imaginings that we as human beings surely have no cause to censure" (LAC 332:3). Nevertheless, the diatribes in the papers with their attacks on Gielgud and their "great paragraphs of indignation saying that all homosexuals are insane and ought to be tossed out of society," revolted him. If he had imagined cosmopolitan London as a far cry from Toronto's bigotry, he was wrong. According to biographers Sheridan Morley and Jonathan Croall, John Gielgud was devastated by this public scandal. He suffered a nervous breakdown and would never allow the subject to be raised in the future. In the immediate present of October 1953, however, the great actor rallied to perform in the opening of *A Day by the Sea* at the Haymarket, and the show went on.

What with the Gielgud scare and bouts of bronchitis, October ended on a mixed note. Findley enjoyed a car trip through the English countryside with Dick Easton, and he continued to read seriously and prepare, as best he could, to meet Beaumont. As his twenty-third birthday approached, Guinness suggested that he call home. Long-distance phone calls were rare at this time, so when the call finally went through on November 1, he was thrilled; talking with his parents, who were almost four thousand miles away, was "madly homesick making but truly wonderful." He received presents from the Guinness family and a "wonderful letter" from Janet Baldwin, whom he missed greatly. But then "disaster" struck. At a party he "drank scotch straight" and made a spectacle of himself by leaving "in shirt sleeves and [with] a complete loss of memory." He was later told by Dick Easton and the Guinnesses that a taxi driver "found [him] in a gutter" and brought him home. To say he was ashamed of himself is to put it mildly. Guinness was "wonderful about the whole thing," but Findley knew he had let the family, and himself, down, and he realized that a pattern had begun in which he experienced highs of happiness followed by despair and crushing lows, which were often followed by a binge. Despite his acute shame over this "disaster," and his recognition of a destructive pattern to his drinking, he did not pause (as he surely should have done) to analyze his behaviour in his journal or to consider what caused him to make such a "spectacle" of himself: was he drowning his sorrows (feeling lonely and rejected), showing off his taste for scotch, simply being foolish, or, once he had started to drink, was he unable to stop?

Over the following week he wrote at length about his "battle over faith" in himself. He went through a litany of recriminations: he was stupid; he lacked knowledge; he was "failing to sacrifice [his] private wants and desires ... to the creative me—the important me" (LAC 332:3). Laments like these occur frequently in his London journals at times of self-doubt and depression. Nevertheless, he believed absolutely that he was destined to be an artist, and he resolved to take full advantage of every opportunity to learn and find his way. He attended Peter Glenville's lectures to RADA (Royal Academy of Dramatic Art) students, he observed Guinness at work filming scenes for *Father Brown* at the Riverside Studio, and the Guinnesses took him to Salisbury to see its historic sites. All this pleased him, and he was grateful. In the middle of one page in his journal, he wrote this warning: "Your depression is a weakness." Had Guinness said this? Had Janet Baldwin scolded him in a letter? She had already warned him not to "self-dramatize or indulge in self-pity" (LAC 332:3). More likely he recognized his depressive tendencies and was talking to himself, as he so often does in these journals. A high point occurred on 20 November 1953 when he, Merula, Dick Easton, and Matthew (the Guinnesses' son) saw Benjamin Britten's *Peter Grimes* at Covent Garden. As far as I can determine, this was his first major opera experience and, although he was disappointed that Peter Pears was not performing the role of Grimes that evening, he was full of praise for the production. "A wonderful opera," he wrote, "that deserves many more performances and certainly it should last as one of the very best of the modern works," which it has (LAC 332:3). A few days later, jealousy over Dick Easton's good fortune crept into the journal because Easton had landed a film role, while he was still waiting for something to come his way, but as November drew to a rainy close, he prayed for patience and success with Beaumont, took the Guinnesses' dogs for walks, and listened to Guinness reading aloud to the family from the Gospel of the Nazarenes. Findley admired Guinness's voice and reading skill but made no comment on the reading material, a Jewish/Christian apocryphal gospel account of the original teachings of Christ.

The fateful day of his meeting with Hugh Beaumont at Tennent's was December 10. For weeks he had worked himself into a state of anxiety and apprehension, so he was surprised to find Beaumont "a very kind man." The interview went smoothly and proved to be something of an anticlimax, although he left Beaumont's office still uncertain about which roles he might be offered, and he would not hear further until the new year. Findley was hoping for a small part in a production of Bridget Boland's *The Prisoner*, in which Guinness had the leading role, but even as he fretted over the audition, he hesitated about committing himself to an acting career. In Canada, he suspected, "one just settles down to '*being* an actor,'" and Findley already knew he wanted "something bigger to work for." This thought led him to his first serious assessment in these journals of the state of creativity at home: "There are still films to be made in Canada. I am sure. There is an untapped quality there. And our playwrights are still in the grey unknown. Oh yes there is a future, but they are all so damned lazy over there about doing something. And so afraid to be bold, and to take chances. Damn it, there is too little creative life, too little going forward" (LAC 332:3). Canada was always in his thoughts, and comparisons between a centre of artistic life like London and what existed at home were stark; moreover, he was beginning to doubt that his artistic ambitions could be met by acting.

As his first Christmas away approached, he began to send cards home and to plan the gifts he would give if he could afford them. He wanted a bound set of Beethoven's sonatas for Dick Easton, and he made a "record," which has not survived, to send to his parents; for them he read poetry—T. S. Eliot's "Journey of the Magi," Robert Frost's "Stopping by Woods on a Snowy Evening," and "three of mine." "I must confess," he noted, that "I read my own better than the Frost or the Eliot" (LAC 332:3). Christmas day was lonely, despite the warmth and generosity of the Guinness family, their gifts (Guinness gave him a cigarette case and silk pyjamas; Merula's gift was a recording of Britten's *The Rape of Lucretia*), and a splendid dinner. His thoughts, understandably, were of his parents, Janet Baldwin, and the family. But at the end of 1953 he reflected on his good fortune: he had completed the classes at the Central School, had seen and heard some magnificent works of art, survived his first audition with the formidable Binkie Beaumont, and taken trips around London and other English cities to explore the layers of history such places offered. Although he was still waiting impatiently for news of an acting contract, he recognized the central role Alec Guinness had played in his life over these few months: "I have been living with a great man. I have taken part in his life and he has taken part in mine. He has given me confidence, education and values [and] taught me that I must live my own life" (LAC 332:3). Timothy Findley was maturing, even though he still had a long way to go. In the months and years ahead, periods of depression recurred; self-doubt continued to plague him; and anguish over what career he should choose never left him in peace. But 1954 was about to begin well.

———

The second volume of his journal covers the period from 30 December 1953 to 20 July 1954, and he began by describing his ten-day trip with Dick Easton through Somerset and Devonshire, where he enjoyed their long walks exploring the countryside and the small towns with their pubs. Refreshed and happy, he arrived back in London to the news that he and Dick Easton had contracts with Tennent's. Findley's was for a small part in

The Prisoner, and he was ecstatic.[11] This meant work, a salary of £10 a week, and a role in a play that would tour. Best of all, he could watch Guinness at work. Things should have continued to move along smoothly, and they would have, except for the fact that Findley seemed unable to be satisfied or happy for any length of time. He was writing poems in the journal and had sent Janet Baldwin his script for a ballet, which she praised. Guinness's reading aloud was relaxing, and listening to Mahler's Symphony no. 4 was "a quiet inspiration." Nevertheless, he was slipping into another depression: "But how sad I am" without a close friend, he wrote; "I am so desperately lonely" (LAC 83:7). This familiar lament must have arisen, in part, from his being gay and having to exercise great caution, but the reasons for this acute loneliness include other factors; after all, he was living at the centre of a vibrant theatre community with many gay men, so finding companions should not, in itself, have proven impossible. But Timothy Findley at twenty-three was highly self-conscious, quick to feel a slight, insecure, a colonial boy with no clear place in Britain's intensely classed society where you were instantly identified by your accent, and very ambitious. He was also proud and, as was increasingly clear, extremely needy.

On 23 January, he drew up a list of the possibilities, pro and con, for his life:

An alcoholic wreck?
A dissipated has been of the arts?
A dabbler in all things; a reality in none?
Mad?
A suicide?
A leaf in a cyclone?
Yes all these I still might be.
And on the brighter side how far can I go?
An actor?
A poet?
A novelist?
A playwright?
An exceptional Actor?

A film star?
A poet of note?
A great actor?
Yes and all these I still might be.
And yet how infinitely easier are the chances of my attaining the state
layed out in the first category than in the second. As I stand now I am a
"reality in none." But I *want* the other list. (LAC 83:7)

In an effort to cheer Findley up, Guinness gave him his old makeup box, which he could use on tours. But the doubts, fears, and longings continued, producing extreme shifts in mood.

To my knowledge, Findley was never diagnosed as bipolar or manic-depressive, but he felt deeply the burdens of being "different" (as he put it), of extreme loneliness, and especially of frustrated ambition: "I want I want I want the whole world to see me and know what I have to say." Small parts in modest plays, or even in Shakespeare, could not fulfill such ambition or match his conviction that he was an artist. What's more, his obsessive concern with self was not attracting friends. "I have been too immersed in self," he admitted. Even Merula and Alec Guinness were irritated and advised him to stop complaining. Judging from comments in his journal, he and Guinness had had a falling out and he feared that their "relationship [could] never be the same." Although he doesn't specify what caused this rift, he describes going on a major bender to escape his worry, which resulted in a lengthy, rambling examination of his past, of a few early friends like Dick Cousland, and of his family, who all, in his opinion, ignored and misunderstood him: "Mi [Michael] was separated [from him] by outright masculinity. Mother thru ... the war and poverty and Michael being sick and father being drunk and me being a weakling. Father was just never there." He felt that only Janet Baldwin was a "true friend" (LAC 83:7). Findley wrote to her regularly during his years away and she answered him faithfully with news of his parents, with reports on the arts scene at home, and always with wise words of encouragement: "Oh darling," she wrote on one occasion, "do buck up your mind—I miss you so." His letters to her were his "safety valve." Hers to him were the loving letters of an older sister.[12]

Opening night for *The Prisoner* in Edinburgh on March 2 should have been exciting, but no: "I am a failure ... I am not good enough." Walks in the cemetery and reading the New Testament merely confirmed that he had "nothing firm to hold on to." Although he had been listening to Guinness read religious texts, he was not able to believe in either the Roman Catholic faith or his parents' stern Protestantism. Thankfully, Dublin was a delight—he loved the Irish after the dour Scots—and his spirits soared. His landlady appreciated the theatre, served good food, and, best of all, had a piano that he was welcome to play. During the Manchester run he enjoyed his pleasant digs. Again, there was a piano, a radio, and, this time, hot water. He luxuriated in his "first [bath] in a week and a half! All the dried sweat and make-up gone at last. What joy. I lay in the hot water for almost three quarters of an hour and do you know it's the first time I've been really warm in weeks" (LAC 83:7). But he continued to worry over the rift with Guinness, and he was devastated when Guinness criticized his "too balletic" way of moving on stage: "I'll have to put an end to it if I have to castrate myself," he confided to his journal, in an outburst of self-loathing in which he seemed to attribute his way of moving to his sexuality, instead of to his training as a dancer.

After the company reached Liverpool, he abandoned such self-pitying thoughts. He gave Guinness some of his poems to read; he visited an art gallery; and there was a piano in this rooming house. Together with other actors staying there, he sang and played and, for once, seemed young and carefree. Until, that is, letters reached him from home. One from his father precipitated this journal confession: "Must say that we've probably hated each other's guts more violently than any other 20th-century father and son but at least we were honest and from that has come the basis for a *real* friendship and understanding" (LAC 83:7). That said, anything approaching a *"real* friendship" with Allan Findley was many years away, and some terrible scenes lay ahead. The last stop on the tour was Cambridge, where spring had arrived, and when he was not performing he visited King's College Chapel, noted the names of the war dead, and then rode a bike out to Grantchester to commune with the spirit of Rupert Brooke, visit Byron's Pool, and have tea at the Red Lion, with its picture of Brooke. Years later he drew on his memories of Cambridge for scenes in *The Piano Man's Daughter*. Once back in London, however, he filled the journal with pages of worry and his dislike of hypocrisy, and by the third week of April 1954 he had moved out of the Guinness home and into his "garret," as he called it, at 60 Warwick Road, Earl's Court. Understandably, this move signalled his need to be independent and to not impose on the Guinness hospitality, but his concern with hypocrisy also suggests that he was seriously troubled by his position in their household. Moreover, the pain he observed in the kind of sexual triangle he witnessed in the Guinness home stayed with him, to be explored years later in his fiction.

When his parents wrote to tell him that they had seen the documentary film about Stratford's first season, with the scene of a young Tiff Findley listening to Alec Guinness's advice, and that they were full of pride, he was very pleased. In fact, he was in regular contact with his family, and during 1954 Allan wrote him two or three times a month. For a father-son relationship that the son saw as seriously dysfunctional, these letters are surprising because they are full of news, words of encouragement, and attempts at fatherly advice. Findley could not like this man, but there is no doubt that Allan was trying to be supportive. For his part, he kept his parents informed of his activities and sent them his short stories, in the vain hope that they could get them published. In one letter, after passing along news of family and friends, Allan closed with fatherly advice: if you are depressed, he said, read the Bible—"Proverbs, Romans etc. I found them a great help, especially when I was living like a lard-ass myself" (LAC 96:7). Then he told his son to blame himself, not the Lord, for his problems— advice Findley certainly tried to follow, as his constant pleas for God's help and his repeated confessions of guilt, sin, and failure demonstrate. Not all of Allan's letters were so preachy, however. In another he updated his son on news about Stratford and described his painting classes, his reading, a hockey game, and his work with the Ames Company. News about Michael was unsettling, and in a February letter Allan described a dreadful binge in which Michael smashed furniture and vomited all over his bedroom in his parents' home; he also alerted Tiff to Michael's plan to visit London in the summer. Allan advised Tiff on his health, praised and kept every letter Tiff sent home, inquired about rehearsals and touring, and reported on his and Margaret's social life, including an evening at one of Janet Baldwin's ballets, in which, Allan insisted, Tiff could easily have taken the lead. For a man who had sneered at his son's ballet lessons this surely showed a change of heart. It seems that Allan Findley was beginning to see some hope for this younger son at a time when the elder son was a frightening disappointment.

Findley found life in his garret extremely depressing, and the prospect of Michael's arrival in London was no comfort. He was acutely lonely and ashamed of his need for others; he damned "the worldly popular beautiful people," who he accused of not caring about the future, and he lamented his indulgence in sex and drink: "I am a chosen person who can't help himself," he wrote, as he struggled with the competing claims of his Protestant conscience (which also bolstered his sense of being "chosen") and the temptations the city offered to a young man (LAC 83:7). To distract himself from such thoughts, he prepared a six-page list of his books and records. Shakespeare, the Bible, and the Oxford dictionary were standards, but other items on the list were more unusual: Donne, Swift, Henry James, and T. S. Eliot (*The Use of Poetry*) appear with André Maurois, Dostoyevsky, Gide, Rimbaud, Rilke, Oscar Wilde (*Essays*), Hopkins, Emily Brontë, Shaw, the plays of Euripides and Aeschylus, and John Bunyan's *The Pilgrim's Progress*. He owned a study of autobiography, a book on the life of Teresa of Avila, whom he would recreate in his last big novel, *Pilgrim*, art books, Remarque's *All Quiet on the Western Front*, Orwell's *Animal Farm*, Auden's *The Age of Anxiety*, Isherwood's *Goodbye to Berlin*, and several Waugh novels (including *Brideshead Revisited*). Clearly, he was immersing himself in the literary masters and reading well outside the English canon. His list of records would expand with time, but for now it was short—four Beethoven symphonies and two piano concertos (one by Mozart, the other by Beethoven). All the books returned to Canada with him, and this careful cataloguing helped him define who he felt himself to be and gave him a degree of self-confidence in his growing education. His library also provided him with a badly needed sense of home; it furnished his thoughts, fed his imagination, and held loneliness at bay.

One evening he enjoyed a visit from the Canadian actor Don Harron, and after dinner they returned to the flat and talked for hours.[13] The next day depression struck. Although he was glad to be far away from the Toronto show business scene as Harron described it, he was alone: "I am alone all day each day. I am alone at night—I am alone alone—but saying it doesn't help. But there is nothing sensible that I can do. I'm sick of reading—I can't relax—even writing in this book doesn't help. Nothing helps. Anyway there aren't any words that come anywhere near the horror of my existence alone—Rimbaud was right. This world stinks of death" (LAC 83:7). When Dick Easton landed a role in Thornton Wilder's play *The Matchmaker*, Findley was envious; worse still, when Easton dropped the Wilder for something better, he was "jealous as a baboon." Alec Guinness's report that Noël Coward had praised his performance in *The Prisoner* gave him a small lift, but he was waiting for a new role and on 1 June 1954 he wrote: "Still no news. I am forsaken." Finally, he put into words the crucial insight that he might not, after all, be meant to be an actor. He wondered if "God" was telling him that he had "given [him]self to the wrong profession." Eventually he got a small part in a play that would tour that summer, with the promise of a role in *The Matchmaker*, and by late June he was in Edinburgh again for a brief run before moving on to Glasgow. He saw his first production of Chekhov's *The Cherry Orchard* that summer and knew instantly that it was a great work of literature; so enthralled was he by the play that it became one of his particular favourites. From Glasgow he made a short trip south to the village of Ecclefechan, the ancestral home of the Findleys and the birthplace of Thomas Carlyle. As he later recalled, he knelt there and kissed the earth.

When the news reached him about the role he was assigned in *The Matchmaker*, however, he was "heartbroken" because his part was that of the barber, who has a mere six lines at the beginning of the play, after which he exits, never to be seen again. Barnaby was the role he had wanted, and once more he felt denied his due. In the midst of a long lament, he summed up his acting career thus far: "There have been digs in London and rooms in Glasgow—and rotten eggs in Edinburgh and no money in Manchester and washing strung up on a chair and bugs and lice at War- wick Road [his London garret] and leaking roofs and sordid train journeys and going mad in Sunderland I will never forget. These things too make an artist" (LAC 83:7). Then, pulling up his emotional socks, he concluded that at least he was "not rotting in drink in Toronto." By July 13 he was back in London and staying with the Guinnesses, when his brother Michael arrived in England. Allan had written to his "Dear 'Snifter'" (a nickname he often used), warning him about Mike's situation and urging Tiff not to support his brother with money or other forms of help: "If he does get to you, make him stand completely on his own feet or he has had it." Allan then put the matter bluntly—"the boy feels 100% that the world owes him a living" (LAC 96:7). Although Allan's warnings alarmed Tiff, he could not ignore his brother. Sally Murray, Michael's fiancée, was already in London, so Tiff and Sally met his ship at Tilbury Docks, after which the three went on a serious pub-crawl to celebrate. Nevertheless, Findley flatly refused to introduce his brother to Alec Guinness because he was "apprehensive" about his behaviour—"I'm afraid of the worst in Mike as I am in myself"— and he was also reluctant to spend time with Mike and Sally because every outing ended in a drunken scene. While Michael's arrival and the increas- ing stress of alcohol marred these late summer months, Findley's dis- appointment over the casting for *The Matchmaker* was a source of agony and fuelled his need for booze. "I have never been a happy drinker," he admitted, and he deplored his "dissipation—both by drink and by the hand," and his equally sinful waste of time. On the last page of this journal (LAC 83:7), he wrote bitterly that "this is the end of volume 2. *My*—how impressive that sounds. Volume one and volume two of the Journals of Timothy Findley, the famous actor. Hah! Hah! Hah! Hah! *Hah!*"

His notebooks from this period contain an odd mixture of poetry (his own), drawings (usually of faces), references to Hamlet and Orestes, in- coherent fragments about Cain and Abel, lists of words, and confessional passages about young men whom he found seductive but was too cautious to pursue. He was also writing a play he called "The Last Days," in which a young man, who falls in love with another man and is rejected, decides to kill himself. This play may have evolved into the work that he eventually asked Alec Guinness and Thornton Wilder to read, but both men found the material he showed them lacking in humour and too abstract to be stageworthy. It was also too subjective in its focus on a young man, very like its author, who is living in a "society [that] refuses to let him be what he truly is." At several points in volume 3 of his journal, which covers August to December 1954, he taped pages from a religious calendar to keep track of people's names and his appointments and rehearsal dates (LAC 83:9). Each month's page is dominated by quotations from scripture, religious poetry, and moral maxims. The December page, for example, carries a lengthy quotation from Isaiah, a poem by Laurence Housman, and Christ's words from the Gospel according to John: "I have come that they might have life." At twenty-four, Timothy Findley still seemed to need constant reminders of his faith and his duty to God and himself, but he would soon become completely disillusioned with any form of Christian belief. On a happier, secular note, he also taped a snapshot, labelled "Janet at Cambridge," into the journal; it showed him standing beside an older woman, looking pleased and relaxed. Janet Baldwin made several visits to England while Findley was there, and each time he was delighted to have her company, travel with her, or go to the ballet.

Rehearsals for *The Matchmaker* began on July 31, with Findley in the role of Rudolph, a waiter, instead of the barber with six lines. How this change of role came about he does not say, but he was "still wallowing in a disastrous despair," and Alec Guinness's view that his part was so minor as to be non-existent would not have lifted Findley's spirits. He couldn't help worrying about his brother; he felt uncomfortable as a guest in the Guinness home (he had escaped the garret for a temporary respite); and he suspected he was a disappointment as an actor. And yet, there was much that interested him: he saw a production of Pirandello's *Six Characters in Search of an Author*, a play he had looked forward to, and he was discovering the works of Thornton Wilder.[14] He preferred Wilder's *The Skin of Our Teeth* to *The Matchmaker*, which he analyzed at length before concluding that it was really a comedy in which philosophizing and moralizing don't belong. This caveat notwithstanding, he concluded that Wilder had a "supreme" gift as a writer. As rehearsals for *The Matchmaker* continued, he warmed to the play and most especially to Ruth Gordon in the title role of Mrs. Dolly Gallagher Levi—the matchmaker.[15] Wilder himself showed up for some rehearsals, and Findley found him "wonderful." During these weeks in August, he not only discovered a play that would stay with him for a long time, but he met two people—Gordon and Wilder—whose impact on his future would prove decisive. And there was a new friend, an English actor, who was also in the *Matchmaker* cast and whom Findley mentions for the first time on 16 August 1954: "I have met another Alec—so I will call A.G. 'A' and McCowen I will designate with 'A.Mc.'" (LAC 83:9).

The Matchmaker began its tour on August 18 in Newcastle, where it received rave notices. The cast was large, which meant that most of the actors had minor roles, but Findley became friends with several of the actors, and being part of the team and watching a veteran like Ruth Gordon at work was good experience. For the most part, he was enjoying himself, but as the weeks passed he became increasingly worried about Michael, who was living in London with Sally, refusing to find work, and pestering him for money, just as Allan had predicted. He also became frantic over a young Canadian woman who had fallen in love with him because he could not return her affection and blamed himself: "I can't bear to see anyone falling in love with me. I'm not decent enough to people. I feel like such a shit [because] it adds up to what I am—how do you change yourself? I want to so badly. I'm so fucking proud and so conceited and useless." Deeply insecure, he believed that "everyone" hated him, especially Alec Guinness, and this young woman's affection triggered some of his worst fears: "Now I am afraid of love again—and yet it could be true—but I'll die before I hurt anyone again—or myself" (LAC 83:9). Findley knew who he was thinking of with this reference to hurt, so he did not name names, but such a comment probably refers to one of the young Rosedale women whom his parents had wanted him to date and, equally important, to the fellow male actor he had loved, and been rejected by, while at Stratford. Nevertheless, love was slowly re-entering his life with Alec McCowen.[16] *The Matchmaker* cast spent about two weeks in Edinburgh, which gave Findley time to enjoy some of the festival, visit exhibitions of Cézanne and

Diaghilev collections, both of which delighted him, and take long walks with McCowen. One of these walks, along the River Forth, took them through fields and meadows to a small seaside town, where they lay on the beach and then had tea before returning to the city for their evening performance. His description of their day together is rapturous. What's more, the personal joy seems to have cleared a space for him to reread the poetry he had written over the past year and to conclude that it was childish, full of "such insipid words as 'soul' and 'God.'" This realization, captured in so few words, may seem minor in the larger context of his career, but at the time it was perceptive because it marks a crucial step towards finding his own vocabulary and voice as a prose writer.

The play's next stop was Liverpool, where he took in a production of Marlowe's *Edward II* that disgusted him because Gaveston (Edward's lover) was depicted as a "depraved queer" whom no one could love. His first encounter with Verdi's *Requiem* was an entirely different experience. This *Requiem* would be one of the most important works from the classical repertoire in Findley's life, but on this occasion he was almost speechless. Sir John Barbirolli conducted, Elisabeth Schwarzkopf sang, and in his journal he described it as "an experience I shall never have again." All the same, he was relieved to get away from Liverpool because the actors' boarding house was dreadful, and he was increasingly fed up with his role as Rudolph. Just the act of writing down these feelings brought him one step closer to a decision about his future. Realistically, he could see himself "becoming for Tennent's ... someone who can play the little parts.... There is no growth in that—there is nowhere to go" (LAC 83:9). Where the cast and play were about to go, however, was important and, for Findley, it proved to be a profound revelation.

After stops in Brighton and Oxford, everyone boarded a plane for Berlin, and the shock of what Findley saw there stayed with him forever. He wrote to his family describing aspects of his response to Berlin, and he devoted nine pages of his journal to an emotional, detailed reaction to what he had seen. On 27 September 1954, safely back in London after the week away, he wrote home:

The first sight of the destruction was of course pretty ghastly—in so many places there are *still* heaps of rubble just pushed back from the street and side walks. Every time one sees these things one wants to scream—you feel as though the politicians must be raving madmen— to be in such a position where war could ever be remotely possible. We've had it twice and we can't stand it again. Believe me—the world *won't* survive another one. If you can imagine the cities we love— Toronto and Montreal and Quebec—in such a state. There would be no downtown—no dockland—no Rosedale—it would be flat. I saw the Reichstag—the Brandenburg Gate with its enormous red flag and the Unter den Linden beyond it. There are weeds across the canal yard of the Reichstag. And Hitler's ghost was there—and voices—and the million raised up hands.... If you have read any Rimbaud—you feel him here in the terror dreams at night as you walk down the streets and see the twilit empty windows—and the fingers of ruination crooked up at God in the sky. You feel the whole and great unanswered—never to be known—the enormous <u>WHY?</u> of war. (LAC 97:6)

He drew a picture of the ruined buildings across the bottom of the page to help his parents understand, but his reference to Rosedale in ruins probably drove the point home more effectively.

As blunt and disturbing as these comments seem, what he confided to his journal was more telling and almost certainly would have shocked his parents, given their strong British allegiance:

As we went down the avenue towards the Reichstag—and we stood looking at the Brandenburg Gate and past it down the Unter den Linden I heard distinctly—quite sadly and slowly sung—the brotherhood chorus from [Beethoven's] ninth. Why should such a nation need to be deformed in such a way? Why Hitler? Why the need? What has defeat done—and the war—and here we are again—and there is still hate—and fear—and terrible distrust—perhaps never to be overcome. [...] Such destruction as there has been—this unbelievable and moving sight Berlin—means nothing apparently. [...] I am called impractical when I talk like that. [...] I don't know anything about politics that say there <u>must</u> be another war. [...] I don't understand. <u>When</u>—since we've had two wars and should for humanity's sake KNOW they achieve nothing—(I ASK YOU—WHAT DO THEY ACHIEVE SAVE EARLY AND AN UNJUST DEATH)—why have another?" (LAC 83:9)

His thoughts grew darker still when he, Alec McCowen, and fellow actor Prunella Scales visited the Russian sector of the city. As he told his parents, "the Russian soldiers ... are very sweet and terrifyingly young. Poor things." But in the journal he wrote that East Berlin was "appalling." The Stalin Allee (a mile-long monument built for propaganda purposes by the East German government) was "hideous," a "deadly atrocity." Findley was already opposed to war, but what he witnessed in Berlin that September deepened his anger considerably, not simply about the death and destruction incurred in a war, but more importantly with the politicians who fomented wars, with the industrialists who profited, and with the average person who refused to think for himself. In the broadest sense, he saw war as the annihilation of all that is creative in life. Berlin symbolized that destruction. Witnessing the city in ruins made the imagined facts and reported history real.

———

By October 1954 he had begun writing a new play. Guinness liked what Findley showed him, and, to Findley's surprise, Thornton Wilder agreed to read the completed text. This development was most encouraging but, as so often seemed to happen, with the good news came the bad. As a single Canadian male of the right age living in England, he was eligible for military call-up and "the British army had its eye" on him. The British National Service summoned him to an interview and required him to complete a form explaining his business in the UK and his reasons for requesting an exemption from military service. While he waited nervously for news, he devoted several journal pages to what can only be called a rant. He was "appalled, sickened, and devastated" by the summons and by the thought that two years could be "wrenched" from his life by these "Impersonal bastards." "It's wrong—it's wrong," he wailed; "My god—when the time comes—when the war comes—of course I'll fight—of course I'll die—not bravely, not wanting to—but I'm prepared to face the fact that *then* (but only then) it will be necessary." On November 4, he received their reply: although they had decided that he was "not at present liable to registry," his "case would be reviewed on 1-10-1955" (LAC 97:5). He was off the hook, but only for a year, and he immediately contacted Binkie Beaumont asking for more and better parts; he was damned (he complained to his journal) if he'd do "fucking Rudolph for the rest of [his] life."

Meanwhile, he and Alec McCowen were becoming constant companions, and by the end of October, with his twenty-fourth birthday approaching, he was grateful to be back in London, staying briefly with the Guinnesses, listening to Poulenc, Berlioz, and Brahms, and enjoying "a great hot bath" after eleven weeks on the road with *The Matchmaker*. The thought of this birthday, however, elicited some of the strangest writing in journal 3 (LAC 83:9): he suddenly began writing about Michael and calling himself "It." "It" has a brother who had the most "efficient army" and "was always conquering Its armies," which reduced "It to terrible tears." Now that this brother had grown up, he refused to do anything and expected others to take care of him. But "It feels very badly because It feels that It hasn't been very nice to him—I mean that It let him down morally." Findley continues in this bizarre, disassociated vein for a few more pages before compiling a three-page list of writers, composers, actors, and artists whom "It" admires. As a child, Findley had been dismissed by his older brother, perhaps even called "It," and even now, with both men in their twenties, Michael had the capacity to make Findley feel that he was the guilty failure in the family, a nothing, a genderless It. Once again, a list served to reassure him, as if naming famous people proved his own self-worth, which Michael denied.

Later in November 1954, he found a new flat at 20 Cranley Gardens, in a first-floor room, for £2 10s. per week, and it was close to two tube stations and near Alec McCowen's place. When he received good news about a possible role in the film version of *The Prisoner*, with Alec Guinness as the Cardinal, he excitedly imagined what his parents would think: "They will go into the cinema [...] and there I will be. Me. Tif [sic]. And they will curl up inside and know that I have achieved something and they will be proud of me. At last" (LAC 83:9). A few days later, however, this dream had collapsed and he despaired: the Rudolph role was a waste of his time; the army reprieve was temporary; and Michael was doing nothing but drink. Then the news of his father's poor health reached him. Allan Findley had entered Sunnybrook Hospital for tests, but the doctors had no answers yet about what was wrong. This was the first indication that Allan Findley might have a serious illness in addition to his alcohol addiction. Through these ups and downs and family worries, McCowen was sympathetic. The two spent more and more time together, going to concerts, plays, and films, walking beside the Serpentine, or doing crossword puzzles in the *Daily Mail*. On November 17 Findley told his journal that he and McCowen were looking for a flat to share, and he was "thrilled" by this prospect.

An invitation to spend another Christmas with the Guinness family also delighted him, as did a postcard he received from Thornton Wilder, which he transcribed in his journal.[17] He attended a Khachaturian concert in December at which Aram Khachaturian (1903–78) conducted his own work—a thrilling and unique experience in itself—but the Concerto for Piano and Orchestra in D-flat Major, played by the English pianist Moura Lympany, filled him with rapture: It was "*My* concerto," he wrote; "My life is in that music" (LAC 83:9). Alec Guinness visited him in his new flat to check out his living arrangements and to pick up a typed copy of Findley's completed play, and Findley noted in his journal, almost casually, that he was writing a short story, but he gave no details. At lunch on "Sunday, 12 December 1954," Guinness, who fancied himself as a writer, returned the play with considerable criticism of its faults, but he also told Findley that he could write and would, perhaps, do so one day. Then he gave his protege a radio, which Findley treasured, and advised him on the writers he should read—Tolstoy, Dickens, and Balzac. To say that Findley was grateful would be to understate things: "there is no one I respect more," he wrote. On December 13, Wilder's letter arrived with his critique of the play and the news was not good. Findley copied the entire letter into his journal, as if to inscribe Wilder's discussion more deeply into his own psyche. Wilder told him that his play was a lecture, not a play, and he quoted Henry James at Findley: "dramatize it." But Wilder ended on an encouraging note; "Write lots," he advised. "Don't be so at-a-distance meditative," and read the masters. Was Findley disappointed? Yes. Was he shattered? No. His reaction to the letter was heartfelt but, in the final analysis, grateful and optimistic. Two busy men he respected, reacting separately, were telling him that he had a lot to learn, but that he had potential. Wilder had actually said that he thought "highly of [Findley's] talent and [his] gifts." Their messages were "proof that I have responsibilities to something in me that might kill me all stone dead if it were ignored" (LAC 83:9).

Christmas Eve and Day of 1954 were spent with the Guinness family. They passed two restorative hours at St. Nicholas Church singing hymns and praying, followed, thanks to the Guinness hospitality, by gifts, good food, champagne, games, and long walks. Findley returned to his flat feeling content. The rest of the holiday period, however, was turbulent. He had dinner with Dick Easton and Leo Ciceri (a Canadian actor visiting London), but he was angry and "childishly bitter" about Easton's continued success. As far as Findley was concerned, his friend boasted too much and was a sycophant. There was no long-distance telephone call home this year, which saddened him, but once McCowen had returned to London after visiting his own family, Findley was much happier—until, that is, McCowen was called to audition for a part in Terence Rattigan's *The Deep Blue Sea*. When no call came for him, he "sat in this room and was quite mad. [...] I was right off the deep end. I am afraid. [...] Nothing is worth living for" (LAC 83:9). Even Beethoven's Fourth Piano Concerto failed to cheer him, and an evening with Michael and Sally left him seriously hungover and depressed. On New Year's Eve he listened to a radio program about the First World War—"a most devastating program of reminiscences from 1914" that marked the fortieth anniversary of that first Christmas, when the troops on both sides had called a temporary truce to play football in no man's land, for which they were severely punished. "I can see millions of young men—young like myself—like I am now on this day—lying dead—or hurt—made useless and pointless," he wrote;

"they died for nothing" in that "futile wastage" of the war (LAC 83:9). He dreaded the prospect of another war, and in his journal he described a nightmarish vision of his own body "lying naked in the fly-moving heat of a battle-field." Only truth, hope, and love, he believed, could overcome the forces of warmongering.

The last eight pages of this journal are truly alarming. He seemed nearly hysterical because he had argued with McCowen, who, he said, "denied my talents." In point of fact, McCowen had not denied Findley's talents; in an undated letter, he urged Findley to think of himself as "extremely talented" and to be patient about his career (LAC 100:42). Findley, however, decided to "dispense" with McCowen. "What is the sense of a second year of this [Tennent's] contract?" he wondered, and then he wrote: "I believe now—that I am ill. That I must be mentally ill."

Timothy Findley was not "mentally ill," if by that term one means a clinical diagnosis, but by the end of this first year abroad, he had recognized a pattern in his abrupt swings between periods of happiness and confidence and shattering lows of alcohol and despair. Self-doubt and suspicion that friends and colleagues disliked him or were about to abandon him simply overwhelmed him at such moments and precipitated these bouts of self-dramatizing despair. That said, there were sound objective reasons for his state of mind. He was deeply disappointed by his lack of career progress, jealous of others' success, fiercely competitive, and terrified by uncertainty about his future. Although he was dealing with the challenges of being a Canadian colonial in the heart of the Empire (no matter how weakened it was by the war), of being gay when to be so was illegal, of coping with a brother's destructive influence, and of lacking an education, it would be a mistake to overlook the intensity of Timothy Findley's ambition and fear of failure as the root causes of these attacks of despair. In the fall of 1953, as he set forth on his journey to England, he had told his journal that he would join the "priesthood of the arts," and he sincerely believed he had talent and was duty bound to make something important of himself. He wanted— needed—to be recognized by others as the artist he knew himself to be. But he still had no clear career plan and he was frantically impatient.

CHAPTER FIVE

Actor or Writer?

———

NO MAIL.

NO STORIES RETURNED.

NO PLAY TO PLAY.

NO ONE.

NOTHING BLOODY.

(Timothy Findley, July 1955 [LAC 84:5])

"You are a writer, Findley"

I t snowed heavily in London that January of 1955, and Findley was delighted: "Snow. Beautiful snow. It is a winter from long ago. I am— my window is—the whole of everything is Canada [and] while this Canadian winter is itself—however briefly, I am going to see it." So out he went into the cold, leaving behind the gas fire in his room, which only warmed a small part of him while the rest of the room remained frigid. This marked a nostalgic start to another period of professional doubt and loneliness. "Here we are," he wrote a few days later. "Shit! In this same bloody room—I was here last night too [and] every other fucking night as well." Two letters from Alec McCowen offered reassurance, but Findley was hesitant about resuming their relationship. McCowen advised him to be patient and stop making deadlines for success; he urged Tiff to break free of his self-imposed "Time Factor" and to stop "playing games with [his] life." In another letter, he warned Tiff not to make hurtful comparisons: "it would be awfully nice," McCowen wrote, "if you could think of us as 2 people and not as 2 careers." (LAC 100:42). Findley, however, was in no mood to listen. Instead he launched into a lament about having no new roles and being stuck with Rudolph in *The Matchmaker*.

A Christmas card from Herbert Whittaker, the leading Canadian theatre critic,[1] precipitated a rant about artists wasting their time in Canada: "What's wrong with that lousy place? No pride—no ambition—wake up Canadians." He was only twenty-four, but his analysis of the state of the arts in Canada was perceptive and courageous. "We have accepted as the gift of other nations which have struggled to attain it for themselves— *the right to believe*. But we are wrong. As a whole nation we have neither struggled nor suffered *for* the whole nation" (LAC 83:11). Although he did not use the term "cultural nationalism," he blamed the individual Canadian, especially the artist, for being "tied to his European" assumptions about quality, and he singled out the idea of a national Canadian cultural and artistic identity as the necessary motivation for struggle and success. His exposure to an established, wide-ranging British scene helped him understand what was missing back home, and he decided that "we lack 'aspiration' as a nation. We do not rise beyond ourselves," but stick with the search for material things. And what should be his role in addressing this "lack"? "I see that because *I* reach—*I* must have them reaching with me—or *my* search will be as worthless as their personal complacency" (LAC 83:11). This is one of his earliest formulations of his commitment to his country through his art. He wanted personal success, of course, but he also wanted to contribute to higher artistic endeavours at home.

Once again music cheered him. On January 9 he wrote a detailed and passionate discussion of Verdi's *Requiem*, which he listened to on the radio, and he was utterly enthralled: "it is one of the greatest pieces of music ever written." After attending a live performance of the *Requiem* in February he analyzed the structure of the music in detail, compared Verdi with Mozart and Bach, and explained why Verdi's masterpiece meant so much to him: "It is such a piece of drama that one forgets the meaning of Christianity and is led into a world where God's trumpets herald our destruction rather than our salvation." The Dies Irae filled him with "exultant terror." "As a picture of the end of the world," he wrote, "it is certainly the one which I will carry within me" (LAC 83:11). A radio broadcast of Francis Poulenc's Concerto for Two Pianos and Orchestra in D Minor also made a profound impact on him, and he concluded that "Poulenc is my composer—he says without a flaw—word for word—something which is so deep down [in] my insides that even I can't finally pick it out." If Findley was aware of the parallels between his life and the French composer's struggles with sexual identity and depression, he does not say, but this concerto, despite its more playful moments, has many dramatic, emotionally probing passages.

Toward the end of January, he received a copy of Tyrone Guthrie's *Twice Have the Trumpets Sounded*, Guthrie's sequel to *Renown at Stratford*, about Stratford's second season. Findley was particularly struck by Guthrie's appraisal, critical but not dismissive, of "the Canadian scene" because Guthrie wrote with eloquence and authority about the importance of theatre as a force for good in the world. Guthrie argued that Canadians needed to speak as Canadians, in their own voice and manner, instead of imitating the British. This notion that Canadians needed to find their own distinct voice stayed with Findley as, week by week, he inched closer to a decision about his future career, and he was moved by Guthrie's "astute" comments, which made him "want, very badly, to go back and enter into the soul of the nation."

As these journal entries show, Findley vacillated between arrogant confidence—"conceited to think I should be of the best? Not at all. I am. I know it"—and crushing self-doubt. Although he described "acting as a ghastly profession," he was not yet prepared to abandon the stage or leave England. At this critical juncture, however, Thornton Wilder's advice began to nudge him further toward a career decision and a writer's life. On January 20, he met Wilder in his room at the prestigious Savoy Hotel on the Strand. Over a memorable dinner, which Findley recalled in *Inside Memory*, Wilder told him—"You are a writer, Findley. That's a certainty"—and advised him to discard his draft play and start afresh: "Pay attention, Findley. Pay attention. That is all you have to do" (IM 31). Findley was exhilarated. When Wilder questioned him about his personal life, he found Wilder to be "a great psychologist" because he suggested that there were "psychotic reasons for a good ninety percent" of the early illnesses that had kept him from school (LAC 83:10). If Findley discussed the trauma he had faced by being gay with Wilder, he made no mention of it in his journal. Instead, he recorded that Wilder tackled his "lack of faith in [him] self" and his need to hear others tell him something was worthwhile and that he urged Findley to forgive himself for being human, to recognize the common failings of the human race, and to embrace his "brotherhood with mankind." Struggling to recall and savour every word, Findley wrote: "He said that I *had* to stop punishing myself" for perceived failures and guilt. This recollection of Wilder's comments resonates clearly with the self-portrait that emerges from Findley's England journals of a young man pursued by the furies of sexual guilt, despair, pride, alcohol, and frustrated ambition. What he does not yet seem able to confront, even though Wilder's advice pointed in that direction, is the role that his family and upbringing most certainly played in his fear of failure. As we shall see, many years later Wilder would return to Findley's problems with his family and advise him to move on with his life.

Wilder was equally blunt about Findley's writing: "he said that I wrote with a bridle on my pen as if I was ashamed of the stage as a medium for presenting my ideas," and that what he needed to understand was that "in writing—the craft is all" (*IM* 31). The meeting ended with Wilder's gift of four Swiss cigarillos and a walk to the theatre, where Wilder left him with this message: "You know my address. Write to me" (LAC 83:10). And he urged Findley to cultivate a sense of humour and find joy in life. Later that night, with another performance of Rudolph behind him, Findley concluded his journal reflections with his first honest acknowledgement that he had to make a choice between acting and writing: "I feel in my heart that day coming [...] when such a choice must be made within me. [...] However—now—I have no worry. I am not (I said it just now) ready yet for such a decision" (LAC 83:10). He had his contract with Tennent's for another year and he was determined to make the most of the time.

Through February and March, he continued to attend concerts and plays, visit art galleries, and read *War and Peace* and *Moby Dick*, which he found boring. He was able to glimpse "the vision" he knew existed "inside" him when at the theatre, or in some paintings, music, poetry, and ballet, and in his "recurrent dreams of Southern Ontario." However, the familiar worries about his career and his family plagued him. Although he did not identify the people he was thinking about, or describe his behaviour, he saw himself as wasting time and as "tormented by lust," which he felt got in the way of his honesty in relationships and tarnished his sense of self-worth. He expressed his frustration by attacking the page with heavy, multiple underlinings, large black capital letters pushed into the paper, and emphatic punctuation. He understood that it took years to become an actor of Ruth Gordon's calibre; therefore, he was, in a sense, screaming at himself from the journal page. When I held this journal, I was struck less by what he said (the complaints were familiar) than by the violent way he said it; this was one of those moments when a biographer encounters his or her subject directly, when Tiff Findley came alive for me, in all his passionate frustration, on the physical pages in my hands.

In addition to this professional anxiety, Findley was deeply troubled by his brother's behaviour. Allan had warned him that Michael must not be catered to, but the reality of dealing with him, on the spot, in London, was another matter. Michael would call Tiff in the middle of the night, drunk, desperately lonely, and asking for money, but Tiff felt powerless: "I just can't help him—I want to—God the Father knows I want to—but I can't" (LAC 83:10). And this inability to help exacerbated his guilt complex. "I do love him," he wrote in his journal, but they were two very different types of men, and Findley, who placed great value on personal appearance and on making his flats, however bare and humble, into orderly homes with books and music, was disgusted by Michael's "swollen face," "nicotine hands," "drinking," squalid living conditions, and childish demands. The Findleys, increasingly concerned about their older son's mental health, planned to bring Michael home in the spring, and Allan wrote Tiff to say that they knew Michael was "a terrific problem" and that they hoped to find out what was wrong with him (LAC 96:7). This was a truly heartbreaking assessment for a father to make, but there is no indication in this letter to Tiff that Allan recognized his responsibility for raising a son who was spoiled as a child, was indulged as a man, and was now emulating the worst aspects of his father's behaviour.

When Findley received an exciting offer to join the Shakespeare Memorial Company, albeit in minor parts, he had to decline because of his Tennent's contract. Although he would have toured Europe with John Gielgud and Peggy Ashcroft and learned much, this disappointment was probably for the best because Dick Easton was also going and with better parts to play. Findley was convinced that Easton's good luck had more to do with whom he knew, and how, than with talent. The thought that his friend traded sexual favours for roles in plays was not a kindly one; therefore, Findley dropped the insinuation and turned instead to a lengthy critique of his own abilities, failures, and fears, not least his fear of flying, which a European tour entailed. Between his utter terror at just the idea of flying—"I am dead, the minute I enter an aeroplane"—and his jealousy over Easton's good fortune—"if Dick is in the company playing grand-dame parts I shall die of mortification"—he was much better off on terra firma in London as the hapless Rudolph (LAC 83:11). Nevertheless, he was angry and bitter, and he used his journal for a combination of prayer and confession. This time the "you" was less the journal itself, although that interlocutory role always hovers over the written page, than a more conventional address to God. Findley believed that he had come before God in the right frame of mind: "I have come <u>NEEDING</u> you—isn't that enough. I have come <u>unconditionally</u>—isn't *that* enough. [...] I keep asking for your help and you are forever silent [which] makes me doubt your existence" (LAC 83:11).

What did help was art. He was swept away by Hemingway's *The Old Man and the Sea* ("a real little classic" and "I will always have this book to read"); and he was deeply impressed by Akira Kurosawa's films *Seven Samurai* (1954) and *Rashomon* (1950). He found Toshiro Mifune's body breathtaking for its muscularity and effective use, and he explained at length that this had nothing to do with sexual attraction because the artistry of these films and Mifune's acting transcended the physical realm and appealed to "something inspiring." Moreover, he was trying to write, and he listed nine ideas for projects he had started or wanted to attempt, including several poems, a "fantasy novel" about poets, and a play about the "un-born."

By the end of the month, Findley received word that his father had left the Ames Company and been offered a job with Bache & Co., a New York firm with a Toronto office, and the promise of $25,000 a year, a tidy sum in 1955 (in the end it was $15,000). He was pleased for both parents and relieved to think that his mother's life might become easier after many years of hardship. Allan had undergone tests at Sunnybrook during the fall that ruled out multiple sclerosis or a brain tumour, but he continued to feel "shakey" and apologized for his handwriting. For the rest of 1955, at least, his parents' fortunes seemed to be on the rise. They sold the Whitehall Road house and moved to a more prestigious address at 7 Strathearn Road, just west of Bathurst Street, with a garden backing on to the ravine. For the moment, Findley put aside his concern for his parents' welfare. However, during March his professional worries increased. He was discouraged by his writing and shattered by the success of his fellow actors. In a journal entry he threatened to kill himself. He shouted at God: "HAVE YOU <u>NO MERCY</u>!!" (LAC 83:11) He described confusing dreams about ruins, nightclubs, war, and Hitler, whom he killed in one dream, and he was exhausted and ashamed by a "week-long" struggle "with my body." When a rumour circulated that *The Matchmaker* would not only continue its English run but tour to New York, he was distraught because this meant another year playing Rudolph, which was "too much to bear."

But these crises paled in comparison with another dilemma. As I noted in chapter 4 in connection with the Gielgud scandal, Findley's presence in the Guinness home during the fall and winter months of 1953–54 involved Alec Guinness's expectation of sexual favours.[2] Now, after a year had passed, this matter surfaced again. In volume 5 of his journals (LAC 83:11), Findley reflected at some length on a traumatic episode that clarifies their relationship. In early March 1955, he recorded that Alec Guinness asked him "To-spend-the-night" (the quotation marks are Findley's) and that he refused, but the request and his refusal caused him acute distress because he worried about hurting Guinness, about being misunderstood, and about losing his affection and support. Nevertheless, he was certain that this was the only ethical decision, and he set forth his reasons in the journal, less to convince himself that he was doing the right thing, than to identify, as precisely as possible, his motivations. He carried on this discussion with himself for twelve pages, including what amounts to a prayer: "Please. Because I am afraid and because I don't know what to do—except that my head has told me what I must not do. Amen." On March 16 he had supper with Guinness in a pub, said what he "had to say because it was absolutely right," and thought Guinness understood his decision, but then sank into despair because Guinness ended the evening abruptly, told his chauffeur to drop Findley at his Cranley Gardens flat, and simply said, "Well—goodbye Tiff."

Although there are no details of tormented reflection in journal entries that Findley wrote after this meal, clearly he had been invited to have sex with Guinness. It is also clear that Merula knew about the arrangement and that this was not Guinness's first such invitation. Regardless of what had (or had not) taken place in the past, what is important here are Findley's feelings and principles. He believed that such intimacies created a "beastly and horrible ... false relationship between us"; "He is *my* friend—he has been my teacher—and is still my guide. I respect and love him." For Findley, such dishonesty threatened all concerned because it involved a degree of ethical equivocation and self-deception that he could not live with: "I cannot be false about this—I can no longer be false. It would only hurt him more and more. And her—she is his true guidance and his companion—there is love and need and trust between them. If I am to interfere with that—then I shall never be able to see them, either of them again." This decision was also based on his concern for Merula, for whom he cared deeply, and for himself. "It would destroy me" because "only unfaithfulness to ourselves can destroy [us]" (LAC 83:11). He feared losing Guinness's friendship by having said no, but he could not "lose her love and esteem" by breaking Merula's trust in him. There were no dire consequences, however, and, despite his fears, neither Alec nor Merula abandoned him. For Findley at twenty-four, however, on his own at the centre of a demanding, competitive theatre scene, where such liaisons were tolerated but never openly discussed, his decision required courage and honesty. He needed to be free from what he called his "bondage" to a fundamentally dishonest relationship, and he also wanted Alec and Merula Guinness to be free. He believed, emphatically, that his decision and his reasons were correct: "I have done the right thing. The Honest thing." Over the years ahead, Findley continued to struggle with the reality of such complex sexual triangles and with the degree to which they compromised his sense of identity and honesty and inflicted pain on the woman married to a bisexual or homosexual husband. In his last novel, *Spadework*, he would present a starkly negative picture of an exploitive relationship between an older, more powerful director and a young, ambitious actor, and in his play *The Stillborn Lover* he examines a similar marital arrangement and the anguish it causes for everyone involved.

"The readiness is all."

Findley's last year in England was crucial for his development as a writer. During the spring months of 1955 he surprised himself by completing three fine stories, "The Name's the Same," "War," and "About Effie," and it was in these stories that he found his own voice by listening to the way he wrote in his journals and heeding the passages that told him he was a writer. Guthrie's advice to Canadians—find your voice—and Wilder's assertion that he was a writer were taking effect. Moreover, it was time to go home. He had been homesick almost from the day he arrived in London, but he had persisted, had had some modest success, and was now weary of the struggle to advance an acting career. His parents had a new home, which he was keen to see—he even dreamt of building a little house on their property in which he could live—and he believed they needed him because Michael was in ongoing crisis and Margaret required surgery for what turned out to be cancer. He also sensed his country pulling at him to return, so he began to save his money and consider all the things he would have to take home with him, for which he joked that he "needed an ark" for the journey.

After Easter he planned to vacate the Cranley Gardens flat, which he had come to loathe, and move into a rented room in the home of theatre colleagues Michael and Elizabeth Hallifax and their children. He was delighted with this prospect: "It will be so wonderful to live amidst a family again" (LAC 83:11). The room itself was charming, with a window looking out on trees and a garden, and there was a piano. Easter itself he spent with the Guinness family in their beautiful new country home, Kettlebrook Meadows, near Petersfield. In other words, he was happy, comfortable in his friends and surroundings, working, reading, and ecstatic over his purchase of a recording of Verdi's *Requiem*: "it literally leaves me weakened of all resistance to death." Michael's circumstances, by comparison, were appalling. Sally had returned to Toronto, leaving Michael alone, and he took to calling Tiff at all hours to beg for money, cigarettes, and food. Findley devoted many journal pages to an analysis of Michael's problems and to a heart-wrenching description of inviting his brother out for dinner to mark his birthday, only to have him refuse food and demand one gin-and-tonic after another. When they returned to Michael's room, he was stunned by the squalor: "Well—I started to cry—like an idiot because I suddenly got this feeling of loving him and he wouldn't have understood that so I said it was the room that upset me ... [and] you feel as if that's the only way he's capable of living" (LAC 83:12).

What Findley saw was a mess of broken furniture, rows of empty liquor bottles, a shelf with a few "lousy books," and piles of scrap paper with bits of writing. Nothing worked. The gas fire sputtered and died; the other lodgers were coarse and unpleasant; there was no food in sight. This squalor reminded Findley of the way he had lived in Kingston during 1951–52, so seeing Michael's room and his drunken condition struck him with the added shock of personal recognition (a there-but-for-the-grace-of-God moment) and revulsion. He wondered what he could do, how he could best help, and why his brother was so lazy, so unwilling to do anything to help himself. He was by turns filled with anger and resentment at being used by Michael and then overwhelmed by grief at his own helplessness and Michael's abject failure in life. How utterly dreadful he thought it must be for his parents: "Imagine having two children like Michael and me!! Two failures." While such a remark has an element of self-dramatization, it also provides insight into Findley's internalized fear—terror really—at the spectre of failure that goes right back to Grandmother Findley's Presbyterian values and stern disapproval of her younger son (Allan) who could never measure up to her dead husband and war hero son (Irving). Unlike Michael, however, Timothy Findley was driven to overcome this spectre, but the emotional cost was high.

If the extraordinary anguish and analysis in these journal pages did not lead him to any practical answers for helping Michael, they did lead directly to a different kind of response to personal tragedy. On 26 April 1955, he told his journal that he had written "a very strange story and so Canadian (the writing and the dialogue) that I was quite staggered that I should write something in this style" (LAC 83:12). Michael, with his sordid room and wasted life, had inspired Findley to use his own voice, to listen to his and Michael's conversation, and to create from immediate experience and from his heart two believable characters and a moving story that he called "The Name's the Same." He carefully copied the story by hand and presented it to Ruth Gordon, to whom he had promised a story, and the next day she told him she was having it professionally typed and would try to get it published. He was overcome with gratitude: "Miss Ruth is the kind of person God grows flowers for," he wrote. She and her husband Garson Kanin gave him a typewriter and their strongest encouragement to write. Ruth was, he noted in the journal, "the third person to intimate that my career (not my career, my real *place*)—is as a writer not an actor." As if some barrier had given way, he seemed released from his tortured obsession with acting and let loose, at least temporarily, into a space where he could imagine a real future. By 13 May 1955, he had completed two more stories—"War" and "About Effie." Findley always called "About Effie" his first short story because it was the first to be published, in the 1956 inaugural issue of *Tamarack Review.* "The Name's the Same" would not appear until 1987, two years after Sally's death from cancer and Michael's hospitalization with Korsakoff's syndrome, and "War" made its first public appearance when Mavor Moore read it for CBC's *Anthology* on March 4 in 1958.

Together with its companion stories, "The Name's the Same" represents a decisive breakthrough for Findley. For the first time, he created fiction using his own voice and several narrative features that would become staples of his mature style. The story has a first-person narrator who is remembering the events he recounts for the reader in the casual, colloquial style of a conversation. The reader is frequently addressed—"I wish I could describe that room to you" (*Stones* 136); "I wish you could have seen Bud's bottles" (137)—and the plot is so simple, so basic and slice-of-life, that it seems as if nothing happens. The narrator, Neil, visits the London flat of his brother, Bud, where Bud's girlfriend, Katie, is preparing supper. Bud arrives, but is drunk and aggressive, and when Katie tries to stop him from attacking another lodger, he strikes her, knocking her down. Appalled, Neil intervenes: "I'll tell you right now," he says, "I really hated him then. I never wanted to see him again" (140). Later in the story, Findley draws on his journal description of taking Michael to dinner for his twenty-sixth birthday and returning to Michael's squalid room to create the final scene between Neil and Bud. Like Tiff, Neil begins to cry—"I cried from way down inside—you know, where it hurts you to cry" (146)—and, like Tiff, Neil feels he is to blame for his brother's desperate condition. Although this scene of drunken squalor and brotherly concern has its roots in personal experience, the story is a fiction in which Findley uses his journal for the details that enhance the realism of his characters' lives and as a way to remember and recreate his feelings of sorrow and guilt. This path from lived experience to the journal record and then to the fiction is one he would follow in most of his future writing. Although Findley never understood his brother and was never able to help or change him, by writing this story he acknowledged their kinship: both men were Findleys and susceptible to alcohol, loneliness, bouts of self-indulgent reliance on others, and extremes of self-loathing and pride. For the first time, Timothy Findley was paying attention, as Wilder insisted he must, to the world around him, to his memories, and to the lives of people close to him.

For "War" and "About Effie" Findley shifted the setting from London to Ontario, with Neil as a youngster who, as in "The Name's the Same," recalls events. In both stories, Findley captured the child's perspective on life and on those around him with remarkable skill. The vocabulary and prose are uncomplicated; the sentences are direct, often no more than fragments or brief statements, and Neil addresses us directly. For example, in "War" he describes the day he threw stones at his father, who had enlisted in the army without telling him, and in "About Effie" he begins quietly, as children often do when recounting something they find mysterious and important: "I don't know how to begin about Effie, but I've got to because I think you ought to know about her. Maybe you'll meet her one day, and then you'll be glad I told you all this" (*DAA* 82). This voice and the narrative style Findley uses to sustain the child's perspective are deceptively simple because what we read is not a child's unmediated voice, but an artist's creation of the illusion of that voice. There is nothing simple about this artistic feat, and it is astonishing that Findley discovered this voice so suddenly over a matter of weeks in April and May of 1955. Astonishing, yes, and for the biographer who has been tracing his steps and missteps, his detours and dead ends, it is exciting to see him emerge on the journal page and to produce a story like this—in his own voice. This was only the beginning, of course, but it marks the moment when he found himself and his vocation.

This encouraging period of creativity, however, was followed by yet another bout of self-doubt and despair. This time, incidents that seem inconsequential were enough to shatter his fragile self-confidence: Thornton Wilder had not written to him for some time and Ruth Gordon had passed him in the theatre without speaking; therefore, he blamed himself for offending them and devoted several pages of his journal to excruciating self-analysis in which he begged for mercy, success, and a clear direction in life. All he possessed, or so he claimed, was "you"—the page? the journal? the alter ego he so often dreaded? God? "I am alone with you—I know that," he wrote, and "I want to go home" (LAC 83:12). He believed he was "hated" and "cursed," while others were "blessed," and he sensed he was teetering on the brink of collapse: "Sometimes I really feel scared because I think that nervous break-down is coming back like I had before I went to Switzerland." By the end of the fifties he would once more have reason to "feel scared," but that's a story for the next chapter. My point here is that Tiff continually struggled against a slough of despair that, at times, threatened to pull him under—despair over his sexuality, which he saw as a curse, yes; but despair also, and more acutely, because he saw himself as an artistic failure with no future.

Predictably, when a letter from Wilder arrived a few days later, his spirits soared. When Ruth and Garson gave him presents—a toaster and a leather overnight bag that had belonged to Spencer Tracy—he rejoiced in the knowledge that they supported him. News from home gave him further comfort: Allan wrote to say they were enjoying the Strathearn house and gardens, which he sketched for Tiff, and this letter made him long to go home to the family, his books, and the piano. In this more positive mood, he started lessons in French and typing, and he slowly typed out a clean copy of "War," which Ruth and Garson planned to send to prospective publishers together with "The Name's the Same." "Remember how blessed you are," he told himself, how "fabulously lucky and privileged you are. Think it over" (LAC 83:12). This was advice he needed to remember but all too often forgot in the months ahead.

It is important to note that thoughts of Canada were constantly on his mind at this time. He listened to Sibelius's Symphony no. 1 in E Minor and felt "this would serve as a Canadian symphony [because] no one has arisen yet to give us these things." Although he greatly enjoyed a weekend visit to Kettlebrook Meadows, the spring gardens and countryside also prompted thoughts of home: "I miss the trilliums in Ontario. That is the most exquisite flower of all." The temptation to go home was "terrible": "I am deeply homesick for Canada" and "long to be a Canadian again" (LAC 83:12). In addition to this longing, another dark cloud gathered over him during these weeks of spring and summer. *The Matchmaker* closed its run on July 2, and, much as he had wanted free of the play, he grew distraught over his lack of future work and listed all the negatives facing him:

No mail.
No stories returned.
No play to play.
No one.
Nothing bloody.
[...]
There is no consolation in mediocrity.
There is no safety in second best.
There is no surety in the middle of the way.
There is no life in half a human being.
There is no point in an unpracticed art.
There is no hope without hope. (LAC 84:5)

By June 28 he had cheered up a bit because he was called to audition for *Hamlet,* and he turned down a request from American theatre producer David Merrick to stay with the cast of *The Matchmaker* as Rudolph for an American tour.

When he received a callback on July 3 to read for the part of Osric (the self-important courtier in *Hamlet*) with the director, Peter Brook, in attendance, he was apprehensive and delighted; however, this audition was a nightmare because there was no one to read the parts that support Osric's scene, and he had to struggle, unaccompanied, through Osric's lines. Brook was only five years older than Findley, but he was already something of an *enfant terrible* in the theatre community. For anyone auditioning before such a famous director, especially a young actor facing such a person for the first time, the experience must have been harrowing. As he waited for Brook's decision, he tried to maintain equilibrium and perspective. Janet Baldwin was coming for another visit, and that would be "wonderful." The practicalities of finding a new flat because the Hallifax family needed the room he had been renting were a distraction, and once more the Guinnesses invited him back to Kettlebrook Meadows for two weeks and then to their London home. If Findley still had doubts about Alec Guinness taking offence at Findley's rejection, these invitations reassured him. And despite his panic over the audition with Brook, he secured the role of Osric (with rehearsals to begin in the fall), and he renewed his relationship with Alec McCowen.

For vague, unspecified reasons, however, he began to feel haunted, shadowed by a "you" who never left him alone, a "'you' that apprehend[ed] and accompani[ed]" him with some vaguely threatening "mystery." The last page of his sixth journal is filled with a stylized drawing of the crucifixion (LAC 83:12). His money had run out and he was "suffering a kind of torment by demons." Concentration on anything was impossible when these attacks by "evil people" inside him occurred because he heard them talking to him, luring him away from work in pursuit of drink and sex. Journal passages like these make one wonder if Findley was, in fact, on the brink of a breakdown, or if hearing voices like this was merely a sign of an overactive imagination rather than something truly serious. On 1 August 1955 he received a very sharp letter from Alec Guinness who criticized his whining and egotism: you are so much better off than most other young men, he told Tiff—"RELAX!" This reprimand served to snap Findley out of his depression so he could focus on his acting and writing.

In August of 1955, rehearsals began for Wilder's new play, *A Life in the Sun* (later *The Alcestiad: Or a Life in the Sun*), which premiered in Edinburgh, and Findley was hired as an understudy. But letters from home brought a mixture of alarm and disappointment. Michael wrote with pompous advice on how Tiff should live, and Margaret wrote to say that she could not, as she had hoped, afford to come to England. Michael had been through "an electric brain-wave test," but neither his father nor mother provided Findley with a context for this medical step. He knew that the shadow of Aunt Ruth's mental health, with a possible genetic link, worried his parents, as it must have worried Tiff, both for Michael and himself. As the day approached for his return to London, he tallied up all the things he had acquired and declared that somehow it must all be taken home to Canada—the books, records, and pictures, "to say nothing of all the note-books and writings—the letters etc. which I mustn't part with." But his chief reason for excitement was that McCowen was meeting his return train from Edinburgh, and they would find "a flat for us to share. I am much *too* excited, I suppose." The move into their new flat at 44 Tedworth Square, in Chelsea, that September, inspired ten journal pages of delighted description of the place, with its two rooms, two beds, a coal-burning fireplace, space for his books, and best of all, a grand piano (LAC 84:5). So pleased was Findley that he drew a floor plan of the flat with a list to identify each object. What with candles to supplement the two light bulbs, a pot of yellow flowers, and a "beautiful gilt mirror," this little flat felt like a home. Sharing it with McCowen brought a new degree of serenity into his life.

In May 2013, when I arrived at Alec McCowen's South Kensington apartment, I was warmly welcomed by one of the few people still alive who had known Timothy Findley in his early years. We had first talked by telephone in June 2012, so I knew he had many clear and cherished memories of the mid-1950s and his time living with Tiff at Tedworth Square. What's more, the two men remained close friends for the rest of Findley's life. They exchanged audio-letters for years, sending cassettes back and forth with their news.[3] On that day in May 2013, McCowen served tea and biscuits as he reminisced amidst art works, theatre posters, and photographs—some of a very young Tiff—displayed in the elegant rooms. And of course there was a piano. McCowen kept a diary during the 1950s and he read me the entry for 19 July 1954, when he first met Tiff at their rehearsals for *The Matchmaker*. Over the next three weeks, they went out regularly after work, and one evening—he remembered this vividly—Tiff came back to his flat. They lay on the floor looking at art books and listening to a record of Muriel Smith singing "Bali Ha'i" from *South Pacific*; gradually their heads came closer together, then touched—and that was the start of their intimate relationship. Timothy Findley was twenty-three and a long way from home; Alec McCowen was twenty-eight, with many of the same interests in art and theatre, and a gentle manner. Both were good-looking, intelligent, sensitive, and ambitious. Would their relationship have lasted had circumstances been different? Probably not. Timothy Findley would not have made a good expatriate transplant, and he needed a degree of looking after that few people would be willing to provide, but their enduring friendship testifies to Findley's ability to retain such friends.

Living with Findley could be great fun or alarming and unpredictable. McCowen returned to the flat one night to find broken glass scattered about the room from a smashed bottle, but there was no sign of Tiff. The next day, after he had sobered up, Tiff explained that he had heard the news of James Dean's death in a car crash on a California highway and, because he identified with Dean, he "felt guilty" about the accident for some bizarre reason. His response to the news was to get drunk; McCowen's response, recalling that night almost sixty years later, was summed up in one word: "extraordinary!" But then he paused in the story to remember that in those days Dean was a cult figure and that Tiff adopted the Jimmy Dean look in his hairstyle, clothes, and pose. On another occasion, Alec was "furious" with Tiff's behaviour. The two had gone to dinner with friends, and Tiff frequently left the table to go to the men's room, where he drank scotch from a bottle he carried with him. After dinner Alec was tired and ready to go home. Tiff was not; he went off into the night on his own. At about one a.m., Alec was wakened by the police calling to say that a man at St. Stephen's Hospital needed him. He raced to the hospital expecting to find something terrible had happened, but he found Tiff giggling and pleased with his escapade. The police had found him, very drunk and wobbling along a parapet overhanging the Thames. He looked like a potential suicide, so they picked him up and admitted him to hospital. Alec was not amused, but he eventually forgave Tiff, took him home, bought him some flowers, and they carried on. This was the second report I had had of Tiff's misadventures on bridges, so I asked McCowen if Findley was ever serious about suicide. His answer was an emphatic no. There were also, of course, many happy outings and adventures, like the time in Berlin with *The Matchmaker*, when Findley and McCowen spotted Binkie Beaumont sitting in a restaurant with a young man in drag. They were astonished, but when Binkie told them that they should be back at the hotel sleeping to prepare for the next day's rehearsal, they beat a hasty retreat. As McCowen told me, in their circle no one ever spoke about being gay, and it would have been in "bad taste" to gossip about what they had seen. Back in London, after their evening performances in *The Matchmaker*, they ran over to the Globe on Shaftesbury to catch Bea

Lillie's second act.[4] They got in free, thanks to Binkie, and they stood at the back laughing with everyone else.

Apparently Findley never discussed his family or Canadian friends with McCowen. McCowen did meet Janet Baldwin on one occasion and realized that she and Tiff were close, and he believed that Tiff and Dick Easton were wary of each other and mutually jealous. About Alec Guinness, McCowen refused to speak. He acknowledged that Findley's relationship with Guinness had been strained, but he would not elaborate. McCowen was "shocked" by his one and only encounter with Michael Findley, and he recalled thinking that if he had had a brother he would have behaved differently from the way Tiff did. This meeting with Michael took place one day when Findley and McCowen were out walking and met Michael in the street. The two brothers greeted each other coldly and with formality: "It wasn't a brotherly meeting," McCowen told me, but he was unaware of Tiff's fear that Michael would be drunk and do or say something rude, and that Tiff felt awkward around this brother when he was with a male friend because Michael mocked Tiff's homosexuality and was quite capable of saying something insulting.

Over the next few months Findley enjoyed his life with McCowen, but rehearsing with Peter Brook was a constant challenge, as well as a golden opportunity to learn and to meet illustrious, experienced actors. Paul Scofield as Hamlet was "a most striking person," and it was during this production that Findley met "Mr. Thesiger ... scented and dressed to the nines." His reminiscences of Ernest Thesiger, who played Polonius, are among the best stories in *Inside Memory*. Thesiger, who had known Oscar Wilde, had been seriously wounded in the Great War but loved to make his colleagues laugh about it with his cavalier and ironic remarks: "*The noise, my dear—and the people ...*" (*IM* 40). Rehearsals were hard work, but Brook commanded Findley's "devout respect," and they agreed that Osric must be played without what Brook called "effeminate inclinations" (LAC 84:5). This was Brook's first crack at a Shakespeare tragedy, and he wanted a minimalist production—a bare stage, with few props, and none of the histrionics he disliked in other productions of *Hamlet*. Brook's request that Findley play Osric without affectation may have simply come from his vision for the play, but he may also have been warning Findley, the gay actor, to play the role straight.

News from home continued to trouble him, however. Margaret was still waiting for her operation and his father sent him the equivalent of £40 (the largest amount he had sent thus far), so Findley could begin to save for the journey home. Between rehearsals, he continued to read and attend plays and films; his first experience of kabuki theatre impressed him as "impeccable" and beautiful. He was reading Francis Parkman's *Montcalm and Wolfe* (1884) and was "amazed that no one—no novelist or poet has taken this story and made a great work around it" (LAC 84:5). Although he would not turn to this founding story of Canada himself, he was clearly struck by the possibility and by the country's need for fiction that explored Canadian history. After he saw the English-language premiere of Beckett's *Waiting for Godot* at London's Arts Theatre with Janet Baldwin, he told his journal that the evening was "an overpowering experience: This is a real play. Could take this sort of thing in great doses."

When confirmation arrived that *Hamlet* would tour to Brighton, Oxford, Birmingham, and then, via Berlin, to Moscow, before opening in London, Findley was ambivalent. He longed "to drop everything and go home," but he also hated to leave McCowen and "our lovely home—this flat. It is beginning to take on and give out great atmosphere" (LAC 84:5). After the play opened in Brighton on October 22, however, things began to unravel. Findley does not say what went wrong, but Brook was displeased with his Osric. In response, and true to his pattern, Findley got very drunk at a party and then worried that he was treating McCowen, who had come to see a performance, "pretty badly—and must stop. I love him and [...] he doesn't know this." On October 26 he made a real mess of Osric (again, there is no explanation in the journal), and Brook took him aside, discussed his expectations for the role, and helped him with "a brilliant touch." Fortunately, his performances improved, along with his confidence, so that by the time Janet Baldwin joined him in Brighton to celebrate his birthday and see the show he was more relaxed. When the tour reached Oxford, however, Findley hit another low: "acting is a ghastly profession," he wrote, and as the departure for Moscow drew closer his anxiety level rose steadily. Birmingham was "a ghastly city" and, when the cast arrived in London, there was only time for a hasty goodbye with McCowen, who was leaving for New York to play Barnaby again in *The Matchmaker*. Findley feared he might not return and missed him greatly. But there wasn't much time to mope; the *Hamlet* cast flew to the continent on November 20.

Findley kept careful notes, with dates and details about the flight and his arrival in Berlin, in a small notebook (LAC 84:1) that provides his only account of the trip and how he felt about Berlin on this brief stopover. He was, as always, terrified about flying, especially the takeoff, but after his initial fear he found "the rest of the flight a sheer delight." They landed at the Tempelhof airport at sunset and were taken by bus through the darkening city to the Casino Hotel in Wannsee. This time the experience hit him hard—harder, in fact, than his longer visit in 1954 had done. As the bus wound its way through damaged streets, he sensed—

> The rush and current of the dead—the blasts of forgotten horrors—the smell of emptiness and ghosts and the old sound of bells, of air-raid sirens, thudding bombs and the feel of fear. And it truly seemed as though people cried out from these massive tombs. I felt desperately as though I were the only one who had heard them—because everyone chattered away like school-children and most did not even look.

The night in the Casino Hotel was a relief because from the balcony he could "smell the air and it was like Canada—cold and hard and pined [with] the smell of fresh water and dead leaves." The next day's bus trip to the airport shattered this temporary calm, and his response to the sight of the city, written while in the bus, says it all: "This drive I shall never forget. This time desolation showed itself as more than ruin. It left you panic stricken—you wanted to get out and touch it because you didn't want to believe it was true." He never did forget that bus ride through the broken city. The memory of those sights shaped his thinking about humanity's predilection for destructive violence against which the artist must throw up the protective shield of creativity.

Moscow was a pleasing contrast. There were parties and a champagne reception to celebrate the first time since before the revolution that Russians had seen a British production of Shakespeare. He visited the Bolshoi Ballet to watch children rehearsing and attended a performance of Tolstoy's *The Fruits of Enlightenment* (1889). During the intermission at a Stanislavsky Theatre production he was mobbed by people wanting his autograph, and on the night of November 24 he reported that the cast's "reception was simply overpowering—with the lights up and the audience standing—and flowers everywhere and photographers taking pictures. [...] It was the kind of reception you dream about" (LAC 84:5). Sandwiched between performances of *Hamlet* and other activities, he visited Red Square and watched in astonishment as long lines of Muscovites waited in the cold to pass by the mausoleum, where the embalmed bodies of Lenin and Stalin lay in state. Lenin struck Findley as a great man, ruthless but wise; Stalin, however, had the face of inhumanity and "calculated terrorism." Findley was nauseated by what he witnessed and wrote a long diatribe against the brutality of Soviet-style totalitarianism in his journal. It was on this trip that he met the Canadian ambassador to the USSR, John Watkins, who would later be brought back to Canada on suspicion of treason and interrogated by the RCMP and the CIA in a Montreal hotel room in 1964. Findley chose Watkins to serve as one of the historical figures behind the character of Harry Raymond in his play *The Stillborn Lover*.

After the success of *Hamlet* in Moscow, things should have been shipshape for the London opening. But no. Apparently, Peter Brook again found fault with Findley's Osric, hurled "a stream of abuse" at him in front of the cast for feminizing Osric and, in what sounds to twenty-first-century ears like a nasty homophobic slur, threatened "to feed my carcass to the Leather Queens of Brighton" (IM 275). This infuriated Findley, who protested in his journal that he had been singled out because he hadn't "bought my way with gifts of fucking-love." He does not reveal who might have wanted sexual favours from him, but such a protest suggests that attempts had been made, if not during this tour of *Hamlet*, then at another time. Brook, who was happily married in the fifties and decidedly heterosexual, would not have been the culprit (see Kustow), which leaves the mystery regarding the identity of the predator in this theatrical sub-plot unsolved.

On a more pleasant note, Herbert Whittaker had published his interview with Findley, called "Flamboyant Personality an Aid to Russian Actor," in which Findley described his experiences with *Hamlet* in Moscow and commented on the theatre scene and the political situation. This was Findley's first interview, and his parents were delighted, although judging from Allan's letters, they were increasingly anxious for him to come home. Margaret was recuperating well from her surgery and Allan was busy in his new position with Bache & Co., but there were disturbing undercurrents to some of his letters to Tiff during the fall of 1954 and the early months of 1955. In one, Allan grew downright maudlin over his past behaviour, calling himself a "fraud" and Margaret a "handmaiden of Christ." In another, he went on for ten pages about God and how Tiff must control and redirect his sex life. Then he assured Tiff that he had never hated him, but that he would never understand his son's "feminine streak," "the make-up," and his "damn-fool relationships" (LAC 96:7). These letters are not fully dated, so determining an exact sequence and their impact on Findley is difficult because he does not comment directly on this letter in his journal. Precisely when he made a trip to Caux is unclear, but references in Allan's letters indicate that Findley had visited there again that fall. News of this visit made Margaret happy, and Allan hoped the MRA regimen would help Tiff. As far as his father was concerned, Tiff "wouldn't have got [himself] in so much trouble if all had been well at home." Although Allan does not say this in so many words, it also appears from this letter that he was blaming himself—specifically his absences, his drinking and infidelities, which hurt and worried Margaret, and possibly his criticism of Tiff when he was a teenager—for his son's homosexuality and unhappiness. Despite his sincere concern for his Tiff's welfare, however, Allan persistently thought and wrote about his sexual orientation as an aberration, an illness, even a sin, and, therefore, as cause for guilt and blame. Although he was no longer rejecting his son, he was most certainly criticizing him, something that must have hurt Findley deeply.

The year 1955 had been eventful and often positive, but it closed on a dismal note. Findley was drinking heavily once more and full of despair over his future career and his sexuality. He admitted in his journal to feeling "terrible bouts of homesickness when I can no longer stand on my own two feet but long to see that new house [on Strathearn] and to meet mother and father and Michael again" (LAC 84:5). But he was profoundly torn. Although he missed his family and his country, he knew he would face many of the old challenges, misunderstandings, and the need for subterfuge when he returned. He was increasingly disillusioned with the religious beliefs of his family (no doubt exacerbated by his second visit to Caux), and he despised the social moralizing and hypocrisy he had witnessed during the Gielgud scandal. He loved the theatre but was fed up with the life of an actor in London. He had not yet given up the profession, but he was on the verge of making a commitment to writing. His affection for McCowen was genuine, but their relationship was often difficult, in no small part because of his own behaviour. All he needed was one definite push to make him leave, and he did not have long to wait. The journal entry for 1 February 1956 reads: "On Monday the National Service and I am too sick with its details to be able to draw even on [enough energy] here to set it down. This is all in letters—I will leave it there. I must leave England by Easter. Good Friday, I note is the 30th March. We close [Hamlet] on the 24th which gives me a week to get out. And farewell England. Shit." (LAC 84:5).[5]

Predictably, this event led to depression and another bout of heavy drinking. He was plagued by sexual urges that wasted his time and energy and was disgusted with himself. He recalled "that ghastly winter [of 1952–53] in Toronto when [he] began to drink" so heavily, and felt he had sunk to similar depths. He could not even focus on simple things like getting up in the morning, and he exhorted himself to make an effort to stop smoking, drinking, and biting his nails. He must also have complained to Alec Guinness about his rage against the army and the unfairness of his fate because in a 1 February 1956 letter, which Findley copied into his journal, Guinness admonished him in no uncertain terms: "Do try not to take an hysterical attitude about it all—you will receive so little sympathy from people ten years older" who fought in the Second World War or from "chaps who have done their N.S." (LAC 84:5). He reminded Findley that many young men had suffered far worse than he and had much more to resent. Moreover, he warned Findley not to claim he was a pacifist before he thought very carefully about what that meant and about what duties such a stance might entail. Findley made no comment on this tough, honest letter, but the very fact that he inscribed it in his journal shows how important he considered it to be.

He turned instead to the many things he needed to do in preparation for the journey home and to contemplating what he would do after his return. On February 2 he wrote to his parents announcing that he was returning home to escape the clutches of the British army. "As to actually *getting* home," he confessed, "I am terrified" (LAC 97:6). He would have to borrow money from them and get professionals to pack his things so they would survive the trip, and he worried about which ship and route he could book. The suddenness of this decision left him little time to contact people in Toronto about possible work, and the prospect of having nothing to do troubled him. Because he wanted to reach Toronto alone, to re-enter his country gradually, he asked his parents not to meet his ship. He was even afraid, or so he told them, of meeting them again face to face: "just the thought of coming home really does put me in such a frenetic frame of mind" (LAC 97:6). And he instructed them not to open his trunks until he was there to do it with them so they could all share in the delight of unpacking the records, books, and his gifts for them. Through most of February, *Hamlet* played to near empty houses, so he did not feel much regret about leaving the play. He wrote at length in his journal about the acting opportunities that might await him in Toronto, possibly with television or radio, at the Crest, or with the Straw Hat Players, but he also noted that his writing was "stagnating." And he compiled another of his lists, this one of all the people and places he must see for the last time, and he described with delight his gift for Janet Baldwin—a pair of ballet slippers, purchased in Moscow, which had been danced in by the great Vera Volkova. A final, glorious weekend was spent at Kettlebrook Meadows with the Guinnesses. Whatever personal tension existed in his relations with Guinness, this family had brought him happiness and provided him with support and an education. And he fully understood this.

March flew by, but he made time to read Tennessee Williams for the first time, and, though he offered no discussion of specific plays, he found the American playwright's portrayal of homosexuality "interesting." Packed in his steamer trunk, along with Williams's plays and his considerable library, was a book Alec Guinness had given him in which he had written a line that Findley had heard at every performance of *Hamlet*: "The readiness is all." Years later, in an interview with Richard Ouzounian, Findley recalled this advice: "The readiness is all. Hamlet. And that's the truth. You have to be ready for it to happen. [...] You have to be willing to give your whole life to what your talent asks of you" (*Stratford Gold* 49). The English journals end with Findley and McCowen listening to Rachmaninov and Brahms, and in a tiny notebook entry for 28 March 1956, Findley wrote, "I haven't had a drink since the Sunday before Lent." And so the curtain descended on a peaceful close to the eventful, by turns wonderful and terrifying, London years. When his ship pulled away from the Southampton dock on the morning of April 5, Timothy Findley was ready to go home.

CHAPTER SIX

Beginning Again—and Again

CANADA! JUST NOW—IT IS WHERE I BELONG.

(Timothy Findley, 11 April 1956)

Coming Home

On 5 April 1956, Timothy Findley sailed from Southampton for New York on the *Queen Mary*, whose route began with a stop in Cherbourg Harbour and a view of the Normandy beaches, which reminded him of Canadian troops landing there on D-Day in June 1944: "Many lives," he wrote, "and now so peaceful." Fate, in the guise of a ship's route, had carried him on this brief detour, before heading across the Atlantic, to within sight of a place that reminded him of the Second World War and beaches still redolent of memory. Even if he wanted to, he could not forget or ignore that war and would often return to it in his writing. The ocean crossing itself was uneventful; however, he was lonely and anxious about meeting people in case they found him dull or dismissed him as a heavy drinker. Two Faulkner novels, *The Unvanquished* and *Sanctuary*, which he had bought to read during the voyage, did not raise his spirits. In his journal he praised Faulkner's prose as "inspiring," but he felt "demoralized" by *Sanctuary* and found the Popeye character "confusing." He did not elaborate on his views and Faulkner was never among his favourite writers, but he may have recalled Popeye when creating the rape scene in *Not Wanted on the Voyage*.[1]

By April 11 he was on the train from New York to Toronto and felt over-whelmed by conflicting emotions: "It is great to be back on my own con-tinent. It is where I belong. [...] And yet the thought of Toronto depresses me horribly." Findley's attitude about the city of his birth and youth would always be ambivalent, so it is not surprising to find him expressing such a feeling. He was, after all, returning to a place where he had no prospect of work and few close friends. When the train crossed the border at Niagara Falls, he noted the moment: "CANADA! Just now—and so I'm back" (LAC 84:4). The natural beauty he could see from the train window as it headed for Toronto filled him with delight. The reunion with his family, and his first tour of their house at 7 Strathearn Road, was wonderful. Granny Bull, he noted with pleasure, was still full of life at eighty-six. Nevertheless, he knew he would have to behave, as he put it, with "kid gloves." There would be no drinking to excess and certainly no expectation that they would accept his homosexuality.

Two letters from Alec McCowen awaited him and these brought much joy, as did the Sunday dinner at Aunt Marg's to celebrate Michael's twenty-seventh birthday. His father's family was smaller now, and Tiff missed his late grandmother Findley, so to re-establish "communications" with her he went to her bedroom, where, as a boy, he had often retrieved her bottle of sherry, and "she was there to say 'hello.'" Being home again included living with the dead. He felt impatient and extremely nervous about the immediate future and the temptation to drink, but he told him-self that "tomorrow my new life takes its first step." He began by calling up old friends and acquaintances: Janet Baldwin, Herb Whittaker, CBC tele-vision producer Bob Allen, Don Davis, who co-founded Toronto's Crest Theatre in 1953, and Bill Hutt. However, there was no work with either the theatre or the CBC. He then turned to John Drainie and Andrew Allan, who both described work prospects as grim.[2] As the days drifted by with no sign of an acting job, he took dance lessons with Janet to improve his physical strength, and he spent hours sorting the family's records. His father and brother had treated them with "dreadful neglect," and care of such important objects mattered greatly to Findley. But these activities were simply filler; he desperately needed work and financial independence.

Six weeks into his new life he was still unemployed, living with his parents, and dejected. On July 9, after another six weeks of treading water, and a long gap in the journal, he scolded himself for his lethargy: "I know it is an effort to keep track of events in here but somehow I must make myself—because there will come a time when I shall want to refer to them" (LAC 84:4).

Although acting opportunities had failed to materialize during June, he had continued to write. The editor and broadcaster Robert Weaver met with him to discuss his stories, and Bob Allen agreed to read "Cain," the play Findley began in England. But these endeavours, while good signs of his persistence, did not bring him money. He enjoyed the gardens at Strathearn and described the hill sloping down to the beautiful Cedarvale Ravine in detail, but he nonetheless felt that he was "suffocating" in his parents' house, and he mourned his lack of a partner with whom he could share his life and thoughts. By July 17, however, his prospects had improved and this period of waiting came to an end. His first live theatre work at home was with the summer stock company called the Straw Hat Players, a company he worked with again in 1959.[3] They were performing in the town of Port Carling in the beautiful Muskoka Lakes area of Ontario, and they attracted young actors. Findley was impressed by their energy and enthusiasm. He felt happy and relaxed in this small-town environment, where he was finally earning some money and regaining his sense of independence. Music provided a spot of inspiration that summer when he first heard Gould's "Goldberg Variations." "I am enchanted," he wrote, "and will buy it at once" (LAC 84:4). By the end of August his luck had taken another turn for the better. Robert Weaver accepted "About Effie" for the *Tamarack Review* and "War" for CBC radio's *Anthology* program, with a contract for a very welcome $150. Bob Allen helped behind the scenes and encouraged Findley to work further on "Cain." He was deeply grateful to both men and especially pleased to be appearing in the first issue of the *Review*. "Cain," however, brought on a "complete breakdown" in his ability to revise, and he wisely decided not "to force the issue." He was also re-invited to join *The Matchmaker* cast in New York—as Rudolph—and he accepted. After a five-month run, the play would tour several other American cities. Instead of groaning at the prospect of resuming his Rudolph role, he was "overjoyed at the thought of five months in N.Y." He would work with Ruth Gordon again, but not with McCowen, who had left the cast and was acting in London.

This joy at the opportunity to make contacts and meet people, however, was short-lived. His train left Toronto for New York on August 28, but the trip was not straightforward. "Typically," as he noted several times in his journal, he encountered delays and problems: his visa was sent to Niagara Falls, but the train was routed through Buffalo and he could not cross the border; he was booked into the wrong roomette and then yanked off the train in Black Rock; at one in the morning he finally got a sandwich in a bar, but it was raining hard and he was down to his last few dollars. By the time he was cleared by immigration and put on another train, it was impossible to sleep, but he found the situation funny and enjoyed his view of the Hudson River as the train approached New York City. A week later, his good mood had soured: "I have been through more hell than ever got loose in Toronto." He does not note any details, but he clearly felt lost and very lonely, and he had begun drinking heavily again. Ruth Gordon and Garson Kanin were there, of course, but he seems to have spent little time with them, apart from performances, and he writes nothing at all about the play or its reception by New York audiences. What's more, his self-confidence started to evaporate; he knew what he wanted—"not just fame [but] a place. A RIGHTFUL ONE" (LAC 84:4)—but Timothy Findley's "place" would never be on the stage or in New York.

It is also clear that he felt seriously troubled by an intense relationship with Meg Hogarth, a young Toronto woman and an actress with the Straw Hat Players. They had met in Port Carling and apparently fallen in love. Judging from her letters to him during his months in New York, she not only loved him but also accepted the fact that he was gay.[4] I have not located his letters to Meg, so it is impossible to say how honest he was with her or himself; nevertheless, it is clear from his journal that he believed he returned her love but was afraid to consider marriage because he could not face the responsibility of trapping her in a "sterile," childless life. Their long-distance relationship dragged on over the following year while Findley was in the USA, and during this time he continued to grapple with his sexual identity, his fear of hurting someone he cared for, and the pressure he felt, and resented, to conform to society's norms. And his binge drinking worsened. Either the drinking precipitated the depression or vice versa, but either way he was feeling suicidal again, and this time he connected drink and depression with what he called his "alter-ego," which had first shown up when he was wobbling along the parapet beside the River Thames. He recollected that this alter ego was rude and had contributed to Alec McCowen's irritation when he was summoned in the middle of the night to retrieve a giggling Tiff from hospital. Although McCowen, when I spoke with him in 2012, dismissed the idea that Findley was ever serious about suicide, a passage in Findley's 1956 journal from September 16 suggests that Findley was deeply alarmed by his feeling of "incredible & haunted aloneness" in New York and by the fear that he was "in great danger of annihilation" (LAC 84:4). He felt on the verge of insanity and sorely tempted to do something drastic: "I can't go on," he concluded, and he did not resume his journal for another month.

When he returned to his journal, he wrote about international politics and the November 1956 American election, which he followed closely. He faulted the Americans and the United Nations for their failure to help Hungary during the 1956 uprising against the Soviet-controlled government or do anything concrete as the Suez crisis escalated and fighting erupted in Egypt. Moreover, he was disgusted by American electioneering strategies, the propaganda, and the mudslinging. But there were bright spots during the late fall, including a visit from Alec McCowen, who came to New York for two weeks. It was also at this time that he burst unannounced into Ruth Gordon's dressing room, while she was pulling on her stockings, waving his copy of the *Tamarack Review* with "About Effie." She forgave him this indiscretion, praised him in front of the cast, and joked that, when he next came to tell her that his work was published, she hoped she would be stark naked (Brooks, Hobbs, and Meyer, 28).

The Matchmaker began its six-month tour in January 1957, but Findley rarely commented on the performances, so consumed was he with the challenge of writing—how to write, the need for disciplined work, and the wealth of advice in Thornton Wilder's letters. He began a lengthy process of quoting from one of Wilder's letters and reflecting carefully on what Wilder meant by each recommendation and on how he could apply the advice to himself (LAC 84:4). Abandoning the "Cain" play was necessary, said Wilder, because "one must have lived long in and with the problem of evil" before one was capable of writing about it. He also stressed Findley's need for craftsmanship and for "concrete expression," instead of vague abstractions (surviving fragments of the play are rambling and lack cohesion), and Findley never returned to this early attempt at a play. Above all, Wilder told him, *observe* the people and the world around you, and Findley followed this advice to the letter, filling his journal with lists and meticulous descriptions of everyone and everything he encountered. He exhorted himself to "read—study—work—write—write—write—write." "*My* job is to be [...] as creative [...] as I and only I can be" (LAC 84:4).

During January he read Hart Crane and Gertrude Stein, at Wilder's suggestion, and quoted from these authors' works. Crane frightened him, not because of his writing, but because of his life, with which Findley identified: homosexuality, alcohol, alienation, and suicide. Stein, by contrast, inspired him. He devoted several pages of his journal to quotations from *The Autobiography of Alice B. Toklas* and was delighted to discover that Stein (like Guinness and Findley, himself) "was devoted to Ste. Theresa of Avila." This interest in Stein also prompted him to experiment, over several journal pages, with the Stein style of short repeated statements and sentence fragments. The result of this effort was boring, which he must have realized because he dropped the attempt. His mature strengths as a prose stylist are radically different from Stein's, but the attempt to pare down his language, à la Stein, to a few basic nouns and verbs may have helped him achieve concrete precision in his writing. Equally important was his realization that he could take lessons from the actor's craft to improve his writing because an actor had to control the expression of emotion or risk losing his audience. As he told himself, if an actor "allows himself to be 'moved' during the course of a performance," the audience has no role to play, no need to feel anything. This was, in part, what Wilder meant when he insisted on the importance of objectivity and control in writing, but, as we shall see, the lessons Findley learned from his theatre work proved valuable for many other aspects of his writing.

Personal problems travelled with him on the tour, but Wilder's insights into these encouraged him to identify his shortcomings and accept his responsibilities. Gone, thankfully, were his long, anguished railings against God and his tormented confessions of "sin" and "guilt," which preoccupied him during the London years. At one point, he told himself that his "incessant & morbid drinking" made it next to impossible for others to put up with him; "only a very interested person is going to bother to go through that with you," he wrote (LAC 84:4). True, of course, if also hard to accept. Nevertheless, Findley's acute loneliness, combined with his need for love and sex, which he never simply equated, continued to be persistent and debilitating distractions. Meg may have thought she could be one of the people who could go through life with him, but his nagging concern about his ability to make her happy was a warning. At some level he knew he could not continue the relationship simply because he was lonely or because his parents wanted him to marry. Before he returned to Toronto in 1958, she had found someone else, so he was spared the ordeal of disappointing her in person. He would try once more, in 1959, to love a woman fully and sexually by marrying, but the result proved heartbreaking and disastrous.

Sadly, during these years his family's expectations and negative influences continued to stalk him; he found himself wrestling with the pressure to conform and struggling to help a brother who was already beyond help. When *The Matchmaker* reached Detroit in early February 1958, Michael reappeared in Tiff's life. Michael was in Windsor, just across the border, with members of a Moral Re-Armament team, and he came over to Detroit, ostensibly to visit with Tiff, but immediately used the visit as an excuse to drink. When Tiff went to Windsor the following day to check on him, he found his brother in a fragile state, which left him bewildered and distressed by what seemed to be Michael's automatic recourse to alcohol when they were together. But this time, unlike those occasions in London, Tiff did not accuse himself of encouraging the drinking or blame himself for Michael's behaviour. This time he resisted the desire to match Michael drink for drink because he knew he had to fight his own battle with alcohol. "I would like to be a true brother," he wrote in the journal, but he was resigning himself to the fact that his love would never be enough to make a difference in Michael's life. After his own experience with MRA types, whom he found aggravating and dishonest, he also doubted their capacity to be of any help to Michael.

While he was still in Detroit he compiled an alphabetical list in his journal, putting the members of "*The Matchmaker* Company" in one column, their professions (actor, actress, stage manager, dresser, etc.) in the next column, and the actors' roles in a third column. The purpose of this list became clear weeks later, when he reorganized these people into groups of offstage relationships by studying how they interacted in "real life" to see where friendships formed or died and where hostilities arose. Here was an example of Findley the writer putting his journal to work because the propinquity and stress of this long tour gave him ample opportunity to analyze the world outside himself, instead of brooding on his private concerns. During the next stop, in Cincinnati, he bought several used books, including a collection of Gertrude Stein's "word portraits" in *Geography and Plays* (1922), with her prose portraits of friends and famous acquaintances. He read these aloud and found them amusing, moving, easy to understand, and always perceptive. A few days later he created Stein-like experimental sketches of his fellow actors in his journal. About Peter Bayliss, he wrote: "He is one who has been hurt. [...] He is one who has been very hurt. [...] Not everyone is one who has been very hurt." Then he changed his angle of observation to note: "He is one who likes music. He is one who loves some music. He is one who shares music. He has shared it with me" (LAC 84:4).

In St. Louis the audiences were disappointing, even rude, but Chicago, where they had the longest run, was the worst period of the entire tour for Findley. His weeks there "were the most gruelling since leaving England," he felt; "worse than New York, [Chicago] offered the free way to the bottom." And by "bottom" he meant the depths of degradation and violence. He was shocked by three murders and an abduction, all of "a sexual nature," that occurred in Chicago at this time, and he found the city to be permeated with a kind of soulless, "post-war era" frenzy for sensation and "thrills." Ironically, despite his disgust with the seamy side of the city, he quickly succumbed to this urban corruption and began frequenting a particularly disreputable bar, which he described in almost demonic terms as swarming with "queers and fairies," not to mention the alcoholics and the bartenders, who were "trade." He was lucky to escape unscathed: "I only got drunk. Nothing ever really happened to warrant hanging around" (LAC 84:4). But hang around he did, night after night, sliding "faster and faster towards the bottom of alcohol & self-degeneration & bitterness." When he was well clear of Chicago, he asked himself why he drank so heavily in such places and decided that part of the answer lay in the temptation of sex or, as he described this, sex "to be indulged in for the purest animal motives." Another answer lay in what he called his "compulsion" to drink due to his inability to identify with other human beings and his desperate desire to communicate: "That is the first indication of my compulsion-to-drink's root. I am afraid that I will miss making & establishing contact with the world" (LAC 84:4). Yet another reason was pure fear: "I drink because I am afraid" of failure and loneliness.

As so often happened with Findley, he felt himself teetering on the edge of an abyss of fear, alcohol, and sex just when things seemed to be going well. He was working hard at his writing, and he was by no means alone. In addition to Arthur Hill, an older Canadian actor in *The Matchmaker* who had been with the show in London and whom Findley admired, he was becoming more and more friendly with Sheila Keddy, an understudy with the play. Moreover, Pascal Covici, an editor with Viking Press in New York, had written to ask him for "a 30,000 word novel along the lines 'Of Mice and Men.'" Findley started work on this novel but confessed that he was worried about finding a style that would "turn out to be 'me.'" For his subject, he turned back to his interest in Cain and Abel, while planning to incorporate "Cassandra (as kitchen help). God—as a travelling preacher— Lilith as the local belle with whom Cain has his first 'affair.' God travels with Angels who are his hymn-singers" [LAC 84: 4]. It is hard to see how he could make sense of such a mixture, let alone impress Covici, but some of these characters would surface in mature works like *Can You See Me Yet?*

and *Not Wanted on the Voyage.* By May 21 the tour had stopped in Washington, D.C., and Sheila Keddy was typing up a completed draft of the long short story "Harper's Bazaar," which Findley considered sending to Covici because he was pleased with it and saw its completion as "a real victory."

Before leaving Washington, he attended some HUAC sessions to observe Arthur Miller being questioned. The House Un-American Activities Committee was pursuing Americans they suspected of being Communists or holding Communist sympathies, and during the postwar decade they persecuted artists, intellectuals, and homosexuals in Hollywood and in the New York theatre world. Miller, a man Findley admired, was on trial for a second time during May 1957, and Findley got a firsthand look at what political persecution was like for an artist. Miller had refused to co-operate with the Committee when he was first called before it in 1956, and now he reiterated his refusal to name other artists whom he knew to have Communist leanings. As Miller noted in his autobiography, *Timebends*, the United States had "the tiniest Communist Party in the world" (311) and yet many Americans, like the infamous Senator Joseph McCarthy, were rabidly anti-Communist. Findley did not dwell on the questions put to Miller at this second trial, but he was impressed by "the dignity with which Arthur Miller endured the badgering" to reveal the names of Communists in the film and theatre industries (*J* 275), and he would later read *Timebends* shortly after it was published in 1987.

The cast boarded a train for San Francisco on June 3 for their second-to-last stop on the tour, and the long train ride was a welcome relief for Findley. He spent much of his time in the dining car watching the landscape change and recording descriptions of the scenery, wildlife, mountains, and stars in his journal. If *The Matchmaker* was well received in San Francisco, he did not say. Instead, he copied a passage into the journal from an interview Ruth Gordon gave to the *San Francisco Chronicle* on 19 June 1957. She had praised his abilities as an actor and gone on to say that she had read "Harper's Bazaar" and found it "greater than Tennessee Williams or Faulkner." Findley was bowled over by such public praise and was immensely grateful for her faith in him. Thirty-three of Findley's letters to Ruth Gordon and her husband, sometimes just brief notes or cards, survive from this period, and in them his trust, respect, and affection for the couple is clear. He often thanked her for giving him tickets to concerts and plays he could not otherwise afford, and he always wrote with his deepest appreciation of their steady advice on his writing and on how to get published.[5] Several weeks later in Los Angeles, where *The Matchmaker* closed, she and Tiff were in a restaurant when she quietly slipped him an envelope containing $500 in postdated cheques so he could give up earning a pittance in two-bit acting jobs and devote himself to writing.

Hard Lessons
Hell in Hollywood and Disaster in Toronto

By July 19, Findley had moved into a rented house in Santa Monica with a new friend, Wesley Russum, and other visual artists, and he began meeting with people at the film studios in hopes of finding work as an actor or a scriptwriter (*IM* 144). Money was running out fast, however; he was down to thirty dollars, but he did not consider returning to Toronto or asking his parents for money. As he recalls in *Inside Memory*, he was scraping by on packages of dried soup, avocados he filched from neighbours' gardens, and good dinners with the artists on Fridays, after which "one of them would bed me" (144). In retrospect this period in his life was "Madness and glory," but it was not making a better writer out of him. He was reading Joyce's *Ulysses* and labouring away on his "masterpiece" for Covici, this time about "three inverted artists" (*IM* 144), instead of the less-than-promising Cain and Abel material he had mentioned in his journal. He also had several stories he wanted to write before he lost them. One was called "Stones," which may have been an early title for "Harper's Bazaar," given the role played by a stone in this story and in Findley's developing set of symbols. "Yes. Yes," he told himself, "there is much much much to do" (LAC 84:4). The journal ends, however, not with drafts of his stories, but with some lines of his own poetry, many quotations from Stein and Emily Dickinson, and a discouraging note that he had received no letters from home, except from his mother, and no news at all from Covici.

It seems that he must have sent something to the New York publisher—an outline? a chapter? a full manuscript of "Harper's Bazaar"? He does not say what he had sent, but it might have been the one about his fellow "inverted" artists, which he would soon be advised to destroy.

Finally, he was down to his last dollar with "no prospects whatsoever." He could not even afford to drink. In his London years, such a dismal state of affairs would have thrown him into despair and a crisis of faith. This time his response to adversity was more measured. There was even room for a wry touch of humour: two months earlier he had splurged on a new grey suit, but now he found it ironic that he could go out looking very respectable when he had "nothing to [his] name."

Once more, Ruth Gordon and Garson Kanin proved helpful because through them he met a literary agent called Stanley Colbert, and it was Colbert who came to the rescue. He and his wife, Nancy, took Findley in, and he spent several months living with them, free of charge, in their Westwood Village home along with two other impecunious artists and the Colberts' young daughter, to whom he enjoyed reading stories.[6] This was, in fact, the start of an important relationship for Findley. After the Colberts moved to Toronto in the seventies, Nancy became his literary agent and a dear friend. At this early stage, however, they provided a home, a typewriter, emotional support, an environment in which he could write, and some tough, practical advice. When he showed them the manuscript he was working on for Covici, they told him honestly that it was dreadful. As Findley recalled in *Inside Memory*, Stan Colbert accused him of writing trash and perpetrating a crime against his talent as a writer. He described the manuscript as nothing better than a "play for meaningless notoriety," and he asked Findley what should be done with it. After a pause Tiff said: "Burn it." But since he was not quite steady enough to burn it by himself, Colbert stayed with him and they "burned it together" (*IM* 146).

A story called "Lemonade" got a more positive reception from the Colberts. According to Nancy, an American television drama program became interested in it, and it would eventually be published as "Harper's Bazaar" before Findley included it in *Dinner Along the Amazon* as "Lemonade," where he dedicated it to Ruth Gordon. In his introduction to this

Beginning Again—and Again

collection of his stories, he described the peripatetic life of the story, which he began in the Tedworth Square flat in London, finished in Washington, D.C., where Sheila Keddy typed it for him, and further revised while living with the Colberts. This long short story is a moving account of a boy's attempt to get his mother's attention and then to understand and help her. Eight-year-old Harper Dewey lives alone in an elegant home with Bertha Millroy, the maid, and his beautiful, widowed mother Renalda Dewey. His father died on the Normandy beaches in the battle for Caen in August 1944, when the child was just a year old, and his mother never recovered from her husband's death. Now, in 1951, she has withdrawn to her bedroom, where she drinks and becomes increasingly remote and self-destructive. Bertha is left trying to hold what remains of this family together and to provide affection and a home for Harper. Although he is only eight, Harper knows something is very wrong and he longs to win his mother's attention, to be seen and acknowledged by her, and to help her in some way. When he realizes that his mother has been pawning her jewellery to buy this substance that she likes to drink, he sets up a lemonade stand—a lemonade bazaar—on the front lawn to raise money for new jewellery. But Harper is too late. Renalda Dewey shoots herself with her husband's Colt revolver, and she is found dead, holding the stone that Harper had just thrown through her open window to tell her he was there, helping her.

This tragic tale, captured in some of his finest, most delicately controlled prose, is classic Findley. Despite its lengthy genesis from 1955 to 1958, it belongs with those early 1955 stories—"The Name's the Same," "About Effie," and "War"—and demonstrates that he had already, at the start of his career, mastered the art of storytelling. Twenty years before *The Wars,* "Harper's Bazaar" displayed many basic elements in Findley's fictional world: the house, with its gracious, sun-filled, claustrophobic rooms; the summer gardens; the disintegrating family behind the walls and curtains; the alcoholic, reclusive mother; the absent, dead father; the maid who is the only source of safety and love for a child; and that sensitive child's heartbreaking bewilderment with the adults around him, plus the animals and birds living in the garden, the shadow of war, and the gun hidden in a dresser drawer in his mother's room. Much of this story's power lies in its understated simplicity and the absence of authorial interference to explain events. We see things from the child's perspective, and that perspective is limited to what he sees and feels but only vaguely understands and cannot articulate. Findley has expertly withheld emotional interpretation and trusted the reader to play his or her role in understanding the story.

Although Findley already knew something about loss and violent death, he had not, as Wilder had pointed out, lived with evil. However, before he left L.A. in 1958, he had an experience (albeit vicarious) of evil that shaped the rest of his life and influenced his art profoundly. This happened when he and an actress friend from *The Matchmaker*, Patricia Cutts, were invited to the home of Ivan Moffat, a well-known producer and screenwriter whom Findley greatly admired.[7] After dinner, as Cutts and Moffat retired to renew a previous romance, Moffat handed Findley a bottle of brandy and told him he was welcome to explore the records, books, and scripts in the living room. "When they had gone, I revelled in what—to me, in that particular place, in that particular time—seemed absolute paradise" (*IM* 309). Then he opened an album of photographs:

> Of course, I could give the pictures a context. I'd already heard and seen what everyone else had seen; *had been allowed to hear, allowed to see*. But nothing—not my nightmares, not the worst of my imagination, not the worst of my experience—had opened the door on the remotest possibility of what I saw that night.
> I was looking into hell—and hell was real.
> I never recovered from what I saw that night. (*IM* 310–11)

What Timothy Findley had stumbled upon was a collection of Moffat's photographs, taken when he was an official army photographer with the American army as it liberated Dachau. Today it is scarcely necessary to describe what happened behind its gates and wire, but in 1957–58 the horror of the concentration camps had not been fully revealed to the public. Facts and images had been censored and survivors' stories had yet to be told. Like others, Findley had seen the images broadcast during the

Nuremburg trials, but Moffat's eyewitness photographs were something else. Confronting these images of atrocity forced him to accept the fact that human beings are capable of pure evil, and to understand, at last, his connection with the human race. "This was a kind of epiphany" that "told me that I was just like everyone else. We are all a collective hiding place for monsters" (*IM* 311).

There, in that "absolute paradise" of California, in a glamorous home owned by this famous man, *there* Findley looked into hell, confronted evil, and understood that he would never relinquish his hold on—or be freed from—such difficult knowledge. This twenty-seven-year-old man from Rosedale, who had decided to become a writer, accepted the fact that he was a member of a species capable of monstrosity. No single experience makes a great artist, of course. No single trauma from childhood or adolescence made Timothy Findley the writer he became, and this severe shock is not the only one he experienced. However, this staring into hell, into this heart of darkness, was for him a seminal experience. He could not recover from what he saw because he chose not to forget; instead, he responded to such evil in his art.

———

When Findley returned to Toronto in late 1958, his parents were still in the house on Strathearn Road, but all was not well. Allan's health continued to be precarious, he was drinking again, and his position at Bache & Co. was about to implode. Nevertheless, life for Findley was by no means bleak. He found acting work with CBC radio and television in adaptations of the classics; he directed Roger MacDougall's *Escapade* for the Straw Hat Players; and he had a small role in the Crest Theatre's March production of John Osborne's *The Entertainer*. His own work received some attention when Mavor Moore read "War" for Robert Weaver's CBC radio program *Anthology*, and, when Stan Colbert informed him that Playhouse 90 had decided to do "Lemonade" and wanted him in L.A. to write the film script, he was excited. However, his terror of flying was exacerbated when a spectacular crash occurred on the day he was scheduled to fly to Los Angeles. The 21 April 1958 daily transcontinental flight from L.A. to New York (United Airlines 736) collided mid-air with another plane over Nevada, and both planes crashed, killing all on board. The crash made sensational newspaper headlines with horrifying photographs of the wreckage, and many other flights were delayed that day. Findley did make it (with white knuckles and the help of several drinks) to L.A. on a flight the next day, but he returned by train, vowing never to fly again. In the end, Playhouse 90 dropped "Lemonade" in favour of another piece about alcohol—*Days of Wine and Roses*.

By far the most important events in his life at this time were his role in a play called *Sanctuary* and his last attempt to conform to his family's expectations by performing as a heterosexual male and marrying the play's female lead, a lovely young actress from Winnipeg who had trained at RADA in the late 1940s, Janet Reid (1930–2004).[8] With her long blonde hair and large eyes, Janet looked younger than her years, and she had performed ingenue roles in several plays before she met Tiff, including the 1957 Crest Theatre production of J. B. Priestley's *The Glass Cage*. Although her role was a minor one (daughter in a wealthy Toronto family), this production went on to considerable success in London's Piccadilly Theatre and earned Janet an aura of success to complement her ethereal beauty. During rehearsals for *Sanctuary*, which was aired on CBC television on 9 November 1958, she and Tiff fell in love. To the observer they must have looked like an ideal couple, and they had much in common. Like Findley's mother and aunts, Janet came from a well-to-do family and had attended a private girls' school; like Findley, she had lived in London while studying acting, and, like him, she loved the theatre. They were married at Grace Church on-the-Hill on 17 January 1959, followed by a lavish reception at Toronto's Park Plaza Hotel. But six months later Janet Reid filed for divorce. In March 1960, the marriage was declared "null and void" for "non-consummation," with no need for a further court appearance. Findley was ordered to pay costs, but the full cost was enormous emotionally, psychologically, and physically.[9] As he admitted in his 1984 lecture "How Would *You* Like to Be Called Gay?" the first court appearance was so appalling that "it was the only time in [his] life when [he] gave any truly serious thought to suicide in the light of [his] homosexuality."[10] He then sank into the longest, darkest period of drink and despair in his life, and he was institutionalized. Janet suffered a nervous breakdown.

In the only interview to include a brief segment with Janet, Ann-Marie MacDonald's 1999 CBC program "Life and Times: Timothy Findley," Findley explained that he had "loved Janet and wanted to be with her." He insisted that he had wanted a family and that she had agreed. She said they had loved each other and believed they could make things work, even though they both knew he was gay. At the time of this interview, Janet and Tiff had not seen each other for almost forty years. They were not brought face to face for the program, but they expressed affection and concern for each other, and Janet, who was living in Toronto and working for the CBC, said she would like to see him again.

They never did meet, but they did correspond briefly in the early 1980s. Janet first wrote him to correct some of the misinformation about her life in his 1982 interview with Jack McIvor for *Quest* and to tell him how to reach her. He had not known how to find her; therefore, his description of her in the *Quest* piece as "happily married" with two daughters was out of date. Like Tiff, she harboured no resentment about their breakup, congratulated him on his success, and wrote him again in December 1982 with her condolences on Allan's death [LAC 96: 11]. His 12 September 1983 response to her is remarkable for what it reveals about the divorce proceedings, his subsequent collapse, and his memories of a marriage few people knew had taken place. He began by apologizing for his delayed reply and then turned to their shared past:

THANK YOU FOR WRITING. It meant—and still means—a good deal to me. I've spent a lot of years feeling guilty about our marriage—and a lot of years, more recently, feeling that, in spite of everything—I am happy with it, in the sense that I look back and am grateful we knew each other—loved each other and spent, however briefly, some time happily in one another's company. If we had been wiser—of course we would not have married. But I think we became "pig-headed" about it and went ahead with it because we wanted to prove something. In the end, it didn't work out—but *now* that doesn't matter the way it did then. We lost sight of one another and we weren't honest about saying "look—if we stop the tension, we might find answers." There was too much pride involved where pride had no business. I really did love you—and was confused to the point of panic when I discovered that loving you didn't solve my problem. It was probably the worst time of my life (not the marriage—or the time with you—but the time of that confusion). I can only assume that it must have been one of the low points of your life, too. I wish it hadn't happened to us—but it did. I needed your help—you needed mine—and we didn't or couldn't help each other. But I must stress this—I loved *living* with you—I loved *being* with you—and I loved *you*. I only regret the end of it. I can still see—very vividly—you in your tailored coat and that grey hat standing in the snow & slush outside the old City Hall saying to me: "well—it's over—and I'm sorry it was rough on you. But I'm glad it's *done* and I'm going to go home and drink a whole bottle of gin!" Then you laughed—smiled—and we shook hands. Then we said "good-bye" and we kissed each other and you went away with your lawyer (whom I *hated*).

I hated him because in the court he petitioned for annulment because I was a homosexual and the other people in the court turned and stared at me and the Judge said: "Silly man. He doesn't know what he's missing!" And everyone laughed. Do you remember that? *You* did not laugh. In fact I think you looked at me and mouthed the words: "I'm sorry."

Something funny happened, too, I've never told anyone—but Bill. You might be amused and also appalled (as I was). Just before we went into the court I was standing with my lawyer and psychiatrist (who had been called to testify, if need be) and your lawyer came over and excused himself and took my lawyer & psychiatrist aside and mumbled with them. Then, his face white and urgent, my psychiatrist crossed back to me and took me by the arm and said: "come." We went whizzing off down the great corridor until he found a washroom and I had no idea what in God's name was happening. He said, "let us go into the urinal together. I just have to relieve myself." (It sounds like a scene from a Peter Sellers movie!) I did *not* have to relieve myself—but he said; "do come over and try ... ." I wondered crazily, if he was trying to seduce me. Anyway—I went and stood beside him and I noticed he wasn't peeing—but was just standing there. I undid my flies and took it out—knowing I wouldn't pee—but thinking I can't stand here doing *nothing*. What if someone comes in?

Then the psychiatrist—who was really a very gentle and considerate old man and charming—said; "Look—I'm sorry—but I just have to take a look. Just one quick *look* ... ." And he leaned to look at it and I had to "flash" on him by turning to face the lights. It was an insane moment. Truly crazy. I was really very frightened. Then he straightened up and said, "all right, put it away—that's all." This done—we left the washroom and back in the corridor he said; "you probably wonder what that was all about ..." and I said; "I sure do, Buster." Then he told me your lawyer had implied there was something "wrong" with my plumbing—and might introduce this as "evidence." The Psychiatrist said—"I had to *know* so that I could deny it," and then he apologized. He was really rather wonderful. When we got back to the others, he turned to your lawyer and said; "you are preposterous!" The subject never came up.

Yes—I was always nuts about animals. I adored "Sam"—but he was, after all, your dog. The cat thing didn't really happen until I was living with Bill in Richmond Hill. We both like cats—but I had never had one. So we had *eleven*. Now we have *29*. They live, of course, out of doors. Only four of them are house-cats.

I thought the *Quest* article was splendid. Jack McIvor came and spent time here with his wife and so the interviews were relaxed and fun. I *loved* the photographs.

There couldn't be better research about you—because I didn't know your married name. I'm very sorry that didn't work out. The last I heard was that you were, indeed, very happily married and the mother of two girls. We should both have done better about keeping in touch—but now we can.

It's impossible to think of you as being 50—not that being fifty is the end of the world—but only because I have an indelible image of you before. Also time. How quick it is.

Yes. I do not envy your passing through menopause—and I hope it's not being too harsh. How is your health otherwise? How are your daughters, and what sort of lives have they chosen? I'm truly sorry if you are lonely—or are having to face too much of this bad period alone. _Don't_.

You've been very generous about my work & its consequences. Thank you for that. I hope you will read *The Wars*—and definitely *The Last of the Crazy People*, just published as a Penguin paperback.

Thanks for your kind words about dad. It was a hard and dreadful death—extended. But he was *wonderful*—and died with great, quiet courage. I came to love him in the last years and we had some super times together. Ma is currently well—but only after a bad time with cancer of the bowel (now completely cut out—the cancer—not the bowel). She is quite remarkable—81. Michael is still locked in to the bottle and that's a sad story. But Sally (his wife) is in good shape and one of my best friends.

I only feel "old" mid-winter and early mornings. I enjoy my work—and am currently writing about the cat on *Noah's Ark*: Lot's of fun, this time.

Very sorry to hear about your brother (Don?) whom I remember vividly. Wonderfully alive and enjoyable, and he kept saying to me: "Don't worry. Stop worrying ... ." He was very good to me.

I still have the beautiful photo of you—against a black background, your hair pulled to one side. I was always so proud of you—NOT just of your beauty—but of your strength and your bravery and your humour. When all is said and done, dear one, that is how I remember you and think of you. For my part—I can only say I got lucky and I'll never regret knowing you. This, with love, from

This moving letter sheds more light on the man, his marriage, his love for this woman, his fundamental kindness, his anguished struggle to conform to society's norms, and the reasons for his major collapse after the court appearance than dates or mere facts can do.

In his 1984 address to the Ontario Psychiatric Association ("How Would *You* Like to Be Called Gay?"), he explained that when he was a teenager, his parents "flung [him] at girls and they flung girls at [him]." He grew up with his family's and society's expectation that he would marry and have children. Sexual relations between a man and a woman in love were simply a given; any other type of relationship was inconceivable. For Findley, however, such relationships were not only conceivable, they could be very worthwhile. "I have never loved by gender," he told the audience attending the Psychiatric Association meeting; "I fall in love with people." That said, he had tried to conform, to meet mainstream expectations, right up to the age of twenty-nine. When his marriage failed, he did not at first see it as a mutual failure, or basic incompatibility, but as his personal, individual failure to belong, to be accepted, to fulfill others' and, to some degree, his own expectations. He had failed to make someone he loved happy; in fact, he had broken her heart. All those old fears so often expressed in his journals became a devastating reality. To be scorned, laughed at publicly, and humiliated by lawyers and a judge was more than he could bear.

Due to this trauma, he lost the better part of a year. He was seriously depressed and drinking so heavily that he would wake up on the floor of a hotel room with no idea how he got there. Finally, he admitted himself to the Toronto Psychiatric Hospital (TPH) for treatment, but that experience proved shattering in other ways. He recalled wandering "around in a nightgown watching people die or having alcoholic seizures. [...] You're screaming mad because you're so afraid of death and *nothing* can stop it" (qtd. in E. Cameron, 1985, 29). For follow-up treatment, he lived briefly at a clinic for recovering alcoholics run by the Alcohol Research Foundation (later the Addiction Research Foundation) on Bedford Road.[12] As if things were not bad enough, he ended up in the care of a psychiatrist who believed homosexuals could and should be cured. This man's method (quite popular at the time) was to use heterosexual pornography on the grotesque assumption that looking at such material would stimulate "normal" sexual desires.[13]

Somehow Timothy Findley survived this abyss in his life, and he kept himself on the wagon by taking Antabuse, a drug that induces vomiting and severe headaches if combined with alcohol. Between late 1960 and 1962, he landed some acting jobs while living, on and off, with his parents, and during the winter of 1961–62 he rented a room in the home of Ann and Michael Tait on Roxborough Street East after performing in a production of *Volpone* at the Ryerson Institute of Technology. Then his luck changed. Three exceptional people entered his life at this crucial moment: William Frederick Whitehead, Jean Roberts, and Marigold Charlesworth. Jean and Marigold became close friends. Bill became the lover, friend, partner, and life's companion that Findley had sought throughout his late teens and twenties. By February 1962 his new life was about to begin.

Three

CAN YOU SEE ME NOW?—

1962 TO 1989

Early,
morning,
at night
kitchen
table
writes......

CHAPTER SEVEN

Becoming a Writer

———

NOW I MAKE CERTAIN EVERY DAY THAT I NEVER TAKE

ANYONE CLOSE TO ME FOR GRANTED. NO AMOUNT OF TIME

IS LONG ENOUGH. [...] HOW STUPID IT IS TO TRY TO GET

THROUGH LIFE ALONE. BECAUSE YOU CAN'T.

(Timothy Findley, *Inside Memory* 75)

WFW and a First Novel

The Last of the Crazy People

The story of Timothy Findley, the writer, cannot be told without introducing "WFW"—as Findley often called Bill Whitehead—because he made so much possible. This is a large claim, but it is one I have come to believe. As Len Collins, a Cannington neighbour and close friend of Findley and Whitehead's, told me: "I don't know what would have happened to Tiff without Bill," or, in Bill's words: "Tiff needed someone to look after him, and I needed someone to look after."[1] Over the course of their forty-year-long relationship, Bill had to learn about alcohol and the demons that pursue a binge drinker, while Findley had to struggle with his insecurities, his fears about his art, and his need for Bill's attention. William Frederick Whitehead was born on 16 August 1931 and grew up in Regina, where he lived with his mother and grandparents. Like Findley, Bill realized he was gay while quite young, but there the similarity ends because Bill's sexual orientation never confused or tormented him. He did not suffer the agonies of guilt or experience the family rejection that Findley had, and while he had many close women friends, he vowed as a teenager never to attempt a marriage. He also differed from Findley in that he had a university education, with a BA and a master's degree in biology, for which he conducted research on the musculature of the black widow spider. Although he won a National Research Council scholarship to do his PhD at Yale, Bill hesitated about devoting himself to scientific research because he disliked experimenting on animals and had already fallen in love with the theatre: In 1953, rumours reached him about a new festival starting up in Stratford, and a few years later, after attending productions by the touring company, Canadian Players, his mind was made up. He resigned his research position at the University of Saskatchewan and caught a bus for Toronto, where he found occasional work with the CBC and picked up several acting jobs touring southern Ontario with amateur companies before being hired for the 1958 Stratford season to perform small parts.

After Stratford, he met Jean Roberts (1926–2012) and Marigold Charlesworth (1926–2015), a couple who would be among his closest friends and later be important in Findley's life.[2] When I spoke with Roberts, who first met Findley in 1959 when he had a bit part in *The Entertainer* at the Crest Theatre, where she was the production manager, she remembered him with great affection and warmth. At that time, she called him Timothy because "[she] didn't know about 'Tiff' until [she] met him with Bill." Two years later, when Jean, Marigold, and Bill decided to present Toronto with its first true repertory season at the Central Library Theatre, Findley auditioned and was hired. Each man noticed the other immediately, so when Findley complained that a play he was in, called *Crawling Arnold*, was being aired on CBC television but that he had no television on which to watch it, Bill offered to help.[3] Certainly watching the play at the Findley parents' home was out of the question. Margaret had joined an MRA march protesting the playwright, Jules Feiffer's, perceived attack on so-called family values. (She later apologized to her son for this.) Bill owned a television, so he invited Tiff to watch the broadcast at his place. Findley arrived, handsome and elegantly groomed, but Bill had nothing to offer him except a beer, which he declined because he was taking Antabuse. What followed—with no drink, no food, and an absurd love scene on the screen—was a real romance unfolding in Bill Whitehead's apartment. Once the broadcast had ended Bill asked if it weren't time for Tiff to go home, but Timothy Findley had decided to stay. And thus began their life as a couple.

The rest of 1962 was busy and very happy for Findley. He performed well in three plays for the Central Library Theatre season—Sheridan's *The Rivals*, N. F. Simpson's *One Way Pendulum*, and Genet's *The Balcony*.[4] That winter, he and Bill moved into their first home together—a basement apartment in a house near Yonge and St. Clair, and Bill met Allan and Margaret for the first time. At one point during this visit, Allan took Bill aside, ostensibly to show him some artwork in the hallway, but in fact to warn him about the shameful family secret: "My son is queer, you know," he whispered in a lugubrious tone. To which Bill could only whisper back: "Yes, I believe he is" (*WLB* 114). What Allan understood, if anything, from that exchange must have been minimal, but Bill grasped the situation clearly. With just six words Allan Findley had revealed his character and his attitude towards his thirty-one-year-old son, and he seems not to have grasped the fact that his son and Mr. Whitehead were a couple. Bill told me that Tiff merely laughed when he told him what Allan had said, but Bill was shocked and Tiff must have been angered and deeply hurt by his father's continuing disapproval. In the spring he and Bill took their first holiday together, camping in Muskoka, north of Toronto, and that summer they joined Jean and Marigold for another Red Barn season, when Findley performed in *For Love or Money* and created an excellent Tom in *The Glass Menagerie*. In alternate weeks, he performed at Jackson's Point and at the Orillia Opera House, and for the only time in their theatre years the two men acted together, in *The Rivals*, when Bill stepped in to replace an actor who had left the company.

As the season drew to a close, Findley realized he must make a firm decision about his career. Acting was enjoyable, but he desperately wanted to write and the idea for a novel was taking shape in his mind. Acting was also an energy-sapping distraction and a constant source of tension, with the uncertainty about roles, the poor pay, plus the lack of any clear future, which he did not handle well. Moreover, his and Bill's combined income from the theatre was pitiful. They discussed the possibilities and took the leap together. That fall they rented the small house in Richmond Hill that was owned by Findley's parents and meant for their retirement, and they went to work: Bill with the CBC; Tiff part-time with a local radio station and part-time on his novel. In this way a pattern was quickly established that they retained for many years to come. Bill Whitehead would travel to his CBC office in downtown Toronto, and Tiff Findley would spend much of each day at home writing.

Findley's first job at this time was with CFGM, a Richmond Hill radio station devoted to country and western music. His task was to prepare advertising copy for the station, and this allowed him time for his own work. Bill's CBC work was more demanding and marked the start of his twenty-year career with the CBC developing science programs, first for *The Learning Stage* (today's *Ideas*) and later for *The Nature of Things*, as well as many award-winning documentaries. It was not long before he managed to land a CBC job for Findley as well, thereby rescuing him from the country and western folks. Findley's first CBC assignment, for *The Learning Stage*, was to conduct a series of interviews with Canadian writers and composers and sometimes with visiting theatre artists like Alec Guinness; he also enjoyed accompanying Bill to Montreal to observe his work on documentary films for CBC's program *Umbrella: We Cover the Arts*.

In retrospect, everything seemed to be going well for Findley: he finally had the stable home he had longed for, with a loving, interesting partner, and he was writing. He had nearly finished drafting his novel *The Last of the Crazy People*, and by August 1963 he had found Dr. Edward Turner (1926–2006), the psychiatrist who would help him for most of the rest of his life. Turner was a forensic psychiatrist with the Clarke Institute, but he was also an enlightened scientist and a human being who accepted Timothy Findley as he was—an extremely sensitive man from a difficult family with addiction problems, a gifted artist who was gay and had suffered from the social prejudices and legal constraints of the period and from the early rejection and ongoing criticism of his father.[5] The only obvious cloud on Findley's horizon at this time was the death of his beloved Grandmother Bull. Nevertheless, something further must have been amiss to trigger a frightening binge (reminiscent of the London Bridge one that Alec McCowen described), which alerted Bill to what life with Timothy Findley could involve. One evening in January 1964, Findley suddenly disappeared. It was Robbie Burns Day (January 25), and Findley apparently joined the parade as it passed the house—and did not return. "When I couldn't find him, I was distraught, then appalled," Bill recalled, because a few hours later "the police appeared with a Timothy Findley I could barely recognize. Drunk. Dishevelled. Belligerent" (*WLB* 128). Findley did not, or could not, explain himself to Bill or to his journal; indeed, there was no rational explanation for such episodes. Loneliness, amounting to a sense of existential aloneness, which produced depression, and persistent fears about his success as a writer, were part of who he was. Fortunately, over the years ahead such extreme episodes were rare, but they were nonetheless terrifying.

As 1964 unfolded, they bought a second-hand car and began searching for their own place in smaller towns northwest of Toronto. For the most part, Findley hated urban life with its conspicuous consumption, noise, crowded streets, cold anonymity, and, of course, temptations. Toronto was no easier to cope with than London, New York, Chicago, or Los Angeles, and that dark period from 1959 to 1961 had left him with scars and ugly memories of life on Toronto's streets and in Toronto's psychiatric institutions. Bill, however, had to be within reach of the CBC offices and his work. The car gave them the flexibility to put distance between their home and the city, and on one jaunt they got lost and ended up on a lovely country road just south of the town of Cannington in Brock Township. They saw *For Sale* signs, and a local realtor introduced them to Nelson Purvis, who was selling a property with fifty acres and an old farmhouse dating from the 1830s. Off they went to examine the place. It was not precisely love at first sight—Bill worried about the condition of the old house—but it came close and Findley was ecstatic. They both fell in love with the gardens, which were full of "lilacs and mock-orange, peonies, del-phiniums, hollyhocks, day lilies, lily-of-the-valley ... [and] scarlet lychnis" (*WLB* 131). Back they went to Mr. Purvis to discuss the price, and on the way Bill begged Tiff to be quiet and let him do the bargaining. Findley was hopeless with money; when he had it he cheerfully spent it, and Bill had already watched him fall in love with a second-hand piano they hoped to buy and loudly proclaim that "he had to have it" regardless of cost. But the price of $9,000 (roughly $75,400 in 2020 dollars) for the farm was right, so they left Cannington that day as the owners of a beautiful property about two hours' drive from downtown Toronto, with enough money left to install a furnace.

The "boys," as their Cannington neighbours called them, moved in later that summer and quickly went out of their way to become part of the community. They hired local craftsmen to carry out major renova-tions, and during the summers and on weekends they paid local teenagers to help with the yardwork, the gardens, and the animals. In addition to the cats, Max and Mouse, and their five kittens, they had brought two dogs with them, Maggie and Hooker, to begin what rapidly grew into a full menagerie. They shopped in local stores, relied on a local barber, and called on the services of local veterinarians. They participated in local fairs and festivals, supported the local high school with gifts, and much more. The idyllic setting of small-town Ontario in the mid-1960s had its limits, of course, and not everyone was welcoming. On rare occasions, there were ugly incidents: drunk teenagers would drive by hurling both homophobic insults and bottles at the house. But for the most part, with the wider goodwill of the town and Tiff and Bill's commitment to the community, they fit in because they "neighboured well."

For Timothy Findley, this place, soon christened "Stone Orchard" in homage to Chekhov and in recognition of the fact that stones were the chief harvest from their fields, was *home*, his paradise, his safety, his writ-ing place, his spiritual sanctuary. Located in this area of old Upper Can-ada, just south of Beaverton and Lake Simcoe, close to Jackson's Point in Georgina Township and the former haunts of Grandfather Findley, it was part of his ancestral past and his family's roots. Beginning with *The Last of the Crazy People*, which was polished and published after the move, all of Findley's major works were created in, at times inspired by, that place with its farm house, its fields, its domestic and wild animals, the country road, the neighbours, and the seasons.

———————

1964 was an important year for Findley. By far the dominant notes in his 1964–65 journal (LAC 84:15) were positive, even buoyant. He enjoyed his work for the CBC, learned a lot from his work on documentary films, took great interest in the repairs and redecorating of the farmhouse, and began his next novel, *The Butterfly Plague*. Central to his happiness and security was Bill, and after one evening in Montreal on CBC work, when he had drunk too much, he noted: "without Bill I would be in ruins." However, this peace of mind was badly shaken by a terrible scene that took place during a visit to his parents' home in October. When he described what happened in his journal, he concluded that it "represented a true crisis in my relationship with my father." The backstory is that a Cannington neighbour's half-wild dogs had attacked another farmer's pig. Findley heard the ruckus and rushed to save the pig. He managed to scare off the dogs, but the pig was so badly injured that it had to be killed. Apparently, when he recounted these events for his parents, Allan went berserk: he called the pig a "stupid noisy animal" and accused Tiff of preferring pigs to dogs. This quickly developed into "an absolutely hysterical political tirade" in which Allan threatened to get his gun out of the safe and shoot anyone—presumably including his wife and son—who tried to "de-ball" him. Margaret explained to her husband that he had missed the point of the story, which was that Tiff had bravely fought off the marauding dogs, but Allan became fixated on the mistaken idea that now all dogs would be shot because of the pig. Bill tried to reason with the man by explaining that the dogs in question were notorious for attacking cattle, but Allan kept going on about people wanting to shoot all dogs until Tiff exploded: "You're a fine one to talk about shooting everyone when you're the one who boasts about his damn gun all the time" (LAC 84:15).

What is remarkable here is less the argument itself, which was clearly irrational and angry, and more the detail and length of Findley's record of it. He set up the main exchange in eight pages of dialogue, as if this were a scene for a play, with asides from himself in brackets:

> FATHER: "I won't let anyone tell me anything. No one is going to get me. I'm my own man. I will not be de-balled. Everyone has been de-balled. And I'd tell them that at the office too." [This last again throws everyone—why has he said it?]
>
> MOTHER: "Well. I have a right to an opinion—and if I think you are wrong about this animal thing I *must* say so—without being afraid of you. I want you to know I am shaken to my roots."
>
> FATHER: "Fine."
>
> MOTHER: "All Tiff wanted was to tell you how he'd saved the pig, and you wouldn't let him. You got all mixed up about the dogs."
>
> FATHER: "Yes. Every time the boys get going you defend them. You've de-balled them. No woman will de-ball me or Barry Goldwater. Those dogs were only playing ..." (LAC 84:15)

As Allan's tirade escalated, Tiff became angrier. He finally retaliated against his father's rant about Tiff's generation being "brainwashed [and] de-balled" by saying, "Thank god I live far away from you in Cannington and write books."

A mistake. Findley should not have mentioned his writing because this sent Allan off on another tirade. Clearly, his parents had read a manuscript version of *The Last of the Crazy People* and Allan disapproved. As far as he could see, Tiff was defaming his own family. Michael, who was not present at this ugly encounter, also saw the novel as a personal attack. Margaret, however, defended the book and her son's motivation in writing it. If Findley's memory can be trusted on the details as recorded in his journal with his thoughts inserted in brackets, this is what was said that day in his parents' living room, and the degree to which the exchange hurt him can only be imagined:

FATHER: "That book of yours ..."

TIFF: "Oh, God. Here we go on the book again."

FATHER: "That's right ..."

TIFF: "I wish you'd make up your bloody mind about that book."

FATHER: "I've tried, like a man, to take the slap in the face you gave me
    in that book. It's only Margaret. I won't have her suffer."

TIFF: "She isn't going to suffer unless I lie ..."

FATHER: "I won't have it!"

TIFF: "Margie is treated very well in the book ..." [which is incidentally
    true]

MOTHER: It isn't really *Margie* anyway ... or any of us. Anyone who
    writes has to have *some* basis in reality." (LAC 84:15).

The "Margaret" Allan refers to here is his sister, not his wife, and the portrait of the aunt in *The Last of the Crazy People* is complex but hardly
insulting.

Before telling this story and writing down the dialogue, Findley
summed up what he had learned from the experience. To do this, he
resorted to lists—one for the basic issues, as he understood them, and
one for what he had learned about himself and his father. He saw that
he had come to the argument—entered the scene, so to speak—afraid of
his father, anxious to have Allan's "approbation," but unable to understand him, and highly critical of the man's character: "I thought him 'two-
faced'" and a "poor judge of character." After the confrontation, he was
"no longer *at all* afraid of him," a heartbreaking, if necessary, admission
for a thirty-four-year-old man to make, but one that taps into the core of
Findley's anxiety and insecurity. He claimed that he no longer needed or
wanted his father's "approbation," and that he feared for his father's sanity.
What's more, he concluded that Allan had always lacked good judgment
and that being "two-faced" was Allan's problem, not his. For a person who
took honesty, openness, and personal integrity so seriously, this last point
amounted to an ethical repudiation of the man, if not also of the father.

His mother's situation, however, caused Findley increasing concern.
On their first trip to the farm, when Bill's family was also visiting, Allan

behaved inexplicably badly and ruined the weekend. Findley was keen to show his parents the house and the fields, but Allan was sullen and childish and refused to participate in conversations or join in a family breakfast. Then he startled everyone by announcing that he and Margaret must leave immediately instead of staying through the weekend as planned. "It was heartbreaking," Findley wrote: "she had relaxed & had been able to enjoy herself—and then she had to go home with him." He knew that his father's health was poor and that his setbacks in business were serious, but he realized that his mother was taking the full brunt of Allan's temper and demands.[6] She always had, of course, and he had seen this even as a youngster. But this time Allan had gone too far to redeem himself in his son's eyes:

> I give him up. He is a waste of time. He'd have us all dead—or ruined to keep him safe and comfortable. [...] For sheer, unadulterated self-centredness he is without an equal anywhere. His real problem this weekend was that he refused to tolerate not being the absolute centre of everyone's attention. And for his complete lack of concern for mother, for me, for Bill, for the Thomsons [Bill's mother and her husband] I cannot forgive him. [...] He has come awfully close to losing my respect in the past—this time he finally has. (LAC 84:15)

Findley resolved to talk to his psychiatrist about his father because he finally understood that the root of his own problems lay, in large part, with this selfish, dysfunctional man.

Parental disapproval, however, was not the only cloud hanging over *The Last of the Crazy People*. Through the fall of 1964, Findley waited in vain to hear from Grace Bechtold, the senior editor with Bantam Books in New York, about a possible hardback edition. Bechtold had already accepted a greatly revised manuscript of the book, but only for a paperback format and on condition that a hardback publisher could be found. Although she was not a literary agent as such, she was diligently shopping the manuscript around in an effort to find a publisher; Doubleday had said no, as had Simon & Schuster and Lippincott. On November 17, Findley told his journal that he hated the book. By December 6, with continuing silence from New York, he found things "heartbreaking." The revisions he had made in response to Bechtold's criticisms were substantial; as he reported in a 6 March 1964 letter to her, "I have torn it apart (literally) and am now in the process of rewriting" (LAC 92:3). He had reduced the length by at least one hundred pages; cut two peripheral characters; refocused the story so that events are "heard and observed" by his central character, the eleven-year-old boy Hooker Winslow; provided more motivation for the boy's mother's withdrawal from the family; and shifted a crucial suicide to Hooker's older brother, Gilbert. Gilbert is the character who owes a lot to Michael Findley, so Findley's description of the character in his letter to Bechtold is worth noting: "it seems to me," he explained, "that Gilbert has far more cause" to kill himself than the uncle who was dropped from the story because "his whole mode of life is negative. He is tired. He has overextended himself (his world of fantasy and inaction has been completely exploded; its revealed emptiness leaves him with no future, even as a dreamer)." By shifting the narrative point of view, so that readers experience events as young Hooker does, Findley made a sound decision, one that drew upon his success creating children in "About Effie" and "War."

However, there were limits to what he would agree to change. He told Bechtold that he could enhance the Toronto-ness of the setting to make the book more Canadian, but that he would not cut Gilbert's use of the word "fucking." While it is difficult now to imagine a writer being told to delete the F-word from a novel, Bechtold was not the only editor to object to this profanity. When the British publisher demanded the deletion of "fucking," which Gilbert uses twice, Findley was livid. This was his first personal brush with censorship, something he strenuously opposed and, in any case, "THE word" was integral to Gilbert's character. As he told Bechtold in an 8 April 1967 letter, small changes like this would damage his prose: "I have worked *very hard* to achieve some of these rhythms. A 'damn' will *not* do where I have put a 'god damn.' I am not a 'style nut,' but a good sense of rhythm is as basic to good writing as choice of words and 'sense of taste'" (LAC 92:3). Rhythm, cadence, movement, and gesture—all of them qualities of music, dance, and acting—were essential aspects of his writing, which is why Bill read drafts out loud to him so he could hear his sentences. From *The Last of the Crazy People* onwards, Findley was an obsessive reviser at such fundamental levels as narrative structure, point of view, prose rhythm, and the choice of characters. Nothing was ever tossed off or written quickly. He was equally determined to keep every page of his writing, just as he had always preserved his journals "in case [he] might need them." There would eventually be so many drafts of each novel, story, and play that Bill needed a special desk with multiple storage slots to keep track of them all.

The Last of the Crazy People finally appeared in 1967, and it explores many of the themes from his earlier story "Harper's Bazaar," except that most of the family members who die in the novel are murdered by Hooker Winslow, the eleven-year-old protagonist. To Findley's disappointment, the novel was not well received in Canada. One of the hurdles it faced was the ludicrous objection that children, especially middle-class kids from well-to-do homes, did not do such violent things in this country and, therefore, that no one would read such an ugly, incredible tale. Dismissive reviews like Robert Fulford's (he found the novel to be derivative of Faulkner and Styron and one of "unrelieved gloom," [Fulford, 1967]) were both hurtful and infuriating for Findley. And yet, one of the sources for the plot came from an actual account of a Toronto boy who shot several members of his family because he loved them. Findley was so taken with this real-life catastrophe that he realized that this is what Hooker would do. He confessed to his journal that he did not "know it would end this way [...]. It just swept over me. [...] *He will kill his family to save them from themselves*" (qtd. in *IM* 70). As far as Findley was concerned, Hooker's actions followed "the logic of innocence [...] battered by too much reality" (*IM* 70).

The basic plot is quite simple in the same way that a Greek tragedy is simple—inevitable, straightforward, and relentless. The story is set in the family home just outside of Toronto in 1963, and the Winslow family consists of the parents, Jessica and Nicholas, a stockbroker with his office on Bay Street; two sons, Gilbert and Hooker; Nicholas's unmarried sister,

Rosetta; and their maid, Iris. The house is gracious, with a stable, a library, fine furnishings, and attractive grounds. However, behind this facade of comfort and gentility lies a series of tragedies that haunt the family and will, during the course of a long, sweltering summer, destroy it. Jessica has withdrawn to her bedroom, locked out her husband and children, and rejected the roles of wife and mother. Her husband is bewildered and helpless, unable even to talk to her or comfort his children. In his wife's eyes he is a failure. Rosetta has moved in to run the household, help with Jessica, and see to the children.

As Allan Findley realized, Rosetta closely resembles his sister, Margaret: she is unmarried, has suffered a stroke that has left her disfigured, and is trapped in a patriarchal past. Her office is filled with Winslow family photographs, and what Hooker sees, when he studies these ghosts from the past, recalls the actual photographic display that Grandmother Findley kept in her living room to remind her family of who they were and of the husband/father and heroic brother to whom Allan and his sons could never measure up. Indeed, the description of Grandfather Winslow is clearly modelled on pictures of Thomas Findley (*LCP* 253–54). Iris, the maid, is Rosetta's positive counterpart, a wise and loving woman who holds the family together and provides Hooker's sole human comfort and connection in life. She owes much to the maids Findley knew while growing up; as he told the late Graeme Gibson (1934–2019), *"that was my childhood,* I spent my whole childhood with maids, sitting in kitchens" (138). Iris provides the emotional centre and ethical compass of the narrative. She is always there when Hooker needs her, and she is there to comfort him at the terrible climax and again at the quiet close of the story. Although Gilbert Winslow had "undeniable ties with Michael," Findley realized that he couldn't "write about Mike" because "the mystery [of the man] defies me. But Gilbert I can grasp, because a part of him is me and I can get him all the way to the page intact" (*IM* 69). While this makes sense because Michael was always beyond Findley's comprehension, it is also fully consistent with his creative instincts—always to work from actual reality into a fully imagined fictional reality. Gilbert, however, more closely resembles a twenty-year-old Michael than Findley realized. He may not be as violent with others or as heartlessly selfish as Michael, but he is a maudlin fail-ure, an alcoholic, a frustrated would-be poet, and an embittered young man who spends most of his time lying on a couch drinking and reciting poetry. Gilbert finally kills himself by driving his Jaguar across a fairway, down a hill, and into a stand of trees, where it bursts into flames as Hooker watches.

Hooker is the focal point of the story and one of Findley's best child observers. Tormented and confused by the tragedy surrounding him, he decides to shoot the remaining members of his family. The day after the inquest into Gilbert's death, he loads the gun, climbs into the loft of the stable (as Neil did with his stones in "War"), and waits for his family to look for him. Then, as if on cue, they come out into the backyard call-ing his name, and he shoots them one by one. The scene is horrifying because of the cool, objective way in which Findley presents it. We cannot see Hooker, but we see what he is aiming at, and we watch as each adult falls to the ground. It is not until Iris finds him that we understand the boy's condition: "She reached the gun out of his hands. 'There, honey,' she said. 'There now. There. There now. There you are. There.' He accepted her embrace. 'You're all right now,' said Iris. 'You've done it. It's over.'" (280). There is no further comment, no explanation or analysis. We learn that Hooker goes to a mental hospital and would probably not recognize Iris if she visited him. The rest is left unsaid.

In the conversation with Graeme Gibson, Findley accepted the description of the novel as Gothic, but stressed that it is "Southern *Ontario* Gothic. And *that* exists" (138); in other words, he was not writing about the American South but about a part of Canadian society that he knew personally. The term *Gothic* is helpful, however, because it identifies the novel's mix of haunting by the past, present fear of danger that lurks around the corner, and a suffocating atmosphere of closed rooms behind heavy drapes, where the living, even the children, must move and speak in hushed tones. There is something rotten in this society or, if not rotten, then repressive, hidden, unspeakable. All the characters are trapped; so is the reader. The novel opens on the night before the murders as Hooker lies unsleeping on his bed with his cat Little Bones: "the first shadows of morning began to lift themselves out of the corners and up from behind the chairs. The curtains—or something in the curtains—motioned and moved and waved" (3). And that's it precisely—the Gothic touch of dread, of something not quite right—before we even know who Hooker Winslow is, before we have finished reading further than the opening lines. The fact that this scene takes place in a "Prologue" means we can expect a shift into some unprepared-for action and can anticipate a possible "Epilogue." And an "Epilogue" is there, at the end, with its completion of this September morning, when one sees what happens, understands what those portentous shadows and waving curtains gestured towards, and reads about the aftermath. Everything between the prologue and epilogue builds toward the tragic outcome.

As Findley noted in his 1964 journal, the story is about "the journey of a child through a nightmare that is not ever garish but which is dim and peculiar. [...] The nightmare is the ultimate arrival at adult life—which he knows is coming and which he tries to fend off [...]. *Crazy People* must be a short, swift plunge through the fog and terror of people who do *not* cry out when they should or move when they should" (qtd. in *IM* 73–74). The boy is basically abandoned, not just by his mother, whose response to her nightmare is escape from the demands of family reality, but by his father, who refuses to see his young son or to remember how old he is or why he might be anxious, and by a brother who cannot cope with the facts of life and withdraws into booze and suicide. Hooker is desperate for someone to shed light on why his family is called crazy and why no one in his family does anything about their lives. Hooker's love for his family, his confusion and despair, his acute sense of being betrayed by them into something so terrible no one will speak of it, leads him to conclude that he must act. The theme of violence complicated by love, loss, and fear will become a constant Findley subject, but here it is developed slowly, almost surreptitiously, from a child's perspective and with the "logic of innocence" through small references to the Great War, the Second World War, political assassinations, and to Oscar Wilde's *The Ballad of Reading Gaol* and the folk song "Frankie and Johnnie," which both tell stories of love, betrayal, and murder.

The question of autobiography is an unavoidable and reasonable one with *The Last of the Crazy People*. Findley is on record as saying that he drew extensively on his own childhood sitting at the kitchen table with the maid for his characterization of Hooker as a child who feels betrayed. In the interview, he told Gibson that "there is certainly a great deal of betrayal in the book," but "that was so personal [that] I will never go into that" (137). But Hooker Winslow is not Timothy Findley, and although he knew he was working from Michael's life when he created Gilbert, Gilbert Winslow is not Michael Findley. Findley's creative ability to ground his fictions in reality, in places, people, and events he knew or had researched, to combine fact and fiction, and to blend real people with fictional characters, is partly what makes a Findley story so powerful. The Winslow house owes much to houses he knew intimately, like Grandmother Findley's, with her portrait gallery of Findley men and Great War memorabilia. The long, hot summer recalls the kind of heavy, stifling, humid summers typical of southern Ontario. Rosetta does resemble Findley's Aunt Marg, but Nicholas is more diffuse, both as a character and as an identifiable family reference. Fathers are troubling figures in the Findley fictional world, and Nicholas's work as a broker reminds one of Allan's, but his character is much gentler than Allan's. Jessica, however, owes a great deal to Aunt Ruth, or rather to Findley's imagined Ruth and to family stories about her life and fate. Like the character Jessica, Ruth withdrew from married life into the seclusion of her bedroom with her books and notebooks. She is the woman who haunted Findley and would, as he told Gibson, "probably be in all my books" (139).

The Butterfly Plague

Improvements on the farm, work for the CBC, and new creative projects kept Findley busy between 1965 and 1967, and there were Cannington friendships to develop and old friends to entertain. Janet Baldwin made her first visit to what she called the "Bifftill Homestead" in June 1965, and their neighbours, Nelson and Phyllis Purvis, gave them a booklet about

Cannington's history, dating its settlement back to the 1830s. They discovered that their house was over one hundred years old by the 1960s, with the oldest section of it built by an eccentric English chemist, Mr. Alfred Wyatt, who established his dispensary there in the 1840s. This was definitely not Rosedale, but it represented Ontario history of an earlier, humbler, and, for Findley, more genuine kind. When the well dried up, they turned for help to the man who was repairing the chimneys, brickwork, and cistern because, as Findley noted with delight, he "'witches' for water [and has] *absolute* faith in this method & in himself as a 'douser'" (LAC 84:15). Findley also had faith, and high-quality water was found. Gradually, as work progressed and they settled in, he grew to love the house, and walking in the fields and woods brought him relaxation and pleasure. His radio and television work from this period introduced him to new people in the arts, and the interviews that he conducted with Québécois artists—Jean Gascon, Gratien Gélinas, Anne Hébert, Claude Jutra, Ulysse Comtois, and Françoise Sullivan—were stimulating and led him to reflect, in his journal, on how important the next decade would be for the arts in Canada. Furthermore, the documentary film work motivated him to try his hand at writing film scripts, taught him a lot about how films are made, and influenced certain ways in which he constructed scenes in his fiction and plays.

Stimulated by his foray into scriptwriting, he tried his hand at creating his own scripts, one of which, *The Paper People*, brought him both frustration and disappointment. This, together with slow progress on *The Butterfly Plague* manuscript, increased his depression and need for drink, which came to a head one evening when choreographer Grant Strate (1927–2015) and his partner, the dancer Earl Kraul (1929–99), were visiting Stone Orchard. Bill hid the wine because he feared that Tiff was drinking too much. But Tiff needed a drink. Tiff needed several drinks. He confronted Bill, who was busy in the kitchen, to demand the wine. Bill refused to divulge its whereabouts, and all hell broke loose. As Bill recalled the scene for me, he "was still learning how to deal with [Tiff's] alcoholism, and so [he] made a serious mistake":

I locked all our alcohol supplies in the trunk of the car. When Tiff discovered this, he was furious. And thus it was that Grant and Earl, hearing an uproar in the kitchen, came upon this farcical scene: Tiff, with his hands around my neck, was banging my head against the door that led to the pantry, while I was pounding his head with a saucepan. The sight of our guests, frozen with disbelief and horror in the doorway, was too much for either of us. We both collapsed in helpless laughter. I went out, got the bottles—and we all had a very pleasant time.

In his version of events, Bill managed to put a comic spin on the scene. In his journal Findley was brief and vague, although he was certainly repentant. "There is a story to tell," he wrote, but he did not, in fact, confide anything further. Instead, he focused on the positive because he believed that "we had improved our friendship (or perhaps 'proved' it, more simply) and I feel much closer to G. and E.—because they know me now—and did not desert me—but seemed to understand" (LAC 84:15). Above all, he recognized and appreciated how Bill managed his bad behaviour and the entire weekend. That said, this appalling scene cries out for the backstory Findley did not provide in his journal. His desperate need for drink that evening was almost certainly brought on, in large part, by his frustration with his work and with the violent, disturbing subject matter of that work. Whatever precipitated his outburst, it revealed his capacity for violence and obliged him to recognize that he was, indeed, a "hiding place for monsters" (*IM* 311).

When *The Paper People* premiered on CBC's *Festival* series on 13 December 1967, viewers were shocked or confused.[7] For a television drama ostensibly about artistic life in Toronto during Canada's centennial year, it was anything but celebratory. In fact, it was a savage condemnation of English Canada's failure to produce meaningful Canadian art. In this television play, CBC's first foray into a feature-length drama in colour, Findley portrayed things as he saw them—a contemporary Canadian art scene that was hollow, derivative, nasty, and second-rate. The play's title refers to the life-sized papier mâché "dolls" that Jamie Taylor creates to represent his friends, lovers, and wife, and then burns in a variety of staged events.

The title also implies that Jamie, his circle, and contemporary Toronto society have no more substance than paper people, throwaways, lacking in identity and value. Taylor is an angry young man, a James Dean figure, with a cult following, whose cause is vague and self-centred. He is estranged from his Rosedale mother, separated from a long-absent father, cruel to his ailing wife, and seemingly consumed by the sixties' obsession with disposable art and pop art culture. Fire and paper are his tools of choice; his misanthropic, decidedly misogynist view of life motivates his desire to reduce art and life to ashes. Filmmaker Janet Webb decides to make a documentary about him; hence, the film-within-the-film structure of the drama, as she follows Jamie around, interviews friends and associates, and films his bonfires. Webb, however, is also an artist, and, unlike Jamie who indulges in disposable autobiography and denies his relationships with others, she creates a perceptive documentary biography. The ethical judgment on Jamie is left to another character, who tells him: "You burn us with your anger, but you never burn yourself. Anger all by itself can't generate life. It can only take it away" (*The Paper People* 153).

Sadly, the play was never rebroadcast and has been largely forgotten, despite its 1983 publication in *Canadian Drama*. In his introduction to this publication, Findley noted problems with the script, which "is still overwritten," but he stood by what he had created and praised CBC's executive producer Andrew Allan for daring to use the piece and David Gardner for his imaginative direction of it. He recognized what he called his "Findley's rhythms" in the production as rhythms he developed in his prose, and he claimed he was still frightened by his portrayal of the sixties: "It was a very ugly age, an age of rhetoric and bullets" (61). When asked about *The Paper People* as a commentary on Canada and Canadian identity, his reply was categorical and reminiscent of his 1954 journal laments about the state of the arts in Canada. We, as a country, avoid accepting who we are because "we don't like it and we don't know how to get away from that person" (61). And yet, he insisted that he was "not utterly despairing but utterly fed up" with the violence and death that characterized his era. He understood that making art was a dangerous vocation; artists can be monsters, killers, fascists. They can also show humanity its soul, speak truth to power, make others pay attention, but only when they put themselves on the line and risk burning themselves.

First published in 1969, *The Butterfly Plague* has become, as Bill told me, the "damaged child" in the family of Timothy Findley's novels because it is the least read and not well understood. Only time will tell if this remains true, but it is without question an ambitious work with a lot to say about the world during the thirties, and, because of its historical reach, political themes, and allegorical qualities, it is an interesting early example of the mature fiction he created in *Famous Last Words*, *Headhunter*, and *Pilgrim*. It is also historical fiction in a distinctly Findley-esque style: while written from a fictional present that is set in a recent past, it warns about a future nightmare, which we know really happened with the Holocaust and the Second World War, and about further possible catastrophes that lie ahead in the reader's present.

The Butterfly Plague takes place in Hollywood between August 1938 and April 1939, during that short, tense period before the start of the Second World War.[8] The story develops almost like a diary or a journal with four "Books," each of which contains units called "Chronicles," and each of these units contains subsections that are dated by month, day, often with the time, and year. There is a plot through-line that a reader can follow, but the narrative intention lies more in juxtapositions of scenes and events, contrasting references to the fantasies of beautiful movie stars and the horrifying fantasies of racial purity, and comparisons between, for example, Nazi anti-Semitism in Berlin and underground Nazi activities in Los Angeles in 1938–39. This striking format has prompted some critics to call the novel postmodern,[9] but the primary impact for a reader who opens the novel for the first time and must struggle to hold the material together is to be repeatedly thrown into the midst of an immediate present action without explanation. Each of the main characters, and a few minor ones, gets their own chronicle, but a key question hovering over the entire story is: if this is a journal or a diary, then to whom does it belong? Who is recording this information about the characters' lives and the deadly world they inhabit? To the extent that the novel functions like a film, with scenes, dialogue, and camera shots from different actors' perspectives, one is still left wondering who the director is and to whom the narrative voice-over belongs.

These are precisely the questions that most troubled Findley in the spring of 1967. He knew he needed to shake himself free of *The Last of the Crazy People* and "come to grips with the new people" who would become Ruth Damarosch, her brother Adolphus (called Dolly), their father George, and their mother Naomi Nola Damarosch. All these characters are adults, and this was his first attempt to write "exclusively about adults—no child's-eye view of things to fall back on" (*IM* 107). Locating the right narrator and narrative point of view were always difficult for Findley. In a 1967 notebook he wondered: "Why am I so concerned about the innocent watcher here? I guess the answer has to be that I want to show the evil aspect of this story without the sophisticated overlay of people's excuses for doing what they do. [...] To do this I must create a character whose innocence—or do I mean naïveté?—can cut through the red tape of psychology" (qtd. in *IM* 107–8). The evil he wanted and felt ready (as Wilder had told him he must be) to portray was widespread, from Hollywood greed and corruption to the rise of Nazism and anti-Semitism, not only in Germany but also in the United States, notably in Los Angeles and within the Hollywood film industry.[10] For his innocent watcher, he created the character of Ruth Damarosch, a young American swimmer who was taken to Germany by her trainer, Bruno Haddon, to compete in the 1936 Berlin Olympics. Ruth was closely based on Janet Baldwin, who had performed in the ballet competition at the 1936 Olympic Games; like Janet, Ruth has white-blonde hair, large blue eyes, and long, elegant limbs, and, like Janet, she is a carrier of hemophilia and must not bear children. Ruth marries her much older, brutal, dictatorial teacher-trainer, just as Janet had married Boris Volkoff, and Ruth lives to regret the marriage and returns to her California home, to her hemophiliac brother, the filmmaker Dolly, and to her mother, Naomi, who has passed the disease on to both of her children. Being in Germany from 1936 to 1938 allows Ruth to watch the Nazis at work. She performs dangerous swimming feats for them, accepts gifts from the likes of Hermann Göring, and worries about the people she calls "they" or "the Others"—the Jews of Germany, whom she saw being persecuted in the streets and removed to camps. On one especially significant occasion, a Jew had reached out to her for help.

As her mother will tell her, for all her Aryan beauty Ruth is part Jewish because her father's mother was a Jew. But she remains a troubling invention because she does not seem to grasp the consequences of the evil surrounding her. She seems confused, and confusing, in her pursuit of a pregnancy and in her choice of a father for the perfect child she hopes to conceive. The least successful aspect of *The Butterfly Plague* is the silent blond German who follows Ruth from Germany to California, watches her on the transatlantic crossing, follows her on to the train across the States, stalking her but refusing to speak, even when they have sex. He is called "Race," meaning that he embodies the Nazi ideal of a perfect Aryan male to match what Ruth appears to be—the perfect Aryan female. Except that Ruth is far from perfect, and the silent German, who may be a Nazi spy, is an abstraction. Findley would manage the complexities of prejudice, violence, complicity, and haunting masterfully in *Famous Last Words*, but here in *The Butterfly Plague* they do not cohere in an ethically clear way. That said, there are other ways in which the character of Ruth rises to the challenge of her time and place successfully. She is the only character in the novel to be granted a first-person voice and story. In "The Chronicle of Nightmare," Ruth addresses the reader directly: "America is not the Nightmare. It will be. The Nightmare is Europe. I went there in 1936. I can tell you that all parts and portions of this Nightmare belong, fit or can be wrenched away from the period between 1936 and 1938" (67). In this chronicle, she bears witness to her experiences in Europe and describes her encounter with a man who seeks her help to escape Europe and gives her his yellow star, telling her that "it will remind you of where you are and of what you do not know" (78).

"The Chronicle of Nightmare" is Ruth's report on her time then and of what she saw for the reader, but as a story of bearing witness to the Western world on the edge of an abyss, it owes much to Findley's response to the devastation he saw in Berlin on his two trips there in the fifties and to his horror when he discovered Ivan Moffat's Dachau photographs. The necessary next step, however, is to wake up from such a nightmare, to address and identify it as racism and genocide; the consequences of failing to do so compromise an individual's integrity as a witness. Although Ruth demonstrates her integrity in some ways after her return to America, she is not a strong enough character to bear the burden of truth, vision, and honesty that Findley and the evils of Nazi ideology require. The character who comes closest to articulating this honesty is Ruth's mother, who warns her daughter to accept reality and reject lies and self-deception: "This is one of your flaws, Ruth," she says. "Not to cope with truth [...]. But the greatest flaw of all, the very worst, the most destructive, and [...] the seat of all our woes and pain, is this *dream*—this impossible quest for perfection" (160). Findley challenges the reader to distinguish perfection from reality, to understand that the plagues and fires in California are warnings of the disaster about to engulf Europe, and to pay attention to what Ruth witnesses.

When Findley revised *The Butterfly Plague* for the 1986 edition, he cut the last chronicle in the 1969 edition and ended the novel on an apocalyptic note. Even the sentences, brief and repetitious—"And she spread the ashes. And they were mud. And there was nothing to do but turn around and go"—echo the Bible and are heavy with foreboding and dread. This editorial decision was wise because it closes the second edition with a confident narrative gesture that leaves questions unanswered and conclusions up to the reader. In the preface to the 1986 edition, he admits that he was a "neophyte writer" in the late sixties with too many ideas and theories: "Every paragraph was twice as long as it needed to be. The characters, not unlike the butterflies, arrived on the pages in droves. The events were about as large as events could get: there were murders, flaming forests, movie making, the Olympic Games and [...] I threw in World War II" (iii). In short, the first *Butterfly Plague* was overwritten and too ambitious: "It was a good idea, but its time had not come. Or rather, its writer had not made sure of his craft" (iv). He was correct, but this assessment overlooks the fact that the author learned his craft through the writing of this book. He honed his style and understanding of narrative structure, and he developed some of his most enduring themes. What he learned with *The Butterfly Plague* made *Famous Last Words* possible.

In 1968, however, Grace Bechtold was still not happy with the manuscript. Findley travelled alone to New York in April to deliver his manuscript in person and to consult with her, but he began drinking on the train, and, after checking into the Meurice Hotel, he went out to buy flowers for Bechtold and two bottles of gin for himself. By the time he reached her office, he was very drunk and accompanied by an inebriated taxi driver, who had helped him capture his manuscript pages after they flew out of his hands in the street. Bechtold was furious and ordered him out. According to the story Findley recalls in *Inside Memory* (122–27), she threw the flowers on the floor and told him she hated him and never wanted to see him again. Over the course of the next two days, he lost track of where he was and what he was doing, until he found himself in the New York home of a friend. Bill tracked him down and arranged for him to be bundled on to a train to Toronto. By May 6 he was heading home to face Bill who, he feared, might also want to be rid of him.

Why had Findley behaved like this on such an important occasion? Because he was alone, desperately anxious about his new novel, terrified by the city, and off his Antabuse. His calendar entry for May 5 reads: "Shameful—awful—frightening. Nothing real" (LAC 85:3). This was another instance of his self-defeating behaviour, much like similar episodes during the fifties in London, when he risked career and personal relationships by drinking. Safely back home, he wrote a CBC radio play called "Walls," which consists of a *Krapp's Last Tape*-style monologue dated 24 June 1968, and performed it himself: the effect is chilling. For thirty minutes, a writer who is alone and drinking heavily becomes increasingly desperate, talks to himself, laments his state, and attempts to reach friends and his psychiatrist by telephone. He is terrified, doesn't know where he is, but insists that he is surrounded by walls and can't get out. Finally, in near hysteria, he tells his doctor that "the walls are endless and real." He hangs up, a phone rings, he says "Hello"—silence follows and the monologue ends.[11] This type of fear recurred for Findley, and as late as 1982 he confessed to Dr. Turner that he felt "reality closing around me—instead of being an 'opening' process"; then he reflected on the possibility that he had missed some aspect of maturing that had to do "with being connected to reality" (LAC 106:11). When Findley said that Hooker in *The Last of the Crazy People* was "battered by too much reality," he was clearly describing a sensation that he recognized in himself, but unlike the frantic narrator in "Walls," Findley had an excellent doctor who would listen and support him through such crises.

Happily, neither Bill nor Grace Bechtold left him. Bill saw him through the ordeal, and Bechtold called another meeting for June. This time everything went smoothly, despite the assassination of Robert Kennedy that plunged Americans into grief and unsettled both Findley and Whitehead. And there was good news: Harvey Ginsberg at Viking was going to publish the hardback, and Bechtold was still on board for the Bantam paperback. To ease the reconciliation with Bechtold, the two men took her to dinner and then to see *Jacques Brel Is Alive and Well and Living in Paris*. Findley was back on his medication and abstained from alcohol. Gradually Bechtold relaxed, and, after the show, Findley realized that all was well when she "took my arm and the three of us walked back over to 12th Street—silent" (*IM* 132).

In the final years of the decade, Findley's life became increasingly hectic. While getting his second novel published was marginally easier than his first, the ultimate fate of *The Butterfly Plague* was little short of ludicrous. Shortly after it appeared in the States, Findley visited a Canadian bookstore to see how *The Butterfly Plague* was selling at home, but it was nowhere to be seen. When he asked the clerk why no copies of his novel were on its shelves, she explained that it was not the type of book her readers wanted because of its rather strange sex and its sordid portrait of Hollywood. Then he asked her what was selling, whereupon, as Bill recalled, she happily reported that the bookstore was "having a terrific season with *Myra Breckinridge* and *Portnoy's Complaint*."[12] This was a classic (if hilarious) case of Canadians in the sixties devaluing and ignoring their own artists, and it must have reminded Findley of his opinion, as far back as 1953 in London, that Canadians lacked confidence in their own culture, were "lazy [and] afraid to be bold," and were prepared to promote the work produced in other countries. Even Canadian correspondence sent to Macmillan Canada was routinely forwarded to New York, as if Findley had no identity or presence in his own country.

Findley's dramatic work for television and film fared no better. *The Paper People* had been panned and forgotten, and a feature film he made with the NFB, *Don't Let the Angels Fall*, premiered at Cannes in 1969 but was dismissed at home, and Findley's creative role as the writer went unacknowledged. The subject of the film, however, is worth noting because it represents another of Findley's early attempts to create fiction from closely observed domestic experience. The protagonist, Robert, is a Montreal insurance broker with a wife and two sons. He is dissatisfied with his marriage and his sons, and he is failing professionally. Unable to cope, he has an affair, and the entire family begins to fall apart, causing the younger son, who is frightened by this crisis, to feel increasingly insecure, skip school, and dream of running away. The parallels with Findley's family are clear, but he could barely recognize his script by the time others had edited and modified it into the finished film. This was a painful lesson in the importance of authorial control.

Meanwhile, Bill was working hard for the CBC, travelling constantly, and trying to handle the business end of Findley's life—correspondence with publishers, contracts, the typing of multiple drafts of works in progress—and Findley was sending Bechtold his ideas for a "theatre novel," in which he planned to use *King Lear* and explore the dissolution of an actor's marriage. She was cool about this project but encouraged him to focus on the marriage and drop the actor-theatre business. Nothing further came of this novel until Findley returned to the basic material and characters thirty years later for *Spadework*. But the friendship with Grace Bechtold continued to develop. She visited them at Stone Orchard, they met again in New York in February of 1969, when Alec McCowen was performing there, and they exchanged gifts at Christmas. After 1970, however, the correspondence tapered off because once he was established in the Canadian publishing scene with his Toronto literary agent Nancy Colbert, he no longer needed to maintain the personal connection. When *The Wars* appeared in 1977, however, Bechtold wrote to congratulate him, and after *Famous Last Words* she wrote again to say that he had proven he was the major writer she knew he would be. Although Grace Bechtold's practical role in Findley's life was over, she followed his career and continued to praise his work. It was she, as he never forgot, who had helped him at a critical stage, when few others believed in him and no one in Canadian publishing or reviewing cared.

Despite the hard work and serious discouragements, the summer of 1969 marked a high point for both men, and Findley discovered a part of his country that impressed him profoundly and renewed his faith in the natural world and his conviction that twentieth-century urban life was corrupt and destructive. As their income increased (by the late sixties Findley was bringing in between $6,000 and $12,000 a year and Bill steadily earned over $12,000) and the initial repairs to the house and farm were complete, they could afford a better car—a green Citroën—and a real holiday. In the early summer of 1969 they set off on an eight-week road trip, with Bill driving and Findley, as usual, recording the trip in meticulous detail in his journal. They travelled to Maine for ten days at Atlantic House, and from there began the long drive west via upper New York State to Chicago, through South Dakota and Wyoming, then north into Alberta to Calgary, Edmonton, and, finally, further north to Fort Smith in the Northwest Territories (NWT). They camped at Pine Lake in nearby Wood Buffalo National Park, which is now a UNESCO World Heritage site for the protection of endangered species such as the whooping crane and the wood bison. As they made their way west, Findley noted the rural poverty of Americans, which struck him as worse than in Canada, and they had problems with the car which, comfortable and capacious as it was, was a foreign make and a challenge to repair or service. By the time they reached the Black Hills in South Dakota, Findley had become disgusted by all the mobile homes they were passing and by what he called a beer-guzzling class of American men. This reaction was not so much a response to poverty itself—he did not judge the poor and on occasion quietly supported people less well off than himself—as it was a visceral reaction to what he saw as aggressive masculinity, coarseness, and ugliness, reminiscent of his devastation when faced with his brother's squalid flat and drunkenness in London. Worst of all, he noted, was the American despoliation of the countryside through the spraying of herbicides, and some of these observations found their way into the story "E.R.A." and into a radio play called "The Journey."[13] He found Yellowstone National Park and the Devil's Tower in Wyoming beautiful, and he took great interest in place names, elevations, graffiti, prairie dogs, and the spiders that Bill discovered along the route. He gathered samples of wildflowers new to him, many of which still lie, flattened and dried, between his journal pages.

One of the highlights of the trip occurred in a campground in the South Dakota Badlands on the night of July 20. The American Apollo 11 spacecraft landed on the moon that night with Neil Armstrong, the first man to walk on the moon's surface, and the two listened to the car radio as a moment-by-moment account of the landing was broadcast. What most impressed Findley, however, was the uncanny parallel between the descriptions of the moon's surface and the lunar landscape of the Badlands that surrounded him on earth. After an overnight camp in Montana's Glacier National Park, they crossed the border into Canada on July 21 and stopped in southwest Alberta's Waterton Lakes National Park with its breathtaking scenery. Seeing such splendour for the first time left him deeply moved and marked the start of his appreciation of Canada's natural beauty and belief that Canadians had a responsibility to protect, not despoil, such richness. They continued north through Banff, Jasper, and Edmonton, and the last leg of their journey took them to Fort Smith and "the mysteries," as Findley put it, "of Farther North" (LAC 86:1). Although he was appalled by the commercialism of Banff, he was impressed by the grandeur of the Columbia Icefield, and the farther north they went and the farther they travelled from civilization, the more lyrical he became in his descriptions and the more thoughtfully he wrote about the meaning, for him, of what he saw. The living conditions of the First Nations people they encountered as they travelled north troubled him, however, and he blamed European settlers for destroying Native culture and dignity. Comments about Canada's Indigenous peoples are infrequent in Findley's work because he rarely had opportunities to meet or know them. Certainly, in 1969 the history of settlement, treaties, and residential schools was scarcely acknowledged by non-Aboriginal Canadians and was not addressed in school curricula or the media. In his journal Findley concluded that the "White man's [...] fear of Indians is really the fear of having treated them badly so that their resentment is justified." "This country was never conquered," he wrote; "We just walked in and said it was ours" (LAC 86:1).

The few settlers he met also caught his attention because he sensed in them a spirit of adventure and creativity lacking in urban Canadians, but he was skeptical enough to see through their "romantic separation from civilization" and careful not to confuse their lifestyle with an unproblematic rejection of modern, technological life. In fact, he began pondering ideas for stories about men who thought they could escape but ended up bringing the worst aspects of civilization with them—noise, garbage, aggression, technology, and the destruction of the environment. Timothy Findley was neither an environmental activist nor a poet, but on this occasion he turned to poetry, and the recent moon landing, to express his view of human stupidity:

> Poem
> I who have walked on the moon
> So lightly
> Did not learn
> To use my toes
> So sparingly
> At home. (LAC 86:1)

On July 30 they found a "perfect" spot on the shore of Pine Lake for their camp and Findley was "ecstatic." Here they enjoyed their "idyl," something so unique and precious that he knew, from the start, it could never be recaptured. They swam every day, took the kayak out, went into Fort Smith for supplies, and were "thrilled" by their first sighting of a buffalo: "incredible—huge & *healthy*—and with a sprig of fir tree caught behind his horn like a <u>*Caesar*</u>" (LAC 86:1). Bill fished, while Tiff sketched and wrote. In one draft story, he created a character who finds himself in a pristine wilderness by a lake and kills himself rather than return to civilization. However, suicide was not the answer to real problems and the world could not be kept entirely at bay. Contented as he was to be with Bill, surrounded by natural peace and beauty, delighted by his first glimpse of whooping cranes, the antics of a grey jay that had adopted them, and the haunting cry of the loons, his spirits sagged. The "death of The Butterfly Plague" depressed him, and when he contemplated man's propensity to destroy other forms of life, he became discouraged. You cannot, he felt, "bring *people* into a wilderness without them wanting to destroy it," and he included himself and Bill in this criticism because they were there, with cameras, a stove, and a car.

As their idyll drew to a close, Findley hurried to fill the journal with notes on everything they encountered. When they got caught on the water by a sudden storm and had to shelter on an island, Bill identified huge wolf tracks and bear tracks, but once they were safely back at the tent, Findley noted with glee that it was "the best day & the best time yet." Although the wilderness interlude was coming to an end, he wrote: "I cannot complain. This place has been marvelous" (LAC 86:1). From this point on, Timothy Findley noted any news item concerning the Canadian north with interest (such as when the American oil tanker *Manhattan* traversed the Northwest Passage in August of 1969 without Canadian authorization), and years later he followed American threats to Canada's Arctic sovereignty with a passion.

There were a few experiences in Findley's life of such importance that they marked significant points in his growth, experiences from which he learned about his identity, clarified or confirmed his beliefs, and sometimes located his spiritual centre. This trip, especially the three weeks in the NWT, camping at Pine Lake, visiting Fort Smith and Yellowknife, gaining some insight into the life of Indigenous people, testing himself physically with swimming, kayaking, and hiking, was one of these experiences. Not only was he gathering information for future work, but he was also incorporating everything into a personal philosophy—a pantheistic reverence for the natural world and all its creatures, among which human beings are, as he saw things, the most destructive species. One day, after stopping the car to watch a buffalo lumber across the road and then disappear into the trees, Findley sensed that this animal was a messenger of sorts, turning its back on them in their ugly vehicle and choosing to live in its own superior realm. "I'll never be the same again," he wrote, "never. Never. Never … God forgive us—but we are the wreckers of the Universe" (LAC 86:1).

At the beginning of the sixties, the odds that Timothy Findley would thrive—or even just survive—over the decade ahead seemed slim. Despair over his failed marriage, which intensified his general fear of failure as an artist, undermined his fragile confidence and reinforced his self-destructive behaviour and resort to alcohol. Although the supportive presence of Bill Whitehead and the psychiatrist Dr. Ed Turner in Findley's life did not erase this pattern of behaviour, these men made it easier for him to climb back on the wagon after he fell off. Moreover, they helped restore his belief in his work and in his confidence that, despite frustrating cycles of depression, he was a writer well worth publishing, with important things to say. Inspired by the example of friends like William Hutt, Janet Baldwin, and Margaret Atwood, he was encouraged to build a successful career at home, in Canada. Furthermore, now in his thirties, Findley had gained financial and domestic independence of his parents. Most important of all, he finally had a stable home with a partner he loved in a setting where he could write and know that he belonged.

While so much else was falling into place, however, Findley's relations with his father remained difficult until the summer of 1969, when this key relationship in Findley's life changed for the better. In a 5 May 1967 letter, Thornton Wilder had reminded Findley that it was less important to "forgive fathers [and] society's obtuseness" than to accept, understand, and "finally see through and beyond them" (LAC 107:8). Then Wilder had warned him not to endanger all he currently enjoyed in his private life and work "by regurgitating [...] past monsters." This sage, caring advice from his old mentor bolstered Findley's sense of his life's work in a secure home. Moreover, the knowledge of Allan's serious illness with Parkinson's disease and Tiff's lessened need for his father's approbation enabled him to respond more positively to Allan's efforts at reconciliation. This father-son relationship could never be fully repaired (one cannot take back cruel words and a deliberate rejection), but it did improve. Findley wrote regularly to his father, describing his and Bill's travels, the beauty of the NWT, and what he was learning from this adventure. In one especially interesting letter dated August 1, he reported that he had inscribed Allan's name in indelible ink on a piece of driftwood and set it afloat "on the river going North." Findley knew that the waters of the Athabasca River eventually discharge through the Mackenzie River system into the Arctic Ocean; hence, while this gesture is impossible to interpret with certainty, it was clearly of symbolic importance. It may have signified Findley's attempt to release himself from his father's negative influence, to move beyond "past monsters," or it may have represented a loving attempt to release his troubled, ailing father into a northern space of peace. Perhaps it signified both.

Findley certainly meant his father to read the gesture positively. Margaret had called him with the bad news of Allan's diagnosis on 20 December 1968, and after her call, Findley had gone for a long walk before returning to the farm to write in his journal that he felt "badly" for his father and realized that the family must rally "to keep him productive & useful & secure" (LAC 85:7). This was a surprisingly muted response to such serious news, but then he must have had a rush of conflicting feelings to work through, and there was a great deal of unpleasant history with his father to process. As he noted on a loose piece of a cigarette pack with his journal (LAC 86:11), he needed to write about his years of experience as "not existing in [his] father's eyes [plus Allan's] demand that [he] *be* someone else—which made [him] shrink from who [he] really was." Nevertheless, he was now doing his best to show love and support, which Allan appreciated. Sadly (but it is revealing), while he was still able to write legibly, Allan wrote to his son, not about his own feelings or life, but of his brother Irving, the First World War hero whose exploits and early death condemned Allan to live forever in his elder brother's shadow, a disappointment to his mother and himself. Allan repeated for Findley the family stories about how Irving's plane was shot down, about how Irving was rescued by French soldiers, and how Irving was celebrated by the military and at home. Allan also gave his son Irving's military medal, which Findley treasured more for what it signified about his father's faith in him than what it said about his uncle. Furthermore, Allan promised to entrust Findley with the family's treasured scrapbooks and memorabilia dating back to 1874.

As the end of the decade approached, Findley made lists of books he had read to sum up his reflections on the last year—from history and letters (Chekhov's) to Goethe, Cocteau, Waugh, Bellow, and Hellman. He commented emphatically, however, on his reaction to Conrad. After returning from the NWT trip, he read *Heart of Darkness* for the first time and decided that this masterpiece taught him never to repeat or recycle what a great writer had already accomplished: "I thought, instead, that what I *should* do was publish a one-page book, between neat, blue covers. And on that single page it would say: 'In lieu of writing his own book, the would-be author respectfully draws your attention to *The Heart of Darkness* by Joseph Conrad. In it, all that he would say—is said. The End'" (LAC 75:9). Despite this statement about the importance of Conrad's work (to which he returned in the early nineties), the sixties closed with Findley finally devoting himself, full time, to his own work. Although some aspects of his CBC commissions were satisfying—especially his work with Bill on "The Trial of Oscar Wilde" for CBC's *Ideas*—Findley had just won his first Canada Council grant to write a play called "Missionaries," and he found the CBC contract work debilitating: he could not write when the sole purpose was to earn money. Bill understood his position, which meant that they would rely on his salary for the time being. Findley needed to be at Stone Orchard, concentrating on his own creative work and free from other demands.

The only drawback to this writing life was his loneliness when Bill was travelling and away for days. At such times, he resented some of Bill's friends who, he feared, absorbed Bill's attention and were his rivals for Bill's affection. Nevertheless, even as he confided these fears and grievances to his journal, he understood that he was living the way he had to in order to create. His withdrawal from the daily distractions of an urban life, he said, was "really a withdrawal to a vantage point from which I hope to gain a truer-wider-hopefully, more positive perspective on a race of beings that, close to, I have grown to hate, and must learn to love" (LAC 85:5).

CHAPTER EIGHT

The Golden Age of Canadian Writing

ONCE BEFORE I DIE, I HOPE TO *KNOW* I'VE BEEN HEARD.

THAT'S ALL.

(Timothy Findley, 1976 journal [LAC 88:4])

From Stone Orchard and on to the Klondike

*A*fter the NWT trip, when Findley resolved to love people again, he could not have been better placed to do so than by living among the people of Cannington, and years later he remembered and celebrated the town and his Stone Orchard home in a collection of short vignettes. Some of these were written over the years for his *Harrowsmith* column; others were new, rather Proustian, rememberings of the past. The collection is called *From Stone Orchard*, and there is a certain irony about this title because, by the late nineties, when he published the book, Findley and Whitehead no longer lived at Stone Orchard. They had purchased the farm in 1964 but sold it in 1997, when they moved to Stratford and also bought a small writing retreat in southern France. I consider *From Stone Orchard* now, however, because it reminds us of the importance that nature, ancestors, human connection, and local community held for Findley and reveals many details of the place and the people that, beginning in the 1970s, he drew upon for his writing. The farm, the surrounding fields and landscape, and the security of home provided the peaceful stability and inspiration he needed to create his finest work. It was in his study at one end of the house that he wrote late into the night and early morning, often playing his records loudly. It was at the kitchen table, over food, tea, or wine, that he discussed his drafts with Bill the next day and where he so often met with his agents, editors, and research assistants. It was during his long walks with his dogs through the neighbouring fields that he found many of the images and locales for scenes in his novels. And some of Cannington's history and people made their way into his fiction. *From Stone Orchard* reveals much about the man behind the writer and portrays a valued way of life, lived by many Cannington families, that nurtured Findley's personal philosophy, which is grounded in love of home, respect for ancestors, and concern for a natural world threatened by those humans who treat it as a commodity.

The volume has brief opening and closing essays, "To Stone Orchard" and "From Stone Orchard," which contain the retrospective pieces, rather like a vintage frame around a collage of cherished family photographs. The vignettes are often shaped by autobiography, although each focuses upon individual people, local sites, loved animals, and significant events rather than upon Findley himself. Other people form the figures in a ground of his remembered landscapes, and by collecting these verbal pictures Findley created a community of memory that forges connections—with the fields, the farms, the house, the neighbours, the road running past the front gate—thereby keeping everything alive. "We found it because we had lost our way" (5), he begins, in a simple sentence that captures a reader's attention. "We will always live there in our hearts," he admits as he closes his reminiscences (*FSO* 170). These two direct statements characterize the gentle prose of this book and testify to his ability to love people and place, in contrast with the darkness and anger that so often surface in his novels and plays.

Near the beginning of *From Stone Orchard*, he wrote: "I said then, and I still believe it: *we have come home*" (6), and one of the people who helped make Stone Orchard a home was Len Collins, to whom the volume is dedicated. Collins did many of the renovations and improvements to the house and managed the property with his wife, Anne, when Bill and Tiff were away.[1] Len Collins, more than anyone else, made it possible for them to live at Stone Orchard; hence, Findley's "prime rule" for anyone from the city who moves to the country: "choose a property across the road from Len Collins" (109). Over the years, *home* expanded to include the animals—six dogs and dozens of cats—the gardens, the fields, the Beaver River, the farm across the road, called Sprucevale, many friends (locals and visitors), and those people who came before him at the farm, whom he began to see as his symbolic ancestors. Family had always been very important to Findley, but as the years passed and it was clear that he would never have children of his own (which, as we shall see, he regretted), he found his roots in extended family and in the material, visible connection with human presence. Len Collins uncovered some of these symbolic ancestors in the writing revealed on the beams and walls when he began a renovation; Findley found others in the ancient bottles and shards of glass discarded in a midden near the house.

In the early eighties, he and Bill went into debt to buy Sprucevale, the Georgian-style house and farm across the road from Stone Orchard, to save it from developers. This is the house, renamed "Arkwright" by Findley, where he lived from January 1984 until October 1986, when Len Collins finished the new wing on Stone Orchard, and where Findley worked on *Not Wanted on the Voyage*. Bill remained at the farm to oversee the renovations and to carry on the increasing work of typing Findley's drafts and most of his correspondence. Tiff would cross the field carrying his precious rough draft, Bill would type it up and bring it back, and the two men continued this practice through all weathers, including heavy winter snow. Len Collins visited Findley from time to time, tended the animals in the barn (which was painted blue because, along with its many positive associations, Findley called it his colour of hope), and answered questions on animal husbandry. Otherwise, Findley spent his time alone, listening to music and writing through the night and into the early mornings. When the time came for him to vacate Arkwright, they sold it to the Collinses, who had become extended family for both men. Perhaps most significantly, when they sold Stone Orchard in 1997, Findley's precious piano crossed the road to join the family. Few gifts could be more meaningful in Timothy Findley's eyes. In the fall of 2002, it was Len Collins who helped Bill scatter Findley's ashes at Stone Orchard beside a pathway where he had walked the dogs. Bill and Tiff's agreement with each other (and with whoever owned the farm) was that, when the time came, Bill's ashes would also be scattered there so he could join Tiff and the other ancestors whose lives are integral to the Stone Orchard story.

Chief among the first ancestors was the original owner of the farm, pharmacist Alfred Wyatt. Alfie Wyatt arrived from England in the 1840s, and by 1848 he had purchased the property and set up his pharmacy in what became Stone Orchard's dining room. This explains the midden of bottles and phials that Findley and Whitehead unearthed in one of their fields. But it does not quite explain Findley's belief that he had *seen* Alfie and his wife one day near a split-rail fence when he was walking the dogs: "I could see them in my mind, quite whole—the way one might remember a photograph" (16). Apparently his mind's eye was surprisingly accurate because, when he was shown an old photograph in 1967, he immediately recognized "our pharmacist"—"short and sharp-featured [...] and greatly old" (19). Other Cannington residents who were important in Findley's daily life and included in his group of extended family were Islay Lambert and Nora Joyce. Lambert was the local historian, and Findley would ride his red scooter into town to collect this elderly lady and bring her back to the farm for lunch and conversation. Curious neighbours, wondering what on earth such a pair had in common (or what gossip Lambert might be sharing), watched his comings and goings from behind their lace curtains, and sure enough Lambert's stories informed some of his fiction. Nora Joyce was Tiff and Bill's housekeeper for twenty-five years, and Findley obtained her permission to change her husband's name from Al to James for the sake of a vignette in *From Stone Orchard*. Mrs. Joyce was ninety-two in 2012 when she and I sat down together, but she remembered those twenty-five years vividly. She cleaned the house weekly, always being careful to put Findley's personal things back on the dresser where she found them because he was so particular. Just as he had been in those humble digs in London, Findley kept all his possessions carefully; every object had its place and must not be disturbed. Mrs. Joyce also did some cooking, mended clothes, and made brightly striped nightshirts for "the boys." One of her favourite memories was listening to Findley at the piano, which "he played wonderfully."

And so it was that Findley's concept of ancestors grew beyond his own and Bill Whitehead's family to include cherished friends in their present and *those who came before*, who prepared the way, and who were still comforting presences on the farm and in the area. Finding an extended family in the neighbouring towns in that area just north of Toronto and south of Lake Simcoe strengthened the sense of belonging that he had longed for during the fifties in London and later in the States. Grandfather Findley had grown up in Sutton West; his summer home was at Jackson's Point, a short drive from Cannington. Whitehead's great-grandfather had owned an inn in the nearby town of Vallentyne. Haunting the area, just a little to the west, were Lucy Maud Montgomery, Mazo de la Roche, Stephen Leacock, and friends associated with the Red Barn, and to the east there were Susanna Moodie and Catharine Parr Traill. Moodie made her presence known one day when Len Collins's mother found an old picture at an auction and brought it to Findley. It was a watercolour and the poem on the back of the picture was signed: "S. Moodie." Findley called in the Moodie expert from Trent University, Michael Peterman, who confirmed that it was an original poem and a painting by Susanna Moodie, a literary ancestor who appears in many contemporary Canadian works, including Findley's *Headhunter*. Margaret Laurence also joined his list of literary ancestors because, before her death, she and Findley had become close friends and she had made some memorable visits to Stone Orchard from her Lakefield home. On one occasion, she insisted on being driven back home when she spotted a sign (it was a joke) by their pool calling it the "R. B. Bennett Memorial Pool." Laurence blamed Bennett for the Depression and refused to stay anywhere near such a memorial (*FSO 33–34),* so they explained, removed the sign, and Laurence stayed for lunch.

Much of a writer's personal life is solitary and spent in his or her imagination; it is only accessible to a biographer through letters, diaries, journals (a rich source in Findley's case), and the published work, but many of the anecdotes in *From Stone Orchard* provide glimpses into his daily routine. The inclusion of them in the volume illustrates his sense of humour and the kind of detail that captured his attention. For example, he delighted in telling the corpse-in-the-field story, which involved his playing the part of a dead Metis man for a shot needed by a CBC film crew who were making a documentary series about the 1885 rebellion, prepared by Findley and Whitehead and based on Pierre Berton's *The National Dream* and *The Last Spike*. This had to be a winter shot with snow on the corpse and a frozen hand raised in death, and no breath could be seen rising into the cold air from the corpse. The group trudged off into the field across the road and Timothy Findley, dressed in a buckskin jacket and a red sash, took up his position on the ground, raised his hand, and held his breath, but instead of filming the twenty-two-second sequence that Bill Whitehead needed, Rudi Kovanic, the cameraman, began considering other possibilities for the shot. Meanwhile, curious passersby on the road had stopped to watch what they assumed was a murder investigation. Back on the cold ground, the corpse had to breathe, and he protested volubly that he was "not about to become a real corpse, even for the sake of art." You can still see Findley—"the living dead"—whenever *The National Dream* is aired (*FSO* 69).

One mouse lived happily in the kitchen at Stone Orchard because the cats lived outside, but there were many other mice in the old farmhouse and they could be heard, day and night, scurrying about behind the walls. Given his sincere concern for all living creatures, Findley refused to use a lethal trap. Instead, he set up an old Pyrex coffee pot on the kitchen floor, placed cheddar cheese inside, and created a ramp made of books that allowed the mice to enter the pot. In the morning he would release the well-fed mice outside; however, Bill told me that he could see them running from the pot back towards the house and heading straight for the basement. So much for Findley's catch and release. Finally, at Bill's insistence, they sought help from Len Collins, who disposed of one good-sized rat (which accounted for some of the noise in the walls) while Findley was travelling. From the mid-1970s on, there was one cat that lived indoors—the unforgettable Mottle, who was blind and unable to catch mice. Nevertheless, "she became the star of the place" (90); she was filmed in documentaries about Findley and appears in photographs with him. On many nights he played silver-paper hockey with her on the kitchen floor, using bits of foil from cigarette packages that she could smell and hear to bat back at him. And she loved the piano. She would "sit beside me," he recalled, "her front paws resting near the keyboard, as she purred out her own vibrations to meet those she could apparently feel as well as hear" (*FSO* 91). For many years, Mottle was Findley's constant companion, and in *Not Wanted on the Voyage* he recreated her as Mrs. Noyes's beloved pet.

One unusual and especially interesting aspect of *From Stone Orchard* is the inclusion of recipes: they would be time-consuming to prepare but delicious, and they establish a connection with Findley's descriptions of planting and nurturing his herb garden. Recipes and this garden, which was an extensive affair of about twenty-five square feet, link Findley with the earth, with living things, and above all with his mother. For many years, Margaret Findley belonged to a women's gardening society in Toronto and her specialty was herbs. She studied them, grew them, cooked with them, and shared her passion for them with her son. On visits to Stone Orchard she enjoyed his herb garden, appreciated his experimentations with plants like sorrel, and enjoyed Bill's exotic soups. Tucked away in Findley's archive are four sets of Margaret's typescripts titled "Reminiscent Recipes," in which she explored her family's history through descriptions of the Bull family's favourite recipes (LAC 332:5). She lovingly recalled the old country roads, the fences built of stones and boulders cleared from the fields by pioneer farmers, the horses and buggies used by her grandfather, and the fruit-picking expeditions to harvest supplies for desserts, jellies, and jams. Without putting this in so many words, she expressed her personal philosophy in these "Reminiscent Recipes"—the importance to her of memory and family loyalty, of food and social gatherings around a crowded table, and, above all, of her faith in the restorative power of nature, gardens, and the countryside with its traces of a pioneer past—her family's past—its stability and continuity.

Findley read and preserved her typescripts, and it is clear from her recipes and from his descriptions of his recipes, the garden, and the Cannington neighbourhood, that he shared much of her philosophy. The affection and trust between mother and son had deepened with the years. He had matured to the point where he could understand her life and choices during the difficult war years when she was fighting to save her marriage and trying to create the home her children needed. Without question, this mother-son relationship had developed to the point where Findley cherished this parent as a friend (see "My Mother, My Friend," in chapter 3), and one of his ways of expressing his love was through food, gardens, and recipes. On a more symbolic level, these gardens and recipes represented his longed-for connection with his ancestors. For years as a young man he had felt isolated—a Richard III figure, "myself alone"—but here at Stone Orchard he knew he belonged, and this connection, through and with his mother, strengthened this sense of belonging. When Margaret died he scattered her ashes at Stone Orchard to commemorate her as one of his most cherished friends and ancestors.

At several points in *From Stone Orchard*, he identified moments in time and place with direct links to his fiction. Among the most important of these are the various writings on the walls of the farmhouse and the drive shed that were uncovered by Len Collins during his renovations. Findley was impressed and moved by these ghostly messages from the nineteenth century and the literal way in which they connected now with then, himself or Len Collins with the first occupant or carpenter. Moreover, as he explained, "the walls of this house have witnessed almost all of my own activity as a writer," and at an early stage of drafting *Famous Last Words* (see chapter 9) his "writings were once spread across an entire wall of [his] study" (27). To keep track of this cast of more than thirty characters, he prepared a filing card for each one "detailing their life histories, their roles in the novel, [and] their relationship with other characters" (28), then he pinned the cards to the wall. Working from this mass of notes (confusing to anyone but himself), repositioning scenes, discarding others, Findley crafted the elegant life story Mauberley writes on the hotel walls in *Famous Last Words*. As far as I can tell, he did not compose this way with any other novel, but the idea of writing on walls had clearly captured his imagination. He was almost certainly remembering the Grand Hotel in Switzerland, where he had stayed before starting his farm work for the Henchoz family in 1950, with the writing on its walls, and he was imagining a writing-on-walls scene in the caves of Altamira which would, in time, acquire enormous significance for Findley and for *Famous Last Words* because such writing connects the individual, in the present, with the past of the human race.

As Findley notes in *From Stone Orchard*, *Not Wanted on the Voyage*, which I discuss in chapter 9, owes many concrete details and some of its characters to the neighbourhood and the farm. An elderly neighbour provided the original inspiration for Mrs. Noyes, Mottle became Mottyl, the ark was inspired by the blue barn at Arkwright, and the woodlot where the fairies and unicorns shelter in the novel resembles the woods Findley regularly visited with his dogs and where he found "a kind of peace [...] that I can carry home up the hill" (24). The idea for "E.R.A.," the story about destroying vegetation by using toxic sprays, draws on things he saw while driving with Bill Whitehead across the United States in the summer of 1969, but it can also be traced to an Ontario municipal attempt to control weeds by spraying pesticide along the shoulders of country roads, including the 11th Concession Road that runs past Stone Orchard. The pesticide killed the milkweed on which monarch butterflies depend, thereby virtually eliminating the monarchs, and this practice infuriated Findley, who undertook a variety of conservation activities through the 1970s. Chief among these was the preservation of the Beaver River, with a Beaver River Nature Trail, and the creation of a wetlands sanctuary. This concern for the environment, local and global, was a constant and consistent part of his approach to life: "When the frogs, turtles, birds and bullrushes are gone," he warned, "we will go next" (*FSO* 113).

Some of the family names in his work can be found in Cannington's history, even if the local families are not fictionalized. Thus, the Wakelin name given to Cassandra in *Can You See Me Yet?* belongs to a Cannington pioneer family; members of the Ross clan lived in the area (and Findley believed the Findleys were part of that clan), so naming Robert Ross was easy; the Wyatts in *The Piano Man's Daughter* have a namesake in old Alfie Wyatt, the pharmacist; McCaskill's Mills, the village in which the travelling piano salesman meets Lily's mother in the novel, was what Cannington was called until 1878. And these links between fact and fiction, physical place and imagined landscape are never merely casual with Findley. In *From Stone Orchard* he explains that the field in which Lily was conceived and born in *The Piano Man's Daughter* exists across the road from Stone Orchard on the Sprucevale (Arkwright) property. He once watched a calf being born in a corner of that field, and "it was also where her character entered my mind. The field was the centre of Lily's childhood, and it remained with her as an image until the day she died" (67). *The Piano Man's Daughter* was not written until the mid-1990s, so when Findley says that this field remained with Lily, he is also saying that it, with the memories it evoked, remained with him.

He does not use the word *sacred* to describe the farm (he does call it "a kind of paradise" and a "Peaceable Kingdom" [54]), but *From Stone Orchard* conveys something of that quality. Today the ashes of several family members lie there—the Findley parents, Allan and Margaret; Bill Whitehead's mother and stepfather; Michael; Tiff himself; and Bill. The graves of six noble dogs—Maggie and Hooker, Belle and Berton, Casey and Minnie—are there, along with generations of cats. Among the locals, a "stone orchard" is a graveyard, so the farm was aptly named and is, in a sense, hallowed ground. Without question, Timothy Findley's spirit lingers there, above all in the old herb garden where, as he promised, he left a part of himself, "a spirit-memento of [his] happiness" (49).

Nevertheless, daily life for Findley was rarely one of unalloyed happiness, and the years between 1969 and 1977 were tough: his energies were scattered across several projects, a major novel he had struggled with for years had to be abandoned, and his first play was panned by critics, leaving him crushed. He often discussed his depression and thoughts of suicide with Dr. Turner, and in some scrawled notes for Turner he confessed that he was "filled with apprehension" about his work and "the fear of commitment to what I put on the page" (LAC 106:11). Such a dilemma—to be a writer and yet to fear the words you write—must have been a torment that would only be exacerbated by the spectre of publication followed by negative reviews. For solace he resorted to making lists—"lists hold the greatest fascination for me" (Journal 1971–72, LAC 86:8)—of the people he considered "friends" (his mother, Islay Lambert, Dr. Turner) and those he could not see as friends (like his father). That he made such a list is hardly surprising. He had used lists to bolster his self-confidence and confirm his identity for years. What is surprising is his exclusion of Allan Findley from his list of "friends," a term of singular importance for Findley. As we have seen, he was trying hard to reach out to his father, to heed Wilder's advice about moving beyond hurt and anger, and to understand and support a man struggling with Parkinson's disease, but he could never trust his father enough to be fully at ease with him. And this degree of trust is what he experienced with those he called his friends.

References to suicide have occurred several times in this story of Findley's life, and yet both Alec McCowen and Bill Whitehead, the two men who knew him most intimately, told me that Timothy Findley was not a seriously suicidal person. So why did he discuss it with his doctor and why would he say that he would "never contemplate suicide" (LAC 86:8) when, in fact, he did contemplate it enough to discuss the idea with Dr. Turner? A definitive answer is impossible, and mere speculation is pointless. It is quite likely, however, that as a writer (his type of serious, prophetic writer) he was intrigued by the idea of suicide and its symbolic potential, which he would explore in both his fiction, notably in *Pilgrim*, and in the play *The Stillborn Lover*. And it is equally possible that as a performer he experienced some theatrical satisfaction from discussing the subject and capturing his doctor's attention. No, Timothy Findley did not seriously contemplate suicide, even during his darkest periods of despair. Although he analyzed the "act of suicide" and listed what he would miss if he killed himself—Bill, his garden, Mottle, and his work—Timothy Findley loved life, and during the painful years prior to the success of *The Wars* in 1977 he struggled to resist these crippling bouts of despair, despite the fact that his published work to date, even his existence as a Canadian writer, was ignored by reviewers and readers. He clung to the belief that he had work to do and things to tell us and, as he said in his 1976 journal, he hoped that once before he died he would "know I've been heard."

Sometime after their move to Stone Orchard (Bill could not recall when and Findley's journal is no help), the two men began sleeping in separate rooms. There were several reasons for this, including the fact that their sexual relationship had waned because, according to Bill, Tiff took ages bathing and preparing to join him in bed, by which time Bill had fallen asleep. A few close friends would later wonder about their living arrangements during those two-plus years (1984–86) that Findley lived at Arkwright because they knew that in the early 1980s Bill had begun an intimate relationship with a younger man, who died a few years later in a motor accident. As Bill told me (and as is clear from *Words to Live By*), he and Findley were not sexually "compatible," but they were honest with each other, which left Bill free to have other relationships and Findley able to find occasional partners. Nevertheless, this understanding was very difficult for Findley to reach; he had always needed someone to love absolutely, someone who would love and be there for him. Bill Whitehead was that person, but he had clearly placed conditions on their relationship. In an undated letter from the mid-1970s (written while Findley was living in Ottawa and Bill was back at the farm or travelling for work), he apologized to Bill for his past selfish possessiveness and promised that he had "released [Bill] from that terrible thing in me that was holding on" (LAC 107:2). In another letter from the early eighties, he stressed how much he loved Bill, how he wished he could make Bill as happy as Bill made him, and he insisted that his love did not mean he wanted to "possess" Bill (LAC 107:3). Although they did not want to be seen as, in Bill's words, the "poster boys" for gay marriage, Bill insisted that he had had no intention of leaving Findley, that he loved Tiff, and that the move to Arkwright was a practical decision to assist Findley's writing. As the years ahead proved, Tiff did come to terms with Bill's needs and it was Bill's turn to stay—for the rest of Tiff's life.

Findley reassured Phyllis Webb that all was well when she wrote to him with her concern about his shift to Arkwright. Moreover, there is no indication in his journals that his and Bill's sleeping arrangements or his time at Arkwright indicated a breakdown in their relationship. Findley was a nighthawk and Bill needed to retire in good time so he could rise early for his commute to work. Moreover, as Findley's insomnia worsened, he began to encourage late-night phone calls. Bill would be asleep by one in the morning when the phone rang for Tiff, who was eager to chat with or listen to the caller—Marian Engel, Margaret Laurence, Glenn Gould, Margaret Gibson, or Ken Adachi. At first, Bill tolerated these interruptions of his sleep routine, but after a while it became clear that Tiff had to have his own phone in a separate room so Bill could get his rest. Ultimately, the renovation created a study and bedroom for Tiff at the other end of the upstairs hall from Bill's room.

When Whitehead had to be away for a weekend or longer periods on CBC assignments, Findley was left alone and lonely, and he tended to drink heavily. On two extreme occasions, this drinking, combined with angry frustration over his own work, nearly cost him Bill's love and the affection of close friends. Although the late-night phone calls were disruptive, Bill usually got back to sleep, but one night (almost certainly in 1971) the racket coming from the kitchen grew alarming. When Bill investigated, he found that Findley had, as Bill told me, "gone totally berserk." He had smashed all the dishes he could lay hands on, and was lying, very drunk, in the midst of the broken glass, cut and bleeding. On this occasion, he lashed out at Bill when he arrived to help, struggled violently, and bit Bill's arm. Neither Findley's cuts nor the bite on Bill's arm was serious, but Bill was, understandably, horrified. Eventually, he was able to calm Findley, clean him up, and get him to bed. What caused this violent outburst and why did Bill tolerate such behaviour? The answers are as complex as they are for all couples, and the dynamics of any long-term relationship, when addiction and abusive behaviour are involved, can be confusing even for the people themselves. But in this instance, despair over his current work had produced rage and extreme frustration, which in turn led to the drinking. Bill, like many partners of people struggling with addiction—not to mention the dread of artistic failure that had dogged Findley for so many years—ended up being a target of Findley's wrath simply by being there. Bill also confessed that, at times like these, he felt suicidal himself and considered walking out because he could not understand the drinking or how best to manage Findley's drinking. In the last analysis, he stayed because he loved the man, refrained from judging him, cherished their good times together, and believed absolutely in Findley's talent. Despite his own moments of despair over such behaviour, Bill stayed because he knew Tiff needed him; as he told me: "Tiff needed someone to look after him and I needed someone to look after."

I have placed this crisis at the end of 1971 because that was when Findley was faced with the rejection of a manuscript on which he had worked for several years and for which he held high hopes. The novel causing him such grief was called "Whimper," and the manuscript has survived, along with a December 1971 letter that Findley sent to the New York editor Harvey Ginsberg, who had rejected it. "In the hurry and rush and fury—in the *rage* of failure itself," he wrote, "all things, including failure itself seem to be absolute" (LAC 86:8). Although he believed that the book contained some of his best writing and that his subject—the collapse of contemporary civilization—was honest and important, he agreed with Ginsberg that, "as a *novel* ... it is too cerebral," and that he was struggling with a "barrier" between himself and his audience. But all this post-mortem reasoning, all the lessons he said he learned from this failure could not hide the fact that he was "desolate." I suspect that Findley's acute frustration with this manuscript, combined with Ginsberg's rejection, precipitated the drinking that led to this terrifying midnight scene in the kitchen. Nevertheless, Findley believed there were good things in the manuscript, notably three haunting characters, Michael, Olivia, and Claire, aspects of whose stories he would eventually tell in *Headhunter* and in "Dinner Along the Amazon." He did not burn the manuscript, as he had the earlier one that Stan Colbert advised him to destroy, but, painful as it was, he was right to abandon the shapeless work and move on.[2]

Fortunately for Bill, he was in Toronto in September 1973 for the press launch of their CBC series *The National Dream* when another appalling scene took place. Bill's absence, however, was not fortunate for Findley. That September was especially difficult for him; he had returned from a visit to Toronto—"it really does destroy me," he noted in his journal, "and I hate everyone" (LAC 87:3)—and was drinking to avoid another trip into the city, which is why Bill went alone. Not long after Bill left, the Canadian writer Scott Symons suddenly showed up, uninvited, at the farm, where-upon the drinking escalated and a scene of extraordinary proportions began to unfold.[3] Timothy Findley, who was severely depressed about his work and already drinking, was extremely vulnerable on that September day, and a person like Symons, intent on creating a disturbance, could not have turned up at a more unfortunate moment. The two men had known each other slightly in the past, and Symons, who had published the sensational, openly gay novel *Place d'Armes* in 1967, followed by his critical meditation on Rosedale in *Civic Square* in 1969, was fearless about his identity as a gay man and was enjoying considerable notoriety in literary circles. Piecing together events from Bill's recollections, from a long rambling letter of apology by Findley, and from oblique references to a disaster in his 1973 journal, it appears that matters unfolded like this. Symons encouraged Findley to keep drinking and insulted him about his sexuality. Although I have no proof of what Symons said to Findley, it is not hard to imagine him confronting Findley, who would never be the kind of aggressive gay man or writer that Symons was, accusing Findley of concealing his homosexuality, hiding away from the city and the public eye on a farm, and of failing as a writer. But Symons did not stop there.

For some inexplicable reason, Symons dared Findley to telephone Margaret Atwood, Graeme Gibson, and Bill Hutt and invite them to Stone Orchard on the pretext that Atwood wanted to write a play for Hutt and that Hutt wanted Atwood to write a play for him to perform. Improbable as it may seem, Symons succeeded in goading Findley into deceiving his friends with this cheap trick, and all three accepted the impromptu invitation. When they arrived in the early evening, however, they found Findley drunk and lying on the grass, babbling about his writing shack in the garden, about Symons, and about St. Teresa, who, he claimed, was sitting in a tree (an image so vivid that he remembered it for *Pilgrim*). Scott Symons had vanished from the scene. Perhaps at first glance this situation might have seemed melodramatic, even hilarious, except that Timothy Findley had been reduced to a pathetic spectacle. They got Tiff to bed, rustled up some dinner, and spent the night. Hutt was especially disgusted by this deception and drunkenness, and the next morning he lectured a badly hungover Tiff about his self-destructive behaviour. The story Bill told me, as reported to him after the fact, was that Hutt yelled at Tiff that he had "more talent than anyone [he] knew," and that he was wasting it. "To hell with you!" Hutt shouted and stormed to his car and drove away. Atwood and Gibson left quietly, without upbraiding Tiff, but they recalled the entire business as "marvelously bizarre."

It is a tribute to all involved, especially Bill, that Findley lost no friendships over this incident. Amends had to be made over the ensuing days and weeks, of course, and he wrote a rambling letter, dated 14 September 1973, to "Peggy" and "Graeme" that began as an apology and expanded into a description of the images he remembered as flooding his mind—of Graeme's "beautiful hands" lifting him up; of his teddy bear, Sebastian; and of people and voices "floating" across the garden (LAC 91:26). He went on about his copy of *The Edible Woman*, planting marigolds, his beloved St. Teresa, and his memories: memories of meeting Graeme in the late fifties in Michael Tait's Rosedale home; memories of attending a stage adaptation of Carson McCullers's *The Member of the Wedding* at the Royal Alex with Hutt and watching his disapproving parents across the foyer. This letter, and the entire event, was indeed "marvelously bizarre," but it was also tragic because it revealed the persistence of Findley's painful memories of his family's past rejection and of the deep-seated insecurity he still felt, despite his home with Bill and his chosen work, about his sexuality.

Most disturbing, however, were his memories of Symons's cruel taunts. In his letter to Atwood and Gibson, he recalled having a stone in his pocket and Symons reminding him that Virginia Woolf committed suicide by drowning in the River Ouse, her pockets weighted with stones. It is not clear from Findley's letter, or his journal, why such a topic came up during this dreadful visit, but if Symons had gone so far as to encourage Findley to drown himself in the Beaver River, which flowed close to Stone Orchard, he failed. This extraordinary letter to Atwood and Gibson closes with Tiff's "Thank you" and "love" and a postscript: "Stone Orchard is in my pocket—but—I can't get it down to the River" (LAC 91:26).[4]

Stones had already acquired symbolic importance for Findley, but at this critical point, when he had abandoned the "Whimper" manuscript, could not see a way forward, and was on the verge of sending in the clowns, Bill staged a private performance to illustrate what Timothy Findley, the writer, needed to understand (see *J* 198). He sat Tiff down, put a stone in his hand, and told him to imagine other people sitting in the room. Then he went from chair to chair asking these imaginary people for specific things—a carrot, a piece of wood, and so on. When he reached Tiff, Tiff could not give him any of those objects because all he had in his hand was a stone. But when Bill went around asking for a stone, only Tiff had one: "That was connection. When they ask for a stone and you have a stone, then something happens, and for me, that something was a book called *The Wars*. That was my stone" (*J* 198). "Connection" is the key term here. Timothy Findley needed to reaffirm the connection between himself and others—beginning, in this living room scene, with Bill—with reality, with his work, and with this potent symbol: the stones of Stone Orchard, the stones Neil throws at his father in "War," the stones of remembrance on the beach at Dieppe. Now, thanks to Bill, a stone also signified his need for patience and belief in the promise of future success. Findley saw that he had to remain true to his own vision; he could not produce genuine carrots when stones were his gift.

A welcome distraction from these personal trials and disappointments with his writing were successful CBC projects like the *Jalna* series and *The National Dream*. Even in his London years, Findley had criticized his country's neglect of its own stories and history, and focusing on these CBC projects rekindled his sense of cultural nationalism. He worked alone on the script for the twelve sixty-minute episodes of *The Whiteoaks of Jalna* and enjoyed preparing for his work by reading the entire sixteen-volume series of Mazo de la Roche's popular novels. His enjoyment is understandable because, even today, her stories about the once affluent and proud Whiteoak family are easy, romantic reading. Findley was familiar with such old Ontario families and Maisie Roach held a warm spot in his heart. She had lived not far from Stone Orchard; he had seen her walking in the Rosedale streets when he was a boy; and her hero, Finch Whiteoak, resembled him in many ways—Finch loves the piano and the theatre, despite his family's disapproval, and he is bullied by an older brother. The series ran on CBC television from 23 January to 9 April 1972, and although critics considered it weak, Margaret Findley and her circle of friends loved it, which was some comfort for its creator. The seventies were a prime period for CBC television adaptations of Canadian classics, and the decade remains a pinnacle of national pride and success in the arts. Moreover, Findley learned a lot about writing for television through the *Jalna* work, and he began to see a role for himself as a contributor to the national arts scene.

The next CBC assignment, *The National Dream*, was a more ambitious, more successful adventure than *Jalna*. The program aired in March and April of 1974, winning both Whitehead and Findley ACTRA Awards, and it entailed a lot of work, as well as leading to Findley's lasting friendship with Pierre Berton (1920–2004).[5] He and Bill began work on the eight-part series in late 1971 with Bill in charge of documentary aspects and film editing and Findley writing the dramatic sequences. Production began in July 1972 and continued through 1973. Berton, one of Canada's most respected and prolific writers, was born in Whitehorse and raised in the gold rush town of Dawson City, Yukon, but by the time Findley met him he was a popular CBC television personality, famous for his wit and his bow ties on shows like *Front Page Challenge* and *The Pierre Berton Show*. Berton would publish fifty books by 2004, most of them on Canadian history and many of them written for children at a time when Canadian history was not well taught in the schools. A Companion of the Order of Canada, a Second World War veteran, and the winner of many awards (including three Governor General's Awards for Creative Non-fiction and a Stephen Leacock Medal for Humour), he became an authority on Canada and a presence to be reckoned with. Berton was consulted on all Findley's scripts, and in many instances he was displeased. The series was based on his work, and he insisted time and again on remaining true to the historical record and downplaying the drama. In an undated, ten-page, single-spaced memo to Jim Murray, the executive producer, he picked away at details and language in the dramatizations of Prime Minister Macdonald's behaviour and flatly stated that "some of Tiff's best scenes will have to be toned down and in several cases sacrificed" (Berton fonds, B236-F28). His complaint was always the same: what makes for good theatre is "bad history" and "in this documentary series history must win out over theatre."

One disagreement had more than a touch of poetic justice about it, however, and it ended with Findley winning the argument over a scene in which he called for Sir John's wife to persist in having her husband wear white gloves to a formal reception. Macdonald, according to Findley, hated white gloves and hid them; she retrieved them and he put them on. The couple left the room with Macdonald wearing the gloves, but a moment later the door opened and the gloves were tossed back inside. Berton was not amused. He wrote to Findley assuring him that nothing in his exhaustive research on the prime minister suggested that Macdonald disliked white gloves: "Please remove all references to same" (Berton fonds B236-F28). Findley refused and consulted Donald Creighton, Macdonald's biographer, who found a way around the impasse. Creighton dug out a photograph of the PM in formal attire but with bare hands and suggested that the photograph proved Macdonald's aversion to white gloves. In the meantime, Bill Hutt, who played Macdonald, had persuaded Berton that the scene needed that stage business and that the gloves were unimportant. The scene stayed, and Berton came to enjoy it.

Findley admired Berton, the man and his achievements, and once he got over Macdonald's white gloves, Berton became a warm supporter of Findley's work and a friend. Moreover, Findley eagerly embraced the kind of national pride that Berton's work represented. In 1974, he and Bill were contracted to prepare a television documentary based on Berton's books *Klondike: The Last Great Gold Rush, 1896–1899* (1958) and *The Klondike Fever: The Life and Death of the Last Great Gold Rush* (1958). Unfortunately, budget cuts eventually caused the cancellation of the project, but in the summer of 1974 the CBC sent them, with a film crew, to the Yukon to explore the route taken to the Klondike by prospectors during the 1896–99 gold rush. Thanks in large part to Berton's books, the Klondike stampede has become a Canadian story of near mythic proportions, despite the fact that most of the protagonists were American prospectors.

2   Thomas Findley (ca. 1920), Findley's grandfather, taken when he was president of
     Massey-Harris and already suffering from the cancer that killed him in 1921. The
     resemblance between grandfather and grandson is striking. Massey Harris fonds,
     Archival and Special Collections, University of Guelph Library (XA1 RHC A0394,
     Box 6).

3   *Above*: Phoebe Findley, Findley's grandmother "Goggie,"
    ca. 1925. Reproduced courtesy of Bill Whitehead,
    with thanks to Trevor Greene.

4   *Right*: Uncle Tif in uniform with his family, Kingston,
    24 May 1915. Left to right: Allan (TF's father);
    Phoebe (his grandmother); Thomas Irving Findley;
    Margaret (TF's Aunt Marg); and Thomas Findley
    (TF's grandfather). Reproduced courtesy of Bill
    Whitehead; Timothy Findley fonds, Archival and
    Special Collections, University of Guelph Library
    (2016-019. 2-2).

5   Uncle Tif, ca. 1916. This formal
    photograph of Thomas Irving Findley
    in uniform sat in his mother's parlour
    before it joined Timothy Findley's
    private collection. It recalls the
    description of Robert Ross's
    photograph in *The Wars*. Reproduced
    courtesy of Bill Whitehead.

6   Edith Maude Fagan Bull (ca. 1907),
    Findley's maternal grandmother and
    beloved "Granny Bull." Library and
    Archives Canada: R4441-339-File 3
    [E-011435512]. Reproduced courtesy
    of Bill Whitehead.

7 A rare photograph (ca. 1922) of Frederick Bull, Findley's maternal grandfather, with his daughters Ruth Bull Carlyle (centre) and Margaret Bull (Findley's mother, right). This old photograph appears in the bottom left corner of the endpapers of *The Piano Man's Daughter*. Library and Archives Canada: Findley/Whitehead fonds MG31-D196, Vol. 125-1. Photograph reproduced courtesy of Bill Whitehead. See page 12.

Last morning on "the

8 *Facing page*: Detail from the endpapers of the first edition of *The Piano Man's Daughter*, showing a selection of family pictures from Findley's albums. Not all can be identified with certainty, but a few of importance can: top left, the Thomas Findley family summer cottage at Jackson Point; top right background, Grandmother Phoebe Findley (ca. 1900); centre right, "Last Morning on the *Minnetonka*" shows the Thomas Findley family returning to Canada from their 1913 trip to England; bottom right, a photograph of special significance for Tiff, shows a family picnic in 1914 with Margaret (Tiff's mother) seated second from left, Aunt Ruth at back left holding out her hand, Isabel McLaughlin seated centre, and Alan Bull on the right. Allan Findley labelled this image "The Guns of August," and Findley said that this picture inspired a "whole series of scenes" in the novel. Finally, at bottom left is the picture of Frederick Bull with his daughters Ruth (centre) and Margaret.

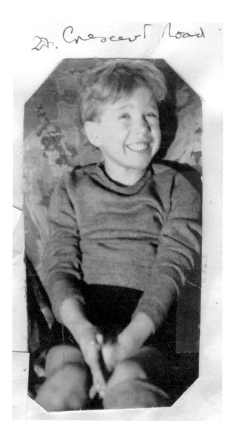

9 Timothy Findley at the Crescent Road home in Rosedale, ca. 1937. He spent his happiest childhood years in this house and garden, which bordered on the ravine, a short distance from a riding stable. Reproduced courtesy of Bill Whitehead.

This photograph shows my mother
father as they were in 1944. T
are standing in the back yard of d
(then) house at 27 Crescent Road
Toronto. Dad was about to be se
overseas — and this picture, amo
others, was taken expressly so t
he would have family photos t
take away with him.

10 *Facing page, top*: Timothy Findley, front row, second from right, in Grade 5 at Rosedale Public School, 1942. His friend Dick Cousland is in the second row, third from right. Reproduced courtesy of Bill Whitehead, with thanks to Trevor Greene.

11 *Facing page, bottom*: Findley often annotated his family's photographs. He has drawn a blue frame around this 1944 picture of his parents; blue was his colour of hope. Reproduced courtesy of Bill Whitehead; Timothy Findley fonds, Archival and Special Collections, University of Guelph Library (2016-019, 3).

12 *Above*: An image Findley often alluded to. Taken in 1944 with Allan in uniform; Tiff on his right and Michael on his left. Reproduced courtesy of Bill Whitehead; Timothy Findley fonds, Archival and Special Collections, University of Guelph Library (unprocessed material 2016-19, 2-2).

13 Janet Baldwin (ca. 1950). Janet was a lifelong friend of Findley's and, in the late 1940s, his ballet teacher. Photograph reproduced with permission of the Special Collections Department, Toronto Reference Library. John Steele Photography.

14 Timothy Findley at 23 as an officer in *All's Well That Ends Well* for the 1953 Stratford Festival. The painting (watercolour on paper) is by Grant Macdonald, who worked in a sweltering space under the festival tent. Reproduced with permission of the Agnes Etherington Art Centre, Queen's University, Kingston. Bequest of Timothy Findley 2008 (51-010).

15 Janet Baldwin and Timothy Findley, Cambridge, England, ca. 1954. He took great pleasure in her visits, when they could travel together and attend the ballet. Photograph reproduced courtesy of Bill Whitehead, with thanks to Trevor Greene.

16   Timothy Findley as Rudolph (standing back left) in the London 1954 Theatre Royal
      production of Thornton Wilder's *The Matchmaker*. Seated, left to right: Arthur Hill,
      Eileen Hurlie, Rosemund Greenwood, and Alec McCowen. Reproduced with
      appreciation, courtesy of the late Alec McCowen. See detail on page 86.

17   Alec Guinness gave Findley this makeup box in 1954. It clearly shows both their names
      (Findley's label on the left with Guinness's name showing behind Findley's), and
      Findley used it every time he travelled to perform. The box is one of the treasured
      memorabilia from his personal collection. Timothy Findley fonds, Archival and
      Special Collections, University of Guelph Library (XZ1 MS B019019).

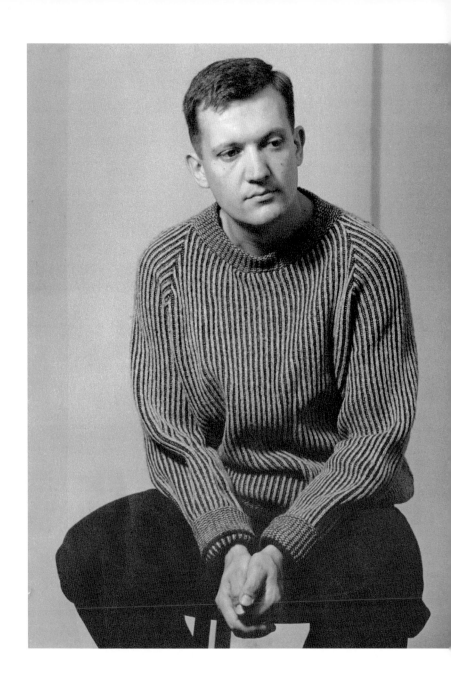

18 Bill Whitehead as "Fredric Whitehead," his official ACTRA name, ca. 1960.
    Reproduced courtesy of Bill Whitehead; Timothy Findley fonds, Archival
    and Special Collections, University of Guelph Library (2011-025 1-4).

19 A rare staged photograph of actors in the field beside the Red Barn Theatre, summer 1961. At left is Bill Whitehead (a.k.a. Fredric Whitehead), with Janet Amos on his left. Tiff is reading to the cow, and Marigold Charlesworth is reclining on the grass. Reproduced with appreciation, courtesy of the late Jean Roberts.

20 Dr. R. Edward Turner (ca. 1975), Findley's long-time trusted
    psychiatrist and friend. Photograph reproduced courtesy of
    CAMH and with thanks to John Court.

21 *Facing page, top, left to right*: Timothy Findley, composer Louis Applebaum, and Bill Whitehead working on the CBC television series *The National Dream*, which aired in 1974. Reproduced courtesy of the CBC Still Photograph Collection.

22 *Facing page, bottom*: Tiff and Bill in the Yukon, June 1974, to prepare for the filming of Pierre Berton's Klondike story. The series was cancelled, but Findley cherished his trip north. Bill is at the left behind sunglasses; Tiff is snuggled down in his warm jacket, cigarette in right hand; centre, Richard Lambert; right of centre Len d'Agostino; far right, Peter Kelly. Reproduced courtesy of Bill Whitehead, with thanks to Trevor Greene.

23 "Early morning, all night kitchen table writer." Findley frequently illustrated his journals. He made this self-portrait sketch while working on *The Wars*, and it depicts him seated in the kitchen at Stone Orchard with tea mug and cat companion. Reproduced with permission of the Findley Estate; courtesy Bill Whitehead. See page 174.

24 Nancy Colbert (1983). Colbert was Findley's literary agent. She was praised for her support of writers, but in Findley's case she became a much-loved and trusted friend. This photograph appeared with an article by Margaret Mironowicz, who described Colbert as "the cream" of Toronto's literary agents. Reproduced with permission: Dennis Robinson/*The Globe and Mail*.

25   William Hutt in the role of Sir John A. Macdonald in Findley's play *John A.— Himself!*,
performed at the Grand Theatre in London, Ontario in 1979. Hutt has inscribed
this photograph: "My dear Tiff—with a heart full of love, admiration and
gratitude—Bill." Reproduced with permission: William Hutt fonds, Archival
and Special Collections, University of Guelph Library (2011-025, 13-1).

26 *Top*: Cannington friends at Stone Orchard in 1980 (left to right): Bill Whitehead, Len Collins, Anne Collins, and Timothy Findley. Reproduced with thanks, courtesy Anne Collins.

27 *Bottom*: The old root cellar at Stone Orchard, as it appeared in 2011. In the 1970s, Len Collins restored the simple log structure so that, during warm weather, Tiff could write and sleep here. Photograph: S. Grace.

28   Findley receiving his honorary degree, Trent University Convocation, 1982.
Left to right: Beverly Northcott Smallman, Malcolm M. Ross, Chancellor Margaret
Laurence, and Timothy Findley. Reproduced courtesy of Trent University Archives.

29 *Facing page*: Martha Henry as Marian Raymond and William Hutt as Harry Raymond in *The Stillborn Lover* (Stratford Festival, 1995). Photograph by Cylia von Tiedemann.

30 *Above*: Findley with his French translator, Nésida Loyer (front centre), at Stone Orchard, 1996. Left to right: Alain Loyer, Bill Whitehead, and Findley seated. Reproduced with thanks, courtesy of Nésida Loyer.

31 Findley's desk in the study of his Stratford condominium, 2001. On the desk to
the left is a framed photograph of him with his parents; leaning against the wall
at the centre of the desk is a picture of Elizabeth Taylor (a childhood icon); to the
right of the desk is a photograph of Ezra Pound, who haunted and puzzled Findley.
Hanging on the wall above the desk are several images of note: Peter Rabbit cards
and calendars, pictures of butterflies and flowers, one tiny shoe, and on the left
a striking painting by Ken Laughton. The photograph is reproduced with thanks,
courtesy of Terence Macartney-Filgate. See detail on page 320.

32   The little house in Cotignac (2001), from the back, which faces
      the valley and opens onto patios and terraces. The house is yellow
      with blue trim and shutters and a red tile roof. Photograph
      reproduced with appreciation, courtesy Bill Whitehead.

33   Findley in his study at "Mots Maison," Cotignac, 2001. He had brought with him
     some of his precious photographs and objects, like the puppet, unicorn, and
     butterfly, and the colours in the room are vibrant Mediterranean yellows and
     blues. Photograph reproduced, with appreciation, courtesy of Bill Whitehead.

34 "Tiff and Bill Laughing." Kitchen in the Stratford condominium, 2001.
Photograph courtesy of Terence Macartney-Filgate.

35   A field and pathway at Stone Orchard where Tiff walked the dogs and where his
      ashes, mixed with Bill's, were scattered on 30 April 2018. Photograph: E. Grace.

The route north was punishing and extremely dangerous. It is roughly 717 kilometres (445 miles) from Skagway to Dawson City, and the passes rise to elevations of nearly 4,000 feet. Many died en route, crushed by snow slides on the Chilkoot and White Passes, drowned in ice-choked lakes or the raging Yukon River, or driven mad and frozen to death in the appalling conditions of the placer mines. A few made spectacular fortunes; most did not. Approximately three thousand pack horses and mules died on the White Pass trail alone during that first winter, and their corpses littered the sides of the trail and were visible, for years afterward, on the slopes down to the Skagway River. Once the men reached the top, they usually wintered over at Lake Lindemann with their supplies, then rushed out on rafts and scows as the ice broke to continue into the Yukon on the Yukon River and north to Dawson. From there they set forth to dig for gold along Bonanza Creek, Eldorado Creek, and the Klondike River.

Today tourists can make the journey in comfort, but in the mid-1970s it was a different story. Now there is a highway, mostly paved, that leaves from Skagway, crosses the Skagway River, goes over the White Pass, and continues up to Dawson City. Although there are many parking lots and other amenities along the White Pass route, the Chilkoot Pass must still be traversed on foot, packing your own gear and food. But Tiff and Bill went up the Chilkoot and down the White in 1974, before any luxuries were established. They travelled by train to Winnipeg, then Jasper, then on to Prince Rupert on the northwest British Columbia coast, where they joined the CBC television crew, and boarded a ferry for Skagway. After two days in Skagway, they left on horseback for Dyea and Sheep Camp at the base of the Chilkoot Pass. Findley notes that it was "a nightmare journey with highlights of beauty" (LAC 87:9). They crossed the pass on foot, stopping at Lake Lindemann on June 7 before continuing to White-horse, where they stayed in a motel, bathed, and ate decent food. From Whitehorse they continued with the film crew to Dawson and spent three days exploring the town, its historic buildings, and the nearby creeks. The return trip began on June 15, with a stopover at the top of the White Pass, where they spent a memorable night, before returning to Victoria and starting the long trip home.

The ferry trip north up the Inside Passage was spectacular, but it was also useful. A young couple planning to homestead in Alaska had brought their animals and a beehive with them, and when the ship stopped off-shore to deliver mail and supplies to small communities, they brought the hive up on deck so the bees could fly to the land and feed before returning to their hive. Years later Findley remembered this couple and their bees, which inspired his creation of a similar scene near the end of *Not Wanted on the Voyage*. In Skagway, the film team met up with local wranglers hired to get them by horse over the Chilkoot Pass. For Bill and Tiff, neither of whom had been on a horse for years, the real adventure was about to begin (*WLB* 159). Due to the treacherous rivers, boulders, snow, and dense underbrush, it took them two days to get over the pass. They finally reached the top exhausted, bearded, and filthy, and carried on by foot from Lake Lindemann to Bennett Lake. When the helicopter transporting them to Whitehorse arrived and each man had to lighten his pack so the machine could take off, Findley dumped his spare hiking boots and kept Sebastian.[6] A wise decision where weight was concerned, of course, but Sebastian mattered more than mere practical considerations. This small teddy bear was a personal totem, a patron saint, an alter ego, a bearer of happy memories.

The group reached Whitehorse without incident, rested, and travelled up to Dawson City, which offered great possibilities for filming. Through all of this travel, Findley kept careful journal notes (LAC 87:9). He felt he was "Walking: through Time, Wilderness, Self," and he sensed ghosts everywhere. The saddest places he saw were the cemeteries in Dawson, which were badly neglected and in disrepair. A visit to Pierre Berton's family home was more uplifting. He found the house small but "charming," with an air of "individuality" about it, and seeing the home gave Findley "a new understanding of the man [Berton] and a sense of the loneliness he must have felt (despite his parents) for someone he could match wits with." He and Bill noted Robert Service's cabin, where today's summer tourists can listen to actors performing Service's poetry, and they hiked out of town to some of the famous creeks. When they climbed the Midnight Dome in Dawson, he finally sensed the history of the place that had been cheapened or erased in the town itself: from up top, he wrote, "there is a genuine feel of the past and of its beauty and of its sadness that is heartbreaking" (LAC 87:9).

However, it was on the return trip during their stopover at the top of the White Pass that Findley had the experience that moved him most deeply and stayed with him the longest. He already knew that three thousand pack animals had been sacrificed to human greed and cruelty during the gold rush, and he knew the pass was called the Dead Horse Trail, but before they caught the train down to Skagway he made another discovery. Near the railway line there was a small cemetery with the graves of two hundred horses killed in the gold rush, and he spent a quiet hour alone there to reflect and remember. Later he sent a postcard to his parents that showed a bronze monument to the three thousand, with a relief depicting two heavily laden pack animals; the inscription reads: "THE DEAD ARE SPEAKING. In memory of us three thousand pack animals that laid our bones on these awful hills during the Gold Rush of 1897–1898. We now thank those listening souls that heard our groans across this stretch of years. WE WAITED, BUT NOT IN VAIN." For his message Findley wrote: "This monument is only a bare indication of what took place in this savage valley—which was a sort of *Auschwitz* for horses. Yet it is greatly beautiful—and Bill and I came down part way on foot from the summit— and then the rest of the way by train. More beautiful than the Alps—more spectacular than the Rockies—I have never seen sights like these" (18 June 1974, LAC 97: 8). In his journal he wrote that "all through the Pass, the horses cried and I could hear them and I will never forget their place—or forgive us for what we have done." "I think my true pilgrimage is made & fulfilled in this place," he concluded (LAC 87:9).

His choice of the word *pilgrimage* here is important, especially as he had increasingly eschewed his Presbyterian upbringing, indeed rejected it in anger, as his London journal cries for religious support and protests against the God of his family and ancestors reveal. This pilgrimage affirmed his spiritual connection with the non-human world of animals and nature and his conviction, as he stressed in his 1992 interview with Terence Macartney-Filgate, that all living things are "sacred." He was already convinced that human beings were destroying the environment, and the evidence provided by the gold rush of men's greed and disregard for the animals they relied on contributed to Findley's mature critical view of contemporary society. But this trip, and what he learned from it, was crucial in other ways, and once more the key term for understanding this knowledge is *connection*. Although Findley remained firmly rooted in his southern Ontario, Stone Orchard, landscape, he was, as he had been on the NWT camping trip, expanding and deepening his connections with the wider landscapes and history of his country. He would never be a nationalist in any narrow sense; however, this gold rush exploration—the stories, the history, the images of stunning beauty he witnessed, juxtaposed so sharply with the horror of silent graves and animal bones still visible in the undergrowth—remained with him for the rest of his life. As we shall see, some of these remembered images would appear—ghostly presences—in the novels he had yet to write.

The critical importance of the seventies for the rise of cultural nationalism in Canada cannot be overemphasized. It was during these years that Findley met other writers who shared his ambition for the country's artistic future, and he described this period as "the golden age of Canadian writing" ("Golden Age" 6). Among the most important literary people in his life at this time were Phyllis Webb, whom he had first met through Bill and the CBC in the mid-1960s, Margaret Laurence, and Marian Engel; they became his close friends through their work to establish the Writers' Union of Canada.

Webb was a regular correspondent and confidante by the seventies. In an interesting February 1970 letter Findley apologized for not visiting her on Vancouver Island after the summer 1969 trip to the NWT, described his "revulsion & horror" with American life in the Midwest, and praised this camping experience to the skies.[7] He told her that this was how and where he wanted to live—in "some kind of rustic homestead" in this "most incredible country." Over the years, as their friendship and correspondence developed, he and Webb discussed ideas, literature and the arts, contemporary politics, love of nature, and various issues facing Canadian writers. At key moments in the years ahead, Webb's poetry would inspire Findley's writing in important ways. He first wrote to Margaret Laurence on 8 February 1970, when she was writer-in-residence at the University of Toronto.[8] Winner of the 1966 Governor General's Award for Fiction for *A Jest of God*, Laurence was already a major presence in Canada; therefore, his letter of introduction was formally addressed to "Dear Mrs. Laurence" and signed "Sincerely—Timothy Findley" (Laurence fonds 2:64). He told her about his published work and radio portraits of artists, stressed his concern for the environment (an interest she shared), and described Stone Orchard. Then he issued an invitation: since they both disliked the city, could she visit him and Bill in the country on the weekend of March 7–8? He explained that they would drive in, pick her up at Massey College, at the University of Toronto, where she was staying, and then bring her back. By April their friendship was launched. In an April 4 letter, she was "Dear Margaret" and he signed himself "Tiff" (Laurence fonds 2:64). Moreover, he had now read *A Bird in the House* (1970) and was full of praise for it. He promised to get *The Fire Dwellers* (1969) from the library and was eagerly looking forward to her permanent return to Canada from England and her relocation near Peterborough, just fifty miles away from Stone Orchard. By 1972 he was discussing the idea of a writers' union with her, and in one letter he described a meeting that fall with Graeme Gibson, Margaret Atwood, Alice Munro, Marian Engel, Andreas Schroeder, himself, and Bill to explore the possibility.

The Writers' Union of Canada was the brainchild of the small group that had gathered in 1972 at Graeme Gibson's urging. The general situation for fiction writers in the country was dismal at that time. There were few publishers interested in Canadian fiction, and the practice of having a Canadian editor or literary agent was virtually unheard of. As Findley and others had discovered, one had to go to England or the United States, where it was a tough sell to interest foreign editors who did not recognize Canadian writers or Canadian settings. And there were many other practical challenges facing aspiring Canadian writers in the seventies—

economic issues of lending rights, copyright, and tax reform, and ethical questions regarding freedom of expression and censorship. Today's union has tackled all these problems, and more, with considerable success, and they also administer awards and contests, hold the Writing for Children competition, and provide legal and editorial advice. None of these benefits and resources existed in the early seventies. In a lively and important 1984 essay called "The Tea Party, or How I Was Nailed by Marian Engel, General Booth, and Minn Williams Burge," Findley recalled that first brainstorming meeting, on 16 December 1972, at Ryerson College (now University) in Toronto. An ad hoc committee of about fifteen had gathered, at Graeme Gibson's invitation, "to explore the idea of a union for prose writers" (30). Marian Engel was one of those attending, and Findley was "very nervous" about meeting her because she had reviewed *The Butterfly Plague* for two Toronto newspapers and had been decidedly lukewarm. They came face to face in the kitchen of the Jorgenson Building, where she was making tea. "You're Findley, aren't you," she said. "I suppose you want to shoot me." Thus began their close and loving friendship, but Engel was a complex, troubled person, an insomniac, and a heavy drinker, and her conversations with Findley often took place late at night when neither could sleep and both had been drinking. Several letters survive that capture aspects of their friendship, but much was lost forever when they hung up their telephones at three in the morning.

During those heady days in the mid-1970s, however, many of the union meetings were held in Engel's living room. "Sometimes, I'd arrive early at these meetings," Findley recalled—

and sit with Marian Engel in the kitchen, while my friend Bill Whitehead was ensconced behind a glass door in the study—where he would set to work on the Engel typewriter, completing a television script. Graeme Gibson and Margaret Atwood lived in the country (as Bill and I did) and they would arrive in a dreadful, mud-encrusted truck with mysterious bits of machinery lumped in the back. Beer was got from the fridge. Matt Cohen would arrive, Sylvia Fraser (on a motorcycle, sometimes wearing evening clothes), Rudy Wiebe (who might be staying at the

Engels'), others. It was wonderful. That's how the Union was born. Over
bottles of beer and cups of tea in Marian Engel's living room on Brunswick Avenue. ("The Tea Party" 37)

Findley served as union chairperson for 1977–78, when the fights of the
day were book dumping (importing of remaindered Canadian books for
sale at lower prices than the Canadian edition) and censorship, which he
took very seriously.

When Margaret Laurence's Governor General's Award-winning novel
The Diviners came under attack in 1978 by a right-wing religious group that
accused Laurence of obscenity and corrupting youth and lobbied school
boards and politicians to ban the book, Findley was furious. He felt great
concern for Laurence, who lived alone with few resources and little support, in the face of such attacks, and he saw this as symptomatic of current
trends of bigotry in Canadian society. In an angry riposte, "Better Dead
Than Read? An Opposing View," he critiqued Paul Stuewe's remarks in
his October report (called "Better Dead Than Read?") on book-banning in
Huron County as "cant ... peppered with inaccuracies," and he named the
ringleaders of the Huron County "Concerned Citizens" lobby group as an
Evangelical minister, the Reverend Kenneth Campbell, and his American
co-religionist Anita Bryant.[9] The Writers' Union of Canada, represented
by Alice Munro, who lived in Huron County and had, therefore, a right to
speak out, had also been attacked for protesting the discrimination fos-
tered by Campbell and his ilk. Findley rose to Munro's defence as well.
On Laurence's behalf, he declared that if he were Laurence, he would sue a
pharmacist called Elmer Umbach for slander when he claimed that young
people would contract venereal disease from the free love she advocated
in her book (which Umbach had not read). Findley did not mince words:
"As a pharmacist, [Umbach] is only required to sell prophylactics; he is not
required to become one" (4).

In Findley's mind, the larger issue extended beyond a single book or an
isolated incident, and he feared that a censorship mentality was spreading
across the country. He wrote that the Campbell movement was "riddled
with fake oral indignation and fake concern for the hearts and minds of

our children [and] a truly evil manipulation of people's genuine fear and uncertainty about the world we live in" (5). Great works of literature like *The Diviners* espouse compassion and understanding, tolerance and love, he insisted. To ban books was to sink into the mire of fascism. This essay, "Better Dead Than Read? An Opposing View," was by no means Findley's last word on censorship, and his reference to fascism was not casual. He saw censorship as a tool of bigots who were intent on forcing a rigid view of human identity, including sexuality, on society, and the catastrophes of twentieth-century history that he knew so well proved the point.

Breakthrough
Can You See Me Yet? and *The Wars*

When he was not writing scripts for the CBC and helping to establish the Writers' Union, Findley was struggling to find a new focus for his work. He needed something completely different from the failed "Whimper," and he found it in his CBC radio play called "Missionaries," which was broadcast in the spring of 1972. Although the play was not well received, he knew he had found the right material and he believed in the Canadian family story and setting. All he needed now was a goal to aim for, which arrived in the shape of Jean Roberts and Marigold Charlesworth. In 1971, Roberts had become the founding artistic director of the theatre division at the newly opened National Arts Centre (NAC), and she invited Findley to be a playwright-in-residence, which brought him to Ottawa and back to live theatre. Bill had already agreed to assist Jean in her new position, which meant that he was often living in Ottawa with Findley (with periods at home in Stone Orchard or travelling for CBC work), and between 1973 and 1976, Findley worked on revisions, eventually developing a slight work into a complex, haunting piece of theatre with a new title—*Can You See Me Yet?*—that premiered at the National Arts Centre on 1 March 1976 with a stellar cast.[10] To celebrate the opening, Bill gave him a ring with a dark-green BC jade stone, which he wore on his left hand for the rest of his life.

Findley's journals from 1973 to 1975 reveal his revision process and the decisions he made as he rewrote the original play. In the fall of 1973, he told his journal that he was "re-thinking 'Missionaries'" because he believed it "could (should)" be a good play (LAC 87:3). He decided to cut several scenes, drop some of the motifs that cluttered up the through-line, and have Cassandra's story begin in an asylum and unfold backwards in time. The character of Edward (Cassandra's domineering father) needed to be made "real"—that is, more three-dimensional and convincingly human—and he wanted photographs to play a part, which a stage play, as distinct from a radio play, allowed: "One idea that appeals more and more," he wrote, "is the idea of photographs. Introducing characters and situations through a 'freeze frame' photograph." Although he did not say more about the freeze-frame method, he gave Cassandra a family photograph album, which she carries with her. On 15 January 1975, he recorded having "trouble with the play," but a few weeks later he was jubilant: "the whole play fell into place in my mind. Once I started writing—I didn't stop until it was done" (LAC 87:8). The next hurdle was a read-through with Jean and Marigold, a prospect he found daunting. Despite his fears, the reading went well, and he could hear that his characters, especially Cassandra, read by Jean, worked. Jean not only liked the play, she wanted to produce it at the NAC. Findley was overjoyed—"*numb* with relief—and pleasure and expectation."

Reflecting on the psychology of the writer in his journal, he went on to conclude that "writers [unlike actors] are schizophrenic ... but have found a way of controlling the illness by writing it down.—writing out the symptoms ... by working [their] way out methodically ... through the madness itself" (LAC 87:8). Was Timothy Findley schizophrenic or "mad" in the clinical sense? No. Volatile, intense, super-sensitive, perhaps obsessive-compulsive? Yes. Nevertheless, the idea of madness and the reality of schizophrenia, and their possible connection with artistic genius, fascinated him. His beloved Aunt Ruth was never far from his mind and his memories of her informed his creation of the Cassandra character. He understood himself well enough, however, to say that "to write well—

one must be in the hold of a kind of despondent-elation that only another writer [...] would understand" (LAC 87:50).

The play opens in *"the Asylum at Britton, Ontario"* on a hot summer day in 1938. Scene 1 begins in the asylum garden, but no one is present; there are offstage sounds of radio music and the barking of a dog, then three loud "whacks" before wooden croquet balls roll across the stage. As the action unfolds, these sounds, and the balls, recur, becoming increasingly ominous each time we see or hear them. The central character, Cassandra Wakelin, enters in scene 2, carrying *"an antique album covered in velvet"* (37) that holds the story of her past life and the photographs of the Wakelin home and her family; throughout the play, she will clasp it to her breast or show it to God and her fellow patients as proof of who she is. Almost immediately, she begins to conflate her fellow patients with members of her family, and the action of the play shifts between the present in the asylum and Cassandra's memories of her family, especially of her father, her brother, of the First World War, and of her younger sister. As Cassandra's mind conjures up this past, the patients assume the roles of Wakelin family members, and we witness the impact on the present as past trauma comes to life onstage. She is also a failure as a missionary because she had reneged on her promise to accompany a missionary friend to China. Although Findley does not develop this aspect of Cassandra's personal guilt, it is clear enough from what she does say that she has lost her Christian faith, as had her creator, and can no longer find anything else to believe in.

In his author's note for the house program, Findley was at pains to explain that his characters were not "real," in the sense of people he knew. "The people in this play exist," he wrote, "but only as themselves. I met them in my mind" (3). He also explained that "the word ASYLUM" means "a place of safety," and that in 1938 almost everyone in the world was looking for "sanctuary": "By 1938, the twentieth century had already gone through a revolution in Russia—the Great War—the 'flu' epidemic of 1919 (killing more than had died in the war)—a decade of cynical despair and then the Great Depression—Mussolini—Ethiopia—Hitler—the Civil War in Spain. And China falling to the ground ... So there was just cause then, to seek asylum (just as there might be now)." The main point of the story and of Cassandra's warning, however, is that there is no safe place left in this world and that one cannot escape the insane asylum to go home, as she longs to do, because they are the same place. As happened with her Greek namesake, Cassandra's warning is ignored by everyone. "The world is ending all around us," she pleads, "and we need each other now. And yet there is no sanctuary. Nowhere. None" (162). But no one responds. No one sees or hears her. There is no God to turn to. Cassandra speaks for Timothy Findley when she warns us that the world is increasingly unsafe and that only love, forgiveness, and imagination can save us.

Findley was honest with his audience when he insisted that his characters existed only in his mind. Nevertheless, they are familiar *people*. We encountered them in *The Last of the Crazy People* and *The Butterfly Plague*, and they owe much to actual people like his Aunt Ruth and his father, and to Findley and Bull stories about the First World War that were part of his childhood. The most poignant connection between this play and Findley's biography develops when Cassandra invokes her brother, whom she sees in her fellow patient Franklin, and prompts him to reveal the wound that has tormented and traumatized the entire family. Franklin and Cassandra grew up in the shadow of their elder brother, Patrick, who was killed at Ypres and idolized by their father as a hero, but Edward denigrated his other children, who could never measure up in his eyes to his first-born: "He made it impossible for us to live," she says, and he "doomed [us] to failure" (114); "My father was a BASTARD" (98). In one of the most excoriating confrontations of the play, Franklin accuses Edward of castrating him and asks why his father wishes that he and Cassandra were dead instead of Patrick, and Cassandra then pushes the confrontation a step further when she accuses Edward of being responsible for Patrick's death (157) because he encouraged his son to go to war. In many ways, this is the story of the Findleys, of Uncle Irving, the war hero, worshipped by Findley's grandmother and preferred over her surviving son, Allan, and her two grandsons. It is also Findley's first articulation of his view—to be explored in *The Wars*—that the fathers, men like Edward, killed a generation of sons in the First World War. Cassandra is considered crazy for warning others of the looming danger of another war, even as Hitler's voice can be heard on the offstage radio and enthusiastic shouts of "SIEG! HEIL!" greet his speech at a Nuremberg rally (123). And she is considered dangerous for insisting that the world is on fire and that something drastic must be done to halt the conflagration. Ironically, perhaps fittingly, she dies "in September of 1939, [when] the Asylum at Britton was destroyed by fire" (166)—the month (on the 3rd) and year when Canada declared war on Germany.

When the play was published a year later, it carried a dedication to Frances Hyland, who had starred as the lead character, to Marigold Charlesworth, who had directed it, to Jean Roberts, who had believed in it, and to the "memory of my grandmother, E. M. Fagan Bull." All four women were important players in Findley's life, but his grandmother had a name to conjure with. Here, for the first time in print, he identified the family connection with the name Fagan, which he returned to in *The Wars*, *Headhunter*, and *The Piano Man's Daughter*. The published text also carried a thoughtful introduction by Margaret Laurence, who called it "an astonishing work," "compelling," and "a triumph," and an epigraph from an early Margaret Atwood poem, "Evening Trainstation, Before Departure":

> I move
> and live on the edges
> (what edges)
> I live
> on all the edges there are.
>   (*The Circle Game* 16)

These lines certainly refer to Cassandra, the main character in the play, but they also describe Timothy Findley who, in 1976, was still living on several edges—of despair, sobriety, and identity—as well as on the brink of success.

Although all involved had high hopes for the play, his first major work since *The Butterfly Plague* and his first produced stage play, most drama critics and reviewers were unimpressed. Simply put, the production flopped, not because anything about it was poor but because most of the initial reviews were scathing, and negative reviews will kill a play. Some writers will claim that they never read reviews of their work, but Timothy Findley was not among them: he followed reviews closely, took them to heart, and was deeply affected by them. In this case the negative reviews were simply wrong. *Can You See Me Yet?* is gut-wrenching theatre about a mad woman in an asylum reliving her traumatic past and bearing witness to a threatening future. When I saw this unforgettable production, I had no idea who the playwright was, but I was deeply moved by the acting and the story. Canadian reviewers, however, were not interested in this kind of serious, emotionally and ethically demanding play. Findley was devastated by Gordon Stoneham's dismissal of the play as an "insipid mess," with "tacky symbolism," but he was infuriated by John Fraser, at the time the theatre critic for the *Globe and Mail* (with considerable clout), who described the play as "a mighty bore ... written with the sort of special high endeavor which has become a national mania."[11] There were positive reviewers, such as Myron Galloway, who called it "a work so stunning that it will take Canadian audiences and some critics a bit of time to appreciate," but the pain Findley experienced over the play's failure—his failure, as he saw it—was overwhelming. On his 1976 calendar for March 2 he wrote: "I am heartbroken."

To make matters worse, Islay Lambert, whom Tiff and Bill had invited to attend the premiere with them, had died two days earlier. Bill, who had planned to bring her with him from Cannington to Ottawa for the occasion, made excuses for her inability to join them, saying that she was quite ill, which had been all too true. He did not tell Tiff the truth until after opening night. Tiff's response was shocked silence; he had no words to express his sense of loss. Lambert's memorial service took place in May and was attended by both men, but by that time Findley was sinking into a severe depression. In his journal he wrote that he could not even confess his feelings to Dr. Turner. He could not face his friends, who knew he had failed again, he believed that everything he was working on would be "unread and useless," and he could see no future for his work.

It would be a mistake, however, to ignore *Can You See Me Yet?* Myron Galloway's prediction that "audiences and some critics" would need time to appreciate it was true. It is a strong, well-crafted play about serious issues that have not lost their relevance. Moreover, to create it Findley dug deep into personal experiences and his abiding interest in themes of family, madness, and war—which means that this play tells us much about the man who wrote it. *Can You See Me Yet?* is about bearing witness, and Timothy Findley believed in an artist's responsibility—to a reader or viewer, to society—to be a witness and to communicate what he or she sees as honestly as possible. He also believed in the power and function of memory, of never forgetting the past, and of maintaining a living grasp on personal and social history. Witnessing and remembering are the two forces propelling the verbal and emotional action of the play, and he hit upon precisely the right dramatic structure to convey this type of internal (as distinct from external, physical) action when he decided to tell Cassandra's story backwards so she could delve into her family's past, reveal its connection with world events in Europe and China, and then bring the meaning of those events forward into the bright light of a summer day in an asylum garden in southern Ontario in 1938. If it is madness to bear witness to the horrors of the past and to warn about looming cataclysm, then Cassandra is mad. She has, Findley suggests, been driven mad by a society, beginning with her family, that refuses to see her or take her seriously and locks her away. Her vision is uncomfortable, disturbing, and she asks us to pay attention, to remember, to change our ways, to accept responsibility for the future. Other Findley characters will also make such demands and be driven to extremes by the seemingly unstoppable violence of the twentieth century, and the most famous of those characters was waiting in the wings.

———

Robert Ross, dressed in his officer's uniform, rode into Findley's life, and his story had to be told. On one memorable morning in May of 1976, Bill got the news. Findley emerged from his bedroom in their Ottawa apartment to tell Bill that he had "a glorious idea for a new novel. It was not to be the dark and dreary stuff of the three earlier attempts, he said, but a strong and positive story. What he excitedly described to me was the story of a young Torontonian who goes off to World War I, is horribly maimed by fire, and dies" (*WLB* 172).[12] Bill met this announcement with "stunned silence." But as he began typing the early drafts, he realized just how positive and powerful this novel was going to be, and he recalls that it took Findley "just three months" to complete a first draft. *The Wars* was published to general praise in 1977 and won the 1978 Governor General's Award for Fiction. Many consider it his best novel. Certainly, it is his best loved and one of the finest novels about the Great War in the English language. At the age of 47, after many years of struggle and despair, Timothy Findley finally received the attention and acclaim he had sought for so long.

Although *The Wars* was written more quickly than any of his other novels, it nonetheless went through several drafts, many revisions, and a major restructuring. The journals and workbooks record the hard work and strategic decisions he made about the structure and point of view, and they provide glimpses into his extensive research on the history of the war and the kind of cultural detail he needed to bring the civilian world of the period to life. The characters arrived in his imagination first; he claimed to see them and hear their story. The difference between *The Wars* and the failed novels was that Robert Ross and his story arrived together. Findley already knew—from childhood memories, family stories, Grandmother Findley's photographs, and the mythology of Uncle Irving, who had such a profound influence on his imagination and memory—a great deal about the First World War. Not its facts, perhaps, but its feel, its lasting impact, its historic role in Canada's history. He had witnessed the war's influence on two specific soldiers—his uncle Irving and Brainerd Carlyle (Aunt Ruth's husband)—and on their families and their generation of young men and women. He owned one of the family's most treasured heirlooms, the leather-bound journal of his uncle's letters home, and he remembered the photographs on Goggie's mantelpiece. The emotional groundwork for Robert's story was already in place.

Nevertheless, one journal and a workbook from 1976–77 reveal the depths of his post–*Can You See Me Yet?* fear of failure, the psychological cost he experienced from delving into his family's war trauma, and the sheer effort it required to channel intense emotion into the writing of *The Wars*. The workbook (LAC 88:6) is titled "The Dark" and is half empty. The pages on which he did write carry brief, cryptic comments, almost like poems or epigraphs, about his failures and fears, about hell, lack of love, ugliness, and loss. The last entry is disturbing: "I AM AFRAID OF MY NAME. _____." This blank, where no name appears, represents a metaphorical erasure of himself, as if he were unwilling to acknowledge his personal investment in this work, his past failures as an artist, his commitment (as he had told Dr. Turner) to the words he put on the page, and the traumas he associated with the Findley name. A journal dated 1976 is more informative (LAC 88:4). He was reading Proust (and was "addicted" to his rhythms), Barbara Tuchman (*The Proud Tower*), David Jones (*In Parenthesis* and *The Anathemata*), Leon Wolff (*In Flanders Fields*), Greek plays, and Uncle Irving's letters. Through this reading he was "steeping himself in the times." And he was listening to Joan Sutherland sing: "Glorious," he wrote. But if the reading and opera-listening suggest optimism and progress, the long sequences of blank pages in this journal suggest otherwise: he was blocked, unable to write anything, and in despair. On his 1976 calendar for May 17, however, in the midst of depression and as if to prod or motivate himself, he wrote: "Begin new book" (LAC 87:15). By September, the book had a name—"The Wars"—and he was working hard to finish a first draft. Finally, on October 7—"*Breakthrough*. Good day writing. Over tension." Ten days later he encountered fresh obstacles. Across three days, from October 18 to 20, he wrote: "WARS—Difficult! The bridges won't come." On October 24 he found "the first 21 pgs ... stilted" and that "Robert [was] not revealed quickly enough" (LAC 88:4). These first pages would soon be changed, but for the time being he was optimistic. In a sketch he made of himself at work (ill. 23), he sits, the "Early morning, all night kitchen table writer," with Mottle on his right and a coffee mug on his left (LAC 88:4). On October 31, a slightly belated birthday present arrived in the shape of another breakthrough: "photographic scheme of Wars—Today the final penny dropped—and I think, now, I have the book in hand" (LAC 88:4).

There were more lows as he worked feverishly to make the novel perfect, but he was ready to think about a publisher, which meant letting someone other than Bill or Ellen Powers (the executive secretary for the Writers' Union of Canada, who helped with typing) see the manuscript. He turned to his old friend Stanley Colbert, who had arrived in Toronto that winter to begin his work with the CBC, and Stan was very positive. They met in October and again in early November, and Stan agreed to take him on as a client (Nancy Colbert became his literary agent after she arrived in 1977 to join her husband), but he insisted on changes to the novel. As Colbert said, he had read about the Ross family, Rosedale, and the factory downtown, but after fifty manuscript pages there was still no war. He'd been promised wars; after all, the book was called "The Wars." His example of what he wanted was *Goldilocks and the Three Bears*; he asked Findley to imagine him as a trusting reader waiting for the bears but getting pages of Goldilocks. "Bring on the Bears!" he told him, so Findley made a sign to hang above his typewriter: "BRING ON THE BEARS" (*IM* 147)—which he did, by an inspired restructuring of a final scene with Robert, the black mare, the train tracks, and the war. *The Wars* now begins with this striking scene and the narrative returns to this scene near the end after readers learn who Robert is and what he has done.

In addition to reading widely for an understanding of the war and the pre-war period, he used other research methods. One of the more extreme was fieldwork. In November he decided to spend twenty-four hours in a muddy, water-clogged ditch beside a field at Stone Orchard in an attempt to experience something of what soldiers in the trenches endured. Soon enough he realized how foolish this was: "No one was firing at me—I was not being shelled. The mud was only ankle deep" (*IM* 148). But he persisted and "stayed there long enough [...] in the freezing rain and wind" to shave in cold water, light a fire, eat cold beans, empty his bowels, and pee: "Peeing—in itself—was agony," he recalls, because all his muscles were "telling [him] not to let in the cold" (*IM* 149). Sleeping was impossible, so he gave up and returned to the house—"defeat." However, he had learned something basic about human nature under duress—the sense of "being alone" and utterly vulnerable. Another research method came more naturally to Findley's kind of imagination and memory in the form of a friend, Juliet Mannock.[13] Originally from England, she had emigrated and become a researcher with Bill at the CBC. She and Bill loved to cook and do batik; she and Tiff loved gardens and cats. She recalls helping him with details on London and its history for *The Wars*, but he recalled her as a presence: "she appears in the mind as an image on film" (*IM* 141), and her image, together with her qualities of bravery and survival, her sherry and cigarettes, and her Englishness began "to filter onto the page in the sketch of a woman who perhaps [would] play an important part in [*The Wars*]" (*IM* 142). In our conversation, Mannock dismissed the notion that she inspired the character of Lady Juliet d'Orsey in the novel. In her view, Timothy Findley had a romantic view of women and did not understand them, but her accent and manner of speech, her gestures, her toughness and intelligence did carry over into his writing as he worked from remembered sounds, images, and his imagination to create the character his novel needed.

By early May 1977, Stanley Colbert had introduced Findley to John Pearce, an editor with Clarke, Irwin, who played an important role in Findley's life over the next several years.[14] Pearce had liked *The Butterfly Plague* but was, as he told me, "stunned" by *The Wars* and believed "it would be the best and most important novel published in Canada that year." He wanted some revisions, however, but with the green light from publisher Bill Clarke, he told Findley that if he could deliver a polished manuscript in time it could be published in the fall. Findley was excited: "this will be my first book published in Canada. *Crazy People* went to all the houses and was turned down" (LAC 303:1). He was also apprehensive: "What if I should now fail in my own country? To date, I have written nothing better than 'The Wars'—but I have no basis for trusting any single Canadian critic for believing I can write at all—let alone well" (LAC 303:1). Once again the archives, with drafts of the penultimate typescript, illustrate the effort he invested in getting his novel right.[15] Dates and names needed checking: Was the *Mail and Empire* being published in 1915? (It was.) Was St. Paul's on Bloor Street in use by 1898? (It was, but not in the

1913 structure.) Could Robert have read *Boys' Own Annual* between 1904 and 1910? (Yes.) The details seemed endless.

And there were many revisions, in addition to the restructuring, that helped to "Bring on the Bears." For example, when Robert and his men find themselves stranded in dense fog on a crumbling dike, Findley made many cuts to tighten the action and simplify his prose; the final effect is a heightened sense of impending danger with an urgent need for action. He made a similar decision to increase the dramatic impact on the reader when he cut a poem from the closing sequence of the novel. What remains—Mr. Ross attending Robert's burial and Lady Juliet choosing the words for his gravestone—intensifies the poignancy and sense of waste that haunt Robert's story. Here, less really is more. He made cuts to the brothel scene, clarified Robert's relationship with young Harris to make his death more meaningful for Robert, and moved the position of the rape scene after Pearce suggested it be shifted to an earlier point in the story so as not to overshadow the climax or seem like the only motivation for Robert's actions. Margaret Laurence, who found the book brilliant, feared the rape scene might sink the novel with critics and the public.[16] When she called Findley to explain her concern, she asked him to tell her why it had to be in the novel. He replied that, "it is my belief that Robert Ross and his generation of young men were raped, in effect, by the people who made that war. Basically, their fathers did it to them" (*IM* 151).

In his journal Findley quoted the Wilfred Owen lines that Benjamin Britten used in his *War Requiem*: "the tenor and the baritone sing together—Abraham and Isaac—

> *Lay not thy hand upon the lad,*
> *Neither do anything to him,* the Angel of God commands.
> *But the old man would not so—and slew his son....*
> *And half the seed of Europe, one by one....*
> And slew his son and half the seed of Europe, one by one.
> It *was* rape. (qtd. in *IM* 151)

The basic idea of the sins of the fathers was not new, but this explanation for his insistence on keeping this scene arises from his hatred of war, his fear of violence (including his own capacity for violence), and his horror at the violation of a person's identity that rape represents. His diatribe against the British National Service in his London journal is unequivocal. Wars and the aggressive masculinity that supports them were anathema to him, as were those individual men—fathers, brothers, religious extremists, ideologues, and fascists—who sought to control the world. Cassandra makes precisely this point in *Can You See Me Yet?* but Findley needed to emphasize his point: the rape scene stayed.

Findley's journals show how carefully he planned *The Wars*. He made a list of key "Thematic Symbols" and their associations—Fire, Water, Glass, Cover (meaning "skin, sheets, clothing, bandages"), and Shelter. Small notes to himself are scattered among the pages of the journal: "Don't Be Afraid" and "Keep Going" (LAC 88:3). But one of the most fascinating notes involves the title itself and the character of Nicholas Fagan. Fagan, who is identified at the end of the novel as "the Irish essayist and critic" (*TW* 191),[17] has a closer connection with the novel's author than generations of curious critics and readers have realized. On one page of this journal, Findley printed the title backwards as it would appear in a mirror and wrote "by Nicholas Fagan." On another page, he wrote the title properly and added: "Nicholas Fagan is the pseudonym chosen by the brother of a well known but 'By No Means Famous' Canadian writer" (LAC 88:3). Brother, instead of aunt? Is this a camouflage gesture on Findley's part because in 1976 he was not ready to reveal that Nicholas Fagan was Aunt Ruth's pseudonym and an actual ancestor? Perhaps. What is clear is that this family connection, first hinted at in the dedication to *Can You See Me Yet?*, was slowly maturing in his imagination. Nicholas Fagan, the ancestor, was mutating into a character that, as we shall see, is inextricably associated with Ruth and with Findley himself.

He delivered his "cut and edited (with additions)" typescript to John Pearce in July 1977. Clarke, Irwin, especially Bill Clarke and his mother, Irene, were enthusiastically behind it.[18] The dedication was already in place: "For my Father and Mother and P. M. [Phoebe Margaret] Findley and in memory of T. I. F.," followed by Euripides: "Never That Which Is Shall Die." In his journal he wrote: "Once before I die, I hope to *know* I've been heard. That's all" (LAC 88:4). With the publication of *The Wars* he knew. By all accounts the launch party at Toronto's then-famous Park Plaza Hotel on October 13 was extraordinary. Often such events are awkward and constrained, but this one was full of laughter, genuine affection for the author, sincere praise for the book—and singing. Allan, Margaret, and Aunt Marg attended and were proud; Margaret Laurence, Margaret Atwood, Graeme Gibson, Robert Weaver, who had recognized Findley's talent years earlier, Gwendolyn MacEwen, Nancy and Stan Colbert, Bill Clarke and his wife Marie, and an ebullient John Pearce, among others, were there. It was Pearce who played the piano and led the singing of period songs—"It's a Long Way to Tipperary," "When You Wore a Tulip," "Pack Up Your Troubles," and "Keep the Home-Fires Burning." About fifty people attended, and the tables were decorated with red poppies. As Findley told Marian Engel, who could not be there, everyone wore "smashing clothes" and was "beautiful"; Margaret Laurence wore a velvet gown, which made him feel "extraordinary" (Verduyn and Garay, 179).

Findley wrote to thank Bill Clarke for the "beautifully produced" book and said, "It's a privilege to be with you and I hope it will be a long and flourishing relationship with many more books to come" (Clarke, Irwin fonds B24-F5).[19] He described the party, organized by Catherine Wilson and paid for by Clarke, Irwin, as "unique, as parties of that kind go—and marvelous." "I felt *safe*," he wrote, an odd thing to say perhaps and yet reflective of his personal insecurity and fear of failure or disapproval from reviewers and his own family. He made a special point of thanking Bill Clarke for his attention to his parents and his aunt: "The publication of the book—with all its implications of private memories and its gestures of honour—has meant a lot to them" (Clarke, Irwin fonds B24-F5). Allan Findley was unequivocal in his praise—"the dead stand up and salute you" he told his son, and in a letter he wrote: "I am very proud of you and your achievements" (LAC 96:8). After so many years of dismissal and criticism, finally this praise from an ailing father.

With the euphoria of the launch party behind him, Findley set forth on his first cross-Canada tour to promote the book. Before he left for the West Coast, with Bill doing the driving, the Canadian reviews began to appear. Writing in the *Globe and Mail*, Donald Jack criticized his "distortion" of the war, but Margaret Laurence made a spirited response to his rather pointless remarks. Findley hardly knew how to thank her for rising to the book's defence, so in a card to her (30 October 1977) he underlined his words: "From here—there is no way back into silence. And no way back into the old insecurity that allowed me to retreat into self-concern and self-censorship. You have offered me that rarest privilege of paying attention from the heart" (Laurence fonds, 2-64). Other reviews were glowing. Lorne Parton called *The Wars* "simply one of the best novels of the Great War, to be ranked with Remarque and Sassoon." General James M. Gavin (quoted in *Playboy's Choice*) called it the "most powerful and most moving book [about] war" he had ever read. Thanks to Nancy Colbert, who had arranged foreign rights and speedy translation, German reviewers were similarly impressed, despite the unfortunate German title—*Der Krieg und die Krote* (*The War and the Toad*). Hans Butow in *Die Welt* called it a "masterpiece," and Heinz Albers in the *Hamburger-Abendblatt* described it as "an extraordinary piece of prose [about] the spiritual decay of the times."[20]

The review that most pleased him, however, came at a low point during the book tour. He was in Edmonton, tired and keen to get home, when Bill brought him a copy of the *Financial Post* with Margaret Atwood's lengthy review. Atwood began by saying that there were at least three reasons for calling the publication of *The Wars* "a major literary event." The first was the state of Canadian publishing, so she had high praise for Clarke, Irwin's taking a gamble on a less-than-"discreet" book and making an investment in a serious writer. Her second reason was that the novel cast an important light on the state of reviewing in Canada; she went on to tear a strip off Donald Jack's review and she questioned the *Globe and Mail's* wisdom in choosing Jack, a popular humorist, to do the review: it was, she said, "like choosing Red Buttons to review *Hamlet*" (5). But, of course, the main reason for celebrating *The Wars* was its quality and, although she did find faults, notably with Findley's near sentimentality about animals, she was the first of the novel's readers to appreciate what he had accomplished with his complex narrative structure and his approach to the subject of war. She called Robert Ross "an essentially Canadian hero [...] neither bloodthirsty nor much of a patriot," and a man whose last heroic act of protest leads to his court martial. She concluded by describing the novel as an example of "Southern Ontario Gothic, Rosedale variation." Findley was full of relief and joy because another writer, one whom he respected, had paid attention and seen what he was doing. In a short letter, reprinted in *Journeyman* (200), he thanked her with a sheet of yellow paper dotted with "blobs" of ink in the hope that these would express what he could not find the words to say: "I hope you will accept it in lieu of whatever other expression I might have mustered to articulate the whoops—shouts—smiles and dances that were performed ad lib on the terrace of an Edmonton hotel this morning after Willy returned with your piece in the *Post*." Pierre Berton's response was also positive, and Findley wrote to tell Berton how grateful he was that Berton had found time to read the novel: "Your praise will do a lot to draw attention to 'The Wars'" (Berton fonds, B164.F8).

In her review, Atwood wrote that "*The Wars* is about the function of memory and our persistence in time. The researcher is haunted and Robert Ross is the ghost, fixed in the mind at the moment of his fiery sacrifice and self-destruction" (5). And she was absolutely right. The "researcher," who is actually Robert's biographer, is haunted by Robert, as we will be, and he must rely on archival evidence and the memories of people he interviews to tell Robert's story. In this telling, he makes us care about one young Canadian soldier, his tragic fate, and his family's loss and grief. He invites us to think carefully about the madness of war, its causes, its social cost, and its violence, and he urges us to remember the past.

The first time the biographer speaks, as if thinking out loud and addressing us, he establishes the context for much of what follows:

> You begin at the archives with photographs. Robert and Rowena—rabbits and wheelchairs—children, dogs, and horses. Barbara d'Orsey—the *S.S. Massanabie*—Magdalene Wood. Boxes and boxes of snapshots and portraits; maps and letters; cablegrams and clippings from the

papers. All you have to do is sign them out and carry them across the room. Spread over table tops, a whole age lies in fragments underneath the lamps. *The war to end all wars.* All you can hear is the wristwatch on your arm. Outside, it snows. The dark comes early. The archivist is gazing from her desk. She coughs. The boxes smell of yellow dust. You hold your breath. As the past moves under your fingertips, part of it crumbles. Other parts, you know you'll never find. This is what you have. (11)

Although he never reveals his name or why he wants to find Robert and tell his story, or why he seeks to remember and understand the war through these archival fragments of the past, we sense how intensely he cares and we too hold our breath. These are the givens: one young man's ordeal in that war matters; remembering him and the enormous human cost of that war matters. Research and biography, however partial the evidence and difficult the reconstruction of the story, matter. Memory matters. So does breath. And because this is a Timothy Findley novel, we must *"pay attention"* (11).

Robert Raymond Ross is one of four children in the wealthy Ross family. The Rosses live in Rosedale and own the Raymond/Ross farm machinery factory that is producing trucks for the war. Before 1915 is over, Robert will have enlisted, trained, and become a second lieutenant, and will be "ripe for the wars." He is nineteen years old. The area of his military action is concentrated around Bailleul in northern France, near the Flemish town of St. Eloi, south of Ypres. Robert endures some of the worst aspects of the war, from near drowning in filthy mud and water on a collapsing dike, to a chlorine gas attack while he and his men are trapped in a corpse- and water-clogged crater, to the Germans' first use of flame-throwers at St. Eloi. His dugout is shelled. His soldiers and friends die. And he receives inane orders from his commanding officer, Captain Leather.

These scenes are certainly graphic and powerful (Findley brought on the bears with force); however, *The Wars* is not only about soldiers and battlefields. Major portions of the story belong to Robert's parents and to two women who knew Robert and agree to be interviewed by the biographer: Marian Turner was the First World War Canadian nurse who cared for Robert when his badly burned and disfigured body was "received" in her nursing station at Magdalene Wood on 18 June 1916, and Lady Juliet d'Orsey, now in her eighties, first met Robert when he visited her family's estate in Cambridgeshire. Nurse Turner insists that Robert "was a hero" because he rejected the war by doing what "no one else would even dare to think of doing" (16). Lady Juliet calls the times "unique" and warns the biographer not to judge the past or the people who fought that war and lived on after it. In her view, Robert clarified who he was through his repudiation of military authority, and she expects his biographer—and us—to respect his decision. Her principles, like Marian Turner's verdict, reflect Findley's views, of course, but by creating the fictional biographer with access to interviews, diaries, and archives he distanced himself from the story, while simultaneously using his favourite narrative strategies—journals, diaries, memory, and archival research.

As the dedication to the novel makes clear, and as Findley said when thanking Bill Clarke for his attention to his family during the launch, his family members and their history bear an important relationship to *The Wars*. His Uncle Irving ("T. I. F." in the dedication) was especially significant, not because he was a model for Robert, but because Findley relied heavily on his uncle's journal for many details about the war, from soldiers' names to specific battles.[21] By drawing on this journal, he was remembering an important ancestor and the lasting impact of that man's life on Grandmother Findley, Aunt Marg, and his own father. Although Irving Findley did not respond to the war as Robert does, his postwar suffering and the terrible price the war inflicted on the family obliged Findley to handle this subject with great care. He also drew inspiration from other family members to create the Rosedale Rosses. Mrs. Ross is a formidable presence, often viewed as cruel and unbending by critics, but she was one of Findley's favourite characters, the kind of strong, honest woman and mother he knew and respected. As he told Karen Mulhallen, he felt great sympathy for Mrs. Ross and gave her some of the characteristics of his own mother (34–38). In one of the most powerful home-front scenes in the book, Mrs. Ross stands up in the middle of the bishop's Sunday address in St. Paul's Church and marches down the aisle to the doors to sit outside on the snow-covered steps with her companion, Davenport. She drinks from her flask and rails against God and clergymen: "I do not understand. I don't. I won't. I can't. Why is this happening to us, Davenport? What does it mean—*to kill your children*? Kill them and then … go in there and sing about it! What does it mean?" (54). When she and Mr. Ross receive the news that Robert is missing in action, she refuses to dress or leave her room. "The sound of [her] cries to heaven [rise] up" through the entire house (178), and she goes blind. The tragedy of the war is hers as well as Robert's.

After a brief medical leave, Robert had returned to the front in June of 1916, shortly before the start of the Somme Offensive. On the way to rejoining his convoy at St. Eloi, he stopped at Bailleul for a bath at an asylum reserved for officers, and this is where he was raped, in a scene that Findley presents with a blunt descriptive economy that is, in itself, shocking. Robert reached his convoy just as the Germans commenced a major assault on the St. Eloi district, and after a week of this nightmare he was trapped at battalion headquarters, with a supply of fresh horses and mules, when a German barrage hit the signals office and the barns. He decided to retreat with the animals to save them from burning to death, and when Captain Leather refused him permission to do this, Robert shot him "between the eyes" (178). From the army's point of view, this was an act of insubordination, treason, and murder. From Robert's it was the necessary execution of a dangerous madman. He then killed the injured and dying animals, tore the lapels from his uniform, and walked away. When he found 130 horses held in railway cars, he freed them, and led them into the countryside, to seek asylum in an abandoned barn, where a military posse found him, ordered him to surrender, and set the barn on fire. By the time Robert escaped the inferno, he and the mare he was riding were engulfed in flames. In her interview with the biographer, Nurse Turner recalls receiving him at the nursing station, his terrible burns, his dreadful pain, and his silence. She also confesses that she offered him a lethal dose of morphine, but that he refused with just two words—"Not yet." "There," she says, "in those two words, in a nutshell—you have the essence of Robert Ross" (189). Robert is arrested, tried in a military court, found guilty, and sent to St. Aubyn's to recover sufficiently to face execution, but he dies of his wounds before reaching his twenty-sixth birthday.

Although *The Wars* is rich in imagery and symbolism, fire is the dominant symbol. It appears in its positive guise as welcomed warmth in a freezing dugout or in an elegant Rosedale or Knightsbridge living room, but it is as a destructive force that fire sweeps through the text killing, maiming, and laying waste to everything it touches. Through the fire imagery, Findley creates vivid scenes that burn on after a reading of the novel is over—the image of Robert and the mare on fire as they break out of the burning barn, fires erupting after shelling along the front, and the almost unimaginable scene of Bailleul as a holocaust. It is the first of these images, however, that haunts us because it is simply evoked and left to linger in the imagination. While fire is *the* Findley element, recurring constantly in his work, the fate of animals and aspects of the Findley and Bull family histories are equally important to this text. Findley's memories of those horses sacrificed to human greed and violence during the gold rush inform the scene with the injured horse aboard the troopship, the bombing of the barns and yard, and Robert's futile attempt to save the horses trapped in the railway cars at Bailleul. Family allusions, especially to the Findleys, strengthen the referential fabric of the story, extending it beyond the fictional tragedy of one character. Descriptions of Toronto before and during the war owe a lot to Findley's intimate knowledge of the city's streets, churches, houses, and the Massey-Harris factory, which inspired the Raymond/Ross farm machinery factory. Robert attends St. Andrew's College, like all the Findley men; he holidays at Jackson's Point on Lake Simcoe, as the Findleys did; and the Ross family travels to England before the war on the same ship that Phoebe did with Irving, Margaret, and young Allan. The Fagan-Bull family is less visible (they are central to *The Piano Man's Daughter*, the companion novel to *The Wars*), but they surface in the words quoted at the end of the novel and attributed to the fictional Nicholas Fagan: *"Nothing so completely verifies our perception of a thing as our killing of it"* (191).

Archives and photographs also play important roles in the novel, as they did in Findley's life and working methods. Both can be seen as symbols of history and the documents that bear witness to events and people long dead, but a Findley archive carries more than symbolic significance.

It is the source of memory, the foundation of personal and cultural identity. The biographer, however, is the key contributor to the novel. Without him we would not have Robert Ross, Mrs. Ross, Marian Turner, and Lady Juliet. He talks to himself in the second person and to us, much as Timothy Findley does in his journals; his "you" is flexible and inclusive. He is also the researcher in the archives, the custodian of memory, the initiating presence who is haunted by Robert's fiery image. He decides to reconstruct Robert's life and to bear witness to the devastation wrought by the war to end all wars. He makes the reader an accomplice, or a sharer, in the bearing of witness, and he functions as a moral compass, not only for an understanding of the past, but also for insight into the present in which we live and about which we must make informed decisions. Among the most important things Robert Ross's archive tells us is that, for Findley, the artist's responsibility is to be a witness, to tell others what they might not want to hear, and to give articulate voices to those without them or those denied a voice. When Nurse Turner offers Robert a quick death, his reply could easily be dismissed and lost, but she remembers and repeats his words, thus enabling the biographer and us to hear them: he said, "Not yet."

The Wars appeared on the literary scene when Canadian literature was beginning to be taught in schools and universities, and its subject spoke to a young generation of readers who would have read about the war in Vietnam but knew little about Canada's role in the Great War. Because of its unusual narrative structure, it has also appealed to scholars who find it an analytical gold mine: is it realist or postmodernist? (Findley always rejected the latter label.) Who tells the story, or what priority should be given to its several narrators; which of them can be trusted the most? How does a reader, who is directly addressed at times, reconcile conflicting opinions about what Robert did? In 2007, it was adapted for the stage, where it has reached new audiences and prompted people to return to the novel or read it for the first time.[22] Years after its publication, *The Wars* still richly rewards rereading and speaks powerfully to a contemporary generation that lives in the context of international conflict, terrorism, and war.

Without question, the happiest event in Findley's professional life was winning the 1978 Governor General's Award for Fiction for *The Wars*. Even the telephone call from Rideau Hall was dramatic. April 15 of that year began with a "cold-dark-stormy" morning and he was depressed. Work on a new novel was going badly; he wasn't sleeping well; and one of the cats was in labour. She had been brought inside because she was having difficulty, but eventually three tiny kittens were born in his rocking chair. When the phone rang it was a gentleman in Ottawa calling to congratulate him on winning a GG for *The Wars*. Findley stammered his thanks and promptly named the last kitten to be born "Gee Gee." The rules about such awards are strict, of course, so a winner can only tell family and very close friends. Formal announcements are the prerogative of the Governor General's office. Findley called his mother first, then Nancy Colbert and Margaret Laurence, and an hour later Ken Adachi called to inquire about the rumours he had heard. Tiff could not keep the secret from Ken, but Adachi waited for the right time to report the good news in the *Toronto Star*. The award was presented in an elegant ceremony at Rideau Hall on May 18, and Nancy Colbert hosted a party for him at Ottawa's venerable Italian restaurant called Mamma Teresa. Another special event was the invitation to read from *The Wars* to the congregation at Bloor Street United Church, which he described for Laurence as "like a homecoming" because Grandfather Findley had belonged to that congregation and was warmly remembered by a former minister of the church. He greatly enjoyed the music, but "the main thing," he said, "was to touch the past that way." The experience, and the memories of those who attended the reading, brought his ancestors, especially Grandfather Findley and Uncle Irving, "back, *real* again and that was fascinating."[23]

A less happy episode in the saga of *The Wars* was the film adaptation, which was released in Toronto and Ottawa on 11 November 1983 after many delays. Although the final product was well done, disagreements behind the scenes resulted in a set of professional and legal problems that persist, and the film is not currently available for commercial distribution. Nielsen-Ferns International, which had purchased the film rights in March 1980, co-produced the film with the NFB, and shooting began in the spring of 1981 with release slated for January 1982. Robin Phillips directed with a stellar cast, including William Hutt (Mr. Ross), Martha Henry (Mrs. Ross), and Brent Carver as Robert.[24] Findley wrote the screenplay, making numerous modifications along the way, and Glenn Gould agreed to select and perform music for the soundtrack once he was assured that no animals would be harmed in the making of the film. By January 1982, however, the NFB and Torstar Syndicate (the distributor) disagreed over licensing, which sent Robin Phillips into a panic, and Findley's calendar for 1982 carries several entries about the film: the soundtrack recording work with Gould on June 1 was splendid, but a few weeks later the NFB suddenly cancelled a meeting and a preliminary screening of rushes; it was not rescheduled until September (LAC 89:6). By 1983, Findley became increasingly angry over the delays and the way he felt he and Phillips had been treated by the NFB. Particularly annoying were comments reported to him criticizing the amount of time devoted to the Ross family, because this was a sensitive point. Such comments recalled Stanley Colbert's "Bring on the Bears" and all the changes he had made to the novel's structure to place more emphasis on the war. For Findley the home front was as important as the battlefront in both film and novel.

Margaret Findley attended the premiere with Tiff and wrote to tell him that "being taken by you and being with you at the Toronto opening of 'The Wars' was one of the most tremendous moments and hours of my life. I salute you" (LAC 96:15). Remembering the film for me thirty years later, Brent Carver was very positive. The cast and Phillips were a "treat" to work with; Findley was always a constructive presence at shoots; and the film itself captured a unique atmosphere and intense emotion. When Carver attended the Ottawa premiere on November 11 with his father, a Second World War veteran, who approved of the film, the audience was enthusiastic and embraced it. In my 2011 interview with Martha Henry, she described Mrs. Ross as a woman with "vision and a spine of steel, one of the most revealing and ingenious characters any writer has ever written." I vividly recall seeing the film shortly after its initial release and believe it deserves to be available now because it is beautifully acted, well scripted, and very well designed and produced. The soundtrack alone is worth experiencing. Gould's playing of a Brahms intermezzo (in E-flat Major, op. 117, no. 1), for example, is perfectly suited to the scene in which Taffler throws young Harris's ashes into the Thames, and when Mr. Ross (Bill Hutt) sits down to play "Abide with Me" after his daughter's funeral, an entire period is captured in a few brief moments—a period when such families attended church, sang hymns, played the piano at home, believed in God and that He was on their side during the war, and wore black for months, if not years, after a death in the family.

Before the 1970s were over, however, and before Findley saw the film come to fruition, he had served as chairman of the Writers' Union in 1977–78, been appointed writer-in-residence at the University of Toronto for 1977, and won a senior Canada Council grant in 1978. All these accomplishments pleased him, of course, but his work with the union meant the most. As he told Jane Rule in May 1978, he was relieved to have his term as chairman behind him and deeply honoured to have been chosen to serve.[25] At the annual banquet, which Rule could not attend, he wore his "Jane-coat"—a special present, which she had made for him, that gave him confidence—and, in his 15 May 1978 letter to her, he described sitting with Audrey Thomas, Margaret Laurence, Sylvia Fraser, June Callwood, Leo Simpson, and Bill: "we had a *marvellous* time. So much laughter. Such a sense of good companions" (Rule fonds). Finally, after so many years of work, fear of failure and actual rejection of manuscripts and his first play, lack of recognition from readers and reviewers, and a biting sense of isolation, Timothy Findley had found his professional place in what Margaret Laurence had famously called the Canadian writers' "Tribe." By the end of the decade, CanLit was in the limelight, with Findley a major voice on that stage.

January 1979 began with rehearsals for his new play, *John A.—Himself!*, at the Grand Theatre in London, Ontario. This play grew out of his work on Berton's *National Dream* documentary, but Findley's Macdonald, with white gloves, was far removed from Berton's. The play is part history, part political satire, and part vaudeville, with songs, cross-dressing, and comic spectacle, written for two types of Macdonald: the live actor (William Hutt) and a large puppet/ventriloquist's dummy, used when the prime minister speaks to the press.²⁶ All this theatricality underscores the serious assertion that governing is a constant performance meant to deceive the public, and the hanging of Louis Riel is the grimly serious focal point of the play. Although Bill, Tiff, and Hutt liked the play, Tiff did not enjoy leaving Stone Orchard to attend rehearsals in London. In his journal, he noted his anxiety walking through a London shopping mall, where he feared being attacked as a "queer"; just because he was now a famous, award-winning author he was not immune to society's homophobia or free from his memories of persecution. He lamented, at length, being separated from his home, the animals, and the land: "Stone Orchard has become my life," he wrote, "the air of where I live" (*IM* 103). He desperately missed the comfort of his house, its ghosts, paintings, music, flowers, even its noises and smells. "And when I'm broken off and swept away in the car, the fragmentation is terrible" (*IM* 103).

In addition to beginning work on a new novel, which would become *Famous Last Words*, his play about Macdonald, and segments for a CBC series about immigrants called *Newcomers*, he was increasingly in demand for reviews and readings, forms of literary service that he took seriously. One of these pieces was a review of Farley Mowat's Second World War memoir *And No Birds Sang*, which he described as "profound and wondrous," a reading experience as "compulsive" as a Hitchcock film, that told him a lot about the Italian campaign of 1943–44, when the Allies pushed the Germans north out of the country. By late 1979, Findley's imagination was increasingly consumed with the Second World War and with what Bill Hutt had told him about his experiences during the Italian campaign. Mowat's memoir and Hutt's stories would enrich the context for the narrator/protagonist of *Famous Last Words*, who is caught up in this scramble to escape Italy ahead of Allied troops. At the end of the year he published some autobiographical reflections in *Chatelaine* called "Christmas Remembered," and for Findley that meant the Christmas of 1942, when the war was raging in Europe, his father was in the RCAF and had left home, his parents' marriage was in trouble, and he and Michael "were increasingly left in other people's houses" (43). Here, for the first time, he publicly revealed this traumatic period in his life, that his father had been "seeing another woman" and not sending any money home for his family, and that his mother had been away so much because she was struggling to save her family and win back her husband. The Findleys survived that war, if at considerable cost, and by 1979 Timothy Findley was transforming that cost and those war years into his masterpiece—*Famous Last Words*.

CHAPTER NINE

The Second World War and the Faces of Fascism

———

I WAS STARING, THROUGH PHOTOGRAPHS, INTO THE HEART

OF DACHAU, [AND] IT CANNOT BE TOLD WHAT IT MEANT TO SEE

THOSE PHOTOGRAPHS THAT NIGHT. [...] I WAS LOOKING

INTO HELL—AND HELL WAS REAL.

(Timothy Findley, *Inside Memory* 310)

Famous Last Words

The "golden age of Canadian writing" may have begun in the seventies, but it continued through the eighties and, with the success of *The Wars*, Findley was well positioned to make the contribution he had envisioned for himself back in the 1950s. He was gaining a greater understanding of Canada—its landscapes, history, artists, and cultural institutions—and an increased confidence in his role as a writer with an important voice. Finally, he could see himself, and be seen, as a creative force to be reckoned with, and the 1980s were his most productive and illustrious decade. The issues that concerned him, however, remained constant and grew out of his earlier work and his conviction that twentieth-century violence was an ongoing threat in need of urgent attention. From the moment Allan Findley enlisted with the RCAF, leaving his family to feel like refugees huddled in Grandmother Findley's home during that forlorn Christmas of 1942, the Second World War obsessed Findley. Its impact and significance for history, safety, and world culture were clear to him from his first glimpses of postwar Berlin in the fifties and his discovery of Ivan Moffat's Dachau photographs in 1958.

When he and Bill were contracted by the CBC to prepare the script for a film about Dieppe, his exposure to the specifics of that calamity revived his childhood memories of a Dieppe survivor who had collapsed at the Findley dinner table, and the combination of such memories with work on the film underscored his belief that war was a prime arena for lies, propaganda, and the suppression of historical fact. *Dieppe 1942*, the two-part documentary film based on Bill and Tiff's script and directed by Terence Macartney-Filgate, was broadcast on CBC television on 11 and 12 November 1979. It is a powerful work that does not shrink from exposing the propaganda promulgated by Allied reporters and governments, who loudly proclaimed the raid a success and the hundreds of dead soldiers strewn across the stones, or washed back and forth by the waves, as "heroes." By contrasting archival images of what transpired that day with how it was reported in Canada and England and how it was remembered by survivors, it exposes the shocking discrepancy between actual events and the propagandistic claims of victory and heroism.[1] Findley was deeply angered by what he had learned through his work on this film, and he addressed the catastrophe again in the story "Stones" and in his essay "A Small Town in Normandy," where he insisted that Dieppe "was a callous, brutal waste of youth—a kind of massacre—and it must never be forgotten—or forgiven" (*J* 121). By 1979, however, his attention was increasingly focused on his new novel about the Second World War and on questions raised by the ideology and impact of fascism during that war.

Central to the story he wanted to tell was the problematic figure of an artist who, swayed by this ideology, betrays his ethical responsibilities, his friends, and his country and must then be judged by posterity either as a traitor to be condemned or as an artist to be forgiven for the sake of his art. Findley's model for such an artist was the American poet Ezra Pound

(1885–1972). The dilemma presented by Pound's artistic talent, on the one hand, and his anti-Semitism and pro-Fascist Italian radio broadcasts during the Second World War, on the other, intrigued Findley. How, he wondered, could an artist, who many claimed to be a great poet, say and believe the things he did, and could such a man be forgiven for being a fascist and a traitor because he was an artist? In 1946, after Ezra Pound was declared unfit to stand trial for treason and sent to St. Elizabeths Hospital, some of his friends forgave and supported him; others did not. William Carlos Williams, a friend and a fellow writer, condemned him because he did not believe Pound was insane and felt that he should have been shot for treason: "No one forgives you for what you did," he wrote to Pound, but "everyone forgives you for what you are. [However,] there is a point in all controversy beyond which a man's life (his last card) is necessarily forfeit. A man accepts that and goes on with his eyes open. But when the showdown comes he loses his life" (qtd. in Torrey, 221). As Findley knew, Pound was by no means the only artist of the day to be anti-Semitic, pro-Nazi, or an actual Nazi party member. Klaus Mann's *Mephisto* is based on the true story of his brother-in-law, the actor Gustaf Gründgens, who advanced his career by selling out to the Nazis; Leni Riefenstahl made propaganda films for Hitler; Elisabeth Schwarzkopf, the legendary soprano, was a Nazi party member in the early 1940s; the famous pianist, Alfred Cortot, was a Nazi collaborator and a Vichy supporter; Louis-Ferdinand Céline, considered a major twentieth-century writer, was a virulent anti-Semite who denied the Holocaust, fled France, was tried and convicted *in absentia*, then later was granted amnesty, returned to France, and resumed his career; and the most infamous example is Knut Hamsun, the Norwegian pro-Nazi author who was arrested and convicted of treason after the war. Moreover, in addition to Pound, English-speaking pro-Nazi and fascist sympathizers, with anti-Semitic views, included some of the giants of literary modernism—T. S. Eliot, William Butler Yeats, Wyndham Lewis, and D. H. Lawrence. But Pound held Findley's imagination because he had escaped a trial and punishment on the grounds, which Findley did not accept, of insanity.

In a 1986 interview, Findley told Eugene Benson that he was "a dedicated anti-fascist writer and thinker" (113). When Benson then asked him about the prevalence of violence in his work, and if he was "personally attracted to violence," Findley's response was unequivocal—"No way"—but he went on to explain his position on violence: "I've been affected greatly by violence," he said, the violence of society, the police, and the judiciary system "against my kind" (113). Violence, he told Benson, appalled him, including the violence he acknowledged within himself but that he controlled (most of the time) through his writing, and he added that, in his view, fascism fosters violence by providing both an outlet for human violence and the ideological crutch to support and sanction its use against all those not considered the correct "kind"—that kind being heterosexuals and, in Findley's mind, sexist, masculinist males. He saw fascist thinking, seduction, and behaviour all around him, from the transformation of a young lad who had worked at Stone Orchard before joining the army and had returned for a visit boasting about his capacity to torture or kill those with the wrong views, to Brian Mulroney, then prime minister of Canada, whom he considered a dangerous charmer with fascist leanings and a killer instinct (Gabriel, 1986, 36). Rightly or wrongly, he found fascist tendencies everywhere: "I'm very concerned politically about fascism, fascism as it shows itself in the larger sense [Hitler and Mussolini]. And also in the smaller sense, in the more personal sense in the way one person will attempt to control another person's life, which is another form of fascism" (Hough, 56). He saw it as his task to explore and expose the emotion and the thinking behind the fascist attraction. As he told Barbara Gabriel, *Famous Last Words* confronts the "whole question of how artists [who are thinkers] can ally themselves with the great horrors of their time" (35).

Famous Last Words is a work of fiction on an epic scale. Although *The Wars* remains his most widely read, translated, and loved work, *Famous Last Words* is his most ambitious, complex, yet structurally unified, and challenging novel. Set during the years leading up to and during the Second World War, it nevertheless spoke directly to the 1980s when it was published, and it has not lost its impact and relevance. On the surface, the story is about a small group of people—British, German, American,

Italian, and Spanish (with a Canadian and a Frenchman)—for the most part powerful, wealthy, aristocratic, or high-ranking politicians, many of whom are either Nazis or fascist sympathizers. Their common purpose is to manage the outcome of the war after Germany has defeated Great Britain and seized control of Europe. Among these characters are several historical figures, including the Duke and Duchess of Windsor, Joachim von Ribbentrop, Sir Harry Oakes (the token Canadian connection), Charles Bedaux (the wealthy French-American businessman), Rudolf Hess, Ezra Pound, Charles Lindbergh, and Walter Schellenberg. Introduced into this mix of the famous and infamous are the fictional characters who propel and tell the story. Chief among them are Hugh Selwyn Mauberley (a name Findley borrowed from Pound and a fact I return to), an American novelist and fascist fellow-traveller, and two officers with the US Seventh Army—Captain Freyberg, an intelligence officer and company commander, and Lieutenant Quinn, a demolitions expert. Surrounding these three invented characters and those based on historical people are a number of fictional figures who play minor but important roles: Isabella Loverso, Edward and Diana Allenby, Harry Reinhardt, and Lorenzo de Broca.[2] This is a very large cast of characters, but it is less their number than the way in which they are portrayed as interacting within the fiction that produces the rich complication of the story. Findley deliberately blurs the distinction between the real characters and the fictional ones, between historical facts and invented stories, between so-called truth and lies, and he expects us to suspend our disbelief that Mauberley could know Wallis, the Duchess of Windsor, sit with her at lavish dinners, and be taken into her confidence. We are also asked to listen carefully to Freyberg and Quinn as they argue about the trustworthiness of a writer like Mauberley, whose last words constitute an autobiographical explanation of his life. Freyberg condemns Mauberley as a liar who is trying to excuse his behaviour; Quinn believes Mauberley's story and forgives him. At stake are matters of ethical urgency because, while the multiple stories woven into the narrative overlap and interconnect, they all explore the seductive danger of fascism, the difficulty of winnowing facts from the fragmentary evidence of history, and the enormous challenge faced by anyone who attempts to separate truth from lies or to distinguish fascist traitors from mere bystanders or sympathizers.

The main evidence—Mauberley's life story—is inscribed on the walls of a suite in an abandoned luxury hotel in the Austrian Alps at UnterBalkonberg called the Grand Elysium Hotel, where Mauberley seeks refuge in the spring of 1945. He is hiding there to escape an assassin, who is pursuing him because he knows too much about an Anglo-German cabal and their plot to keep the Duke of Windsor in Europe, and he carries his incriminating notebooks and journals with him. But it is not only secret agents working for the Germans who want to find Mauberley. Along with Ezra Pound, his mentor, he has been denounced as a traitor; if the Americans find him, he will be arrested and tried for treason. His private archive of journals and papers will provide valuable evidence against him and those with whom he associated. Before the American army pushes north into Austria and finds the hotel, however, Mauberley is assassinated by the Nazi hit man Harry Reinhardt, who tracks him down and murders him by driving an ice pick through his eye and into his brain. Then Reinhardt finds Mauberley's journals, notebooks, and letters and burns everything: "The complete destruction of the man [...] and of all his words" (388). Mr. Mauberley, novelist, fascist sympathizer, traitor to his own country and the Allied cause, murderer, and a witness to the wartime machinations of those in power, has been eradicated. Only his gruesome corpse and a bathtub full of ashes remain for the American soldiers to discover when they reach the hotel. Or so it seems, until Lieutenant Quinn, who identifies the dead man as Hugh Selwyn Mauberley, an important artist, discovers Mauberley's writing on the walls. This is what survives of Mauberley's story, his *apologia pro vita sua*, his revelations about the conspiracies and plots of the Anglo-German cabal, and his confession of his role in these clandestine events.

How faithfully the story on the walls represents the information in the burned archive, no one will ever know. It is up to Quinn, Freyberg, and the reader—like the biographer in *The Wars*—to work with the surviving evidence. Mauberley's autobiographical story is his "famous last words," a recounting of his life from 1924 up to the hour of his death in

April 1945. We read this story along with Quinn, who wants desperately to give Mauberley the benefit of the doubt, and with Freyberg, who damns the man and judges his words as an attempt at self-justification and a plea for forgiveness. Readers of the novel receive Mauberley's story partly from Quinn, who is ordered to transcribe it, but also from the frame narrator, who stands back from Mauberley, Quinn, Freyberg, and the wider context of the war and the private lives of many characters and provides information to which Mauberley had no access. It is this narrator who reports on Quinn's and Freyberg's reactions to Mauberley's text and establishes their reasons for thinking as they do. It is also this narrator who supplies some background details about Mauberley's lonely childhood and troubled family, thereby eliciting sympathy for the adult man. If this summary makes the novel sound like a wildly inventive murder mystery set against a backdrop of the Second World War—a sort of *Foyle's War* or a le Carré thriller—it is not. To be sure, it is an enthralling tale of intrigue with multiple assassinations among glamorous elites and aristocratic families, but it seizes our attention less because we want to know whodunit than because we feel compelled to search for answers to disturbing questions. What exactly did Mauberley know? Why did he hang out with the Windsors and become infatuated with the Duchess? When and why did he begin to publish pro-fascist propaganda? Of what use was he to such people as von Ribbentrop or Wallis? And why should his famous last words be trusted? After all, as Quinn reports, Mauberley warned anyone who found his writing on the wall that *"All I have written here is true; except the lies"* (59). And therein rests one of the novel's key challenges—distinguishing truth (however defined) from lies, fact from fiction, when much of what seems outrageous, too far-fetched to be true, is historically accurate.

By the time Findley began work on *Famous Last Words* he had thirty-five years of voracious reading under his belt, and he did extensive research for this novel. He knew where the Duke and Duchess had been and when, and he built the plot line on the foundation of these facts. Where research alone could not fill in the narrative gaps, he relied on his imagination and informed speculation to connect the dots. For example, in the late seventies it was known, if not widely discussed, that the Duke of

Windsor admired Adolf Hitler and agreed with many aspects of Nazi ideology. Coverage of his and Wallis's October 1937 tour of Germany and their meeting with Hitler, which was arranged through the Duke of Coburg, a German relative of the royal family and a Nazi, and the wealthy pro-Nazi industrialist Charles Bedaux, at whose chateau in France the couple was married that summer, was in all the newspapers. Edward was fluent in German and related by blood or marriage to many of the royal houses in Europe; Queen Mary, his mother, was of German parentage. Many of these aristocrats saw Fascism as a bulwark against Communism, held fascist views, or were pro-Nazi and anti-Semitic. Since the publication of *Famous Last Words* in 1981, more historical information has emerged that confirms both the existence of an Anglo-German cabal and the role envisioned for Edward if Hitler won the war.[3] Findley's seemingly exaggerated story about Edward, Wallis, and a cabal of Nazi conspirators working with English collaborators has been proven historically accurate.

Famous Last Words represents four years of drafting and revision, and the genesis of the novel can be followed through thousands of pages preserved in Findley's archive. These include handwritten notes, manuscript fragments, typed pages with annotations and comments, pages of "outs," masses of notes on research, plus annotated photocopies of materials he needed for the history and geography of the story. His copy of William Shirer's *The Rise and Fall of the Third Reich* is falling apart and was clearly read and consulted heavily; his copies of published articles on Sir Harry Oakes reveal his curiosity about the Canadian mining tycoon and his unsolved murder; and he drew extensively on Ralph Martin's 1973 book about the Windsors, with its portrait of a charismatic Wallis, called *The Woman He Loved.*[4] As Findley told Stephen Overbury, he "read all the books [he] could find on the Windsors" to learn more about their connection with Charles Bedaux, but he was cautious: "some books were very sympathetic and others were overly damning. A good researcher has to learn to recognize an author's bias" (61). In a 5 November 1981 letter to Michael and Sally (his brother and sister-in-law), he enclosed a copy of the novel for them and reflected on the fun he had had "with hidden people in the book: some of whom you will recognize—by which I mean, hidden real, historical figures."[5] And he went on to comment on some of the other "obscure, but frightening things [...] that [he] didn't put in the book," such as the Duke of Windsor's visits to Miami, where Charles Bedaux was incarcerated on suspicion of murder. Up to this point, Findley had always incorporated real people in his fiction or drawn upon his family members for certain characters, but in *Famous Last Words* he pushed this strategy much further to complicate the distinctions between truth and lies and illustrate the challenge faced by anyone attempting to understand the nature of truth.

There are many literary and artistic intertexts in the novel, from Ezra Pound's poem *Hugh Selwyn Mauberley* to W. H. Auden's poetry, from biblical quotations to refrains from popular songs and allusions to films of the period. One especially significant reference, however, only shows up in the dedication to the "memory of Thornton Wilder" and in the epigraph quoted from Wilder's novel *The Ides of March*: "one does not know what one knows, or even what one wishes to know, until one is challenged and must lay down a stake." While he was working on *Famous Last Words*, he reread Wilder's novel twice to reflect on his mentor's exploration of the assassination of Julius Caesar. Wilder presents his story through a first-person narrator who has an archive of letters and other documents exchanged among the ruling families of Rome in 45 BC. He calls the group plotting Caesar's overthrow the "Company of Twenty," which includes actual figures, such as Catullus, Brutus, and Cicero, and fictional ones, and this cabal distributes broadsheets across Rome attacking Caesar as a tyrant who must be removed from power. Propaganda, a secret cabal, elite conspirators, preparations for war (in the Roman case, with the Parthians), and an archive of private documents—all these aspects of *The Ides of March* have parallels with *Famous Last Words*. That said, there are significant differences between the two novels. Wilder's Caesar is not a monster like Hitler or Mussolini, and his laws are more just than unjust. Moreover, unlike Wilder, Findley creates an active role for the reader, who is encouraged to take responsibility for weighing the ethical consequences of human actions and for remembering what happened during the Second World War. *Famous Last Words* can be described in many ways—as a historical novel, a murder mystery, a postmodern metafiction, a modernist critique of fascist aesthetics, or a study in human psychology, guilt, and the shared capacity of the human species for evil. But it does not masquerade as an allegory about Fascist Italy set in the distant past; it confronts the recent past to warn against real socio-political threats in the 1980s and the future.

The novel had three different titles during its gestation. Its first was "Alligator Shoes," a reference to the sinister Harry Reinhardt, who survived from the earliest draft—with his alligator-skin shoes—to murder Mauberley in the final text. The next working title was "Fabled Times: A Novel of the 1940s," but from the start Findley knew this title was no more than provisional. By 1980, he had found the right, inevitable title in "Famous Last Words" because he had found the voice and personal-point-of-view character he needed to tell the story-within-the-story: Hugh Selwyn Mauberley, the writer who must die when he has finished his story. Nevertheless, in 1980 Findley was floundering, and he considered abandoning the novel. "Alligator Shoes" was a false start; he cut most of the characters from his original cast and, at his editor, John Pearce's, urging dropped hundreds of pages set in the Bahamas. As the drafts of his fiction show, Findley often faced this kind of problem because by trying to incorporate so many minor characters, each with a separate story, into a novel, he lost his focus and then struggled to find the narrative structure he needed to control the remaining material. "Fabled Times" was a weak hook on which to hang such a serious story, and his journals and notebooks from these years show how frustrated he was: "Against despair" comes up repeatedly on journal covers, on the first pages of notebooks, and on his personal calendars.

Although Findley had read Pound's poetry, including *Hugh Selwyn Mauberley*, he did not make the connection between Pound, this poem with its figure of the failed artist, and his novel until late in its development. Notes held in the Clarke, Irwin fonds (B 24-F4), illustrate his struggle to develop his ideas effectively and some aspects of John Pearce's effort to assist Findley at this stage in the drafting. The character of Mauberley was the problem. Among other things, Pearce suggested that he "re-work" and enhance Mauberley's first-person voice and develop his interaction with Reinhardt. He also asked Findley to be clear about Mauberley's notebooks: has Mauberley preserved all of them? Does Reinhardt burn all of them? But Findley grew increasingly frustrated with the pressure to produce a revised manuscript quickly, and at one point he yelled at Pearce that he could not be expected to produce as fast as Mozart. Pearce then gave a copy of his suggestions to Bill Clarke, Findley's publisher, who had become concerned about delays in completing the novel, and, after reading the 1981 draft, Clarke flew to Maine to discuss the book's progress with Findley at the Atlantic House hotel. As Clarke recalled, he found Findley very discouraged, but he made suggestions, reacted to Findley's responses, and boosted his confidence in the work; by the time he left, Clarke told me, Findley was "all energy and no hesitation."

Findley proceeded to compile a list of things he still needed to develop, and chief among these was his character of Mauberley. He realized that he had "failed to fully 'see' the character" and only gradually understood what he wanted to convey. His Mauberley "is not ... a greatly successful writer (as I had thought at first) like Maugham—but a writer of initial genius which he fails to realize" (Clarke, Irwin fonds 24-4). Apart from Mauberley's novels, "Crowd Invisible" and "Stone Dogs," "the rest of his work is muddied with 'pronouncements' and politics and 'crowd pleasing.'" He is not wealthy but lives on some money inherited from his mother and plays the role of the "man in the white suit"; he is a "penny-pincher," who spends money to advance his "performance." He survives by cultivating the rich and "battens on the Ezras and the Eliots of this world." Most important for Findley was his realization that Mauberley "is definitely *not* a great writer and knows it." His sole claim to "stature as an artist" is what he writes on the Grand Elysium's walls; only his last words deserve to be read and taken seriously. Aspects of what he writes echo Pound's critical self-portrait in *Hugh Selwyn Mauberley* insofar as the young Pound, like the poem's Hugh Selwyn Mauberley and Findley's Mauberley, was "out of key with his time" and unmoved by "the march of events."[6] Findley's character shows comparatively little interest in the tragedy of the Great War, when a generation "walked eye-deep in hell" believing "old men's lies," behaviour Pound criticizes in his poem. Pound creates a bitterly sarcastic portrait of his younger self in his Mauberley, who is a failure, unable to respond to "current exacerbations" and capable only of "maudlin confession" (Pound 131–32). His epitaph is pathetic: "I was / And I no more exist; / Here drifted / An hedonist" (133). The Mauberley of *Famous Last Words* is more complex and manipulative than the man Pound consigns to oblivion, and much more important. To dismiss him as merely a hedonist, a hanger-on, and a third-rate writer, is to miss Findley's point. Once he found Mauberley's voice and renewed his confidence in his work-in-progress, he moved ahead quickly to create a writer who realized his crimes and endured suffering and isolation long enough to prepare his last words and leave them where they could be found after he and his archive had been destroyed. Then he accepted the fact, as Williams said Pound should have, that his life was "necessarily forfeit."

To carry him through the final moments of his writing and his life, Mauberley listened to Schubert's Sonata in B-flat Major, D 960, the composer's last work, because "Schubert's 'last words' would do very nicely. This, after all, was Schubert's country—not only the place, but the ending of things" (385). *Things.* Vienna, where Schubert died; Austria, which lost its empire and its glory after the First World War, and then succumbed to (many would say welcomed) Hitler's Anschluss in March 1938. With the war over, Mauberley knew the American army was moving north into the mountains. Germany, and with it Austria, had lost, and the atrocities committed by the Nazis in places like Auschwitz and Dachau were finished. It would not be long before he was discovered and arrested, and he wanted to add an epilogue to his story. While writing he listened to Schubert's "perfect music, played by the perfect fingers of Alfred Cortot. [...] Schubert's last words—endings" (386), and the last movement ended as Mauberley concluded his epilogue with his warning to the future that something "*from the other side of reason*" lies out there in the sea, waiting. The epilogue completed, he left the rooms with his story on their walls and returned to his own rooms. There, Harry Reinhardt was waiting for him with the ice pick.

Findley chose this music and the pianist who performs it with care. The Swiss-French pianist Alfred Cortot (1877–1962) had an international reputation before the war, but during it he was a collaborator who held important positions in Pétain's Vichy France, played at the 1942 exhibition of Nazi artist Arno Breker, and toured Germany with the Berlin Philharmonic. He was arrested on 2 September 1944 but was released after pleading that he had devoted his life to French music, and he moved to Switzerland to escape the recriminations of the French. By 1949 he was welcomed back to continue his career. He was, in short, forgiven. The curious aspect of Findley's combination of the Schubert with Cortot is that there is no mention of Cortot recording the B-flat Major sonata in his extensive discography. It seems that Findley deliberately connected the artist-collaborator and anti-Semite with the sonata. In 1945 Mauberley could not have known that the great Cortot played such an infamous role during the war or that he would be rehabilitated after it because he was an artist. But Findley must have been aware of the man's past and may even have attended a Cortot recital in London in the 1950s. Given the horrors perpetrated by the Nazis in the quest for perfection, the irony of Mauberley describing Cortot's "perfect fingers [making their] perfect impact" (386)—Cortot was known for making many mistakes with his fingering—is profound. It reverberates back through the novel to Freyberg and Quinn's earlier argument about Mauberley (155), when Freyberg broke the record in two to stress his suspicion that Mauberley wrote only half of the truth on the walls, and forward to Quinn's saving "the two dusty halves of the Alfred Cortot recording of the Schubert Sonata" at the end (394).

There are many ways to approach the narrative and ethical challenges of *Famous Last Words*, all of them valid and rewarding.[7] The last Schubert sonata is a productive one, however, because of its strategic role and because Findley's love and knowledge of classical music are beyond question; like Mauberley, he often played his records at night while he was writing. Most forms of music pleased him, but classical music influenced the rhythms of his prose and the structure of his narratives, and it provided a rich source of image and allusion in his work. The Schubert sonata haunts the entire novel, both the narrative frame and Mauberley's testimony. It functions as a persistent reminder of the beauty of art and its danger, when linked with the pursuit of perfection, which is another name in Findley's lexicon for evil and madness. By returning to Cortot's perfect fingers performing the sonata as the novel closes, Findley reinforced this thematic through-line across narrative time and space and connected his three protagonists. Mauberley chose this recording of the last sonata; Freyberg listened to and then broke the record to make his point about art and deception, or half-told stories; and Quinn, sentimental to the end, kept both halves of the record, along with Mauberley's scarf, when the army vacated the hotel.

Freyberg also has a collection of memento mori to weigh in the balance with Quinn's keepsakes, but Freyberg's archive explains why he is obsessed with remembering and unable to trust or forgive people like Mauberley. Freyberg and Quinn were with the American army that liberated Dachau. Both were appalled, but for Freyberg the experience was shattering. As an intelligence officer, his job was to take photographs, make lists, and gather evidence, but the horror of what he saw and documented in Dachau led him to assemble an archive of this evidence so that what took place there could never be forgotten. In their final confrontation, Freyberg forces Quinn to scrutinize the pictures, and the effort nearly breaks Quinn, who insists that he does not need to look at these images of torture, burned corpses, and starved children to remember what he saw because he can still see them in his mind. "But do you remember?" Freyberg demands. "Remember?" "But do you remember it?" Finally, Quinn screams, "YES! [...] Yes, God damn you" (391). In the face of such atrocity, however, it is easier to forget, to move on, to rationalize, even to forgive, and Quinn, unlike Freyberg, finds extenuating circumstances for Mauberley, wants to forgive him, and, above all, wants to let go of the trauma of Dachau. Mauberley's scarf and the broken Cortot recording of Schubert's sonata are his trophies, his private talismans of artistic value.

No narrator in *Famous Last Words* tells the reader how to interpret the symbol of the broken record or weigh the comparative evidence in these officers' collections, but Timothy Findley had seen Ivan Moffat's photographs of Dachau after the liberation. Like Freyberg, Moffat, an official army photographer, had to gather evidence for use in the Nuremberg trials. Like Freyberg, he had kept an archive, and for Findley these photographs were proof of human evil beyond anything he could believe. Echoing Conrad's *Heart of Darkness*, he described seeing Moffat's photographs as "staring [...] into the heart of Dachau": "I was looking into hell—and hell was real. [...] I never recovered from what I saw that night" (*IM* 310–11). He realized that part of his epiphany on seeing Moffat's photographs meant accepting that each of us is responsible for violence and evil, that "we are all a collective hiding place for monsters" because we are all part of the human race (*IM* 311). But in *Inside Memory*, he went further to insist upon mourning death and celebrating life. "How can monsters bring white flowers to Dachau?" he asked. "Because, in spite of our complicity, we must. Or there will be no reconciliation" (312).

Famous Last Words is Findley's offering of white flowers and reconciliation. In many respects, Freyberg's response to Dachau reflects his own: we must remember and never be too quick to forgive. But Quinn's response also has merit because Mauberley's story can be interpreted as bringing white flowers of grief and mourning to Dachau, to the war, and to his own complicity with fascism and atrocity. Although Mauberley struggled against Reinhardt in the hope that he would not be slaughtered, "death itself was welcome" (387). He was ready to pay the price of his sins—unlike Ezra Pound. He admitted that he too was "a hiding place for monsters," and he achieved a degree of reconciliation with his own nature and guilt by bearing witness. Through this novel, which means through an examination of both sides of the ethical argument represented by Freyberg and Quinn and through careful reflection on Mauberley's confession, Timothy Findley, the artist, asks us not only to not forget humanity's evil, destructive past, but also to preserve the broken record as a symbol of creative promise, whether or not we are able to forgive.

The phrase "famous last words" can express many things, from disbelief, rejection, or error, to a warning about impending disaster, and there are several portentous warnings in the novel. The most significant of them is a scene that connects the title of the novel with Mauberley's autobiography and the Book of Daniel. On 4 July 1941, Findley has his young Italian poet, Lorenzo de Broca, fly over Nassau in a small plane to drop a "blizzard" of bright green papers onto the crowd of five hundred leading members of Bahamian society who have gathered on the lawns of the government mansion where the Duke and Duchess are celebrating her renovations in an extravagant garden party. The message on these papers is brutally direct: "DEATH TO FASCISTS EVERYWHERE!" (285). While these fall to the ground, alarming the guests, the plane writes a message across the sky in inky smoke: *"mene mene tekel upharsin,"* which is "the ultimate graffiti ... *thou art weighed in the balance—and found wanting"* (287). Mauberley also inscribes this warning from the Book of Daniel (5:25) in capital letters on the hotel room's walls as one of two epigraphs to his story: "IN THIS SAME HOUR CAME FORTH FINGERS OF A MAN'S HAND, AND WROTE [...] UPON THE PLAISTER OF THE WALL ..." (52). His second epigraph, *"All I have written here is true; except the lies,"* is also a warning, "like a bear trap to catch the reader unaware" (59), because, as Freyberg maintains, Mauberley may well be lying to us and he is by no means a god with the divine right to judge others. Nevertheless, Mauberley's citation of Daniel is chilling; it testifies to his self-judgment while alerting us of the need to examine our own consciences because one day we too may be found wanting.

Mauberley leaves one further warning on the walls and one more way to interpret his last words. In 1938, in a bombing raid during the Spanish Civil War, he and Isabella Loverso took refuge in the caves of Altamira, where Mauberley saw the paintings and handprints of humans from the Upper Paleolithic Period. He read these images as messages from the past affirming the longevity of individual human identity and artistic imagination. Today these caves are closed to the public, but they exist outside the novel and are one of the fictional world's many intersections with external reality. Back inside the story-within-the-story of *Famous Last Words*, Mauberley has drawn birds, stars, and animals on the ceiling, and he has traced his own hand with candle smoke (51), as if to say: this is my final signature, the real me as creator of these words, and my proof of connection with the human race. Whether or not we agree with Mauberley's understanding of Altamira, Findley did. He often recited this passage from *Famous Last Words* to conclude his public readings, and he chose this description of the caves as one of his endings for *Inside Memory* because it represented, for him, the "final hours" of prehistoric people and a warning to all who come after of their impending demise. This warning, then, is not from a god or from a fanatical anti-fascist like Lorenzo de Broca, but from the long distant past of human existence. This writing on the walls speaks, or so Findley wants us to believe, as one human being to another across millennia and urges us to remember the past and cherish human imagination. Mauberley's imitation of the signs at Altamira doesn't ask us to forgive Mauberley; rather, it asks us to reflect on our capacity for violence and evil, our pride and weakness, our lies and submission to power—and also our shared humanity, our creative potential, our ability to think and imagine a better world.

Famous Last Words was launched on 22 October 1981 and Findley read from it at Harbourfront's International Festival of Authors in Toronto that evening. Allan Findley was too ill to attend, but he wrote, in what was his last letter to his son, that "it is not every father who can call his son a genius," and he called the novel "another masterpiece" (LAC 96:6). In his review for the *Toronto Star*, Bruce Blackadar described the novel as having "sweeping historical insights, grand ironies, and enough riveting scenes to fill more than a few movies." Then he asked Findley about his Mauberley character. "Mauberley is in everyone," Findley replied; "we're all fascists [and] I needed to find out why people like Mauberley needed to be so repressive." By December the novel was on the *Toronto Star* bestseller list, and he noted on his calendar that this was the first time a first edition of his work had been so successful; he was "very pleased" (LAC 89:6). The most thoughtful of the novel's reviews, however, was by Keith Garebian, who maintained that, despite the central position of Mauberley, the novel's chief concern was with "the sense of history as theatre" (93–94). And he had a point. From slight touches, as when Quinn puts a match "in his upstage pocket" (*FLW* 45), to the extended metaphor of life as a performance by both Wallis and Mauberley, *Famous Last Words* builds from one dramatic scene to the next and turns the reader into an audience member who shares the stage of history with the rest of the cast.

Despite this glowing reception in Canada, the publication of *Famous Last Words* was not without its disappointments and problems. The novel should have been considered for a Governor General's Award, but Findley refused to submit it because he had accepted the invitation to sit on the jury and would be in a conflict of interest. John Pearce has told me that he tried to change Findley's mind but that Findley could not "face the nervous strain" of waiting for a decision. It is even more likely that he could not face the risk of failure because to fail was one of his most deep-seated fears. Then Peggy Fox, associate editor with New Directions Publishing Corporation (the Trustees of the Ezra Pound Literary Property Trust), wrote in 1982 to draw his attention to a mistake in his final summation of the lives of the real figures in the novel. He had written that Pound was tried and convicted, and she asked him to correct this factual error in reprints or new editions of the book. Her letter is both generous and positive; she had read *Famous Last Words* "with a great deal of pleasure" and was not threatening him in any way, but Findley was mortified. He replied immediately to assure her that all forthcoming printings in Canada and the United States would be corrected. Worse still, no publisher in the UK would touch the book until after the Duchess of Windsor had died, and Nancy Colbert had to arrange for author's insurance to protect the American publisher, Delacorte Press, and Findley against a possible libel suit.

Timothy Findley had high hopes for this novel, believing it would establish him as a major writer on the international scene, which it should have done. When *Famous Last Words* was finally released in the UK in 1987 after Wallis had died, however, the reviews were so vicious that he and Bill, who had gone to London for the occasion, withdrew to France, where Findley consoled himself with a few days at Dieppe. He and his publisher (Macmillan) were accused of "cashing in" on the Duchess and "waiting like vultures" for her death. Who was this "overpraised" colonial anyway? His words would have been "better left unspoken." The respected critic and Pound expert Frank Kermode dismissed the novel as "pure tosh," worthy of nothing more than a "tin wreath" (qtd. in Adachi, 1987). Findley was deeply hurt and embarrassed by this public rejection, as much for old friends like Alec Guinness and Alec McCowen, as for himself.

None of these loud negative reviewers had paid any attention to the novel as a serious work of art. When his adaptation of *Famous Last Words* was produced for CBC radio's *Sunday Matinee* during January and February of 1988, however, reviewers were enthusiastic. Directed and produced by Damiano Pietropaolo, with music by Dennis Patrick, both Findley's adaptation and the production were praised as a "soaring drama" that should be "required listening" (Robert Crew), and Findley won an ACTRA Award for best writer. Steven Bush, who played Freyberg, told me that in the process of reworking the novel for this radio script, Findley said he had come to sympathize more with Freyberg than when he wrote the novel. He wanted Freyberg's voice, his warning, and his judgment of history to be heard and remembered.[8]

Not Wanted on the Voyage

By the end of 1981, *Famous Last Words* had won Findley great praise at home; his next novel, the "Cat Story" (*Not Wanted on the Voyage*), was already underway; and he had a contract with Clarke, Irwin to publish it. Many accolades followed: his first honorary doctorate in 1982 from Trent University, where Margaret Laurence was chancellor, had special meaning for him. In 1983 he won another Canada Council grant, which freed his time for the final work on *Not Wanted on the Voyage*. In 1984 he was named Author of the Year by the Canadian Booksellers Association, awarded another LLD (from the University of Guelph) and published both *Not Wanted on the Voyage* and a collection of stories, *Dinner Along the Amazon*. All this professional success, however, did not bring him peace of mind. Things were not going well on the personal front, and by 1983 he had entered another period of depression, of regular sessions with Ed Turner, of increased medication and heavy drinking. His relations with Bill, who had retired from the CBC to help full-time with Findley's career and run Pebble Productions, the company they set up to manage their finances, were strained; Bill had to adjust to his new routine, and several events precipitated Findley's personal crisis. His beloved Mottle had died;

a few months later his father died; the filming of *The Wars* (described in chapter 8) caused frustration and disappointment; the subject of his new novel disturbed him; he and Bill could just get by on Findley's royalties and they were nearly broke; and he lost the Canadian publisher who had championed him and on whom he had relied for six years.

When Mottle died on 14 October 1981, Findley was heartbroken. As was his habit when someone he cared about or one of his closest animal companions died, he would print their names in large letters with black ink and a cross beside the date in his calendar. Allan Findley's death on 6 January 1982 was a much more complicated matter. Findley's calendar entries for the week of January 4 speak volumes:

> Monday the 4th: *Dad* in dreadful shape. Two tumors—one in lung—and one on neck. I am trying to clean up work room. *Can't.*
> Tuesday the 5th: *WFW* [Bill] home—both in low spirits.
> Wednesday the 6th–Thursday the 7th: MY FATHER HAS DIED. IN THE NIGHT. ✚ HE WAS IN HIS EIGHTIETH YEAR. *WFW* drove me to Toronto in dark. We stay with *Mother.* [...]
> Yesterday we visited the Mausoleum/Crematorium and looked at Chapel. Sad. *Numb.* [...] Sad, sad day & last night I did not sleep.
> Friday the 8th: *Father's Funeral.* [...] Over a hundred people. Minister dreadful—syrupy. [...] Reception went well. Then *WFW* & self home.
> (LAC 89:6)

The only entry for each of the next three days is *"Drinking."* On January 12 he wrote: "stopped drinking fear dreadful."

He had little time to mourn because the next several months were booked solid: there was a promotion tour for *Famous Last Words* and reading engagements, one of which was at St. Andrew's College, where he was warmly welcomed and read from *The Wars* and *The Last of the Crazy People*. Crises with the filming of *The Wars* distracted him, as did the planning for a CBC series about the War of 1812, numerous interviews, a seminar on Canadian fiction and film at McMaster University at which he gave the after-dinner speech, and several short writing projects.[9] One of these projects began as a speech on censorship at the 1983 annual banquet of the Ontario Association of Teachers of English in which he compared Hitler's persecution of the Jews to contemporary racism, the banning of books, and pornography ("Censorship by Every Other Name"). Another was his 12 November 1983 address at Conrad Grebel University College at the University of Waterloo called "Artists: Prisoners of Conscience"; this time he spoke about repressive governments and the work of Amnesty International. Both talks explored issues of contemporary violence and oppression that harkened back to *Famous Last Words* and motivated his thinking in *Not Wanted on the Voyage*. As if he did not have enough on his mind during this time, his mother was diagnosed with bowel cancer and had emergency surgery (successful); Glenn Gould died (a keen personal blow for Tiff); Bill's close friend, Jim Lumley, died in a car accident; and June Callwood's son was killed by a drunk driver. His own health began to suffer from the constant personal strain, increasing back problems, excessive drinking, and anxiety. He was fifty-two, writing a book that was emotionally draining and, for the first time in his life, dangerously close to a state of exhaustion. "Horrendously tired," he noted on January 26; "We are now living through 18 or 20 hour days" (LAC 123:4).

To make matters worse, he lost his trusted publisher Bill Clarke. In the late sixties, when the Ontario government relaxed the rules on how school boards spent their money and on which books they could buy, Clarke, Irwin and Company had lost much of its main source of income and was forced to reduce its staff. It became dependent on a government loan guarantee program, and by 1983 their debt to this program, established as a temporary fund to assist struggling publishers, was $1.5 million (about 3.4 million in 2018 dollars). The Ontario government rejected their request for more time to recover their losses or for further financial support, and the company was forced into receivership. Having the high-profile Timothy Findley and the popular detective-novel writer Howard Engel among their authors was not enough to save the company. John Irwin Jr. purchased a majority of Clarke, Irwin's inventory for the Book Society of Canada, which left authors who had been loyal to Bill Clarke with no choice but to move on.

It was at this point, in 1983, that Findley shifted to Penguin Canada, but not before protesting loudly and publicly over Clarke, Irwin's fate. He organized a letter, dated 13 May 1983, that he sent to William Davis, the premier of Ontario, urging the government to "preserve the Canadian integrity of Clarke, Irwin." Signed by himself for Margaret Atwood, Pierre Berton, June Callwood, Matt Cohen, Marian Engel, Graeme Gibson, William Kilbourn, Margaret Laurence, Dennis Lee, W. O. Mitchell, Farley Mowat, Al Purdy, and Charles Taylor, this appeal, which fell on deaf ears, is worth quoting at length:

> On Friday, May 13th … we were suddenly made aware that Clarke, Irwin is in imminent danger of completely disappearing as an independent Canadian publishing enterprise. We are shocked and alarmed to hear this news because we believe it is essential that your Government maintain its commitment not only to Clarke, Irwin but to the concept of Canadians publishing for Canadians.
>
> We take pride, as writers, in all our presently remaining Canadian publishing houses, whether large or small. Clarke, Irwin is among the pre-eminent and internationally recognized names in the publishing industry and is identified with essential and important publishing accomplishments in this country—in particular those that deal with the education, history and creative representation of our people. (W. O. Mitchell fonds, 679/00.10, 7-22)

At stake was much more than one publisher. Most of the co-supporters were not Clarke, Irwin authors, but as the next few decades proved, their shared concern for the future of Canadian publishing was well placed.[10]

Despite Findley's strong personal loyalty to Bill Clarke, Nancy Colbert's job was to look out for his best interests, both financial and literary. After John Irwin's Book Society of Canada (soon renamed Irwin Publishing) bought up the major portion of Clarke, Irwin, it made an effort to keep Findley. In September of 1983, John Pearce, now the editorial director with Irwin, replied to Colbert's request for a release from the contract Findley had signed for his next novel, the "Cat Story," with the return of the

$3,000 signing advance (about $7,100 in 2020 dollars) that Findley had received. Pearce agreed to do this, but then he made a strong pitch to be Findley's Canadian publisher. He offered a more generous advance and promised a three-week tour to promote the book, and he assured her that the Book Society of Canada believed that Penguin Canada was the right publisher, but only for paperback rights. A continuing relationship with Pearce and Clarke, Irwin through Irwin Publishing, however, was not in the cards. Other publishers (Jack McClelland and Louise Dennys, for example) approached Findley directly; they praised his work and told him how "honoured" and "delighted" they would be if he came to them. Bill and Tiff replied carefully but left negotiations to Colbert.[11] *Not Wanted on the Voyage* would be published by Penguin.

His 1983 calendar is mostly empty except for his appointments with Ed Turner, but his journal bears eloquent witness to his inner turmoil. The first page has a decorative label with poppies and his name, but above this he printed "Against Despair" (LAC 123:4). Although the journal is marked for 1983, he devoted much of it to reviewing 1982 and several pages to the repercussions from Allan's death in January. "I don't think I have come to terms with dad's death even now," he wrote, but it was his father's negative influence on him that he would not confront for many years. He described his disgust with Michael, who left him to "cope alone" with the funeral and disappeared "into a bottle of private reactions," and he realized that he had had no "room" to grieve, "so I haven't caught up with it." There had been a disturbing family dispute about where Allan's ashes should rest. Allan's sister, Tiff's Aunt Marg, wanted them placed in the Mount Pleasant Cemetery plot beside their brother, Irving, but Tiff and his mother had other plans. Although Allan Findley's name appears on the plot marker, Tiff had replaced the ashes with sand so he could scatter some of the ashes at Stone Orchard, and he carried the rest to a place Allan had loved from childhood—the Atlantic House hotel in Maine. On "Friday, August 27th [1982]," he recorded in his 1983 journal that he had "scattered father's remaining ashes in the ocean" (LAC 123:4). Bill captured this moment on camera, but the photograph he showed me is blurred and grainy and I could just make out the figure of a man standing knee deep in the water with one arm extended. This scattering of ashes off the hotel's beach was of more than passing importance to Findley. It was symbolic, a ritual performed because his father had requested it and because only Tiff, the son with whom he had bitterly disagreed for years, would carry out the request. Allan's death, distressing as it was, was not unexpected, and over the last two years of his life he had reached out to Tiff, praised him, and reassured him of his love and admiration—the very things Findley had longed for from his youth. Although his lifelong addiction to alcohol, exacerbated by the Parkinson's disease, led to gangrene and extreme pain over the many months he spent in and out of Sunnybrook Hospital, Allan died with dignity, patience, and a humility that Findley respected.

Eventually Findley recreated this father-son relationship in the story "Stones" and then in *You Went Away*, but privately he remembered and struggled to forgive the person in his life who had caused him the greatest anger and most persistent pain. His capacity to forgive came through a deeper understanding of Allan, which he reached in part by writing about his father and in part through contemplating his father's "emblems"— Allan's RCAF identity disc and his miniature football from the SAC championship game of 1921, in which, Findley noted, he had "played a starring role" (LAC 276:1). Mixed in with his notes and early drafts for *Pilgrim*, which he was working on in the mid-1990s, is a single, undated page, marked with an asterisk, which reveals how profoundly this relationship haunted him. He kept his father's "emblems" hanging above his desk, where he saw them every time he sat down to work. As he contemplated these simple objects, he realized that they had mattered to his father: "I hated the war and I hated football—but it mattered to him that he was able to take part in a war, as Tif [Allan's brother, and Findley's uncle, Irving] had done—and it mattered that he was a supreme (which he was) player of the game." Then Findley acknowledged that his opinions were irrelevant, that he had "no right to judge" because "it was his [father's] life." Regret followed quickly upon this thought when he wished he had been able "to *say* this—and to ask his understanding" (LAC 276:1). In a scrawled line at the bottom of this loose page Findley wrote: "At least—in the end—we spoke & settled."

Glenn Gould's death on 2 October 1982, after a massive stroke, was a shock to all Canadians and to his fans around the world. He had lived a reclusive life in his latter years, so Findley had been deeply honoured when Gould agreed to work on the film of *The Wars* and was greatly saddened that he had not lived to see its completion in 1983. At Gould's memorial service, held in St. Paul's Anglican Church on Bloor Street, Maureen Forrester sang from the St. Matthew Passion, then the mourners stood and "shouted hymns." When silence fell, Findley recalled that "hundreds of us, each one sitting alone—heard the first painfully haunting notes of the *Aria da capo*, the melody from which Johann Sebastian Bach extrapolated The Goldberg Variations" ("The Gould Standard" 72). It was, of course, Gould playing, and his familiar "humming gave him away." Timothy Findley wept at Gould's memorial. For him it marked another dark time in a period of loss. When he moved out of Stone Orchard and across the road to Sprucevale in January of 1984 to work on *Not Wanted on the Voyage*, he took all his Gould recordings of Bach with him. The hymns he had sung at Gould's service, and several selected by Gould for the film, would surface in the new novel when Mrs. Noyes and her sheep sing forth their joy and praise—at least until such singing ceases forever. When Findley wrote to Ed Turner later that year (27 September 1984) he confessed that "since last January [...] I feel as if I have been putting everything down in a pit somewhere—like atomic waste—and that it is beginning to make strange noises: warnings" (LAC 106:11). Warnings indeed. Turner saw Findley on October 30 (his forty-fourth birthday and a date he associated with his father's absence during the war), so this warning prepared the doctor to find Findley in a state of deep distress because of his unresolved feelings about Allan's death and his trepidation over the challenge he faced with his new novel.

Findley said that in *Not Wanted on the Voyage* he saw this world becoming a concentration camp because human beings confine what is useful to them and destroy everything else. The "cat story," however, did not begin as a damnation of the Old Testament or of twentieth-century society. In its early version, Findley created a farming story inspired by a local Cannington family in which the farmer was abusive and his wife, a decent soul, liked gin and played the piano. For his story he gave the wife a blind cat and subjected the couple and their neighbours to the kind of blizzard often experienced in farming communities around Stone Orchard. But then he stalled. This story was going nowhere, and he resorted to decorating his early drafts with coloured pictures of cats and flowers. He wanted to create a happy ending in which the farm family came together again, but the words refused to come. Then, in May 1983, he heard Phyllis Webb read her poem "Leaning" at a gathering of writers, and Bill recalled Tiff telling him that "the whole book fell, all at once, into his mind [and] the blizzard was transformed into the Flood—with the wife and her blind cat representing the better half of human attitudes to the rest of this planet's inhabitants." In the poem, the poet is caught half-way up the Leaning Tower of Pisa and the reader is there with her, along with "smelly tourists." Why should anyone "ever come down," the poet asks? Then, in the final three lines, come the words that inspired Findley: "And you, are you still here / tilting in this stranded ark / blind and seeing in the dark" (58–59). Because "she had used the words *ark* and *blind* and *dark*," Findley later explained, "I knew who all my people were and what their predicament was" (*IM* 220). He saw the "whole of modern civilization crowding into" the Tower of Pisa (*IM* 219), and so it is with *Not Wanted on the Voyage*, except that only those creatures permitted by Yaweh's divine fiat and Noah's earthly tyranny are allowed into the ark. The rest of creation is not wanted and drowns.

Over the twenty years since they had first met, he and Phyllis Webb had become good friends. He shared her interest in symbols of the imagination, like the unicorn, and he read and enjoyed her poetry. His letters to her, especially between the fall of 1981 and the fall of 1984, shed considerable light on his state of mind as he searched for a way to channel his anger into the writing of this new novel, which refused to be more optimistic than his last. By February of 1983, he told her, the unicorns of his own imagination had still not shown up and he was deeply depressed.[12] His journal entries for January and February 1984 reveal his reactions to what he was creating. His drinking had increased. He would call Phyllis at three a.m. (midnight on the West Coast) protesting that he "hated" the book and Noah. He would go to Bill and tell him he could not write this book. Both of them understood his panic and urged him not to stop writing. In a "pep-talk" to himself, he said that he had "absolutely no justification" for retelling the Great Flood story unless he could "tell" something new, which he ultimately did (*IM* 222). Bill had bought him a stuffed toy unicorn for encouragement, and Findley settled on his title after Bill suggested the label used on luggage not needed on a sea voyage—"not wanted on voyage"—by adding "the" to achieve the right rhythm. Then, on July 30, he wrote to Phyllis, his "Dear Lady P," to announce that the book was finished, copy-edited, revised, and ready to go. For the epigraph he chose those last three lines of "Leaning" and asked for her permission to use them. Writing this novel, he declared, had changed him, and by the end he had become "deeply involved and attached to *all*" the characters. Gradually, his dreams grew peaceful once more and he stopped waking up weeping.

To help Findley get through the ordeal of writing this book, Dr. Turner had put him on a controlled regimen of Antabuse, painkillers for a shoulder problem, and sedatives to help with depression. The move, in January 1984, across the road to Arkwright (Sprucevale) with its blue barn also helped; in fact, it was essential. Although they had to remortgage the farm to manage the expense, extensive renovations were underway at Stone Orchard to create, among other things, a new study and bedroom for Findley. Typically, he planned this relocation with care, making lists and sketches showing where everything, right down to towels and toiletries, must go. Several hundred books went with him—all his books about the North and Canadian history, three shelves of criticism, the plays of Shakespeare, Shaw, Chekhov, Pinter, Bond, Albee, Tennessee Williams, Wilder, and some Greek plays. Both his Oxford and Canadian English dictionaries accompanied him, as did volumes of poetry by twenty-six poets (many of them Canadian), and dozens of novels and story collections (Atwood, Cheever, Conrad, Davies, Engel, Hodgins, Munro, and Woolf among them). He spent a night in the barn with the animals to experience the darkness and their noises and then settled in to work. For their holiday in 1985, he and Bill took a long road trip and visited Saltspring Island, where

Phyllis Webb was living and where they spent several idyllic weeks. This time away was restorative, and despite the work, deadlines, pressures, and his bouts of panic and depression over *Not Wanted on the Voyage*, he persisted and moved back into his new space at Stone Orchard in the fall of 1986 with a completed novel.

Not Wanted on the Voyage is a fable for our times that retells biblical myth by bringing it down to earth. It is a tall tale full of fantasy and spectacle, with animals that talk to each other, sheep that sing, a drag queen called Lucy, and a Yaweh who is dying. There are dragons and unicorns in the woods, but the only miracles are cheap magician's tricks performed by Noah to amuse his God. It is the penny and bottle trick that gives the dull-witted Yaweh his idea for a flood (95–96) because a penny placed under a bottle seems to disappear when the bottle is filled with water.[13] The novel is a far cry from the historical fact and plausible reality of *Famous Last Words*, and yet the world of *Not Wanted on the Voyage* is familiar. Violence, deception, war, and a patriarchal thirst for absolute power over women, children, animals, and nature are prevalent in Western culture, and have been so from the time of the ancient Greeks to today, with roots in aspects of human nature that Findley vehemently rejected. Where Margaret Atwood located oppression and sexism in the future with *The Handmaid's Tale* (1985), and Yann Martel later imagined a present-day animal holocaust in *Beatrice and Virgil* (2010), Findley used the mythic past to throw light on present concerns about environmental degradation, prejudice, and religious terrorism.

Reality, then, is never far from the surface in such texts, and in *Not Wanted on the Voyage* it emerges in the dedication: "FOR THESE ESPE-CIALLY Mottle and Boy; Maggie and Hooker—and the horses who shared the days. And for The Two Hundred. *Against Despair.*" These are two beloved cats, two beloved dogs, and the Stone Orchard horses. The "two hundred" are some of the horses sacrificed to man's greed during the 1898 Yukon gold rush; Findley did not forget their small graveyard beside the White Horse Pass. *Not Wanted on the Voyage* was his labour of writing against despair over man's inhumanity to man and all life besides. This novel is not only about inhumanity, however; there is much love, generosity, humour, and kindness portrayed in its pages. Mrs. Noyes is a wonderful character, one of Findley's most endearing, feisty, big-hearted women. Mottyl, her blind cat, is a delightful creation, but she is also a realist; mice exist to be hunted and eaten, going into heat (against one's wishes) must be endured, kittens are a blessing to be kept away from Noah Noyes's experiments, and Mrs. Noyes is a source of comfort and safety in a terrifying world. Ham, Mrs. Noyes's favourite son, is a gentle, imaginative scientist, quick to analyze but not to damage the world around him. Apples are sweet, sunsets are beautiful, gin is ready to hand, as is the piano. Before the flood, there is much to be thankful for, despite Noah's cruel tyranny. After the flood, life becomes a fascist nightmare, a biblical final solution. Before we are swept up in Yaweh's plan and Noah's collaboration, we see the antediluvian world through the eyes of Mrs. Noyes and from her cat's perspective, which helps us understand the extent of the catastrophe about to descend on the earth and the scope of the beauty and life to be lost. The alarm bell rings at the start of the prologue with an epigraph from Genesis 7:7 stating that Noah, his sons, his wife, and his son's wives entered the ark *because of the waters of the flood.* Then the first sentence of the novel dismisses this biblical claim as a lie: "Everyone knows it wasn't like that. [...] It wasn't an excursion. It was the end of the world" (3). There was panic, screaming, pushing and shoving, and a massive *auto-da-fé* ordered by Noah to destroy as many creatures as possible in a display of his power. It is Mrs. Noyes who realizes, with horror, the meaning of this voyage as she watches those sacrificed to the flames *"heaving up through waves of smoke, like beasts who broke the surface of a drowning-pool, then sank and broke again. And again—and then were gone"* (4).

The story proper begins with the announcement that Yaweh is about to visit his faithful servant Noah. Such an event—an honour in Noah's eyes—is unprecedented, and the entire family is recruited to prepare for this divine visitation. But Yaweh is not the only heavenly visitor to Noah's farm. Lucy, the "rogue angel" Lucifer, in the shape of a beautiful seven-foot woman with a "moon-white face and jet-black hair" (59) is already on the scene, and Ham has fallen in love with her. Lucy knows that Yaweh plans to destroy the world and she has joined the Noyes family with Ham because she wants to "survive the holocaust in heaven" and, if possible, "prevent the holocaust on earth" (110). She is unable, however, to prevent the holocaust that precedes the boarding of the ark, and once the family and chosen animals are all on board, she is powerless to stop the ensuing nightmare. Noah makes a sacrifice of one of Mottyl's kittens, treats his wife as a slave, and, in one of the most appalling scenes in the story, rapes Japeth's young wife with the unicorn's horn, killing the creature, and reducing the girl to a shuddering heap. When Mrs. Noah, Lucy, and Ham rebel, he locks them below deck and confiscates their sources of light, and Japeth warns his mother that he will kill her if she dares to resist. "We are truly captives here," she realizes, "every one of us—and yet they have called this: *being saved*" (251). As the weeks of torment and incarceration on the ark drag on, Mrs. Noyes begins to fear that if this voyage ends, human tyranny, bigotry, and violence will once more take over the world, and she says "No!" Then she prays to the absent clouds and empty sky for rain ... and the novel ends. Cold comfort, perhaps, and small hope, but she is still alive and Mottyl, old, blind, and weak, is safe in her lap. Noah, however, remains in charge, still exacting his tribute and enforcing his will.

Timothy Findley had indeed told a new story about Noah's flood by turning the biblical account inside out and upside down. What Christianity preaches as the annihilation of a corrupt, degenerate world and the salvation of a select few, pure beings in preparation for a better, more obedient postdiluvian world Findley condemned as propaganda, censorship of all dissent, the silencing and abuse of women, and the oppression of memory and imagination. No wonder he despaired of bringing a modicum of hope out of this vision. No wonder he experienced rage as he brought his story of the flood to a close. As he told Alan Twigg, he suffered acutely before finding the right plot for *Not Wanted on the Voyage* and he was left in a rage when he had finished it (87). Human indifference to the destruction of the environment and to "whatever else is alive in this world" was akin to a holocaust in his eyes because people could have paid attention to what was happening around them and protested, but they didn't. In a letter to Pierre Berton dated 8 October 1984, he wrote: this is "the harshest thing I've ever written. And the hardest. The book is a kind of blasphemy" (Pierre Berton fonds B236-F13). If there is any solace to be gleaned from *Not Wanted on the Voyage* it must be found in the telling of the story, in its wry touches of humour, and in its life-affirming characters. Mrs. Noyes is a force of nature, brimming with love for all living things and feisty as hell. Lucy is wonderfully transgressive, charming, witty, and certainly on the positive side of Findley's argument with the powers that be. His Yaweh is nothing more than a petulant old man who is dying, and Noah is a human fascist who claims the words of this false God as divine sanction for his ambition, cruelty, and lust. The scenes of fire, drowning, panic, lying, murder, and rape that punctuate the narrative hearken back to *Famous Last Words* and *The Wars* and forward to novels Findley had yet to write. The Second World War may not be named in *Not Wanted on the Voyage*, but it is impossible to miss the parallels Findley draws between his novel and the Holocaust and his view of that war. It is equally impossible to gloss over his condemnation of organized religion and society's treatment, sanctioned and promoted by right-wing religious doctrine, of nature and of those human beings—women, children, gays— who do not conform, who are not the correct "kind."

The post-publication life of *Not Wanted on the Voyage* was rich and varied. Findley toured the country to promote it and read to listeners who were, more often than not, positive, despite the novel's criticism of Judeo-Christian tradition and its damning portrayal of Yaweh and Noah. The novel became a bestseller, won awards, and would be adapted as a stage play. Early reviews and articles were uniformly positive. Marianne Ackerman quickly grasped the scope of the novel and drew attention to the fact that it was much more than an audacious retelling of the Genesis story about the flood. She called it "an amazing feat of imagination" that was a "strong indictment of our secular values" and a "brilliant" morality tale for modern times. David Staines devoted his review to an interview with Findley by stressing some of the background to the novel and Findley's firm view that the "Ark is a concentration camp" and that "we all live in concentration camps." John Moss called the novel "a thing of wonder, one of the truly great books" ("Timothy Findley" 113). Writing a year later and at greater length, George Woodcock published the first in-depth analysis of the novel, and he began by noting the motto, "Against Despair," and its relevance for a story about humanity's capacity to survive against the odds. *Not Wanted on the Voyage* is, Woodcock claimed, "a combination of fable and prose mock epic, which performs the same kind of bold and illuminating outrages on revealed religion as *Famous Last Words* performed on history" (233), and he placed Findley's vision in the tradition of Gnosticism, last practised in medieval Europe by the Cathars, who were brutally repressed as heretics by Simon de Montfort. For both the ancient Gnostics and Timothy Findley, Yaweh is a diabolical imposter and Lucifer is an "'eternal messenger,' the emissary from the 'world of Light'" (236).[14]

Opposition to Findley's heretical vision struck when the novel appeared as a stage play. A co-production by Necessary Angel and the Manitoba Theatre Centre, it was performed in Winnipeg and Toronto in the spring of 1992, but reactions from the critics were cool.[15] The public response to the Winnipeg premiere was more emphatic; some audience members objected to the attack on Judeo-Christian tradition and were outraged by the scene in which Emma is raped with the unicorn's horn. The Manitoba vice squad arrived in the theatre to judge things for themselves but decided against laying charges. Whether a success or a failure on stage, adapting the novel for live performance presented problems. Findley worried that dressing up actors as animals would merely look cute, and the hybrid mix of fantasy-musical-spectacle with a story about survival in a world that is portrayed as a concentration camp seems an unlikely proposition.

The promotion tour began on 23 October 1984 in Oshawa. Six weeks later he and Bill had covered seven thousand miles, stopping in twenty-three towns and cities, and he had read in dozens of schools, universities, and bookstores. In his essay, "Alarms and Excursions," Findley recalled such marathons with good humour, considering the toll it took on him and Bill, who did the driving when they could not take trains. "Uprooting and disorientating, tiring and fraught with alarming confrontations, touring is dreadful," he complained. Dreadful "but mandatory" because "if you write books, it goes with the territory." Interviewers who had not read the book ahead of time could be insulting bores, and he would later discover that some of them disliked the book and said so in reviews. Nevertheless, Findley did not blame his publishers or the interviewers; a writer had to learn how to manage these situations when a publisher had gone to the trouble and expense of getting their writers and their books across the country. "If your book has been lucky enough" to be chosen for a tour, out of the hundreds published in a given season, he believed a writer should be grateful. Findley *was* grateful, but by the time the tour ended and he finally arrived home, he was very tired. From this point on, as his success grew and demands on his time and energy increased, he became seriously exhausted. Being famous and much sought after exacted a heavy price.

CHAPTER TEN

Staring Down Despair

Stories, Lectures, and *The Telling of Lies*

———

NOTHING IS HARDER, NOW IN THE PRESENT TIME, THAN

STARING DOWN DESPAIR. BUT STARE IT DOWN WE MUST.

(Timothy Findley, *Inside Memory* 318)

Dinner Along the Amazon and *The Telling of Lies*

I n the years immediately following the publication of *Not Wanted on the Voyage*, Findley suffered several personal losses. Aunt Ruth died on 2 September 1984, Marian Engel died on 10 February 1985, and his sister-in-law, Sally, died on May 21 that year. Findley had rarely visited Ruth in her final years, perhaps because she existed so vividly in his imagination as a young woman and as Nicholas Fagan, but his calendar entry for September 2 was a heavy cross, followed by "Ruth Bull Carlyle. My beloved aunt, Nicholas Fagan. She was 91 years old and, mercifully, died asleep" (LAC 89:12). Marian and Sally died relatively young after battling cancer, and Findley grieved deeply for both. He had long been appalled by Michael's treatment of his wife and his refusal to believe she was ill, but after Sally died he found his brother in the house, near death in deplorable conditions, and admitted him to hospital. Michael was suffering from acute alcohol poisoning (as well as Korsakoff Syndrome) and remained in hospital until his death ten years later.

Dinner Along the Amazon, Findley's first collection of short stories, appeared in 1984 and was dedicated to Marian Engel. In his brief introduction to the volume he confessed to his shock at realizing how many images, characters, and situations from his "CATALOGUE OF PERSONAL OBSESSIONS" recurred in his work: photographs, dusty roads, letters, revolvers, rabbits, stones, darkened rooms, and troubled people who communicate, when they do at all, indirectly, tangentially, or even with cruelty. Some of the stories connect directly with his novels, and several of them draw upon his personal experiences and his recollections of family and friends or explore persistent themes of interest to him. "Lemonade," for example, developed into *The Last of the Crazy People*, and "Sometime—Later—Not Now" is based on his friendship with Jo Dibblee during the fifties and the complications, similar to Findley's at that time, caused by the male protagonist's homosexuality. "The People on the Shore" is set at the Atlantic House hotel in Maine and provides a glimpse into the world portrayed in *The Telling of Lies*. In "Hello Cheeverland, Goodbye," set in a wealthy neighbourhood overlooking Long Island Sound, he recalls his experiences while staying in the area to write a screenplay for *The Last of the Crazy People* and explores the kind of selfish, ignorant world anatomized by John Cheever, a writer he admired. "Losers, Finders, Strangers at the Door," about a wife whose husband is bisexual and seeks rough sex with young men, examines the kind of ménage à trois Findley had observed during his London years and the pain it produced. This theme is one he treated later in the Minna and Bragg stories and in his last novel, *Spadework*, but he could never convincingly resolve what he saw as an untenable situation (I shall return to these stories and the novel). In "Daybreak at Pisa," he examined the figure of Ezra Pound, who represented such a serious ethical dilemma for an artist, in the attempt to see the fascist poet as a suffering human being, instead of as a monster.

Several stories from *Dinner Along the Amazon* demonstrate the degree to which Findley thought of narrative structure in dramatic terms. They start like opening scenes for short plays, capture a moment of action or dialogue, and end ambiguously, leaving the reader troubled at times, even shocked, and always uncertain about what might happen next. The cliffhanger ending is at no point more effective than in "Dinner Along the Amazon," where, at long last and after wrestling with these characters for more than twenty years, Findley put the married couple Michael and Olivia into a long short story, set it on prestigious North Seton Drive in Rosedale, and introduced other characters and allusions that would surface again in *Headhunter*. His savage portrayal of Rosedale socialites, who gather for a dinner party, is fraught with tension, accusation, animosity, and jealousy and is a fine precursor to the horrifying vision of Toronto in the later novel. When Patrick Sisam made a television film based on this story, Findley was delighted with the result; he believed that Sisam had captured the dramatic tension and scenic dynamics of the story and wanted Sisam to make more films of his work.[1]

Among the unpublished public talks that Findley gave in 1984 and 1985, two stand out because they so clearly demonstrate his role as an advocate for human rights, education, and the arts in the last quarter of the twentieth century. That he was asked to write such essays and give public lectures on a range of subjects shows not only his generosity with his time and his strong commitment but also the respect he had earned as a writer and public intellectual. On 28 January 1984, he gave an important talk called "How Would *You* Like to be Called Gay?" to the Sexology Section of the Ontario Psychiatric Association (OPA). To the best of my knowledge, this is the first time he discussed being gay in a public forum, and his autobiographical message was, by turns, funny, angry, and very moving. His opening joke about Joan of Arc telling the Inquisition not to throw more faggots on the fire because she wanted to die alone drew much laughter, but he followed this with a sobering revelation: "I am a walking, talking joke. I am a faggot. I am one of the Boys in the Band. I am gay."[2] He went on to describe being pointed at, ridiculed, insulted, even persecuted, and explained his discomfort with the terms "gay" or "homosexual writer": "*I am a writer. I am a man*," he insisted. Then he recounted his childhood, his youth, his growing up in a family that rejected his sexuality, and his early experience with psychiatrists, who *mis*treated him, in "a society which refused to have me as I was." He recalled the trauma of his divorce from Janet Reid and confessed that this was the only time in his life when his homosexuality almost drove him to suicide. And then he declared an important fact about himself: "I have never loved by gender. I fall in love with people." He closed with a challenge to the audience and a warning: "a society that defines itself by its sexuality alone has lost its freedom."

Findley may well have been encouraged to give this speech to the OPA by Ed Turner, who was a member of the Ethics Committee of the Association at this time. Turner, an enlightened psychiatrist who argued that homosexuality was neither a mental illness nor a disorder to be cured, had served Findley well for years as his psychiatrist and friend, respected him, and appreciated his artistic talent, intelligence, and eloquence. Turner must have calculated that if anyone could convince those in the medical profession—and there were many in the 1980s who still needed convincing that a gay man was not a criminal or mentally ill or in need of a cure—it was Timothy Findley.[3] Although I have not located any notes or marginal comments made by Findley about this lecture, it is clear that this speech reflects years of thoughtful consideration about his damaging experiences with his family, with psychiatrists and lawyers in the late fifties, with social prejudice that persists to this day, and his conversations with Ed Turner. That he "never loved by gender" is abundantly clear from his life story. That a society cannot be free if it lumps individuals into groups to be kept or discarded on ideological grounds is the powerful message of *Not Wanted on the Voyage*.

The Vancouver Institute lecture on 2 February 1985 is memorable for different reasons. To get to Vancouver and home again in the midst of a busy schedule, he had to fly, but he had refused to fly for thirty years, and the prospect terrified him. Bill took him in hand: the promised fee was worthwhile, and they were now living on what Findley earned; the Institute was prestigious; and flying had improved greatly since the fifties. Findley finally agreed, Bill arranged for them to stay overnight at a Toronto airport hotel (with good wine) before the flight, and the lecture, called "Matter over Mind: The Imagination in Jeopardy," was a success.[4] Several of those who were there that night recall it as spellbinding, one of the best lectures ever given in the Institute's long history. Findley's topic, however, was not a lighthearted one and he did not simply give a reading. He spoke about the state of education in the arts and humanities in a climate of censorship and began by summoning up the spectre of the Dark Ages: "we can read—we can write: we can speak and we can hear. And such capabilities as these are also among the weapons we use against dark ignorance." Then he went on to explore a variety of threats facing Canada and the rest of the world, from war, to cutbacks in education, to environmental degradation, to the British Columbia battle over logging on Meares Island. He had written a furious diatribe against the B.C. government in his 1984 journal (LAC 123: 11), and the Meares Island controversy was close to his heart. But his chief concern was censorship, which, he argued, served the purposes of those in power who wanted to keep the general populace, at home and abroad, in the dark of ignorance. He warned that another "Dark Age" was at hand.

He did not, however, end on a note of gloom. He made an eloquent pitch for greater government investment in education and for a future in which art, literature, music, history, and philosophy are celebrated in schools and universities instead of attacked and subjected to cutbacks. This was a speech championing the arts and humanities, and the audience loved it. He also made his pitch for the importance of the imagination and for not playing it safe by choosing careers bound by rules and the certainty of making money. Safety first, he reminded his listeners, produces the "politics of fear," and Germany in 1938 had used just such a politics. He wrapped up his lecture by discussing Joy Kogawa's *Obasan* and Margaret Laurence's *The Diviners*, novels that explore fear, repression, and prejudice in Canadian society, and he concluded with a personal anecdote about a Cannington girl who had wanted to be an artist and whom he and Bill had helped. After she had married and experienced some adversity, she had turned to a right-wing church and lost all her courage, ambition, and imagination. This young woman, once so full of promise, came to Stone Orchard one evening to chastise him for having so many books when the only one he should have was the Bible. "That night, I saw an imagination—not just in jeopardy—but so closed in, it was immobilized. Useless."[5] Timothy Findley despised such religiosity; he had experienced it in his own upbringing, in the MRA's influence on his mother, and in the attempt to censor literature like *The Diviners*. And he had damned it in *Not Wanted on the Voyage*.

Not all of Findley's assignments from the early eighties were as personal or portentous as these two unpublished lectures. One of his more interesting published essays from 1985 is his piece on Isabel McLaughlin: "Comparing Notes." Izzy, or "Doodle," as the Findleys called her, was an old family friend, but she was also an accomplished painter whose works are now held in the Robert McLaughlin Gallery in Oshawa. Findley admired her work, her way of seeing, and her attention to form and detail, but in this article he focused on his interest in her sketchbooks and on the importance, to her, of memory. Keeping such books—journals in his case—as a way of recording what one sees and remembers, was a practice the two artists shared. "For the writer and for the artist," he explained, "such sketchbooks and journals may contain images that never worked, but their importance is never forgotten" ("Comparing Notes" 54). True to form, Findley kept one such journal during the two glorious months, from late August to late October, that he and Bill spent on an extended road trip that took them to Saltspring Island. He treasured these quiet hours with Bill, and he started a new journal with a unicorn motif and titled it: "To the West, August 1985, from Stone Orchard and Arkwright//WFW & Tiff" (LAC 123:15). This journal is almost like a diary because he made daily entries noting the names of people they met, places they passed or stopped in, the cost of meals and what he ate, the heights of mountains, and the distances covered. On September 30 they bade farewell to Saltspring, to Phyllis Webb, and to the white horse that Findley called the unicorn, and began the long drive east. They stopped in Winnipeg for his writer-in-residence assignment to teach a creative writing course and attend a round of literary activities before starting for home three weeks later to face piles of mail and several deadlines. Findley ended this journal on an intimate note: "It has been a gift—these two months with WFW. I have truly loved being in his company. We love each other absolutely. How rare that is. How fortunate we are—how fortunate, above all, *I* am." (LAC 123:19).

During this first stay on Saltspring Island, they rented a house on Sunset Road, where Findley settled down to work on *The Telling of Lies*. All the novels from this highly productive period explore aspects of fascism, twentieth-century history, and the complex boundaries between fiction and reality, truth and lies, and *The Telling of Lies* is no exception. Although he did not struggle to find the narrative voice, as he had with *Famous Last Words*, or experience the rage and despair that he had while writing *Not Wanted on the Voyage*, he was nevertheless nervous about this new novel. "I don't know what I think of it yet," he wrote in his journal; "I have not enjoyed writing it—not really understanding the form it demands ... the terseness of one who tells a tale without appearing to—" (LAC 124:2). But the "one who tells" this tale turned out to be a splendid invention. *The Telling of Lies* comes from Vanessa Van Horne through the medium of a journal that she keeps during her last annual summer holiday at the Aurora Sands Hotel in Maine. Vanessa, who was a child prisoner in a Japanese POW camp, is now an award-winning landscape architect by profession and an amateur photographer. It is her photography and her journal that stand her in good stead as she unravels the mysterious murder that occurs on the beach in front of the old hotel. Findley first thought of the basic plot for this novel while holidaying at the Atlantic House hotel, and the Aurora Sands and its rooms, guests, and beach are closely modelled on Atlantic House. The story is set in July and August of 1986 and the Aurora Sands, better known to its habitués as the ASH, has been sold to developers, as was the Atlantic House hotel. This is the final summer for the ASH and all the regular guests are heartbroken. The character of Vanessa was inspired by an old friend of the Findleys, an American who was a regular guest at Atlantic House: Dorothy Warren.[6] Nevertheless, it is not Dorothy Warren who comes so vividly alive on the pages of *The Telling of Lies*. Vanessa is a uniquely Findleyesque creation who not only succeeds in discovering why and how the villain met his end, but also uncovers other evils in the process. And she keeps the reader dangling until the very last pages of her journal.

As Findley explained to Joel Yanofsky, one of the chief challenges he faced in writing this kind of novel was to sustain narrative interest without letting the cat out of the bag. Another challenge—all too typical of Findley—was to maintain a firm grip on the main characters and resist being "swept away by minor characters" (32). Using Vanessa as a journal writer who makes chronological entries allowed him to reveal information as she discovered it and to keep the reader in the dark along with her. Moreover, the voice and personality of Vanessa are engaging because she is a complex, interesting first-person narrator with keen powers of observation, a healthy sense of irony, and a set of past experiences that shape her ethical response to the events unfolding around her at the ASH. She begins her journal "on the first day of the last summer" that she and the other guests will ever spend at the hotel. She then recalls being brought there in 1926 as a baby and that, "barring the years of my imprisonment, I have returned incessantly ever since" (1).[7] With one succinct phrase—"barring the years of my imprisonment"—Findley establishes a major theme of the novel, which he explores in passages of Vanessa's journal that run in tandem with her recording of present events at the hotel. She is haunted by these lost years because she and her mother spent them in a Japanese POW camp at Bandung in West Java, where she witnessed the murder of her father at the wire fence of the women's compound. Vanessa also recalls her memories of the Japanese officer in charge of the camp, Colonel Norimitsu. During her imprisonment, an understanding of sorts arose between the soldier and the teenage girl, who stood barefoot on her side of the fence as her father's blood pooled around her feet. Norimitsu had watched her there; as she bore witness to her father's murder, he bore witness to her pain. He later secretly passed medicines for the women prisoners to Vanessa at this same fence, and she never forgot his words that *even monsters are not always monsters*" (203). Vanessa's powerful memories of the camp, and her haunting by those Second World War horrors, have taught her much about human nature, and she now brings the lessons learned there to bear on the violence and sinister plots surrounding her on the tranquil beach stretching for miles on either side of the ASH.

For *The Telling of Lies*, Findley conducted extensive research into Canadian and American Cold War activities to expose specific medical abuses that occurred during the period. These abuses are represented in Calder Maddox, an elderly pharmaceuticals tycoon, who is discovered dead on the beach and who owes his wealth and reputation to the invention of drugs that induce deep sleep and wipe the memory clean of all past experiences. Real drugs like these were actually used in CIA-sponsored experiments on patients suffering from depression or mental illnesses under the supervision of Dr. Ewen Cameron at the Allan Memorial Institute in Montreal during the late fifties and early sixties.[8] This so-called research into psychic driving, mind control, and behavioural modification went under the acronym MKULTRA, and the damage caused to patients subjected to such treatments amounted to a form of soft torture. Findley, who always followed the news closely, was aware of investigations into CIA activities in Canada, and his long personal interest in psychiatry and the treatment of troubled patients, like Aunt Ruth or even himself in the late fifties, reinforced his wish to expose the clandestine experiments at the Allan through the fictional portrayal of Maddox and his murder. After several twists in the plot and thanks to Vanessa's keen observations, we learn that Maddox has been murdered by Meg Riches, a friend of Vanessa's and the wife of Michael Riches, a former Canadian diplomat who had been treated for depression at a Montreal hospital and reduced to a childlike state of mental and physical disability. Meg has brought her husband to the ASH for this last summer holiday, and she uses the opportunity to poison Maddox. When confronted by Vanessa, Meg confesses, but Vanessa still needs to know why, and Meg's explanation is horrifying: an ambitious Canadian doctor working at the Makin Memorial Institute in Montreal accepted funding from the CIA to conduct brainwashing experiments on his patients, one of whom was Michael: "Absolutely secret [...] and absolutely illegal," Meg insists (346). Using electroshock, sensory deprivation—*"psychic driving"*—and the drug called *Maddoxin*, this doctor destroyed Meg's husband and his capacity to remember what he knew about Canadian political activities during the Cold War.

The Telling of Lies is, then, a revenge story based on historical facts. Vanessa's role, once she has learned the truth, is an ethical one. She must decide what to do with her knowledge, and in this she is a true Findley narrator. She decides on silence to protect Meg "for now," but like Mauberley she confides the full story to her journal, where she preserves the traumatic memories of her own life, the tragic events at the ASH, and the facts about what happened at the Makin Memorial Institute, for future reference. Vanessa's first ethical decision is to protect Meg by remaining consistent with a form of human justice that lies beyond the law: because Calder Maddox was a killer, he deserved his death—his, as it were, execution. Her second ethical decision is to allow the publication of her journal in the form of this novel. Now it is our turn to read Vanessa's journal and take heed of the frightening connections she makes between torture in war and secret crimes against humanity in peacetime.

Findley dedicated *The Telling of Lies* to "The Atlantic House Hotel and all who sailed in her." The ASH becomes a character in the novel, and his chapter about the background to the novel in *Inside Memory* is a portrait of Atlantic House and the friends he knew there, like Dorothy Warren and Joellen Knight, the daughter of the owners, but he saw the novel as "a tribute to the generations who made the Atlantic House such a wondrous place—as an 'exercise' in storytelling—as a look at some of the tensions between my country and America. [...] The milieu was a gift. I only had to close my eyes and I was there" (*IM* 240). He also used two epigraphs, one from Thornton Wilder's journals to the effect that a writer must never be surprised by the evil in human nature, and the other a quotation from Cheever: "the telling of lies is a sort of sleight of hand that displays our deepest feelings about life." Cheever gave him his title, and Wilder advised him to use journals and pay attention. To bear witness, as Findley often said, was a writer's duty, and Vanessa is his surrogate watcher, who records the truth as she sees it in photographs and words, and bears witness. With *The Telling of Lies* he completed his trilogy of novels about the Second World War, fascism, the international twentieth-century scene, and the storm clouds he saw threatening the future. Unlike its companions, it has often been overlooked when Findley novels are discussed.[9] This neglect, however, is unjustified because it is a fine example of Timothy Findley at his best—telling a powerful story in which private lives and public events collide, with a cast of memorable characters, a vividly realized setting, and serious themes worthy of our attention.

Stones of Remembrance, Anger, and Hope

The last few years of the 1980s were consumed by travel and public duties, with little time to concentrate on his creative work. Findley received several honours in 1986, but the one that meant the most to him was his appointment as an Officer of the Order of Canada in a ceremony at Rideau Hall on April 9. In his calendar for 16 November 1986, when he first received the news, he wrote that he felt humbled: "Cannot believe— wonderful" (LAC 94:6). Despite such accolades, which confirmed his stature within Canada, his ambition, plans for a new novel, the pressure of publishing deadlines, and frequent requests to give talks or assume public duties did not permit him to relax. In 1986, as president of PEN Canada, he started a correspondence with a political prisoner in Ethiopia that resulted in a victory for human rights and a lasting friendship. Kuwee Kumsa was a journalist who had been arrested in February 1980 during the country's long civil war and thrown into prison in Addis Ababa. Her case was taken up by Amnesty International and brought to the attention of PEN Canada, whose members began writing to her with messages of hope and encouragement. However, Martha Kumsa, her Canadian name, rarely received these letters and there was no word of her until 4 December 1986, when her hand-drawn Christmas card reached Canada. After three years of silence, this was the first sign that anyone had that she was still alive. When Findley opened the card he was ecstatic. He immediately called Jan Bauer, the executive director of the English-speaking centre of PEN Canada: "We've found her! She's alive!" For obvious reasons, none of his letters to her have survived, but some of her letters to him from prison have. "Dear Mr. Kindly" she wrote at first because she could not decipher his handwriting, but the mistake was perfect.

Several more years would pass before Martha was released from prison and able to reach freedom; she arrived in Toronto, with her children, in September 1991.[10] Mr. Kindly supported Martha in many ways and welcomed her and the children to Stone Orchard and into the Tiff-Bill family. He and Bill bought bicycles for the children and the family regularly visited the farm for Thanksgiving holidays. In quiet moments,

Tiff and Martha discussed politics, the Free Trade Agreement, which he abhorred, and literature; *Heart of Darkness* was much in his mind at this time and he wanted her views on it. For the official celebration of her freedom at the December 1991 PEN International benefit at Toronto's Winter Garden Theatre, he wrote a short play called "Martha and the Minder." He read the role of "the Minder" and Judith Thompson read the role of Martha in her Addis Ababa prison. At the end of this duologue, Thompson left the stage, and Findley turned to the audience to tell them Martha had been released, announcing, "Here she is." Whereupon she entered and ran across the stage into his embrace. Tears, laughter, and a standing ovation. To this day, Martha Kumsa remembers the closing words on his lost letters to her—"Hope against despair."

He also accepted the increasing invitations to lecture, read, and promote his books abroad, and in the spring of 1986 he and Bill travelled to Australia for the Adelaide Writers' Week. As always, he kept a detailed calendar plus journals to record his experiences. The long flight to Australia and New Zealand began on 24 February and he and Bill were away for close to six weeks. His list of what to pack for so many weeks was extensive, from medications to several personal items like "Sebastian pictures" (the bear stayed home this time, so his image had to suffice as a guardian spirit), Grandmother Bull's crucifix, and Grandfather Findley's watch. Copies of his own books were, of course, essential in light of the festival and his invitations to read and speak, but he also needed other reading: Patrick White's novel *Voss* (1957) went in his hand luggage to be read on the plane, along with Elizabeth Jolley's short story collection *Woman in a Lampshade* (1983). Although he did not comment on either work in his journal, in his 1986 essay "Legends" he expressed his admiration for White, whom he was sorry not to meet in Australia.[11] Len Collins drove them to the Toronto airport, with Findley in a nervous state. He was flying; he was coping. But the prospect alarmed him.

The Writers' Week itself was interesting, if not an unqualified success. After their arrival, visiting writers were housed in an "estate hotel" surrounded by an impressive landscape, but some of Findley's fellow writers put him off. He noted, with distaste, that Alain Robbe-Grillet and his wife kept apart with a francophone group and refused to mix, and he described the Canadian writers, Naïm Kattan and Josef Skvorecky, as unfriendly. When they reached Sydney for Canada Week, arrangements for his visit collapsed. They were not met at the airport as planned; they had no idea which hotel to go to until Bill called the Canadian consulate; and no one in the English Department at the University of Sydney had been informed of Timothy Findley's supposed reading there. To add insult to injury, the woman at the consulate was rude and flippant. These glitches prompted Findley to write a lengthy letter to Joe Clark, the foreign affairs minister in Brian Mulroney's cabinet, outlining the fiasco (Writers' Union of Canada fonds 107-2). What he did not mention in his journal or note on his calendar was the frightening episode in Adelaide when Bill could not find him for five full days because he had gone on a monumental binge. Probably Findley could not remember what had happened during this binge, but his journal is silent on what precisely pushed him off the deep end: fury over his cavalier treatment by the consulate, fatigue and the stress of travel, anger—all made worse by his constant fear of being neglected? It is as if he refused to analyze his behaviour, and this silence—a gap in the manuscript, an aporia—is disturbing because the episode was dreadful for Bill. "When he finally appeared," Bill told me, "he was sober—but belligerent [and] it took another half-day for him to return all the way." Findley did manage finally to give his reading, and before returning to Canada they escaped for a restorative holiday in Cairns and Brisbane. As soon as he was alone with Bill and away from a big-city setting and the pressure to perform, he began to relax. They took a boat to see the Great Barrier Reef and rented a car to travel into the hills. Findley described, at length, the birds, fish, blue butterflies, fragrant flowers, and beautiful harbour. Brisbane, where they were warmly welcomed by Alan Lawson, a University of Queensland professor, was their favourite Australian city, and his description of the sights, scents, and sounds helped him create the setting for the "Bragg and Minna" story in *Stones*. Moreover, as Findley noted, their Brisbane hotel, called the Park, had a sign that read "ARK Hotel which, after Noah's Hotel in Christchurch [New Zealand] is no less than our due" (LAC 124:2).

Binges like the one in Adelaide were now rare—there would be one more, of lesser proportions, in England during the disastrous UK publication of *Famous Last Words* in March 1987—but, more importantly, the signs of physical and emotional exhaustion were becoming worrisome. As he told his journal, he felt old. He badly needed the peace and quiet of home, but staying home was growing more and more difficult. By the mid- to late 1980s, he was seeing several doctors for everything from back and shoulder problems to arthritis and high blood pressure, and each shock to his system—the death of a family member, friend, or beloved animal, or a hurtful review—intensified his anxiety and tension. He took the rise of right-wing politicians like Ronald Reagan and Brian Mulroney so seriously that he expounded at length in his journals on the danger they represented. He was appalled, for example, by the 1988 election and the free trade debate, and in a 1988 interview with Laura Busheikin he brought up the free trade issue and told her that he "believe[d] fervently in our country.... where we can, if we don't screw it up, use the best civilization has to offer. That's why I'm so concerned about the free trade deal." As he saw it, the deal meant selling out to the United States and allowing "rotten American culture [to] follow American businesses into Canada." Threats or damage to the environment also troubled him; reports on the destruction of rainforest habitat in British Columbia and headlines about whales trapped in the arctic ice infuriated him. *"Pray for the whales,"* he wrote on 14 October 1988, and he concluded the journal by quoting, in full, Yeats's "The Second Coming" (LAC 124:8). In short, he lived with exposed nerve ends, and events of the day, about which many caring citizens worried, signalled extremes of social evil and looming disaster for Findley. Moreover, he was extremely sensitive to perceived slights and so uncompromising about his work that success, awards, stature, and achievement could not supply the inner calm he craved, satisfy his ambition, or bolster his confidence in his work.

The routine of Stone Orchard, where he was surrounded by everything he loved, was essential to his well-being and his creativity, and yet, even there, he began every journal from this period with "Against Despair." At one point he actually became angry with Ed Turner for, on the one hand, not prescribing enough sleeping pills, and on the other, not understanding how much he craved a drink. Nevertheless, it was with Dr. Turner that he could unload his resentments, fears, and anger, confess his exhaustion and tension, and admit that he felt "guilty because [he] was angry at everyone [he] loved" (LAC 90:1). Although it may seem odd in the context of so many deaths (his father, Aunt Ruth, Marian, Sally), the fact that his elderly horse, Flicka, had to be put down a week before his fifty-fourth birthday was especially distressing. He could not be with the animal due to a reading engagement for the Writers' Development Trust and he was deeply upset. After two pages describing his feelings, he concluded: "I loved her beyond words—as I did Boy and Mottle—Hooker and Maggie, and the others. Gone. Against Despair."

Apart from Stone Orchard, the only place where he could rest and enjoy nature was Saltspring Island. The journals he kept during their second holiday there in 1988 confirm his attraction to island life. Phyllis Webb was there, and he and Bill often visited with her. There were good restaurants, a library, other writers and artists, and a strong sense of community. They made interesting side trips to Galiano Island to see Jane Rule, and, on one occasion, they visited William Head Institution, the minimum-security facility for men near Victoria on Vancouver Island, where Findley read and found the prison audience no different from others. An especially delightful treat was a visit to the home of Robert Bateman, an artist Findley admired, and he wrote to Mary Lou Finlay describing the shoreline setting and beauty of the place.[12] And then there was the "Unicorn," the solitary white horse that he insisted recognized him from year to year and for which Bill would buy apples. They even considered buying property on Saltspring: "one day, if it is right—and if we *ever* have some money, this is what we would do: buy waterfront land on one of these islands—and, with Len, build a house, over time—as a retreat, not as a home. *We will never leave Stone Orchard*" (LAC 124:6). Famous last words.

During their island break, he wrote every day, read constantly, and kept abreast of the radio and television news. Surprisingly, given his aversion to sports, he followed the 1988 Summer Olympics avidly, was ecstatic when Ben Johnson won gold in the 100-metre race, and then was disgusted when Johnson, disqualified for doping, lost the medal to a boastful American. And he was constantly thinking ahead. He feared he would not have another big novel for two or three years (it was five years before *Headhunter* appeared), and he was immersing himself in *Heart of Darkness*, which he described as "one of the finest pieces of writing ever achieved in English" (LAC 124:8). Together with Bill and Phyllis, he discussed Conrad at length because he believed they would help him understand the novel. Here was that old self-doubt again: "to be nearly 58—and know so little." And he told his journal that he loved Phyllis, "this extraordinary woman [who] has, at heart, the real integrity that others only claim to have" (LAC 124:8). Through the late eighties his regular letters—to his mother, to other family members, to Isabel McLaughlin and friends like Mary Lou Finlay and William Hutt, and to Nancy Colbert—show how faithfully he kept in touch. Many of these letters are handwritten, and those typed by Bill always carry Findley's handwritten notes, signed "Tiff." In one long letter to Margaret Findley (with Bill's private papers), he described Saltspring for her—"rolling vistas ... blackberries in profusion," and the "Unicorn with blue eyes and white marble hooves with blue veins. He comes when I whistle and I feed him apples and sugar. It is magical." But then he gave her stern advice: "*If you don't let go of Michael NOW*—he won't ever let go of you. [...] Those are Michael's hands twisting your insides [and] *No* one has the right to do that to *anyone. PERIOD.*" Precisely what Michael was expecting from his elderly mother is unclear, but he often called her (and Tiff) when he was drunk, to shout and complain.

When Margaret Laurence died in 1987, Findley was shocked and grief-stricken. He prepared a special obituary for her that he read on Peter Gzowski's *Morningside* program on CBC radio, but this was a painful task because he had known her well and cherished her deeply. He shared many of her values, her "espousal of peace," her obsession with a writer's duty, and her concern with getting the words, characters, time, and place exactly right. He was aware, as few outside her immediate circle were, that she had been battling writer's block as well as cancer and cataracts, and he praised her courage: "Brave, braver, bravest." In his article "Margaret Laurence: A Remembrance," he mixed personal memories of her as chancellor at Trent, when he received his LLD, with recollections of her role in establishing the Writers' Union of Canada; "it was there, in those founding meetings, that she coined her now famous definition: 'writers are a tribe'" (15). Gwendolyn MacEwen also died that year, so it seemed that death was stalking the Canadian tribe. But if Findley was once more struggling against despair, he also recognized (*pace* Samuel Johnson and Malcolm Lowry) that sunshine keeps breaking through. The chief source of Findley's sunshine was Bill, and some of their shared sunshine was food. Findley loved good food and wine; Bill loved to cook and did so extremely well. Findley often recorded restaurant menus and meals they had enjoyed, along with recipes, in his journals. He also published some favourite recipes after Bill had proved their value by preparing them. "Timothy Findley's Summer Peaches" appeared in *The CanLit Foodbook* (120), and it is a simple recipe, as ingredients go, but not easy to prepare. His "Coquilles St. Jacques from Dieppe" was published in *Descant*, complete with a note on the French town and the tragic Allied raid of 1942 and some personal history: "We retreated [to Dieppe] after the lesser 'disaster' of the critical scorn received in England by my novel, *Famous Last Words*." But his most delightful journal entry on food was the menu for a dinner held in his honour at the home of John and Barbara Craig on 28 October 1987 (LAC 241:12):

The Dream Menu

The Last of the Crazy Hors d'Oeuvres
—

Butterfly Salad Plagued with
Orange and Almonds
—

Matchmaker Sorbet
—

Warsfowl avec sauce normande
The Telling of Rice
The Green/Orange Oaks of Moore Park
—

Famous Last Words

—

Can You See Me Yet? Brandy

By September of 1988, Findley was worrying about the critical reception of his collection of stories, *Stones*, but the reviews were positive. The
volume won the prestigious Trillium Book Award in 1989, and "Almeyer's
Mother," one of his most interesting family biography stories, won the
1988 Periodical Distributors of Canada Award for its first publication in
Saturday Night. Several of the stories in the collection rank among his
finest, and all of them explore territory close to his own experience—the
love of a gay man for a straight woman; the streets of Toronto, with specific Toronto institutions; Rosedale life; family relationships—and each
employs familiar Findley images and symbols. As a group, these stories
inhabit his unique fictional and personal world and reveal a great deal
about his life, his family, and his attitude toward the city he loved to hate
and would anatomize in *Headhunter*. The two Bragg and Minna stories,
"Bragg and Minna" and "A Gift of Mercy," are his first published examination of marriage between a heterosexual woman and a bisexual man
(who prefers same-sex partners) and they should be read in conjunction
with two stories about this couple in *Dust to Dust* ("A Bag of Bones" and
"Come as You Are"). In "Bragg and Minna," which is dedicated to Charlotte Engel, Marian's daughter, Minna dies from cancer in Australia, and
Bragg travels there to throw her ashes "like an offering upon the stones"
(24). In that gesture, with that simple phrase, Findley combines two of
his favourite symbols—ashes and stones—and one of his most significant,
recurrent gestures—the scattering of a loved one's ashes.

Minna is a character inspired by Marian Engel and, like all Findley fictional writers, she is an obsessive keeper of journals. In "A Gift of
Mercy," she suffers from a deep-seated sense of insecurity laced with
despair, something Bragg cannot understand until he realizes that she
keeps a "journal of despair" about other people (suicides, the homeless,
the mentally ill), who reflect her inner life. As if to flout her upper-middle-
class Rosedale family, Minna starts bringing these people into their home,

which prompts Bragg to bring the first of his male lovers home. Bragg, however, is definitely modelled on Findley himself; he is a writer who attributes his bitter sense of humour to "the fact of his homosexuality," and he rages against those family members who reject him or deign to forgive him, like his brother and his father, who "urged him to seek a 'cure'" (49). Although such a situation never occurred with Marian Engel and Timothy Findley, he was exploring an aspect of real life rarely addressed in fiction or drama of the time but familiar enough to him from the lives of others. He was also remembering his own disastrous marriage, his father's rejection, his love for women, and the marriages of theatre people he had known in England or knew in Stratford and Toronto. Moreover, he doubted that such marital triangles brought happiness and he could not imagine a satisfying ending for them in these stories or in the play (*The Stillborn Lover*) and novel (*Spadework*) he had still to write.

"Foxes," "The Sky," and "Dreams," which is dedicated to Ed Turner, are interesting for what they convey about city life, the world of a Rosedale couple, and professional psychiatrists, at least as Findley imagined them, but they seem rather occasional, less rooted in lived experience. The last four stories, however, are more satisfying, and they are central to an understanding of Timothy Findley, the son and brother. "The Name's the Same" is the first story he wrote, the one about himself and Michael that he showed to Ruth Gordon back in 1954 and the one in which he realized he could write fiction that drew upon his personal experience in a recognizable Canadian voice. "Real Life Writes Real Bad" could not be written or published until after Sally had died and Michael had reached his point of no return. It is a devastating portrait of Michael at the time of Sally's death that belongs with the Cable stories ("War" and "The Name's the Same"), with Bud based on Mike and younger brother Neil based on Tiff, and it hews close to actual events. Michael Findley did behave as Bud does, and Findley's effort, like Margaret Findley's, to reason with him failed. Like Bud, he refused to believe his wife was dying, refused to allow home care providers into the house, and after Sally (Katie) was taken to hospital, he withdrew into alcohol and refused to visit her. Michael would shout at Tiff and his mother for always taking Sally's side against him, and after her death he called constantly to complain. Then, some months later, the phone calls suddenly stopped. When Findley checked the house, he found his brother exactly as Neil describes finding Bud. Moreover, Michael Findley died, as Bud does, on 7 November 1994 in York Regional Hospital, and Findley, like Neil, was left to clean up the house and try to come to terms with the failure of his brother's life. At the end of the story, Neil describes what he found in Bud and Katie's home after the ambulance took Bud away, and the mess resembles what Findley found: filthy or smashed dishes, rotting food, empty liquor bottles, unmade beds, and the half-starved family cat. Neil also finds Katie's note pinned to her pillow; it is her farewell message to Bud telling him that she is dying, that she has hidden one hundred dollars for him in the hall closet, and that she wants him to come and see her in hospital. Then she writes: "*I will always love you, honey. Thank you for everything. Katie*" (168). Findley found just such a note pinned to his sister-in-law's pillow.

In telling this story, Findley portrayed the actions of a man he loathed and a brother for whom he felt some love and compassion. He also celebrated the loyalty and goodness of Sally, a woman he adored and respected. In a journal entry, two weeks before Sally died, he wrote: "*Mike* in *appalling* condition—drunk. Phone calls abusive and ugly. All he thinks of is self." Sally's condition was "dreadful," and he admits that he had "finally shut the phone off—to stop Mike's calls" (LAC 90:3). He would never understand Michael or fathom how Sally put up with such a man, but *Stones* is dedicated to "Michael and in memory of Sal." Does real life write real bad? Yes. But one has to hope that this fiction, which is beautifully crafted, honest, and brave, brought Timothy Findley some peace with his family's past.

In "Almeyer's Mother" and "Stones," he drew upon aspects of his parents' lives to create characters who attempt to deal with childhood trauma. In "Almeyer's Mother," Peter learns something about his mother's past that astonishes and disturbs him, something that will help him understand who his mother is as a person. This knowledge centres on an old family photograph, which he had never seen, until his mother, Edith, visits his farm to show him the picture and tell him her story. The photograph is of a family group, in which Edith is a teenaged girl standing beside her father, the grandfather whom Peter had never heard her talk about and whose pictures, she claimed, did not exist. "Now, there he was and the sight of him—gazing down at his daughter—was so disturbing, Almeyer looked away. *Photographs that reveal such intimacy should not be taken*, he thought. *It isn't right*" (184). Then Edith begins to explain who is in this photograph and what happened to them. The year was 1926 and Edith had two brothers, both of whom were killed in a car accident shortly after the photograph was taken. Her parents never recovered from this tragedy: "My father begged my mother for another child," especially a son, but "my mother refused to sleep with him. [...] She locked her door" (187). Her father began living a secret life, and then, one day, he took Edith with him to a little house with flowers and a garden swing (just like the one Findley creates for Peter's garden), and left her alone for quite a while. She sat there on the garden swing, wondering why she had been brought to this place, until her father appeared with a young woman of about her age who was obviously pregnant. He introduced the woman, Lily Jerrold, to her and announced that he was divorcing his wife to marry Lily because "*the child would need a name*" (189).

Like Fred Bull, he had found a way to have another child and wanted a divorce from his wife. But that is not the end of Mrs. Almeyer's story, any more than it was all that Margaret Findley told Tiff. On her visits to Stone Orchard after Allan's death, Margaret often slipped away in the afternoons, but neither Tiff nor Bill knew where she went until the day she summoned the courage to explain. In a corner of the Stone Orchard garden there was a swing reminiscent of the one on which Fred Bull had left her to wait so many years earlier. She retired to that place to remember, and what she remembered and told Tiff is close to what Edith Almeyer tells Peter: she has destroyed pictures of herself with her father except for this one family photograph because she "couldn't bear the way he looked at [her]" (190). "If it hadn't been for Lily Jerrold—what might have happened to me?" she asks (190).

As Timothy Findley's biographer, the unanswerable question I find hovering over this story is: Why did he choose to fictionalize this material?

Maude and Fred Bull's only son, Alan, did die young from the Spanish flu. Maude did refuse to sleep with her husband or have more children, and Fred Bull did ask for a divorce when he learned that his lover, Amy Maude (Peggy) Douse, was pregnant. Then he married Peggy, and the shock of their father's behaviour made a lasting impact on all the Bull women. But Findley ends "Almeyer's Mother" in his customary fashion—with many unanswered questions and no sense of closure. Peter Almeyer wonders if his grandfather ever realized how much his daughter had feared him and why, and if his second wife, Lily, ever became his mother's friend. After her confession, Peter realizes that his mother "would always be alone" and that he could not change her past (191). Like Peter, Findley had no idea if Fred Bull realized his negative impact on Margaret, but he made sure she was never alone; his bond with her was very strong and they kept in constant touch. During her final illness, Margaret needed home care, so a nurse, whose name was Peggy Fortune, was hired to visit her apartment daily. Margaret did not dislike her nurse, but then Tiff never told her what he had learned: by some bizarre coincidence, this semi-retired nurse was once the young woman for whom Fred Bull had left his wife and daughters in 1926. Perhaps by writing this story, Timothy Findley granted his mother some degree of emotional restitution for past trauma. Possibly this was his way of saying that he understood and sympathized, his offering of reassurance that she was not entirely alone. Whatever his personal motivation, he knew an interesting real-life story when he heard one, and he transformed it into a compelling work of fiction.

"Stones" is also a memory story, set in May 1987 but recalling the years before, during, and following the Second World War. Findley drew upon what he had heard about his Uncle Irving's post-First World War life, the lives of other war veterans, and what he had seen from his father's post-Second World War life. After a brief evocation of pre-war life in Toronto, with its "perfect winters, heavy with snow and the smell of coal" and the summers smelling "of grass being cut in the park and burning tar from the road crews" (197), the first-person narrator, Ben, recalls how it all ended, when he was just five: "the end of summer 1939 is a line drawn down through the memory of everyone who was then alive. We were all about to be pitched together into a melting pot of violence from which a few of us would emerge intact and the rest of us would perish" (198). The story that unfolds from this point on is about the war, a destroyed father, a shattered family, and a lost childhood. Although the details do not correspond exactly with Timothy Findley's personal life, the story depicts a father's failure and a son's need for reconciliation. David Max, the father in the story, returned to his family on 14 February 1943, roughly six months after Dieppe. He has been "destroyed [because] his mind [is] severely damaged and his spirit [...] broken" (203), and he is violent and abusive to his wife and young Ben. After he nearly kills his wife in a drunken rage, he is incarcerated in "the Asylum for the Insane on Queen Street" (214), a place that haunted Findley and to which he would return in his fiction in the 1990s. When Ben begged his brother to explain what had happened to their father, Cy's answer was one word: "Dieppe" (205). And *Dieppe* is the word that hangs over this family like a curse. On 19 August 1942, Captain Max failed to lead his men from the landing craft to the beach; terrified, he stripped off his uniform and swam out to sea to be rescued, while his men were blown to pieces by German shells. He was "dishonourably discharged and sent home to us" (217). Ben's memory of the family's life is that "the rest was all a nightmare" (210). After his father's death in May 1987, Ben carries out the man's final request to have his ashes scattered on the beach at Dieppe so he could, in death, join the men he had failed: "*Why not*, I thought. *A stone among stones*" (218). In the present time frame of Ben's storytelling, we watch him on the beach as he releases his father's ashes to join the ghosts of Dieppe: "The red stones look as if they have been washed in blood and the sight of them takes your breath away. I hunkered down above them, holding all that remained of my father in my fist. He felt like powdered stone—pummelled and broken. I let him down between my fingers, feeling him turn to paste—watching him divide and disappear" (219–20).

This is one of Findley's most accomplished stories. It portrays in miniature what novels like *The Wars, Famous Last Words, The Telling of Lies, The Piano Man's Daughter,* and *You Went Away* explore at length: the controlled intensity of emotion; the narrative framing of memory;

the first-person voice of a narrator who searches the past for the ghosts that haunt him or her; and the desire for reconciliation with our shared, complex, and deeply flawed humanity. While this story is not about Allan Findley as such, it most certainly plumbs the depths of Timothy Findley's feelings for a father who he felt had abandoned him by joining the RCAF and then rejected him because he was gay. Moreover, Allan wallowed in self-pity when the war was over, drank constantly, was abusive, and denied Tiff a father's love and approbation until late in his life, and yet it was Tiff who scattered Allan's ashes as he had wished. In real life and in his work, Timothy Findley was not finished with this father figure, but in "Stones" he achieved a remarkable sense of a son's peaceful reconciliation with a father. Stones and ashes are what Findley offers the reader in this story, and they are his most profound symbols of remembrance.

———

By the end of the decade Bill and Tiff were volunteering at Casey House, the AIDS hospice created by June Callwood and named for her son. Callwood was a friend, as well as a distinguished author, journalist, and activist, so in 1988 they stepped up to support her. They attended her first fundraiser, and for two and a half years they devoted one day a week to help at Casey House.[13] Bill manned the telephone switchboard and Findley met with patients, talking with them or reading to them and always bringing them comfort. As Bill recalls, the work was "wonderful therapy" for Tiff because it helped him overcome his fear of death. On a few occasions they invited the hospice staff, with those residents capable of travelling, to Stone Orchard for summer parties. Guests swam in the pool or relaxed in the sun, and Bill cooked for more than fifty people: "great pots of curried shrimp, chicken stew, corn on the cob and tomatoes— all from our garden—served with endless numbers of fruit-topped cream pies and homemade ice cream" (*WLB* 203). This hospice work may have been "wonderful therapy" for Findley's fear of death, but the suicide of Ken Adachi in 1989 (in the wake of accusations of plagiarism) was nevertheless a terrible shock; he and Findley had often talked by phone late at night,

Ken had publicly supported Findley's work, and his death left a host of questions unanswered.[14] Silence, Findley wrote, was "his most grievous fault": "Speaking to others after the event, I found that my rage against his silence was echoed again and again. But the silence, after all, was Ken's, and we have to accept it now as having been deliberate and [...] a generous example of his integrity. He wouldn't have troubled us for all the world" (*IM* 300).

One of the most important and positive assignments Findley accepted that year was to host a CBC radio series called *Lost Innocence: The Children of World War Two*. *Lost Innocence* won a Peabody Award for distinguished achievement in broadcasting, and it represents a fitting coda to Findley's thinking about the impact of the war, the state of world affairs, and his own work during the 1980s. Karen Levine, the author of *Hana's Suitcase* (2002), did the research and wrote the script for the series, which involved interviews with people who had been children during the war, notably those who had survived the Holocaust. She was nervous about approaching Timothy Findley; after all, he was a star. He was also extremely busy, but that war meant more to him than she realized. At first he declined, but after he agreed to help her, they added an episode to the series called "Children on the Home Front," which allowed him to reflect on Adachi's experiences as a Japanese Canadian interned during the war. The series aired in September to mark the fiftieth anniversary of the start of the war, and in her review of the production Antonia Zerbisias called it "an emotional hurricane" and a "superbly produced mix of very personal interviews" with a powerful soundtrack that included children singing "The Maple Leaf Forever" and Lorne Greene's "Voice of Doom" war broadcasts. Part 3, "Children of the Holocaust," she said, "will tear your heart out," and part 2, about the home front, reminds Canadians about what children here experienced and how Canada, as a nation, behaved towards Jewish refugees and Japanese Canadians. *Lost Innocence* was rebroadcast in the fall of 2014, when it was met with silence and largely ignored, but the program deserves better. As Findley insisted, repressing or ignoring the past produces forgetting, and forgetting is dangerous.

In January 1987, he gave an address to the Philosophical Society at Trent University called "My Final Hour" (*IM* 301–19). In it he told the audience that he believed in the power of imagination to save us and this earth, and he concluded his remarks with two quotations: the last words in Dr. Johnson's final journal—"Against despair"—and several lines from Phyllis Webb's "I Daniel." Like Webb's Daniel, he said, he had tried to pose urgent questions in his work, the kind of questions that warn readers to pay attention. But Dr. Johnson's admonition led him to urge his audience, composed largely of students, to resist despair and never abandon hope: "Nothing is harder, now in the present time, than staring down despair. But stare it down we must. Unless we do, there can be no reconciliation" (318). With the benefit of hindsight, it is clear that his work from the eighties uses imagination masterfully to stare down despair and memory to bear witness to human violence and corruption, but Timothy Findley was far from finished remembering and imagining, and several major works lay just ahead.

Four

STILL PAYING ATTENTION—

1990 TO 2002

CHAPTER ELEVEN

The Canadian Findley

WHERE ARE WE GOING? AND WHAT COMES AFTER?

HAVE WE FORGOTTEN SOMETHING? WILL WE BE REMEMBERED?

HAVE WE BEEN SEEN? *YES.*

(Timothy Findley, *You Went Away* 5)

1990 to 1993

From *Inside Memory*
to *The Stillborn Lover*

Four major concerns preoccupied Findley during the 1990s: the important role of memory for his imagination; recreating the lives of his ancestors; exposing what he saw as the corruption of twentieth-century society; and death. The decade began with the publication of *Inside Memory* in 1990 and peaked with the premiere of *The Stillborn Lover* and the publication of *Headhunter*, both in 1993, followed by *The Piano Man's Daughter*, which appeared just two years later: four major works in less than five years. The demands on his time and energy had reached an unsustainable level, however, and to follow his steps through his calendars is to see that he was on a collision course with collapse. He continued to win prestigious awards; he increased his travel, both at home and abroad; and he accepted several invitations to give lectures. The pressure of constant deadlines, not least with his publisher HarperCollins, plagued him, and he neglected his health. Despite his lifelong hypochondria, he refused to listen to his body because thoughts of serious illness and death haunted him and his mind was teeming with ideas for new work, which he was desperate to complete while he still had time. To add to this stress, by 1996 he and Bill were preparing to leave Stone Orchard for good and, however practical and necessary this move was, for Findley it was emotionally and psychologically traumatic. Two deaths in September of 1990 were a further blow. Although the timing of such losses can never be good, these deaths occurred when he was frantically busy and heavily burdened with commitments. Once again, as with his father's death and Aunt Ruth's, he had no quiet, private time to grieve. The promotion tour for *Inside Memory* began at the end of September. It lasted for nine weeks, taking him and Bill from Halifax to Vancouver and landing him in hospital twice. Margaret Findley died on September 26, at the age of 88, as he was preparing to leave on the tour. He had written to her on 1 January 1990 to tell her how much her letters meant to him, to tell her she was his "splendid, courageous, and thoughtful friend" and that he felt "privileged and endlessly grateful that we are each other's people."[1] In essays, stories, and finally in *You Went Away*, he acknowledged his mother's strength and intelligence and recognized the pain she endured in her marriage and from her family's past. When she died, he did not record in his journal any reflections on her life or death that compare with his complex reaction to Allan's death; there was no need to because of their clear, steady love for each other and mutual trust.

The other person he loved and lost that September was Janet Baldwin, who died on the twenty-eighth, just two days after his mother. Janet had been a presence in his life since his childhood. She had boosted his morale during the London years, visited Stone Orchard regularly, and was with him and Bill at Atlantic House. Patricia Brennan's terracotta bust of Baldwin occupied a place of honour in his home, beside a bust Brennan had made of Findley. As he became increasingly busy during the eighties, however, he saw less of Janet, and after her hospitalization with dementia, he visited her on rare occasions. Nevertheless, Janet mattered enormously to him and she occupied an important place in *Inside Memory*, where he described seeing her once in hospital shortly before she died and recreated her visit to Stone Orchard in 1974, after Boris Volkoff (her former husband) died. Remembering the hospital visit, Findley recalled the woman he knew when he was a child and the way she stood "poised without intensity" (*IM* 111). By 1990 she no longer recognized him but responded to his smile and suggestion that they go for a walk. He pushed her wheelchair along the corridor to a window, where she could see the sunlight and the frozen lake in the distance. These memories were bittersweet because the woman in the wheelchair was no longer the young Janet Baldwin whose grand entrances had always delighted him. His other memory reads more like a scene for a play and captures a younger Janet with all the distress of her marriage to Volkoff. When she visited Stone Orchard after his death, she told Findley about his dying and her role in it. He, in turn, created a story within *Inside Memory* about her visit, recounting how she met Volkoff, her performance at the 1936 Berlin Olympics, and her refusal to bear children because of her hemophilia. Then he recreated the final scene of her departure from Stone Orchard, after she confessed her continued love for Volkoff and that she had remarried him on his deathbed. Finally, he wrote the stage instruction: "She walked away. She didn't even say goodbye. [...] A lesson in perfect timing" (*IM* 121). This mode of remembering as dramatic storytelling, in what can only be called vividly realized scenes embedded in the larger narrative remembering of his life, makes *Inside Memory* the unusual memoir that it is—a form of narrative performance in which the narrator plays a minor role, a fifth business, in his own autobiography.

By the end of 1991, Findley had received two awards for *Inside Memory* and had been named to the Order of Ontario. The year 1992 was largely devoted to work on *The Stillborn Lover* and *Headhunter*, but he made time to begin teaching at Humber College and on December 10 he gave the CBC's Graham Spry Lecture on Culture and Society. The Humber College connection started with a one-week summer course for a writers' workshop, and after three summers he shifted to a post-graduate correspondence course, which helped pay the bills and continued until he died. According to Joe Kertes, Findley was a "brilliant teacher" and loved by his students.[2] At the end of the 1997 summer workshop, Humber College awarded him their Calliope Prize for Excellence in Writing and Teaching. One essay he wrote at this time, "Point-Counterpoint: Ethics in the Media," illustrates his continuing concern about the dangers of censorship and the importance of writers, books, and archives for the preservation of democratic freedoms. These concerns date back to the 1950s, but by the nineties he had the profile and celebrity status to reach wider audiences. In the "Point-Counterpoint" essay (repr. in *J* 168–71), he took up his cudgels in defence of Brian and Terence McKenna's television series about the Second World War, *The Valour and the Horror*. As is clear, the war was a sensitive subject for Findley, and he had high praise for the balanced and moving way in which the McKennas explored the courageous feats, the agonies, and the atrocities committed in Europe and the Pacific by the Allies as well as by the Germans and Japanese. What prompted his speaking out was the reactionary response to the series by veterans' groups, and others, who succeeded in forcing the CBC to halt further broadcasts. His chief target in the essay was the deception practised during the war, as in news reports claiming that Dieppe was an Allied success. The first casualty in war, he reminded his readers, is "truth," the same point he had made in *Famous Last Words* and *The Telling of Lies*. To pretend that the Allied forces always did what was necessary and right, a mantra that the series challenged, was to spread propaganda. Remembering the devastation of Berlin that had shocked him in 1955, he wrote: "I personally witnessed the results of what can only be called Allied barbarism" (*J* 169). He concluded by accusing the Canadian government of reaching inside the CBC, "where government has no business," to stage a coup by damning *The Valour and the Horror* (170). To keep repeating that "we meant well" was, for Findley, to produce a cover up—the big lie.

The Graham Spry Lecture, named for the co-founder of the Canadian Radio League, which persuaded the government to establish the CBC, gave Findley a further opportunity to expand upon the points he had made regarding the fate of *The Valour and the Horror*. He gave this lecture at the University of Toronto as part of CBC's *Ideas* program, hosted by Lister Sinclair. Sinclair introduced him as "a champion of Canadian

culture" and Findley went on to perform the lecture as a one-man dialogue.[3] The audience enjoyed this performance; there was much laughter
and a very warm response. Findley's argument, however, was deadly serious. He assured them that he was not a pessimist, but he asked them to
reflect on the survival of the written word, with all it conveyed of human
creativity and imagination, in an age of television, censorship, and political correctness. His voice heavy with irony, he pronounced that one must
never offend the oil companies, which is precisely what he would do in a
speech before the oilmen of Calgary in 2001. And he thanked God that
television, which "precludes imagination," and Walt Disney, who degrades
books for children, "never got his hands on *The Tale of Peter Rabbit.*"[4] He
then stressed the importance of two books that he valued: John Hersey's
Hiroshima and Ray Bradbury's *Fahrenheit 451.* These books, he insisted,
told the truth, through fact and fiction, and provided urgent warnings
about past lies and contemporary threats to democracy for anyone willing
to read them and pay attention. Literature, he told the audience, confirms
the human spirit: "All literature is a singing."

Had Findley lived into his eighties to see the rise of social media, communication by tweet, and the online management of the news, he would
have been critical, but he was not totally averse to electronic media. He
always watched television, listened to the radio, and even tinkered with a
computer, until Bill took it away because he was not getting on with his
writing. And he resorted to the tape recorder, instead of the written letter,
to connect with a few close, but distant, friends. One of these recorded
letters from 1993 has survived on tape and a remarkable one it is. On September 7, after a long day's writing, an exhausted Findley sat down at the
machine to talk to Michael Tippett, who had visited Toronto in the late
eighties and asked to meet the author of *Not Wanted on the Voyage.*[5] A
warm friendship had developed from that first meeting. The transcription
of this letter runs to seventeen pages, but the tape itself cannot be reproduced in written form because that is where one hears Timothy Findley talking and thinking and chuckling as he reaches out to someone so
far away. The words and his form of address are informal, even intimate.
"Hello Michael," he begins, confessing that he knows he needs "to stop"

writing and not rush his work. He recalls Tippett's advice to him: put your best work "out there" and move on to the next stage. Then he tells Tippett that he has "written what I think is the best piece of work *I* have ever produced [*Headhunter*,] a very *harsh* book. But one that I wanted and knew I must write."[6] He also promises to send Tippett a copy of *The Stillborn Lover*, of which he is very proud, and he describes the play's premiere at length. The recording ends with pauses, as if he is reluctant to let go of this spoken connection with Tippett: "how good it is *for me* ... to have thought of you there ... that I can speak to you, that you are a voice in my heart and in my life. [...] This comes to you with love, Michael."

Findley had good reason to be proud of his new play because *The Stillborn Lover* is arguably his most powerful and perfectly crafted work for the theatre, and the process of writing this play is nicely captured in an important documentary interview he gave in 1992. By the early nineties, he had been interviewed many times in print, on radio, and on television, but Terence Macartney-Filgate's documentary film *Timothy Findley: Anatomy of a Writer* is by far the most intimate, informative, and enjoyable of all his interviews. It was primarily shot at Stone Orchard and Macartney-Filgate was an old and trusted friend, as well as a gifted documentary filmmaker, so the Tiff Findley captured in this film is relaxed and at home. The film opens with a short scene in which Findley plays two roles—that of a snarky interviewer in dark glasses and an ugly tweed jacket, with a Donald Trump hairdo, who asks rude questions of the writer Timothy Findley: are you a *Canadian* writer? Are you a *homosexual* writer? When the camera shifts to a relaxed Mr. Findley, Tiff answers calmly that he is a *writer* who is Canadian and a *writer* who is homosexual. Then Mr. Findley turns the tables on the interviewer: do you ask about sexual orientation when you interview heterosexual writers? Macartney-Filgate had proposed this little skit and Findley loved the idea. In this way the stage is set for what follows: an autobiographical account of his life, family history, childhood memories—notably that traumatic moment in 1942, when his mother left him alone at St. Andrew's College (she took Michael, who was ill, back to Toronto)—and his views on writing or, at least, on how he writes. Other people appear in this story through old photographs or in real life, and they are key to the way Findley thinks about life. Bill appears in several sequences, and Marilyn Powell (a friend) plays a brief role when Findley describes his visceral approach to writing—"I am not an intellectual writer."

The most powerful presences, however, are the winter roads beside Stone Orchard, the fields, gardens, and rolling landscapes of the area, and, of course, the animals. We see Timothy Findley walking the dogs, with one or two cats trailing along, and cradling one favourite cat: "everything that lives is holy," he says. We see him at the kitchen table with Bill as he reads Tiff's daily work back to him so he can hear the rhythm and cadence of the sentences. We see him at the piano playing "Smoke Gets in Your Eyes" and recalling how his parents played this music from the thirties at their parties. And we see him in his study surrounded by his notebooks and journals explaining how his characters and their stories come to life for him. An especially fascinating sequence concerns *The Stillborn Lover*, on which he had just begun to work. Bill Hutt and Martha Henry, who would star in the premiere, perform three possible versions of a key confession scene for the film, while Findley searches for the right way to handle the exchange. He rejects the first take as wrong and the second as "too explicit," but the third time he likes the result, which is the version he kept for the play. This rehearsing process reveals the complex emotional depths of the plot and sheds light on how he worked through ideas and drafts to create his art. After the documentary shoot was finished, Martha Henry inquired about the play because she wanted to stage it at the Grand Theatre in London, Ontario, but Findley had not yet finished it; he set to work immediately and in three weeks he had a complete working script for the director and actors.

Although *The Stillborn Lover* was not polished and performed until 1993, Findley's interest in two men, Herbert Norman and John Watkins, whose stories inspired the play, dates back to the 1970s. He was well aware of the Cold War persecution of homosexuals and people with Communist sympathies (described in detail by Kinsman and Gentile in *The Canadian War on Queers*), and by June 1978 he had completed the draft of a television script called "The Norman Affair," about the life and death of

Canadian diplomat Herbert Norman (1909–57).[7] Norman, who had been briefly attracted to Communism in the thirties, ended up on the blacklist of the RCMP and the CIA. He was interrogated more than once, fully exonerated, and in 1956 appointed Canadian ambassador to Egypt by Lester B. Pearson, then Minister of External Affairs. Nevertheless, the RCMP and the CIA continued to hound him until, on 4 April 1957, Norman stepped backwards from the roof of a Cairo apartment building. His suicide was a *cause célèbre*. According to Charles Taylor, whose book *Six Journeys: A Canadian Pattern* Findley owned and drew upon for his play, "old friends saw Norman's suicide as neither cowardly nor as an admission of guilt, but as a brave gesture of defiance to his enemies. [...] He took the ultimate step which would affirm his own integrity, while passing the burden of shame and guilt back to his adversaries" (Taylor 148). This Herbert Norman is, in part, the man who inspired Findley's creation of Harry Raymond, the main protagonist in *The Stillborn Lover*. The other influence on the backstory of the play and on the Harry Raymond character is John Watkins (1902–64), whom Findley had met in 1955 when he travelled to Moscow with the production of *Hamlet*. Watkins served as Canadian ambassador to the USSR from 1954 to 1956, but because he was gay he was considered a security risk, vulnerable to coercion and blackmail by the KGB. He died in 1964 in a Montreal hotel room, ostensibly from a heart attack, but the RCMP later admitted that he had been secretly detained and was undergoing police interrogation when he died.

Harry Raymond, Canadian ambassador to Moscow, is the "stillborn lover" of the play for reasons that become clear as the plot unfolds. The action begins in the fall of 1972; Harry and his wife Marian have just been recalled from Moscow to Ottawa and taken to a "safe house" overlooking a steep ravine that drops down to a river below. Their daughter, Diana, joins them to create an important dimension in the developing drama. The first question driving the plot is: why has the couple been suddenly recalled? The next question is linked to the first: why are two RCMP officers stationed in this so-called safe house, watching the Raymonds? These questions expand to include many others: What is the connection between Harry Raymond and a young Russian called Mischa who was found murdered in a Moscow hotel room? Who murdered this young man and why? Has Harry betrayed his country and his old friend, Michael Riordan, the external affairs minister, by giving in to KGB blackmail? And what role does Marian Raymond, who is suffering from early onset Alzheimer's, play in this complex story of love, intrigue, and betrayal? Their daughter is the concerned witness to her parents' ordeal, and she must learn to accept her father and help her ailing mother. The RCMP superintendent is there to interrogate Harry and Marian, and he has an archive of incriminating photographs with which to confront Harry and force him to admit he is a homosexual and a traitor. The Riordans, Michael and wife Juliet, are long-time friends of the Raymonds, but this friendship is about to be sacrificed to Michael's political ambitions because Michael's goal is to become prime minister, and a scandal involving the Raymonds would harm his career. For anyone familiar with Canadian Cold War history and government homophobia, the play's parallels with Pearson's career and the fates of Watkins and Norman are clear.

In the confession scene that Hutt and Henry performed for Findley in *Anatomy of a Writer* and that he chose for his play, Marian stands quietly to one side while Harry tells his daughter that Mischa was his lover. It is a stunning moment, after which the three characters freeze, the stage is silent, and the lights fade to black. In act 2, father and daughter confront each other in one of the most wrenching scenes of the play. Her father's confession has left Diana feeling betrayed: "I don't know who you are," she throws at him in anger; "all my life you've lied about who you are" (*SBL* 78). "What am I going to do with this information, Father? Not that you're queer—who gives a damn! But that you lied. You lied" (79). This is a core theme in the play and a deeply personal issue for Findley, who knew what it meant to lie about his identity, to pretend, and then to be rejected by loved ones and by society. However, Harry refuses to sympathize with Diana's confusion and anger: "You don't know me because you do not want to know *me*. You want to know a stranger. An invention" (81). And he explains that he had to hide his sexual orientation because his work demanded it and his government insisted that he *"not be a homosexual"* (80). Consequently, he did what was necessary to survive: "I killed what stood in my way, Diana. Stone dead. [...] I killed myself" (83). During this emotional scene, Harry comes downstage to the edge of the garden, with its sharp drop into the ravine, and this movement is not idle stage business. Audience members, and readers, should keep that movement and that drop in mind.

Just how much Marian knows or remembers, however, remains a puzzle throughout the play. She has startlingly lucid moments and remembers a young man called Mischa, whom she introduced to her husband, and that she had found other lovers for Harry. She will not, however, tell the RCMP that Harry is homosexual or that he had a liaison with Mischa. Despite her illness, she is capable of protecting Harry from the police by pretending she recalls less than she does, and she understands that she and Harry are caught in a political game beyond their control. In the prelude to the play, Marian's voice is heard describing the ancient game of Go, which is played by two players with sets of round, smooth, black and white stones on a square board. Once stones have been set in place they cannot be moved, unless they are captured and removed; as Marian explains: "Their positions are locked, irrevocable. Like the moves and gestures we make with our lives" (1). However, the game can be lost if a player resigns, and, according to some rules for the game, such a resignation is tantamount to committing suicide. When Harry tells her that he has been her stillborn lover, "passing through [her] life on a diplomatic passport" (148), she understands that they are saying goodbye to each other and "*hands him one of the stones*": "Here," she tells him. "It's your move" (150). And the play ends. The audience, or reader, does not know what Harry will do but this game of Go has left him only one ethical choice: suicide. That steep drop into the ravine beckons, and, like Herbert Norman, Harry will stay true to himself by choosing death with honour and integrity, rather than life with more lies.[8]

In a thoughtful interview with Patricia Black, Findley discussed the importance of the Second World War for the play and mentioned two books that had influenced his thinking (John Hersey's *Hiroshima* and Anthony Cave Brown's *Bodyguard of Lies*). He also expressed admiration for Alan Turing, the man who had broken the Enigma code at Bletchley

Park, and for Hugh Whitemore's play, *Breaking the Code*, about Turing's life and suicide, after he was convicted of being homosexual. But as he was quick to point out, *The Stillborn Lover* is not about Turing or the war, as such, any more than it is about Herbert Norman or John Watkins. It is, he tells Black, a play about memory, politics, ruthless politicians, and love. The theme that brings these issues together is betrayal, "and what people will do. They'll throw even their most beloved friends over to achieve what they want" (44). *The Stillborn Lover*, which won an Arthur Ellis Award in 1994 and a Chalmers Award in 1996, offers a distillation of Findley's themes—identity, memory, love, and betrayal—and in it he creates credible, moving characters who command our attention. Furthermore, he presents the story in a tight, elegant, Aristotelian structure, with the layers of meaning and symbolism of great tragedy. It is his most deeply personal and his most Canadian play, steeped as it is in his understanding of identity politics and the history of his country. It is also his most sensitive, and convincing, exploration of the price paid for being gay in a prejudiced, rigidly heterosexual world.

Headhunter and the "Fascination of the Abomination"

On Nancy Colbert's advice, Findley had moved from Penguin to Harper-Collins in 1990. All his work, from *Inside Memory* onward, was published with HarperCollins, and, beginning with *Headhunter*, Iris Tupholme became his primary editor.[9] She had met him a few years previously through Cynthia Good, his Penguin editor, but Timothy Findley was a star, hence a serious responsibility, and any new Findley book was a "big deal." She was nervous, but recalls him as always amiable and open to a dialogue about whichever manuscript he was working on, and she often visited Stone Orchard, where she, Tiff, and Bill would sit at the kitchen table discussing the work-in-progress. Her role was to give feedback and ask questions, while Bill took notes and recorded the sessions. Productive and agreeable as these sessions were, *Headhunter* was not an easy novel to handle. She found it "a very dark vision" and told me that Findley found it "terrifying to write." Without question, this is his most disturbing novel. It is an unflinching study of the vicious underbelly of contemporary society that exposes Toronto, Rosedale elites, the abuse of children, and the maltreatment of psychiatric patients. It is not called *Headhunter* lightly, and Conrad's *Heart of Darkness* is its chief inspiration and literary intertext. The two novels are closely connected but, if anything, Findley goes where Conrad refused to go and is explicit about "the horror," where Conrad leaves much unsaid.

In August 1992, when he had finished his second full draft, he allowed a few trusted friends to read the manuscript and waited anxiously for their responses. Nancy Colbert did not reply quickly, which worried him, but David Staines, Iris Tupholme, and Phyllis Webb sent him their responses promptly. They praised the book, but with some reservations and suggestions, among them that he reduce the overt references to Conrad. He summarized everyone's remarks in his 1992 journal, but it is his own reaction that screams from the page. Not since the 1950s in England had he condemned himself with such a *cri de cœur*. He hated *Headhunter*:

> Could not read at first—"badly written"—"dreadful premise"—"characters don't work". *Very, very* negative reaction. Stopped reading [...] Begin again—thinking "you were tired, the first time, too close to be able to see it"—depressed etcetera—Second reading same if not worse than first. Actively *hate* the book. [...] How can I have made something I hate? I am afraid to launch the book. Fear of being misperceived—old fear of lack of intellect [...] I feel too much and know too little. I had wanted—*desperately* a final success—a book that would widen the reputation of my work—increase readership abroad. That was supposed to be *FLW*—shot down in flames. Now this. I am lost—and don't know what to do. [...] I fear—(rightly or wrongly is not the point, here)—that it is flawed beyond redemption. [...] *What I fear most is the next step that must be taken—which is the salvaging of a good idea by lifting the book all the way to its potential*—and I cannot achieve the confidence that is required to do that. But I MUST try. (LAC 124:13)

Perhaps only Bill and Iris would ever know what it cost him to revise and publish *Headhunter*. But revise it he did, so that when he recorded his letter to Michael Tippett, he could say the novel was "the best piece of work" he had produced.

Headhunter had, in fact, gone through many stages of development and only gradually taken its final form. Some of the secondary characters in the very large cast had been in his mind since the sixties and appeared in "Dinner Along the Amazon," "Duel in Cluny Park," and in the story from *Stones* called "Dreams," about two psychiatrists called Drs. Everett and Mimi Menlo. According to his 1990 journal (LAC 188), on July 22 he had made his first big "epiphany" about the work-in-progress while shaving and ran, stark naked, face lathered, razor in hand, into the dining room to tell Bill. He had made the psychiatry connection and would give the name Everett Menlo to the doctor at the Queen Street Mental Health Centre; he would model this man on Ed Turner, to whom the novel is dedicated, and make himself one of Menlo's patients and, thus, a character in the story. These developments helped him understand how to design the narrative, and at this stage Menlo was to be a first-person narrator. Findley also knew he wanted to create an institution called the Parkin and have it presided over by a powerful figure whose early name was Janos Kordas.[10] Other sources of inspiration were also falling into place. In the fall of 1990, while on tour for *Inside Memory*, he saw a Calgary exhibition of paintings by Attila Richard Lukacs and was utterly captivated, albeit horrified, by his large, homoerotic pictures of violent skinheads in Doc Martens boots, and when he reached Vancouver he arranged to see more of the artist's work at the Diane Farris Gallery.[11] In his journal, Findley noted that "his work says on canvas what I am trying to say in [the] new book" (LAC 188). Lukacs and his paintings from the late 1980s inspired the artist character Julian Slade in *Headhunter*, and the Slade painting, *The Golden Chamber of the White Dogs*, closely resembles several Lukacs pieces. Other characters were already identified in the journal, including the photographer John Dai Bowen; Emma, the surgeon's wife with the white limousine; Lilah (not yet a major character); and one of the most corrupt Rosedale men, Ben Webster. The initial working title was "Heart of Darkness in

Rosedale." This changed on 28 July 1990, when he decided to call the novel "Asylum," an evocative title recalling *Can You See Me Yet?*, and one that reveals his shift in emphasis from Rosedale to the Parkin Institute. The precise parallel with *Heart of Darkness* did not emerge, however, until he decided to call his evil doctor Kurtz and his good doctor Marlow. On 29 June 1991, he had another "epiphany": the Marlow character, first cast as a journalist doing research on child-abuse cases in London, Ontario, should be the psychiatrist, and he dropped the Menlo character.[12]

The background sources, research, and literary influences informing *Headhunter* were extensive. Findley enjoyed this basic research because grounding fiction in the world of fact was always important to him. As the journals show, he was reading widely, taking copious notes, and preserving newspaper clippings relevant to the novel, such as reports on violence in High Park and on Finch Avenue West in Toronto. Susan Sontag's "The Pornographic Imagination" (1967) impressed him greatly, as did George Steiner's "To Civilize Our Gentlemen," George Grant's *Technology and Empire*, and T. S. Eliot's *The Waste Land*;[13] these last three were works he had first read years before and they warned against the dangers facing contemporary society. However, it was the difficult issue of pornography that obsessed him, and he linked pornographic practices to society's general appropriation of youthfulness and, from there, to the exploitation of children, and, ultimately to the destruction of the planet. Even AIDS, he argued, encouraged the sexual abuse of children. He railed in his journal about the connection between AIDS and child abuse because he feared the disease encouraged some men to think that "the only truly *safe* sex is the sex you have with 'virgins.'" "The whole situation," he continued, "is pornographic. It is the penultimate phase of the demise of the social contract. The final phase will more than likely involve universal plagues far worse than AIDS—and/or environmental catastrophe which will decree that we can no longer care for one another" (LAC 322). Which is why Conrad's Kurtz and *Heart of Darkness* were so important to him. He believed that "Kurtz is gaining ground on us and the fabric of our everyday 'civilized' lives is woven from the very horror we imagine we reject. [...] Kurtz is in all of us, endlessly weaving a circumstance for holocaust" (LAC 322).

As Findley saw it, *Headhunter* "is a book about witness," and in it he bears witness to the corruption of society by paying attention—and calling his readers'.attention—to the world around him. Unlike *Not Wanted on the Voyage*, this novel is not presented as myth or fable; it more closely resembles *Famous Last Words* and addresses Freyberg's warning that to forget Dachau and to forgive evil is to allow the horror to recur and produce the "demise of the social contract." Mr. Kurtz was not simply back, he had never gone away, but Findley chose to balance the corruption he represents with good in the form of three characters: Dr. Charlie Marlow, Professor Nicholas Fagan, and Miss Lilah Kemp. The novel opens as Lilah Kemp "inadvertently set[s] Kurtz free from page 92 of *Heart of Darkness*" (*H* 3).[14] A schizophrenic, a spiritualist (who communes with Susanna Moodie), an ex-librarian, and a lover of books, Lilah is quietly reading on the main floor of the Metropolitan Toronto Reference Library beside the rock garden and pool with its plants, when suddenly there he is—"a tall, pale man" with "dyed black hair"(4–5)—watching her. She recognizes him instantly as Dr. Rupert Kurtz, head of the Parkin Institute of Psychiatric Research, and she orders him back inside the book. But he moves away and disappears through the Yonge Street doors: "Kurtz, the horror-meister. Kurtz, the headhunter" (6). In this way, Findley established the extended metaphor of the novel: Toronto is another "heart of darkness." As Lilah has intuitively understood, this Dr. Kurtz is the evil genius of the tale; Conrad's African river, with its deadly jungle, is the St. Lawrence River leading to Lake Ontario and to the urban jungle of Toronto; the abominations and primitive rites glimpsed in *Heart of Darkness* are transposed to the Parkin and to the pornographic rites of a local group of men. Dr. Kurtz sits, as does Conrad's Kurtz, deep within the precincts of his empire, controlling everyone around him for his own ends. Or almost everyone. As long as Lilah stays off her medication, she retains her psychic powers, and when the new doctor, Charles Marlow, arrives to work at the Parkin, they will both actively resist Kurtz's power. Only the mad and those rare individuals with integrity, who understand the wisdom of the mad as artists do—or so *Headhunter* tells us—can appreciate the danger facing contemporary society and take steps to address it.

Findley's plan for the novel was a bold one, and its success depends on a reader's willingness to accept the initial analogy between *Heart of Darkness* and *Headhunter* and to believe the perceptions of someone like Lilah. It is not until near the end of the story, when Charlie Marlow has the information he needs to confront Kurtz, that the analogy with *Heart of Darkness* surfaces with full force. Not only has Charlie come into possession of Kurtz's personal reflections on his ambitions for the Parkin—to expand it and enhance his reputation—and the ruthless steps he has taken to meet them, but he has also found files full of incriminating evidence that reveals what is going on behind the scenes at the Parkin and what Kurtz is capable of. These files contain patient records, names, transcripts, and photographs that prove the existence of a wealthy Club of Men that gathers to indulge in the psychological and sexual abuse of children, who are drugged with *Obedian* to ensure their compliance and who end up in psychiatric care at the Parkin. By the time Marlow visits Kurtz, however, the man is ill with sturnusemia, the disease he had tried to deny, and like Conrad's Kurtz, Findley's lies dying as Marlow listens to his appalling confession. Worse still, the man shows no remorse. As Kurtz wrote in the document outlining his ambitions for the Parkin: *"Access to the personal obsessions of the élite equals access to the pockets of the élite … psychiatry is my mode, psychiatric research is my delivery system"* (493). His confession to Marlow that he knew about the Club of Men and facilitated their activities with experimental drugs is rendered moot by his rationale for such behaviour. Not only did he blackmail his wealthy patients, he excused them and insists that "none of these children was forced" because just as their fathers lusted after them, so the children "craved their fathers [...] their attention—their approval" (499). All Kurtz did was give the men "permission": "We made a pact," he whispers to Marlow, "a fair exchange. The Parkin got its new wing—I got my research funds—and they got …" what they wanted—their children (502). When Marlow asks Kurtz what, beyond ruthless ambition, motivated him, the answer he receives is shocking and personal—"I wanted to be … my father" (503)—and completely incommensurate with his crimes.

If the reader hopes that the truth about the "fascination of the abom-ination" connecting Kurtz, the Parkin, and the Club will bring resolution or redemption, let alone restore safety and sanity to Toronto and to the victims of corruption and violence, he or she will be disappointed. Findley could not wring any hope, let alone redemption, from his heart of dark-ness. Violence, corruption, sexual deviance, pornography, madness, and the abuse of children exist in the all-too-real heart of darkness that is Toronto. What's more, as Findley was at pains to stress, these forces are steadily undermining the social contract that supports civilization.

Although there are many interesting minor characters in *Head-hunter*, each with his or her troubled backstory, Toronto itself is the most imposing character. Much more than a setting or a backdrop, the city is the dark heart of the novel; most of its characters merely inhabit its spaces while furthering its moral contamination. Here Findley explores his long hatred of cities and the corruption he felt was synonymous with them. The portrait he creates of Toronto is sufficiently complete for a reader unfamiliar with the city to find their way around, from the Metropolitan Toronto Reference Library, south on Yonge Street and west along Bloor to St. George Street, south past the University of Toronto's Robarts Library, or downtown to the Bay Street offices and law firms, to various restau-rants, some with fictional names, and to the Queen Street Mental Health Centre, then back up further north and east of Bathurst to the Annex. Lapin Lanes, where Lilah and Marlow live, bears a name that hints at the long-lost natural history of the city and the fact that small animals, like rabbits and hedgehogs, still survive in its hidden corners. Furthermore, the name links Lilah and her place in the city with one of her favourite fic-tional characters, Peter Rabbit, whose lost shoes, her talisman, she keeps wrapped in tissue paper in her handkerchief drawer or purse. Rosedale comes alive with all its history, elegance, and manicured lawns. Its streets and landmarks are named—Crescent Road, South Drive, Cluny Drive, Beaumont Road, Glen Road, and the Glen Road Bridge—and its wealthy families entertain, drive their posh cars, and pursue private affairs and deals behind closed doors or in the Beaumorris Corporation office tower downtown. The parks Findley evokes are there, real; one can walk in them, or cruise them after dark. Toronto's private schools are also there, and in one of them, located "on the city's outskirts" (*H* 100) but not named, twelve-year-old Warren Ellis was sexually assaulted by an older boy while "a dozen of [this boy's] acolytes gathered to watch" (98); he is now Kurtz's patient at the Parkin.

Among the minor characters in *Headhunter* there is a special one whose role is instrumental in linking this portrait of Toronto with Conrad's vision of corruption and with Findley's personal archive of ancestors: Nicholas Fagan. This time Fagan is cast as a professor emeritus of Trinity College, Dublin, and a specialist in English literature. Lilah Kemp had been one of his students, whom he taught about life, ethics, and the role literature and language play in sustaining human imagination and, thereby, the highest principles of civilization. As if in answer to Lilah's need for guidance, he accepts an invitation to give the Appleby Lecture at the University of Toronto, and he travels to Montreal by ocean liner and then up the St. Lawrence to Lake Ontario and the city. At a gathering in his honour Dr. Fagan describes his journey upstream toward Toronto as a personal voyage of discovery, but what he reports finding is scarcely flattering. "This place [Canada] was once perceived as nothing more or less than a place in which to survive. A place to live," but now, he believes, "there is little beauty left—but much ugliness. Little wilderness—but much emptiness. No explorers—but many exploiters. There is no art—no music—no literature—but only entertainment. And there is no philosophy. This that was once a living place for humankind has become their killing ground" (299). When Lilah tells him that Kurtz has escaped from *Heart of Darkness* into Toronto's streets, he reminds her that "Kurtz is with us always [...]. He is the darkness in us all" (302).

Is Kurtz then mad, a monster, a psychopath, a man utterly devoid of conscience? Or does Kurtz represent something terrible in the human psyche, something his creator, Timothy Findley, recognized from his own childhood? Kurtz's theory that children crave a father's "attention [and] approval" points to one of the buried sources of the novel's power: the impact of Allan Findley on Findley and his need for his father's attention and approval. Which is not to imply that Allan did anything physically abusive to his son, but to understand that his absence, drinking, and criticism of the boy and young man had injured Tiff deeply. As Dr. Richard Isay argues in *Being Homosexual*, fathers who withdraw from their homosexual sons can cause loss of self-esteem and much suffering (32–35), and Findley fathers are either withdrawn and absent, or cruel to the point of fascist tyranny. Father-son relationships in Findley's works are always troubled, complex, and, more often than not, destructive, and his personal experience informs his perspective on Kurtz, the fathers in the Club of Men, and the heart of darkness in *Headhunter*.

In his 1992 journal, Findley had written that he hated this new novel and feared it was a failure. Nevertheless, a year later, with revisions behind him, he could tell Michael Tippett that he believed *Headhunter* was his "best piece of work." Despite several translations, however, it has not yet helped to secure his reputation abroad, as *The Wars* and *Famous Last Words* have done. The problem with the novel is twofold: it rests on a too obvious analogy with *Heart of Darkness* and has an overly large, complex cast of characters. Findley's use of Conrad's novel as a source of allusion is effective for the portrayal of Toronto as a contemporary, homegrown heart of darkness, but having Kurtz escape, even in Lilah's imagination, from *Heart of Darkness* is heavy-handed, especially considering the clear allusion signalled by the names of Dr. Rupert Kurtz and Dr. Charles Marlow. The large number of characters, many of which are excellent cameo portraits, obliged Findley to provide some resolution to their stories and this meant creating several distinct endings to the multiple plot lines instead of focusing on the key Kurtz-Marlow plot. Perhaps *Headhunter* should have ended sooner, with Kurtz's death. Or perhaps it should have ended after Marlow's visit to Fabiana (Kurtz's "Intended"). As it stands, the last ending, with Lilah, Fagan's letter, and Peter Rabbit's shoes, lifts the ugly reality of the Kurtz–Marlow–Parkin–Club of Men story out of real world darkness into the light of fantasy, and this is not convincing. After all, Professor Fagan is a fiction; Peter's shoes are still in Mr. McGregor's garden, where he lost them; Lilah must resume her medication if she is to cope with the real world, and, as Grendel, Marlow's dog, knows, there is a "beast" lurking in the cellar, waiting to surface in our lives.

In interviews with Jeffrey Canton (1993) and Laurie Kruk (1996), Findley explained some of the background and anguish that he brought to the creation of the novel.[15] He had come to see the abuse of children, which plays a key role in the story, as much more than sexual: "it's like cannibalism," he told Canton, and it signifies contemporary patriarchal society's propensity to use anyone and anything for its own selfish ends (59). Behind this issue lies Findley's quarrel with hyper-masculinity and male violence and, as he told Kruk, he understood male violence because he had been "frightened into submission" himself when he realized he might be killed (120), but he also knew that men could be loving and nurturing. Nevertheless, as reviewers and critics have pointed out, and as Findley understood, most of the male characters in this novel are corrupt manipulators intent on advancing their careers at any cost or evil predators who pursue helpless members of society to gratify selfish desires. When members of these two categories of men find a common purpose, the moral fabric of society is destroyed.

After the novel appeared in 1993, it became a bestseller, but the awards he might have hoped for did not follow. Reviews ranged from cautiously positive (and these ones did not dwell on the subjects of pornography and abuse) to cruel and damning. Philip Marchand dismissed the book as "dodgy," "febrile," filled with "stock characters," and too obviously indebted to *Heart of Darkness*. John Bemrose, however, called it Findley's "finest novel yet." Others were more measured in their comments: Susan Cole pressed Findley about his personal experience with abuse, and he admitted that as a teenager he had sought sex with older boys and men but insisted that he was not abused as a child; Andrew Clark, who put *Headhunter* among Findley's "most disturbing best," nevertheless criticized it for having too many characters; and David Helwig stressed the successful portrayal of Toronto as a dying city but suggested that Findley had tried to do too much. The most interesting review came from an American. Writing in the *New York Review of Books*, James Marcus labelled it "a loose and baggy saga," but he understood the novel's relevance for late twentieth-century North America: "Mr. Kurtz—He Back" put the matter succinctly. And this is precisely Findley's central point. The potential for

Kurtz exists in all of us and we must strive to contain, if not eradicate, what he represents and never let him loose in our lives.

Family History
The Piano Man's Daughter and *You Went Away*

On the evening of 23 June 1993 Findley participated in a forum at the Queen Street Mental Health Centre called "The City and the Asylum—Finding the Balance." The week-long event provided perspectives from art and culture on the history of mental health in Toronto and featured a number of distinguished speakers, art and photography exhibits, music, and a public discussion of homelessness. Findley read from *Headhunter*, and, fortunately, his reading was videotaped.[16] Casually dressed in blue, holding his red bandana as a handkerchief in his left hand, he arrived at the lectern to a standing ovation. He was in an excellent mood because he had just seen a performance of Cirque du Soleil and urged everyone to go; it was magical, "the best therapy," he told them. Then he turned to *Headhunter* and, being the actor he still was, he began his own performance. Few visual records survive of Timothy Findley's live readings from his work, so this one is valuable. He started by explaining that he had often been at the institution, but had never had to "*stay*" there, and he provided a brief summary of the novel's plot. Then, he revealed, with a chuckle, that he had called his fictional Parkin Institute of Psychiatric Research after John B. Parkin, the architect who designed the Clarke Institute of Psychiatric Research at 250 College Street. What he did not tell his audience was that asylums for the mentally ill played an important role in his life and that he was far from finished portraying such places and their methods of treating—and mistreating—their patients. For the reading he selected sections that focused on Lilah Kemp, and he began with the opening pages of the novel, when Kurtz escapes from her copy of *Heart of Darkness*. The audience was spellbound by his deep, resonant voice, careful gestures, and precise enunciation. From there he moved smoothly to Lilah's visit to the Centre for her medication and her invocation of Susanna Moodie.

Mrs. Moodie, he reminded them, had visited the lunatic asylum, as it was called, over one hundred years ago; her ghost, he explained, now inhabits a dark cellar at Queen Street, where Lilah converses with her. During his performance of the dialogue, you could have heard a pin drop. There everyone sat, in the very building where these women—the one a fiction, the other a historical figure called up from the dead—were meeting. It was a chilling, but perfect, close to the evening and a triumph for Findley.

For his introduction to the 1993 publication of *Art for Enlightenment: A History of Art in Toronto Schools*, he was alive with personal memories of Canadian artists he had seen on Toronto's streets as a child or had known as friends. He regretted the loss of this past artistic community in present-day Canada and said so, most emphatically, in the Duthie Lecture he gave in Vancouver that October. This lecture, called "Significant Others," represents one of his more dramatic public performances, which cannot be captured by a published essay. On this occasion, Findley addressed those gathered in Bill Duthie's Vancouver bookstore on the subjects of political correctness, censorship, and the destruction of imagination represented by the banning of books. He blamed religious fundamentalism for Ayatollah Khomeini's "regime of terror" in 1970s Iran, for the persecution of Little Sister's Book and Art Emporium, and even for the rejection of Jane Urquhart's application for a Canada Council grant on the grounds that her proposed book was "too Eurocentric."[17] These examples of "fascist" repression, he argued, were undermining democratic values everywhere. To make his point, he began throwing books on a metaphoric pyre: *Heart of Darkness* hit the floor; followed by all of Dickens, "creator of the dreaded Fagin"; followed by *Othello*, *The Merchant of Venice*, and *Richard III*; followed in turn by Atwood, Munro, McCullers, Faulkner, Urquhart, and David Adams Richards—all these last writers "so appallingly Eurocentric" (158). Down with Toni Morrison, Richard Wright, and Alice Walker—"appallingly Afrocentric." And so it went, until Western society had destroyed most of its great works of literature in the name of political correctness. "I shall be," he proclaimed, "*just another dead white male* in 20 years or so. And a *gay* one! *Eurocentric*! *Middle class*! God! What could be worse?" (157).

If Timothy Findley thought he had twenty years to live, he was wrong, and he would never be dismissed as just another white, male, middle-class, gay writer. He would, however, have to confront an attempt to censor *The Wars*. A few days before Remembrance Day in 1994, he received a letter from Michael J. Lindop, head of the English Department at Bowmanville High School. Mr. Lindop wrote to tell him that *The Wars*, which had been part of the senior curriculum for six years, was "under attack" by members of a group called "Parents Against Pornography," and that he had to present the case for teaching the novel to the Northumberland Clarington Board of Education on November 23. He was furious and enclosed a copy of his statement defending the novel against the parents' accusations; he asked if Findley would read the statement, let him know if he had misrepresented the book, and "write a short note of your own to add weight to my case."[18] Mr. Lindop's defence of *The Wars* was eloquent. He dismissed the argument that certain scenes were in any way pornographic as "fatuous" and insisted that "to condemn a work of this magnitude on the basis of a few passages taken out of context [was] repugnant." Findley replied, thanking this courageous teacher for his "impassioned and insightful and wonderful defence" of the novel, and he marvelled at the idea of anyone imagining Robert's rape as advocating homosexuality. He had heard this type of reaction before but never as grounds for banning the book, and he assured Lindop that his purpose in writing the scene was to emphasize the obscene violence of war as "a rape" that robbed the country of almost an entire generation of young men, thereby impeding Canada's advance into the twentieth century as a nation.

On November 24 Lindop wrote to inform him that the novel was exonerated and would continue to be taught. He thanked Findley for his support and reported some of the charges brought before the appeal panel by parents: the novel "did not represent family values"; it was "tillitating (sic)"; it contained "saddle masolchasm (sic)"; and the homosexual scenes made readers feel "dizzy." For his part, Findley had written an open letter to "Ontario students of English" (17 November 1994), which Lindop presented to the panel, and in the letter Findley described writing fiction as a "rewarding adventure" and stressed the value of reading literature. *The*

Wars is not a pessimistic book or a "downer," he told them, because it shows that life, in all its wonder, goes on despite the horror of war. Findley closed by reminding the students of Samuel Johnson's last words in his journal—"*I must make prayers against despair*"—and offered these words to them: "*Against despair.* Be well, be happy—and above all, be yourself."

The year 1994 was by no means a "downer" for Findley. In addition to the many awards he received, including the Toronto Arts Award for Writing and Publishing, he and Bill had their first extended holiday in Europe.[19] They travelled to Italy, where he gave a keynote lecture at a conference in Venice and visited Pound's grave, before continuing on to Athens and the Greek islands of Paros and Santorini, and then settling down in Provence for several weeks of quiet writing in the village of Cotignac. *The Piano Man's Daughter* was uppermost in his mind at this time, and although he did not mention the novel by name in his Venice lecture, "A Nation of One," he spoke at length about the "mythology" of recent history, the dangers of political correctness, and the importance of family. He admitted his deep regret at not being a parent and that he was concerned because his family line ended with him: "what to do with this gift of history of which I am the sole repository," he mused. "I am the bearer of a nation: a nation of one: How is my nation to survive?" (14). His question was rhetorical, of course, because he was already creating a fictional legacy for his Fagan/Bull ancestors in the new novel, and much of what he told his Venice audience about the Fagans and his Aunt Ruth would appear later in *Journeyman* (74–95). In Venice, however, he stressed the "singer in my blood" who compelled him to sing in prose, and, recalling his dire assessment of the future in his Duthie Lecture, he affirmed his confidence in the future of his songs: "When I am just another dead, white male, my voice will still be here. MY—VOICE—WILL—STILL—BE—HERE—ALIVE."[20] As indeed it is with Lily, Charlie, and the ancestors in *The Piano Man's Daughter*.

Charlie is the chief narrator of *The Piano Man's Daughter*, an autobiographer, a biographer, and the family historian. Near the close of the novel, he writes: "This is the story of everything I know. Of who we are and how we've lived. And where we come from" (537).[21] His purpose is to "pass it on," just as his mother, Lily Kilworth, urged him to do. Lily is the piano man's daughter; she is also the character Findley identified with most closely. However, Lily has inherited an affliction from the Fagan side of the family. That is, from the Fagan side of Findley's mother's family, from Edith Maude Fagan Bull, and to tell Lily's story Charlie must go back to the 1890s and an Irish family, James and Eliza (Fagan) Kilworth, who left Dublin to settle on a farm in the small town of McCaskill's Mills not far north of Toronto and southeast of Jackson's Point. He must also reconstruct the piano man's family, the Wyatts, who settled in Upper Canada, to the east of Toronto, and became successful manufacturers of the Wyatt piano. To create the lives of these two fictional families, Findley drew extensively, and in detail, on the lives of his Bull, Fagan, and, to a lesser degree, Findley ancestors (see Grace 2018). *The Piano Man's Daughter*, he said, was a companion piece to *The Wars* in the sense that for it he drew upon his mother's side of the family, whereas he had drawn on the Findleys for *The Wars*. Uncle Irving was the inspiration behind *The Wars*, but Aunt Ruth was the woman behind the character of Lily, and many specific events in the lives of Findley's ancestors have their fictional counterparts in *The Piano Man's Daughter*. However, the links between the two novels extend well beyond family history. Southern Ontario and Toronto (especially Rosedale) history from 1890 to 1939 are essential to the family saga in this novel, and the Great War sits like an open wound within its story to recall the Ross family ordeal in *The Wars*. The historical scope of *The Piano Man's Daughter* exceeds that of *The Wars* by decades on either side of the Great War, so the later novel seems to contain, or enfold, the trauma of the earlier novel. The Second World War also plays a role in *The Piano Man's Daughter*, casting its shadow back to *Famous Last Words* and *The Telling of Lies* and forward to *You Went Away*.

The general background and many specific events in this novel are historically factual. Findley asked his research assistant Beverley Roberts for everything she could find on seizures and their treatment in the late nineteenth and early twentieth centuries. He kept an audiotape of the CBC *Morningside* program on "Childhood Epilepsy" (4 February 1994) in which Dr. Bernard Rosenblatt, a neurologist at the Montreal Children's

Hospital, discussed seizures, treatments, and some myths about epilepsy. Because Findley saw Lily as autistic, the subject with its wide spectrum of symptoms fascinated him, and he read what he could find on that subject; a heavily annotated photocopy of Oliver Sacks's essay "An Anthropologist on Mars" exists with his files (LAC 111:17). He needed information on brain tumours and home surgeries on kitchen tables during this period, and background on Ontario's psychiatric hospitals. His research files bristle with photocopies of materials Roberts sent him, with notes, dates, details, titles of books, and the names of medical specialists of the day. Pianos—their manufacture, marketing, sales, and importance in the lives of Canadian families sufficiently well off to own one—are central to the Kilworth-Wyatt saga, as they were to the Bull family (see chapter 2), and he investigated many aspects of the business in southern Ontario. He visited the Robert McLaughlin Gallery and the McLaughlin Branch of the Oshawa Public Library to study the history of the Williams Piano Company, and Roberts sent him photocopies of archival photographs of the first Canadian branch of the Piano and Musical Instrument Workers' Union. This history is fascinating in itself, and the material he gathered illustrates the piano's economic and cultural importance before technology, like the Victrola, pushed many instrument manufacturers out of business. Fred Bull appears in one Williams factory photograph, and Brainerd Carlyle appears in another, and on the endpapers of the hardcover edition of the novel there are images of craftsmen at work juxtaposed with Fagan/Bull/Findley family pictures. Using this archival material, Findley created key scenes that take place in the Wyatt factory, which he places in Toronto on the site of Massey-Harris buildings, instead of in Oshawa, where the Williams factory was located. And the encounter that brings the Wyatt and Kilworth families together in the 1890s is based on the fact that piano salesmen had to travel by train to small communities, which is precisely how Fred Bull met Edith Maude Fagan in Collingwood in 1890, and how Tom Wyatt meets Edith Mary Kilworth in the novel's McCaskill's Mills.

To create the period accurately, Findley also required information on Toronto's oldest hotels, especially on the King Edward Hotel, which plays a significant role in the novel: what were the menus like, how did the lobby look in 1910, what music was played at their famous "tea dances"? The Toronto fire of 1904 has its part in the story, so he needed the facts, the streets and businesses affected, and details as reported in the papers. What beer did people drink, and where did they drink it, before the Great War? Which films were playing at the Duke of York theatre between 1910 and 1918? What kind of live music accompanied those old silent flickers? What were the lyrics and provenance for popular songs of the day, such as "Love's Old Sweet Song," "Pack Up Your Troubles," or "The Band Played On"? Exactly which battles took place in 1918, and how were they reported in the papers through editorials, obits, and lists of the missing? And then, how did the press cover the arrival and spread of the Spanish flu pandemic? All of this research informs the densely realized time and place of the novel to create a convincing world in which the characters exist.

Findley's personal archives were even more important for imagining the lives of the characters and the complex, often tragic, story Charlie tells. Here, he turned to his memories of Granny Bull's stories, to actual events from family history and, above all, to Aunt Ruth's personality, talent, and incarcerations. He kept photocopies of twenty-two of her poems, several of them circled as significant, and he searched family photograph albums for individual faces, family groups, and parties at Jackson's Point. These old images stimulated his imagination and spoke to him, but they also provided visual information about how people dressed and how fashions changed, especially when it came to women's hats. Later they were arranged into the tantalizing collage for the hardcover endpapers, where I can identify a few people, but many stare back at me withholding their identity and story (ill. 8). All are frozen in time—haunting, mysterious. Findley was fascinated by such photographs, which appear, usually as descriptions, in almost everything he wrote, and Lily resembles her creator in this regard. She keeps photographs, along with her notebooks and a few totemic items (although not a teddy bear called Sebastian), in the wicker suitcase that she carries with her every time she "escapes" from the demons that plague her, and she and Charlie often pore over them as she tries to identify his father. I have spent hours poring over Findley's family photographs in his archive, in the albums Bill preserved, and on the endpapers of *The Piano Man's Daughter* because these pictures are part of his life and his art. They hold keys to his memory and imagination. In a June 1995 unpublished talk he delivered at the Clarke Institute's annual general meeting, Findley described how he pored over family photographs for inspiration. His specific example was a 1914 snapshot of a group of people having a picnic—Aunt Ruth, his mother Margaret, and Alan Bull, with friends. Allan Findley had titled this picture "The Guns of August," and Tiff explained that this one image inspired "a whole series of scenes" in *The Piano Man's Daughter.* "A single photograph," he told his audience, "can give you almost a whole novel."[22] He placed this old photograph at the bottom right of the novel's endpapers.

For a biographer they are irresistible and dangerous: irresistible because they promise answers to questions I have had about his ancestors; dangerous because photographs, as Findley well knew, can deceive. They can seem to tell a happy story about a boy and his dog or about Aunt Ruth standing between her sister Margaret and their father Fred, with all three smiling broadly. These people look back at me from the endpaper collage and from the original snapshots tempting me to read them as cheerful mementoes of family life. And yet, the stories Findley tells about these people are seldom happy, which implies that these pictures lie, as pictures often do. Nevertheless, handled with caution, they do confirm facts in Timothy Findley's biography, and they are definitely evidence of his creative method and of the value he placed on remembering family.

Lily was present from the novel's conception in 1992–93, when its working titles were first "The Suitcase" and then "Songs," and her name was always Lily; lilies, Findley said, were his "favorite flower" because they fill a room with a "scent that is magical, provocative—warm and sensual" (1997 journal, LAC 304:4). One of the earliest journals in which he recorded his work on the novel shows that in 1993 he called the piano manufacturing family Williams, after the Toronto and Oshawa business for which Fred Bull worked. His shift to the name Wyatt, recalling Alfred Wyatt, the Cannington pharmacist and original owner of the farm, came later when it was clear to him that his Kilworth family, their property, and the village of McCaskill's Mills were inspired by Cannington, its history, and the fields surrounding Stone Orchard. McCaskill's Mills was, in fact, the first name given to the town site in recognition of one of its founding families and early industries. Almost from the beginning, he knew that Lily would be born in a corner of the field he could see from Stone Orchard: "My home and native land," as he called it (LAC 125:1). That the Kilworths and Wyatts would be based on the Fagans and the Bulls was also clear by 1993 because Findley removed family photographs from his albums, taped them into his journal, and sometimes identified which character he related to the picture. One of these photographs is of his maternal grandmother, Edith Maude Bull, in 1908, and she, together with his grandmother Findley, inspired aspects of the character of Ede (Edith) Kilworth Wyatt.[23] Another is the picture of Grandfather Bull with his two daughters, which is reproduced in the lower left corner of the novel's endpapers. He also pasted a photocopied picture of the Massey-Harris staff into this journal and called them the Wyatt factory staff. The journals he kept while writing this novel are unusual, even for Findley, because of the range of photocopied or original material he inserted into their pages and because of the detailed, parallel genealogies he made, with names, relationships, and dates, for the real and fictional families, and his long list of events that occurred during the 1890s. Clearly, he was determined to locate his characters in their time and place and capture the milieu in which his ancestors had lived. However, by 1 March 1994, something unspecified caused him to hesitate: "I have reached critical moment with 'Songs'—and am facing ultimate decision whether it is worth going on with it. Aspects of work are so far promising—but other aspects, which I feel are dominant, not coming to fruition. I would hate to leave it. [...] I must not let go." To make matters worse, he noted, "Lily has fled." His problem with *The Piano Man's Daughter* involved point of view, a narrative decision with which he always struggled. By the end of June he wrote that he was still "trying to get Lily onto pg through Charlie's eyes & memory" (LAC 125:4).

The second "Notebook of Songs" (LAC 125:5) is crammed with information on epilepsy and autism, more details about the Williams Piano factory, the Toronto construction crews of 1911, the makes of cars from the period, and descriptions of Toronto streetcars, bicycles, and clothing styles. But it was Lily who continued to preoccupy him:

> Landscape is the reigning metaphor of 'Songs.' Lives as landscape— Landscape as time. Looking out over the vast terrain of someone's life. Seeing all its features, and also, seeing where those features require the most exploration. Get down from the high place and go walk through someone's life. Lily as landscape. 'I am not I that was—nor I that will be—but only I that am.' Lily Wyatt's creed.

Lily would come to him in his sleep, he complained, but then elude him when he sat down to write, almost as if she refused the page and insisted that he walk in the fields to find her. Between June and September 1994, however, the novel began to take its final shape. Charlie Kilworth's name, voice, and perspective on Lily and the family history became clear and he was able to write a long "Charlie-section" into the workbook. Then, on September 14, the "Title comes—AT LAST!!!" The novel now had its first-person narrator (Charlie), its central character and raison d'être (Lily), its landscape, and its perfect title—*The Piano Man's Daughter* (LAC 125:5). He had been rereading "for the 90th time," he said, *The Great Gatsby*, and Fitzgerald's narrative strategy helped him see Charlie as a Nick Carraway narrator who reports on the lives of others. It is also possible to see in Lily's death by fire the influence of Zelda Fitzgerald's tragic end.[24]

By December 1994 he had finished drafting book 5 of the novel, but he noted in his journal that he was "very tired." In addition to the two years of wrestling with the early stages of *The Piano Man's Daughter* and juggling extensive travel and the constant demands to give lectures and plan future work, he had to deal with Michael's death on November 7. Despite the friction between them, so often manifested in outright antagonism on Michael's part and disgust on Tiff's, he was profoundly saddened by the manner of his brother's dying and described it in detail in the journal. During those final weeks, Michael was *non compos mentis*, suffering from pneumonia and the effects of a stroke; he had managed to pull out the tubes from a tracheotomy, as if to indicate his wish to die. It was a terrible spectacle, and his death was a relief. "I love him still," he wrote, "with great sorrow—he has had such a very sad life. But he is quiet now and no more anguish" (LAC 125:4). Findley scattered his brother's ashes at Stone Orchard. And then he and Bill left for a few days and a change of scene in New York, where friends and some theatre outings provided a welcome distraction from grief and the final push of work on his novel.

The Piano Man's Daughter was published on 4 March 1995. It is dedicated to his friend, the writer Margaret Gibson (1948–2006), who was bipolar and whose vision and courage as a single mother informed his concept of Lily, and to his cousin Isobelle Guthrie, Ruth's daughter and the woman who described her mother's life for Findley in the taped conversation from 1993. It is also written "in memory of my Aunt Ruth," followed by a succinct quotation from Oliver Sacks on autism: "It is their fate to be isolated and thus original" (*The Man Who Mistook His Wife for a Hat* 230). Although it was well enough received, some reviewers found fault with the emphasis on family history and domestic details, and it did not create the controversy or elicit the excitement that accompanied *Famous Last Words*, *Not Wanted on the Voyage*, and *Headhunter*.[25] With hindsight, one can see why its arrival on the scene created less of a stir and why this novel, one of his finest, may have disappointed readers who expected a Findley novel to be overtly political and sensational. *The Piano Man's Daughter* is a capacious, gentle book, a family/historical novel reminiscent of *Buddenbrooks*, *The Forsyte Saga*, or *Whiteoaks of Jalna*. But Charlie Kilworth is a more complex and interesting narrator than is usually found in such fictions, and Lily is a character like none other—a life force, tragic, talented, beautiful, seductive, loving and wise, generous, haunted, and ultimately dangerous, to herself and others. Their story, which combines fictional autobiography, biography, fact, and fiction with twentieth-century Ontario history and the lives of people trapped between two world wars, is more relevant to contemporary readers than the term historical fiction might imply. Moreover, in this novel Findley addresses the same ethical issues that he always found important, while grounding them in family life, as he had in *The Last of the Crazy People* and, to a degree, in *The Wars*. Such questions are timeless. Foremost among them are the challenges of recreating another's life, accepting the fact that one's own life story is inseparable from the other's story and that memory may not always be reliable, and distinguishing truth from lies. Although the focus is on the daily life of women, men, and children through whom Findley traces the history of southern Ontario from the late nineteenth century to the Second World War, this in no way obscures the impact of national and international events on the lives of these people.

Charlie is the character who opens the novel and carries the narrative forward. Through Charlie we see Lily and come to understand her as a unique person with an enormous impact on the lives of those around her. Findley's struggle to locate Charlie testifies to the complexity of this character and his role; even his name presented a challenge, until he describes in his journal landing on the name Charlie when he connected his character, as Lily's son, to her love of Charlie Chaplin's movies. To Lily her son is like her sidekick, a movie character on the silver screen, and it is not until near the end of her life, when she recognizes the grown man and individual in him, that Charlie is able to see himself as a three-dimensional human being instead of as a confused child who is yanked from pillar to post by a demented, beloved mother.

After her death and after his service in the Second World War, Charlie recreates the family story, establishing his perspective on past events, his motivation for writing, the central images of the novel—fire, notebooks, photographs, madness—and its governing metaphors of music and memory. He recalls that on 16 July 1939, he was visiting his mother at the Asylum for the Insane at Whitby, Ontario, and, as they walked through the grounds, Lily talked about the young man she had loved, whose death in the Great War precipitated her collapse twenty years before, her hospitalization, and her subsequent incarceration. She also raised another spectre from the past—Charlie's father. Lily cannot remember who he was, and this mystery is one of Charlie's motivations for telling her story, and his. The day after this visit, Lily died in a fire that damaged the asylum, and when Charlie was called to identify her remains, he was given her wicker suitcase with her notebooks, photographs, and other mementoes, which will help him remember his early life with her, their desperate escapes "from her demons" and from the temptation of fire (*PMD* 7), and the many times they studied her photographs to identify his father. "Some of what follows, I lived," he explains, "and some was told to me" (*PMD* 6).[26] Charlie feels compelled to tell this story about the person he most adored and feared, this woman who cannot speak for herself and who, he believes, has been betrayed by society, her family, the medical profession, war, and even by himself. Through his story, he gives Lily a voice, as Findley wanted to give Aunt Ruth, so he could "give her back her life" (*PMD* 13).

Charlie Kilworth was born on October 30 (Findley's birthday) in 1909, while Lily was studying in England, but due to her seizures she cannot recall who fathered her child. When she returns to Toronto with her son, she is rejected by her family and obliged to live in hotels until they settle in "Eccelfechin," a boarding house for ladies at 84 St. George Street that recalls "Iverholme," where Edith Maude Bull (Findley's maternal grandmother) lived in 1927 after her divorce. Charlie remembers his terror, escaping from hotel rooms in the night with his mother when she was threatened by her demons, and he vividly recalls overhearing her speak to a presence that appeared within the flames in her bedroom fireplace at St. George Street; she would be frantic, protesting, and call this presence "John." The final crisis in their life together occurs in 1918 when Lily received the news that the man she loves has been killed in the war. She collapses, abandons Charlie, and tries to kill herself by setting fire to the cinema where she had met her lover and enjoyed many movies with her son. After her rescue, she is committed to the Queen Street Lunatic Asylum, and Charlie is sent to a private boarding school. Lily's attempted suicide and her incarceration in different institutions, where she can rarely see her son, parallel what happened to Aunt Ruth, what Findley remembered about his boyhood visits to see his aunt in the Whitby Asylum, and what he later learned about her life from his cousin Isobelle Guthrie's story about finding her mother, after Ruth's attempted suicide, and calling for her father's help, which led directly to her mother's hospitalization.

Although Lily's problem is never named as schizophrenia, epilepsy, or autism, her seizures and voices, her fascination with fire, and her obsessive attachments, are traced back to a distant relative, John Fagan, in

Dublin. If Lily Kilworth's life, like Ruth (Bull) Carlyle's, is a tragedy, it is because there could have been alternatives to this trajectory. To be sure, Lily and Ruth were handicapped by mental illness, possibly inherited, but they were also victimized and betrayed by social prejudice and ignorance. In another time, closer to the present day perhaps, women like Lily and Ruth would survive to live reasonably normal, productive lives. They were gifted artistically; they were wise, with the visionary understanding of life associated with artists and philosophers; they longed for the freedom to be themselves; and they were remembered as loving and generous. Above all, neither the actual woman nor her fictional counterpart was simply mad, unless one sees madness in protests against patriarchal authority, war, destruction of the natural world, and medical ignorance.

Like Findley's Fagan and Bull ancestors, James and Eliza (Fagan) Kilworth emigrated in the mid-nineteenth century to settle in Upper Canada, and part of Charlie's task is to recount the history of these two generations of Kilworths. Ede Kilworth Wyatt (Lily's mother and Charlie's grandmother), is central to Charlie's recreation of Lily. Insofar as the character of Ede is inspired by Findley's two grandmothers, she becomes, with age, more like Phoebe Findley than Maude Bull, more severe, more repressed, and more concerned with social status than love. Her husband, Frederick Wyatt, who is determined to become a successful businessman, owner of the Wyatt Piano Factory—the best pianos in Toronto—and a member of Rosedale's elite, is ominous from the start: cold, uncommunicative, ruthlessly ambitious, certain that he is right, and always determined to control everything and everyone around him. He is another domineering and cruel pater familias in the Findley fictional world, and he is not Lily's biological father. Lily's father was Frederick's brother, the travelling piano man Tom Wyatt, who came to McCaskill's Mills to sell Wyatt pianos, fell in love with Ede on first sight, and then was killed by a Toronto streetcar before he and Ede could marry. Thus, he remains forever the lost, mourned, idealized lover and father, whose musical talents are passed on to Lily and Charlie. Apart from the facts that his only son dies in the Spanish flu pandemic after the war (as Alan Bull did), that he owns a piano business, and that the Wyatts, like the Bulls, have five musical brothers,

Frederick does not resemble Fred Bull, who was a generous man and never abandoned his daughter Ruth when she became ill and was rejected by Brainerd Carlyle. If Frederick Wyatt's personality resembles any member of Findley's family, it is Brainerd Carlyle, the uncle by marriage, the Williams piano manufacturer, Ruth's husband, and a man Findley despised.

The Piano Man's Daughter is one of Findley's best novels; it is also his most biographical, and its quality owes much to the biographical sources, which are deeply buried in the narrative until one studies the endpaper photographs and realizes the importance of Aunt Ruth. To write this novel, he plumbed his family background, his ancestors' stories, and his deep love for key people and places in his life, and this personal dimension gives the story an energy and immediacy that carry the plot forward. A brief summary of this long, complex story and of the extensive background research he conducted to create it scarcely captures the historical scope of the book, the richness of its city and rural landscapes, and the three-dimensionality of its main characters. Above all, *The Piano Man's Daughter* is a beautifully crafted narrative, with its large cast of characters carefully situated within the controlling frame of Charlie Kilworth's post-Second World War present and his convincing narrative voice. Although Findley often claimed that he was an emotional, rather than a cerebral, writer, the power of this novel arises from the seamless blending of emotion and intellect, his sincere love for Lily, Charlie, and many of the minor characters, and his rigorous attention to historical fact and accurate detail. A case in point is the scene in which young Lizzie [Lizgard] Wyatt dies on the Kilworth's kitchen table during an operation to remove a brain tumour, while Lily, who adores him, has been banished from the room and must watch through a window (*PMD* 331–43). To create this scene, Findley recalled the appalling story handed down in the Findley family about his father's brother, Stuart Eadie Findley, who had died in 1907 during a primitive operation on a kitchen table to remove a tumour from his brain. For his fictional account, however, he required medical history about such procedures, which is why his research was imperative, but he also relied on his imagination and skill with descriptive language to present the operation from both an omniscient narrator's perspective and that of the terrified Lily. The result is one of the most memorable, realistic scenes in the novel.

Many aspects of *The Piano Man's Daughter* reiterate and resonate with Findley's personal values and previous work. McCaskill's Mills, Munsterfield, and the landscape that still exists around Cannington and Stone Orchard are the heart and soul of the novel, which is his elegy for home, ancestors, and roots. The themes of madness, war, and trauma are all here, as is his abiding fascination with notebooks, journals, photographs, and memorabilia. Like his creator, Charlie relies on Lily's archive in that wicker suitcase to piece together their story. Like his creator, Charlie is a biographer, an autobiographer, and a historian, who makes fiction from the basic facts and from personal memories. And like Tiff, Charlie is appalled by mental institutions. As in *Can You See Me Yet?*, *The Telling of Lies*, and *Headhunter*, in *The Piano Man's Daughter* they resemble prisons, torture chambers, fascist venues for social control, and symbols of what is most destructive in society. What's more, Timothy Findley was not yet finished with such places, as we shall see with *Pilgrim*. It is also a story about fathers, one of whom is a Bluebeard figure, two of whom are long dead but haunt the living, and only one of whom assumes a loving fatherly role. Charlie is the kind father figure and loving son and partner that Findley tried to be in life and that he had wanted Allan Findley to be. Despite the many horrors depicted in this novel, it is finally a love story about mothers and children, and, in the technical sense, it is a comedy because it ends with Charlie's marriage, the birth of a child, a return to the fields of Munsterfield, and hope for the future. Here, Findley finally achieved a happy ending.

It is always wise to be cautious about taking autobiography and biography literally, especially in fiction, because the novel's art lies in what Findley did with the materials at hand and in his ability to tell a complex, compelling story, set in a recognizable time and place, that becomes larger than life because it rises from "a country of invention" (*J* 5). When the novel was being translated into German, he faxed Doris Janhsen, his German editor with Claassen-Verlag, to explain that the "most pertinent" autobiographical aspect of the novel was the piano, which "played a role in the whole of my life" (LAC 282:11). He allowed that his maternal grandfather had owned a piano factory and had travelled around southern Ontario selling pianos, and that he had an aunt who was schizophrenic. "Otherwise," he insisted, "the characters in the book are *themselves*— completely fictional. Lily is not my mother's sister any more than I am Charlie. Though I love the piano, and play it, I couldn't tune one if my life depended on it." A neat sidestepping of the autobiographical question, to be sure. For his German translator, Sabine Roth, it was the musicality of the language in the novel that impressed her. She recalled for me her effort to translate a story-within-the-story about the history of the Kilworth family, which was cast as a fairy tale, that has stayed with her because she worked hard to convey both the poetry and the implicit threat in Findley's description.[27]

———

The Piano Man's Daughter had an unusual launch. Jane Rowland, who was in charge of publicity for Canadian books from HarperCollins, wanted to do something different than the standard bookstore signing routine for Findley's new novel. She suggested that he give a reading, but not in a bookstore, and Bill immediately ran with the idea. He called Veronica Tennant, who had been a close friend for years, and asked her if she might consider performing while Tiff read. She said yes and brought Canadian jazz pianist Joe Sealy into the plan. The launch took place in Trinity-St. Paul's United Church on Bloor with Tiff reading, Veronica dancing, and Joe playing. Eager people lined up outside and along the street in hopes of getting a seat. It was a magical evening, and it led to what would become the 1997 touring show called *The Piano Man's Daughter and Others*.

Before Findley took to the road with this show, however, he had other travels to complete and several commitments to meet. One of the most interesting of these commitments was the lecture he gave in Stratford's Avon Theatre on 30 July 1995. It was published as "Everything I Tell You Is the Truth Except the Lies," and in it he confessed that he was still obsessed with Ezra Pound—"a figure who won't let me go [...] the icon of a paradox"

(25). He explained why he had written Pound and his poetry into *Famous Last Words* and created a radio play, *The Trials of Ezra Pound*, about this fascist anti-Semite who was also a famous poet. The Pound he portrayed in his novel has a minor role as a thoroughly unlikeable human being who is cruel to his wife, is contemptuous of Mauberley, and torments a neighbour's cat, and yet Findley was fascinated by, even attracted to, this troubling figure. He named one of his favourite cats Ezra, as if to exact a form of poetic justice for his character's nastiness while acknowledging his admiration for what he saw as the separate beauty of a poet's art. On his 1994 trip to Venice, he had insisted on visiting Pound's grave in the cemetery on the island of San Michele, and such a visit was a form of pilgrimage, even though what especially impressed him was a small lizard that appeared on the headstone and hissed at him, as he imagined Pound might do. His most important treatment of Pound, however, is the play, which was first produced as a CBC radio play in 1990 and staged at Stratford in July 2001. In his preface to the published script, Findley explained that, although he had based his play "in part, on transcripts" from the 1945–46 hearings to determine if Pound was fit to stand trial, his chief aim was to explore what Pound "did not say" during these hearings.[28] The only thing Pound said at the hearings was that he had never believed in Fascism; therefore, Findley drew on transcripts of the pro-Fascist, anti-Semitic broadcasts Pound made during the war to create the play's dialogue. He also created a role for William Carlos Williams and quoted from the letter Williams sent to Pound telling him that he could never be forgiven for what he did and that his life was "necessarily forfeit" (*TEP* 111) but that "*everyone* forgives you for what you *are*" (113).

Given that this was Findley's last word on the subject of a person who represented the paradox of a great artist and a dangerous bigot, it seems that he resolved the paradox, at least in this play, by forgiving the poet. Another way to view this resolution, however, is to say that in Pound Findley saw and accepted the reality that we are all potential hiding places for monsters; that no one is exempt, that to hide or deny this reality amounts to a failure to face and resist the evil symbolized by Kurtz, and this view is consistent with his personal philosophy and perspective on human nature, which had been confirmed so many years earlier in Hollywood when he saw Ivan Moffat's Dachau photographs. As he told Robert Reid, he saw Pound as "emblematic" of the twentieth century because "there is a fascist in everybody [and] to deny that is to deny what Ezra was about."

His travels in 1995 were extensive. In February, he and Bill visited Australia again for a writers' conference and, on August 5, the day after attending opening night for *The Stillborn Lover*, they flew to Stuttgart, where Findley gave another lecture at a writers' conference and held a seminar on *The Wars*. In between these long trips, he had received more awards, had several appointments with Ed Turner, and found some peace and quiet at Stone Orchard. In July 1995 he was one of four prominent Canadians invited to contribute their views on the state of the nation on its 128th birthday to *Maclean's* magazine. For his "Reflections on Nationhood," he contemplated the country's history from the first inhabitants and animals to the early European immigrants, who, he argued, cared for each other and their new country. The present sorry state of affairs, he said, resulted from a loss of that original dream of community and "a slow erosion" of any sense of relationship with others, the environment, and this place. Hardly an optimistic view of Canada, this was very much in line with his thinking and recalls the words he gave Professor Fagan in *Headhunter*.

By late September he and Bill were ensconced for their second time in Cotignac, where they had rented the same little house. Back home later that fall, two exciting things occurred: *The Piano Man's Daughter* was nominated for a Giller Prize (it did not win, but Findley was pleased with the nomination), and Bill surprised him with the announcement that they had bought the house in Cotignac. They were in the kitchen preparing dinner when the phone rang in the other room. Bill answered, and when Findley asked who had called Bill explained that the little house had just been sold. He was "devastated" until Bill finished his sentence: "To us." At this news, Findley's response was, to say the least, positive: "I don't remember exactly what he was holding at that moment," Bill recalls in *Words to Live By*, "but whatever it was left a dent in the kitchen ceiling that was still there when we ultimately sold Stone Orchard" (217). They had been looking for a writing retreat for some time. Saltspring tempted them, as did Guelph and Stratford, but Provence was further away from distractions, Findley's work was receiving enthusiastic attention in France, and Jean Roberts and Marigold Charlesworth were already there urging them to come. In any case, they had fallen in love with the house, the valley, the village, and the fine food. At first this was only meant to be a retreat, where Findley could write for a few months at a time. There was no talk, yet, of leaving Stone Orchard for good. Findley was focused on several deadlines he had to meet and on the daunting amount of work on his desk. The novella *You Went Away* was contracted for 1996 and a collection of short stories, *Dust to Dust*, was due for 1997. Meanwhile, simmering in the background was the tour idea, which was taking on a life of its own and expanding beyond *The Piano Man's Daughter* to include the novella and the stories. The push to complete work was intense.

You Went Away is a continuation of the intimate world Findley portrayed in *The Piano Man's Daughter*, but this time he moved directly into his parents' generation. The novella is the closest he ever came to writing a fictionalized autobiography about his life from 1939 to 1942 and his parents' troubled marriage during those years. Many of the scenes portrayed in the novella are familiar from interviews he had given over the years.[29] Other details and, of course, the names are fictional. The interesting question is why he felt the need to give fictional form to this critical period in his life because, after *You Went Away*, his attention turned away from realistic personal stories to historical characters, philosophical issues, and allegory, and from Ontario settings to European ones. One answer is that his father was still unfinished business for him; another is that the Second World War remained one of the most disturbing experiences of his life. In the novella, these two concerns converged as he recalled the trauma of that time.

The book begins with a nameless first-person narrator sifting through an old shoebox filled with photographs and speculating about who the people in the pictures were and what story they might tell. None of these photographs is reproduced in the text, but several are described—pictures of soldiers between 1914 and 1918, scenes on busy city streets, crowded trams, tree-lined residential avenues, flowerbeds, a wedding, one of a young man in shorts and running shoes with the prairie *"spread out behind him"* (3), a group of children, a father and son with hockey sticks.[30] A key moment, over which the narrator lingers, is captured by several photographs of men in uniform. War has returned, *"the ever present war that began with the Boers in 1899 and ran its course until 1945"* (YWA 3). From these undated, unidentified fragments, the narrator constructs a story about the silent lives and the era captured in the photographs that begins on *"3rd September, 1939."* The Second World War is about to be formally declared; lives in Canada are about to be changed forever; many lives in Europe have already been destroyed. Matthew, the young protagonist, will have his ninth birthday on 30 October 1939, the day Findley turned nine.

The fictional Forbes family in *You Went Away* comprises Graeme Forbes, the father; Michael Maude Forbes (called "Mi"), the mother; Matthew, their only son; and a daughter, who dies in 1941. Grandmother Ellen Forbes, a "domineering" matriarch, lives on Foxbar Road with her daughter, Isabel, and maintains a shrine of photographs and memorabilia to her dead husband, Tom, and her eldest son, Ian, whose plane was shot down in 1918 and who died a decorated war hero. When Graeme and his family visit the Forbes matriarch, she scrutinizes them with a severe eye, smokes cigarettes, and sips sherry from her teacup. As far as she is concerned, her surviving son is a failure, an alcoholic womanizer, who can never live up to his dead father and elder brother. Isabel, who has never married, is a more sympathetic figure. These three generations of the Forbes family closely resemble the Findleys, from Grandmother Phoebe and Aunt Marg, who lived on Foxbar Road surrounded by memories of their dead men, to Graeme, who is a recognizable portrait of Allan Findley, to young Matthew, who experiences many of the same hurts and challenges faced by Findley at the same age. Matthew's mother, who plays a crucial role in the story, is not a precise recreation of Margaret Findley, but there are many parallels between the real and fictional mothers who fight to save their marriages.

Matthew is another of Findley's child watchers, who observes the adults around him. He is both angry and hurt by this father, who has abandoned him, and yet he longs for fatherly recognition and affection. He cannot forget the night his father arrived home drunk, full of glee over his enlistment in the RCAF, and having forgotten his son's birthday and the bicycle he had promised as a present. Shortly after this, he is posted to Halifax, where he begins an affair, fails to write home, and forgets to send money to Mi. Allan Findley carried on very much like this, and Findley never forgot the scene of his father's enlistment, Allan's childish eagerness to escape, and his being left with relatives when his mother followed her husband to Halifax in an attempt to save their marriage. As was Allan, Graeme is demoted from flying officer to pilot officer because of his drinking. Although he pulls himself together long enough to be promoted and posted to RCAF Station Trenton east of Toronto, like Allan he will only, as Tiff and Bill often said, "fly a desk." Many of Matthew's other memories draw directly on Findley's experiences. Like young Tiff Findley (*IM* 5–6), he enjoys looking over the backyard fence at his grandmother's Foxbar home into St. Michael's Cemetery, and Findley's early title for the novella was "The Fence."[31] In 1941, Matthew is sent to St. Andrew's College at Grandmother Forbes's expense (as were Tiff and Michael); however, he feels followed around the school by his male ancestors because their faces appear in photographs hanging on the walls (as the Findley men's did), mute reminders of Forbes status and achievements. Whether he is in his grandmother's parlour or at this private boys' school, he cannot escape this patriarchal legacy and burden.

You Went Away paints a damning picture of a father, a marriage, and a father-son relationship, and the autobiographical elements are painfully convincing. As the story draws to a close, Graeme Forbes tries to regain a degree of adult dignity; however, Mi reflects that "*it's too late*" (242). Too late for her to respect and forgive him. Too late for him to rescue his career and pride. Too late because the damage he has inflicted on his wife and son can never be undone. The implication is that for Timothy Findley in 1996 it is also too late, but the story does not explore the consequences of this belatedness. The characters called up from the box of old photographs simply disappear. Just when a reader might expect to follow the family into the future to see how they deal with the aftermath of these watershed years, the narrator stops. The summer vacation is over; Matthew will return to SAC and Mi reminds herself that she is *"alive"* and has *"a son to prove it"* (245). Perhaps that is all that can be said. Real life may not always "write real bad," but it rarely provides tidy, conclusive endings or transformations of human nature. On a note stuck into his workbook for the novella (LAC 116:20), Findley asked himself: "is this a happy story?" On balance, the answer is no. After Allan Findley's death in 1982, Findley wrote that at the end of his life he and his father had reconciled, but *You Went Away* tells a different story, one in which a son still feels, and expresses, the pain of rejection by a self-absorbed, largely absent, uncaring father.

As a work of fiction, *You Went Away* displays all the qualities one looks for in a Findley work. The writing is elegant in its simplicity and evocative in its imagery. The familiar themes of loss, haunting, marital breakdown, memory, and war that are integral to the fabric of the Findley world are all here. Songs and piano playing recur through the story. The creation of a child's perspective on pain, fear, adult complexities, and the simple pleasures of life is masterful. The story is always moving, yet understated. The atmosphere is tinged with sadness, even nostalgia, for a peaceful happiness now lost. The novella is dedicated to friends—Al and Nora Joyce in Cannington, Agnes Mortson, and Edna Mott: "This is not their story—but it was their war." Its title comes from the popular Second World War song "You'll Never Know" by Mack Gordon and Harry Warren:

> You went away and my heart went with you.
> I speak your name in my every prayer.
> If there is some other way to prove that I love you,
> I swear I don't know how.
> You'll never know if you don't know now.

No song is more appropriate for the meaning of the novella than "You'll Never Know," which is, after all, about love, absence, going away, and remembering. In this novella, Timothy Findley wrote a farewell to his family, his mother and father, and his own childhood.

The year 1996 brought other farewells. Findley noted several deaths in his calendar (his cousin David Carlyle, Aunt Ruth's son; the writer, Sinclair Ross; and the painter, Yvonne McKague Housser), and his dreams were so filled with death that he became afraid of sleep. "If the dreams don't stop, I don't know what I'm going to do," he told his journal in March that year: "Oh, please make them stop. Everything dead and dying & me always helpless. Pills and drink no help at all. [...] If life is reduced to this, I won't be able—*But I must*" (LAC 304:1). The decision to sell Stone Orchard was momentous, and even though he settled into the Cotignac house with pleasure, he was depressed by the impending loss. In January 1997, he admitted that his dreams were "totally horrifying—Death all the time [...] children—animals—friends. Myself, of course, dying every night [in] a sickness of nightmares" (LAC 304:3). He attributed his desperate state, at least in part, to his grief at leaving Stone Orchard, but he also knew that his health was failing, and he was "very tired," drinking too much, and constantly on the road. For a person who craved his home and needed quiet to work, the situation was untenable. But his old, recurrent fear of death has even more to do with the work he needed to produce and was terrified he would not. He was trapped in a vicious circle of physical pain, medications, and alcohol, which he recognized and yet from which he seemed unable to free himself. The dislocation of moving was the last straw because it rendered him unable to work and triggered his nightmares. I also think that this extreme mental distress invoked the spectre of his ending up in an asylum like so many of his characters, including the one, Mr. Pilgrim, he was trying to create at this time.

You Went Away was published without fanfare and his last collection of stories, *Dust to Dust*, appeared a year later. He had "hated" writing some of these death-haunted stories, or so he confided to his journal, but he met his contractual deadlines. Of the many awards he received at this time, one stands out—being named a Chevalier de l'Ordre des Arts et des Lettres, the highest award for artistic distinction awarded in France. His week in Paris in April for the "Belles Étrangères" festivities was great fun. He and Bill stayed in the Hotel Lutetia (famous for its Nazi occupation during the war, and the setting for a story in *Dust to Dust*), visited the Louvre (which he recreated for a dramatic scene in *Pilgrim*) and the Musée d'Orsay, and enjoyed fine meals with Jane Urquhart, Carol Shields, and Lorna Crozier, who were also on the reading tour. The summer and fall of 1996 marked his last extended period of time at the farm. He was trying to focus on his new novel, *Pilgrim*, but he was beset by the disruptions of moving, packing, making decisions about what to sell, keep, take to France, or put in storage for the condo they had bought and were renovating in Stratford. Circling an illustration of rabbits in his "Peter Rabbit Diary," he wrote: "I hate what I'm doing. I hate leaving here and I hate *not* leaving here. I hate limbo" (LAC 304:1). On September 26, he and Bill left for a short holiday on Saltspring, but by early October they were "home" again and "both ill." The week of October 7 was crazy: they went to Ottawa, Montreal, Kingston, Toronto, London, and Kitchener, with readings or talks in each city. On November 23 they shipped more of his papers to the National Archives—another divestment of the "stuff" they had to deal with as they downsized their lives in preparation for leaving—and on December 3 they arrived in Cotignac for four months of comparative calm.

That calm dissipated after they returned to Canada in the early spring, but for the most part Findley enjoyed the rest of 1997 because two special events buoyed his spirits: in April he embarked on the tour for *The Piano Man's Daughter and Others* and, in October, Trent University held a conference in his honour. The Trent conference, called "Can You See Me Yet?," the first such event to celebrate Timothy Findley and his work, took place on the weekend of October 19 to 21 and was, in Michael Peterman's words, "part conference, part gathering of writers, and part celebration."[32] Many old friends and fellow writers attended, and the conference revenues, augmented by a silent auction, enabled Trent to establish a trust fund in support of The Timothy Findley Creative Writing Prize, which was a fitting outcome for an event at which everyone recognized Findley "as a source of creative inspiration and mentorship" (Peterman and Eddy 5). One of the most interesting papers presented at the conference was by Findley's translator, Nésida Loyer, who discussed some of the challenges and rewards of translating *Headhunter* into French as *Le Chasseur de têtes*. She had many interesting things to say about the difficulties presented by such a complex novel and the generosity of its author, who met with her, answered questions, and, at a few points, allowed her to modify what he had said in English so that French readers would better appreciate the nuances of expression or the subtlety of certain references. Often, during her work with him, Findley would explain what he meant by acting out his answers, and she told me that the deeper she delved into Findley's world, the more she understood it: "Because I had access to the author; his help in answering a long list of queries became an asset for the quality of the finished product."

When Findley left Stone Orchard for *The Piano Man's Daughter and Others* tour that spring, he was setting out on an extraordinary adventure. The occasion was the publication of *Dust to Dust* and the tour included readings from *The Piano Man's Daughter*, from *You Went Away*, and from four of the stories in the collection. Paul Thompson created scenes to support Findley's readings, with Veronica Tennant, her dance partner Michael Sean Marye, actor and musician Jack Nicholsen, Joe Sealy, and Sylvia Tyson all performing. It was a celebrity cast, and Thompson, who directed the show, had worked with Findley before and knew his performance style well.[33] Bill went along as the assistant stage manager. They spent almost two months on the road, living out of suitcases and giving one-night-stand performances in schools, churches, and local community centres, in what Thompson described for me as their "Canterbury Tales with Timothy Findley as our Chaucer." For Findley this tour was a great joy. Bill told me that it was "one of the final and most cherished highlights" of his life, and "one of the last times [he] saw Tiff completely happy." He acted, read, sang, danced with Veronica Tennant, and played the piano. He was in his element, accompanied by artists he loved and respected, and performing to live audiences.[34]

The tour began in Blyth, Ontario, and took them to twenty-two stops from Prince Edward Island to Vancouver. Sylvia Tyson sang "Chocolate Cigarettes," a song about Edith Piaf, while Findley leaned on the piano and puffed away; Sealy and Tyson performed "You'll Never Know," which they later recorded for Bill and which she sang at Findley's Toronto memorial. His reading of an excerpt from "Kellerman's Windows" in *Dust to*

Dust was superb. Given the subject of this story—a middle-aged writer's
return to Paris and his death there from a heart attack—this reading is,
in retrospect, uncanny, even prophetic, because Kellerman is exhausted,
struggling with writer's block, and grievously ill; his collapse (wineglass
in hand) is "Not a shock. No surprise. It had been half expected" (*DD*
45). As well as dancing, Veronica Tennant read opposite Findley from *You
Went Away* and *The Piano Man's Daughter*, and her performances worked
well. She was a convincing Lily beside his Charlie, and she danced Lily's
birth in the field while Findley performed the words. After the troupe had
disbanded and everyone returned home, Findley and Bill sent Tennant a
special card of thanks. Bill drew and coloured a cover picture of leaves
and berries, and Findley wrote: "Well now—what can a person say? Here
we are—*thank God*. What a joy—what a wonderment it has been. No end
to the possibilities—none."[35] He was in "awe" of her acting ability, he said,
and he declared that from now on he would boast of having danced with
Veronica Tennant.

This tour energized Findley, despite his worsening health. To be supported by some of the finest artists in the country for such a length of time
on a cross-Canada gig was exceptional. Thompson remembers the show
as "magical" and Findley as "terrific." He had returned to his first great
love, live performance, and the enthusiastic audiences that attended the
performances renewed his strength and stimulated his imagination for
the work he would do on *Elizabeth Rex*. But the high did not last. He and
Bill finalized the sale of Stone Orchard, completed the packing up and distribution of their belongings, and found good homes for the last few cats
and dogs. The piano went across the road to Len and Anne Collins, and
what couldn't be given away was auctioned. From now on they would live
part-time in France and part-time in Stratford, but they insisted on having
a clause in the deed of sale that allowed their ashes to be scattered at Stone
Orchard when the time came. In every other way it was a final goodbye.

CHAPTER TWELVE

Not Yet

WE PLAY SO MANY ROLES BEFORE WE DIE—AND THEN ... WE DIE.

I'M NOT READY. NOT YET.

(Timothy Findley, *Elizabeth Rex* 5)

Last Works
Dust to Dust, Pilgrim, Elizabeth Rex, and *Spadework*

uring the last four years of his life, Findley suspected that he was being stalked by death, and he was right. The warning signs were urgent and undeniable: very high blood pressure, shortness of breath, and trouble walking for any distance. Inevitably, his deteriorating health produced increased anxiety about his work and affected his choice of subjects and perspective on life. Most of the stories in *Dust to Dust* deal with death, and he emphasized this focus in his three prefacing sentences for the book, which are less a statement of acknowledgement or an epigraph than a form of reassuring address to the reader: "We humans, dead and alive, are not and never have been alone. Some of this dust is dog-dust, horse-dust and cat-dust—the dust of beloved animals. For those who have shared my life, my thanks."[1]

The title story, "Dust," establishes this theme dramatically. When a boy drowns in a hotel swimming pool, Oliver, the narrator, is left to feel guilty because he had threatened the child, who had constantly screamed for help, with the story of the shepherd who cried wolf, and then he had ignored the boy's genuine cries for help. Oliver believes that death is only for adults: *"Children should not die like that,"* he thinks (31). And now there is nothing left for him to do but carry on, "from death to death" (34) because finding meaning in the boy's death is impossible. "Kellerman's Windows," one of the best stories in the collection, closes on a similar note of abrupt death, from which little purpose or consolation can be gleaned. Kellerman, the writer, has returned to Paris, with his wife and an unfinished manuscript, to die. He cannot cope with his publisher's deadlines; he grieves the death of his son in a gay bashing; and he cannot write. On the night of his demise, he drinks glass after glass of Côtes du Rhône, watches the nightlife of others from his hotel window—then collapses and dies. In "Abracadaver" Findley strikes a somewhat lighter note by reintroducing the intrepid Vanessa Van Horne, last seen in *The Telling of Lies*, who solves a mysterious death in the Hotel Lutetia in Paris. Her first-person narrative is refreshing and witty, and her thoughts and speech are lively and touched with irony, even as she surveys the legless corpse of the dead man with her matter-of-fact detective eyes. The two Minna and Bragg stories continue the death theme. In "A Bag of Bones," Minna becomes obsessed with what the wreckers discover when demolishing the house next door—a baby's bones hidden in a wall—and in "Come As You Are" she goes to bed alone mourning the dead and the unborn.

Of the last four stories—"Hilton Agonistes," "Americana," "Infidelity," and "The Madonna of the Cherry Trees"—the first three are interesting but slight; the last one is excellent. It is the most complex and thought-provoking story in the collection and belongs with Findley's explorations of the Second World War, the consequences of atrocity and betrayal, and the haunting of the present by the past. The story takes place in 1996 and is set in the fictional town of Villeverger in the Hautes-Pyrénées region of southwestern France. It represents Findley's first attempt to locate characters and a story in the south of France in regions he was coming to know through his visits to neighbouring Provence, the village of Cotignac, and the Var. Although set in his own present, the plot involves events that took place during the war and the revenge exacted by a survivor of the concentration camp near Villeverger. This geographic and historical context strongly suggests that he had the city of Pau in Aquitaine, the famous Lescar Cathedral, and the nearby internment camp at Gurs, in mind for the setting.[2] But the opening scene of the story had a more benign source. "The Madonna of the Cherry Trees" begins with three elderly women, the Vergerine sisters, dusting the floors and sculptures in the town's cathedral. They do this by "gliding in from the vestry, skating across the stones in mop-soled shoes, their pockets full of dusters" (193). He had seen women doing this kind of cleaning in a Greek church during a 1994 holiday and the delightful image had stayed with him. The sisters still live in the house where they were born, but since the end of the war they have rented out rooms, and one day a Spanish woman, Rosa Fuentes, arrives seeking accommodation. There is a younger woman, Cristabel, with her, whom Rosa introduces as her daughter.

After the women settle in, Rosa begins to work at the local hospital, where three elderly French women suddenly die. By the time the third woman is found, the doctors and coroner have become suspicious. The three dead women had one thing in common, apart from their nationality and age: they had all worked in the nearby camp during the last year of the war. Moreover, they were viciously cruel to the women prisoners in the camp. Now, fifty years later, they have something else in common: the coroner confirms that all three have been murdered. Their murders are explained by Rosa, who tells the Vergerine sisters that from 1942 to 1944, she had been interned in France in the camp outside Villeverger with a large number of Jews. When German guards took charge of the camp, women were forced to be sex slaves, until 1944, when Jewish prisoners were sent to Drancy, the detention camp for Jews outside Paris and, from there, to Auschwitz. With the end of the war and the retreat of the Germans, the French guards took over and decided to kill surviving inmates to stop them from telling the world how they had been abused: *"In those last days,"* Rosa says, *"before the liberation, women were lined up and shot down. The ill were poisoned. Troublemakers, certain to point fingers and name names if they survived, were hanged. I ... was silent. I saw nothing—heard nothing. Knew nothing"* (220–21). She did, however, rescue the newborn infant of a raped Jewish girl, who was shot by three French women guards. Cristabel is the baby she rescued and the three French women Rosa has killed were the guards. The Vergerine sisters are appalled by this confession, and they protest—"We did not do this" (223)— which is literally true. But as Rosa insists, they *knew*, they *saw*, they *heard*, and did nothing. Findley, however, does not conclude the story with Rosa's revenge. Instead, she takes responsibility for her actions and will either kill herself or surrender to the police. Her final request of the Vergerine sisters is that they shelter and protect Cristabel. By welcoming Cristabel into their lives, the sisters signify their atonement for doing nothing and their acceptance of the responsibility to remember, in an ending that recalls the message in *Famous Last Words*: to forgive is important, but to remember is essential. Although this story closes with a life-affirming movement toward a future made bearable through remembering and accepting responsibility, it is small wonder that Findley confessed in his journal that, while writing these stories, he was afraid to sleep because his dreams were constantly about death: "totally horrifying—death all the time" (LAC 304:4). What's more, his two works-in-progress, *Pilgrim* and *Elizabeth Rex*, were also death-haunted.

The fall and winter of 1997–98 left no room for writing. He and Bill had their hands full with moving, and Findley needed time to settle into his new part-time life in France and to explore the history, culture, and language around him. The little house on Ancien Chemin de Salernes, outside the village of Cotignac, was a delight, and it is still much as it was when he and Bill lived there. The exterior stucco walls were yellow, the shutters were blue, and these colours were picked up inside the house as well. One entered the property from the road, descended the driveway to the first level, where there was a garage that they converted into Findley's *"atelier,"* and Findley christened their retreat "Mots Maison." The house itself was not large, but it had the spaces they needed: two bedrooms, two bathrooms, a small living room with a fireplace, a good kitchen, also painted blue, and a dining room that opened out onto the first of four terraces overlooking the valley and descending down the hillside towards the road leading to the nearby village of Entrecasteaux.

With the help of John Bertram, an expat Englishman who worked as their handyman, they made improvements. Following Findley's instructions, Bertram converted the garage into a study by adding a door and windows; he also built a desk and installed a small sink so Findley could make tea. The walls were painted blue—the colour of hope, Tiff's favourite colour—and the colour that had surrounded him at Stone Orchard. In this compact study, he had everything he needed—many of his books and files, several of his puppets and dolls, Sebastian, his family photographs, a comfortable chair, a CD player, and complete privacy. Many ornaments and memorabilia from the farm were unpacked and displayed, and when I visited the house in 2013, a framed dust jacket for *Dust to Dust* still hung on the living room wall. The first terrace, where Bill and Tiff would sit sipping pastis before dinner, cried out for gardening attention, so a small pond was installed for goldfish and koi, the steps to the lower terraces were repaired, and they found small sculptures to adorn the garden or to perch on the balustrades. Stray cats arrived almost immediately and took up residence. A garden statue of Peter Rabbit, given to them by Carol Roberts, arrived intact from Stone Orchard and was placed by the main door. Photographs of the house show it glowing in the sunlight, surrounded by cypress and olive trees, flowers, and a variety of plants, with a view out over the valley that is still serene and uninterrupted by other buildings. From the terraces he and Bill could listen to the bells on the goats in the valley below or the sound of the church bells ringing out from the town.

Cotignac is one of thirty-nine villages in the region of Provence Verte. It is best reached by taking the train to Toulon, or by flying into Marseille, and driving northeast to Brignoles, the largest city in the area. The country roads are narrow, winding, and hilly. The scenery of cliffs, valleys, olive groves, and vineyards is beautiful. The village itself is nestled up against eighty-foot cliffs of tuff (rock formed from volcanic ash), topped by ancient ramparts and containing troglodyte caves. Its buildings, fountains, and clocks date from the fifteenth and sixteenth centuries. The tiny Place de la Mairie has a war memorial, a bench, and an antiquarian bookshop whose owner remembers Timothy Findley. The name Cotignac, according to some, derives from the *cognassier* tree that produces quinces (*coings*), for which the town has been famous since the time of Louis XIV, but the town site dates back to Roman times, when it was called Cotinacco. Today one can buy quince jellies and candies as souvenirs, or jars of the local honey. Tourists come every summer and fall, and their arrival increases the population from just over two thousand residents to well over nine thousand. They come for the quiet beauty of the town's pinkish buildings that glow in the sun, its good restaurants, the local wines, the history, and the festivals, one of which is the *Fête du Coing* held in late October. A significant number of Cotignac's residents are expats who have settled there from more northerly parts of Europe, the United Kingdom, and North America, so Findley and Whitehead found that some of their neighbours spoke English and could advise them on local matters.

Shopping was an adventure. They drove into nearby Salernes for its market and to Brignoles for a variety of household and garden supplies. On the days when Findley had enough energy, they walked (with stops to rest) to the village of Cotignac, to enjoy a drink beneath the plane trees in the main town square of Cours Gambetta beside the fountain in front of Findley's favourite spot, Phil's Bar. On one of his early visits to the local barber, his attempt to explain what he had come for was hilarious: his French was far from fluent, but the barber understood that this chap who was asking to have his *"chevaux"* (horses) cut was actually there to have his *"cheveux"* (hair) trimmed. With time, they discovered restaurants. Cotignac had some good ones, so did Salernes, but their favourite was "La Fourchette" in the village of Entrecasteaux, which was owned and operated by Pierre and Léa Nicolas. This young couple became friends with Tiff and Bill, who dined there often, enjoying superb food and the view from the restaurant's balcony.[3]

As they had in Cannington, the two men made friends with many local residents and they occasionally visited with Canadians who had moved to France or spent part of their year in Provence. When one of their neighbours invited them for a meal, they happily accepted; however, Findley then found himself in a very awkward position because he had dietary taboos, one of which was rabbit, no matter how deliciously prepared. Confronted with a rabbit stew, he was too polite to refuse the dish, but he was horrified at having to eat one of his dearest literary icons: "Oh—God!" he later wrote in his journal, "what to do—? but I ate—closing my mind against it" (LAC 304:4). The cheeses and flan were, by contrast, "splendid." They also spent time with Jean and Marigold, who were close by in Bagnols-en-Forêt, and Bruce Westwood, Findley's agent, had a place in Saint-Paul-de-Vence, where Tiff and Bill spent the 1996 New Year's holiday with the Westwoods and Alberto Manguel. Canadian friends sometimes came to Cotignac, among them Nicholas McConnell, Phyllis Webb, and Len and Anne Collins, whose visits Tiff described in his journal with pleasure. He was never cut off from friends or business connections back home because Bill set up an office with the computer, a printer, and a fax machine, and these devices, plus the telephone, radio, and television, meant that, while they had put distance between themselves and Canadian distractions, they were in easy communication with the world.

Their new life in Stratford was more social. They had many theatre friends and associates in the city, and it was an easy place to reach from Toronto, so there was a regular flow of visitors. However, the condo was not ready for them to occupy until 8 May 1999, so they established temporary homes in rented places, first an apartment on Albert Street and then a house on Cambria Street, which provided the setting for *Spadework*. In Stratford they could see old friends like Bill Hutt, whose 1998 performance in a modern-dress production of *Much Ado About Nothing* greatly appealed to Findley. In a July 1998 letter to Alec Guinness, he listed the plays in the festival season, which was a rich one—four Shakespeare plays, Chekhov's *The Cherry Orchard*, Beckett's *Waiting for Godot*, Williams's *The Night of the Iguana*, and several lighter pieces—but he described *Much Ado* in some detail. It is "delightful—quite, quite wonderful," he told Guinness,

> though you might quarrel with some of the effects of having it set in the 1920s. Don't panic. It works. Post World-War I, Italian Riviera (hints of Coward flapper mode, '20s music, fashion, etc.)—a sense of tired

bravura in an aging generation which has managed to survive slaughter. Interestingly, Beatrice and Benedict are played in their fifties (!) by Martha Henry and Brian Bedford—and Bill Hutt is a superb tiddly-on-martinis Leonato. Great, great fun—and will play in New York in the fall.[4]

The rest of this letter to his old mentor is surprisingly formal in tone, even reserved. He included observations on the lack of serious theatre in Canada, noting that "Webber-style" musicals, while popular, did little for "local playwrights," but he said nothing about his own plays except that one of them (*Elizabeth Rex*), which he neither named nor described, would premiere in 2000. He did, however, take the opportunity to revisit an old wound—the British rejection of *Famous Last Words* in 1987—when he was dismissed as an *"upstart colonial who dares to besmirch the name of our beloved Duchess of Windsor."* And he enclosed a colour photograph of himself, dated July 1998, dressed in black with his signature red bandana around his neck and his glasses in his right hand. Timothy Findley at sixty-eight, with his white hair, moustache, and neat beard, was a handsome man, distinguished, successful, serious, and he was making a point that Guinness could not have missed: this man in the photograph is no colonial upstart, but an artist of stature and a person of substance.

Between late 1997 and late 1998, he had several new, positive experiences to allay his persistent fears about his health and his work. Atom Egoyan had written to Richard Monette praising *Famous Last Words* and wondering about a film adaptation; Whoopi Goldberg renewed her option on the film rights for *The Piano Man's Daughter*;[5] and he won a Banff Centre School of Fine Arts Award, which included the Donald Cameron Medal, $10,000, and a residency at the centre, which he took up in 2001. He even dared to be optimistic about his novel manuscript (*Pilgrim*), confiding to his journal that, "the curve of a great novel is possibly within my grasp. [...] *A gift. Be grateful. Praise. Give thanks*" (LAC 304:4). Interspersed with such high notes, however, were his ongoing references to death—anniversaries of deaths in his family, the deaths of beloved pets (Ezra, the cat, died of cancer while he and Bill were in Cotignac), and the deaths of public figures such as Diana, Princess of Wales, on 31 August 1997. He was also very disturbed by a television series about the Battle of Verdun in the Great War, and chilled by Alec Guinness's autobiography, *My Name Escapes Me*, and by the man's ability to withdraw into his private self and shut others out. In his journal, he recalled an "alarming episode" he had witnessed in the Guinness home in the 1950s, when Guinness ridiculed his mother to elicit sympathy for himself. Whatever his public statements about Guinness, and he was always quick to praise his mentor, privately Timothy Findley was reassessing the man Alec Guinness and not liking what he perceived. Listening to a CD of Wilhelm Kempff playing Beethoven sonatas, he criticized the pianist's "astringently maintained distance between the artist and the viewer" (LAC 304:4) and remarked that both Guinness and Kempff, despite their great talents, had this cold quality, which he neither approved of nor shared.

Late in December 1997, he noted in his journal that he was "in very deep trouble with alcohol, other drugs and sleeping pills." He was doing his best to hide his state of mind and his drinking from Bill, and he marked this admission "Private" because he did not want Bill to know that he was getting "booze" or where he was hiding it. This comment caught my attention because I had not seen similar concerns about keeping secrets from Bill in Findley's journals, and this time he even considered hiding the journal, or at least the eight pages of confession that it held. "I grieve for him," Findley wrote, "because I cannot do better than I do. He *gives* so much—and I give so little" (LAC 304:5). Above all, he did not want to become a "burden." He wished that the seemingly unending nights filled with terror and despair could be exchanged for unending days with Bill and the joy he felt when they were together. He blamed his feeling of distance from Bill on his self-absorption, intense ambition for his work, and "profound mourning for Stone Orchard" (LAC 304:4). At one point in this journal, he reminded himself of "Ruth," his aunt—rather than the character "Lily"—telling Charlie that he must learn to manage his talent instead of being consumed by it: "This is a terrible, terrible time—and I have drunk too much and raged too much and wept too much. I feel so badly for WFW, who has invested so much love and care and hard work in making *this* heavenly haven—and I'm dragging him down" (LAC 304:4).

Although he was not dragging Bill down, he was being very difficult. Bill told me that, when they were packing up Stone Orchard for the move, he was shocked by the number of empty wine and liquor bottles he found hidden behind the books in Tiff's study, but when I read Tiff's "Private" journal confession to Bill he was distressed by Tiff's need for secrecy, for trying to hide his faults and weakness from him. But surely this desired secrecy was a symptom of the guilt so often expressed in his 1950 journals and a behaviour learned from the pressure he had felt, during his formative years, to hide his identity. He was doing his best but sometimes failing to perform as a successful writer and a companion to the person he most loved and needed, and in whose eyes he could not bear to be shamed.

From late 1997 and through 1998, Findley worked hard on *Pilgrim*, which was published on schedule in 1999, but it would not be the major novel he had hoped was within his grasp. Among the reasons for this were his failing health, the loss of Stone Orchard, the disruptions of moving, and the pressure of deadlines; however, another problem with the novel arises, I think, from the distance between the main character and his creator. Ironically, given his criticism of Guinness and Kempff, the journals reveal that Findley found it difficult to release a believable human being from the cold marble of intellectual abstraction and that he needed more time and energy to feel his way into Mr. Pilgrim's life. Certainly the effort to combine classical myth, and an allegorical figure like Pilgrim, with the realities of early twentieth-century life and historical people was, as he admitted, "proving difficult"; he had many "unproductive, useless days wondering how [he] could achieve this book" (LAC 304:5).

As early as 1954–55, he had toyed with the idea of writing about a character he called Tiresias; he was reading Greek literature at the time and absorbing all he could from Guinness and Wilder. At one point, he had tried to write poetry about the Tiresias figure; at another he began a play with Greek characters, one version of which Wilder rejected as too abstract for good theatre and unconvincing as a piece of writing. But the concept of Tiresias stuck in Findley's imagination, and it is clear from a series of notes in his 1997–99 journals that the Tiresias character was central to his plan from the start. Although the novel's "possible title was

PILGRIM," the first-person narrative parts of the story would be in "the voice of Tiresias" (LAC 292:7). Moreover, this character "was condemned to live forever," and "each new *regeneration* begins with his eighteenth year—the year which, during his first incarnation, he committed the sins for which he is cursed" (LAC 292:7).[6] Here Findley outlined his decision to introduce his Tiresias character in the early twentieth century at his home in London, have him committed to a psychiatric hospital, and then conclude with this character protesting the approach of the First World War by attacking great works of art: "Art has always embraced and defined humankind's highest ideals and brought out the best of its creative abilities," Findley reasoned; "Destroy it—and people might turn away from war and the mass destruction of humankind in order to create more art" (LAC 292:7). Tiresias's "targets" would be the *Mona Lisa*, the Cologne cathedral, the Christian saints, and the works of Shakespeare and Mozart. In the finished novel, no works of art are destroyed, the Cologne cathedral is changed to the cathedral at Chartres, and Shakespeare and Mozart are left alone. His rationale for Tiresias's/Pilgrim's destructive behaviour is this notion that only the destruction of great works of art will force human beings to confront their actions and recognize in art "a gesture at survival" (LAC 292:7).[7]

At first glance, *Pilgrim* seems to stand alone in Timothy Findley's oeuvre, but thematically it belongs with *The Butterfly Plague, Can You See Me Yet?, Famous Last Words*, and *Headhunter*. At its centre sits another dreaded psychiatric institution, presided over by another controlling (albeit not evil) doctor. Moreover, this late novel draws upon his reading and interests from over fifty years. It is by no means a personal or autobiographical work like its immediate predecessors, but it rests on images, memories of actual places, and ideas dating back to July 1950, when he made his first trip to Europe, visited Paris, and spent several weeks near Rossinière in Switzerland. It draws explicitly on his years in London in the mid-1950s, and it is informed by his research and travels between then and the early 1990s. In other words, *Pilgrim* represents a summation of Timothy Findley's philosophy, experiences, and creative goals. It may not be his best novel, but with it he attempted to present his vision of human nature—its cruelty, violence, arrogance, compassion, capacity for love, and creativity—and of what, in his view, thousands of years of human evolution and civilization have produced ... and failed to produce. It is an ambitious novel that combines myth and fantasy with history, psycho-analysis, cultural memory, realistic settings in Zurich, London, and Paris, and a mixture of actual and fictional characters. The verdict passed on human nature by the title character, "Mr. Pilgrim," who has no first name, is, to say the least, bleak. There is no Charlie Marlow here to provide a counterbalance to a Kurtz, and the women who might resist masculine vanity and destructiveness, as Lilah Kemp did in *Headhunter*, either die or are marginalized. The psychiatrist in *Pilgrim* is none other than Dr. Carl Jung, who, as Findley imagines him, may not be as evil as Dr. Kurtz but has many of the same failings and is not up to the challenge that his patient, Pilgrim, presents.

In an interview with John Bemrose, Findley said that the original idea for the novel came from his observation of the alcoholic, ailing Ameri-can author John Knowles (1926–2001) on the beach at Atlantic House in the 1980s being followed around by his keepers ("Still Angry"). Findley had read Knowles's novels about the Second World War, *A Separate Peace* (1959) and *Peace Breaks Out* (1981), and the sight of this writer reduced to such a state troubled him deeply. He pondered what could have pro-duced such despair and decided it had to be the persistence of war, which convinced him to tackle this subject once more because he feared that art and all attempts to counter humanity's destructive impulses through creativity seemed doomed to fail. War, as he had long believed, and as he told Bemrose and others after *Pilgrim* was published, always seems to win because a majority of people refuse to heed the warnings of artists, philosophers, scholars, and scientists. The motivating question posed in *Pilgrim*, then, is: what will it take to get your attention? What will it take to make you understand that the human race is headed into yet another war, or the destruction of the environment, or the end of civilization as you know it, when the "your" and "you" includes psychiatrists, historians, pol-iticians, industrialists, parents, and the general public—in short, all of us? The novel's, or at least Pilgrim's, answer seems to be that nothing less than a massive shock, in the form of a wholesale destruction of great works of art, will force humanity to cease their violence and turn to creative action. Mr. Pilgrim, who has lived several lives over hundreds of years and by 1912 knows another war is coming, has had enough. He wants to die, and yet, despite several suicide attempts, he survives. After he is brought to the Burghölzli Clinic in Zurich and left in the care of Jung, he tries to warn this doctor about the future. Jung, however, refuses to believe his patient, except insofar as Pilgrim appears to corroborate his theory of the collective unconscious, and Pilgrim escapes the clinic to exact what revenge he can on an unresponsive world. The rest of the characters simply drift toward the cataclysm of the Great War. If there is any hope for the future in this novel, it lies not in Jung's theories but in the survival of Pilgrim's seven private journals, parts of which are transcribed within the main narrative so that a reader may consider what this man, who could not die and who has lived as both a man and a woman, had to say.

When the novel opens on 17 April 1912, Mr. Pilgrim is about to hang himself in his Chelsea garden. Previous suicide attempts have failed, but this time he almost succeeds. Two doctors declare him dead before he revives, after which a friend, Lady Sybil Quartermaine, takes him to Zurich for help. Pilgrim at first refuses to speak to anyone, including Dr. Jung, and what is learned about his past lives comes from his journals, which Lady Sybil entrusts to Jung, who asks his wife Emma to read and summarize for him. All Jung knows for certain about his patient is that he is a well-known English art historian with a major book on the life of Leonardo da Vinci. As Emma reports what she discovers in Pilgrim's journals and as Jung confronts his patient with this material, which he insists is no more than fantasies and dreams, Pilgrim begins to speak. Not that this does him much good. Jung rejects what his patient writes and says about his past lives or about the looming threat of war. Emma, however, is deeply moved by his autobiographical journals, with their accounts of Pilgrim's earlier lives. They humanize Pilgrim to a degree and provide a context for his despair and longing for death. They also serve to bring Emma Jung alive as she reads and responds to his first-person account of things he has endured and witnessed. We are positioned beside her, reading over her shoulder, and we gradually become interested in this compelling voice from the journals because Pilgrim's symbolic status as a Tiresian seer fades behind the personal stories of suffering and of the rage with which he has reacted to key events in his past lives. *"Herr Doktor Blockhead"* (*P* 621) or the "useless prick" (483), as Pilgrim calls Jung, may dismiss the journals as unreliable testimony to his patient's experiential truth, but Emma does not. And it is Emma's perspective on Pilgrim that carries the day.

Among the journal stories, two stand out as particularly important: an encounter with Leonardo da Vinci and a friendship with Teresa of Avila. The first, set in 1490s Florence, when Pilgrim is living as a young woman, tells of such horror and violence that it explains why Pilgrim calls Leonardo his "enemy," why his "definitive" book on Leonardo (60) presents the great artist as almost a monster, and why, after his escape from the clinic, Pilgrim's first task is to steal the *Mona Lisa* from the Louvre. From Emma's reading of the journals we learn that the identical twins Angelo and Elisabetta Gherardini were contemporaries of Leonardo and that Pilgrim *was* Elisabetta. As the teenaged Elisabetta, Pilgrim dressed as a man to accompany her brother on escapades into the city streets and bars. After her brother's death from the plague, she continued to dress as a man and enjoy the public freedom denied to a woman of her time and class. On one such outing, she went to Leonardo's rooms because Angelo had been his friend and model, and she wanted to meet the artist who knew her brother. When Leonardo, who mistakes her for Angelo, discovers her disguise, he is enraged and rapes Elisabetta so violently that she almost loses consciousness. She is made pregnant by this rape and gives birth to a son, who dies in infancy. Later, after her marriage, her portrait is painted by Leonardo and becomes world famous as *La Gioconda*. Emma discovers this tragic story in a letter, which exists in the journal and is signed "Elisabetta Giocondo, The Florentine Woman. April 12, 1519" (287). Emma weeps over this letter because her heart aches for the woman who suffered such pain, and she believes in the truth of the letter. For Jung, however, such a tale is little more than a fabrication, a fantasy, at most the dream of a sick man.

Pilgrim's friendship with Teresa took place in sixteenth-century Spain, when he was an eighteen-year-old disabled shepherd called Manolo, who lived a solitary life with his dog and flock of sheep in the hills northwest of Avila. One day Manolo became aware of broad white wings up in the highest trees, and he believed this apparition to be an angel. When he went closer, however, the angel asked for guidance in getting down from the tree and introduced herself as Teresa de Cepeda y Ahumada. In his simplicity, Manolo believed Teresa had supernatural powers and could heal him, but she rejected his appeal for a miracle to make him strong and whole. Nevertheless, Manolo continued to love Teresa, and she never forgot him or the lessons he taught her about simplicity, faith, and patience. Pilgrim writes in his journal that this experience encapsulates *"those certainties which I hold to be the centre of all my beliefs,"* and that the story about Manolo and Teresa *"is literally true, drawing as it does on my memories of life as a poor shepherd, and on scholarship of later times"* (396–97). The "certainties" Pilgrim writes of are the positive values of love, compassion, and acceptance of the self and others—the core beliefs that make his life (like Findley's) worth living, regardless of illness, disability, and social stigma. Moreover, Manolo's experiences with Teresa contrast sharply with Elisabetta's treatment by Leonardo: Teresa is a force for good in the world; Leonardo, his great art notwithstanding, is a force for cruelty and power over others, instead of kindness and love. Pilgrim wants this message of love to be passed along to future generations as one way of mitigating the aggression and egotism that cause wars and are associated, in his mind, with Leonardo and Jung.

With these stories from Pilgrim's past, Findley achieved some important goals for his novel. Not only had he humanized Pilgrim to a degree, but he also invited the reader to question the actions and the accountability of an artist and the unquestioning value placed on that artist's work by later generations, who forget or do not know about his behaviour. (Here again is Findley's old problem with Ezra Pound and the ethical dilemma represented in *Famous Last Words*.) And there is a further aspect of Findley's portrait of Leonardo that begs for attention: although he does not discuss this in his journal, he knew that Leonardo is believed to have been gay and that fifteenth-century Florence was famous as a playground for homosexual activity (see Ross King, 75–76). Was Findley, then, deliberately creating a hateful picture of a gay artist? The novel *Pilgrim* does not provide an answer, but Findley would return to the question of an artist's ethics in his last novel.

Although Findley did not explore his personal response to Jungian concepts in his journals, he made several references to reading Jung, and he quoted Jung in an epigraph to *Headhunter*. To create his fictional portrait of Jung, he consulted Jung's letters, books (notably *Memories, Dreams and Reflections* [1963]), and biography, and for the most part he stayed close to the facts of Jung's life. The Zurich clinic Findley imagines, however, is more elegant than the actual psychiatric hospital where Jung worked, which Findley had visited during a brief stopover in Zurich in 1997. Jung's private life was by no means admirable—he had affairs and proclaimed his right as a man to have them—and he exploited and marginalized the woman he married, with whom he had several children, and on whose talent for research he relied. As the couple's story unfolds in *Pilgrim*, the character of Jung that Findley imagines becomes less and less deserving of respect and more and more like the ruthless Leonardo. It is Findley's use of fictional journals, however, that is especially noteworthy. Not only do they contain the most powerful scenes in the novel, but they also confirm, yet again, his reliance on the journal as a narrative genre that can open windows on the interior truth of a person's life—or perhaps I should say, on the version of the truth that the journal writer wants his or her reader to have. Apparently, Pilgrim's journals contain no caveat, such as Mauberley's warning about truth and lies, but then we only have access to those parts of his journals that Emma gives us. She is the conduit, the witness to Pilgrim's inner life, his despair, rage, and Cassandra-like warnings of disaster. We are implicitly asked to believe in her integrity, as well as in Pilgrim's sanity.

Findley puts his most important lesson in Emma's care because it is she who finds Pilgrim's crucial warning in the journals: "PAY ATTENTION! he had shouted in capital letters, over and over. But no one had listened" (609). After his escape from the clinic, Emma knew he would go to Paris because "he was on a campaign to destroy" great works of art in the belief that by doing so he could "draw attention to [art's ...] double message of compassion and reconciliation" (610). In Paris, Pilgrim goes to the Louvre to steal his portrait, the *Mona Lisa*, but instead of destroying it he gives it to an Italian workman, who promises to return it to Florence.[8] Then he heads to Chartres, where he tries, but fails, to burn down the entire church. After Chartres, Pilgrim and his valet, Henry Forster, head south into the Loire Valley, and it is there, on July 4, that Pilgrim releases the brake on the Renault and the car rolls, with him in it, into the Loire River. Clearly, he thinks that he will finally die by drowning, but we will never know because his body is never found. Pilgrim's last words for Jung are that we have *"rejected the truth"* of our *"collective memory,"* and Pilgrim insists that he has been *"aware over the past few years of yet another conflagration standing in our immediate path. [...] Sooner rather than later, we shall be impelled to embrace it"* (622).

Psychiatry and psychiatric institutions, subjects of long-standing concern for Findley, receive intense scrutiny in *Pilgrim*, and despite his reading of Jung and his personal relationship with Ed Turner, they do not come out any more favourably than they did in *Headhunter* or *The Piano Man's Daughter*. The subject of war is even more important to this novel than psychiatry; it drives the plot. War is factual and specific in his work—the Somme, Passchendaele, Dunkirk, Dieppe, the Holocaust, Japanese POW camps—as well as a metaphor for human aggression, destruction, pride, and greed. Is there something in our genes, Findley asks, or in our psyches, that makes us choose war over peace and repeat ourselves so disastrously? The other important theme in *Pilgrim* is death. Pilgrim longs to die: "Nothing can kill me," he complains. "Not even myself. And I am tired. I am tired of being captive to the human condition. Of being so endlessly a human being" (314). Findley's work, like his waking thoughts and his recent dreams, can be described as death-haunted, but nowhere else does he focus so relentlessly on the death wish, not even in *Dust to Dust*. And yet, despite the evidence in his journals and his life that by the late 1990s he was exhausted and constantly in despair over work, world affairs, and his health, he continued to choose life and more writing.

To help him face down the temptation to despair he always turned to imagination and memory, which he drew upon heavily for *Pilgrim*. References that seem casual are signs of his remembered past, such as Zurich (with its yellow wagon [500], no longer in use), Rossinière (350), Tedworth Square (369), or the name Brainerd (329). Research was also essential. His journals are replete with facts and dates, and at one point he noted that Virginia Woolf's essays were "invaluable for [details on] daily life in London ca. 1900" (LAC 304:4), but his research for the novel tells only part of the backstory about his intellectual and emotional sources. Some of these sources are identified in his "Author's Note" at the end of the book, most notably his reading about Jung, St. Teresa, and Leonardo da Vinci. But behind these obvious ones lie many others, from passing references to *The Magic Mountain, Much Ado About Nothing, Hedda Gabler, War and Peace, The Picture of Dorian Gray, Hamlet, The Tale of Peter Rabbit*—"*Possibly the finest novel written in the English language*" (P 330)—to Michael Tippett's reflection on war, *A Child of Our Time* (1944). The novel is dedicated to Tippett's memory, and Findley's epigraph is from *A Child of Our Time*: "*Here is no final grieving, but an abiding hope.*" But *Pilgrim* is saturated in loss and grieving, with very little room for optimism about the human condition. Some hope can perhaps be found at the novel's end, when Jung suffers a severe depression and experiences terrible dreams about a looming catastrophe, as actually happened to him in the summer of 1913. Tormented by this dream, he seems prepared to admit that Pilgrim's warning to pay attention was serious. Furthermore, in Jung's dream about the Old Man archetype, Pilgrim appears and holds a stone out to Jung. As we have seen, stones are important Findley symbols and this one is no exception. It is "*a building stone. Squared and fired and red with life*" (638), and in the dream Pilgrim places it in Jung's hand. This stone, red like the stones on the beaches of Dieppe in "Stones," purposeful like the stones Neil throws at his father in "War," is a Findley symbol of memory and imagination that says pay attention, remember, create something new.

Pilgrim was shortlisted for the Giller Prize in 1999, but it did not win, and Findley was deeply disappointed. He had hoped that this novel, which he sensed was his last major work of fiction, would be, and would be recognized as, his best. Given his extreme sensitivity, he was cut to the quick by early reviews, which were mixed or downright poisonous; Kevin Bolger, for example, called the novel "an overblown drugstore paperback." During the two months he spent touring Canada to promote the book, however, interviewers were positive, and *Pilgrim* reached number one on the *National Post* bestseller list. Findley told Linda Richards that Jung had always fascinated him, but that he might "never write a book with the scope of [*Pilgrim*] again," and that it was "the deathbed book." She did not press him on that last point, but this description—a "deathbed book"— was not casual. Findley knew this was his last big book and through Pilgrim he delivered his judgment on the world as he saw it: *Pilgrim* is his requiem for a species hell-bent on destruction. In his conversation with Linda Frum, he mentioned his views on psychiatry and psychoanalysis and, while praising Ed Turner, stressed his belief that a person cannot— *should not*—be "cured of their life." Jung's determination to cure Pilgrim is, he said, misguided, just as those early attempts to cure his homosexuality or normalize people like Aunt Ruth were, to put it mildly, misguided. Writing in *Maclean's*, John Bemrose, who had reviewed several Findley books with insight and sensitivity, found the title character unsympathetic. Pilgrim, he told Findley, is dominated by anger and "becomes a force of pure destruction," and Findley agreed: "Pilgrim is the person I try to avoid in myself," he admitted, before launching into a protest against war and the fact that "we're still killing everything in sight. We're still killing one another. We're still not solving our problems. It's endless" (Bemrose, "Still Angry" 63). The trouble is that Timothy Findley, the artist, had not distanced himself enough from Pilgrim's anger, and the novel's flaw lies in what Pilgrim espouses and does.

It is difficult to sympathize or agree with this character's violently negative response to the world around him in 1912, and I do not think Findley intended his readers to do so. Even if one accepts the fictional premise that Pilgrim has lived and suffered acutely in previous lives and witnessed centuries of war and atrocity, then one is stuck with the ethical problem of revenge on one hand—are his attacks on others and on art ethically defensible?—and a more purely narrative dilemma on the other—how does one reconcile a symbolic pilgrim figure with the believable, suffering human being created through Emma's perspective and the journals? Most reviewers sidestepped these questions, but Craig Stephenson called the novel "a cautionary tale" with an allegorical Pilgrim, reminiscent of Bunyan's, and he focused on Pilgrim's valet, Henry Forster, and on Emma Jung as the human "heroes" of the main story. Jung, he said, was portrayed as "convincingly arrogant and selfish—and Findley is our Euripides."⁹ I too focus on Emma, but for slightly different reasons. As Findley's biographer, I find it impossible not to reflect on his portrayal of biographer characters who have access to private archives, like Emma, Charlie, Marlow, and, of course, Robert Ross's biographer, and to compare their challenges with my task as the biographer of a writer who kept, and preserved for posterity and his future biographer, thousands of pages of private journals. But I have another reason for stressing the role of Emma Jung, and I wish Findley had given the last words to her because she is the most positive presence in the story and a reliable witness to Pilgrim's life and his journals. In his interview with Linda Richards, he said of Emma: "I adore her. If there is someone strong [in my writing] it is usually a woman. Women don't flail in the presence of danger" (6). Findley's Emma represents the strengths of the novel: the value of love, emotional intelligence, an ability to perceive truth in Pilgrim's journals, the willingness to heed his warnings, and a determination to live, which is, after all, a gesture of hope.

———————

After the publication of *Pilgrim*, Findley turned his attention to his first love—the theatre. Several things conspired to make this the right decision: the move to Stratford immersed him in the life of actors, plays, and productions; he had been thinking about a new play for at least two years and, at one point, even considered inserting a play about Queen Elizabeth I into *Pilgrim* (an idea he abandoned as the novel grew increasingly complex); and he was tired. Writing a long novel requires years of solitary commitment, but a play is shorter and requires the collaborative process with actors and a director that Findley enjoyed. Moreover, he placed great importance on the craft and discipline of playwriting, and he had long believed that experience as an actor was the best training a writer could have. As he told Sandra Martin, many prose writers lack a sense of rhythm, cadence, and an appreciation of scenic structure that comes with acting and writing for actors. So, he returned to the theatre with renewed energy and pleasure.

Elizabeth Rex was, in some respects, his most successful stage play. It opened to a sold-out audience on 29 June 2000 at Stratford's Tom Patterson Theatre, with Martha Henry directing a stellar cast, including Diane D'Aquila as Elizabeth, Brent Carver as Ned Lowenscroft, and Peter Hutt as Will Shakespeare. Reviews of the premiere were enthusiastic, and the play won the Governor General's Award for Drama that year. Since 2000, it has been produced in Canada, the UK, and the USA, but later reviews have been mixed. Colin Thomas, for one, found the script "simplistic" and lacking in credibility. In the context of Findley's biography, however, this play is significant for what it shows about his life and philosophy and for its links with the novel *Spadework* and the unfinished play *Shadows*. To create *Elizabeth Rex*, he drew on his love of Shakespeare and gave final expression to some of the personal issues that had troubled him since his youth. "To thine own self be true," he said, quoting Polonius, in his "Playwright's Note"; "All that matters is that you become yourself," he insisted, quoting Glenn Gould. In his own words he told readers and audience members that from the creative process he had learned "that neither gender nor sexuality, politics nor ambition, are as important as integrity" (xi). Finding oneself, being true to that identity, and living by a strict code of personal integrity—Findley's ethical position and the lives he gave many of his characters can be summed up in these terms.

The play opens with a prologue, in which Shakespeare speaks about his life and impending death. The time is *"night, April 22, 1616,"* and Shakespeare died on the morning of April 23; the place is a barn in Stratford-upon-Avon. There is a *"ghostly LIGHT"* and offstage noises: a tolling bell, a barking dog, the sound of a stone hitting water, and boys' voices calling "Will! Will!" (2). Ghosts from his past begin to appear; Will, like Findley, knows he must deal with them before he dies, and he is "not ready" for death—"Not yet" (5). So he puts on his scholar's cap, in which he always writes, and the play proper begins by returning to Will's memories about the night of Shrove Tuesday, 1601, in another barn, where his actors' company welcomed Queen Elizabeth as she waited out the night before the morning when, on her orders, Robert Devereux, the Earl of Essex, would be executed for treason. The actors had just performed *Much Ado About Nothing* to entertain their sovereign in one of her palaces, and they had retired to the barn, where they stayed until after the next morning's execution had taken place and the curfew was lifted. Amidst much banter among the actors, Will takes out his notebook and starts to write. Enter the Queen. During the hours ahead, Elizabeth challenges Ned Lowenscroft, a star performer of women's roles, who has just played the role of Beatrice for the Queen, to reveal his true self. Ned, who is dying of syphilis, contracted in an affair with an Irish captain in the Queen's army, is bitter about his own fate and the death of his captain, and he challenges the Queen to pardon Essex, because Essex is the man she loves. The main action of the memory play-within-the-play is this confrontation in which she will try to release the woman within the monarch if Ned can release the man within the actor of women's roles and confess his love for the captain and mourn that love. Meanwhile, Will is making notes for the play he was forbidden to write in 1601 but will create in 1616, and his characters—a queen, her courtiers, Ned, and the actors—will re-enact what took place in that barn in 1601. The queen will perform her womanhood and Ned will perform his manhood. However, there are problems with this concept.

Findley was constrained by the facts: Essex was not pardoned; he was imprisoned in the Tower of London and executed. Moreover, Findley appears to be falling back on gender stereotypes that undermine the characters' attempt to be true to themselves. To be a true woman and a true man, it seems that Elizabeth must give in to her love and save her lover's life and that Ned must face his and his lover's death with courage and his queen's stubbornness with a show of aggression. Therefore, a true woman is governed by emotion and compassion, while a true man is brave and forceful—or so the play suggests. When morning comes, however, the bell tolls, announcing the execution, and Elizabeth leaves. Despite admitting her love for Essex and showing grief over his death, she remains the monarch. In history, and offstage in the real world, she is Elizabeth *Rex*, a Prince of Europe who orders executions, and Ned is still a dying actor. With a shift in lighting, the tolling of a passing bell, and other offstage sounds, the action returns to Stratford-upon-Avon on the early morning of 23 April 1616 and William Shakespeare's death.

Reflecting upon the evolution of the play, Findley had only praise for the creative team. Paul Thompson workshopped the script between 1997 and 2000, and Findley appreciated his guidance. For his part, Thompson described the entire process as "exhilarating" because Findley and the actors were willing to make a leap of faith, which in practice meant adjusting, even rewriting, the script as it developed. Findley was delighted with Martha Henry's directing and Brent Carver's creation of the role of Ned, and the actors with whom I spoke—Carver, D'Aquila, and Peter Hutt— were impressed with Findley's understanding of the theatre and moved by the experience of working with him on a powerful script. As Findley told Patricia Black, he had long been intrigued by the fact that, in Shakespeare's day, women could not appear on stage, and he wondered how a boy could play mature women like Lady Macbeth or Cleopatra. This prompted him to imagine Ned Lowenscroft, a mature man who is expert in such roles. Then, after reading Lytton Strachey's *Elizabeth and Essex*, in which Strachey claimed that *Antony and Cleopatra* was really about Queen Elizabeth and her lover, Essex, "I just gave a whoop of joy because I found my play" (Black, *"Elizabeth Rex"* 1). Findley thought that if *Antony and Cleopatra*, which Shakespeare was writing in 1601, was his cover for a play about the British queen and her lover, then he could have his Will character create a play about Elizabeth that portrayed a fictional version of the night in 1601 before the execution of Essex and still have room to explore other matters important to him.

In an interview with Keith Garebian, Findley said that he had reached an age when he felt he had a responsibility to explore aspects of sexuality that he had experienced among actors, playwrights, and directors but had "been afraid of trying to articulate" up to this point (Garebian,

2000). As is abundantly clear from his life, his journals, and some of his work, Findley had wrestled with these matters for decades, but this is the first time he openly admitted his reluctance to foreground homosexuality in his work. At seventy he finally felt ready to address AIDS through the character of Ned, who is dying of the pox, by drawing on his experience volunteering at Casey House and his concern for Alec McCowen, whose partner had recently died from HIV/AIDS. He was also prepared to foreground homosexuality in *Elizabeth Rex* and examine it further in *Spadework*, and he told Garebian that his thinking about the connection between homosexuality and the theatre dated back to the 1950s, when he had known "extremely famous, very happily married men, with children," who had homosexual affairs. He called their situation "accommodating sexuality." He was acutely aware of the dangers faced by these men and the private pain they experienced by hiding their true identity; this is, after all, the point of *The Stillborn Lover*. But if he was recalling Alec Guinness, among others, he did not tell Garebian how much the pain felt by their wives and children had troubled him.

In *Spadework*, Findley examined the price paid by a wife and son when an actor husband gives in to blackmail to advance his career. The novel is set in Stratford during the 1998 summer festival. The main characters are Jane and Griffin Kincaid; she is a festival set designer and artist and he is a rising star. They have a seven-year-old son, Will, a dog, and a housekeeper, Mercy Bowman. Life seems to be going well, with career success, a gracious home, and plenty of love, until raw ambition disrupts their domestic bliss in the form of an older, predatory theatre director, Jonathan Crawford, who denies Griffin the roles he wants for the festival's next season until the actor agrees to sleep with him. Griffin believes he deserves those roles, and nothing—not his wife, his home, his son, or his integrity—matters enough to stop his agreeing to Crawford's deal. Although this picture of the theatre world is far from flattering, the town of Stratford is presented in loving detail.[10] The theatres, streets, and restaurants, and the Avon River, which Findley knew well, are all there. One could walk the streets he describes (although the exact number of the Kincaid house does not exist), find good pizza at Pazzo (still flourishing), enjoy dinner at Down the Street (now closed) and watch the actors who hung out there, or dine in style at the former Church Restaurant (now Revival House). Southwest of Stratford is the town of St. Marys and the Westover Inn, called the Pinewood Hotel in the novel, where Jonathan Crawford stays and where Griffin joins him for their trysts.

There are several subplots in *Spadework*, one of which involves a handsome young telephone repairman, who arrives at the Kincaid home to fix a cable severed by the gardener, Luke. The character of Milos Saworski is based on an actual repairman who arrived at the Cambria Street house that Bill and Tiff were renting in the summer of 1998 while their condo was being renovated. Matt Mackey, their friend and a landscape gardener, had accidentally cut the line, and Findley was so impressed with the beauty of the repairman that he decided on the spot to make him a character in a story with the gardener, who was inspired by Mackey. What he needed after that was a story about why this accidental loss of telephone communication would have consequences and who his main characters would be. He also needed more time than he had to develop and polish his material before publishing the book. As it stands, *Spadework* is a recognizable Findley novel with potential, but it does not work. Griffin's relationship with Crawford, no matter how closely modelled on "accommodating" sexual practices that Findley had witnessed, is not convincing. Crawford is worse than unsympathetic as a realistic character and unconvincing as a great director or a charismatic man. He is a ruthless sexual predator, who shows no regard for Griffin's family or for his own abandoned wife and son. Griffin's supposed acting talent is not demonstrated, and he seems little more than a cad. Jane's fling with Milos is also unconvincing because this aspect of her story is not well prepared for or established as a credible aspect of her character.

So why did Findley write *Spadework*? The bottom-line answer is that he had a contract to honour, an advance on royalties to earn, and therefore a novel to produce. But there are other reasons. Judging from the novel's links with *Elizabeth Rex* and the unfinished play *Shadows*, Findley's move to Stratford brought him full circle back to the 1950s and his memories of theatre experiences in England, Toronto, and Stratford, and on his

American tour with *The Matchmaker*. Much as he loved and respected the theatre and individual theatre people, from Alec Guinness, Ruth Gordon, Thornton Wilder, and Alec McCowen to William Hutt and Martha Henry, Findley retained emotional scars from the fifties and viewed aspects of offstage theatre life with a jaundiced eye. *Spadework* is his version of *Noises Off* (Michael Frayn's hilarious 1982 play about behind-the-scenes theatre life), except that the happy ending Findley gives his main plot is forced. Once Griffin has secured the roles he wants for the next Festival season, he walks back into the Cambria Street house, is welcomed by Mercy, Jane, his son, and the loyal dog, and resumes his happy family life. Jonathan Crawford disappears from the story, and no one's feelings, doubts, or questions about what Griffin has done are explored. The Kincaid family is last seen the following spring, when the Stratford community gathers beside the river to watch the ritual return of the swans after their long overwintering in a nearby barn. Spring, the parade of beautiful birds rediscovering freedom outdoors, and the reunited, happy family all suggest the restoration of hope, love, and domestic order: all's well that ends well. Except that there is no reason to believe that Griffin Kincaid has learned anything, least of all about integrity.

An important clue to Findley's motivation for writing *Spadework*, however, lies in the epigraph and quotations he uses from W. H. Auden's poem "Detective Story." The crucial lines appear well along in the story: "when the truth, / The truth about our happiness comes out / How much it owed to blackmail and philandering" (*Spadework* 103). Here is the key to the novel, not the severed telephone cable, the repairman, or the swans, but issues of "blackmail and philandering," and to stress his point, Findley quotes Auden's closing lines at the end of the novel, just before the swans are released to the applause of the observers and the Kincaid family: "someone must pay for / Our loss of happiness, our happiness itself" (*Spadework* 311). The problem with *Spadework* is that no one is held to account; no one pays for the loss of happiness, unless perhaps one can say that all three Kincaids pay: Griffin by sacrificing his integrity, Jane by losing her confidence in a secure future, and Will, who will carry the scars of a father's betrayal and abandonment for life—as Timothy Findley did.

According to Iris Tupholme, who went to Cotignac to work with Findley on *Spadework*, he never spoke of it as his "gay" novel and he wanted the novel to be entertaining, but if he was trying, late in his career, to explore matters of sexual identity and behaviour that, as he told Garebian, he had been reluctant to consider, then why shine such a harsh light on these aspects of life and why associate betrayal with gay men in the theatre? Neither his journals nor his interviews help to answer these questions, but this book, while certainly not as angry as *Headhunter* or *Pilgrim*, is scarcely an entertaining read. There are ghosts that continued to haunt him, none more so than those husbands, like Allan Findley and Brainerd Carlyle, who betray their wives and those fathers who abandon their sons. And there may be two other ghosts here: one, an actor from Findley's first Stratford summer who, he believed, had betrayed him along with the sacrosanct value of personal integrity by sleeping with men who could further his career; and one, possibly a director in England, who tried to bribe him with a desired part in a play in return for sex. On the identity of these ghosts, however, Timothy Findley is silent.

Wrestling with the unresolved anger stirred up by these ghosts was not made easier by the health problems that plagued him during the winter and spring of 2001. He was suffering from constant back pain and weak legs, and he fell ill with pleurisy, followed by pneumonia. It was not until the publication of *Spadework* and the Stratford premiere of *The Trials of Ezra Pound* were behind him that he was finally able to take up his residency at the Banff Centre. Once there, he began writing *Shadows*, but this one-act play, commissioned by Stratford, did not open in the new Studio Theatre until 24 August 2002, two months after his death, and before he had found a satisfying conclusion to the piece. As with *Spadework*, this play needed more time plus the important input provided by actors during rehearsals on a new script. Nevertheless, *Shadows* is an interesting example of autobiographical theatre, in which the characters, six of whom are playwrights, gather at the home of the manipulative director, Ben Singer, for a dinner party, where they watch a lunar eclipse, which gives the play its title, and participate in a game called "Storytime." Each guest must tell a personal story that may be true or false as long as it convinces the others that it is actual autobiography. The shadows, then, also involve the secrets lurking in the dark corners of their private lives.[11]

Singer is testing these writers to see who can come up with the best new play for him to direct, but Findley is testing the borders between truth and lies, fiction and reality, the world onstage and the realm of the audience. He is also playing a game with the expectations we bring to autobiography and to realist theatre—that what we get will be true and factual. Pirandello was on his mind as he was writing this play, but where Pirandello creates six characters in search of an author, Findley creates six authors trying to convince a director to choose their plot for a play. He also invokes Brecht's alienation effect, or distancing technique, when Singer shatters the theatrical illusion of a fourth wall separating an onstage performance from an audience by asking the audience what they think of what they're watching. After a round of often nasty and brutal personal disclosures, Singer calls an end to the dinner party and sends everyone home. *Shadows* could have ended right there, leaving Ben Singer alone on a set cluttered with dirty dishes, wine bottles, and discarded napkins, but Findley had wanted more, some further twist, to wrap up his play and his playing with truth and lies, theatre and the real world. So Bill, drawing on what he knew of Tiff's ideas for a conclusion, wrote the last speech of the play, in which Singer addresses the audience: "Why don't you decide how this whole thing plays out. I'm going home. Oh, and keep in touch with the truth. You'll fail, of course. We all do." (71).[12] This injunction to "keep in touch with the truth," even though we all fail, rings true for a play by a writer who always asked how we can distinguish illusion from reality, truth from lies, but to end the play with this throwaway line is disappointing. Brent Carver, who performed the role of Singer at the premiere, knew the play was unfinished and did his best to bring off the closing speech, but the entire cast was worried about the script, and Findley's death left them uncertain and sad.

Bill notes in his introduction to the published text that Findley "built a lot from our own lives into the play," from a dinner party at Stone Orchard, when guests went outside to watch a family of deer, to "a word-for-word duplication of an argument Tiff and I had on more than one occasion" (55); however, Findley also drew on many other events in his earlier life, most of them sources of pain. When one of the characters in *Shadows* describes a marriage that failed because he was gay and could not consummate it, Findley was remembering his failed union with Janet Reid. He also returned to other traumatic experiences during the fifties—his effort to become an actor, his resentment at being exploited and betrayed by certain directors and fellow actors, his fear of rejection by the theatre world—and these provide moments of emotional credibility by informing the anger and despair of the characters' stories. Instead of focusing on his happy years with Bill, which were personally supportive and professionally successful, and dramatizing a loving gay relationship in a stable home, or imagining a story about a productive theatre world with talented actors and generous, gifted directors (like Tyrone Guthrie, Robin Phillips, and Martha Henry), in *Spadework* and *Shadows*, he dug down into some of his most disturbing memories to anatomize an ugly world of jealousy, ruthless ambition, and betrayal. It is impossible now to imagine how he might have concluded this play or whether he could have laid his own ghosts to rest, had he lived. Ben Singer's last words, given to him by Bill, were the words Findley often used to close a speech or a reading—"Be well. Goodnight." But Timothy Findley was not well in 2001, and by the play's premiere in August 2002, this "goodnight" was heartbreaking.

Not Yet

During the last months of 2001, Findley made the news with a speech he gave in Calgary. The occasion was the annual luncheon to honour his winning of the 2001 Bob Edwards Award, and he seized this opportunity before a captive audience of 450 to berate those involved with oil and gas extraction for polluting the environment and behaving like terrorists. He urged the audience to "think of the consequences if the corporate world continues to rush headlong, and heedless of the danger, into the exploitation of global gas and petroleum reserves" (qtd. in Blakey). Not surprisingly, the oil-patch executives were insulted by his remarks and shocked by his comparison of their activities with the 9/11 terrorists. Some of them walked out; others heckled him. And newspapers put the story on their front pages. David MacInnis from the Canadian Association of Petroleum Producers repudiated Findley's remarks: "we're not going to even dignify his remarks with a response," he said (qtd. in Wattie). Did Timothy Findley go too far? Perhaps. It is doubtful that his warning and angry accusations had any positive impact. Nevertheless, he was being true to himself, and he was not yet ready to give up the fight for a better future. He cared passionately about the environment and he wanted people to pay attention and connect the dots between local and global behaviour. History since 9/11 suggests that he was right to link oil and gas extraction with environmental degradation and with the complex and largely clandestine network of global terrorism.

Other activities that autumn were happier. On October 14 he met with Eleanor Wachtel for an interview on her CBC radio program *Writers & Company*. This was the last interview he gave, and it was informative and cordial. A week later, on October 22, he received a public tribute at the annual Festival of Authors held at Toronto's Harbourfront. He had given a special tribute to William Hutt on a similar occasion the previous year; now it was Hutt's turn to praise Findley, which he did in glowing terms. Early the next year, Veronica Tennant asked him to participate in a fundraising gala she was organizing, and he could not refuse a dear friend and an artist he greatly admired. This gala, called *Dreams Come True*, was held on 11 February 2002 at the Princess of Wales Theatre to celebrate the opening of the Al and Malka Green Artists' Health Centre at Toronto Western Hospital. Tennant had persuaded many star artists to attend—Pinchas Zukerman, Karen Kain, and Brent Carver, among them. When the moment came for Findley to take the podium, however, he needed help, so Brent Carver walked with him, holding his hand. Then he read from *Pilgrim*, and the passage he chose could not have been more appropriate or poignant. When the once-famous ballet dancer, Countess Blavinskeya, enters the therapy baths at the Burghölzli Clinic with her caretaker, ghostly music is heard—no words, just a "liquid line of melody" as she steps into the water. However, Findley concluded this reading by telling the audience that later in the novel this dancer leaps to her death from a balcony at the clinic. Thus ended his last public appearance. On February 22, a few days after celebrating their fortieth anniversary, Bill rushed him to Emergency at the Stratford General Hospital.

Findley spent most of that week in hospital, at first in Intensive Care and then in a semi-private room. As soon as he was able, he began what would be his last journal; he titled it "Hospital Journal" and added his familiar motto: *"Against Despair"* (LAC 333). This document has several remarkable features, not the least of which are the details he remembers and records: each nurse is named; the meals are described as very good, which is astonishing, given his criteria for good food and the usual state of hospital fare; his fellow patients are named and commiserated with; and his doctors are praised. Wayne Parsons, his GP, visited him every day, and his specialist, David Tamblyn, checked him frequently. However, to Findley's dismay, Dr. Tamblyn admitted him to Intensive Care within moments of examining him on the twenty-second and would not hear of his going home for one last cigarette or a glass of wine. And small wonder. His blood pressure was appalling (220/110) and the oxygen level in his blood had dropped to 75 percent, when it should have been 90 percent or higher. "That I survived this episode," he wrote, "is due to them [his two "terrific" doctors]—to WFW—to the hospital staff—and—to my own interest in the process of survival" (LAC 333). This interest in the "process of survival" is manifest on every page of the journal. Assembled after the fact, with get-well notes and a photograph pasted into its pages, this journal was clearly intended for some further use. The entries are all dated, and the opening pages, headed "Friday, 22 February 2002. Stratford General Hospital," are labelled "Prelude"; he describes work on *Shadows*, Veronica Tennant's gala, and Sylvia Tyson's hosting skills: the "Queen of Serene" is his new name for her. But he admits that he knew he was "fading." He could not breathe, stand, or walk without help, "and was clearly in a new kind of trouble."

At this point in the journal, Findley shifts into the present tense to note down each stage in his treatment—his hospital gown, the tubes, needles, pills, and machines he is hooked up to—and he immediately thinks of Michael and of his death, after which he writes: "I want a glass of wine." This comment aside, he does not complain; he is grateful to the staff and fully co-operative. His chief regret is that he and Bill will have to cancel their trip to France, for which Bill has already purchased tickets using frequent-flyer points. He describes the patient sharing his room with sensitive concern, and he notes how tired Dr. Tamblyn is and how hard he works to save lives. The last thing he wants, he writes, is to become a burden for Bill, but he realized how dependent he was under these circumstances. "I have to die first," he writes. Bill came several times a day, bringing the *Globe and Mail*, fresh clothes and toiletries, and egg-salad sandwiches to supplement the hospital diet because, without the chain-smoking, Findley's appetite soared and he was constantly hungry. True to form, he watched the television news and made notes on items in the newspaper; he was still, as always, paying attention, and still angry with politicians and distressed by world events. Music, however, brought him comfort and hope: "And yet—as I write this—I am listening to Chopin's First Piano Concerto—played by Richter." And he went on to note that he identified with Chopin as an artist and political figure who is remembered, unlike the forgotten politicians of his day. Findley continued to write this journal after his release from hospital on February 27, and he included a description of his ride home with Bill, which reminded him of his bus rides home from St. Andrew's College as a boy because of the stark contrast between home and an institution. Then he reminded himself that he must return to the hospital on March 15 for further tests and that he has been ordered to rest, avoid wine and cigarettes, and not push too hard on work deadlines. Easier said than done, of course. Upon reaching their Ontario Street address, the first thing he did, even before going up to the condo, was to have lunch at Pazzo's with wine and a cigarette.

It is not difficult to understand why Timothy Findley wrote this journal; he had kept journals since his youth, had recorded much of his life's story in them, and had drawn on them for his work. Journals were his connection with himself, his method for embracing experience, and his way of living his private life through words. What is impossible to know is how he might have used his near-death account in a new novel, a new play, a short story, or for a chapter in a second memoir. As it stands, this last journal testifies to his generous concern for others, his need for the written word, his curiosity about life and death, and his strong survival instinct. Like his characters Robert Ross and Will Shakespeare, he said "Not yet" to death. On March 15 he was cleared for travel to France, and he and Bill left on the twenty-seventh. He was planning to write an adaptation of *The Trojan Women* for Stratford, but a week after their arrival in Cotignac, he suffered the fall that put him in the Brignoles hospital. This time he did not recover. Timothy Findley was gone before his seventy-second birthday, with much work left unfinished, but he had died first, as he hoped, before becoming a burden.

Back to Stone Orchard

———

Timothy Findley was a private person. As an author he protected himself by performing, and he was very good at these performances: readings, lectures, interviews, meeting strangers on book tours and at social gatherings. He let his guard down with a few close friends, possibly in those midnight phone calls of which there is no record, and with Bill, the person who knew him at his worst and his best. His journals, however, provide remarkable access to much of his inner life—his terrible battles to create his work, to make it perfect; his fear of failure and death; his profound love of home and of some family members and of Bill; his effort to love a brother who was often a violent failure, and a father who rejected him in his early, formative years but whose approbation he never ceased to long for; and his constant struggle against despair. The roots of this despair lay in his need to be recognized for who he was—a homosexual human being who should not have to masquerade as a person he was not—and in his fierce ambition. From 1950 on, he knew he was an artist, that he would make his contribution as an artist, and he was desperate not to fail in this work. He manifestly did not fail, of course, either as an artist or in being accepted, and yet he was tormented to the end of his life by the spectre of failure. He was driven and, as such, could never be satisfied that his work was good enough or that his warnings were heard. But he was also blessed, and he knew it, by a companion who supported him all the way; those sometimes frantic pleadings for someone to love him, for a companion, that recur through his journals from the 1950s were answered.

If he had been sufficiently conscious to know how and where he died, he would have been appalled. He had wanted to die at home, at Stone Orchard, but by 2002 he had left the farm, never to return—with one notable exception. Although he had written "none" in the space provided on the living will for his final instructions should he be incapable of making decisions, he and Bill had a private agreement: a portion of his ashes would be set aside and, when Bill died, his ashes would be mixed with Tiff's. Then their combined ashes would be scattered at Stone Orchard.

April 30, 2018, was a beautiful day in southern Ontario. It was warm for the season; the sun was shining; the cloudless sky was a delicate, pale blue—the colour of hope. It was a perfect day for the quiet ceremony about to take place at Stone Orchard. My daughter, Elizabeth Grace, drove Trevor Greene (Bill's companion in his final years) and me north to Cannington and then to the farm. We were expected by one p.m., and the current owners, Terry and Kelly Sellers, welcomed us as we waited for Len and Anne Collins to arrive. When the four of us (Trevor, me, and the Collinses) were ready, we set forth, Trevor carrying a box with the mixed ashes of Tiff and Bill. We first visited the herb garden (now just a ruin) and then set out along the path through the field where Tiff had walked the dogs. We stopped at several spots to scatter ashes, and at the top of a hill Trevor read a passage from Bill's memoir *Words to Live By* and then released the remaining ashes. There was a slight breeze and the ashes were picked up and carried out across the winter-grey field with its small spring shoots of green beginning to appear. This was a simple ceremony without much talk or expression of grief because this was, in fact, a happy, positive occasion. Tiff and Bill were once more together, and they had returned to the home they loved.

In his 1994 journal, Findley had reflected on the importance of landscape and memory. He was thinking of *The Piano Man's Daughter* and of his character Lily, who seemed to be eluding him. But I am sure he was also thinking about himself. "Landscape is the reigning metaphor" of the novel, he wrote: "Lives as landscape—Landscape as time. Looking out over the vast terrain of someone's life." And he reminded himself that to write a life one had to "get down from the high place and go walk through someone's life" (LAC 125:5). Timothy Findley as landscape. Now, with his return to the fields of Stone Orchard, the landscape of his life is complete. There is no despair, only hope for the future in the human imagination and in nature's renewal.

Timothy Findley Chronology

1929
- APRIL 14: First son born, Thomas Michael Findley, to Allan and Margaret Findley

1930
- OCTOBER 30: Second son born, Timothy Irving Frederick Findley ("Tiff")

1932
- JANUARY 22: Third son born, Allan Gilmour Lyon Findley (d. 23 February of same year)

1933
- AUGUST 17: Uncle Tif (Thomas Irving Findley) dies
- TF hospitalized for double mastoid infection

1934-35
- Family live with Phoebe Findley (paternal grandmother) at 27 Foxbar Road

1936-42
- TF attends Rosedale Public School

1937-46
- Family rents 27 Crescent Road, backing on riding stables and ravine
- TF in hospital at various times with appendicitis and whooping cough

1940

- Allan Findley enlists with the RCAF; spends time in Trenton, then Barrie, Kingston, Halifax, and stationed at Trenton

1942

- SEPTEMBER: Michael and TF sent to St Andrew's College (SAC) in Aurora
- Margaret and boys move in with Maude Bull (maternal grandmother)

1943-46

- JUNE 1943: TF leaves SAC after Grade 6; wins an English prize
- Returns to Rosedale Public School for Grades 7 and 8; graduates in 1945
- Allan Findley spends six months of 1945 in England; he is discharged and returns home on 30 October 1945
- SUMMER 1945 AND 1946: Spends a few weeks each summer at Camp Kagawong on Balsam Lake in the Kawarthas

1945-47

- Attends Jarvis Collegiate, Toronto, with periods of time away from classes due to illnesses; leaves high school in Grade 10 (does not complete the year); ill with mononucleosis; kept at home with private tutor and begins writing journal-scribblers

1947-48

- Works at Massey-Harris Company (manual labour) to pay for ballet lessons at Margaret Fulton School; summer work at a Michigan hotel (near Detroit) as a gardener; studies briefly with Boris Volkoff, then switches to Janet Baldwin

1948

- Stops ballet due to fused disc; begins acting with the Earle Grey Players; works at the Stock Exchange for cash and flexible hours

1949-50

- Struggles with illnesses and a nervous breakdown
- 26 JULY 1950: Sent to France and then Switzerland by parents for recuperation; visits Caen in Normandy; stops in Paris; spends three days in Caux, Switzerland, during MRA "World Conference on Moral Re-Armament"
- Stays with the Henchoz family on a farm in Rossinière (near Geneva), Switzerland; begins first serious extant journal
- NOVEMBER: Returns to Canada

1950–51

- Studies speech with Clara Baker at the Royal Conservatory of Music, Toronto, and theatre with the Sterndale Bennetts at the Sterndale Bennett School of Theatre; meets Bill Hutt and Kate Reid

1951

- Joins the International Players and works with them from summer 1951 to winter of 1951–52; has roles in Sidney Howard's *The Silver Cord*, directed by Hutt, at Leaside Collegiate, Toronto; J. B. Priestley's *Dangerous Corner* in Kingston; and Robertson Davies's *At My Heart's Core* in Kingston

1952

- Plays Peter Pupkin in CBC television production of Leacock's *Sunshine Sketches of a Little Town*

1953

- Shares apartment #8 at 21 Avenue Road in Toronto with Hugh Hood and others
- Becomes a charter member of the Stratford Shakespearean Festival, Ontario; acts in first Festival season and meets Alec Guinness, Amelia Hall, and William Needles
- SEPTEMBER 6: Sails to England on the RMS *Scythia*
- OCTOBER: Starts classes on voice and speech at London's Central School of Speech and Drama
- OCTOBER 12: Paternal grandmother Phoebe Constance Smith Findley ("Goggie") dies

1954–56

- Contract player with the H. M. Tennent Company; lives for periods with Guinness family; meets Ruth Gordon and Thornton Wilder; 19 July 1954, meets Alec McCowen; performs in London West End, at Edinburgh Festival; tours to Berlin, Moscow; contacted by British military for national service; writing journals, plays, and fiction

1956

- APRIL 5: Sails for home, via New York, on the *Queen Mary*; train to Niagara Falls and then Toronto; stays with parents at 7 Strathearn Road; summer acting in Port Carling
- NOVEMBER: In NYC for *Matchmaker*
- First published story—"About Effie" in *Tamarack Review*'s Autumn issue

1957

- FEBRUARY 3: Begins USA tour of *Matchmaker*; corresponds with Meg Hogarth
- MAY 5: Attends HUAC hearings in Washington
- JULY: *Matchmaker* closes in Hollywood
- Stays on in Hollywood and meets Nancy and Stanley Colbert; moves into the Colbert home and burns a novel manuscript on Stanley Colbert's advice

1958

- Sees the Dachau photographs by Ivan Moffat; TF drinking heavily
- Returns to Toronto; acts in TV production of *Sanctuary* (with Janet Reid)

1959

- JANUARY 17: Marries Janet Reid at Toronto's Grace Church on-the-Hill; present are Allan and Margaret Findley, Leonard and Jessie Reid; witnesses are Michael Findley and Toby Freedman
- MARCH: Has minor role in John Osborne's *The Entertainer* at the Crest Theatre
- JUNE: Janet files for divorce and marriage is annulled

1960

- MARCH 28, 1960: Decree nisi is registered and signed; marriage "null and void" for "non-consummation"
- TF has psychological crisis: depressed and drinking; treated at the Toronto Psychiatric Hospital and the Bedford Road Clinic
- Asked to do screenplay for "Lemonade" in Hollywood (script dropped)

1961–62

- Acts in Ionesco's *Rhinoceros* at Toronto's Civic Theatre; performs title role in *Volpone* at Ryerson Institute of Technology
- FEBRUARY 1962: *Crawling Arnold* broadcast on CBC TV; moves in with Bill Whitehead (WFW)
- Meets Jean Roberts and Marigold Charlesworth
- Spring/summer 1962: Performs in three plays at Central Library Theatre— *The Rivals, One Way Pendulum, The Balcony*—and in *For Love or Money* at the Red Barn Theatre
- TF and WFW move into the Findley parents' house in Richmond Hill; TF gives up theatre for writing

1963

- TF works as Arts/Music copywriter for local country and western radio station CFGM; WFW works for CBC; TF begins writing *The Last of the Crazy People*
- Maternal grandmother Edith Maude Fagan Bull dies
- Begins treatment with Dr. Edward Turner

1964

- TF and WFW buy Stone Orchard and move to Cannington area

1965

- SUMMER: TF and WFW take a trip by car through parts of USA and Canada, including Canadian Rockies

1966

- Seeing Dr. Ed Turner regularly; working on *LCP.*

1967

- Publishes *The Last of the Crazy People*; TF works for CBC and NFB; CBC broadcasts his film script *The Paper People*; writing *The Butterfly Plague*

1968

- Disastrous meeting in NYC with Grace Bechtold; performs "Walls" monologue for CBC radio's *The Best of Ideas*

1969

- Publishes *The Butterfly Plague*; summer road trip through USA and up to the NWT; the film *Don't Let the Angels Fall* opens at Cannes

1971-74

- 1971: Wins Armstrong Award for "The Journey" on CBC radio's *Ideas*
- Writing for television and collaborating with WFW on *The National Dream* series; reading *Jalna* novels and writing scripts

1972

- Sets up Pebble Productions and now all copyright is in this name
- JANUARY 23–APRIL 9: *The Whiteoaks of Jalna* twelve-part series broadcast on television
- Buys Sprucevale ("Arkwright") near Stone Orchard

1973

- Founding member of the Writers' Union of Canada

1974

- MARCH–APRIL: CBC TV broadcast of *The National Dream*
- JUNE–AUGUST: Trip to Yukon for research on the Berton *Klondike* television series (cancelled)
- Playwright-in-residence at National Arts Centre for three months at end of year

1975

- WFW and TF win ACTRA Award for television film series *The National Dream*

1976

- MARCH 1: *Can You See Me Yet?* premieres; Islay Lambert dies

1976-77

- Nancy Colbert establishes literary agency in Toronto and becomes TF's agent

1977

- Publishes *The Wars*
- OCTOBER 13: Launch party for *TW* at Park Plaza; wins 1978 GG for Fiction; wins City of Toronto Book Award
- Serves as chair of Writers' Union of Canada from 1977 to 1978
- Appointed writer-in-residence at University of Toronto

1978

- Wins Canada Council grant to work on *FLW*

1979

- Premiere of *John A.—Himself!* starring William Hutt, at Grand Theatre, London, Ontario.

1980

- WFW and TF win Anik Award for Best Television Documentary for *Dieppe 1942*
- TF chairs GG Award Adjudication Committee for English-language Fiction for 1980–81

1981

- Publishes *Famous Last Words* (except in the UK—see 1987)
- OCTOBER 14: Mottle dies

1982

- Receives LLD from Trent University
- JANUARY 6: Allan Findley dies in Sunnybrook Hospital

1983

- Film made of *The Wars*, directed by Robin Phillips, with Brent Carver and Martha Henry
- WFW retires from CBC and devotes full time to TF
- Early in the year TF enters a period of depression that continues through to 1985 while writing *NWV*; sees Dr. Turner regularly and is on medication
- Wins Canada Council grant for *PMD*; uses it to complete work on *NWV*
- Clarke, Irwin closes; TF moves to Penguin

1984

- JANUARY: Moves from Stone Orchard to Arkwright
- Named Author of the Year by Canadian Booksellers' Association
- Publishes *Dinner Along the Amazon*
- Receives LLD from University of Guelph
- Publishes *Not Wanted on the Voyage*
- Aunt Ruth Bull Carlyle dies

1985

- Wins Canadian Authors' Association Award for Fiction for *NWV*
- FEBRUARY 2: Flies to Vancouver to give the Dal Grauer Lecture at UBC; first time on a plane since 1968
- FEBRUARY 10: Marian Engel dies
- MAY 21: Sally Findley dies
- Michael Findley found near death and admitted to hospital in Newmarket

1986

- Publishes *The Telling of Lies*; new edition of *BP* published
- APRIL 9: Made Officer of Order of Canada in ceremony at Rideau Hall
- Serves as president of PEN Canada, 1986–87
- Receives CNIB Talking Book of the Year Award for *NWV*

- Delegate to the Congress of PEN International in Lugano, Switzerland
- Spring tour to Australia and New Zealand for Adelaide Festival
- OCTOBER: Returns to Stone Orchard from Arkwright
- DECEMBER 10: Sells papers to LAC

1987

- *Famous Last Words* is published in the UK after the death of the Duchess of Windsor
- JANUARY 5: Margaret Laurence dies
- MARCH 13: Flies to UK for *FLW* promotion in UK; reviews of *FLW* are harsh
- MARCH 22: Flees to Dieppe
- NOVEMBER 29: Gwendolyn MacEwen dies
- Wins Periodical Marketers' Award for Best Paperback Fiction

1988

- *Stones* published, with story "Dieppe"
- Five-part radio adaptation of *FLW* is broadcast; TF wins ACTRA Award for Best Writer
- Begins volunteer work at Casey House
- Wins Periodical Distributers' of Canada Award for Best Magazine Fiction (for "Almeyer's Mother")
- Wins Western Magazine Award for Fiction

1989

- Wins Trillium Book Award for *Stones*; wins Mystery Writers' of America award for best original paperback for *The Telling of Lies*
- Receives LLD from York University
- Ken Adachi dies
- Hosts the five-part CBC series *Lost Innocence: The Children of World War Two*
- JUNE: Travels to Scandinavia for writers' conference in Lahti, Finland

1990

- *Inside Memory* is published and wins a Canadian Authors' Award for Non-fiction
- Wins Gabriel Award for radio broadcast of *The Trials of Ezra Pound*
- MARCH: Wins Peabody Award (Best Documentary) for *Lost Innocence: The Children of World War Two*
- SEPTEMBER 26: Margaret Findley dies
- SEPTEMBER 28: Janet Baldwin dies

1991

- Wins Canadian Authors Association Award for *Inside Memory*
- Named to the Order of Ontario
- Wins City of Toronto Book Award for *Inside Memory*
- Martha Kumsa arrives in Canada

1992

- *NWV* adapted as a play and premieres in Winnipeg
- Begins teaching writers' workshop at Humber College
- DECEMBER 10: Gives 1992 Graham Spry Lecture on Culture and Society (CBC)

1993

- Premiere of *The Stillborn Lover* at the Grand Theatre, London
- Publishes *The Stillborn Lover* and *Headhunter*
- JUNE 23: Reads from *H* at Queen Street Mental Health Centre for "The City and the Asylum: Finding the Balance" event
- SEPTEMBER–OCTOBER: TF and WFW on Saltspring Island
- OCTOBER: Gives Duthie Lecture (later published as "Significant Others")

1994

- Wins Canadian Authors' Association Award for Drama (*SBL*) and City of Toronto Book award (for *H*); wins Toronto Arts Award for Writing and Publishing
- TF and WFW travel to Venice for conference (TF gives keynote lecture, published in 1997 as "A Nation of One") and continue on to Florence, Athens, and Greek Islands (Paros and Santorini)
- JUNE 1–MID-AUGUST: TF and WFW rent Cotignac house for first time
- NOVEMBER 7: Michael Findley dies
- NOVEMBER: *TW* threatened with censorship on curriculum of Bowmanville High School (resolved)
- *SBL* wins Arthur Ellis Award (awarded by the Crime Writers of Canada)

1995

- Receives LLD from Lakehead University
- *The Trials of Ezra Pound* published by Blizzard
- WFW buys Cotignac house
- FEBRUARY 27: TF and WFW fly to Australia

- MARCH 4: Publishes *The Piano Man's Daughter*; receives Gemini Award (Margaret Collier Award) for body of work for television
- AUGUST 4: *SBL* opens at Stratford
- AUGUST 5: TF and WFW fly to Stuttgart
- SEPTEMBER 26: TF and WFW arrive at Cotignac
- OCTOBER: *PMD* nominated for Giller Prize

1996
- Publishes *You Went Away*
- Receives Harbourfront Prize for Lifetime Achievement
- Receives LLDs from Memorial University and University of Toronto
- Wins Chalmers Award for *SBL*
- To France for "Les Belles Étrangères"
- Named Chevalier de l'Ordre des Arts et des Lettres

1997
- Publishes *Dust to Dust*; does "the travelling show"—*The Piano Man's Daughter and Others* promotion tour with Sylvia Tyson, Veronica Tennant, et al.
- APRIL: Visits Paris, Dieppe, London
- SUMMER: Receives Humber's Calliope Prize for Excellence in Writing and Teaching
- Sale of Stone Orchard is finalized; packing for move to Cotignac and Stratford
- OCTOBER: Trent University holds conference to honour TF

1998
- Receives Banff Centre School of Fine Arts Award and Donald Cameron Medal
- TF and WFW move to Stratford; rent apartment #179, 59 Albert Street and house at 224 Cambria Street; renovation of condominium
- Begins *Spadework*

1999
- Publishes *Pilgrim*, followed by book tour; *P* shortlisted for Giller; move into condominium at #210, 72 Ontario Street, Stratford

2000

- Stratford premiere of *Elizabeth Rex*, published by Blizzard
- Receives Libris Lifetime Achievement Award
- Wins GG Award for Drama (*ER*)
- Winter in Cotignac

2001

- Receives LLD from Wilfrid Laurier University; publishes *Spadework*
- Stomach and low back problems; exhaustion
- JULY: Ill with pleurisy, pneumonia
- *TEP* opens in Stratford; begins *Shadows*
- AUGUST: Takes up National Arts Award and Banff residency
- SEPTEMBER: Writer-in-residence at University of Calgary; Bob Edwards Award
- OCTOBER 14: Interview with Eleanor Wachtel on *Writers & Company*—his last interview
- OCTOBER 22: Festival of Authors tribute for TF at Harbourfront in Toronto

2002

- FEBRUARY 18: Reads from *P* at "Dreams Come True" gala; health failing
- FEBRUARY 22–27: Hospitalized in Stratford for a week
- LATE MARCH: WFW and TF leave for Cotignac
- MARCH 31: TF falls and cracks pelvis; admitted to Brignoles hospital on April 4; sent home on April 29; infection sets in and he is transferred to Toulon on May 3 unconscious; May 27, has tracheotomy
- JUNE 21: Dies in hospital in Toulon (at 00:50 hours); cremation held on June 26 in Vidauban, France
- JULY 12: WFW returns to Canada; Sunday, July 14 memorial service held in Stratford; September 29, second memorial in Convocation Hall (University of Toronto)
- AUGUST 24: *Shadows* premieres at the Studio Theatre, Stratford
- WFW scatters TF's ashes at Stone Orchard in early September, and later at Cotignac

APPENDIX II

Family Tree

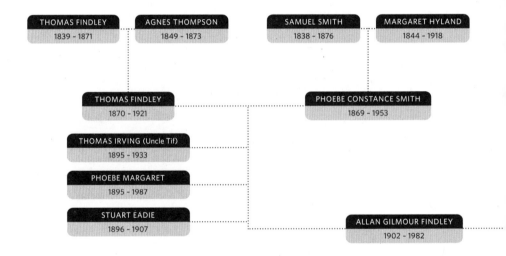

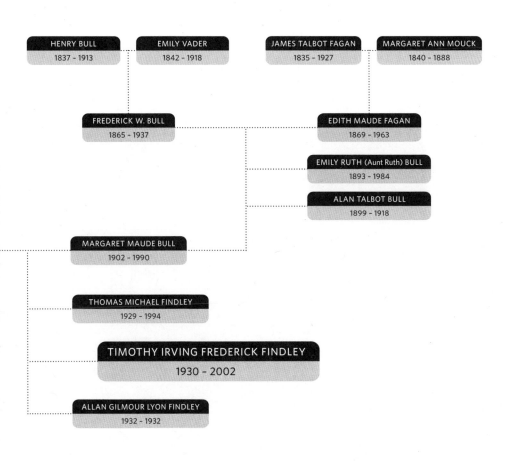

HENRY BULL
1837 – 1913

EMILY VADER
1842 – 1918

JAMES TALBOT FAGAN
1835 – 1927

MARGARET ANN MOUCK
1840 – 1888

FREDERICK W. BULL
1865 – 1937

EDITH MAUDE FAGAN
1869 – 1963

EMILY RUTH (Aunt Ruth) BULL
1893 – 1984

ALAN TALBOT BULL
1899 – 1918

MARGARET MAUDE BULL
1902 – 1990

THOMAS MICHAEL FINDLEY
1929 – 1994

TIMOTHY IRVING FREDERICK FINDLEY
1930 – 2002

ALLAN GILMOUR LYON FINDLEY
1932 – 1932

NOTES

CHAPTER ONE | **Inside Findley's Memory**

1   My thanks to Dr. Wayne Parsons for sharing this document with me.

2   Quotation and medical details are from my September 2013 interview with Drs. Wayne Parsons and David Tamblyn.

CHAPTER TWO | **Living with the Dead**

1   I read the small diary with Bill's private papers in September 2013. Irving described his school work, friends, sports activities, church attendance, holidays at Jackson Point, and a July 1913 trip to England. He had pasted a photograph of his mother on the last page.

2   The original journal, which was inherited by Tiff, is held with the Findley papers at LAC (332:2) and a copy exists in Special Collections at the University of Guelph (Findley/Whitehead Collection XZ1 B019000-011.4). The family preserved Irving's letters, letters from others about Irving, and his war diary, but the documents in the journal have been typed, organized (possibly edited by Irving), and collected into this final unpaginated form. It has leather covers and a photograph of Lieutenant T. I. Findley, M.C., as a frontispiece. Letters cited or quoted here are from this journal, courtesy of WFW.

3   The inclusion of this letter indicates that the journal was carefully constructed after the fact to present a coherent narrative of Irving's war.

4 Bill discovered these letters with his files and sent me photocopies, which I cite here courtesy of WFW.

5 See Terence Macartney-Filgate's *Timothy Findley: Anatomy of a Writer.*

6 My thanks to Joann Guthrie (Ruth Bull Carlyle's granddaughter) for giving me this interesting letter. John Bull was putting together a history of the Bull family and had contacted Findley for information.

7 My thanks to Eric Bull, Findley's second cousin and, like him, a great-grandson of Henry Bull's, for his assistance with dates and details on the Canadian Bull lineage.

8 The R. S. Williams & Sons piano business was one of the most important in Canadian history; see Ladislav Cselenyi-Granch. At its peak, it had stores across Canada, with international outlets by 1906; by 1921 it employed 275 workers.

9 In 2014, Bill gave me two boxes, containing sixty audiotapes, from his files, and one of these tapes is the recording he made in 1993 of Tiff in conversation with his cousin (Ruth's daughter) Isobelle Carlyle Guthrie. This tape provides much insight into Ruth's life and illness. See also *Journeyman* 85–91. I am grateful to Joann Guthrie for clarifying some details of Ruth's life and sharing Ruth's poems with me. Titled "The Writings of Emily Ruth Bull," the typescript was prepared for the family by Carolyn Guthrie-Stone, and it contains an undated photograph of Ruth (ca. 1911), a brief preface, a few biographical facts, and fifty-four poems.

10 The school was housed in "Ellesmere Hall," a stately residence originally owned by T. N. Gibbs and located on extensive grounds in central Oshawa. By 1895 it had forty-five pupils in grades from kindergarten to matriculation; it closed in 1932. Records and photographs for Bishop Bethune College are held in the Oshawa Library archives, and some materials are available online. See also olivefrench.wordpress.com.

11 Edith Maude Bull appeared before the Senate Committee on Divorce in December 1926 and under the "Act for Relief" requested that her marriage "be dissolved" and that "she be divorced" from Frederick Bull. Her petition was granted on 31 March 1927.

12 The Queen Street facility, now CAMH (the Centre for Addiction and Mental Health), opened in the 1850s as the Provincial Lunatic Asylum. The Ontario Hospital for the Insane in Whitby, known as the Whitby

Psychiatric Hospital, was built on a 624-acre site beside Lake Ontario, where it provided a home-like environment on beautiful grounds with gardens, a farm, and a recreation centre. The hospital closed in 1995.

CHAPTER THREE | Going up to Rosedale

1 Camp Kagawong was founded in 1908 on Manitoulin Island by Ernest Chapman, for many years the sports director at SAC. It later moved to Balsam Lake, northeast of Lake Simcoe, in the Kawartha Lakes district, and it closed in 1970. My thanks to Dick Cousland for sharing with me his photographs of the boys at the camp in 1944–45 and his memories of Tiff.

2 This scribbler (LAC 82:1) is undated and unpaginated, but it does have daily entries from June 2 to 18, which, if accurate, confirm 1944 as the year. He was originally meant to stay for one week, but his family allowed him to extend the visit.

3 Thomson's shack now sits on the grounds of the McMichael Canadian Art Collection in Kleinburg, Ontario.

4 Allan Findley's RCAF file, with the personnel records of Veterans Affairs at LAC, contains his application to enlist, the RCAF's Special Reserve Report, a list of his postings (with dates), his identity card and regulation photographs, and his discharge papers. He achieved the rank of flight lieutenant, was "honorably released," and received a Canadian Volunteer Service Medal, with clasp, and a General Service Medal.

5 These photographs were preserved in the Findley family's albums and were sometimes decorated by Tiff. Bill shared these albums with me, and Trevor Greene made copies of selected pictures for my use.

6 Phoebe Findley paid for Tiff's education at SAC and helped with Michael's fees for his six years there. She took the family in several times when they were between rental houses and had no other place to go.

7 Two of these girls were Anne Comfort (Charles Comfort's daughter) and Ann Lawson, who Findley considered friends. Joyce Diblee, another Rosedale girl of whom he was especially fond, was a talented young pianist, and Findley recreated her in the story "Sometime—Later—Not Now," where she is called Diana Galbraith and the narrator, Davis Hart, "grew up loving" her.

8 Buchman (1878–1961) and his "Buchmanites" changed their organization's name from the Oxford Group to Moral Re-Armament (MRA) in 1938. The MRA movement became discredited due to its links with fascism, and after Buchman's death its membership dwindled.

9 Margaret Findley's letters and most of Findley's letters to Isabel McLaughlin are held in the McLaughlin fonds in the archives at Queen's University. Isabel, called "Darling Doodle" (by Margaret) and "Aunt Doodle" (by Findley), was a significant painter in her day, and she helped create the Robert McLaughlin Art Gallery in Oshawa.

10 Findley left from Montreal on July 26 and returned via Quebec City on October 25. The journal (LAC 332:3), a large, hardback book (14 by 18 inches) with unlined, unpaginated pages, is devoted entirely to this journey. He completed it after returning home, adding maps he drew and coloured of France, Switzerland, and the English Channel. With this journal he began the practice of inserting documents, such as the telegram informing his family of his passage home, into the text. He also wrote poems in this journal (one was about his great-uncle John Fagan, who drowned at age twenty) and noted down the conversations he had with or overheard among the sailors.

11 Ernest Sterndale Bennett (1884–1982) and his wife taught classes at the Toronto Conservatory of Music, and they established their Canadian Theatre School, dedicated to training professional practitioners, in 1949.

CHAPTER FOUR | Leaving Home

1 The words "Against Despair" appear at the end of Johnson's journal, after his entry for 31 October 1784 (*Diaries, Prayers, and Annals* 414), but he frequently warned himself against despair, which was a serious sin demonstrating a lack of faith in God. Samuel Johnson (1709–84) drank heavily and suffered from depression, anxiety, and many ailments. He was an assiduous journal-writer, who chastised himself in his journals for lists of sins and failures and repeatedly resolved to improve.

2 Hugh Hood (1928–2000) was a Canadian writer of stories, essays, and novels exploring Ontario life through the twentieth century.

3 *The Member of the Wedding*, published as a novel in 1946, was adapted for the stage in 1951. Set in a small town, in the home of the Addams family,

the son is about to marry and his twelve-year-old sister, Frankie (Frances), has developed an obsessive love for her brother and his fiancée. She feels rejected and excluded from the "we" unit represented by the couple, runs away, and contemplates suicide. Frankie spends much of her time in the kitchen with the maid, who tries to comfort her.

4   See Ouzounian's *Stratford Gold*, and Pettigrew and Portman on the first thirty years; for memories of the early Stratford years see Mavor Moore's *Reinventing Myself* (214–26), two volumes of reminiscences by Tyrone Guthrie, and Garebian's *William Hutt* (1988, 84–95).

5   Vincent Massey (1887–1967), a member of the wealthy Massey family, was Canada's first Canadian-born Governor General, and his brother, Raymond Massey (1896–1983), was a successful actor.

6   The chief distinction between the journals and the notebooks or diaries is that the entries in the latter two are terse and occasional, unlike the lengthy, descriptive passages in the journals. The journals have titles and are numbered, with dates but no pagination.

7   "D" is probably Richard (Dick) Easton (1933–), whom Findley met at Janet Baldwin's School of Ballet. In 1953 Easton danced and spoke lines written by Findley for the ballet "Theme Primeval," which was presented at the Fifth Canadian Ballet Festival in Ottawa. Mr. Easton did not reply to my requests for an interview.

8   Findley's reference is to Radclyffe Hall's novel *The Well of Loneliness* (1928) about an Englishwoman who falls in love with a female ambulance driver during the Great War. Hall's allusions to the Old Testament (notably to Cain) may have influenced his use of Cain in the play he tried to write while in England, and her descriptions of horses sacrificed during the war would have distressed him.

9   Sir Alec Guinness, the illegitimate son of a working-class woman called Agnes Cuffe, never knew who his father was and admitted in his autobiography, *Blessings in Disguise*, that he searched for this man all his life (224). His mother drank heavily and moved frequently, taking young Alec with her and leaving unpaid bills behind. This life of "flitting," as Guinness called it, closely resembles the life Findley portrayed in *The Piano Man's Daughter*. Guinness married Merula Salaman in 1938 and insisted she drop her acting career; they had one son. He is remembered for his roles

in films like *The Ladykillers* (1955), *The Bridge on the River Kwai* (1957), and *Star Wars* (1977).

10 After we met in December 2011 to discuss TF and her friendship with him, Mary Lou Finlay sent me this letter and nine others from her personal papers. These letters, which span the years 1985 to 1991, testify to their close friendship. The 26 September 1985 autograph letter runs to fourteen transcribed pages and was written over several days while Tiff and Bill were en route to Saltspring Island. Tiff signs himself "Tiff/d'Arte"—a private joke between himself and Finlay. It is my special pleasure to thank Finlay for preserving these letters and sharing them with me.

11 The play is based on the life of the Hungarian Cardinal József Mindszenty, who was accused of treason. Guinness played the Cardinal; Findley was the Prosecutor's clerk.

12 Incoming letters between 1953 and 1978 from Janet Baldwin are with the Findley fonds (LAC 91:33–34). Findley's London letters to her do not appear to have survived; three of his letters from the 1970s are with the Janet Baldwin fonds.

13 Don Harron (1924–2015) began acting at the University of Toronto after the war and became a well-known performer at Stratford and on CBC radio and television. Findley and Harron first met when *Sunshine Sketches* (for which Harron was a scriptwriter) aired on CBC television in 1952–53, and they were both in the acting company for the 1953 Stratford season.

14 American writer Thornton Wilder (1897–1975) is best remembered for his 1938 play *Our Town* and his 1927 novel *The Bridge of San Luis Rey*. The British production of *The Matchmaker*, directed by Tyrone Guthrie, was very successful and later toured the United States. In 1964, it was adapted for the musical *Hello, Dolly!*

15 Ruth Gordon (1896–1985) was an award-winning American actor and a writer of plays, film scripts, and memoirs. Among her best-known films are *Rosemary's Baby* (1968) and *Harold and Maude* (1971).

16 Alexander Duncan McCowen (1925–2017), CBE, was born in Tunbridge Wells, attended RADA, and began acting in 1942. He had a successful career with the Old Vic Company and in film and television; see his two-volume memoir, *Young Gemini* and *Double Bill*.

17 Most of Wilder's papers are held in the Beinecke Library at Yale, but my inquiries about Findley letters to Wilder have turned up nothing, although one Findley letter is published in Wilder's *Selected Letters* (654–55). Wilder's sister, Isabel, controlled her brother's literary estate and supervised what would be preserved. A 1992 catalogue of the papers Findley was preparing for deposit with LAC notes that all his letters from Wilder are being held back; Findley kept twenty originals in his safety deposit box.

CHAPTER FIVE | Actor or Writer?

1 Herbert Whittaker (1910–2006) was a staunch supporter of Canadian theatre and for many years a regular reviewer with the *Globe and Mail.*

2 In a 23 October 1954 diary entry, Guinness recorded his anger with "Dicky Easton," who had refused an invitation to stay the night because Easton seemed to feel his "virtue would be in danger." Guinness wrote, and then destroyed, an "indignant letter" to Easton, but he refers (with no details) to things that took place during the months in 1953–54 when both Easton and Findley lived with the Guinness household (Alec Guinness fonds MS89015/1/2/3). My special thanks to Kel Pero who consulted this diary for me after restrictions were lifted in 2018 and I was unable to travel to London.

3 Findley developed this method of corresponding with a few close friends. He would talk into the tape recorder for as much as an hour, reviewing various subjects, from the view out his window to politics and his current work. McCowen would tape his reply over Findley's letter and return the tape. Although this method was less tiring for Findley after a long day's writing, it means that these letters to McCowen do not survive.

4 Toronto-born Beatrice Lillie (1894–1989) was famous in England and North America for her stage performances as "Bea Lillie," the lovable funny-woman whose parodies and arch innuendos delighted audiences.

5 His letters to his family about this National Service call-up are in his fonds, with his National Service form (LAC 97:5).

CHAPTER SIX | Beginning Again—and Again

1   First published in 1931, *Sanctuary* remains a controversial novel for its depiction of violent rape. Popeye, a terrifying character, rapes a young woman with a corncob and later keeps her in a brothel to watch her having sex with other men.

2   John Drainie (1916–66), a popular actor on CBC radio, narrated the 1952 television broadcast of *Sunshine Sketches* in which Findley performed. Producer, director, and writer Andrew Allan (1907–74) was the national head of CBC Radio Drama from 1943 to 1955.

3   The Straw Hat Players was launched in 1948 by Donald and Murray Davis and their sister, playwright Barbara Chilcott. The group performed in Memorial Hall in Port Carling, which became a popular venue for summer theatre in Ontario.

4   Only a few letters from Meg survive (LAC 99:21), and I have not located any of Findley's letters to her from these years.

5   My thanks to Martha Wilson, who oversees the Garson Kanin Papers in New York, for her help in locating Findley's letters to Ruth Gordon and Garson Kanin.

6   Nancy Samuels Colbert (1931–) and Stanley Colbert (1927–2010), with their children, moved to Toronto in 1976 when Stanley was invited to join the CBC as Executive Producer of Film Drama. She opened her literary agency, Nancy Colbert and Associates, in 1977; in 1984 her husband and son joined her to form The Colbert Agency. In 1989, they became part owners of HarperCollins Canada, a position they maintained until 1995. Nancy Colbert began representing Timothy Findley with *The Wars*, and they remained close friends for the rest of Findley's life.

7   Ivan Moffat (1918–2002), a British screenwriter and film producer, made films to promote the war effort. In 1943 he joined the United States Army Signal Corps and filmed the activities of the American army as it moved across France into Germany. After the war, he moved to Hollywood to work with George Stevens at Paramount Pictures.

8   John Whelan's one-hour television play *Sanctuary*, aired in the General Motors Presents series, was a historical romance set in the wilderness of Upper Canada during the 1812–14 war. Two American soldiers trapped

behind British lines hide in an abandoned homestead, where a young blind woman called Laura (Janet Reid) also seeks refuge. The wounded soldier, Danny (Tiff Findley), and Laura fall in love.

9   Janet Reid filed a writ of summons to begin the legal process with the Supreme Court of Ontario on 1 June 1959. The court appearance for the plaintiff, Janet Mary Findley, and the defendant, Timothy Irving Findley, took place on 8 June 1959. A notice of discontinuance was filed on 2 July 1959 indicating that no further court appearances were required. The final document annulling the marriage was signed and recorded on 28 March 1960 and declared that the marriage "was and is null and void to all intents and purposes in law whatsoever by reason of the non-consummation of the said marriage due to the physical incapacity of the defendant to consummate the same, and that the parties hereto be free of bond of the said marriage." The defendant was ordered to pay the plaintiff's costs of $100. Janet Reid continued to act for the CBC and later remarried, raised two children, and directed children's plays for Cottingham Junior Public School in Toronto until her retirement. She died in Toronto on 24 October 2004; her obituary, under Reid-Hunter, Janet Mary, appeared in the *Toronto Star* on 30 October 2004 (B7). Had he lived, Timothy Findley would have been 74 on 30 October 2004.

10   A copy of this unpublished lecture is with the Elspeth Cameron papers in the University of Toronto's Fisher Library (77:15). It is a twelve-page typescript of the talk Findley gave on 28 January 1984 to the Sexology Section of the Ontario Psychiatric Association.

11   This eight-page holograph letter is with the Findley fonds (LAC 96:11) and is reproduced here by permission of Bill Whitehead.

12   Research into possible connections between alcoholism, homosexuality, and mental illness developed during and after the Second World War. In Toronto, this led to the creation of ARF, the Alcoholism Research Foundation, in 1949. During the fifties and sixties, ARF had its clinic at 9–11 Bedford Road in Toronto, with fifteen beds for inpatients; it also treated outpatients. Since 1970, the permanent home for ARF (now part of the Centre for Addiction and Mental Health) has been at 33 Russell Street in Toronto.

13   This form of treatment was popular in the 1960s; see Chenier (159).

CHAPTER SEVEN | **Becoming a Writer**

1   The main source for Bill's biography is *Words to Live By*, but I am grateful for information he provided in our many hours of conversation over seven years. Unless the memoir is cited, quotations are from our personal correspondence and conversations; they appear with his permission.

2   Jean Roberts, OC, was born in Scotland and educated at the University of Edinburgh. She met the English actress Marigold Charlesworth while working as stage manager and assistant director with the Shakespeare Memorial Theatre in Stratford-upon-Avon (today the Royal Shakespeare Company). The two women immigrated to Canada in 1956.

3   Jules Feiffer's play *Crawling Arnold*, a satire on an American family with a domineering mother, aired on 14 February 1962.

4   *The Balcony* (*Le Balcon*), which premiered in London in 1957, is now considered a masterpiece of twentieth-century theatre. Findley played the role of Roger, a failed revolutionary who castrates himself near the end of the play; it was a bold choice for a Toronto audience. See *Words to Live By*, 114–18.

5   Dr. Robert Edward Turner, MD, FRCP, was a pioneer in forensic psychiatry. During his career he held the positions of Director of the Forensic Clinic of the University of Toronto, Medical Director of the Clarke Institute of Psychiatry, Psychiatrist-in-Charge and Director of the Metropolitan Toronto Forensic Service (METFORS), and Professor of Psychiatry at the University of Toronto. While at the Clarke Institute, Turner reported to Dr. Vivian Rakoff, the CEO, and after he retired in 1991, he provided outpatient therapy at the College Street site (the former Clarke Institute of Psychiatry) of CAMH (Centre for Addiction and Mental Health). Dr. Turner's professional papers are in the CAMH archives; his clinical records were almost certainly destroyed when he retired. From 1961, Turner lectured on homosexuality, sexual criminality, depression, and deviancy. He was instrumental in having homosexuality removed from the Ontario Psychiatric Association's list of mental illnesses in the 1970s, but he continued to treat men suffering from the negative social impacts of being homosexual, such as anxiety, guilt, and depression. For his publications, see the bibliography and Court et al. His wife, Dr. Gene Anne (Jan) Turner (1926–2012), was a physician with long service in public health and psychotherapy.

6   After Allan lost his position with Bache & Co., he entered into a brokerage deal with a man who turned out to be a fraud, and Allan lost his investment.

7   According to Mary Jane Miller (1983), *The Paper People* was "one of the most innovative television dramas in [the CBC's] beleaguered prestige series, *Festival*" (49). It was shot in 16 mm, in colour, outside the studio, and the critics "either loved or hated it," but viewers' statistics were negative and the federal government "joined the critics and the public attacking the piece for cost ($300,000) and content" (49); see reviews by Bob Blackburn, Sheila Kieran, Pat Pearce, and Frank Penn. Guy Morris called the film "fascinating," but not meant for viewers who liked to be spoon-fed, and Les Wedman described it as "La Dolce Vita, Canadian style" and praised the acting of Marc Strange as Jamie Taylor, and Marigold Charlesworth as Janet Webb.

8   My quotations are from the 1969 first edition, which is closer in time to the beginning of Findley's career and sheds more light on how he was developing.

9   See Brydon's *Timothy Findley* (2–7 and 39–52) for a discussion of this novel and the appropriateness of labels like *postmodern* and *metafiction* for Findley's work.

10 Findley could not have known the full extent of Nazi infiltration and plans to assassinate Jews in the film industry, but he must have heard about these plots and discussed the Nazi presence in Los Angeles with friends. See Steven Ross, chapter 14, "Slaughter the Hollywood Jews."

11 My thanks to Bill Whitehead for giving me a tape of this tour de force performance. "Walls" was one of six short programs broadcast for *The Best of Ideas* and produced by Phyllis Webb.

12 Gore Vidal's 1968 novel depicts a sleazy Hollywood and a widow (Myra) who claims 50 percent of her dead husband's estate, but Myra is really Myron, and this fictional autobiography acquired cult status. In Philip Roth's *Portnoy's Complaint* (1969), another fictional autobiography, Portnoy describes his sexual life in explicit detail. *The Butterfly Plague* is better compared with Nathaniel West's *The Day of the Locust* (1939), which Findley was reading in 1965 while drafting his novel.

13 "E.R.A." first appeared in the magazine *Cavalier* in April 1970 and was reprinted as "What Mrs. Felton Knew" in *Dinner Along the Amazon.*

"The Journey," broadcast on 3 April 1970 on CBC radio, explores the corruption of contemporary society and humanity's rush to destroy the natural world.

CHAPTER EIGHT | **The Golden Age of Canadian Writing**

1   Len Collins, Anne (Brandon) Collins, and their three children became family for Bill and Tiff. One of the many improvements Len made was to repair the nineteenth-century root cellar behind the house (see ill. 27) so Findley could write and sleep there during the summer. Anne helped with some of his correspondence in the late 1970s, taking dictation and typing letters on behalf of Amnesty International.

2   Copies of the first draft (297 typescript pages) of "Whimper" survive in the LAC fonds and with Bill's private papers. It is a confusing story about a family gathering at an English country estate, but the themes of family dysfunction, death, and alcohol, set in a claustrophobic domestic environment, are familiar Findley material.

3   Scott Symons (1933–2009) was born and raised in Rosedale. He claimed to have been in the Cub Scouts with Findley; he attended Trinity College School in Port Hope, the University of Toronto, and Cambridge University for two years. He married in 1958 and had a son, but he was gay and blamed his family for complicating his sexual identity.

4   Findley sent a more legible holograph version of this letter to Gibson and Atwood, also dated 14 September 1973 (Gibson fonds Ms Coll. 00527, Box 20:21), in which he suggests that their presence prevented his trip to the river. In a 29 December 1978 letter to Gibson, Findley told Gibson that Symons scared him because he needed to destroy others' self-confidence (Gibson fonds 20:21).

5   The main Pierre Berton fonds is at McMaster University, and the Pierre Berton Resource Library opened in Vaughan in 2004. A 27 March 1972 "Status Report" outlines a tight schedule of production details for scripts and shooting locations, and it is clear that Berton was integral to the entire process. Whitehead and Findley signed their contracts with the CBC in 1972 but had begun planning the work in late 1971. For a discussion of the significance of this CBC production, see Monica MacDonald, chapter 5.

6   The name recalls St. Sebastian, a patron saint of homosexuals, and Sebastian Flyte in Waugh's *Brideshead Revisited* (1945), which Findley read during his London years.

7   My thanks to Phyllis Webb (1927–) for permission to consult Findley's letters in her fonds at LAC (LM5-0098).

8   In 1974, Margaret Laurence (1926–87), who had lived in England for several years, moved to Lakefield, Ontario. She served as chancellor of Trent University from 1981 to 1983 and presided in 1982 when Findley received his honorary degree from Trent. She was made a Companion of the Order of Canada in 1972. See James King's biography.

9   To prepare his report for *Books in Canada*, Paul Stuewe visited the agricultural area west of Toronto, interviewed Elmer Umbach and others, and set forth the pros and cons for a school board's decision to remove novels from the curriculum at parents' request. Although he did not support the "Concerned Citizens" attempt at censorship, he did respect a community's right to protect their shared values, and he criticized the Writers' Union for defending the book. Barry Brewer took a harder line; he insisted that a selection of reading material was necessary to education and that the Union was a "pressure group" that overlooked the need for censorship in matters of libel and hate literature and neglected the distinction between child and adult readers.

10 By the late sixties Jean Roberts and Marigold Charlesworth had moved to Ottawa, where Roberts worked for the Canada Council before her appointment as the director of the theatre division at the new National Arts Centre in 1971; see Jennings (95).

11 In *Telling Tales* (86–87), Fraser describes seeing the Ottawa premiere of the play and hating it. In his view he had not been malicious but simply brought "[his] own views on 'mental illness'" into his review.

12 The three works Findley referred to were "Whimper," "Desperadoes," and a play called "Whisper." He tells his own version of this announcement to Bill in *Inside Memory* (135–36).

13 Mannock assisted Findley on details for *The Wars* and with background research for *Famous Last Words*.

14 John Pearce joined Clarke, Irwin in 1976 and worked with Findley on *The Wars* and *Famous Last Words*. When Clarke, Irwin closed in 1984, he

moved to the Book Society of Canada, and in 1987 he joined Doubleday Canada as editor-in-chief. When Doubleday merged with Random House of Canada in 2000, he became executive editor-at-large. Since 2004, he has been a literary agent with Westwood Creative Artists.

15 The Clarke, Irwin & Company Limited fonds is held in the William Ready Division of Archives and Research Collections at McMaster University. There are extensive holdings for *The Wars* and *Famous Last Words*, including page proofs, correspondence, contracts, reviews, and promotional material. See boxes 24, 75, 76, and 81. LAC holds the full set of original drafts of *The Wars*.

16 In an 18 June 1977 letter to John Pearce, who had solicited her assessment of the novel, Laurence wrote that *The Wars* was "a splendid piece of work" with "the inevitability of Greek tragedy." She did not recommend cutting the rape scene but wondered if it could be better integrated into the whole (Clarke, Irwin fonds B24-F5). Marian Engel also read the manuscript and told Pearce that *The Wars* was "an astonishing accomplishment [and] a triumph" (Clarke, Irwin fonds B24-F5).

17 All quotations are from the 1978 Penguin edition of the book.

18 Dr. William H. Clarke (1940–) was a professor of astrophysics at the University of Toronto and a successful businessman with a large computer firm before taking on the family business as managing publisher of Clarke, Irwin & Company Limited in 1966. The company was founded in 1930 and by the sixties, with authors like Robertson Davies and Emily Carr, was an important champion of Canadian literature and one of the three top publishers of creative works in the country. Irene Clarke could be hard to please when a new literary manuscript was being considered, but she read *The Wars* and decided immediately that they had to publish it; she had had two brothers in the Great War and understood the importance of the novel. Bill Clarke admired *The Butterfly Plague* before he heard about *The Wars* or had met Timothy Findley. He was deeply touched when Findley sent him a signed copy of the revised edition of *The Butterfly Plague*. Clarke, Irwin was forced into receivership in 1983. For further information on Clarke, Irwin, see Judy Donnelly, Robert Fulford, and Joyce Wayne.

19 The first edition dust jacket showed a stark title in red over the grey of a Great War photograph with a lone officer walking away from the viewer

across a wasted landscape. A detail of this image was repeated at the beginning of each of the novel's five parts.

20 Undated translations of the Albers and Butow reviews are with the Clarke, Irwin fonds (B24-F5).

21 Certain soldiers' names—Clifford Purchas and Captain Leather, for example—come from the journal, and Findley borrows scenes from his uncle's descriptions but develops them to imbue the facts with humanity and an ethical dimension.

22 For critical discussion, see Bailey, Brydon, Cobley, Davey, Drolet, Hastings, Krause, Kröller, Novak, Pennee, Rhodes, Ricou, Vauthier, and Peter Webb. Dennis Garnhum's *The Wars*, based on Findley's novel, has had productions in Calgary, in Vancouver, and, in 2018, in London, Ontario. It is staged expressionistically from Robert's perspective, without attempting naturalistic battle details or a representation of the rape scene.

23 This quote is from an undated letter to Laurence that was probably sent in January 1980 (Laurence fonds 1980-001/002 [64]).

24 Other roles were played by Barbara Budd (Nurse Turner), Jackie Burroughs (Miss Davenport), and Ann-Marie MacDonald (Rowena). Graeme Gibson appeared in the cameo role of Devlin. Cinematography was by John Coquillon, with editing by Tony Lower, both from the NFB. Most critics dismissed the film; see Rick Groen, Gina Mallet, and Jay Scott. Phillips refused to talk about it, and Findley rarely mentioned it publicly. However, in a 7 November 1983 letter to Graeme Gibson (Gibson fonds 20:22) he praised Gibson's performance as Devlin and told him how pleased he was that the premiere of the film was a benefit event for the Parkinson's Foundation because Allan Findley had died from the disease.

25 Jane Rule (1931–2007), CM, OBC, a novelist and activist for gay rights, lived on Galiano Island with her partner, Helen Sontag.

26 *John A.—Himself!* premiered in January 1979 to mixed reviews. Bale described it as a "potentially fine play that simply needs more work." Ashley criticized the play's "odd mix of styles" and wished Findley had opted for a "more conventional, and therefore comprehensible approach to his subject." Herbert Whittaker approved of this "biographical vaudeville" version of Canada's first prime minister and agreed with the theatrical presentation of Macdonald's life.

CHAPTER NINE | The Second World War and the Faces of Fascism

1   The documentary includes footage from a contemporary newsreel called *Dieppe Heroes in Canada* that shows happy soldiers returning to their cheering families. *Dieppe 1942* won an Anik award for best CBC television documentary in 1980.

2   All references are to the 1981 first edition of the novel. Lorenzo de Broca is loosely modelled on the Italian poet and anti-fascist Lauro De Bosis (1901–31), who flew over Rome in a small wooden plane on 3 October 1931 dropping anti-fascist leaflets to inform citizens about Il Duce. Findley learned about De Bosis from Wilder, who had been a friend of De Bosis, and from his friend Dorothy Warren, who wrote biographies of De Bosis and of Ruth Draper, De Bosis's lover.

3   See, for example, Bloch's *Operation Willi*, Maltby's *Britain's Nazi King—Revealed*, and Urbach's *Go-Betweens for Hitler*.

4   Findley also consulted Alistair Cooke's *Six Men* (1977), which has a chapter on Edward, and he did considerable research on the Bahamas. He tracked Charles Bedaux's story through articles, and he was interviewed in 1995 for George Ungar's documentary on Bedaux called *The Champagne Safari*. Beverley Roberts, a friend of Bill's, became Findley's researcher at this time.

5   My thanks to Trevor Greene for sending me a copy of this letter, in which Findley describes Mottle playing goalie in their late-night silver-paper hockey games and tells Michael that she has just died.

6   In "H. S. Mauberley (Life and Contacts)" Pound writes about himself, people he knew, and his age, mostly in the third person. His younger alter ego, Hugh Selwyn Mauberley, is a passive, minor poet who deserves to be rejected. For a comparative analysis of the poem and the novel, see Scobie. My references are to Pound's *Selected Poems*.

7   See studies by Bailey, Brydon (1995), Duffy, Scobie, Shields, Williams (1991), and Woodcock (1985).

8   My thanks to Bush for recalling his experience with this radio production. Others in the cast were Douglas Rain (Ribbentrop), John Colicos (Oakes), Neil Munro (Mauberley), and Greg Ellwand (Quinn).

9 The CBC had asked Findley and Whitehead to write a series based on Berton's *Flames Across the Border*, and they devoted some time to planning this before the CBC dropped it.

10 See MacSkimming and Dobson and Kamboureli.

11 On 28 December 1983, Findley signed his contract with Penguin for *Not Wanted on the Voyage* (Colbert fonds, LAC 93: 34). This contract included a clause stating their intention to publish a revised edition of *The Butterfly Plague* and a collection of short stories. They also contracted the paperback rights to *Famous Last Words* and *The Last of the Crazy People*. Colbert had negotiated a solid deal for Findley with a guaranteed annual payment of $27,000 ($64,300 in 2020 dollars) in royalties and advances. In a 12 February 1984 letter to Graeme Gibson and Margaret Atwood (Gibson fonds 20:22), Findley said he was happy at Penguin and had felt intimidated by the authors' list at McClelland and Stewart.

12 Letter to Webb, 19 December 1981. My thanks to Phyllis Webb for permission to consult Findley's letters with her papers at LAC (Webb fonds 2: 13a). For her reflections on their friendship and shared interests, see "The Confluence of Imaginations." Webb dedicated "I Daniel" to Timothy Findley, and her volume of selected prose, *Nothing but Brush Strokes*, is dedicated to "Tiff and Bill, faithful friends."

13 All quotations from *Not Wanted on the Voyage* are from the 1984 Penguin edition.

14 See studies by Brydon ("The Dream of Tory Origins"), Dickinson, Nicholson, Pearson, Pennee (*Moral Metafiction*), Tiffin, and York (*Front Lines*).

15 Richard Rose and D. D. Kugler obtained the rights in 1990 after Robin Phillips, who had planned an adaptation for Stratford, left the Festival. An early version of the script was performed on 2 March 1991 aboard the Captain Matthew Flinders cruise ship in Toronto harbour with Ann Baggley (Emma), Rodger Barton (Shem), Peter Boretski (Yaweh), Roland Hewgill (Noah), Richard McMillan (Lucy), Duncan Ollerenshaw (Japeth), Paul Rainville (Ham), and Goldie Semple (Hannah). John Millard composed the score, with set and lighting design by Graeme S. Thomson.

CHAPTER TEN | **Staring Down Despair**

1   *Dinner Along the Amazon* was made for CanWest/Global, directed by
    Sisam and produced by Sisam and Anita Herczeg, with original music
    by Jim McGrath; it starred Arsinée Khanjian, Dan Lett, Philip Craig, and
    Anne Farquhar. The film was nominated for a Gemini Award for Best
    Short Dramatic Program, and it is the best film based on Findley's work to
    date. My thanks to Sisam for lending me a copy of the film and answering
    my questions about it and his friendship with Tiff and Bill.

2   *The Boys in the Band*, an off-Broadway play adapted as a film in 1970,
    portrays a gathering of men, several of whom are gay. It received mixed
    reviews from the gay community because some felt it portrayed gay men
    in a negative light. Findley's comment suggests he did not like the film. See
    chapter 6 for my discussion of Findley's speech "How Would *You* Like to
    be Called Gay?"

3   Despite decriminalization and the advancement of gay rights, debates
    over homosexuality within the psychiatry profession persisted through
    the seventies, eighties, and nineties in Canada and the United States;
    see Carey, Chenier, Isay, Israelstam and Lambert, Kinsey, Kinsman and
    Gentile, McLeod, Nardi, Reilly, Schüklenk et al., Turner, and Ziebold
    and Mongeon. My special thanks to Frances Reilly for sending me her
    doctoral dissertation, which is especially useful for its analyses of the
    Ontario Psychiatric Association, CAMH, and the work of Dr. Turner and
    his colleagues.

4   Findley sent a complete copy of this thirty-page typescript to Margaret
    Laurence; see Laurence fonds (1986-006, 4:147).

5   See *Inside Memory* (81–83) for Findley's happy memories of "Emma."

6   Dorothy Warren (1905–2008) wrote a biography of Lauro De Bosis, *Sac-
    rificio: A Study in Heroism*, and two books about his lover, the dramatic
    monologist Ruth Draper. She was also a successful photographer.

7   All references are to the 1986 first edition of the novel. For information on
    the POW camp, Findley began with a book he had read as a boy—Agnes
    Newton Keith's *Three Came Home* (1947)—but he imagined much of the
    rest of Vanessa's experience.

8   Donald Ewen Cameron (1901–67) began his CIA-funded research at the
    Allan in the late fifties. His method was to subject a patient to a drug-

induced deep sleep and long hours of tape-recorded messages and sounds. In *The Shock Doctrine*, Melanie Klein calls Cameron's work for the CIA a system of torture. Don Gilmor's book *I Swear by Apollo: Dr. Ewen Cameron and the CIA-Brainwashing Experiments* was one of several published in the late seventies and eighties, by which time Cameron's reputation was in tatters. See Gilmor's "The Brain Drain." Several newspaper articles appeared in the *Washington Post* during 1977 and were reprinted in the *Globe and Mail*; see also Weinstein.

9   For reviews, see Bale and Yanofsky; articles of note are by Theo D'haen, Lorna Irvine, and Kenneth McGoogan. See also the discussions of the novel by Bailey, Brydon (1998), Pennee, and York.

10 After her arrival in Canada, Martha Kuwee Kumsa earned a PhD in social work from the University of Toronto and joined the faculty at Wilfrid Laurier University. It was a pleasure to meet with her and hear her memories of Tiff and Bill.

11 Among the writers Findley met on this trip, Janet Frame filled him with the greatest delight. See "Legends," in which he describes standing outside White's house with other writers to pay his silent respects.

12 This letter, dated 26 September 1985, is with Finlay's private papers, and it is the same long letter in which he told her about the Gielgud scandal in 1954 (see chapter 4). Again, my thanks to Finlay for sending me this letter.

13 June Callwood (1924–2007), CC, OOnt, an award-winning journalist with the CBC and the *Globe and Mail*, was also a social activist who founded or co-founded many organizations to assist women and youth, as well as Casey House.

14 Findley greatly valued Adachi's book about the Second World War, *The Enemy That Never Was*. Ken Adachi (1929–89), author and literary columnist with the *Toronto Star*, was also the husband of Mary Adachi (1937–), who was the designated copy editor for most of Findley's work. She prepared a ten-episode version of *The Piano Man's Daughter* that Colm Feore read for the CBC radio program *Between the Covers*, and worked collaboratively with Findley on his manuscripts. She recalls that he could be stubborn about accepting editorial advice, but usually agreed when Bill suggested that the changes were good. My special thanks to Mary Adachi for meeting with me and sharing her memories of Tiff and Bill, and of Ken's death.

CHAPTER ELEVEN | **The Canadian Findley**

1   My thanks to Trevor Greene who sent me this letter, which he found with Bill Whitehead's papers. This is one of several original autograph letters from Tiff to his mother that were with Bill's files.

2   Joe Kertes, Dean of the School of Creative and Performing Arts at Humber College in 2012, when I interviewed him, recalls Findley as an "extraordinary" person, "constructive and generous"; students loved him, which was not the case with other visiting workshop writers. He had "wonderful confidence in young writers" and continued to mentor them after the workshops.

3   My thanks to Bill Whitehead for giving me the box of old audiotapes, one of which has the Spry lecture. Findley's performance was eloquent and powerful. For the text, see "Turning Down the Volume."

4   See "Turn Down the Volume" (A19), where Findley went on to say (but not explain) that he would "hate to think what might happen if a child should ever understand" *The Tale of Peter Rabbit*.

5   Sir Michael Kemp Tippett (1905–98) was a leading English composer, best known for his oratorio *A Child of Our Time* (1944) and *The Midsummer Marriage* (1952). In his latter years he suffered from macular dystrophy, and his near blindness made an oral letter a practical form of communication.

6   All quotations are from Erin Ramlo's transcription of the tape given to me by WFW.

7   The script I saw is a 102-page second draft of a telefilm, dated June 1978, with Bill's personal papers. It opened with a photomontage of archival footage showing the rise of Fascism in Italy, Hitler speaking at Nuremberg, the Spanish Civil War, the bombing of Japan, and the postwar trials. The final image Findley wanted to use was of Lester Pearson with Norman. The story is structured in numerous short scenes introduced by a television host who explores different theories about Norman's death. There are scenes of RCMP interrogation, and at one point the host claims that Pearson "threw Norman to the dogs" and that Norman's suicide was a Japanese-style protest. In this script, his wife, Irene, is not ill, and there is no mention of a homosexual affair in Moscow. Two copies, dated 1977 and 1978, are with the archive at LAC (67:13–20).

8 The play was a co-production of the Grand Theatre and the National Arts Centre, and it opened in London, Ontario, on 26 March 1993 before going to Ottawa. It received high praise; see Reid, and see Lane's 1993 article, "'Not His Own Person.'" Directed by Peter Moss, the play had a stellar cast, and Astrid Janson's set design captured the multi-level house (in which people watch each other), the garden, and the drop to the ravine. Other members of the Grand Theatre cast were Kate Trotter (Diana), Donald Davis (Michael Riordan), Patricia Collins (Juliet Riordan), Hardee T. Lineham (Supt. Daniel Jackman), and Michael McManus (Corporal Greg Mahavolitch). Boko Suzuki created original Japanese-style flute music. Henry and Hutt also starred in the 1993 Stratford production. Shaftesbury Films held an extended option on the play in 1996, but a feature film was never made. Instead, in 1999, Peter Moss directed a CBC television play called "External Affairs," based on *The Stillborn Lover.* This production simplified aspects of the play by making the wife unequivocally ill with Alzheimer's disease, and it introduced into the plot a Russian man who wants to defect to Canada. Victor Garber was excellent as Harry and Kenneth Welsh was convincingly ruthless as Michael. My thanks to Moss for showing me his copy of the program and answering questions about his work with this play as a stage production and a television play.

9 In our 2011 interview, Tupholme told many stories about her work with Findley. He was always willing to listen and discuss any suggestions she made, and she cherishes memories of visiting with him at Stone Orchard and in Cotignac. She recalls *The Piano Man's Daughter* as "a wonderful editing experience" and *You Went Away* as "heartbreaking." She still has the Matinee Super Mild package on which Findley wrote, about "Pilgrim": "he is trying to connect with the future"; it is seen as a special memento of a great HarperCollins writer. My thanks to Tupholme for these memories.

10 The entire 1990 journal is in LAC 188; Findley had a copy made (LAC 322) for safekeeping while he was working. He describes the doctor who ran the fictional Parkin as "the Rakoff character"—a reference to Dr. Vivian Rakoff, who served as CEO and Psychiatrist-in-Chief of the Clarke Institute of Psychiatry from 1980 to 1990—but makes no further mention of his plans for this character.

11 Attila Richard Lukacs (1962–) first came to the Canadian art world's attention in the 1985 "Young Romantics" show at the Vancouver Art Gallery,

and his large 1988 paintings of skinheads and neo-Nazis were sensational. No single Lukacs piece matches the fictional work of Slade, but canvases like "The Young Spartans Challenge the Boys to Fight" (1988) and "Authentic Décor" (1991) clearly echo the painting Findley imagined for the novel.

12 Pedophile rings involving lawyers, doctors, clergy, and police officers in Cornwall, London, and Prescott were exposed in the 1980s, and the abuse received wide coverage in the national media.

13 Findley does not comment on Sontag's work or appear to have read her more widely, but the two writers, close contemporaries, had much in common in their private struggles with family and sexuality and in their themes and socio-political views. See Benjamin Moser's *Sontag*.

14 All references to *Headhunter* are to the 1993 HarperCollins paperback edition. The novel is dedicated to R. E. Turner, and Dr. Turner, with the staff at the Clarke Institute of Psychiatry and the Queen Street Mental Health Centre, are among those thanked in the acknowledgements.

15 See also Bailey, Brydon (1996), D'Haen, Goldman, and Rosemary Sullivan.

16 The forum ran from June 22 to 27. My thanks to CAMH archivist John Court for his help with information on the Mental Health Centre and Findley's connections with it and the College Street facility. Court also saw that Findley's reading from *Headhunter* at the forum was transferred from videotape to DVD for archival preservation and my research use.

17 Vancouver's Little Sister's Book and Art Emporium case began in 1985, when Canada customs seized a shipment of gay literature at the US border, charging that the material was obscene. In 1986, Little Sister's began the fight that took them to the Supreme Court of Canada in 2000. Although the Court found in their favour, no rules or policies were put in place to block customs officials from censoring books in the future. Urquhart's novel *Away* was published in 1994.

18 My thanks to Michael Lindop for permission to quote him, and to Bill for sending me copies of correspondence concerning this attack on the novel.

19 The money Findley received from the sale of his papers to the National Library of Canada (now Library and Archives Canada [LAC]) enabled them to make this trip. In Italy they stopped in Florence, which became an important setting in *Pilgrim*.

20 My thanks to Carol Roberts for a copy of this typescript speech, which Findley sent to her. He first gave this speech in Venice in September 1994, and these words were not included in either the published text, *A Nation of One*, or in excerpts for *Inside Memory*.

21 All quotations are from the 1995 paperback edition of the novel.

22 My thanks to John Court for sending me an audio version of this talk, which is with the CAMH Archives, Clarke Institute fonds (2006 accrual, Box 67).

23 Although Findley often pasted or taped material into his journals, this is the first journal into which he cut and taped actual photographs of his ancestors. Beside one of his grandfather, Thomas Findley, who is holding a big fish he has caught, Findley writes, "already knowing he was dying," and on a picture of John James Fagan, the Fagan brother who drowned, he notes the dates 1870 to 1890 and that John died on October 25. Another photograph shows members of his mother's family and friends dated 1914 with a note in Allan Findley's handwriting: "The Guns of August" (an allusion to Barbara Tuchman's book). This picture is also reproduced on the endpapers of *The Piano Man's Daughter*. Beside a picture of his grandmother Phoebe Findley, Findley wrote that this is "Ede Kilworth."

24 In June 1994, Findley was reading Arthur Mizener's *The Far Side of Paradise* (1951), and he made notes about the life and death of Zelda Sayre Fitzgerald (1900–48), who suffered from mental illness; she died in a fire that destroyed her locked room in the Asheville, North Carolina, hospital. Lily dies in a fire that destroys the fictional Whitby Asylum, but historical records show that there was no such fire at Whitby, so Findley has created a fictional death that loosely parallels Zelda Fitzgerald's and recalls Cassandra's fate in *Can You See Me Yet?*

25 Stephen Smith noted the autobiographical aspects of the novel, and Paul Quarrington praised the "wonderful description" of the land and Findley's portrayal of music. However, Will Aitken disliked the "glamorizing" of madness in the Lily character, and John Bemrose ("Rural Roots") found Charlie's search for his father "forced." Stan Persky wondered why anyone needed "another novel about the First World War," and Philip Marchand ("Findley Weaves Gothic Romance") criticized Findley's portrayal of male characters and his "over-blown prose."

26 All quotations are from the 1995 paperback edition of the novel.

27 My thanks to Sabine Roth for these memories. The scene Dr. Roth recalled is one in which Lily's brother, who is drunk, tells the child a fairy story about an illegitimate baby conceived in a field and the fate that awaits such a child. That child is, of course, Lily. In 2001 Roth translated *Famous Last Words* as *Mauberleys Ende*, and she considers this his masterpiece. She found the rhythms of his prose and his paratactic sentences to be a challenge and a delight for a translator.

28 The play, which takes place in "the mind of Ezra Pound," is a memory play with several characters based on people in Pound's life, including his wife, a lover, his psychiatrists, and William Carlos Williams.

29 "All the characters [in *You Went Away*] are based on my own family and their friends," Findley has said (*J* 47); see also, interviews with Canton, Meyer and O'Riordan, and Twigg.

30 All quotations are from the first edition, but the paperback is consistent with the hardback except for the appearance on the hardback endpapers of Findley's manuscript for the opening pages.

31 "The Fence" persisted as the working title until March 1996, when Findley prepared an episode breakdown using the new title.

32 My thanks to Michael Peterman for sharing his memories of Findley and the conference with me; see the materials published in the *Journal of Canadian Studies/Revue d'études canadiennes*, and Peterman and Charmaine Eddy's introduction, "Can You See Me Yet?" (5). The only other conference, to date, held on Findley's work took place at the University of Toulouse in December 2013 and focused on *The Wars*.

33 Paul Thompson, OC (1940–), a Canadian theatre director, writer, and the founding artistic director of Theatre Passe Muraille, first worked with Findley at the inaugural Vancouver Writers Festival organized by Alma Lee in 1988. He was impressed with Findley's willingness to change his words to facilitate an actor's needs.

34 I greatly appreciate Veronica Tennant's assistance in recalling this tour. She sent me a copy of her DVD of a performance in Calgary to help me visualize what the group was doing.

35 My thanks to Veronica Tennant for sending me a colour copy of this delightful hand-drawn, autograph letter, which is with her private papers.

CHAPTER TWELVE | **Not Yet**

1   All quotations are from the first edition of *Dust to Dust*. Although the book sold well, it was not praised by reviewers; see Lorna Jackson and John Ayre. See also Kruk (2012) and Grace's "Timothy Findley's Wars" (2015).

2   Pau was the birthplace of Philip II of France, whom Findley mentions as born in Villeverger. Gurs is less than an hour's drive from Pau; the internment camp was established in 1939 to hold Spanish refugees.

3   Entrecasteaux is perched above a gorge, with a castle at the top of a steep, narrow road. "La Fourchette," located opposite the castle and nestled against a small, fortified church, has views across the town site and the valley. Tiff and Bill always sat at the same corner table, from which Tiff could watch other diners and listen to their conversations. Although the sign pointing to the restaurant still says "La Fourchette," the restaurant's name is now "Chez Pierrot." My thanks to the Nicolases for answering questions and sending me photographs of Tiff and Bill at the restaurant.

4   This is the only letter from Findley to Guinness currently available in the Alec Guinness fonds in the British Library (MS989015/2/7/7-5030-1). Judging from incoming correspondence in the Findley fonds, the two men corresponded more frequently, and it is clear from Findley's 1950s London journals that he wrote to Guinness during those early years.

5   Nothing came of the Goldberg option, but a film adaptation was made by Kevin Sullivan in 2000.

6   The seven-page typescript outlining the "Scheme" for *Pilgrim* (LAC 292:7) reveals much of Findley's initial thinking about the novel and about what would become *Elizabeth Rex*, but as he worked on his draft his emphasis shifted away from a mythological Tiresias to a more contemporary, human character that recalls figures in Western cultural history who cannot die or who live as both men and women—the Flying Dutchman, the Wandering Jew, and Virginia Woolf's "Orlando."

7   All references are to the 1999 paperback edition.

8   Findley based his description of the theft on the actual story of Vincenzo Peruggia, who stole the painting on 21 August 1911, kept the painting in his Paris flat for a year, and then was caught trying to sell it to a dealer in Florence. See Grace 2019.

9 Other reviewers were less positive; see Archer, Bolger, Evans, Govier, and Rigelhof. In 2008, the University of British Columbia's student opera ensemble performed the premiere of composer Lloyd Burritt's opera "The Dream Healer," with a libretto, based on *Pilgrim*, by Christopher Allan and Don Mowatt. The work is set in the Burghölzli Clinic, and it featured two distinguished professional singers, Judith Forst as Lady Quartermaine, and Roelof Oostwoud as Mr. Pilgrim.

10 The first edition of the novel had a map of Stratford on the endpapers. Findley dedicated the novel to Matthew Mackey, "whose spade began it all," and the people of Stratford. For reviews of the novel, see Oliva and Terauds. My references are to the 2001 paperback edition.

11 Findley was remembering Priestley's play, *Dangerous Corner*, in which he had performed in 1951.

12 Dennis Garnhum directed the premiere; all quotations are from the play as published in *CTR (Canadian Theatre Research)*.

BIBLIOGRAPHY

The bibliography is divided in two parts. Part A is a list of primary works by and about Findley that is as complete as possible. Part B is a selected bibliography of critical studies and other secondary works consulted in my research for this biography.

PART A | Primary Works by and about Timothy Findley

FICTION

Findley, Timothy. "About Effie." *Tamarack Review* 1.1 (Autumn 1956): 48–60. Repr. in *Dinner Along the Amazon*, 82–93.

———. "Almeyer's Mother." In *Stones*, 71–91.

———. "The Ark in the Garden." In *The Ark in the Garden: Fables for Our Time*, edited by Alberto Manguel, 15–23. Toronto: Macfarlane Walter & Ross, 1998.

———. "The Banks of the Wabash." In *Story of a Nation: Defining Moments in Our History*, 144–75. Toronto: Doubleday Canada, 2001.

———. *The Butterfly Plague.* 1969. Rev. ed. 1986. Toronto: Penguin, 1996.

———. "The Dead Can Dance." In *Bizarre Dreams*, 11–17. New York: Masquerade Press, 1994.

———. *Dinner Along the Amazon.* Markham, ON: Penguin Books, 1984.

———. "The Duel in Cluny Park." *Toronto Life* August 1989. F29–31, F43–50.

———. *Dust to Dust*. Toronto: HarperCollins, 1997.

———. "E.R.A." *Cavalier* 20.6 (April 1970): 30–32, 74–77.

———. *Famous Last Words*. 1981. Toronto: Clarke, Irwin, 1981.

———. "A Gift of Mercy." In *Streets of Attitude: Toronto Stories*, 43–66. Toronto: Yonge & Bloor Publishing, 1990.

———. "Harper's Bazaar." *Exile* 7.1–2 (Autumn 1980): 141–200. Repr. as "Lemonade" in *Dinner Along the Amazon*, 1–64.

———. *Headhunter*. Toronto: HarperCollins, 1993.

———. *The Last of the Crazy People*. 1967. Harmondsworth, UK: Penguin, 1983.

———. "Memorial Day." *West Coast Line* 24.2 (Fall 1990): 112–28. Repr. in *Canadian Mystery Stories*, edited by Alberto Manguel, 80–97. Toronto: Oxford University Press, 1991.

———. "The Name's the Same." In *Stones*, 133–47.

———. *Not Wanted on the Voyage*. Toronto: Penguin, 1984.

———. *The Piano Man's Daughter*. Toronto: HarperCollins, 1995.

———. *Pilgrim*. Toronto: HarperCollins, 1999.

———. "Real Life Writes Real Bad." In *Stones*, 149–70.

———. *Spadework*. Toronto: HarperCollins, 2001.

———. *Stones*. Toronto: Viking, 1988.

———. "The Surgeon's Wife" [excerpt from *Headhunter*]. *Saturday Night* April 1993. 52–61.

———. *The Telling of Lies*. Markham, ON: Viking, 1986.

———. "The Unicorn and the Grapevine." In *The Monkey King and Other Stories*, edited by Griffin Ondaatje, 99–103. Toronto: HarperCollins, 1995.

———. "War." Read by Mavor Moore on CBC radio's *Anthology*, 4 March 1958. Repr. in *Dinner Along the Amazon*, 69–84.

———. *The Wars*. Toronto: Clarke, Irwin, 1977.

———. "We Must Prepare for a New Plague." *Globe and Mail* 12 August 2000. A10.

———. "What Mrs. Felton Knew." In *Dinner Along the Amazon*, 116–93.

———. *You Went Away*. Toronto: HarperCollins, 1996.

NON-FICTION

Findley, Timothy. Afterword to *Any Time at All and Other Stories*, by Joyce Marshall, 212–19. Toronto: McClelland and Stewart, 1993.

———. Afterword to *The Diviners*, by Margaret Laurence, 491–94. Toronto: McClelland and Stewart, 1988.

———. "Alarms and Excursions." *Globe and Mail* 13 April 1985. 7.

———. "Alice Drops Her Cigarette on the Floor..." *Canadian Literature* 91 (Winter 1981): 10–21.

———. Anecdotes. In Green and Moore, *Standing Naked*, 85, 93, 104–5, 263, 314.

———. "Beardless Mowat Goes to War." *Saturday Night* November 1979. 40–42.

———. "Better Dead Than Read? An Opposing View." *Books in Canada* (December 1978): 3–5.

———. "The Black Queen Stories." *Globe and Mail* 24 April 1982. 15.

———. "Censorship by Every Other Name." *Indirections* 8.4 (December 1983): 14–20.

———. "Christmas Remembered." *Chatelaine* December 1979. 43, 80.

———. "Comparing Notes." *Canadian Art* (Summer 1985): 54–57.

———. "Coquilles St. Jacques from Dieppe." *Descant* 21.4/22.1 (Winter/Spring 1990/91): 101–2.

———. "The Countries of Invention." *Canadian Literature* 100 (Spring 1984): 104–8.

———. "Critical Reaction No Factor in Award." *Globe and Mail* 1 May 1980. 7.

———. "A Determination to Be Heard." *Graduate* (University of Toronto) 7.5 (May/June 1980): 18–24.

———. "*Elizabeth Rex* and the Search for Self." Program notes. Stratford Festival House Program. 21 June to 30 September 2000. 5–6.

———. "Everything I Tell You Is the Truth except the Lies." In Ziegler, *Rewriting History*, 17–41.

———. "Fail to Hear Artists." *Globe and Mail* 29 May 1990. A6.

———. *From Stone Orchard: A Collection of Memories*. Toronto: HarperCollins, 1998.

———. "From Stone Orchard: Going Going." *Harrowsmith Country Life*. June 1995. 104.

——. "The Golden Age of Canadian Writing Is Here." *Globe and Mail* 8 July 1978. 6.

——. "The Gould Standard." *Saturday Night* April 1989. 71–72.

——. "Growing Up Together." *Canadian Author & Bookman* 61.3 (Spring 1986): 6.

——. "How Did Pinocchio Get into This?" *Globe and Mail* 7 August 1982. 6.

——. *If Stones Could Speak*. With a foreword by William Whitehead and wood engravings by Gerard Brender à Brandis. Pebble Productions: Stratford, ON. 1999.

——. *Inside Memory: Pages from a Writer's Workbook*. Toronto: HarperCollins, 1990.

——. "Insulting to Writers." *Globe and Mail* 8 September 1990. D7.

——. Introduction to *Art for Enlightenment: A History of Art in Toronto Schools*, 1–10. Toronto: Fitzhenry & Whiteside, 1993.

——. "Island." In *The Newcomers: Inhabiting a New Land*, 85–95. Toronto: McClelland and Stewart, 1979.

——. *Journeyman: Travels of a Writer*. Edited by William Whitehead. Toronto: HarperCollins, 2003.

——. "The King and Mrs. Simpson." *Toronto Life* May 1984. 32–33.

——. "Lana Speaks! C-54, Where Are You?" *This Magazine* 21.8 (February 1988): 36–38.

——. "Legends." *Landfall* 159 (September 1986): 327–32.

——. "A Letter to Readers." In *Journeyman*, 892–95.

——. "A Long Hard Walk." In *The Newcomers: Inhabiting a New Land*, 145–55. Toronto: McClelland and Stewart, 1979.

——. "Margaret Laurence." In *The New Morningside Papers*, by Peter Gzowski, 218–20. Toronto: McClelland and Stewart, 1987.

——. "Margaret Laurence: A Remembrance." *Canadian Women's Studies* 8.3 (Fall 1987): 15.

——. "Mature Civil Wars." *Globe and Mail* 27 July 1985. 7.

——. "Mount Pleasant Cemetery." *Toronto Life* April 1982. 60–62.

——. "My Final Hour: An Address to the Philosophy Society, Trent University, Monday, 26 January 1987." *Journal of Canadian Studies* 22.1 (Spring 1987): 5–16.

——. "My First Job." *Toronto Star* 27 July 1982. A2.

——. "My Mother, My Friend." *Chatelaine* May 1985. 46, 47, 91.

——. "Myth and Metaphor." In Ziegler, *Rewriting History*, 43–67.

——. *A Nation of One*. Harbourfront Chapbook 8. Toronto: Harbourfront Reading Series, 1997.

——. "Never Look Down." *Globe and Mail* 10 December 1975. 41.

——. "Of Trunks and Burning Barns." *Writing Home: A PEN Canada Anthology*, edited by Constance Rooke, 61–67. Toronto: McClelland and Stewart, 1997.

——. "Point-Counterpoint: Ethics in the Media." *Journal of Canadian Studies* 27.4 (Winter 1992): 197–98.

——. Preface to *The Tattooed Woman*, by Marian Engel, vii–ix. Toronto: Penguin, 1985.

——. "Queen of the Ages." *Books in Canada* (November 1987): 16–17.

——. "Reflections on Nationhood." *Maclean's* 1 July 1995. 37–39.

——. Review of *The Whole Night, Coming Home*, by Roo Borson. *Journal of Canadian Poetry* 1 (1986): 10–12.

——. "A Sense of Place." In *Inside Memory*, 77–103.

——. "Significant Others." *Journal of Canadian Studies* 28.4 (Winter 1993–94): 149–59.

——. "A Small Town in Normandy." In *Journeyman*, 119–29.

——. "The Sweet Second Summer of Kitty Malone." *Globe and Mail* 3 March 1979. 44.

——. "Syllables of Recorded Time." *Globe and Mail* 22 August 1981. E15.

——. "The Tea Party, or How I Was Nailed by Marian Engel, General Booth, and Minn Williams Burge." *Room of One's Own* 9.2 (June 1984): 35–40.

——. "Through the Looking Glass." *Books in Canada* (June–July 1987): 14.

——. "Timothy Findley Interviews Timothy Findley." In *Journeyman*, 215–19.

——. "Timothy Findley's Literary Recipe." *Financial Post* 8 June 1992.

——. "Timothy Findley's Summer Peaches." In *The Canlit Foodbook*, compiled and illustrated by Margaret Atwood. Edited by Mary Adachi, 120. Don Mills, ON: Totem Books, 1987.

——. "A Trial and a Joy." *Books in Canada* (April 1985): 18–19.

——. "Turn Down the Volume." *Globe and Mail* 1 April 1994. A19.

——. "Turning Down the Volume." *Queen's Quarterly* 100.4 (Winter 1993): 803–21.

——. "The Valour and the Horror." In *Journeyman*, 168–71.

——. "When This You See." *Toronto Life Gardens* Winter 1996. 79–82.

——. "Words on Film." *Globe and Mail* 20 November 1982. L1.

——. "Writing: The Pain and the Pleasure." *Toronto Star* 21 March 1987. M1, 5.

UNPUBLISHED FICTION, NON-FICTION, AND PLAYS

Findley, Timothy. "Artists: Prisoners of Conscience." Talk given at Conrad Grebel College, University of Waterloo, 12 November 1983.

——. "Author's Note." House program for *Can You See Me Yet?* National Arts Centre Theatre Company, 1–20 March 1976.

——. "Blue Is the Colour of Hope." CBC *Ideas*. 15 and 16 June 1992.

——. "Convocation Address." University of Guelph, 1 June 1984.

——. "Everything I Tell You Is the Truth—Except the Lies." Speech given to the Clarke Institute of Psychiatry, Annual Meeting, 22 June 1995.

——. "The First Fable." Play for children. 1988.

——. "Freedom to Read." Talk presented at the Book and Periodical Development Council Freedom to Read Week. Ottawa, October 1986.

——. "How Would *You* Like to be Called Gay?" Address given to the Sexology Section of the Ontario Psychiatric Association meeting, 28 January 1984.

——. "John A., Himself" Unpublished play script 1979.

——. "The Killing of Strangers." Unpublished three-act play. 1974.

——. "Matter over Mind: The Imagination in Jeopardy." Address to the Vancouver Institute, 2 February 1985.

——. "Mute Court: Censorship on Trial." 23 September 1989. Created for PEN International.

——. "The Norman Affair." Television script. 1978.

——. "Other People's Children." Television script. 1978.

——. Presentation talk with readings from *Headhunter*. Clarke Institute Annual General Meeting, 22 June 1995. CAMH Archives, Clarke Institute fonds.

——. Reading from *Headhunter*. DVD. 23 June 1993. At "The City and the Asylum—Finding the Balance" (forum) at Queen Street Mental Health Centre.

——. "Rescue—A Novella." Unpublished TS. 1982.

——. "The Stillborn Lover." Synopsis, undated TS. Hutt fonds.

——. "What Is a Literature: Some Thoughts in Response to John Metcalf's 'What Is a Canadian Literature?'" Undated TS. Findley fonds 213:12.

——. "Whimper." Unpublished draft novel, 1971.

——. "Whisper." Unpublished television script, 1975.

——. "William Hutt." Tribute speech, 16 April 2000, 7 pp. TS. Hutt fonds.

——. "Witness." Unpublished essay on the film of *The Wars*. 3 pp. TS. 1983.

PLAYS, RADIO AND TELEVISION SCRIPTS, FILMS, OTHER
Note: Some CBC items cannot be fully dated.

Findley, Timothy. *Can You See Me Yet?* Vancouver: Talonbooks, 1977.

——. "The Colour of Hope." CBC Radio *Ideas*, 1995.

——. *Le Dernier des Fous*. Film based on *The Last of the Crazy People*. See Achard.

——. *Dinner Along the Amazon*. Telefilm adapted by Timothy Findley. Directed by Patrick Sisam. Protocol Entertainment, 1996.

——. *Don't Let the Angels Fall*. Film script. NFB, 1969.

——. "The Dream Healer." Opera based on *Pilgrim*. Score by Lloyd Burritt. Libretto by Christopher Allan and Don Mowatt. Unpublished opera, premiered at the Chan Centre, Vancouver, 2 March 2008.

——. *Elizabeth Rex*. Toronto: HarperCollins, 2000.

——. *External Affairs*. Telefilm based on *The Stillborn Lover*. See Peter Moss.

——. "Gold." Radio script. CBC *Ideas*, 16 July 1971.

——. "The Journey: A Montage for Radio." *Canadian Drama* 10.1 (1984): 115–40. Broadcast, 1971, CBC.

——. *Lost Innocence: The Children of World War Two*. Five-part series, CBC, 1989. Narrated by Timothy Findley. Produced by Karen Levine.

——. "Martha and the Minder." Playlet, 1991. In *Paper Guitar: 27 Writers Celebrate 25 Years of "Descant" Magazine*, edited by Karen Mulhallen, 431–51. Toronto: HarperCollins, 1995. Repr. in *Journeyman*, 149–61.

——. "Missionaries." Radio script. CBC *Tuesday Night*. 22 February 1972. Rebroadcast, CBC FM *Encore*, 2 March 1972.

——. *The National Dream*. Co-written with William Whitehead. Eight-part documentary. CBC TV, March/April 1974.

——. "The Newcomers, 1872 and 1911." Scripts for *The Newcomers*. Seven-part series, CBC TV, 1980. Directed by Eric Till. Produced by Nielsen Fern.

——. "Other People's Children." Script for CBC TV, 1980.

——. *The Paper People: A Television Play*. 1967. *Canadian Drama* 9.1 (1983): 62–164.

——. *The Piano Man's Daughter*. Film based on the novel. See Kevin Sullivan.

——. "Rivers through Time." Radio script. CBC *Ideas*, 20 April 1973.

——. *Shadows. Canadian Theatre Review* 114 (Spring 2003): 55–71.

——. "Songs." Three drama scripts. CBC TV, 1980.

——. *The Stillborn Lover*. Toronto: HarperPerennial, 1993.

——. *Strangers at the Door. Quarry Magazine* 31.3 (1982): 75–85.

——. "Timothy Findley's Stephen Sondheim." Narrated by Timothy Findley. "Personal Relationships: Part I," "Memory: Part II," "Harmony: Part III," and "Historical Sweep of a Society in Crisis: Part IV." *Arts National Friday Night* CBC-FM Radio, 13 November, 20 November, 27 November, 4 December 1987.

——. *The Trials of Ezra Pound*. Winnipeg: Blizzard, 1995.

——. "Walls: A Monologue." Radio play. *The Best of Ideas*, CBC Radio, 24 June 1968. Written and performed by Timothy Findley.

——. *The Wars*. Film based on the novel. See Phillips.

——. *The Whiteoaks of Jalna*. Drama scripts. CBC TV. 1971–72.

Whitehead, William, and Timothy Findley. Script for documentary film *Dieppe 1942*, directed by Terence Macartney-Filgate, narrated by Douglas Rain. CBC, 1979.

RADIO AND TELEVISION INTERVIEWS

Includes archival tapes with the author's private papers.

Bhabra, H. S., and Marni Jackson. "An Interview with Pierre Berton and Timothy Findley." *Imprint*. TV Ontario, 1997.

Callwood, June. "Timothy Findley." *National Treasures*. Show 11. Vision TV, 29 November 1991.

Drainie, Bronwyn. Interview with TF. *Sunday Morning*. CBC, 21 May 1978.

Gabereau, Vicky. Interview with TF. CBC, June 1986.

Gibson, Graeme. Interview with TF. *Anthology*. CBC, 31 March 1973.

Harron, Don. Interview with TF about *The Wars. Morningside*. CBC Radio, 1977. Rebroadcast in Michael Enright's tribute to Harron, CBC, 20 August 2015. http://www.cbc.ca/radio/don-harron-the-serious-comic-part-2-1.2999879.

Hay, Elizabeth. Interview with TF. *Sunday Morning*. CBC, 10 October 1981.

Hulcoop, John. "A Frame of Fire." Interview with TF. CBC, 26 March 1983.

Macartney-Filgate, Terence, dir. *Timothy Findley: Anatomy of a Writer*. NFB and Tiffin Productions 1991. Premiered on CBC TV *Adrienne Clarkson Presents*, 30 January 1992.

MacDonald, Ann-Marie. "Timothy Findley." *Life and Times*. CBC TV, December 1999.

Rogers, Shelagh. Interview with TF. *State of the Arts*. CBC, January 1987.

Wachtel, Eleanor. Interview with TF. *Writers & Company*. CBC, 14 October 2001.

PUBLISHED INTERVIEWS WITH TIMOTHY FINDLEY

Aitken, Johan. "'Long Live the Dead': An Interview with Timothy Findley." *Journal of Canadian Fiction* 33 (1981–82): 79–93.

Ashenburg, Katherine. "Writers in Residence." *Toronto Life*. February 2000. 86–90.

Benson, Eugene. "Interview with Timothy Findley." *World Literature Written in English* 25.1 (1986): 107–15.

Bissoondath, Neil. "The Illusion of a Spinner of Tales." *Globe and Mail* 19 November 1988. E5.

Black, Patricia. "Dangerous Words: An Interview with Timothy Findley." *Carousel* 10 (1994): 25–44.

——. "Writer Timothy Findley." *Scene* 25 March–7 April 1993. 3.

Brooks, Andrew, Greg Hobbs, and Bruce Meyer. "Interview with Timothy Findley: Bread to a Starving City." *University of Toronto Review* 4 (Spring 1980): 26–32.

Buck, Naomi. "Pilgrim's Progress in Berlin." *Globe and Mail* 5 June 2000. R3.

Buitenhuis, Peter. "The Return of the Crazy People." *Books in Canada* (December 1988): 17–20.

——. "Timothy Findley and the Theatre: An Interview." *West Coast Line* 2 (Fall 1990): 109–11.

Busheikin, Laura. "The Canadian Apocalypse: Timothy Findley Fights Free Trade." *Ubyssey* 4 November 1988. 3.

Cameron, Donald. "Timothy Findley: Make Peace with Nature, Now." In *Conversations with Canadian Novelists*, 49–63. Toronto: Macmillan, 1973.

Cameron, Elspeth. "The Inner Wars of Timothy Findley." *Saturday Night* January 1985. 24–33.

Canton, Jeffrey. "Interview with Timothy Findley." *Paragraph: The Canadian Fiction Review* 15.1 (Summer 1993): 3–7. Repr. as "The Whole Lake Beneath: Timothy Findley" in *The Power to Bend Spoons: Interviews with Canadian Novelists*, edited by Beverley Daurio, 59–68. Toronto: Mercury Press, 1998.

Casselman, William. "Give Up the Imitation American Dream Factory—We Have Ourselves to Observe." *Maclean's* 28 May 1979. 51.

Chessler, Suzanne. "Examining Ezra Pound." *Detroit Jewish News* 29 June 2001. 70–71.

Cornell, Pamela. "The Gentle Master of Violence." *Graduate* (University of Toronto) 7.3 (January/February 1980): 22, 24.

Cusack, Veronica. "Timothy Findley Lives Here." *Toronto Life* April 1993. 74–82.

Dunphy, Catherine. "Timothy Findley Loves the Slow Lane." *Toronto Star* 29 July 1988. D1, 4.

Fitzgerald, Judith. "From *The Wars* to a Blind Cat on the Ark." *Globe and Mail* 2 July 1983. E3.

Gabriel, Barbara. "Masks and Icons: An Interview with Timothy Findley." *Canadian Forum* (February 1986): 31–36.

Garebian, Keith. "'Finding the Note, the Way.'" 15 June 2000. *Xtra!* (Toronto). https://www.dailyxtra.com/toronto/finding-the-note-the-way-56707.

Gibson, Graeme. "Timothy Findley." In *Eleven Canadian Novelists Interviewed by Graeme Gibson*, 113–49. Toronto: Anansi, 1973.

Goldie, Terry. "Timothy Findley." *Kunapipi* 6.1 (1984): 56–67.

Hough, Michael. "Timothy Findley: An Interview." *Public Works* (Spring 1985): 55–59.

Kareda, Urjo. "Adapting 16 Jalna Books Doesn't Faze TV Writer." *Toronto Star* 29 May 1971. 69.

Kruk, Laurie. "I Want Edge: An Interview with Timothy Findley." *Canadian Literature* 148 (Spring 1996): 115–29.

MacGregor, Roy. "Wound Stripes." *The Canadian. Toronto Star* 17 December 1977. 10–11.

MacLeod, Hilary. "Timothy Findley Writes for Peace." *Canadian Author & Bookman* 61.2 (Winter 1986): 3–4.

Manguel, Alberto. "On the Art of Detection: An Interview with Timothy Findley." *Descant* 119 (Winter 2002): 22–32.

Martin, Sandra. "Timothy Findley's Public Face and Private Space." *Quill & Quire* (August 1999): 18–19.

McFadden, David. "The Dead Stand Up in Their Graves." *Quill & Quire* (December 1977): 17.

McIvor, Jack. "Timothy Findley's Private Wars." *Quest: Canada's Urban Magazine* (October 1982): 76–83.

Mellor, W. M. "Timothy Findley's Fictions." *Studies in Canadian Fiction* 19.2 (1994): 77–101.

Meyer, Bruce, and Brian O'Riordan. "Timothy Findley: The Marvel of Reality." In *In Their Words: Interviews with Fourteen Canadian Writers*, 45–54. Toronto: Anansi, 1984.

Minett, Barb. "Findley's Ark." *The Bookshelf.* May/June 1990. 1–2.

Montador, Gordon. "Talking with Tiff." *Body Politic* (October 1984): 27–30.

Mulhallen, Karen. "A Conversation with Timothy Findley." *Descant* 119 (Winter 2002): 33–48.

Mumford, Ted. "Findley Masters Mythic Distance." *Now* (Toronto) 29 January–4 February 1987. 33.

Nothof, Anne. "Timothy Findley: Apocalypse Now." *Aurora* 16.27 (2002): 1–9.

Reid, Robert. "The Findley Business." *Cambridge Reporter* 16 August 2001. B1.

Richards, Linda L. "Timothy Findley." *January Magazine* November 1999. http://www.januarymagazine.com/profiles/findley.html.

———. "Timothy Findley." *January Magazine* 27 June 2002. 1–9. http://www.januarymagazine.com/profiles/timothyfindley.html.

Ross, Val. "High Colour, Deep Shadow." *Globe and Mail* 15 May 1993. C1, 6.

Sandor, Suzanne. "The Mystery of Violence—An Interview with Timothy Findley." *Maclean's* 27 October 1986. 10–12.

Schuck, Paula. "Timothy Findley: Poised upon the Moment." *Canadian Author* (Summer 1995): 10–11, 13.

Siddiqi, Tabassum. "Timothy Findley: An Adventurous Life." *In 2 Print* (Spring 1997): 36–37.

Sparling, Ron. "A World of Consequence: Timothy Findley." *Canadian Forum* (November 1990): 26–29.

Steed, Judy. "It Doesn't Get Better Than This." *Toronto Star* 20 June 1993. D1, 7.

Summers, Alison. "An Interview with Timothy Findley." *Malahat Review* 58 (April 1981): 105–10.

Twigg, Alan. "Timothy Findley." In *Strong Voices: Conversations with 50 Canadian Authors*, 83–89. Madeira Park, BC: Harbour Publishing, 1988.

Whittaker, Herbert. "Flamboyant Personality an Aid to Russian Actor." *Globe and Mail* 7 December 1955. 7.

OBITUARIES

Crew, Robert. *Toronto Star* 22 June 2002. A4.

Cushman, Robert. "A Man of the Theatre." *National Post* (Toronto) 29 June 2002. T9.

Czekaj, Laura. "Timothy Findley Dead at Age 71." *Beacon Herald* (Stratford, ON) 21 June 2002. 1, 5.

De Palma, Anthony. "Timothy Findley, Canadian, Author, Dies at 71." *New York Times* 22 June 2002. B6.

Friscolanti, Michael. "'I Just Write Whatever I Write.'" *National Post* (Toronto) 22 June 2002. A13.

Gatenby, Greg. "Timothy Findley." *Guardian* 25 June 2002. 18.

Goodwin, Carol. "Stratford Friends Mourn the Death of Timothy Findley." *Kitchener-Waterloo Record* 22 June 2002. C16.

Marchand, Philip. "Findley Rejoined Life's Meanness with Tenderness." *Toronto Star* 22 June 2002. A1, 4.

Martin, Sandra. "Canadian Literary Giant Timothy Findley Dies at 71." *Globe and Mail* 21 June 2002. A1.

Monette, Richard. "Pilgrim's Progress." *National Post* (Toronto) 22 June 2002. A12. Repr. *Time* 1 July 2002. 52.

Rérolle, Raphaëlle. "Disparition de Timothy Findley, une grand figure de la littérature canadienne." Le Monde 23 June 2002. https://www.lemonde.fr/archives/article/2002/06/23/timothy-findley_4232179_1819218.html.

Scott, Alec. "You Went Away." *Toronto Life* 1 September 2002. 67–68.

Shypula, Brian. "'Tiff' Fondly Remembered." *Beacon Herald* (Stratford, ON) 15 July 2002. 1–2.

Symons, Scott. "From Rosedale Cub Troops to *Elizabeth Rex*." *National Post* (Toronto) 22 June 2002. A12.

Tesher, Elie. "Tiff Findley: Theatre Giant Beloved by Little People." *Toronto Star* 25 June 2002. A25.

Vallis, Mary. "Friends and the Famous Honour Timothy Findley." *National Post* (Toronto) 30 September 2002. A13.

PART B | Critical Studies, Reviews, and Selected General Bibliography

Abella, Irving, and Harold Troper. *None Is Too Many: Canada and the Jews of Europe, 1933–1948*. 1983. Toronto: University of Toronto Press, 2012.

Achard, Laurent, dir. *Le Dernier des Fous*. Film based on *The Last of the Crazy People*. AGAT Films, Versus Productions, and Rhone-Alps Cinema, 2006.

Ackerman, Marianne. "Findley Spins a Magical Tale with 'New' Noah." *Gazette* (Montreal) 10 November 1984. I1.

Adachi, Ken. "Findley Novel a Sell-Out in London." *Toronto Star* 6 April 1987. B1.

——. "This Author's Finally a Hero." *Toronto Star* 6 May 1975. D5.

Adilman, Sid. Review of *The Whiteoaks of Jalna*. *Variety* 16 February 1972. 47.

Adorno, Theodor. "Commitment." In *The Essential Frankfurt School Reader*, edited by Andrew Arato and Eike Gebhardt, 300–18. New York: Continuum International, 2005).

Aitken, Will. "Piano Man Strikes a Sour Note." *Gazette* (Montreal) 13 May 1995. H4.

Albers, Heinz. "Der Krieg und die Krote." *Hamburger-Abendblatt* 28 August 1978. 11.

Allan, Blaine. "CBC Television Series 1952–1982." https://www.queensu.ca/filmandmedia/other-resources/cbc-television-series-1952-1982.

Anderson, Scott A. "Findley Emerges from the Shadows." 21 Aug 2002. *Xtra!* (Toronto). www.dailyxtra.com/toronto/findley-emerges-from-the-shadows-56006.

Archer, Bert. "Bite." *Globe and Mail* 16 October 1999. D31.

Arthur, Eric. *Toronto: No Mean City*. Toronto: University of Toronto Press, 1964.

Ashley, Audrey. "Odd Mix of Styles Confuses Audience." *Ottawa Citizen* 5 February 1979. 27.

Atwood, Margaret. *The Circle Game*. Toronto: Anansi, 1966.

——. "An Important Book for Many Reasons." *Financial Post* 12 November 1977. 4–6. Repr. in *Second Words: Selected Critical Prose, 1960–1982*, 290–95. Toronto: Anansi, 1982.

——. "Tiff and the Animals." In *Moving Targets: Writing with Intent, 1982–2004*, 275–77. Toronto: Anansi, 2004.

Auden, W. H. "Detective Story." In *Collected Poems*, edited by Edward Mendelson, 151–52. London: Faber & Faber, 1976.

Ayre, John. "Everyday Nightmares." *Books in Canada* (September 1997): 11.

Bailey, Anne Geddes. *Timothy Findley and the Aesthetics of Fascism*. Vancouver: Talonbooks, 1998.

——, ed. "Timothy Findley Issue." Special issue, *Essays on Canadian Writing* 64 (Summer 1998).

Bailey, Anne Geddes, and Karen Grandy, eds. *Paying Attention: Critical Essays on Timothy Findley*. Toronto: ECW Press, 1998.

Baldwin, James. *Giovanni's Room*. 1956. New York: Dell, 1964.

Bale, Doug. "Findley's *Stillborn Lover* Superb." *London Free Press* 27 March 1993. C2.

——. "*John A.—Himself!* Potentially Fine Play." *London Free Press* 1 February 1979. C5.

——. "A Literary Doubleheader." *London Free Press* 26 March 1993. C1.

——. "*The Telling of Lies* a Ground Breaker for Timothy Findley." *London Free Press* 5 November 1986. C4.

Baraness, Marc, and Larry Richards, eds. *Toronto Places: A Context for Urban Design*. With essays by Barry Callaghan et al. Photographs by Geoffrey James and Steven Evans. Toronto: University of Toronto Press, 1992.

Barber, John. "Auction Signals Author's Final Adieu." *Globe and Mail* 29 October 1998. A8.

Barthes, Roland. *Empire of Signs*. Translated by Richard Howard. New York: Hill and Wang, 1982.

Bart-Riedstra, Carolynn, and Lutzen H. Riedstra. *Stratford: Its History and Its Festival*. With a foreword by Richard Monette. Toronto: James Lorimer, 1999.

Belknap, Robert E. *The List: The Uses and Pleasures of Cataloguing*. New Haven, CT: Yale University Press, 2004.

Bemrose, John. "Battlefield of the Soul." *Maclean's* 11 November 1996. 84.

——. "Mortal Thoughts." *Maclean's* 19 May 1997. 62.

——. "Rural Roots." *Maclean's* 15 May 1995. 66.

———. "Sentences That Sing." *Maclean's* 19 May 1997. 62.

———. "Still Angry, after All These Years." *Maclean's* 6 September 1999. 62–63.

———. "Two Spring Hits." *Maclean's* 19 April 1993. 49–50.

Bernstein, Tamara. "An Evening of Magical Storytelling at YPT." *Globe and Mail* 14 December 1988. C12.

Berton, Pierre. *Klondike: The Last Great Gold Rush, 1896–1899.* Toronto: McClelland and Stewart, 1958.

———. *The Klondike Fever: The Life and Death of the Last Great Gold Rush.* New York: Knopf, 1958.

———. *The Klondike Quest: A Photographic Essay, 1897–1899.* Photography research by Beverley Sears. Toronto: McClelland and Stewart, 1983.

———. *Marching as to War: Canada's Turbulent Years.* Toronto: Anchor Canada, 2002.

———. *Vimy.* Toronto: McClelland and Stewart, 1986.

Besner, Neil. "The Heart of Novelness." *Border Crossing* 12.4 (October 1993): 59–62.

Bishop-Gwyn, Carol. *The Pursuit of Perfection: A Life of Celia Franca.* Toronto: Cormorant Books, 2011.

Black, Patricia. "*Elizabeth Rex*—Of Boys and Men and Queenly Plays." *Scene* 27 July 2000. 1.

Blackadar, Bruce. "Findley and the Rise of Fascism." *Toronto Star* 22 October 1981. F1.

Blackburn, Bob. "In Blackburn's View." *Toronto Telegram* 13 December 1967. 37.

Blakey, Bob. "Author Links Oil Patch, Terror: Industry Fuming." *Calgary Herald* 5 October 2001. A1.

Bloch, Michael. *Operation Willi: The Plot to Kidnap the Duke of Windsor, July 1940.* London: Weidenfeldt & Nicolson, 1984.

Bolger, Kevin. "An Immortal Pain." *Toronto Star* 29 August 1999. D24–25.

Bolin, John S. "The Very Best of Company: Perceptions of a Canadian Attitude Towards War and Nationalism in Three Contemporary Plays." *American Review of Canadian Studies* 17.3 (1987): 309–22.

Bonellie, Janet. "A Portrait of Robert Ross." *The Beaver* 80.5 (October/November 2000): 16–21.

Bonnell, Jennifer L. *Reclaiming the Don: An Environmental History of Toronto's Don River Valley.* Toronto: University of Toronto Press, 2014.

Boswell, John. *Christianity, Social Tolerance and Homosexuality: Gay People in Western Europe from the Beginning of the Christian Era to the Fourteenth Century.* Chicago: University of Chicago Press, 1980.

Bourget, Dominique. "Forensic Psychiatry in Canada: A Journey on the Road to Specialty." *The Journal of the American Academy of Psychiatry and the Law* 38.2 (2010): 158–62.

Bower, Jeff. "Village Mourns 'Tiff' Findley." *Brock Citizen* 28 June 2002. 1.

Bowker, Gordon. *Pursued by Furies: A Life of Malcolm Lowry.* Toronto: Random House, 1993.

Bradbury, Ray. *Fahrenheit 451.* 1951. New York: Simon & Schuster, 1967.

Bradshaw, Thomas. "Thomas Findley: An Appreciation." *The Massey-Harris Weekly* 3.40 (24 December 1921): 8.

Branach-Kallas, Anna. "Conflicting Narratives of Obligation: Conscientious Objectors and Deserters in Canadian Great War Fiction." *Journal of War & Culture Studies* 4 (November 2015): 1–14.

Brewer, Barry F. "Licence, Not Freedom." *Books in Canada* (October 1979): 8–9.

Brown, Anthony Cave. *Bodyguard of Lies: The Extraordinary True Story of the Clandestine War of Deception That Hid the Secrets of D-Day from Hitler and Sealed the Allied Victory.* Toronto: Bantam Books, 1975.

Brown, Dan. *The Da Vinci Code.* New York: Doubleday, 2003.

Brydon, Diana. "A Devotion to Fragility: Timothy Findley's *The Wars*." *World Literature Written in English* 26.1 (1986): 75–84.

———. "The Dream of Tory Origins: Inventing Canadian Beginnings." *Australian Canadian Studies* 6.2 (1989): 35–46.

———. "Intertextuality in Timothy Findley's *Headhunter*." *Journal of Canadian Studies* 33.4 (1998–99): 53–62.

———. "'It Could Not Be Told': Making Meaning in Timothy Findley's *The Wars*." *Journal of Commonwealth Literature* 21.1 (1986): 62–79.

———. "'Rogues and Brutes ... in Pinstripe Suits': Timothy Findley's *Headhunter*." *Kunapipi* 18.1 (1996): 192–99.

———. *Timothy Findley.* New York and London: Twayne and Prentice Hall, 1998.

———. "Timothy Findley: A Post-Holocaust, Post-Colonial Vision." In *International Literature in English: Essays on the Major Writers*, edited by Robert L. Ross, 583–92. New York: Garland, 1992.

————. *Writing on Trial: Timothy Findley's "Famous Last Words."* Toronto: ECW Press, 1995.

Bucholz, Garth. "Ship of Fools." *Maclean's* 13 January 1992. 49.

Buitenhuis, Peter. "The Black Within." *West Coast Line* 24.2 (Fall 1980): 129–32.

Bull, Jeoffrey S. "Giving the Sickness a Name: Reading Timothy Findley's *Headhunter* and Walter Percey's *The Thanatos Syndrome* as Diagnostic Fictions." *Journal of Canadian Studies* 33.4 (1998–99): 153–65.

Busby, Brian. *A Gentleman of Pleasure: One Life of John Glassco.* Montreal: McGill-Queen's University Press, 2011.

Caldwell, Rebecca. "Stratford Celebrates Life of Findley." *Globe and Mail* 15 July 2002. A5.

Callwood, June. "Digger House." In W. E. Mann, *The Underside of Toronto*, 123–28.

Cameron, Elspeth. *Earle Birney: A Life.* Toronto: Viking, 1994.

Careless, J. M. S. *Toronto to 1918: An Illustrated History.* Toronto: James Lorimer, 1984.

Carey, Benedict. "Psychiatry Giant Sorry for Backing Gay 'Cure.'" *New York Times* 19 May 2012. A1, 3.

Carruth, Cathy. *Unclaimed Experience: Trauma, Narrative and History.* Baltimore: Johns Hopkins University Press, 1996.

Cavell, Richard, ed. *Love, Hate, and Fear in Canada's Cold War.* Toronto: University of Toronto Press, 2004.

Chamberlin, Edward J. *If This Is Your Land, Where Are Your Stories? Finding Common Ground.* Toronto: Knopf, 2003.

Chambers, Ross. *Untimely Interventions: AIDS Writing, Testimonial, and the Rhetoric of Haunting.* Ann Arbor: University of Michigan Press, 2004.

Chase, Robert. *Dies Irae: A Guide to Requiem Music.* Lanham, MD: Scarecrow Press, 2003.

Chenier, Elise. *Strangers in Our Midst: Sexual Deviancy in Postwar Ontario.* Toronto: University of Toronto Press, 2008.

Clark, Andrew. "Findley Does 'Apocalypse Now' with *Headhunter.*" *Financial Post* 17 April 1993. S5.

Clark, C. S. *Of Toronto the Good: The Queen City of Canada as It Is.* Montreal: The Toronto Publishing Co., 1898.

Clay, Catrine. *Labyrinths: Emma Jung, Her Marriage to Carl, and the Early Years of Psychoanalysis.* New York: HarperCollins, 2016.

Cobley, Evelyn. *Representing War: Form and Ideology in First World War Narratives.* Toronto: University of Toronto Press, 1993.

Cohen, Deborah. *Family Secrets: Living with Shame from the Victorians to the Present Day.* London: Viking, 2013.

Cohen, Mark. "'Singing Our Way Out of Darkness': Findley's Anti-Censorship Argument in *Headhunter.*" *Journal of Canadian Studies* 33.4 (1998–99): 89–100.

Cohen, Matt. *Typing: A Life in 26 Keys.* Toronto: Random House, 2000.

Colburn, John. "Lover Missing Tender Care." *Toronto Sun* 29 March 1993. 1.

Cole, Susan. G. "Timothy Findley: Freeing the Mind inside the City." *NOW Magazine* 17 June 1993. 28–29.

Coleclough, Albert. "Toronto's Pornography: Disease or Symptom?" In W. E. Mann, *The Underside of Toronto,* 314–21.

Collins, Anne. *In the Sleep Room: The Story of the CIA Brainwashing Experiments in Canada.* 1988. Toronto: Key Porter, 1997.

Collura, Thomas F. "History and Evolution of Electroencephalographic Instruments and Techniques." *Journal of Clinical Neurophysiology* 10.4 (1993): 476–503.

Conley, Garrard. *Boy Erased: A Memoir.* New York: Riverside, 2016.

Conrad, Joseph. *Heart of Darkness* and *The Secret Sharer.* Edited by Franklin Walker. New York: Bantam, 1969.

Cook, Peter. *Massey at the Brink: The Story of Canada's Greatest Multinational and Its Struggle to Survive.* Toronto: Collins, 1981.

Cook, Tim, and Andrew Iarocci. "Animal Soldiers." *Canada's History* (October/ November 2013): 20–27.

Cooke, John. *The Influence of Painting on Five Canadian Writers: Alice Munro, Hugh Hood, Timothy Findley, Margaret Atwood, and Michael Ondaatje.* Lewiston, NY: Edwin Mellon Press, 1996.

Court, John P. M., Alexander I. F. Simpson, and Christopher D. Webster. "Contesting Mad versus Bad: The Evolution of Forensic Mental Health Services and Law at Toronto." *Psychiatry, Psychology, and Law* 21.6 (2014): 918–36.

Crawford, Bess Hillery. *Rosedale.* Erin, ON: Boston Mills Press, 2000.

Crawford, Skye. "*Can You See Me Yet?*" *London Reviews: January–June 2008.* www.brockleyjack.co.uk.

Crew, Robert. "*Famous Last Words* Makes Smooth Transition to Radio." *Toronto Star* 9 January 1988. F3.

Croall, Jonathan. *Gielgud: A Theatrical Life.* London: Methuen, 2000.

Crozier, Lorna. "Crossing with Tiff." *Journal of Canadian Studies* 33.4 (1998–99): 27–31.

Cselenyi-Granch, Ladislav. *Under the Sign of the Big Fiddle: The R. S. Williams Family, Manufacturers and Collectors of Musical Instruments.* Toronto: Natural Heritage/Natural History, 1996.

Cude, Wilf. "Timothy Findley." In *Profiles in Canadian Literature,* vol. 4, edited by Jeffrey M. Heath, 77–84. Toronto: Dundurn Press, 1982.

Davey, Frank. "Homoerotic Capitalism: *The Wars.*" In *Post-National Arguments: The Politics of the Anglo-Canadian Novel,* 113–27. Toronto: University of Toronto Press, 1993.

Davidson, Martin. *The Perfect Nazi: Uncovering My Grandfather's Secret Past and How Hitler Seduced a Generation.* London: Viking, 2010.

Davies, Robertson. *At My Heart's Core* and *Overlaid: Two Plays.* Toronto: Irwin Publishing, 1966.

———. *The Manticore.* New York: Viking, 1972.

de la Roche, Mazo. *Whiteoaks of Jalna.* Boston: Little, Brown, 1929.

Dellamora, Richard. "Becoming-Homosexual/Becoming-Canadian: Ironic Voices and the Politics of Location in Timothy Findley's *Famous Last Words.*" In *Double Talking: Essays on Verbal and Visual Ironies in Canadian Contemporary Art and Literature,* edited by Linda Hutcheon, 172–200. Toronto: ECW Press, 1992.

Denison, Merrill. *Harvest Triumphant: The Story of Massey-Harris.* New York: Dodd, Mead, 1949.

Derrida, Jacques. "Archive Fever: A Freudian Impression." Translated by Eric Prenowitz. *Diacritics* 25.2 (Summer 1995): 9–63.

Devine, Lawrence. "*Lover* Is a Majestic Play about Betrayal." *Detroit Free Press* 31 March 1993. C8.

Dewar, Elaine. *The Handover: How Bigwigs and Bureaucrats Transferred Canada's Best Publisher and the Best Part of Our Literary Heritage to a Foreign Multinational.* Windsor, ON: Biblioasis, 2017.

D'haen, Theo. "Timothy Findley: Magical Realism and the Canadian Postmodern." In *Multiple Voices: Recent Canadian Fiction*, 217–33. Sydney: Kangaroo Press, 1989.

———. "Timothy Findley's *Headhunter*, Empire, and Canadian Modernity." In *(Un)Writing Empire*, edited by Theo D'haen, 309–21. Amsterdam: Rodopi, 1998.

Dickinson, Peter. "'Running Wilde': National Ambivalence and Sexual Dissidence in Timothy Findley's Fictions." In *Here is Queer: Nationalisms, Sexualities, and the Literatures of Canada*, 39–68. Toronto: University of Toronto Press, 1999.

Dobson, Kit, and Smaro Kamboureli. *Producing Canadian Literature: Authors Speak on the Literary Marketplace*. Waterloo, ON: Wilfrid Laurier University Press, 2013.

Donnelly, Judy. *The Archive of Clarke, Irwin and Company Limited*. Hamilton, ON: William Ready Division of Archives and Research Collections, McMaster University Library, 1992.

Donnelly, Pat. "Memoir of a Life Shared." *Globe and Mail* 21 February 2004. R5.

Dopp, Jamie. "Reading as Collaboration in Timothy Findley's *Famous Last Words*." *Studies in Canadian Literature* 20.1 (1995): 1–15.

Dowbiggin, Ian. "'Prescription for Survival': Brock Chisholm, Sterilization, and Mental Health in the Cold War Era." In Moran and Wright, *Mental Health*, 176–92.

Drolet, Gilbert. "'Prayers against Despair': A Retrospective Note on Findley's *The Wars*." *Journal of Canadian Fiction* 33 (1981–82): 148–55.

Dubé, Bernard. "The Paper People." *Gazette* (Montreal) 15 December 1967. 28.

Duberman, Martin. *Cures: A Gay Man's Odyssey*. New York: Dutton, 1991.

Duffy, Dennis. "Let Us Compare Histories: Meaning and Mythologies in Findley's *Famous Last Words*." *Essays on Canadian Writing* 30 (1984–85): 187–205.

Eakin, Paul John. *How Our Lives Become Stories: Making Selves*. Ithaca, NY: Cornell University Press, 1999.

Eco, Umberto. *The Infinity of Lists*. Translated by Alistair McEwen. New York: Rizzoli International Publications, 2009.

Edelman, Lee. *Homographesis: Essays in Gay Literary and Cultural Theory*. New York: Routledge, 1994.

Egan, Susanna. *Burdens of Proof: Faith, Doubt, and Identity in Autobiography.* Waterloo, ON: Wilfrid Laurier University Press, 2011.

———. *Mirror Talk: Genres of Crisis in Contemporary Autobiography.* Chapel Hill: University of North Carolina Press, 1999.

Eliot, Ian. "Local Teacher on Front Line of Book War." *Port Hope Evening Guide* 18 January 1995. 2.

Engel, Marian. *The Honeyman Festival.* Toronto: Anansi, 1970.

Evans, Julian. "Questions That Will Not Die." *Weekend Post* 28 August 1999. 7.

Everett-Green, Robert. "Summers of Sand and Shonagon Lend Color to Findley's Lies." *Globe and Mail* 15 November 1986. C1.

Fagan, Cary. *City Hall and Mrs. God: A Passionate Journey through a Changing Toronto.* Stratford, ON: Mercury Press, 1990.

Fagan, Nicholas [Ruth Bull]. "Music." *Mail and Empire* 25 April 1917. 6.

Feiffer, Jules. *Crawling Arnold.* New York: Dramatists Play Service, 1963.

Felman, Shoshana, and Dori Laub. *Testimony: Crises of Witnessing in Literature, Psychoanalysis, and History.* New York: Routledge, 1992.

Fergus, Kyle. "Incidents at the Fire." In *Canada's Greatest Fire: A Souvenir Booklet*, edited by Kyle Fergus and Clyde Forman. Toronto: S. J. Dunning, 1904.

Findley, Thomas. "The Only Way to Reach Every Member." In *Canada's Missionary Congress*, 213–17. Toronto: Canadian Council Layman's Missionary Movement, 1909.

Finlay, Karen A. *The Force of Culture: Vincent Massey and Canadian Sovereignty.* Toronto: University of Toronto Press, 2004.

Fisher, Honey. *From Vision to Legacy.* Toronto: Centre for Addiction and Mental Health, 2000.

Fitzgerald, James. *What Disturbs the Blood: A Son's Quest to Redeem the Past.* Toronto: Random House, 2010.

Fong, William. *J. W. McConnell: Financier, Philanthropist, Patriot.* Montreal: McGill-Queen's University Press, 2008.

Foran, Charles. "Getting Lucky with *The Wars*." *Journal of Canadian Studies* 33.4 (1998–99): 36–37.

———. *Mordecai: The Life and Times.* Toronto: Knopf, 2010.

Forman, Clyde. "Canada's Greatest Fire." In *Canada's Greatest Fire: A Souvenir Booklet*, edited by Kyle Fergus and Clyde Forman. Toronto: S. J. Dunning, 1904.

Fraser, John. "Significance Abounds—but It's a Mighty Bore." *Globe and Mail* 2 March 1976. 14.

——. *Telling Tales.* Toronto: Collins, 1986.

French, William. "Writers' Guardian Angels." *Globe and Mail* 5 April 1982. L1.

——. "Writers Hear Tale of Woe from Findley." *Globe and Mail* 16 May 1983.

Frum, Linda. "Putting Pilgrim on the Page." *National Post* (Toronto) 4 September 1999. B1–2.

Fulford, Robert. "Decline and Fall." *Saturday Night* August 1983. 5–7.

——. "Deep in the South (of Ontario)." *Toronto Star* 29 July 1967. 26.

Full of Sound and Fury: Living with Schizophrenia. Video. Directed by Deborah Magidson. Written by William Whitehead. TV Ontario. New York: Filmmakers Library, 1984.

Gabriel, Barbara. "Performing the *Bent* Text: Fascism and the Regulation of Sexualities in Timothy Findley's *The Butterfly Plague*." *English Studies in Canada* 21.2 (June 1995): 226–50.

——. "'The Repose of an Icon' in Timothy Findley's Theatre of Fascism: From 'Alligator Shoes' to *Famous Last Words*." In Bailey and Grandy, *Paying Attention*, 149–80.

——. "Staging Monstrosity: Genre, Life-Writing and Timothy Findley's *The Last of the Crazy People*." *Essays in Canadian Writing* 54 (Winter 1994): 168–97.

Galloway, Myron. "Findley Achieves Great Play with *Can You See Me Yet?*" *Montreal Star* 2 March 1976. B7.

Gardner, John. *Grendel.* Illustrated by Emil Antonucci. New York: Alfred A. Knopf, 1971.

Garebian, Keith. "Timothy Findley—*Famous Last Words*." *Quarry Magazine* 31.3 (1982): 93–97.

——. *William Hutt: A Theatre Portrait.* Oakville, ON: Mosaic Press, 1988.

——. *William Hutt: Soldier, Actor.* Toronto: Guernica, 2017.

Garner, Hugh. *Cabbagetown.* 1950. Toronto: McGraw-Hill Ryerson, 1968.

Gatenby, Greg. *Toronto: A Literary Guide.* Toronto: McArthur, 1999.

Gavin, James M. "*The Wars*." *Playboy's Choice: The Bulletin of the Playboy Bookclub* July 1978. 95.

Gervais, Marty. "Writing and the Writer." *Windsor Star* 26 February 1983. C10.

Gibson, Margaret. "Writing, Like Mental Illness, Can Be Blinding with Its Visions." *Toronto Star* 19 June 1993. G1, 11.

Gillman, Charlotte Perkins. *The Yellow Wallpaper.* 1892. Edited by Thomas L. Erskine and Connie L. Richards. New Brunswick, NJ: Rutgers University Press, 1993.

Gilmor, Don. "The Brain Drain." *Globe and Mail* 30 May 1987. D5.

Gilmore, Leigh. *The Limits of Autobiography: Trauma and Testimony.* Ithaca, NY: Cornell University Press, 2001.

Gittings, Christopher E. "'What Are Soldiers For?' Re-Making Masculinities in Timothy Findley's *The Wars.*" *Kunapipi* 18.1 (1996): 184–91.

Goddard, John. "Findley Takes to the Road." *Gazette* (Montreal) 3 May 1997. C8.

Goldie, Terry. "The Canadian Homosexual [sic]." *Journal of Canadian Studies* 33.4 (1998–99): 132–42.

———. *Pink Snow: Homotextual Possibilities in Canadian Fiction.* Peterborough, ON: Broadview, 2003.

Goldman, Marlene. "The End(s) of Myth: Apocalyptic and Prophetic Fictions in *Headhunter.* In *Rewriting Apocalypse in Canadian Fiction*, 29–52. Montreal: McGill-Queen's University Press, 2005.

Good, Cynthia. "Timothy Findley—Author of the Year." *Canadian Bookseller* (June/July 1984): 12.

Govier, Katherine. "Pilgrim's Regress." *Time* 4 October 1999. 71.

Grace, Sherrill. "Bearing Witness and Cultural Memory: Canadian Representations of War in the Pacific." In *Bearing Witness: Perspectives on War and Peace from the Arts and Humanities*, edited by Sherrill Grace, Patrick Imbert, and Tiffany Johnstone, 107–20. Montreal: McGill-Queen's University Press, 2012.

———. "Biography and the Archive: Pollock and Findley." In *Sharon Pollock: First Woman of Canadian Theatre*, edited by Donna Coates, 213–35. Calgary: University of Calgary Press, 2015.

———. "Border Crossings in Contemporary Canadian Responses to WWII: *Famous Last Words* and *Burning Vision.*" In *Riding/Writing across Borders*, edited by Waldemar Zacharasiewicz, 369–89. Vienna: Verlag der Österreichischen Akademie der Wissenschaften, 2011.

——. *Landscapes of War and Memory: The Two World Wars in Canadian Literature, Theatre, and the Arts, 1977–2007*. Edmonton: University of Alberta Press, 2014.

——. "Performing the Autobiographical Pact: Towards a Theory of Identity in Performance." In *Tracing the Autobiographical*, edited by M. Kadar et al., 65–79. Waterloo, ON: Wilfrid Laurier University Press, 2005.

——. "Reading the Writing on the Wall: From Malcolm Lowry to Timothy Findley." In *Malcolm Lowry: La Fureur et la Grâce*, edited by Josiane Paccaud-Huguet, 399–415. Paris: Garnier-Classiques, 2017.

——. "Remembering *The Wars*." In *The Great War in Post-Memory Literature and Film*, edited by M. Sokolowska-Paryz and M. Löschnigg, 219–38. Berlin: De Gruyter, 2014.

——. "Timothy Findley, His Biographers, and *The Piano Man's Daughter*." *Text Matters: A Journal of Literature, Theory and Culture* 8.8 (2018): 413–29.

——. "Timothy Findley's Wars." *Caliban* 53 (2015): 17–38.

——. "'Turning the Page': Timothy Findley's *Pilgrim*." In *The Anglo-Canadian Novel in the Twenty-First Century: Interpretations*, edited by Maria Löschnigg and Martin Löschnigg, 95–103. Heidelberg: Universitätsverlag, 2019.

——. "'Uncreative Forgetting': Memory Discourse and the Case of Timothy Findley." In *Narratives of Encounters in the North Atlantic Triangle*, edited by Waldemar Zacharasiewicz and David Staines, 291–308. Vienna: Verlag der Österreichischen Akademie der Wissenschaften, 2015.

Grace, Sherrill, and Jerry Wasserman, eds. *Theatre and AutoBiography: Writing and Performing Lives*. Vancouver: Talonbooks, 2006.

Graves, Robert. *Good-bye to All That*. 1929. Harmondsworth, UK: Penguin, 1957.

Gray, John, and Eric Peterson. *Billy Bishop Goes to War*. Vancouver: Talonbooks, 1981.

Green, Lynda Mason, and Tedde Moore, eds. *Standing Naked in the Wings: Anecdotes from Canadian Actors*. Toronto: Oxford University Press, 1997.

Grey, Charlotte. *The Massey Murder: A Maid, Her Master, and the Trial That Shocked a Country*. Toronto: HarperCollins, 2013.

Groen, Rick. "War Rages in the Mud of Kleinberg." *Globe and Mail* 13 June 1981. E1.

Guinness, Alec. *Blessings in Disguise*. London: Hamish Hamilton, 1985.

Guthrie, Tyrone, Robertson Davies, and Grant Macdonald. *Renown at Stratford: A Record of the Shakespeare Festival in Canada, 1953*. Toronto: Clarke, Irwin, 1953.

———. *Twice Have the Trumpets Sounded: A Record of the Stratford Shakespearean Festival in Canada, 1954*. Toronto: Clarke, Irwin, 1954.

Gutteridge, Robert. *Magic Moments: First 20 Years of Moving Pictures in Toronto, 1894–1914*. Whitby, ON: Gutteridge-Prately Publications, 2000.

Gwyn, Sandra. *Tapestry of War: A Private View of Canadians in the Great War*. Toronto: HarperCollins, 1992.

Hair, Donald. "To Catch the Reader Unaware." *Brick* 17 (1983): 8–14.

Hale, Jennifer. "Findley Fans Flames of Fascination." *Gazette* (Western University) 30 March 1993.

Hall, Radclyffe. *The Well of Loneliness*. London: Jonathan Cape, 1928.

Halperin, David M. *One Hundred Years of Homosexuality, and Other Essays on Greek Love*. New York: Routledge, 1990.

Hambleton, Ronald. "Theatrical Diversion Worth Expansion." *Toronto Star* 13 December 1988. B2.

Harris, Amy Lavender. *Imagining Toronto*. Toronto: Mansfield Press, 2010.

Hastings, Tom. "'Their Fathers Did It to Them': Findley's Appeal to the Great War Myth of a Generational Conflict in *The Wars*." In Bailey and Grandy, *Paying Attention*, 85–103.

Hay, Elizabeth. "In Toronto and Italy with Timothy Findley." Unpublished tribute/recollection of Timothy Findley. 2008.

Helms, Dorothea. "Timothy Findley: Even His Home Is a Masterpiece." *Homes & Lifestyles* (Spring 1996): 15–17.

Helwig, David. "High-Wire Act." *Gazette* (Montreal) 3 April 1993. K1.

Hemingway, Ernest. *A Farewell to Arms*. 1929. New York: Macmillan, 1957.

Henighan, Stephen. "In the Heart of Toronto's Darkness." *Globe and Mail* 10 April 1993. C22.

———. "Literature Survives through Its Variety." In Dobson and Kamboureli, *Producing Canadian Literature*, 130–49.

Hepburn, Allan. "Findley Captures Anguish of Betrayals in Signature Style." *Financial Post* 11 January 1997. 24.

Heron, George. *Child of the Great Depression: Growing Up in Downtown Toronto during the 1930s*. Scarborough, ON: Select Press, 2005.

Hersey, John. *Hiroshima*. New York: Alfred A. Knopf, 1946.

Hill, Douglas. "Unfolding Timothy Findley." *Globe and Mail* 8 October 1983. 13.

Hirsch, Marianne. *Family Frames: Photography, Narrative, and Postmemory*. Cambridge, MA: Harvard University Press, 1997.

Hobsbawm, Eric. *The Age of Empire, 1875–1914*. 1987. New York: Vantage Books, 1996.

Hollenberg, Donna Krolik. "Art for Whose Sake? Reading Pound's Reputation in Timothy Findley's *Famous Last Words* and *The Trials of Ezra Pound*." *Journal of Canadian Studies* 33.4 (1998–99): 143–52.

Hood, Hugh. *Reservoir Ravine*. Toronto: Oberon Press, 1979.

———. *The Swing in the Garden*. Toronto: Oberon Press, 1975.

Howard, Burt. "Findley Finds Inspiration in Peaceful Country Life." *Ottawa Citizen* 12 August 1983. 58.

Howard, Scott. "Cannington Author Fondly Remembered." *Oshawa This Week* 17 October 2011.

Howells, Coral Ann. "'History as She Is Never Writ': *The Wars* and *Famous Last Words*." *Kunapipi* 6.1 (1984): 49–56.

———. "'Tis Sixty Years Since': Timothy Findley's *The Wars* and Roger McDonald's *1915*." *World Literature Written in English* 23 (1984): 129–36.

Hulcoop, John. "'The Intricate Evasions of As': Or the Art of Findley's Sexual Evasions." Unpublished TS. 1994.

———. "'Look! Listen! Mark my Words!': Paying Attention to Timothy Findley's Fictions." *Canadian Literature* 91 (Winter 1981): 22–47.

———. "Timothy Findley." In *Dictionary of Literary Biography: Canadian Writers since 1960*, vol. 53, edited by William H. New, 181–91. Detroit: Gale Research, 1986.

Hunter, Catherine. "Passing It On, or, How I Met Tiff." *Journal of Canadian Studies* 33.4 (1998–99): 38–46.

Hutcheon, Linda. *The Canadian Postmodern: A Study of Contemporary English-Canadian Fiction*. Toronto: Oxford University Press, 1988.

Hutt, William. Unpublished TS of tribute to Timothy Findley at Harbourfront, Toronto, 22 October 2001. Hutt fonds, University of Guelph.

Huyssen, Andreas. *Present Pasts: Urban Palimpsests and the Politics of Memory*. Stanford, CA: Stanford University Press, 2003.

Ingham, David. "Bashing the Fascists: The Moral Dimensions of Findley's Fiction." *Studies in Canadian Literature* 15.2 (1990): 33–54.

Irvine, Lorna. "Crises of the Legitimate: Matt Cohen and Timothy Findley." *American Review of Canadian Studies* 19.1 (1989): 15–23.

Irving, John. *In One Person*. Toronto: Vintage Canada, 2013.

Isay, Richard. *Becoming Gay: The Journey to Self-Acceptance*. New York: Pantheon, 1996.

———. *Being Homosexual: Gay Men and Their Development*. New York: Farrar, Straus, and Giroux, 1989.

Isherwood, Christopher. *The Berlin Stories*. New York: New Directions, 1954.

Israelstam, S., and S. Lambert. "Homosexuality as a Cause of Alcoholism: A Historical Review." *The International Journal of Addictions* 18.8 (1983): 1085–1107.

Jackson, Lorna. "Dust to Dust." *Quill & Quire* (March 1997): 70.

Janoff, Douglas Victor. *Pink Blood: Homophobic Violence in Canada*. Toronto: University of Toronto Press, 2005.

Jennings, Sarah. *Art and Politics: The History of the National Arts Centre*. Toronto: Dundurn Press, 2009.

Johnson, Samuel. *Diaries, Prayers, and Annals*. Edited by E. L. McAdam Jr., with Donald and Mary Hyde. New Haven, CT: Yale University Press, 1958.

Johnson, William. "The Gay World." In W. E. Mann, *The Underside of Toronto*, 322–33.

Jones, David. *In Parenthesis*. 1937. New York: Chilmark Press, 1961.

Joyce, James. *A Portrait of the Artist as a Young Man*. 1916. Harmondsworth, UK: Penguin, 1960.

Keefer, Janice Kulyk. "A Portrait of the Artist as a Political Being." *Globe and Mail* 6 October 1990. C9.

Keith, Agnes Newton. *Three Came Home*. Toronto: McClelland and Stewart, 1947.

Keith, W. J. "Apocalyptic Imaginations: Notes on Atwood's *The Handmaid's Tale* and Findley's *Not Wanted on the Voyage*." *Essays on Canadian Writing* 35 (Winter 1987): 123–34.

Kelner, Merrijoy. "Changes in Toronto's Elite Structure." In W. E. Mann, *The Underside of Toronto*, 204.

Kieran, Sheila. "*The Paper People*: Pretentious, Sickeningly Arty—and Boring." *Globe and Mail* 7 December 1967. 14.

King, James. *The Life of Margaret Laurence*. Toronto: Alfred A. Knopf Canada, 1997.

King, Nicola. *Memory, Narrative, Identity: Remembering the Self*. Edinburgh: Edinburgh University Press, 2000.

King, Ross. *Leonardo and The Last Supper*. London: Bloomsbury, 2012.

Kinsey, Alfred. *Sexual Behavior in the Homosexual Male*. 1948. Bloomington: Indiana University Press, 1998.

Kinsman, Gary. *The Regulation of Desire: Homo and Hetero Sexualities*. Montreal: Black Rose Books, 1996.

———. "'These Things May Lead to the Tragedy of Our Species': The Emergence of Homosexuality, Lesbianism, and Heterosexuality in Canada." In *Sexing the Maple: A Canadian Sourcebook*, edited by Richard Cavell and Peter Dickinson, 413–58. Peterborough, ON: Broadview Press, 2006.

Kinsman, Gary, and Patrizia Gentile. *The Canadian War on Queers: National Security as Sexual Regulation*. Vancouver: UBC Press, 2010.

Kirchhoff, Jack. "From the Page to the Screen: Making the Most of Movies." *Quill & Quire* (May 1988): 8–11.

Kirchhoff, H. J. "*The Stillborn Lover* a Grand Coup." *Globe and Mail* 29 March 1993. C3.

Kirmayer, Laurence J. "Landscapes of Memory: Trauma, Narrative, and Dissociation." In *Tense Past: Cultural Essays in Trauma and Memory*, edited by Paul Antze and Michael Lambek, 173–98. London: Routledge, 1996.

Klovan, Peter. "'Bright and Good': Findley's *The Wars*." *Canadian Literature* 91 (Winter 1981): 58–69.

Knowles, John. *A Separate Peace*. 1959. New York: Scribner, 2003.

Korinek, Valerie J. *Prairie Fairies: A History of Queer Communities in Western Canada, 1930–1985*. Toronto: University of Toronto Press, 2018.

Krause, Dagmar. *Timothy Findley's Novels: Between Ethics and Postmodernism*. Wurzburg: Konigshausen & Neumann, 2005.

Kroetsch, Robert. "A Conversation with Margaret Laurence." In *Creation*, edited by Robert Kroetsch, 53–63. Toronto: New Press, 1970.

———. *The Man from the Creeks*. Toronto: Random House, 1998.

Kröller, Eva-Marie. "The Exploding Frame: Uses of Photography in Timothy Findley's *The Wars*." *Journal of Canadian Studies* 16.3–4 (Fall/Winter 1981): 68–74.

——. "The Eye in the Text: Timothy Findley's *The Last of the Crazy People* and Alice Munro's *Lives of Girls and Women*." *World Literature Written in English* 23.2 (1984): 366–74.

——. "'Sur les rivages d'un autre âge': Timothy Findley et Evelyn Waugh." *Études Littéraires* 27.1 (1994): 29–41.

Kruk, Laurie. "'Double-Voicing' Family in Findley's Short Fiction: Pinking the Triangle, Drawing the Circle." *Canadian Literature* 212 (Spring 2012): 34–48.

——. "Hands and Mirrors: Gender Reflections in the Short Stories of Alistair MacLeod and Timothy Findley." In *The Dominant Impressions: Essays on the Canadian Short Story*, edited by Gerald Lynch and Angela A. Robbeson, 137–50. Ottawa: University of Ottawa Press, 1999.

——. "Mothering Sons: Stories by Findley, Hodgins and MacLeod Uncover the Mother's Double Voice." *Atlantis* 32.1 (2007): 35–45.

Kubrick, Stanley, dir. *Paths of Glory*. Film. Bryna Productions, 1957.

Kustow, Michael. *Peter Brook: A Biography*. London: Bloomsbury, 2005.

LaCapra, Dominick. *Writing History, Writing Trauma*. Baltimore: Johns Hopkins University Press, 2001.

Lacey, Liam. "Excess Baggage on This Voyage." *Globe and Mail* 11 January 1992. C3.

Laing, R. D. and A. Esterson. *Sanity, Madness, and the Family: Families of Schizophrenics*. 1964. Harmondsworth, UK: Penguin, 1970.

Lambert, Islay. *Call Them Blessed: A History of Cannington, 1817–1971*. Cannington, ON: Corporation of the Village of Cannington, 1971.

Lambert, Norman. "The Rapid Rise of Thomas Findley." *Maclean's* February 1918. 18.

Lane, Harry. "'Not His Own Person': Questions of Betrayal in *The Stillborn Lover*." *Queen's Quarterly* 100.2 (Summer 1993): 442–56.

Langer, Lawrence L. *The Holocaust and the Literary Imagination*. New Haven, CT: Yale University Press, 1975.

Laurence, Margaret. *The Diviners*. New York: Knopf, 1974.

——. "Margaret Laurence Talks about *Can You See Me Yet?*" *NAC Stage* 2.3 (March 1976): 1–4.

——. *The Stone Angel*. Toronto: McClelland and Stewart, 1964.

——. *A Very Large Soul: Selected Letters from Margaret Laurence to Canadian Writers*. Edited by J. A. Wainwright. Toronto: Cormorant Books, 1985.

Lawrence, T. E. *The Seven Pillars of Wisdom*. 1926. New York: Garden City Publishing, 1938.

Lederman, Marsha. "Elizabeth, not Elizabethan." *Globe and Mail* 15 July 2013. L6.

———. "Findley's Operatic Epitaph: 'On First Reading, I Heard Music.'" *Globe and Mail* 1 March 2008. R5.

Lee, Dennis. *Civil Elegies*. Toronto: Anansi, 1969.

———. "When I Went Up to Rosedale." In *The Difficulty of Living on Other Planets*, 62–63. Illustrated by Alan Daniel. Toronto: Macmillan, 1987.

Lee, Hermione. *Virginia Woolf's Nose: Essays on Biography*. Princeton, NJ: Princeton University Press, 2005.

Lehmann-Haupt, Christopher. "Books of the Times." *New York Times* 22 June 1982. C10.

Lejeune, Philippe. "The Autobiographical Pact (bis)." In *On Autobiography*, edited by Paul John Eakin, translated by Katherine Leary, 119–37. Minneapolis: University of Minnesota Press, 1989.

Lemon, James. *Toronto Since 1918: An Illustrated History*. Toronto: James Lorimer, 1985.

Levi, Primo. *The Drowned and the Saved*. Translated by Raymond Rosenthal. New York: Vintage International, 1989.

Levine, Allan. *Toronto: Biography of a City*. Madeira Park, BC: Douglas & McIntyre, 2014.

Levine, Elizabeth. "Findley Play Jumps from Stratford to London's West End." *National Post* (Toronto) 15 August 2001. A1, A8.

Lilly, Mark. *Gay Men's Literature in the Twentieth Century*. London: Macmillan, 1993.

Lind, Jane. *Perfect Red: The Life of Paraskeva Clark*. Toronto: Cormorant Books, 2009.

Lorinc, John, Jane Farrow, Stephanie Chambers, Maureen Fitzgerald, Tim McCaskill, Rebecka Sheffield, Tatum Taylor, Rahim Thawer, and Ed Jackson, eds. *Any Other Way: How Toronto Got Queer*. Toronto: Coach House, 2017.

Lowry, Malcolm. "Curse." In *The Collected Poems of Malcolm Lowry*, edited by Kathleen Scherf, 66. Vancouver: UBC Press, 1992.

———. *Under the Volcano*. 1947. With an afterword by Sherrill Grace. New York: Perennial Classics, 2000.

Loyer, Nésida, trans. "L'Agonie du Hilton." *TransLit* 4 (1999): 97–105.

———, trans. *Le Chasseur de têtes* [*Headhunter*]. Montréal: Boréal; and Paris: Le Serpent à Plumes, 1996.

———. "On Translating Timothy Findley: Of Words and Worlds." *Journal of Canadian Studies* 33.4 (1998–99): 166–76.

———, trans. "Une petite ville de Normandie." *TransLit* 3 (1996): 5–13.

———, trans. "Les renards." *TransLit* 6 (2004): 158–68.

———, trans. *Le Verger de pierres: un bouquet de souvenirs*. Montréal: Les Éditions Point de Fuite; and Paris: Le Serpent à Plumes, 2001.

MacDonald, Monica. *Recasting History: How CBC Television Has Shaped Canada's Past*. Montreal: McGill-Queen's University Press, 2019.

Macfarlane, David. "The Perfect Gesture." *Books in Canada* (March 1985): 5–8.

MacGregor, Roy. "Who Killed Sir Harry?" *Books in Canada* (November 1982): 6–8.

MacKay, Gillian. "An Ode to Joy." *Maclean's* 8 October 1990. 74.

MacSkimming, Roy. "Back to the Literary Land." *Globe and Mail* 19 September 1998. D16.

———. *The Perilous Trade: Publishing Canada's Writers*. Toronto: McClelland and Stewart, 2003.

Magris, Claudio. *Danube*. Translated by Patrick Creagh. New York: Farrar, Straus, and Giroux, 1989.

Mallet, Gina. "It's a Reel Battle Filming *The Wars*." *Toronto Star* 4 July 1989. F1, F3.

Maltby, Clive, dir. *Britain's Nazi King—Revealed*. Film. Produced by Simon Rockell. BBC, 16 July 2009.

Manguel, Alberto. "Findley's People." *Books in Canada* (June/July 1984): 13–15.

Mann, George. "The Sterndale Bennetts: The Formative Years (1910–1932)." *Theatre Research in Canada* 14.1 (1993): 1–23.

———. "The Sterndale Bennetts: The Masquers Years (1933–1940)." *Theatre Research in Canada* 21.2 (Fall 2000): 149–75.

Mann, Klaus. *Mephisto*. 1936. Translated by Robin Smyth. Markham, ON: Penguin Books, 1983.

Mann, W. E., ed. *The Underside of Toronto*. Toronto: McClelland and Stewart, 1970.

Manson, Ian McKay. "The United Church and the Second World War." In Schweitzer, *The United Church of Canada*, 59–75.

Marchand, Philip. "Findley Tells an Eerie Fable about Male Menace." *Toronto Star* 10 April 1993. H13.

——. "Findley Weaves Gothic Romance." *Toronto Star* 22 April 1995. H16.

——. "Timothy Findley: Novelist on a High Wire." *Chatelaine* February 1983. 44, 96.

——. "What I Really Think." *Saturday Night* October 1997. 52–59.

Marcus, James. "Mr. Kurtz—He Back." *New York Times Book Review* 5 June 1994. 40.

Marshall, Brenda. "Meta (His)Story: Timothy Findley's *Famous Last Words*." *International Fiction Review* 16.1 (1989): 17–22.

Martin, John. "The Passing of Our President." *The M-H [Massey-Harris] Weekly* 3.40 (24 December 1921): 1–2.

Martin, Ralph. *The Woman He Loved.* New York: Simon & Schuster, 1973.

Martin, Sandra. "Prize Play Hits Close to Home." *Globe and Mail* 17 November 2000. R8.

——. "Tiff: An Appreciation." *Globe and Mail* 22 June 2002. R1, R5.

Martyn, Lucy Booth. *Toronto: 100 Years of Grandeur.* Toronto: Pagurian Press, 1978.

Martz, Fraidie, and Andrew Wilson. *A Fiery Soul: The Life and Theatrical Times of John Hirsch.* Montreal: Vehicule Press, 2011.

Maskoulis, Julia. "Impassioned Play Fails to Reach Ottawa Audience." *Gazette* (Montreal) 3 March 1976. 43.

McCormick, Marion. "Timothy Findley Remembers." *Gazette* (Montreal) 6 October 1990. J3.

McCowen, Alec. *Double Bill.* New York: Atheneum, 1980.

——. *Young Gemini.* New York: Atheneum, 1979.

McCullers, Carson. *The Member of the Wedding.* New York: New Directions, 1951.

McGoogan, Kenneth. "Author's Gripping Tale Began as a Joke." *Calgary Herald* 17 November 1986. C1.

McIntire, C. T. "Unity among Many: The Formation of The United Church of Canada, 1899–1930." In Schweitzer, *The United Church of Canada*, 3–37.

McKenzie, Sister M. L. "Memories of the Great War: Graves, Sassoon, and Findley." *University of Toronto Quarterly* 55.4 (Summer 1986): 395–411.

McLeod, Donald W. *Lesbian and Gay Liberation in Canada: A Selected Annotated Chronology, 1964–1975.* Toronto: ECW/Homewood Books, 1996.

McPhee, Joyce. "'From Bibliographer to Biographer': Carol Roberts Tells Tales of Timothy Findley." *Feliciter* (June 1994): 38–39.

Merivale, Patricia. "The Biographical Compulsion: Elegaic Romances in Canadian Fiction." *Journal of Modern Literature* 8.1 (1980): 139–52.

Metcalf, John. *What Is a Canadian Literature?* Guelph, ON: Red Kite Press, 1988.

Middleton, Peter, and Tim Woods. *Literatures of Memory: History, Time, and Space in Postwar Writing.* Manchester, UK: Manchester University Press, 2000.

Miller, Arthur. *Timebends.* New York: Grove Press, 1987.

Miller, Mary Jane. "An Analysis of *The Paper People.*" *Canadian Drama* 9.1 (1983): 49–59.

———. "Canadian Television Drama, 1952–1970: Canada's National Theatre." *Theatre History in Canada* 5.1 (Spring 1984): 51–71.

Mironowicz, Margaret. "Agent Provides Affection, Protection for Writers." *Globe and Mail* 15 September 1983. CL5.

Moir, John S. *Early Presbyterianism in Canada.* Edited by Paul Laverdure. Gravelbourg, SK: Gravelbooks, 2003.

Moore, Christopher. *Founding the Writers' Union of Canada: An Oral History.* Toronto: Writers' Union of Canada, 2015.

Moore, Mavor. *Reinventing Myself.* Toronto: Stoddart, 1994.

Moran, James E., and David Wright, eds. *Mental Health and Canadian Society: Historical Perspectives.* Montreal: McGill-Queen's University Press, 2006.

Morley, Sheridan. *John G: The Authorised Biography of John Gielgud.* London: Hodder and Stoughton, 2001.

Morris, Guy. "*Paper People* Plumbs Emotions." *Cinema Canada* (Nov–Dec. 1967): 6, 20.

Morton, Andrew. *17 Carnations: The Royals, the Nazis, and the Biggest Cover-Up in History.* New York: Grand Central Publishing, 2015.

Moser, Benjamin. *Sontag: Her Life and Work.* New York: HarperCollins, 2019.

Moss, John. *Still Waters.* Toronto: Dundurn, 2008.

———. "Timothy Findley." In *A Reader's Guide to the Canadian Novel,* 108–18. Toronto: McClelland and Stewart, 1981.

Moss, Peter, dir. *External Affairs.* Telefilm based on *The Stillborn* Lover, by Timothy Findley. Toronto: Shaftesbury Films, Alliance Atlantic, and CBC, 1999.

Murray, Don. "Seeing and Surviving in Timothy Findley's Short Stories." *Studies in Canadian Literature* 13.2 (1988): 200–22.

Nardi, Peter M. "Alcoholism and Homosexuality: A Theoretical Perspective." *Journal of Homosexuality* 7.4 (1982): 9–25.

New, W. H., ed. "Timothy Findley & the War Novel." Special issue, *Canadian Literature* 91 (Winter 1981).

Nicholson, Mervyn. "God, Noah, Lord Byron—and Timothy Findley." *Ariel* 23.2 (April 1992): 87–107.

Niven, Penelope. *Thornton Wilder: A Life*. New York: HarperCollins, 2012.

Noonan, James. "The National Arts Centre: Fifteen Years at Play." *Theatre History in Canada* 6.1 (Spring 1985): 56–81.

Novak, Dagmar. *Dubious Glory: The Two World Wars and the Canadian Novel*. New York: Peter Lang, 2000.

O'Connor, Garry. *Alec Guinness, the Unknown: A Life*. London: Sidgwick & Jackson, 2002.

Oliva, Peter. "Murder Most Foul, Fiction Most Fair." *Globe and Mail* 22 September 2001. D12.

Oliver, Kelly. *Witnessing: Beyond Recognition*. Minneapolis: University of Minnesota Press, 2001.

Olos, Ana. *Timothy Findley: The Writer and His Recent Work*. Baia Mare: Editura Universitatii de Nord, 2001.

Ondaatje, Michael. *In the Skin of a Lion*. 1987. Toronto: Vintage Canada, 1996.

Ouzounian, Richard. *Stratford Gold: 50 Years, 50 Stars, 50 Conversations*. Toronto: McArthur, 2002.

———. "Timothy Findley's Stratford Memories." 2001. Repr. *Toronto Star* 23 June 2002. B3.

Overbury, Stephen. "Famous Last Words." In *Finding Canadian Facts Fast*, 59–64. Toronto: Methuen, 1985.

Owen, Wilfred. "The Parable of the Old Man and the Young." 1920. In *The Collected Poems of Wilfred Owen*, edited by C. Day Lewis, 42. London: Chatto & Windus, 1963.

Parton, Lorne. "The Written Word." *Vancouver Province* 18 November 1977. 28.

Pearce, Joseph. *Literary Converts: Spiritual Inspiration in an Age of Unbelief*. London: HarperCollins, 1999.

Pearce, Pat. "*Paper People* Cut Flimsy Figures." *Montreal Star* 14 December 1967. 62.

Pearson, Wendy. "Vanishing Acts II: Queer Reading(s) of Timothy Findley's *Headhunter* and *Not Wanted on the Voyage*." *Journal of Canadian Studies* 33.4 (1998–99): 114–31.

Pegis, Jessica. "A Farm to Write Home About." *Financial Post* (Weekend) 8–10 August 1998. R9.

Penn, Frank. "S B-B Backfire." *Ottawa Citizen* 14 December 1967. 43.

Pennee, Donna Palmateer. "Imagined Innocence, Endlessly Mourned: Postcolonial Nationalism and Cultural Expression in Timothy Findley's *The Wars*." *English Studies in Canada* 32.2–3 (2008): 89–113.

———. *Moral Metafiction: Counterdiscourse in the Novels of Timothy Findley*. Toronto: ECW Press, 1991.

———. "Trials of the Post-War World." Program Notes. Stratford Festival House Program. Stratford premiere of *The Trials of Ezra Pound*. 8 July to 17 August 2001. 5–6.

Persky, Stan. "The Pain of Lost Parents." *Globe and Mail* 6 May 1995. C28.

Peterman, Michael, and Charmaine Eddy. "'Can You See Me Yet?' Perspectives on Timothy Findley: An Introduction in Two Parts." "Perspectives on Timothy Findley." Special issue, *Journal of Canadian Studies* 33.4 (Winter 1998–99): 3–9.

———, eds. "Perspectives on Timothy Findley." Special issue, *Journal of Canadian Studies* 33.4 (Winter 1998–99).

Pettigrew, John, and Jamie Portman. *Stratford: The First Thirty Years*. 2 vols. Toronto: Macmillan, 1985.

Phillips, Robin, dir. *The Wars*. Film based on the novel by Timothy Findley. Nielsen-Ferns International, Polyphon Film, und Fernsehgesell-Schaft, 1983.

Pirie, Bruce. "The Dragon in the Fog: 'Displaced Mythology' in *The Wars*." *Canadian Literature* 91 (Winter 1981): 70–79.

Pocci, Luca. "History, Parahistory, and the Uses of Memory in Timothy Findley's *Famous Last Words*." *CLIO* 38.2 (2009): 151–72.

Polanski, Roman, dir. *Rosemary's Baby*. Film. Paramount Pictures, 1968.

Popham, A. E. *The Drawings of Leonardo da Vinci*. New York: Reynal & Hitchcock, 1945.

Pound, Ezra. "H. S. Mauberley (Life and Contacts)." 1920. In *Selected Poems*, edited with an introduction by T. S. Eliot, 117–33. London: Faber, 1948.

———. "The Rest." In *Selected Poems*, 100.

Priestley, J. B. *The Glass Cage*. London: Samuel French, 1958.

Pripps, Robert N. *The Big Book of Massey Tractors*. Vancouver: Raincoast Books, 2001.

Quarrington, Paul. "*Piano Man's Daughter* a Novel Full of Music." *Financial Post* 20 May 1995. 29.

———. *The Ravine*. Toronto: Random House, 2008.

Queerstory. http://www.queerstory.ca.

Raytor, Scott. *Queer CanLit: Canadian Lesbian, Gay, Bisexual, and Transgender (LGBT) Literature in English*. Toronto: Coach House Press, 2008.

Read, Piers Paul. *Alec Guinness: The Authorised Biography*. London: Simon & Schuster, 2003.

Reaney, James. "Timothy Findley: Man in Motion." *London Free Press* 2 October 1999. 68.

Reaume, Geoffrey. *Remembrance of Patients Past: Patient Life at the Toronto Hospital for the Insane, 1870–1940*. Toronto: Oxford University Press, 2000.

Reid, Robert. "Findley Is Simply Superb." *Kitchener-Waterloo Record* 29 March 1993. C7.

Reid-Hunter, Janet Mary. Obituary. *Toronto Star* 30 October 2004. B7.

Reilly, Frances. "Controlling Contagion: Policing and Prescribing Sexual and Political Normalcy in Cold War Canada." PhD diss., University of Saskatchewan, 2016.

———. "Leadership at Toronto for De-pathologizing Homosexuality during the Cold War." *CAMH Newsletter* Autumn 2018. 4.

———. "'The Most Common Deviation': The Problem of Pathologizing Homosexuality and the Fear of Masculine Weakness at the Toronto Forensic Clinic." Unpublished paper, 2019.

Rhiel, Mary, and David Suchoff, eds. *The Seductions of Biography*. New York: Routledge, 1996.

Rhodes, Shane. "Buggering with History: Sexual Warfare and Historical Reconstruction in Timothy Findley's *The Wars*." *Canadian Literature* 159 (Winter 1998): 38–55.

Ricard, François. *Gabrielle Roy: A Life*. Translated by Patricia Claxton. Toronto: McClelland and Stewart, 1999.

Ricou, Laurie. "Obscured by Violence: Timothy Findley's *The Wars*." In *Violence in the Canadian Novel Since 1960*, edited by Terry Goldie and Virginia Harger-Grinling, 125–37. St John's, NL: Memorial University Press, 1981.

Rigelhof, T. F. "Pilgrim's Regress." *Globe and Mail* 28 August 1999. D18.

Roberts, Carol. "Bibliographer in Search of an Author." *Canadian Library Journal* 46.4 (August 1989): 253–56.

——. "T. F. Drops His Cigarette on the Floor (Looking over the Biographer's Shoulder)." Unpublished talk. Trent University, 18 October 1997.

——. *Timothy Findley: Stories from a Life*. Toronto: ECW Press, 1994.

——. "The Perfection of Gesture: Timothy Findley and Canadian Theatre." *Theatre Research in Canada* 12.1 (Spring 1991): 1–9.

Robinson, Paul. *Gay Lives: Homosexual Autobiography from John Addington Symonds to Paul Monette*. Chicago: University of Chicago Press, 1999.

Ross, Steven J. *Hitler in Los Angeles: How Jews Foiled Nazi Plots against Hollywood and America*. New York: Bloomsbury USA, 2017.

Ross, Val. "Findley and Co. Hit the Highway." *Globe and Mail* 24 April 1997. C6.

Roth, Philip. *Portnoy's Complaint*. New York: Random House, 1969.

Sack, Daniel. *Moral Re-Armament: The Reinventions of an American Religious Movement*. New York: Palgrave Macmillan, 2009.

Sacks, Oliver. "An Anthropologist on Mars." *New Yorker* 27 December 1993/3 January 1994. 106–25.

——. *The Man Who Mistook His Wife for a Hat and Other Clinical Tales*. New York: Touchstone, 1970.

Sanderson, Heather. "(Im)Perfect Dreams: Allegories of Fascism in *The Butterfly Plague*." In Bailey and Grandy, *Paying Attention*, 104–24.

——. "'What Is There Left to Say?' Speech and Silence in Timothy Findley's *Dinner Along the Amazon*." *Journal of Canadian Studies* 33.4 (1998–99): 75–88.

Schüklenk, Udo, Edward Stein, Jacinta Karin, and William Byne. "The Ethics of Genetic Research on Sexual Orientation." *The Hastings Centre Report* July–August 1997. 6–13.

Schweitzer, Don. Introduction to *The United Church of Canada: A History*, edited by Don Schweitzer, xi–xix. Waterloo, ON: Wilfrid Laurier University Press, 2011.

Scobie, Stephen. "Eye-Deep in Hell: Ezra Pound, Timothy Findley, and Hugh Selwyn Mauberley." *Essays on Canadian Writing* 30 (1984–85): 206–27.

Scott, Jay. "Dialogue on *The Wars*: A Symphony of Firsts." *Globe and Mail* 10 November 1983. E5.

Sebba, Anne. *That Woman: The Life of Wallis Simpson, Duchess of Windsor.* New York: St. Martin's Press, 2011.

Seddon, Elizabeth. "The Reader as Actor in the Novels of Timothy Findley." In *Future Indicative: Literary Theory and Canadian Literature*, edited by John Moss, 213–20. Ottawa: University of Ottawa Press, 1987.

Service, Robert W. "The Shooting of Dan McGrew." In *Songs of the Sourdough*. 1907. Toronto: Ryerson, 1940.

Sewell, John. *How We Changed Toronto: The Inside Story of Twelve Creative, Tumultuous Years in Civic Life, 1969–1980.* Toronto: James Lorimer, 2015.

"Shadows." In *Stratford 50: Background Book*, 40–41. Stratford, ON: Stratford Festival of Canada, 2002.

Shaffir, William. "Remembering the Christie Pits Riot." *Globe and Mail* 10 August 2013. A10.

Shelley, Mary. *The Last Man.* 1826. Edited by Hugh J. Luke Jr. Lincoln: University of Nebraska Press, 1965.

Sherman, Martin. *Bent.* New York: Avon Books, 1979.

Shields, E. F. "Mauberley's Lies: Fact and Fiction in Timothy Findley's *Famous Last Words*." *Journal of Canadian Studies* 22.4 (1987–88): 44–59.

———. "'The Perfect Voice': Mauberley as Narrator in Timothy Findley's *Famous Last Words*." *Canadian Literature* 119 (Winter 1988): 84–98.

Shorter, Edward, ed. *TPH: History and Memories of the Toronto Psychiatric Hospital, 1925–1966.* Toronto: Wall & Emerson, 1996.

Showalter, Elaine. *The Female Malady: Women, Madness, and English Culture, 1830–1980.* New York: Penguin, 1987.

Shuster, Bena. "Lives Lived: Marigold Charlesworth." *Globe and Mail.* 24 December 2015. S8.

Sigvaldason, Ian, and Scott Steedman. *Art for War and Peace: How a Great Public Art Project Helped Canada Define Itself.* Vancouver: Read Leaf Books, 2015.

Sims, Jane. "An Evening of Great Theatre and a Neat Way to Sell Books." *London Free Press* 24 April 1997. B1.

Skidmore. "Timothy Findley Still Fighting the Good Wars." *Gazette* (Montreal) 5 January 2002. 13.

Smith, Neil G., Allan L. Farris, and H. Keith Markell. *A Short History of the Presbyterian Church of Canada*. Toronto: Presbyterian Publications, 1965.

Smith, Stephen. "His Own Place in the World." *Gazette* (Montreal) 7 May 1995. F1.

———. "The Telling of Lives." *Quill & Quire* (April 1995): 1, 24.

Souster, Raymond. *Jubilee of Death: The Raid on Dieppe*. Ottawa: Oberon Press, 1984.

Staines, David. "Montreal Holds Special Memories for Award-Winning Author." *Gazette* (Montreal) 10 November 1984. 11.

Stebner, Eleanor J. "The 1930s." In Schweitzer, *The United Church of Canada*, 39–56.

Stephenson, Craig. "*Pilgrim* Finds Carl Jung in a Peach of a Novel." *Calgary Herald* 4 September 1999. G9.

Stephenson, Jenn. "Setting Free Silenced Autobiographical Voices." In *Performing Autobiography: Contemporary Canadian Drama*, 68–102. Toronto: University of Toronto Press, 2013.

Stevens, Peter. "Warring Spirits." *Ontario Review* 9 (Fall–Winter 1978–79): 107–8.

Stevenson, William. *A Man Called Intrepid: The Secret War*. New York: Ballantyne Books, 1976.

Stoneham, Gordon. "Insipid New Canadian Drama." *Ottawa Citizen* 2 March 1976. 48.

Straight, Annabel, ed. *Exploring Toronto*. Toronto: Architecture Canada, 1972.

Stuewe, Paul. "Better Dead Than Read?" *Books in Canada* (October 1979): 3–7.

Sullivan, Kevin, dir. *The Piano Man's Daughter*. Film based on the novel by Timothy Findley. Directed and produced by Kevin Sullivan. Sullivan Entertainment International, 2000.

Sullivan, Rosemary. "The Private Entertene." *Brick* 46 (Summer 1993): 48–50.

———. "Saying 'Yes' in the Darkness." *Maclean's* 15 July 2002. 51–52.

———. *Shadow Maker: The Life of Gwendolyn MacEwen*. Toronto: HarperCollins, 1995.

Symons, Scott. *Dear Reader: Selected Scott Symons*. Edited by Christopher Elson. Toronto: Gutter Press, 1998.

Szende, Andrew. "Far from the Footlights of Glory." *Toronto Star* 29 July 1967. 26.

Tait, Michael. "The Lost Journal of Timothy Findley." *Globe and Mail* 15 March 2003. R1, 8.

Taylor, Charles. "Herbert Norman." In *Six Journeys: A Canadian Pattern*, 105–51. Toronto: Anansi, 1977.

Taylor, Kate. "Henry and Hutt Carry the Day." *Globe and Mail* 7 August 1995. C3.

Terauds, John. "Stratford Gothic." *Toronto Star* 23 September 2001. D13.

Teresa of Jesus, Saint. *The Life*. Vol. 1 of *The Complete Works of Saint Teresa of Jesus*, translated and edited by E. Allison Peers. 9 vols. London: Sheed & Ward, 1946.

Thacker, Robert. *Alice Munro: Writing Her Lives*. Toronto: McClelland and Stewart, 2011.

Thomas, Colin. "Elizabeth Rex." *Georgia Straight* 18–25 July 2013. 30, 32.

Thompson, Eric. "Canadian Fiction and the Great War." *Canadian Literature* 91 (Winter 1981): 81–96.

Tiffin, Helen M. "*Not Wanted on the Voyage*: Textual Imperialism and Post-Colonial Resistance." *Australian-Canadian Studies* 6.2 (1989): 47–55.

Tippett, Michael. *A Child of Our Time*. 1944. Royal Philharmonic Orchestra, conducted by Andre Previn, recorded in London, 1986. RPO Records, CDRPOS8005, compact disc.

Todd, Douglas. "The Letter of Timothy: Findley Has Spiritual-Ethical World View." *Gazette* (Montreal) 1 May 1993. J5.

Torrey, E. Fuller. *The Roots of Treason: Ezra Pound and the Secret of St. Elizabeths*. Bethesda, MD: Lucas Books, 1992.

Tuchman, Barbara. *The Guns of August*. 1962. New York: Presidio Press, 2004.

———. *The Proud Tower: A Portrait of the World before the War, 1890–1914*. New York: Macmillan, 1966.

Tumanov, Vladimir. "De-Automatization in Timothy Findley's *The Wars*." *Canadian Literature* 130 (Autumn 1991): 107–15.

Turner, R. Edward. "Homosexuality." Unpublished lecture. 10 March 1972. R. Edward Turner fonds. CAMH F27.6-26.

———. "A Review of Homosexuality." Unpublished lecture. 20 January 1959. R. Edward Turner fonds. CAMH F27.6-12.

———. "Services Note: The Development of Forensic Services in Toronto." *Canadian Journal of Criminology* 21.1 (January 1979): 200–209.

Turner, R. Edward, Harry C. Hutchison, and Lorraine O'Donnell. "The Forensic Clinic of the Toronto Psychiatric Hospital." *Canadian Journal of Corrections* 1.1 (October 1958): 15–20.

Tyson, Sylvia. *Joyner's Dream*. Toronto: HarperCollins, 2011.

Ungar, George, dir. *The Champagne Safari*. Film. Narrated by Colm Feore and David Hemblen. NFB, 1995.

Urbach, Karina. *Go-Betweens for Hitler*. Oxford: Oxford University Press, 2015.

Urquhart, Jane. "A Very, Very Uncertain Way to Make a Living." In Dobson and Kamboureli, *Producing Canadian Literature*, 61–74.

Valverde, Mariana. "Pride & Prejudice." *Canada's History* June–July 2019. 48–53.

Van Herk, Aritha. "No Reason to Fool Yourself." In Dobson and Kamboureli, *Producing Canadian Literature*, 111–29.

Vauthier, Simone. "The Dubious Battle of Storytelling: Narrative Strategies in Timothy Findley's *The Wars*." In *Gaining Ground: European Critics on Canadian Literature*, edited by Robert Kroetsch and Reingard Nischik, 1–39. Edmonton: NeWest Press, 1985.

———. "Photo-Drama: *The Wars* de Timothy Findley." Études canadiennes 14 (June 1983): 101–19.

Ventura, Héliane, and Françoise Besson, eds. *Caliban: French Journal of English Studies* 53 (2015). Special number: *La guerre de 14 re-présentée: l'art comme réponse à la guerre / Representing World War One: Art's Response to War*.

Verdi, Giuseppe. *Messa da Requiem*. World premiere. San Marco, Milan, 22 May 1874.

Verduyn, Christl, and Kathleen Garay, eds. *Marian Engel: Life in Letters*. Toronto: University of Toronto Press, 2004.

Verhoeven, W. M. "Naming the Present/Naming the Past: Historiographic Metafiction in Findley and Ondaatje." In *Shades of Empire in Colonial and Post-Colonial Literatures*, edited by C. C. Barfoot and Theo D'haen, 283–99. Amsterdam: Rodopi, 1993.

Vidal, Gore. *Myra Breckinridge*. Boston: Little, Brown, 1968.

———. "Pink Triangle, Yellow Star." 1981. In *The Essential Gore Vidal*, edited by Fred Kaplan, 737–51. Toronto: Random House, 1999.

Wagner, Vit. "The Art of Controversy." *Toronto Star* 8 February 1992. J1, J10.

———. "*Piano Man*'s Author ... and Others." *Toronto Star* 10 May 1997. K12.

———. "Stars Add Depth to Intriguing New Drama." *Toronto Star* 29 March 1993. B4.

Warren, Dorothy. *The World of Ruth Draper: A Portrait of an Actress*. Carbondale: Southern Illinois University Press, 1999.

Wattie, Chris. "Author Compares Oil Industry to Terrorists." *National Post* (Toronto) 6 October 2001. A1, 15.

Waugh, Evelyn. *Brideshead Revisited*. 1945. New York: Little, Brown, 2012.

Wayne, Joyce. "The Evolution of Clarke, Irwin, a House for All Seasons." *Quill & Quire* (1980): 4.

Webb, Peter. "'At War with Nature': Animals in Timothy Findley's *The Wars*." In *Other Selves: Animals in the Canadian Literary Imagination*, edited by Janice Fiamengo, 227–44. Ottawa: University of Ottawa Press, 2007.

Webb, Phyllis. "The Confluence of Imaginations." *Journal of Canadian Studies* 33.4 (Winter 1998–99): 13–26.

———. "I Daniel." In *The Vision Tree: Selected Poems*, 151–54. Vancouver: Talonbooks, 1998.

———. "Leaning." In *Water and Light: Ghazals and Anti-Ghazals*, 58–59. Toronto: Coach House, 1984.

———. *Nothing but Brush Strokes: Selected Prose*. Edmonton: NeWest Press, 1995.

Wedman, Les. Review of *The Paper People*, by Timothy Findley. *Vancouver Sun* 11 December 1967. 26.

Weinstein, Harvey M. "A Story of a Life Destroyed in CIA-Funded Experiment." *Globe and Mail* 28 August 1985. 7.

Weiss, Allan. "Private and Public in Timothy Findley's *The Wars*." *Canadian Literature* 138/139 (Fall/Winter 1993): 91–102.

Weissman, Aerlyn, and Lyne Fernie, dirs. *Forbidden Love: The Unashamed Stories of Lesbian Lives*. Film. NFB, 1992.

Whitehead, William. "Good Grief." In *The Heart Does Break: Canadian Writers on Grief and Mourning*, edited by George Bowering and Jean Baird, 324–29. Toronto: Random House, 2009.

———. [Brock Wilson, pseud.]. "I've Never Felt Guilty about Being Homosexual." In *True to You in My Fashion: A Woman Talks to Men about Marriage*, by Adrienne Clarkson, 92–115. Toronto: New Press, 1971.

———. "A Winter's Tale." *Globe and Mail* 21 December 2013. F7.

———. *Words to Live By: A Memoir*. Toronto: Cormorant Books, 2012.

Whiteson, Leon, and S. R. Gage. *The Liveable City: The Architecture and Neighbourhoods of Toronto*. Oakville, ON: Mosaic Press, 1982.

Whittaker, Herbert. "John A. the Ultimate Ham." *Globe and Mail* 2 February 1979. 12.

Widerman, Jane. "New Protection for the Author." *Maclean's* 16 August 1982. 46.

Wilder, Thornton. *The Bridge of San Luis Rey.* London: Longmans, Green, 1927.

——. *The Ides of March.* New York: Harper & Brothers, 1948.

——. *The Journals of Thornton Wilder, 1939–1961.* Selected and edited by Donald Gallup. New Haven, CT: Yale University Press, 1985.

——. *The Matchmaker.* New York: Samuel French, 1955.

——. *Our Town.* 1938. New York: Harper & Row, 1957.

——. *The Selected Letters of Thornton Wilder.* Edited by Robin G. Wilder and Jackson R. Bryer. With a foreword by Scott Donaldson. New York: Harper-Collins, 2008.

——. *The Skin of Our Teeth.* New York and London: Harper & Brothers, 1942.

Williams, David. *Confessional Fictions: A Portrait of the Artist in the Canadian Novel.* Toronto: University of Toronto Press, 1991.

——. "The Shock of Film and the Transformation of Place: A Case in Point in *The Butterfly Plague.*" In *Imagined Nations: Reflections on Media in Canadian Fiction,* 163–82. Montreal: McGill-Queen's University Press, 2003.

Winston, Iris. "*The Piano Man's Daughter*: Veronica Tennant in Adaptation of Findley's Works." *Performing Arts* (Summer 1997): 36.

Wiseman, Adele. *The Sacrifice.* Toronto: Macmillan, 1956.

Wolff, Leon. *In Flanders Fields: The 1917 Campaign.* New York: Viking Press, 1958.

Woodcock, George. "History to the Defeated: Notes on Some Novels by Timothy Findley." In *Present Tense: A Critical Anthology,* edited by John Moss, 15–28. Toronto: NC Press, 1985.

——. "Timothy Findley's Gnostic Parable." *Canadian Literature* 111 (Winter 1986): 232–37.

Woodrow, Marnie. "Spinach with Nutmeg: A Tribute to Timothy Findley." *Journal of Canadian Studies* 33.4 (1998–99): 32–35.

Woolf, Virginia. *Orlando: A Biography.* 1928. Harmondsworth, UK: Penguin, 1942.

Wyile, Herb. "It's Just a Story: Postmodernism, Politics and Findley's Italics." *Journal of Canadian Fiction* 33.4 (1998–99): 63–74.

Yanofsky, Joel. "Findley Locates the Ache for a Sweeter Time, a Lost Love." *Gazette* (Montreal) 12 October 1996. I1.

———. "Murder He Wrote: Timothy Findley Tackles a 'Howdunit' Novel." *Cross-Canada Writers' Quarterly* 10.1 (1988): 5, 32.

———. "Timothy Findley's Whodunit Is Medium for His Message." *Gazette* (Montreal) 25 October 1986. B8.

York, Lorraine. "Civilian Conflict: Systems of Warfare in Timothy Findley's Early Fiction." *English Studies in Canada* 15.3 (1989): 336–47.

———. *Front Lines: The Fiction of Timothy Findley*. Toronto: ECW Press, 1991.

———. *Introducing Timothy Findley's "The Wars": A Reader's Guide*. Toronto: ECW Press, 1990.

———. "'A Shout of Recognition': 'Likeness' and the Art of the Simile in Timothy Findley's *The Wars*." *English Studies in Canada* 9.2 (1985): 223–30.

———. "'Violent Stillness': Timothy Findley's Use of Photography." In *The Other Side of Dailiness: Photography in the Works of Alice Munro, Timothy Findley, Michael Ondaatje, and Margaret Laurence*, 51–92. Toronto: ECW Press, 1988.

———. "'What It Took and Took/To Be a Man': Teaching Timothy Findley and the Construction of Masculinities." *Journal of Canadian Studies* 33.4 (1998–99): 101–13.

Zemans, Joyce. "Establishing the Canon." *Journal of Canadian Art History* 16.2 (1995): 6–39.

Zerbisias, Antonia. "Superb War Series on Babes in Arms." *Toronto Star* 9 September 1989. J3.

Ziebold, Thomas O., and John Mongeon. *Alcoholism and Homosexuality*. New York: Haworth, 1982.

Ziegler, Heide, ed. *Rewriting History: Proceedings of the Fourth Stuttgart Seminar in Cultural Studies*. Stuttgart: M & P Verlag, 1997.

INDEX

———

"About Effie," 90, 96, 133, 135, 137, 153, 155, 163, 185

Ackerman, Marianne, 290

ACTRA Award, 225, 278

Adachi, Ken, 19, 220, 255, 277, 437n14
    suicide of, 316–17

Adachi, Mary, 29, 437n14

Admiral Road House, 33, 36, 38, 41, 43

A. E. Ames Insurance Company, 44, 63, 112, 131

Aeschylus, 113

"Against Despair" (personal motto), 19, 87, 269, 282, 287, 291, 306–7, 318, 344, 398, 422n1

AIDS, 391

"Alarms and Excursions," 291

Albers, Heinz, 248

alcohol abuse: susceptibility by Findley men, 65, 136. *See also* Findley, Allan; Findley, Thomas Michael; Findley, Timothy Irving Frederick

Alcohol Research Foundation, 171

"Alice Drops Her Cigarette on the Floor" interview, 16–17

Allan, Andrew, 95, 152, 193

Allan Gardens (Toronto), 82

Allan Memorial Institute (Montreal), 301

Allen, Bob, 152–53

"Almeyer's Mother," 312–14

Altamira, caves of, 216, 275–76

Amnesty International, 280, 303, 430n1

ancestors, influence of, 2, 15, 30, 32, 209, 212, 215, 241, 255, 321, 338, 344–45, 354

Ancien Chemin de Salernes house ("Mots Maison"), 371–72

Apollo 11 Space Mission, 202

archives. *See* Findley, Timothy, writing practice

Arkwright, 210, 217, 219, 286, 298

Art for Enlightenment: A History of Art in Toronto Schools, 342

"Artists: Prisoners of Conscience," 280

ashes, scattering of, 2, 21, 29, 211, 215, 217, 257, 282–83, 310, 316, 351, 367, 402

Atlantic House, Maine, 21, 201, 270, 282, 294, 299, 302, 322, 379

Atwood, Margaret, 28, 205, 222–23,
   231–32, 247, 281
   The Circle Game, 238
   "Evening Trainstation, Before
      Departure," 238
   The Handmaid's Tale, 287
   review of *The Wars,* 248–49
Auden, W. H., 101, 113, 268
   The Age of Anxiety, 113
   "Detective Story," 393
audiotapes
   1993 tape of TF and his cousin
      Isobelle Guthrie, 420n9
   recorded letter to Tippett,
      325–26
Aunt Marg. *See* Findley, Phoebe
   Margaret
Aunt Ruth. *See* Bull, Emily Ruth
Auschwitz, 70, 271, 369
autobiography, 5–6, 14, 16, 190, 326
   fictional, 265, 274. *See also*
      *Famous Last Words; Inside
      Memory; Journeyman*

Bach, Johann Sebastian 126, 284
Bache & Co., 131, 147, 165
Bagnold, Enid; *National Velvet,* 67–68
Baker, Clara, 81, 87, 92
Baldwin, Janet, 19, 76, 105–6, 108–10,
   116, 139, 143–44, 149, 152, 190,
   195, 205, 322–23
Banff Centre of the Performing Arts,
   95, 394
Bantam Books, 184
Bateman, Robert, 307
Battle of Vimy Ridge, 40–41
Bauer, Jan, 303
Bayliss, Peter (actor), 158

Beaumont, Hugh "Binkie," 103–5,
   107–8, 121, 142–43
Beaver River, 23, 210, 223
   Beaver River Nature Trail, 216
Beaverton, 180
Bechtold, Grace, 19, 184–85, 198,
   200–201
Beckett, Samuel: *Waiting for Godot,*
   144, 374
Bedaux, Charles, 264, 267–68
Bedford, Brian, 375
Beethoven, Ludwig van, 113
   sonatas, 376
Bellow, Saul, 207
Bemrose, John, 340: "Still Angry,"
   379, 386
Benson, Eugene, 90, 263
Berlin, 118–20, 145, 261
   East Berlin, 120
   Nazi anti-Semitism in, 194
Berton, Pierre, 7, 19, 39–40, 213, 225–
   26, 228, 249, 281, 289–90, 430n5
   Klondike documentary project, 226
Bertram, John, 372
"Better Dead Than Read? An Opposing
   View," 232–34. *See also* Findley,
   Timothy Irving Frederick,
   censorship
biography
   sources for, 3, 6–9, 129
   writing of, 3, 5, 10, 250–51, 340
Bishop Bethune College, 50, 52, 57
Black, Patricia, 330–31, 390
Blackadar, Bruce, 276
Bob Edwards Award, 396–97
Boland, Bridget, 107
   The Prisoner, 107, 109, 111, 114;
      film version, 121–22

Bolger, Kevin, 386
Boys' Own Annual, 245
Bradbury, Ray, 325
Bradshaw, Thomas (Massey-Harris): "Appreciation," 44
Brahms, Johannes, 8–9, 70, 121, 150, 257
Bragg and Minna stories, 294, 305, 310–11, 369
Brecht, Bertolt, 395
Brennan, Patricia, 322
Brewer, Barry, 431n9
Brighton, 118, 144
Brignoles, France, 26, 372–73, 400
British National Service. *See* Findley, Timothy Irving Frederick: British National Service
Britten, Benjamin, 106, 108
    Peter Grimes, 106
    War Requiem, 245
Brook, Peter, 2, 139, 143–44, 146
Brooke, Rupert, 112
Brooks, Hobbs, and Meyer, 88, 93, 94, 155
Brown, Anthony Cave: *Bodyguard of Lies*, 330
Buchman, Frank, 77–79, 422n8
    association with Nazism, 78
Bull, Alan Talbot (uncle), 52, 54, 57, 314, 348, 354
    Spanish flu epidemic, 49, 54
Bull, Edith Maude Fagan (grand-mother), 46, 50, 58–59, 61, 179, 238, 304, 314, 345–49, 353–54, 420n11
    crucifix, grandmother's gift, 9, 59, 304
    Granny Bull, 58, 65, 152
    Roman Catholic faith, 58
Bull, Emily Ruth (Aunt Ruth), 6, 9, 18, 50–57, 61, 140, 237, 246, 293, 301, 307, 344–45, 347–48, 351, 353–55, 364, 386
    as inspiration for *The Piano Man's Daughter*, 50, 54
    mental illness, 56–57, 63
    "Nicholas Fagan" as pseudonym, 52, 53, 55, 57, 338
    poems of, 54–55
Bull family history, 46–49, 50, 344–46, 349, 354
Bull, Frederick (grandfather), 48–50, 53–55, 58, 61, 313–14, 346, 349, 355
    Douse, Amy Maude (Peggy), second wife, 54, 314
Bull, Henry Sr. (great-grandfather), 47–48
Bull, John, 48, 50
Bunyan, John, 113, 387
    The Pilgrim's Progress, 113
Burgess, Guy, 104
Burritt, Lloyd: "The Dream Healer," 444n9
Burton, Richard, 103
Bush, Steven, 278
Butow, Hans, 248
Butterfly Plague, The, 17, 19, 181, 191, 232, 237, 238, 244, 378, 432n18
    depiction of Nazism in, 196–97
    discussion of, 194–98
    ignored in Canada, 199–200
    revision of (1986), 197

Callwood, June, 29, 257, 280–81, 316, 437n13
Cameron, Elspeth, 64, 75–76, 171, 301
Campbell, Kenneth, 233
Camp Kagawong, 66, 421n1
Canada Council for the Arts, 96

Canada Council grant, 207, 278
Canadian Broadcasting Corporation
  (CBC), 89–90, 92, 95–96, 104,
  152, 165, 176, 178–79, 181, 213,
  230, 243–44, 279, 323–24, 358
  Anthology, 153, 165
  Dieppe 1942, 261
  Festival, 192
  Graham Spry Lecture, 323–25
  Ideas, 178, 207
  The Learning Stage, 178
  Life and Times: Timothy Findley, 167
  *Lost Innocence: The Children of
    World War Two. See Lost
    Innocence*
  Morningside, 308, 345
  *The National Dream. See National
    Dream, The*
  The Nature of Things, 178
  Sunday Matinee, 278
  Umbrella: We Cover the Arts, 178
  "Walls" radio play (Findley), 198–99
  *The Whiteoaks of Jalna. See
    Whiteoaks of Jalna*
  Writers & Company, 397
Canadian cultural arts development,
  95–97
Canadian cultural nationalism, 230
Canadian Literature (journal), 16, 96
CanLit Foodbook, The, 309
Cannington, 22, 23, 175, 179–82, 191,
  208–9, 211, 216, 239, 284, 297,
  348–49, 356, 363
Can You See Me Yet?, 16, 159, 216, 241,
  246, 334, 356, 378
  conference, 365
  discussion of, 234–40
  psychiatric institutions in, 235–40

reviews of, 238–39
Carlyle, Alan Talbot, 54
Carlyle, David (cousin), 364
Carlyle, David Brainerd (uncle), 50, 53,
  55–57, 241, 346, 355, 385, 394
Carlyle, Emily Ruth Bull (aunt). *See*
  Bull, Emily Ruth
Carlyle, Isobelle Ruth (cousin), 52–55.
  See also Guthrie, Isobelle.
Carver, Brent, 28, 256, 388, 390, 395, 397
Casey House (AIDS hospice), 316, 391
Caux, 77–79, 147–48
CBC. *See* Canadian Broadcasting
  Corporation
censorship. *See* Findley, Timothy
  Irving Frederick: censorship,
  views on
"Censorship by Every Other Name," 280
Central Library Theatre, 176–77
Central School of Speech and Drama
  (London, England), 95, 101, 108
Centre for Addiction and Mental
  Health (CAMH), 420n12
CFGM radio station, 178
Charlesworth, Marigold, 27, 172, 176–
  77, 234–35, 238, 360, 374, 429n7,
  431n10
Cheever, John, 294, 302
Chekhov, Anton, 16, 180, 207
  The Cherry Orchard, 14, 114, 374
Chicago, 158–59, 179
Chilkoot Pass, 227–28
Chopin, Frédéric, 56, 399
"Christmas Remembered," 72–73, 258
CIA experiments, 301. *See also*
  MKULTRA
"City and the Asylum–Finding the
  Balance, The," 341–42

Clark, Andrew, 340
Clarke, Bill, 244, 246–47, 251, 267, 270,
    280–81, 290, 432n18
Clarke, Cecil, 92
Clarke Institute of Psychiatric
    Research, 341, 348
Clarke, Irwin & Company, 244, 246–47,
    269–70
    demise of, 280–81
    fonds, 432n15
Clarke, Marie, 247
Clarkson, Adrienne, 28
Cohen, Matt, 232, 281
Colbert, Nancy, 19, 162, 200, 243, 247,
    248, 255, 277, 281–82, 308, 331–32
    Nancy Colbert and Associates,
    426n6
Colbert, Stanley, 19, 162, 221, 243–244,
    247, 256
Cold War, 327–29
    Canadian political activities in,
    300–301
Cole, Susan, 340
Coleridge, Samuel: "The Pains of
    Sleep", 103
Collingwood, 48, 50, 346
Collins, Anne, 209, 367, 374, 402,
    430n1
Collins, Len, 175, 209–10, 212, 215,
    304, 367, 374, 402, 430n1
Comfort, Charles, 68
"Comparing Notes," 298
Conrad, Joseph, 20, 207, 274, 334–36,
    338
    Heart of Darkness, 207, 274, 304,
    308, 332, 334–36, 341
"Coquilles St. Jacques from Dieppe,"
    309

Cortot, Alfred, 6, 262, 271–73
Cotignac, 22, 25–26, 29, 344, 364–65,
    369, 371–73, 375, 394, 400
    purchase of home in, 359–60
Court, John, 440n16, 441n22
Cousland, Dick, 65–66, 110
Covici, Pascal, 159, 161–62
Craig, John and Barbara, 309
Crane, Hart, 156
Creighton, Donald, 226
Crescent Road house, 63–64, 67, 73
Crest Theatre (Toronto), 149, 152,
    165–66, 176

Dachau, 20, 22, 164, 271, 273–74, 335,
    359. See also Moffat, Ivan
D'Aquila, Diane, 28, 388, 390
Daniel, Book of, 274–75
Davies, Robertson, 90
    At My Heart's Core, 88–89
da Vinci, Leonardo. See Leonardo
    da Vinci
Davis, Don, 152
Davis, William, 281
Davison, C. M., 41
Dawson City, Yukon, 225, 227–28
Dean, James, 142, 192
De Bosis, Lauro; model for character
    Lorenzo de Broca in FLW, 434n2
de la Roche, Mazo, 31, 67–68, 212, 224
Denison, Merrill: Harvest
    Triumphant, 44
Der Krieg und die Krote, 248
Devereux, Robert, 389–90
Dickinson, Emily, 161
Dieppe, 21, 261, 277, 309, 324, 385
Dieppe Heroes in Canada, 434n1

Dinner Along the Amazon, 70, 137,
    162–63, 278, 294–95
    "Dinner Along the Amazon," 221,
        295, 333
    "Lemonade," 294
Dominion Drama Festival, 95
Donald Cameron Medal, 375
Don't Let the Angels Fall, 200
Douse, Amy Maude (Peggy); Peggy
    Fortune, 54, 314. *See also* Bull,
    Frederick
Drainie, John, 152, 426n2
Drancy detention camp, 369
Dreams Come True gala, 397–98
Duchess of Windsor, Wallis Simpson,
    264, 266–67, 275, 277
"Duel in Cluny Park," 333
Duke of Windsor, 264–68, 275
Duke of York Theatre (Toronto), 347
Dunkirk, 80
Dust to Dust, 310, 372, 384
    "Abracadaver," 369
    Bragg and Minna stories, 369.
        See also Bragg and Minna
        stories; *Stones*
    discussion of, 368–71
    "Dust," 368–69
    "Kellerman's Windows," 369
    "The Madonna of the Cherry
        Trees," 369–71

Earle Grey Players, 76
East Berlin. *See* Berlin
Easton, Richard, (Dick), 94–95, 102–3,
    105–8, 114, 123, 143, 423n7, 425n2
Ecclefechan, Scotland (Findley
    ancestral home), 114
Eccelfechin boarding house, 353

Edinburgh, 111, 114, 140
Edinburgh Festival, 117
Egoyan, Atom, 375
Eliot, T. S., 108, 113, 262, 310
    The Waste Land, 334
Elizabeth I (queen), 389–90
Elizabeth Rex, 17, 28, 367–68, 371, 375,
    392
    discussion of, 388–91
    as memory play, 389
    Queen Elizabeth I, as character in,
        389–90
    sexuality in, 390–91
    Shakespeare as character in, 388–90
Engel, Howard, 280
Engel, Marian, 7, 19, 64, 220, 230–33,
    247, 281, 307, 310–11, 432n16
"E.R.A.," 202, 216, 429–30n13
Euripides, 29, 113, 247, 387
"Everything I Tell You Is the Truth
    Except the Lies," 357

Fagan, Edith Maude (grandmother).
    See Bull, Edith Maude Fagan;
    See also Bull, Frederick
Fagan family history, 47, 50–59, 344–45,
    349, 354
Fagan, James Talbot, 50
Fagan, John James (great-uncle),
    422n10, 441n23
Fagan, Nicholas, 50, 53, 338
    fictional character, 246, 253, 338.
        See also Bull, Emily Ruth
Famous Last Words, 2, 6, 19, 79, 81,
    194, 196–97, 201, 258–59, 279–
    80, 290–91, 299, 309, 315, 324,
    335, 339, 345, 351, 358, 369, 378,
    382, 432n15

adaptation for CBC, 278
archives in, 273–74
composition of, 215–16
discussion of, 263–76
ethical argument in, 274–76
fascism in, 264, 275
fictional autobiography in, 17,
    265–66, 269–71, 274
Hugh Selwyn Mauberley. See
    Pound, Ezra
intertexts in, 268, 271–73
Nazism in, 267, 272
publication, reviews of, 276–77
research for, 267–68
UK reception of, 277–78, 306, 375
fascism, 302
ideology and impact, 207, 261–62
Father Brown, 103, 106
Faulkner, William, 160
    Sanctuary, 151, 426n1
    The Unvanquished, 151
Feiffer, Jules: *Crawling Arnold,* 176
Findley, Allan (father), 4, 9, 18, 33, 43–
    45, 67, 75, 186, 217, 237, 247, 251,
    253, 258, 260–61, 307, 313, 338–
    39, 356, 361, 363, 394, 441n23
alcohol abuse, 61, 63, 73, 122, 283
concern for Michael's health,
    129–130
death of, 167 279, 282–83
health concerns, 122, 165, 276
hostility to TF's homosexuality,
    64–65, 73–74, 82, 98, 110, 147, 177
married life, 60–65, 72–73
Parkinson's disease, 205–6, 218,
    283, 433n24
photographs, collector of, 37, 207, 348
RCAF file, 421n4

relationship with TF, 111–13, 115,
    147, 181–84, 205–7, 247, 316
Second World War, role in, 69–70,
    72, 362
Findley, Allan Gilmour Lyon
    (brother), 45, 62–63
Findley, Margaret Maude Bull
    (mother), 18, 42, 47, 53–54, 75–
    76, 95, 113, 176–177, 181–84, 206,
    217, 218, 225, 247, 255, 256, 308,
    311–14, 348, 361
childhood, 57–58
health concerns, 144, 147, 280
married life, 60–65, 72–73, 183–84
MRA movement and, 77–79. *See
    also* Moral Re-Armament
    movement
philosophy of family and nature,
    214–15
relationship with Allan, 183–84
"Reminiscent Recipes," 214
Findley, Phoebe Constance
    (grandmother), 34–35, 42–43,
    46, 135, 187, 190, 237, 251, 253,
    261, 354, 361, 421n6, 441n23
"Goggie," 45, 65, 241
Findley, Phoebe Margaret (Aunt
    Marg), 33, 35, 42–43, 152, 183, 187,
    190, 246–47, 251, 253, 282, 361
Findley, Sally (sister-in-law), 134, 135,
    267, 293, 307, 311–12. *See also*
    Murray, Sally.
Findley, Stuart Eadie (uncle), 33, 43,
    45, 355
Findley, Thomas (grandfather),
    31–34, 40, 44–45, 75, 180, 187,
    212, 255, 304

"The Only Way to Reach Every
    Member," 44
Findley, Thomas (great-grandfather), 32
Findley, Thomas Irving (Uncle Tif), 9,
    14, 18, 33, 37–41, 43, 62, 63, 80,
    206–7, 237, 241, 242, 247, 251,
    253, 255, 282–83
  Battle of Vimy Ridge, 40–41
  wartime journal, 39–42, 251
Findley, Thomas Michael (brother),
    62, 64–65, 71, 72–73, 117, 121,
    140, 143, 152, 182, 267, 308, 326,
    362, 399
  alcohol abuse, 100, 110, 112–13, 115,
    122, 129, 134–35, 157–58, 217, 258
  death of, 312, 350–51
  as influence on TF's fiction, 185,
    187–88, 311–12
Findley, Timothy Irving Frederick
  "1950 Journal," 80–81
  acting career, 76, 88–95, 103–4,
    107–11, 114–18, 128–31, 139–40,
    143–46. See also Hamlet;
    Shakespeare, William; Wilder,
    Thornton: The Matchmaker
  alcohol abuse, 4, 88–89, 98, 100, 106,
    115, 124, 142, 148, 158, 171–72, 179,
    191–92, 198–99, 205, 220–23,
    278–79, 285–86, 305, 364, 376
  Antabuse, use of, 172, 177, 198–99, 286
  ballet, 75–76, 113
  Berlin, response to post-war city,
    118–20, 145, 196
  British National Service, 120–21,
    148–49, 246
  Canadian culture, critique of, 126
  censorship, views on, 232–34, 280,
    297–98, 325, 343–44

childhood, 62–68
  conservation activities, 216. See
    also Beaver River
  criticism of USA, 201–2, 204
  critique of humanity, 202–4
  death of, 26–27, 29–30, 400
  depression, 106, 109–10, 114, 148,
    171, 179, 217, 239, 278–79, 364
  despair, 87–88, 123–24, 137–38, 148,
    220–21, 242, 385, 401
  early reading, 67–68
  education, lack of, 74, 101, 104
  fascism, views on, 263, 276, 299, 342
  fear of: death, 316, 322, 364, 368,
    371, 375–76, 401; failure, 124,
    128, 135, 179, 205, 242, 277;
    flying, 145, 165–66, 296
  hatred of cities, 179, 221, 231, 337
  health of, 24–26, 306–7, 321–22,
    368, 377, 394, 397–400
  homophobia, struggle with, 76–77,
    146, 171, 258
  homosexuality, 4–5, 15, 64–65, 73–
    74, 76, 82–83, 104–5, 147, 148,
    154–55, 158, 167, 171–72, 222–23,
    295–96, 331, 391, 401
  "Hospital Journal," 397–400
  hospitalization, 25–26
  importance of: journals, 9, 37, 46,
    52, 58, 71, 97–101, 112, 130, 136,
    186, 236, 241, 251, 253, 298, 399;
    landscape, 21–23, 402–3; lists,
    66, 98–99, 104, 113, 121, 155, 158,
    183, 207, 218, 270; memory, 223,
    240, 274, 298, 315, 317, 321, 369;
    music, 20–21, 68–69, 122, 126–
    27, 153, 272–73, 399; photographs,
    9, 39–40, 80–81, 164–65, 235–36,

241, 251, 253, 312–13, 347–48,
360–62, 372; pianos, 69, 111, 180,
210, 257, 367; psychiatric
institutions, 56–57, 235–40, 301,
333, 341, 356, 378, 384; witnessing,
20, 240, 254, 302, 335
job at Massey-Harris, 44
living will, 24
marriage to Janet Reid, 166–67, 171,
295, 427n9
memorials for, 27–29
obituaries, 27
Order of Canada, 28
Osric, TF's role in *Hamlet*, 143–46
personal motto: see "Against
Despair"
radio and film, work in, 191
relationship with Alec Guinness,
102–8, 111–12, 131–33, 148–49
relationship with father, 70, 72–74,
111–13, 181–84, 205–7, 218, 247,
338–39
relationship with mother, 214–15, 218
religious beliefs, 98–99, 111, 113,
116, 130–31, 148, 157, 229
response to father's death, 279,
282–84
Second World War, impact of,
69–70
sexual triangles, 131–33
suicide ideation, 94, 100, 131, 142,
155, 167, 217–18, 223, 296
teaching at Humber College,
323–24
Tiff, as nickname, 4
views on: colonialism and
Indigenous peoples, 202–3;
free trade, 306; Soviet-style

totalitarianism, 146; war, 123–24,
246, 379
Findley, Timothy, personal philosophy
concern for natural world/
environment, 202, 204–5, 209,
216, 229–30, 253, 297, 306–7, 327,
334, 379, 396–97
importance of: arts and humanities
in education, 297; imagination,
297, 318; landscape, 327; social
contract, 334–35
love of home, 2, 23, 29, 179–80,
208–9, 258, 327, 401
"PAY ATTENTION," 383–84
Pilgrim as summation of, 378
Findley, Timothy, writing career, 161–64
Adelaide Writers' Week, 304–5
burning an early manuscript, 162
decision to pursue writing, 177–78
documentary films, 181
early writing and practice, 133, 137,
162–64
failures, 221, 238–39
first story, "The Name's the Same,"
135–38
influences, 18–20, 156, 209–10.
See also Conrad, Joseph; Wilder,
Thornton
lessons from acting/theatre, 156–
57, 294–95, 388
move to Penguin Canada, 281–82
scriptwriting, 191, 224–25, 234, 261
Southern Ontario Gothic, 249
tours, 248, 290–92
Findley, Timothy, writing practice, 20,
209–10, 241, 243–45, 391
child observers in fiction, 188–89,
361–62

depiction of father-son
relationships, 70–71, 190, 237,
283, 316, 338–39, 362–63
fictional autobiographers and
biographers, 344–45, 356–57,
360, 387
fictional journals in, 299–300,
301–2
importance of archives and
research, 250–51, 253–54, 265,
347–48, 387
narrative strategies, 251, 272, 294–
95, 315
playwriting as craft, 388
qualities of good writing, 185–86
theme of death in, 368–69, 371
Tiresias figure in, 377–78
treatment of ménage à trois, 294,
310–11, 391
Finlay, Mary Lou, 104–5, 307–8,
424n10
First World War, 38–42, 52–53, 57, 69,
123–24, 189–90, 206, 236–37, 241,
254, 270–71, 347, 376, 378, 380
Fitzgerald, F. Scott, 350
Fitzgerald, Zelda, 350, 441n24
Fort Smith, 203–4
Fox, Peggy, 277
Franca, Celia, 96
Fraser, John, 239
Fraser, Sylvia, 232, 257
Frayn, Michael: *Noises Off*, 393
*From Stone Orchard: A Collection of
Memories*, 23, 208–17

Galloway, Myron, 239
Garebian, Keith, 88, 93, 276, 390–91, 394
Gardner, David, 193

Garnhum, Dennis, 433n22
Gascon, Jean, 97
Gavin, James M., 248
Genet, Jean: *The Balcony*, 177
Gibson, Graeme, 28, 187–88, 190, 222–
23, 231–32, 247, 281, 430n4, 433n24
Gibson, Margaret, 220, 351
Gielgud, John, 101, 104–5, 131, 148
Ginsberg, Harvey, 199, 221
Glenville, Peter, 103, 106
Globe and Mail, 57, 239, 248
"Goggie." *See* Findley, Phoebe
Constance
Goldberg, Whoopi, 375
Goldilocks and the Three Bears, 243
Good, Cynthia, 331
Gordon, Mack, 363
Gordon, Ruth, 18–19, 117, 129, 135,
137–38, 154–55, 160–62, 311,
393, 424n15
Gould, Glenn, 2, 5, 6, 19, 27–28, 91, 96,
220, 256–57, 280, 284, 388
memorial, 284
"The Goldberg Variations," 153, 284
"The Gould Standard," 284
Grand Chalet, 78, 81
Grand Hotel (Switzerland), 215
Grand Theatre (London, ON), 257, 327
Granny Bull. *See* Bull, Edith Maude
Fagan
Grant, George: *Technology and
Empire*, 334
Great Gatsby, The, 350
Great War. *See* First World War
Greene, Lorne, 317
Greene, Trevor, 402
Guinness, Alec, 2, 7, 91, 94–95, 98–99,
101, 106, 110, 120–22, 134, 143,

178, 277, 374, 377, 391, 393, 423–424n9, 425n2
Blessings in Disguise, 102
criticism of TF's work, 122
influence on TF, 102–8, 111–12, 114–17, 122, 139–40, 148–50
My Name Escapes Me, 376
sexual favours, 131–33
sexuality, 103–5, 112
Guinness, Matthew, 102, 106
Guinness, Merula Salaman, 101–6, 108, 110, 132–33
Gurs internment camp, 369
Guthrie, Isobelle, 351, 353, 420n9
Guthrie, Tyrone, 90–94, 101, 127, 133, 396
Reknown at Stratford, 94, 127
Twice Have the Trumpets Sounded, 127
Gwyn, Sandra, 36
Gzowski, Peter; *Morningside*, 308

Hall, Radclyffe: *The Well of Loneliness*, 423n8
Hallifax, Michael and Elizabeth, 134
Hamlet, 103, 139, 143–44, 150, 248, 385
tour of, 144–47, 149
Moscow tour, 328
See also Findley, Timothy Irving Frederick: Osric, TF's role in *Hamlet*
Hamsun, Knut, 262
"Harper's Bazaar," 160–64, 186
Harris, Lawren, 38
Harron, Don, 114, 424n13
Harrowsmith, 208
Havergal College (Toronto), 50, 52, 57
Headhunter, 2, 22, 194, 212, 221, 238, 295, 308, 321, 323, 326,

331–41, 351, 356, 359, 378–79, 383–84, 394
depiction of Toronto in, 337–38
discussion of, 332–40
father-son relationship as influence on, 338–39
French translation of, 365–66
importance of Conrad's *Heart of Darkness*, 332, 334–36
influence of Lukacs on, 333
issue of pornography in, 334
Nicholas Fagan as character in, 338
publication and reviews of, 340–41
research and sources for, 333
Hellman, Lillian, 90, 207
Helwig, David, 340
Hemingway, Ernest, 130
Henchoz, Daviel and Rachel, 79–80
Hendry, Tom, 97
Henry, Martha, 28, 256, 327, 375, 388, 390, 393, 396
Hersey, John: *Hiroshima*, 325, 330
Hess, Rudolf, 264
Hill, Arthur, 159
Hilltop Acres (Toronto), 57
Hiroshima bomb, 70
Hirsch, John, 97
Hitler, Adolf, 263, 267–68
H. M. Tennent Company, 103–5, 107, 108, 118, 128
Hogarth, Meg, 154, 157
Hollywood, 161, 195
Holocaust, 194, 289–90, 317
homophobia, 76–77, 82, 258, 329
homosexuality, 4–5, 64–65
as criminal activity, 75, 82, 104–5
debates in psychiatry, 436n3
Guinness, Gielgud period, 103–5

persecution for, 327–28
portrayal of, 150
sexual triangle, 112, 133; *see also*
    Findley, Timothy Irving
    Frederick: relationship with
    Alec Guinness
treatment for "cure" of, 1950s–'60s,
    171–72
Hood, Hugh, 89
House Un-American Activities
    Committee (HUAC), 160. *See
    also* Miller, Arthur
"How Would *You* Like to Be Called
    Gay?" 166–67, 171, 295–96
Howard, Sidney: *The Silver Cord*, 88
Humber College, 323–24
Hunter, N.C.: *A Day by the Sea*, 105
Hutt, Peter, 388, 390
Hutt, William (Bill), 2, 28, 88–89, 94,
    96, 152, 205, 222–23, 226, 256–
    58, 308, 327, 375, 393, 397
Hyland, Frances, 238

*Inside Memory: Pages from a Writer's
    Workbook*, 5, 13–24, 30, 45, 70,
    127–28, 146, 161, 164–165, 175,
    186, 189, 192, 195, 198, 243–45,
    258, 260, 274, 276, 285–86, 293,
    302, 317–18, 321–23, 331, 333, 362
    Ernest Thesiger, memories of, 143
    narrative collage in, 17
International Players, 88, 91, 95
Irwin, John Jr., 280
Irwin Publishing, 281
Isay, Richard: *Being Homosexual,* 339
Isherwood, Christopher: *Goodbye to
    Berlin*, 113
Iverholme boarding house, 61, 353

Jack, Donald, 248
Jackson's Point, 36, 37, 38, 43, 177, 180,
    212, 253, 345. *See also* Lake
    Simcoe
*Jacques Brel Is Alive and Well and
    Living in Paris*, 199
Janhsen, Doris, 356–57
Jarvis Collegiate, 64, 74
John A.—Himself!, 257–58, 433n26
Johnson, Ben, 307–8
Johnson, Samuel, 19, 87, 309, 318, 344,
    422n1. *See also* "Against Despair"
Jolley, Elizabeth: *Woman in a
    Lampshade*, 304
Jones, David
    The Anathemata, 242
    In Parenthesis, 242
Jonson, Ben: *Volpone*, 172
"Journey, The," 202
Journeyman: Travels of a Writer, 24–
    25, 31, 47, 51–52, 55, 58–59, 224,
    324, 344
Joyce, James, 20, 101, 161
    Ulysses, 161
Joyce, Nora, 211–12, 363
Jung, Carl, 379, 383–84, 385. *See also
    Pilgrim
    Memories, Dreams and Reflections*,
    383
Jung, Emma, 380–81. *See also Pilgrim*

Kanin, Garson, 135, 154, 162
Keddy, Sheila, 159
Keith, Agnes Newton: *Three Came
    Home*, 436n7
Kempff, Wilhelm, 376–77
Kermode, Frank, 277
Kertes, Joe, 323–24

Kett family farm, 66
Kettlebrook Meadows (Guinness family
   home), 134, 138–39, 149–50
Khachaturian, Aram, 122
King, Charmian, 88
King Edward Hotel (Toronto), 35, 82,
   346–47
King, Ross, 383
King, William Lyon Mackenzie, 8–9
Kinsman, Gary and Gentile, Patrizia:
   The Canadian War on Queers,
   82, 327
Klondike, 226
Knight, Joellen, 302
Knowles, John
   Peace Breaks Out, 379
   A Separate Peace, 379
Kraul, Earl, 191–92
Kumsa, Martha, 303–4
Kurosawa, Akira
   Rashomon, 130
   Seven Samurai, 130

Lake Lindemann, 227–28
Lake Simcoe, 23, 31, 36, 65, 180, 212, 253
Lambert, Islay, 211, 218, 239
Lambton Golf and Country·Club, 42
landscapes, 21–23, 208–9
"Last Days, The" 115–16, 122–23
Last of the Crazy People, The, 22, 43,
   45, 90, 178, 180–85, 195, 199, 237,
   244, 351
   discussion of, 186–90, 279
   "Frankie and Johnnie," 189
Laurence, Margaret, 2, 19, 96, 212,
   220, 230–31, 238, 247–48, 255,
   257, 278, 281, 308, 432n16
   A Bird in the House, 231

The Diviners, 233–34, 297–98
The Fire Dwellers, 231
A Jest of God, 231
Lawson, Alan, 305
Leacock, Stephen, 31, 90, 212; Sunshine
   Sketches of a Little Town, 90
Lee, Dennis, 281
"Legends," 304
Leishman, Greg, 66
Lemaistre, Philippe, 80
"Lemonade," 162; See also "Harper's
   Bazaar"; Dinner Along the
   Amazon.
   Playhouse 90, 165–66
Leonardo da Vinci, 380, 382–83, 385
   as character in Pilgrim, 381–82
   La Gioconda, 381
Letros Tavern (Toronto), 82
Levine, Karen; Hana's Suitcase, 317
Lillie, Bea, 142–43, 425n4
Lindbergh, Charles, 264
Lindop, Michael J., 343–44
Little Sister's Book and Art
   Emporium, 342, 440n17
Liverpool, 111, 117–18
Loring, Frances, 68
Los Angeles, 166, 179, 194
Lost Innocence: The Children of World
   War Two
   "Children of the Holocaust," 317
   "Children on the Homefront," 317
Louvre, 381, 384
Lowry, Malcolm, 6, 20, 309
Loyer, Nésida (translator), 365–366
Lukacs, Attila Richard, 6, 333,
   439–40n11
Lumley, Jim, 280

Macartney-Filgate, Terence, 229–30, 261, 326
   Timothy Findley: Anatomy of a Writer, 326–27
MacDonald, Ann-Marie, 62, 70, 167
Macdonald, Grant, 88, 94
MacEwen, Gwendolyn, 19, 247, 309
Mackey, Matt, 392
Maclean, Donald, 104
Maclean's, 359, 386
MacLennan, Hugh: *The Watch That Ends the Night*, 97
MacMillan, Ernest: *Music in Canada*, 96
"Madonna of the Cherry Trees, The," 22, 369–71
Mahler, Gustav, 109
Mail and Empire, 35, 52, 55, 244
Manguel, Alberto, 374
Manitoba Theatre Centre, 291
Mannock, Juliet, 244
Marchand, Philip, 340
Marcus, James: "Mr. Kurtz—He Back," 340
"Margaret Laurence: A Remembrance," 308
Marlowe, Christopher: *Edward II*, 118
Martel, Yann: *Beatrice and Virgil*, 287
"Martha and the Minder," 304
Martin, Ralph: *The Woman He Loved*, 267
Marye, Michael Sean, 366
Massey family, 15. *See also* ancestors.
Massey Hall, 69
Massey-Harris Company, 32–34, 36, 41, 42, 44, 75, 76, 253, 346, 349
Massey, Hart, 32, 35
Massey/Levesque Report, 96

Massey, Vincent, 38, 96
"Matter over Mind: The Imagination in Jeopardy," 296–98
McCaskill's Mills, 345–46, 348–49, 354, 356. *See also* Cannington
McClelland, Jack, 96
McConnell, Nicholas, 374
McCowen, Alec, 117–18, 120–26, 150, 152, 154–55, 179, 200, 218, 277, 391, 393, 424n16
   relationship with TF, 140–45, 148
McCullers, Carson: *The Member of the Wedding*, 89–90, 223, 422–23n3
McIvor, Jack, 61, 70, 167
McKaugue Housser, Yvonne, 364
McKenna, Brian and Terrence: *The Valour and the Horror*, 324
McLaughlin, Isabel, 61, 78–79, 298, 308
Meares Island, 297
memory, 2, 5, 8, 14, 17, 20, 209, 223, 250–51
Metropolitan Opera, 69
Metropolitan Toronto Reference Library, 337
Mifune, Toshiro, 130–31
Miller, Arthur: *Timebends*, 160
"Missionaries," 207, 234–35
Mitchell, W. O., 281
MKULTRA, 301
Moffat, Ivan, 20, 22, 164, 196, 261, 273–74, 426n7
   photographs of Dachau, 164–65, 196, 261, 273–74, 359
Moiseiwitsch, Tanya, 91
Mona Lisa, 381, 384
   theft of, 443–44n8
Monette, Richard, 25, 28, 375
Mont Gaspé, 77, 80

Montgomery, Lucy Maud, 68, 212
Moodie, Susanna, 212, 335, 341–42
Moore, Dora Mavor, 52, 95
Moore, Mavor, 52, 90, 95, 97
Moral Re-Armament movement
    (MRA), 77–79, 147, 157–58, 176,
    297, 422n8
  adoption of Nazi tactics, 78
  Rising Tide magazine, 78
Moss, John, 290
Mottle, the cat, 19, 21, 29, 213–14, 218,
    242, 278–79, 307
Mount Pleasant Cemetery, 14–15, 42,
    55, 58, 282
  Mausoleum, 43, 45
Mowat, Farley, 281
  And No Birds Sang, 258
Mozart, Wolfgang Amadeus,
    113, 126
MRA. *See* Moral Re-Armament
    movement
Mulroney, Brian, 263, 305
Munro, Alice, 96, 231, 233
Murray, Sally, (sister-in-law) 115, 117.
    See also Findley, Sally.
music; *see also* Verdi, Giuseppe;
    Schubert, Franz
  centrality of, in Bull family,
    47–49, 54
  role of music in Findley's writing,
    20–21, 272. *See also* Findley,
    Timothy Irving Frederick:
    importance of music
Muskoka Lakes, 153, 177
Mussolini, Benito, 263, 268
"My Final Hour," 15–16, 76, 83, 318
"My First Job," 75
"My Mother, My Friend," 67, 72, 215

"Name's the Same, The " 133, 135–38,
    163, 311
National Arts Centre (NAC), 234–35
National Ballet of Canada, 96
National Dream, The, 213, 257
  film project (CBC), 221, 224–30
National Film Board (NFB), 94–95
  Don't Let the Angels Fall (Findley),
    200
  The Stratford Adventure, 94–95, 112
Nation of One, A, 46–47, 50
"A Nation of One" (lecture), 344
Nazi ideology
  Anglo-German cabal, 267
  anti-Semitism, 194–95, 262, 267,
  historical influence, 194–95, 267
  in Los Angeles, 429n10
  pro-Nazi artists and writers, 262
Necessary Angel, 291
New Canadian Library series, 96
New Play Society (Toronto), 95
New York, NY, 151–52, 154–55, 158,
    179, 184, 198, 200
Nicholsen, Jack, 366
Nicolas, Pierre and Léa, 373
Norman, Herbert, 327–31, 438–39n7
"Norman Affair, The," 327–28
Northwest Territories, (NWT), 22,
    201, 204, 206–7
  Pine Lake, 201, 203–4
  Wood Buffalo National Park, 201
Not Wanted on the Voyage, 2, 19, 28,
    79, 151, 160, 210, 214, 216, 228,
    278, 280, 284–92, 293, 296,
    298–99, 325, 335, 351
  "Cat Story," 278, 281, 284
  condemnation of organized
    religion, 290

dedication, 287
discussion of, 287–90
Holocaust, parallels with, 289–90
reviews of, 290–91
stage play, 291
tour of, 290–92

Oakes, Harry, 264, 267
O'Connor, Garry, 102
"Of Trunks and Burning Barns," 29
Olympics, Berlin (1936), 323
O'Neill, Eugene: *Anna Christie*, 90
Ontario Psychiatric Association
    (OPA), 171, 295–96
Osborne, John: *The Entertainer*, 165
Oshawa, 50, 54, 55, 57, 61
Ouzounian, Richard, 92–93, 95, 150
    Stratford Gold, 150
    "Timothy Findley's Stratford
    Memories," 92–93
Owen, Wilfred, 245

Paper People, The, 191, 200
    discussion of, 192–93
    Mary Jane Miller on, 429n7
Parkin, John B., 341
Parkinson's Foundation, 433n24
Parkman, Francis; *Montcalm and
    Wolfe*, 144
Parsons, Wayne, 25, 398
Parton, Lorne, 248
Patrick, Dennis, 278
Patterson, Tom, 90–91
Pau in Aquitaine, 369–70, 443n2
Pearce, John, 244, 246–247, 269–70,
    277, 281–82, 431–32n14, 432n16
Pearson, Lester B., 328–29, 438–39n7
Pebble Productions, 278

PEN Canada, 303–4
Penguin Canada, 281–82, 331
Peruggia, Vincenzo, 443n8
Peterman, Michael, 212, 365
Phillips, Robin, 7, 256, 396
Piano Man's Daughter, The, 2, 22, 29,
    33, 35, 37, 43, 45, 52, 54–55, 57, 61,
    66, 112, 216–17, 238, 253, 315, 321,
    359–60, 366–67, 375, 384, 402
    biographical sources in, 216, 345,
    355, 361
    discussion of, 344–57
    fictional autobiography and
    biography in, 351
    landscape in, 350, 355, 402
    metaphors of music and memory
    in, 352–53
    photographs for, 347–38, 355
    psychiatric institutions in, 57, 356
    publication of, 357
    research for, 345–38, 355–56
*Piano Man's Daughter and Others,
    The*, 28, 357
    tour for, 365–67
Pietropaolo, Damiano, 278
Pilgrim, 113, 194, 218, 222, 283, 356, 365,
    371, 375, 377–87, 394, 397–98
    Carl Jung as character in, 379–81,
    383, 385, 387
    death theme in, 384
    discussion of, 378–87
    Emma Jung as character in, 380–81,
    383–84, 387
    ethical problem in, 386–87
    fictional journals in, 380–81, 383–84
    Jungian concepts in, 383
    Leonardo da Vinci as character in,
    381–83

memory, importance of, 385
research for, 385
reviews of, 386
suicide in, 380, 384
Teresa of Avila as character in,
    381–82; *see also* Teresa of Avila
Tiresias figure in, 378
vision of humanity in, 378–379
war theme in, 384, 386
Pine Lake, NWT, 201, 203–4
Pirandello, Luigi, 116, 395
    *Six Characters in Search of an
    Author*, 116
"Point-Counterpoint: Ethics in the
    Media," 324
Pompes Funèbres Claude Pianetti,
    Vidauban, 26–27
Port Carling, 153–54
Potter, Beatrix, 68
    The Tale of Peter Rabbit, 67–68,
    325, 337, 372, 385, 438n4
Poulenc, Francis, 21, 121, 127
Pound, Ezra, 261–62, 264, 265, 274,
    277, 294, 344, 357–58, 359, 382
    Hugh Selwyn Mauberley, 268–71,
    434n6. *See also Famous Last Words*
Powell, Marilyn, 327
Powers, Ellen, 243
Priestley, J.B., 88
    Dangerous Corner, 88, 444n11
    The Glass Cage, 166
Proust, Marcel, 242
Purvis, Nelson, 179–80, 190
Purvis, Phyllis, 190

Queen Street Mental Health Centre,
    55, 337, 341
Quest, 167

Rattigan, Terence, 90, 123
    The Deep Blue Sea, 123
    O Mistress Mine, 90
Read, Piers Paul, 102
Red Barn Theatre, 9, 95–96, 177, 212
Redgrave, Michael, 101
"Reflections on Nationhood," 359
Reid, Janet, 7, 166–71, 295, 396
    annulment of marriage, 427n9.
    See also Findley, Timothy
    Irving Frederick: marriage
    to Janet Reid
Reid, Kate, 52, 88
Reilly, Frances, 436n3
religion
    condemnation of right-wing
        doctrine, 290
    influence of Alec Guinness, 102
    Presbyterian Church: ancestors, 33,
        38, 44, 65; influence of, 98, 135;
        support of MRA, 77
    See also Findley, Timothy Irving
        Frederick: religious beliefs
Remarque, Erich Maria: *All Quiet on
    the Western Front*, 113
Report of the Royal Commission on
    National Development in the Arts
    (Massey/Levesque Report), 96
Ribbentrop, Joachim von, 264, 266
Richard III (king), 15, 91–93
Richards, Linda L., 97, 386, 387
Richler, Mordecai, 96
Richmond Hill, 178
Richter, Sviatoslav, 399
"Riding Off in All Directions," 31
Riel, Louis, 258
Rimbaud, Arthur, 113–14, 119
Robert McLaughlin Gallery, 346

Roberts, Beverley, 345–46, 434n4
Roberts, Carol, 75, 372
Roberts, Charles G. D., 67–68
Roberts, Jean, 27, 172, 176–77, 234–35, 238, 360, 374, 428n2, 431n10
Rosedale, 22, 60–74, 119, 243, 253, 295, 310–11, 332, 337
Rosedale Public School, 65, 74
Rosenblatt, Bernard, 345–46
Ross, Sinclair, 364
Rossinière, 77–78, 81, 378, 385
Roth, Sabine, 357, 442n27
Rowland, Jane, 357
Royal Academy of Dramatic Art, 106
Royal Alexandra Theatre, 81, 89, 223
Royal Canadian Air Force (RCAF) Station Trenton, 69, 362. *See also* Findley, Allan
Royal Conservatory of Music, 81, 87–88
Royal Winnipeg Ballet, 96
Rule, Jane, 257, 307
Russum, Wesley, 160
Ryerson Institute of Technology, 172

Sacks, Oliver
    "An Anthropologist on Mars," 346
    The Man Who Mistook His Wife for a Hat, 351
Saint-Anne Military Hospital, 26
Saint Sebastian, 431n6
Saltspring Island, 22, 286–87, 298, 307, 308, 360, 365
San Michele, 358
Schellenberg, Walter, 264
Schroeder, Andreas, 231
Schubert, Franz, 6, 21, 271
    Sonata in B-flat Major, 271–73. *See also* Cortot, Alfred

Scofield, Paul, 143
Scythia, 95, 100
Sealy, Joe, 29, 357, 366
Sebastian (teddy bear), 9, 223, 228, 304–5, 372
Second World War, 68–69, 80, 98, 149, 151, 189, 194, 256, 261–62, 266, 268, 290, 300, 302, 330, 345, 352, 355, 360–61, 363, 369, 379
Sellers, Terry and Kelly, 402
Service, Robert, 228
Seton, Ernest Thompson, 67
Shadows, 25, 28, 388, 392, 398
    discussion of, 394–396
Shakespeare, William, 146
    All's Well That Ends Well, 91–94
    Antony and Cleopatra, 101, 390
    Hamlet, 103, 139, 143–44, 150, 248, 385; tour of, 144–47, 149, 328
    King Henry VI, Part III, 83
    King Lear, 101, 200
    Much Ado About Nothing, 374–75, 385, 389
    Richard III, 15, 83, 91–94. *See also Elizabeth Rex*
Sheridan, Richard B.: *The Rivals,* 177
Shields, Carol, 365
Shirer, William: *The Rise and Fall of the Third Reich,* 267
Sibbald Point, 31
Sibelius, Jean, 138–39
"Significant Others," 67
    Duthie Lecture, 342, 344
Simpson, Leo, 257
Simpson, N. F.: *One Way Pendulum,* 177
Sinclair, Lister, 324
Sisam, Patrick, 295
Skagway, 227–29

"Small Town in Normandy, A," 261

Smith, Phoebe Constance, 33, 45. *See also* Findley, Phoebe Constance

Society Blue Book (Toronto), 34, 36, 42, 45

Sontag, Susan, 440n13
    "The Pornographic Imagination," 334

South Dakota Badlands, 202

Spadework, 133, 200, 294, 311, 388, 391, 396
    depiction of Stratford in, 391–92
    discussion of, 391–94

Spanish flu epidemic, 49, 54, 236, 354

Sprucevale, 210, 284, 286. *See also* Arkwright

Staines, David, 290, 332

St. Andrew's College (SAC), 35–36, 38, 42, 43–44, 55, 72–74, 253, 283, 326, 362–63, 399

Stein, Gertrude
    The Autobiography of Alice B. Toklas, 156
    Geography and Plays, 158

Steiner, George: "To Civilize Our Gentlemen," 334

Stephenson, Craig, 387

Sterndale Bennett School, 81, 83, 87–88, 92

Stillborn Lover, The, 133, 146, 218, 311, 321, 323, 326–31, 359, 391, 439n8
    discussion of, 328–31
    game of Go in, 330
    persecution of gays in, 329–31

St. Michael's Cemetery, 24, 45, 362

Stone Orchard, 1, 2, 7, 10, 16, 21, 22, 23, 29, 67, 180–81, 191, 200, 207–11, 213–15, 217, 222–23, 230–31, 234, 243, 258, 263, 282, 284–87, 298, 303, 306–7, 313, 316, 322–23, 326–27, 348, 351, 356, 359–60, 366, 372, 395, 402–3
    as a graveyard, 217
    as "home," 209–211
    loss of, 364–65, 367, 376–77

"Stones," 21, 261, 283, 312, 314–16, 385

Stones, 60, 68, 136
    Bragg and Minna stories, 294, 305, 310–311. *See also* Findley, Timothy Irving Frederick: treatment of ménage à trois
    discussion of stories in, 310–16
    "Dreams," 333

Strachey, Lytton: *Elizabeth and Essex*, 390

Strate, Grant, 191–92

Stratford Festival, 25, 88, 112, 175;
    history of, 90–91, 93–95

Stratford General Hospital, 25, 398

Stratford, ON, 22, 25, 27, 29, 90–91, 208, 360, 367, 374, 387, 394

Stratford-upon-Avon, 389–90

Strathearn Road house, 131, 138, 148, 152–53, 165

Straw Hat Players, 95, 149, 153–54, 165, 426n3

Stuewe, Paul, 431n9
    "Better Dead Than Read?" 233

Sutton West, 32, 212

Symons, Scott, 221–23, 430n3

Tait, Anne, 172

Tait, Michael, 172, 223

Tamarack Review, 96, 135, 153
    See also "About Effie"

Tamblyn, David, 398–99

Taylor, Charles, 281, 328

Six Journeys: A Canadian Pattern,
328
Taylor, Elizabeth, 9, 68
"Tea Party, The," 232–33
Tedworth Square, 140, 163, 385
Telling of Lies, The, 2, 16, 21, 294, 315,
324, 345, 356, 369
discussion of, 298–302
research for, 300–301
Tennant, Veronica, 28, 29, 357, 366–67,
397–98
Teresa of Avila, 102, 113, 385
as character in *Pilgrim,* 381–82
as influence on Gertrude Stein, 156
Thesiger, Ernest, 18–19, 143
Thompson, Judith, 304, 366–67
Thompson, Paul, 390, 442n33
Thomson, Tom, 23, 68
"Timothy Findley's Summer Peaches,"
309
Tippett, Michael, 325–26, 333, 339
A Child of Our Time, 385
Tolstoy, Leo
The Fruits of Enlightenment, 146
War and Peace, 129
Tom Patterson Theatre (Stratford), 388
Toronto, 22, 33, 179, 335, 345
fire of 1904, 347
gay life in, 82
history of, in relation to Findley
family, 34–36
Toronto Psychiatric hospital (TPH), 171
Torrey, E. Fuller, 262
Traill, Catharine Parr, 212
Trent University, 15, 278, 308–9, 365
"Can You See Me Yet?" conference,
365
Philosophical Society at, 318

Timothy Findley Creative Writing
Prize, The, 365
"Trial of Oscar Wilde, The," 207
Trials of Ezra Pound, The, 358, 394,
442n28
Trojan Women, The, adaptation of,
25, 400
Tuchman, Barbara: *The Proud Tower,*
242
Tupholme, Iris, 29, 331–32, 394, 439n9
Turing, Alan, 104, 330–31
Turner, Edward, (psychiatrist) 6, 178–
79, 198–99, 205, 217–18, 239, 242,
278, 284, 286, 296, 306–7, 311,
333, 359, 384, 386, 428n5, 428n5,
436n3, 440n14
Twigg, Alan, 289
Tyson, Sylvia, 29, 366, 398

Umbach, Elmer, 233
Ungar, George: *The Champagne
Safari,* 434n4
Urquhart, Jane, 52, 342, 365

Vancouver Institute, 296
Varley, Frederick, 68
Verdi, Giuseppe: *Requiem,* 118, 126, 134
Vimy Monument, 80
Volkoff, Boris, 76, 195, 344

"Walls," 198–99
"War," 70–71, 133, 135–36, 137–38,
153, 163, 165, 185, 188, 224,
311, 385
Warren, Dorothy, 299, 302, 436n6
Warren, Harry, 363
Wars, The, 2, 3, 10, 17, 18, 19, 28–29, 38,
45, 163, 200–201, 218, 223, 237,

238, 260, 279, 284, 290–91, 315, 339, 345, 351, 432n15, 432n16
adaptation for stage, 254, 433n22
ancestors, influence of, 251, 253
censorship threat, 343–44
conference on, 359
Der Krieg und die Krote, 248
fictional biographer in, 249–51, 254, 265film, 255–57;
Governor General's Award for Fiction, 255
Irving Findley's journal, use of, 39–40, 251
novel, 240–55
photographs in, 242, 253–54
reviews of, 248–49
Washington, D.C., 160, 163
Waterton Lakes National Park, 202
Watkins, John, 146, 327–29
Watson, Sheila: *The Double Hook*, 97
Waugh, Evelyn, 113, 207
Brideshead Revisited, 113, 431n6
Weaver, Robert, 153, 165, 247
Webb, Phyllis, 15, 19, 22, 219, 230–31, 285–87, 298, 307–8, 332, 374
"The Confluence of Imaginations," 435n12
"I Daniel," 15, 318, 435n12
"Leaning," 285–86
Nothing but Brush Strokes, 435n12
"We Must Prepare for a New Plague," 45, 49
West, Nathaniel: *The Day of the Locust*, 429n12
Westwood, Bill, 29
"Whimper," 221, 224, 234
Whitby Asylum for the Insane, 352, 420n12. *See also Piano Man's Daughter, The*

Whitby Psychiatric Hospital, 56–57, 353, 420n12
White, Patrick: *Voss*, 304
Whitehead, Bill, 1, 2, 4, 9, 16, 18, 22, 24–29, 45, 52, 172, 175–177, 179–81, 198–99, 204–7, 217–18, 234, 239, 240–41, 244, 257, 277–80, 282, 286, 296–97, 304–5, 308, 316, 322, 325, 333, 344, 347, 357, 359, 364–67, 371–77, 392, 395–400, 401–2.
handling TF's business, 200, 210, 331
life at Stone Orchard with TF, 208–14
response to TF's alcohol abuse, 191–92, 220–21, 223, 377
sexual orientation, 175
sexual relationship with TF, 219
WFW, 18, 298
Words to Live By, 179–80, 219, 228, 241, 316, 359, 402
work as an actor, 175–76
work for CBC, 178, 200, 207, 213, 220–21, 225–26, 261
Whitehead, William Frederick; "WFW." *See* Whitehead, Bill
Whitehorse, 225, 227–28
White Horse Pass, 227, 229, 287
Whitemore, Hugh
Breaking the Code, 331
Whiteoaks of Jalna, 224–25, 351
Whiteoaks of Jalna, 224–25, 351
Whittaker, Herbert, 126, 152
"Flamboyant Personality an Aid to Russian Actor," 147
Wiebe, Rudy, 232
Wilde, Oscar, 113, 143
The Ballad of Reading Gaol, 189

Wilder, Thornton, 2, 7, 15, 18, 22, 114,
116–17, 120, 122–23, 137, 140–143,
164, 195, 205, 218, 377, 393, 424n14,
425n17
Alcestiad: Or a Life in the Sun,
140–43
Findley/Wilder correspondence, 7,
155–56
The Ides of March, 268
influence on TF, 127–28, 133, 302
The Matchmaker, 114–18, 121, 126,
131, 138–39, 141–42, 145, 158, 164;
American tour of, 153–55; 157–
60, 393
The Skin of Our Teeth, 116
William Head Institution, 307
Williams Piano Company, 49, 346, 348
Williams Piano Factory, 55
Williams, Tennessee, 150, 160, 374
The Glass Menagerie, 177
Night of the Iguana, 374
Williams, William Carlos, 262, 271, 358
Wolff, Leon: *In Flanders Fields*, 242
Woodcock, George, 96–97, 291
Woolf, Virginia, 223, 385

World War I. *See* First World War
World War II. *See* Second World War
Writer's Development Trust, 307
Writer's Union of Canada, 2, 230–34,
243, 257, 305, 309
Wyatt, Alfred, 191, 211, 216, 348
Wyle, Florence, 68

Yeats, William Butler: "The Second
Coming," 306
You'll Never Know, 29, 363, 366
You Went Away, 22, 283, 315, 321–22,
345, 364, 366–67
Allan Findley as inspiration for, 69,
73, 361–62
discussion of, 360–63
as fictionalized autobiography, 360
photographs in, 360–61, 362
Yukon, 226, 287
Yukon River, 227

Zerbisias, Antonia, 317
Zurich, 379, 385
Burghölzli Clinic in, 380, 397